RESEARCH HANDBOOK ON INSIDER TRADING

RESEARCH HANDBOOKS IN CORPORATE LAW AND GOVERNANCE

Elgar *Research Handbooks* are original reference works designed to provide a broad overview of research in a given field while at the same time creating a forum for more challenging, critical examination of complex and often under-explored issues within that field. Chapters by international teams of contributors are specially commissioned by editors who carefully balance breadth and depth. Often widely cited, individual chapters present expert scholarly analysis and offer a vital reference point for advanced research. Taken as a whole they achieve a wide-ranging picture of the state-of-the-art.

Making a major scholarly contribution to the field of corporate law and governance, the volumes in this series explore topics of current concern from a range of jurisdictions and perspectives, offering a comprehensive analysis that will inform researchers, practitioners and students alike. The *Research Handbooks* cover the fundamental aspects of corporate law, such as insolvency governance structures, as well as hot button areas such as executive compensation, insider trading, and directors' duties. The *Handbooks*, each edited by leading scholars in their respective fields, offer far-reaching examinations of current issues in corporate law and governance that are unrivalled in their blend of critical, substantive analysis, and in their synthesis of contemporary research.

Each *Handbook* stands alone as an invaluable source of reference for all scholars of corporate law, as well as for practicing lawyers who wish to engage with the discussion of ideas within the field. Whether used as an information resource on key topics or as a platform for advanced study, volumes in this series will become definitive scholarly reference works in the field.

Research Handbook on Insider Trading

Edited by

Stephen M. Bainbridge

University of California, Los Angeles, USA

RESEARCH HANDBOOKS IN CORPORATE LAW AND GOVERNANCE

Edward Elgar
Cheltenham, UK • Northampton, MA, USA

Published by
Edward Elgar Publishing Limited
The Lypiatts
15 Lansdown Road
Cheltenham
Glos GL50 2JA
UK

Edward Elgar Publishing, Inc.
William Pratt House
9 Dewey Court
Northampton
Massachusetts 01060
USA

A catalogue record for this book
is available from the British Library

Library of Congress Control Number: 2012951752

This book is available electronically in the ElgarOnline.com
Law Subject Collection, E-ISBN 978 0 85793 185 6

ISBN 978 0 85793 184 9 (cased)

Typeset by Servis Filmsetting Ltd, Stockport, Cheshire
Printed by MPG PRINTGROUP, UK

Contents

Figures

Tables

Contributors

Kern Alexander, Chair for Law and Finance, University of Zurich, and Senior Research Fellow, The Centre for Financial Analysis and Policy, University of Cambridge.

Stephen M. Bainbridge, William D. Warren Distinguished Professor of Law, UCLA School of Law.

Laura Nyantung Beny, Professor of Law, University of Michigan Law School.

Stephen F. Diamond, Associate Professor of Law, Santa Clara University School of Law.

Jill Fisch, Perry Golkin Professor of Law, University of Pennsylvania Law School. Professor Fisch thanks Charlotte Newell, University of Pennsylvania Law School Class of 2012, for excellent research support.

Joan MacLeod Heminway, W.P. Toms Distinguished Professor of Law, The University of Tennessee College of Law. Professor Heminway thanks Tayo Atanda and Bobby Ahdieh for reading and commenting on chapter drafts, and Merrit (as always) for his generous support and encouragement.

M. Todd Henderson, Professor of Law, The University of Chicago Law School.

Nicholas Calcina Howson, Professor of Law, University of Michigan Law School.

Hui Huang, Associate Professor, Faculty of Law, Chinese University of Hong Kong; Conjoint Associate Professor, Faculty of Law, University of New South Wales.

Keith Kendall, Senior Lecturer, La Trobe University School of Law.

Sung Hui Kim, Acting Professor of Law, UCLA School of Law. Professor Kim thanks Stephen Bainbridge and Robert Prentice for helpful comments and Jihee Yoo (UCLA J.D. 2013) for valuable research assistance.

Thomas A. Lambert, Professor of Law, University of Missouri Law School.

Katja Langenbucher, Professor of Law, Goethe University's House of Finance; Affiliated Professor at Sciences Po Law School.

Donald C. Langevoort, Thomas Aquinas Reynolds Professor of Law, Georgetown University Law Center.

Henry G. Manne, Dean Emeritus, George Mason University School of Law.

Matthijs Nelemans, Post-Doctoral Researcher, Tilburg University Law and Economics Center.

Alexandre Padilla, Associate Professor of Economics, Department of Economics, Metropolitan State University of Denver. Professor Padilla would like to thank the editor, Stephen Bainbridge, for helpful comments and suggestions on earlier drafts of this chapter. The usual caveat applies.

A.C. Pritchard, Frances & George Skestos Professor of Law, University of Michigan Law School.

J. Mark Ramseyer, Mitsubishi Professor of Japanese Legal Studies, Harvard University.

Michael Schouten, Post-Doctoral Researcher, University of Amsterdam Faculty of Law, Duisenberg School of Finance. Messrs. Nelemans and Schouten thank Elodie Gal, Roan Lamp, Mathias Siems and Anne-Will van der Vegt for helpful comments.

H. Nejat Seyhun, Professor of Finance and Jerome B. and Eilene M. York Professor of Business Administration and Director of the Financial Engineering Program, University of Michigan.

Andrew F. Simpson, The Hong Kong Polytechnic University.

J.W. Verret, Assistant Professor, George Mason University School of Law.

Gordon Walker, Professor, La Trobe University School of Law.

1. An overview of insider trading law and policy: an introduction to the *Research Handbook on Insider Trading*
Stephen M. Bainbridge

In most capital markets, insider trading is the most common violation of the securities laws. It is certainly the violation that has most clearly captured the public's imagination. Surely no other corporate or securities law doctrine has provided the plot line of as many crime thrillers and motion pictures as has insider trading.

Insider trading also long ago captured the attention of academic lawyers and economists to a degree few other topics in corporate law or securities regulation can match. As a result, it attracts scholars in fields ranging from pure legal doctrine to empirical analysis to complex economic theory. This volume collects cutting-edge scholarship in all of these areas by many of the leading experts in insider trading law and economics.

Insider trading jurisprudence is strongly skewed towards US law. This emphasis is not mere academic parochialism or chauvinism, however. The USA remains the world's largest capital market. More important for present purposes, the USA was one of the first jurisdictions to ban insider trading and remains the jurisdiction in which the ban is most energetically enforced. To be sure, insider trading bans are now on the books in many jurisdictions and there is growing global emphasis on fighting the practice. A number of the chapters in this volume focus on these developments. Much of the volume nevertheless is appropriately devoted to US law. The long history and highly developed body of US law on the subject suggest that studying the legal doctrine and policy underpinnings of the US prohibition of insider trading will reward study not only for US corporate and securities law scholars, but for those of all countries. Accordingly, this Introduction provides a foundation for the chapters that follow by setting out the basic US legal rules and the policy debate those rules have engendered.

I. ORIGINS OF THE US PROHIBITION

The prohibition of insider trading originally evolved in the USA as a matter of the state law fiduciary duties of corporate directors and officers. Even after the federal government took primary responsibility for securities regulation, following the adoption of the Securities Act of 1933 and the Securities Exchange Act of 1934, federal law continued to largely ignore insider trading until the late 1960s. Since then, however, a complex federal prohibition of insider trading has emerged as a central feature of modern US securities regulation.

Although the modern insider trading prohibition technically is grounded in the federal securities regulation statutes, most notably Rule 10b-5 promulgated by the Securities and Exchange Commission (SEC) pursuant to the authority granted it by

Section 10(b) of the Securities Exchange Act, the prohibition in fact evolved through a series of judicial decisions in a process more closely akin to common law adjudication rather than statutory interpretation. Indeed, change is one of the key distinguishing characteristics of the federal insider trading prohibition. Unfortunately, this process has been rather ad hoc, which has left the doctrine with a number of problems and curious gaps.

A.   The Statutory Background

The modern prohibition is a creature of SEC administrative actions and judicial opinions, only loosely tied to the text of the key statutory provision—Securities Exchange Act § 10(b)—and its legislative history. Section 10(b) provides in pertinent part that:

> It shall be unlawful for any person, directly or indirectly, by the use of any means or instrumentality of interstate commerce or of the mails, or of any facility of any national securities exchange—
> (b) To use or employ, in connection with the purchase or sale of any security registered on a national securities exchange or any security not so registered . . ., any manipulative or deceptive device or contrivance in contravention of such rules and regulations as the Commission may prescribe as necessary or appropriate in the public interest or for the protection of investors.[1]

Notice two things about the statutory text. First, it is not self executing. Until the SEC exercises the rulemaking authority vested in it by the statute, § 10(b) does nothing.

Secondly, nothing in § 10(b) explicitly proscribes insider trading. To the extent the 1934 Congress addressed insider trading, it did so not through § 10(b), but rather through § 16(b), which permits the issuer of affected securities to recover insider short-swing profits.[2] Section 16(b) imposes quite limited restrictions on insider trading. It does not reach transactions occurring more than six months apart, nor does it apply to persons other than those named in the statute or to transactions in securities not registered under § 12.

If Congress intended in 1934 that the SEC use § 10(b) to craft a sweeping prohibition on insider trading, the SEC was quite dilatory in doing so. Rule 10b-5, the foundation on which the modern insider trading prohibition rests, was not promulgated until 1942, eight years after Congress passed the Exchange Act. The Rule provides:

> It shall be unlawful for any person, directly or indirectly, by the use of any means or instrumentality of interstate commerce, or of the mails or of any facility of any national securities exchange,
> (a) To employ any device, scheme, or artifice to defraud,
> (b) To make any untrue statement of a material fact or to omit to state a material fact necessary in order to make the statements made, in the light of the circumstances under which they were made, not misleading, or
> (c) To engage in any act, practice, or course of business which operates or would operate as a fraud or deceit upon any person, in connection with the purchase or sale of any security.[3]

---

[1]   15 U.S.C. § 78j(b).
[2]   15 U.S.C. § 78p(b).
[3]   17 CFR § 240.10b-5.

Note that, as with § 10(b) itself, the Rule on its face does not prohibit (or even speak to) insider trading. Indeed, it was not until 1961 that the SEC finally claimed that insider trading on an impersonal stock exchange violated Rule 10b-5.[4]

B.   The Disclose or Abstain Rule

The modern federal insider trading prohibition fairly can be said to have begun with the SEC's 1961 enforcement action *In re Cady, Roberts & Co.*[5] Curtiss-Wright Corporation's board of directors decided to reduce the company's quarterly dividend. One of the directors, J. Cheever Cowdin, was also a partner of Cady, Roberts & Co., a stock brokerage firm. Before the news was announced, Cowdin informed one of his partners, Robert M. Gintel, of the impending dividend cut. Gintel then sold several thousand shares of Curtiss-Wright stock held in customer accounts over which he had discretionary trading authority. When the dividend cut was announced, Curtiss-Wright's stock price fell several dollars per share. Gintel's customers thus avoided substantial losses.

Cady, Roberts involved what is now known as tipping: an insider who knows confidential information does not himself trade, but rather informs—tips—someone else, who does trade. It also involved trading on an impersonal stock exchange, instead of a face-to-face transaction. As the SEC acknowledged, this made it "a case of first impression."[6] Although Rule 10b-5 had sometimes been invoked prior to *Cady, Roberts* to deal with insider trading-like issues, those cases typically had involved face-to-face or control transactions rather than impersonal stock market transactions. Notwithstanding, the SEC held that Gintel had violated Rule 10b-5. In so doing, it articulated what became known as the "disclose or abstain" rule: an insider in possession of material nonpublic information must disclose such information before trading or, if disclosure is impossible or improper, abstain from trading.

It was not immediately clear what precedential value *Cady, Roberts* would have.[7] It was an administrative ruling by the SEC, not a judicial opinion. It involved a regulated industry closely supervised by the SEC. Neither the text of the statute nor its legislative history supported—let alone mandated—a broad insider trading prohibition.[8] There was a long line of state law precedent to the contrary.[9]

In this volume, Adam Pritchard argues that the Supreme Court's decision in *SEC v. Capital Gains Research Bureau*[10] could have had a major impact on the development of

---

[4]   In re Cady, Roberts & Co., 40 S.E.C. 907 (1961).

[5]   40 S.E.C. 907, 1961 WL 3743 (1961).

[6]   Id. at *1.

[7]   See, e.g., Recent Decision, 48 Va. L. Rev. 398, 403–04 (1962) ("in view of the limited resources of the Commission, the unfortunate existence of more positive and reprehensible forms of fraud, and the inherent problems concerning proof and evidence adhering to any controversy involving a breach of duty of disclosure, there is little prospect of excessive litigation evolving pursuant to [*Cady, Roberts*]").

[8]   See Stephen M. Bainbridge, Incorporating State Law Fiduciary Duties into the Federal Insider Trading Prohibition, 52 Wash. & Lee L. Rev. 1189, 1228–34 (1995).

[9]   See id. at 1218–27 (analyzing cases).

[10]   375 U.S. 180 (1963).

the law of insider trading post-*Cady, Roberts*. In his account, *Capital Gains* broke ground both in its approach to interpreting the federal securities laws and in its willingness to incorporate fiduciary principles into the law of insider trading. The opinion's influence was short-lived, however, as the Supreme Court reverted to a more textualist approach in securities cases.

In any case, when the Second Circuit turned *Cady, Roberts* into the law of the land in the seminal *Texas Gulf Sulphur* decision,[11] it opted not to rely on fiduciary principles but rather on a purported policy requiring that investors have equal access to information. In March 1959, agents of Texas Gulf Sulphur Co., a mining corporation, began aerial surveys of an area near Timmins, Ontario. Evidence of an ore deposit was found. In October 1963, Texas Gulf Sulphur began ground surveys of the area. In early November, a drilling rig took core samples from depths of several hundred feet. Visual examination of the samples suggested commercially significant deposits of copper and zinc. Texas Gulf Sulphur's president ordered the exploration group to maintain strict confidentiality, even to the point of withholding the news from other Texas Gulf Sulphur directors and employees. In early December, a chemical assay confirmed the presence of copper, zinc, and silver. At the subsequent trial, several expert witnesses testified that they had never heard of any other initial exploratory drill hole showing comparable results. Over the next several months, Texas Gulf Sulphur acquired the rights to the land under which this remarkable ore deposit lay. In March and early April 1964, further drilling confirmed that Texas Gulf Sulphur had made a significant ore discovery. After denying several rumors about the find, Texas Gulf Sulphur finally announced its discovery in a press conference on April 16, 1964.

Throughout the autumn of 1963 and spring of 1964, a number of Texas Gulf Sulphur insiders bought stock and/or options on company stock. Others tipped off outsiders. Still others accepted stock options from the company's board of directors without informing the directors of the discovery. Between November 1963 and March 1964, the insiders were able to buy at prices that were slowly rising, albeit with fluctuations, from just under $18 per share to $25 per share. As rumors began circulating in late March and early April, the price jumped to about $30 per share. On April 16, the stock opened at $31, but quickly jumped to $37 per share. By May 15, 1964, Texas Gulf Sulphur's stock was trading at over $58 per share—a 222 percent rise over the previous November's price. Any joy the insiders may have taken from their profits was short-lived, however, as the SEC sued them for violating Rule 10b-5.

In what quickly became a leading opinion, the Second Circuit agreed with the SEC that Rule 10b-5 had been violated. The court held that when an insider has material nonpublic information the insider must either disclose such information before trading or abstain from trading until the information has been disclosed. Thus was born what is now known as the "disclose or abstain" rule.

The *TGS* opinion rested on a policy of equality of access to information. The court concluded that the federal insider trading prohibition was intended to assure that "all investors trading on impersonal exchanges have relatively equal access to material

---

[11]   SEC v. Texas Gulf Sulphur Co., 401 F.2d 833 (2d Cir.), cert. denied, 394 U.S. 976 (1968).

information."[12] Put another way, Congress purportedly intended "that all members of the investing public should be subject to identical market risks."[13]

Accordingly, under *TGS* and its progeny, virtually anyone who possessed material nonpublic information was required either to disclose it before trading or abstain from trading in the affected company's securities. If the would-be trader's fiduciary duties precluded him from disclosing the information prior to trading, abstention was the only option.

In *Chiarella v. US*,[14] the United States Supreme Court rejected the equal access policy. Vincent Chiarella was an employee of Pandick Press, a financial printer that prepared tender offer disclosure materials, among other documents. In preparing those materials Pandick used codes to conceal the names of the companies involved, but Chiarella broke the codes. He purchased target company shares before the bid was announced, then sold the shares for considerable profits after announcement of the bid. He got caught and was indicted for illegal insider trading.

Chiarella was convicted of violating Rule 10b-5 by trading on the basis of material nonpublic information. The Second Circuit affirmed his conviction, applying the same equality of access to information-based disclose or abstain rule it had created in *Texas Gulf Sulphur*. Under the equal access-based standard, Chiarella clearly loses: he had greater access to information than those with whom he traded.

The Supreme Court reversed. In doing so, the court squarely rejected the notion that § 10(b) was intended to assure all investors equal access to information. The court said it could not affirm Chiarella's conviction without recognizing a general duty between all participants in market transactions to forego trades based on material, nonpublic information, and it refused to impose such a duty.[15]

Chiarella thus made clear that the disclose or abstain rule is not triggered merely because the trader possesses material nonpublic information. When a 10b-5 action is based upon nondisclosure, there can be no fraud absent a duty to speak, and no such duty arises from the mere possession of nonpublic information.[16] Instead, the disclose or abstain theory of liability for insider trading was now premised on the inside trader being subject to a duty to disclose to the party on the other side of the transaction that arose from a fiduciary relationship between the parties.[17] As applied to the facts at bar, Chiarella was not an employee, officer, or director of any of the companies in whose stock he traded. He worked solely for Pandick Press, which in turn was not an agent of any of those companies. Pandick did work mainly for acquiring companies—not the takeover targets in whose stock Chiarella traded. He therefore had no fiduciary relationship with—and thus no duty to disclose to—those with whom he traded.[18]

---

[12] Id. at 847.
[13] Id. at 852.
[14] 445 U.S. 222 (1980).
[15] Id. at 233.
[16] Id. at 235.
[17] Id. at 230.
[18] Id. at 232–33.

C.   Tipping

Chiarella substantially limited the scope of the insider trading prohibition. As such, it posed the question whether anyone other than classical insiders such as directors, officers, and perhaps large shareholders could be held liable for dealing on the basis of insider information. In *Dirks v. SEC*,[19] the Supreme Court confirmed that the prohibition extended beyond classical insiders and started fleshing out the rules applicable to them. The court began by reaffirming its rejection of the equal access standard in favor of a fiduciary duty-based regime:

> We were explicit in *Chiarella* in saying that there can be no duty to disclose where the person who has traded on inside information "was not [the corporation's] agent, . . . was not a fiduciary, [or] was not a person in whom the sellers [of the securities] had placed their trust and confidence." Not to require such a fiduciary relationship, we recognized, would "[depart] radically from the established doctrine that duty arises from a specific relationship between two parties" and would amount to "recognizing a general duty between all participants in market transactions to forgo actions based on material, nonpublic information."[20]

Recognizing that this formulation posed problems for tipping cases, the court held that a tippee's liability is derivative of that of the tipper, "arising from [the tippee's] role as a participant after the fact in the insider's breach of a fiduciary duty." A tippee therefore can be held liable only when the tipper breached a fiduciary duty by disclosing information to the tippee, and the tippee knows or has reason to know of the breach of duty.

What *Dirks* proscribes thus is not merely a breach of confidentiality by the insider, but rather the breach of a fiduciary duty of loyalty to refrain from profiting on information entrusted to the tipper. Looking at objective criteria, courts must determine whether the insider-tipper personally benefited, directly or indirectly, from his disclosure. The most obvious case is the *quid pro quo* setting, in which the tipper gets some form of pecuniary gain. Non-pecuniary gain can also qualify, however. Suppose a corporate CEO discloses information to a wealthy investor not for any legitimate corporate purpose, but solely to enhance his own reputation. *Dirks* would find a personal benefit on those facts. Finally, *Dirks* indicated that liability could be imposed where the tip is a gift, because it is analogous to the situation in which the tipper trades on the basis of the information and then gives the tippee the profits.

Because *Dirks* requires that the tipper receive some personal benefit, it did not prohibit corporate insiders from selectively disclosing information to certain analysts so long as there was a corporate purpose for doing so. In 2000, the SEC adopted Regulation FD to create a non-insider trading-based mechanism for restricting selective disclosure. If someone acting on behalf of a public corporation discloses material nonpublic information to securities market professionals or "holders of the issuer's securities who may well trade on the basis of the information," the issuer must also disclose that information to the public.[21] Where the issuer intentionally provides such disclosure, it must simultaneously

---

[19]   463 U.S. 646 (1983).
[20]   Id. at 654–55.
[21]   Exchange Act Rel. No 43,154 (Aug. 15, 2000).

disclose the information in a manner designed to convey it to the general public. Hence, for example, if the issuer holds a briefing for selected analysts, it must simultaneously announce the same information through, say, a press release to "a widely disseminated news or wire service."[22] The SEC encouraged issuers to make use of the Internet and other new information technologies, such as by webcasting conference calls with analysts. Where the disclosure was not intentional, as where a corporate officer "let something slip," the issuer must make public disclosure "promptly" after a senior officer learns of the disclosure.[23]

In this volume, Jill Fisch traces the development of the SEC's use of Regulation FD to address information asymmetry in the securities markets. She describes the SEC's enforcement policy and notes, in particular the SEC's efforts, through its selection and settlement of Regulation FD cases, to provide guidance to corporations and corporate officials about areas of key concern. Fisch concludes by highlighting current areas of particular importance, including disclosure of information through private meetings and the implications of technological innovations such as the Internet and social media.

D.   The Misappropriation Theory and Rule 14e-3

Dirks did not resolve the significant question posed by *Chiarella*; namely, to what extent does the insider trading prohibition apply where the defendant traded on the basis of market information derived from sources other than the issuer? The classic case is where an insider of a takeover bidder trades in stock of the target company on the basis of information about the bidder's plans. Such a person is not one in whom the shareholders of the target have placed their trust and confidence. Accordingly, under *Chiarella* no liability should arise.

1.   Rule 14e-3

Rule 14e-3 prohibits insiders of the bidder and target from divulging confidential information about a tender offer to persons that are likely to violate the rule by trading on the basis of that information. This provision (Rule 14e-3(d)(1)) does not prohibit the bidder from buying target shares or from telling its legal and financial advisers about its plans. Instead, it prohibits tipping of information to persons who are likely to buy target shares for their own account. Rule 14e-3 also, with certain narrow and well-defined exceptions, prohibits any person that possesses material information relating to a tender offer by another person from trading in target company securities if the bidder has commenced or has taken substantial steps towards commencement of the bid.

Unlike both the disclose or abstain rule and the misappropriation theory under Rule 10b-5, Rule 14e-3 liability is not premised on breach of a fiduciary duty. There is no need for a showing that the trading party or tipper was subject to any duty of confidentiality, and no need to show that a tipper personally benefited from the tip.

---

[22]   Id.
[23]   Id.

2. Misappropriation

In response to the setbacks it suffered in *Chiarella* and *Dirks*, the SEC began advocating a new theory of insider trading liability: the misappropriation theory. Unlike Rule 14e-3, the SEC did not intend for the misappropriation theory to be limited to tender offer cases (although many misappropriation decisions have in fact involved takeovers). Accordingly, the Commission posited misappropriation as a new theory of liability under Rule 10b-5.

In *US v. O'Hagan*,[24] the Supreme Court endorsed the misappropriation theory as a valid basis for insider trading liability. A fiduciary's undisclosed use of information belonging to his principal, without disclosure of such use to the principal, for personal gain constitutes fraud in connection with the purchase or sale of a security and thus violates Rule 10b-5.

The court acknowledged that misappropriators have no disclosure obligation running to the persons with whom they trade. Instead, it grounded liability under the misappropriation theory on deception of the source of the information: the theory addresses the use of "confidential information for securities trading purposes, in breach of a duty owed to the source of the information."[25] Under this theory, "a fiduciary's undisclosed, self serving use of a principal's information to purchase or sell securities, in breach of a duty of loyalty and confidentiality, defrauds the principal of the exclusive use of that information."[26] So defined, the majority held, the misappropriation theory satisfies § 10(b)'s requirement that there be a "deceptive device or contrivance" used "in connection with" a securities transaction.

II. KEY ELEMENTS OF THE MODERN PROHIBITION

A. Inside versus Market Information

Nonpublic information, for purposes of Rule 10b-5, takes two principal forms: "inside information" and "market information." Inside information typically comes from internal corporate sources and involves events or developments affecting the issuer's assets or earnings. Market information typically originates from sources other than the issuer and involves events or circumstances concerning or affecting the price or market for the issuer's securities and does not concern the issuer's assets or earning power. Under US law, the use of either sort is prohibited.

B. Materiality

Liability arises only with respect to trading on the basis of material information. Materiality is defined for this purpose as whether there is a substantial likelihood that a reasonable investor would consider the omitted fact important in deciding whether to buy or sell securities.[27]

---

[24]   521 U.S. 642 (1997).
[25]   Id. at 652.
[26]   Id.
[27]   Basic Inc. v. Levinson, 485 U.S. 224, 231–32 (1988).

C. Nonpublic Information: When can Insiders Trade?

Insiders may not trade whenever they are in possession of material nonpublic information. When the information in question is disclosed, insiders may trade but only after the information in question has been effectively made public. The information must have been widely disseminated and public investors must have an opportunity to act on it. At a minimum, insiders therefore must wait until the news could reasonably be expected to appear over the major business news wire services.

D. The Requisite Fiduciary Relationship

In neither *Chiarella* nor *Dirks* did Justice Powell lay out a convincing doctrinal basis for premising insider trading liability on a fiduciary relationship. His sole direct reference to precedent merely opined that:

> In the seminal case of *In re Cady, Roberts & Co.*, the SEC recognized that the common law in some jurisdictions imposes on "corporate 'insiders,' particularly officers, directors, or controlling shareholders" an "affirmative duty of disclosure . . . when dealing in securities." The SEC found that . . . breach of this common law duty also establish[ed] the elements of a Rule 10b-5 violation . . . .[28]

While Justice Powell's opinion acknowledged that this common-law duty exists only in "some jurisdictions," he went on—without any explanation or citation of authority—to extrapolate therefrom a rule that all "insiders [are] forbidden by their fiduciary relationship from personally using undisclosed corporate information to their advantage."[29]

Even setting aside the question of how a duty recognized only by "some" states, which historically had not applied to impersonal stock market transactions, suddenly morphed into a national insider trading ban, this formulation posed many difficult questions. For example, did one look to state or federal law to determine whether a particular relationship qualified as fiduciary in nature? The latter answer is suggested by Powell's observation "that '[a] significant purpose of the Exchange Act was to eliminate the idea that use of inside information for personal advantage was a normal emolument of corporate office.'"[30] Justice Powell's repeated references to a "*Cady, Roberts* duty" imply that *Cady, Roberts* created a federal duty prohibiting insider trading. If so, however, a conflict arises between the Supreme Court's insider trading precedents and its holdings on federalism elsewhere in the law of Rule 10b-5.

In *Santa Fe Industries, Inc. v. Green*,[31] the Supreme Court held that Rule 10b-5 is concerned with disclosure and fraud, not with fiduciary duties. The court thus held, for example, that Rule 10b-5 did not reach claims "in which the essence of the complaint is that shareholders were treated unfairly by a fiduciary,"[32] which is the very essence of an insider trading complaint. The court justified that limitation, in part, on grounds that it

---

[28] *Dirks*, 463 U.S. at 653.
[29] Id. at 659.
[30] Id. at 653 n.10.
[31] 430 U.S. 462 (1977).
[32] Id. at 477.

was reluctant "to federalize the substantial portion of the law of corporations that deals with transactions in securities, particularly where established state policies of corporate regulation would be overridden,"[33] which is precisely what the federal insider trading prohibition did.

Dirks and *Chiarella* simply ignored this doctrinal tension. In *O'Hagan,* Justice Ginsburg's majority opinion tried to solve the problem by recharacterizing insider trading as a disclosure issue. It is thus the failure to disclose that one is about to inside trade that is the problem, not the trade itself. Justice Ginsburg's approach fails to solve the problem. Ginsburg accepted Powell's holdings that the duty to disclose had to arise out of a fiduciary relationship. If one is to look to federal law to determine whether a particular relationship is fiduciary in character, one is necessarily invoking the sort of "federal fiduciary standards" whose development *Santa Fe* clearly precludes. As a result, the conceptual conflict between the Supreme Court's current insider trading jurisprudence and its more general Rule 10b-5 precedents remains unresolved.

E.   State of Mind

On its face, the connection between insider trading regulation and the state of mind of the trader or tipper seems intuitive. Insider trading is a form of market abuse: taking advantage of a secret to which one is not entitled, generally in breach of some kind of fiduciary-like duty. Donald Langevoort's chapter in this volume examines both the legal doctrine and the psychology associated with this pursuit. There is much conceptual confusion in how we define unlawful insider trading—the quixotic effort to build a coherent theory of insider trading by reference to the law of fraud, rather than a more expansive market abuse standard—which leads to interesting psychological questions as to the required state of mind. Is it always simple greed? What if there is an element of unconscious misperception—or rationalization—at work? My sense is that the causal explanations for what is charged as insider trading are sometimes quite murky and not easily explained as pure greed. Langevoort thus tries to connect the law of insider trading to a more sophisticated approach to state of mind, motivation, and causation.

F.   The Universe of Potential Defendants

Who is an insider? *O'Hagan* confirms that the attorney–client relationship is a fiduciary one. Dictum in all three Supreme Court precedents tells us that corporate officers and directors are fiduciaries of their shareholders. Subsequent cases make clear that the universe of potential defendants is far more expansive, however.

1.   Insiders
Exchange Act § 16(b)'s short-swing profit provisions apply only to officers, directors, and shareholders owning more than 10 percent of the company's stock. One of the many issues first addressed in the seminal *Texas Gulf Sulphur* case was whether § 10(b) was

---

[33]   Id. at 479.

restricted to that class of persons. The court had little difficulty finding that mid-level corporate employees were insiders for purposes of Rule 10b-5. "Insiders, as directors or management officers are, of course, by this Rule, precluded from [insider] dealing, but the Rule is also applicable to one possessing [nonpublic] information who may not be strictly termed an 'insider' within the meaning of [section] 16(b) of the Act."[34] Although *Chiarella's* rejection of *Texas Gulf Sulphur's* equal access test shrank the universe of potential defendants substantially, the court's reference to an "agent" of the issuing corporation as a proper defendant confirmed that the Rule encompassed all corporate employees, rather than just § 16(b) insiders.

2. Constructive insiders

Not all of a corporation's agents are employees, of course. Accordingly, in *Dirks*, Justice Powell held that certain outsiders' relationship with the issuer qualifies as fiduciary for purposes of the insider trading prohibition:

> Under certain circumstances, such as where corporate information is revealed legitimately to an underwriter, accountant, lawyer, or consultant working for the corporation, these outsiders may become fiduciaries of the shareholders. The basis for recognizing this fiduciary duty is not simply that such persons acquired nonpublic corporate information, but rather that they have entered into a special confidential relationship in the conduct of the business of the enterprise and are given access to information solely for corporate purposes . . . .. For such a duty to be imposed, however, the corporation must expect the outsider to keep the disclosed nonpublic information confidential, and the relationship at least must imply such a duty.[35]

Although *Dirks* clearly requires that the recipient of the information in some way agree to keep it confidential, courts have sometimes overlooked that requirement. In *SEC v. Lund*,[36] for example, Lund and another businessman discussed a proposed joint venture between their respective companies. In those discussions, Lund received confidential information about the other's firm. Lund thereafter bought stock in the other's company. The court determined that by virtue of their close personal and professional relationship, and because of the business context of the discussion, Lund was a constructive insider of the issuer. In doing so, however, the court focused almost solely on the issuer's expectation of confidentiality. It failed to inquire into whether Lund had agreed to keep the information confidential. A subsequent case from the same district court acknowledged that this was an error:

> What the Court seems to be saying in *Lund* is that anytime a person is given information by an issuer with an expectation of confidentiality or limited use, he becomes an insider of the issuer. But under *Dirks*, that is not enough; the individual must have expressly or impliedly entered into a fiduciary relationship with the issuer.[37]

Even this statement does not go far enough, however, because it does not acknowledge the additional requirement of an affirmative assumption of the duty of confidentiality.

---

[34] *SEC v. Texas Gulf Sulphur Co.*, 401 F.2d 833, 848 (2d Cir.), cert denied, 394 U.S. 976 (1968).
[35] *Dirks*, 463 U.S. at 655 n.14.
[36] 570 F. Supp. 1397 (C.D. Cal. 1983).
[37] SEC v. Ingram, 694 F. Supp. 1437, 1440 (C.D. Cal. 1988).

3.   Tippers and tippees

Dirks held that tippees could be held liable, provided two conditions are met: (1) the tipper breached a fiduciary duty to the corporation by making the tip; and (2) the tippee knew or had reason to know of the breach. The requirement that the tip constitute a breach of duty on the tipper's part eliminates many cases in which an insider discloses information to an outsider. For example, no fiduciary obligation is violated by making disclosures for a legitimate corporate purpose.

Indeed, not every disclosure made in violation of a fiduciary duty constitutes an illegal tip. What *Dirks* proscribes is not just a breach of duty, but a breach of the duty of loyalty forbidding fiduciaries to personally benefit from the disclosure. Hence, for example, negligently discussing business confidences in a public place may be careless, but it is not a breach of one's duty of loyalty and thus does not give rise to liability.

4.   Nontraditional relationships

Outside the traditional categories of Rule 10b-5 defendants—insiders, constructive insiders, and their tippees—things become more complicated. Suppose a doctor learned confidential information from a patient, upon which she then traded? Is she an insider? As the Second Circuit observed in *United States v. Chestman*:[38]

> [F]iduciary duties are circumscribed with some clarity in the context of shareholder relations but lack definition in other contexts. Tethered to the field of shareholder relations, fiduciary obligations arise within a narrow, principled sphere. The existence of fiduciary duties in other common law settings, however, is anything but clear. Our Rule 10b-5 precedents . . ., moreover, provide little guidance with respect to the question of fiduciary breach, because they involved egregious fiduciary breaches arising solely in the context of employer/employee associations.[39]

In *Chestman*, the question was whether the relationship between spouses was fiduciary in nature. In answering that question, the court laid out a general framework for dealing with nontraditional relationships. First, unilaterally entrusting someone with confidential information does not by itself create a fiduciary relationship.[40] This is true even if the disclosure is accompanied by an admonition such as "don't tell." Secondly, familial relationships are not fiduciary in nature without some additional element.

Turning to factors that could justify finding a fiduciary relationship on these facts, the court first identified a list of "inherently fiduciary" associations. "Counted among these hornbook fiduciary relations are those existing between attorney and client, executor and heir, guardian and ward, principal and agent, trustee and trust beneficiary, and senior corporate official and shareholder."[41] Once one moves beyond these "hornbook" fiduciary relationships, the requisite relationship exists where one party acts on the other's behalf and "great trust and confidence" exists between the parties:

---

[38]   947 F.2d 551 (2d Cir. 1991) (citations omitted), cert. denied, 503 U.S. 1004 (1992).

[39]   Id. at 567.

[40]   Repeated disclosures of business secrets, however, could substitute for a factual finding of dependence and influence and, accordingly, sustain a finding that a fiduciary relationship existed in the case at bar. Id. at 569.

[41]   Id. at 568.

A fiduciary relationship involves discretionary authority and dependency: One person depends on another—the fiduciary—to serve his interests. In relying on a fiduciary to act for his benefit, the beneficiary of the relation may entrust the fiduciary with custody over property of one sort or another. Because the fiduciary obtains access to this property to serve the ends of the fiduciary relationship, he becomes duty-bound not to appropriate the property for his own use.[42]

Because the spousal relationship did not involve either discretionary authority or dependency of this sort, it was not fiduciary in character.

In 2000, the SEC addressed the *Chestman* issue by adopting Rule 10b5-2, which provides "a nonexclusive list of three situations in which a person has a duty of trust or confidence for purposes of the 'misappropriation' theory . . .." First, such a duty exists whenever someone agrees to maintain information in confidence. Secondly, such a duty exists between two people who have a pattern or practice of sharing confidences such that the recipient of the information knows, or reasonably should know, that the speaker expects the recipient to maintain the information's confidentiality. Thirdly, such a duty exists when someone receives or obtains material nonpublic information from a spouse, parent, child, or sibling. On the facts of *Chestman*, accordingly, Rule 10b5-2 would result in the imposition of liability because Keith received the information from his spouse who, in turn, had received it from her parent. The validity of this expansion of liability from fiduciary relationships to those based purely on contract remains unresolved.

5. Legislators

A sharp controversy the US insider trading laws applied to a special class of nontraditional defendants erupted when a study found evidence of insider trading by members of the US Congress. Over time, nobody beats the market. This basic premise of efficient capital markets theory has been confirmed in numerous academic studies.[43] The only important exception to the rule traditionally has been corporate insiders trading in their own corporation's stock.[44] The obvious and generally accepted explanation for insiders' results is their access to and use of material nonpublic information about the company.[45]

A 2004 study of the results of stock trading by US Senators during the 1990s, however, found that Senators on average beat the market by 12 percent a year.[46] In sharp contrast, US households on average underperformed the market by 1.4 percent a year and even corporate insiders on average beat the market by only about 6 percent a year during that period.[47] A reasonable inference is that some Senators had access to—and were using— material nonpublic information about the companies in whose stock they trade:

---

[42]   Id. at 569.
[43]   Bob Ryan, Corporation Finance and Valuation 84 (2006) ("The empirical evidence is absolutely solid, fund managers cannot out perform the market . . ..").
[44]   Hasan Nejat Seyhun, Investment Intelligence From Insider Trading 312 (2000).
[45]   Id. at 74.
[46]   Alan J. Ziobrowski et al., Abnormal Returns from the Common Stock Investments of the U.S. Senate, 39 J. Fin. & Quant. Anal. 661 (2004).
[47]   Jane J. Kim, U.S. Senators' Stock Picks Outperform the Pro's, Wall. St. J., Oct. 26, 2004, available at http://tinyurl.com/nrwm6r.

Looking at the timing of cumulative returns, the senators also appeared to know exactly when to buy or sell their holdings. Senators would buy stocks just before the shares suddenly would outperform the market by more than 25%. Conversely, senators would sell stocks that had been beating the market by about 25% for the past year just when the shares would fall back in line with the market's performance.

The researchers say senators' uncanny ability to know when to buy or sell their shares seems to stem from having access to information that other investors wouldn't have. "I don't think you need much of an imagination to realize that they're in the know," says Alan Ziobrowski, a business professor at Georgia State University in Atlanta and one of the four authors of the study.[48]

Members of Congress can obtain material nonpublic information in many ways. They can learn inside information when, for example, a company confidentially discloses it during the course of a Congressional hearing or investigation. In most cases, however, members of Congress likely trade on the basis of market information. "'Market information' refers to information that affects the price of a company's securities without affecting the firm's earning power or assets. . . . Examples include information that an investment adviser will shortly issue a 'buy' recommendation or that a large stockholder is seeking to unload his shares or that a tender offer will soon be made for the company's stock."[49] In the present context, examples of market information readily available to members of Congress include knowing that "tax legislation is apt to pass and which companies might benefit," being aware "that a particular company soon will be awarded a government contract or that a certain drug might get regulatory approval . . ."[50]

Commentators disagreed as to whether insider trading by members of Congress was captured by existing US insider trading laws.[51] In this volume, Sung Hui Kim revisits the issue. Specifically, she explores a curious distinction that Henry G. Manne made in his influential 1966 book, *Insider Trading And The Stock Market*. On the one hand, Manne defended corporate insider trading because of its potential to increase share price accuracy and its usefulness as a compensation tool for entrepreneurial innovations. On the other hand, Manne denounced the practice of governmental insider trading, seeing no good reason to compensate government officials on the side and warning against "the ease with which inside information can be utilized as a payoff device." Kim argues that such a bifurcated position is unstable. She contends that, just as governmental insider trading should be viewed as a form of public corruption, corporate insider trading should be viewed as a form of corruption in the private sector. Moreover, she argues that if one examines the reasons why public corruption in the form of governmental insider trading

---

[48]   Id. The extent of Congressional trading on material nonpublic information is uncertain. "Just over a third of the senators bought or sold individual stocks in any one year in the study, and the vast majority of stock transactions were less than $15,000." Id.

[49]   U.S. v. Chiarella, 588 F.2d 1358, 1365 n.8 (2d Cir. 1978), rev'd on other grounds, 445 U.S. 222 (1980).

[50]   Kim, supra note 47.

[51]   Compare Stephen M. Bainbridge, Insider Trading Inside the Beltway, 36 J. Corp. L. 281, 285 (2011) ("Congressional staffers and other government officials and employees could be prosecuted successfully for insider trading under the federal securities laws, but the quirks of the relevant laws almost certainly would prevent Members of Congress from being successfully prosecuted"), with Donna M. Nagy, Insider Trading, Congressional Officials, and Duties of Entrustment, 91 B.U. L. Rev. 1105 (2011) (arguing to the contrary).

is normatively problematic, one sees that similar reasons apply to private corruption in the form of corporate insider trading. Thus, if one rejects governmental insider trading, one has good reason to reject corporate insider trading as well.

J.W. Verret's chapter explores the related issue of trading on the basis of political intelligence. Verret examines the Stop Trading on Congressional Knowledge Act (STOCK Act), which was adopted in the USA in 2012 in response to the allegations discussed above of insider trading by members of Congress on the basis of nonpublic information obtained through their elected position. Verret offers a critique of the STOCK Act, demonstrating three key flaws.[52] The STOCK Act grafts a fiduciary duty relationship created in a distinctly different context, corporate law, into the relationship between Congress and the taxpayer in a way that makes enforcement of the Act potentially either under-inclusive or over-inclusive of the behavior the Act's drafters sought to prevent. He demonstrates how these problems also apply to the Act's application to government employees. Verret also shows how the Act's reference to existing law under Section 10b-5 will introduce a raft of uncertainty as doctrines developed therein, such as the misappropriation doctrine, extend the reach of the Act to outsiders, like political intelligence traders, that the Act ostensibly sought to exclude.

G.   Recent Developments

Stephen Diamond's chapter in this volume discusses the dismissal of a senior Facebook employee in connection with the purchase of Facebook shares on a private resale trading platform prior to the Facebook IPO, which raised new concerns about secondary trading in the securities of private companies and insider trading. After exploring those issues, Diamond suggests that startup companies consider adopting a variation on the standard insider trading policy widely adopted by public companies. The case study is especially important in light of new attention being paid by regulators to insider trading as well as an ongoing debate in Congress about barriers to raising capital for smaller companies. Joan Heminway's chapter describes the interrelationship between gender and US insider trading law and explores (anecdotally and through extensions of existing gender studies outside the insider trading realm) the potential roles and significance of gender in that context. Although women have become more visible as participants in the securities markets and as alleged and actual transgressors of insider trading rules, the role of gender and women in insider trading is still poorly understood, except anecdotally. Accordingly, Heminway argues, the portrait of the insider trader as a woman is a work in progress to which targeted research can make significant contributions.

Volume editor Stephen Bainbridge's chapter argues that the narrowing of the scope of insider trading liability effect by the Supreme Court's decisions in *Chiarella* and *Dirks* met substantial resistance from the SEC and the lower federal courts. Through both regulatory actions and judicial opinions, the SEC and the lower courts gradually chipped away at the

---

[52]   Kim's chapter also discusses the STOCK Act, but her analysis deliberately extends beyond trading by members of Congress to consider the liability of state legislators and the relationships between Congressional and private insider trading from a policy perspective.

fiduciary duty rationale. In recent years, moreover, the trend has accelerated, with several developments having substantially eviscerated the fiduciary duty requirement. After tracing those developments, Bainbridge argues that the current unsettled state of insider trading jurisprudence necessitates rethinking the foundational premises of that jurisprudence from first principles. He argues that the correct rationale for regulation insider trading is protecting property rights in information. Although that rationale obviously has little to do with the traditional concerns of securities regulation, he further argues that the SEC has a sufficiently substantial competitive advantage over private parties and state enforcers in detecting and prosecuting insider trading that it should retain jurisdiction over the offense.

III.   GLOBALIZATION OF INSIDER TRADING LAW

Today, all countries with developed capital markets limit insider trading to some extent. In many respects, however, this is a relatively recent phenomenon. A generation ago, the United States was virtually alone in aggressively prosecuting insider trading and even today US insider trading law remains the most restrictive legal regime. Global restrictions on the practice thus have largely come about as other jurisdictions converge on the US model. In this volume, a number of contributors focus on insider trading laws in key securities markets around the world.[53]

A.   Australasia

Keith Kendall and Gordon Walker's chapter in this volume traces the evolution of the present insider trading regime in Australia, highlighting some contentious issues with that regime and noting the aggressive enforcement of insider trading laws in that country. Australia was the first jurisdiction in the world to eliminate the requirement for a connection—fiduciary, contractual, or otherwise—with the subject company. Since the 1990s, Australia has prohibited "any person" from trading on inside information regardless of any connection with the subject company. Thus, Australia can be regarded as the most longstanding of those jurisdictions—others being Singapore, Malaysia, and New Zealand—that have adopted the "any person" regime.

The insider trading laws of one of those jurisdictions—i.e., New Zealand—are described and analyzed by Gordon Walker and Andrew Simpson's chapter. New Zealand's first comprehensive statutory regime banning insider trading was introduced in 1988. This regime, as amended, persisted until 2008. Generally speaking, the 1988–2008 laws on insider trading in New Zealand are regarded as a failure due to the initial absence of enforcement power by the regulator and poor design. In 2008, New Zealand adopted a version of Australian insider trading laws pursuant to which "any person" in possession of inside information is prohibited from trading. Walker and Simpson review the 1988–2008 regime and then outline the statutory prohibitions applying since 2008. They

---

[53]   At the risk of semantic confusion, the term "insider dealing" is used in this volume in lieu of the US term "insider trading" when preferred by authors writing about non-US jurisdictions.

conclude by noting the absence of any prosecutions under the present regime and suggest some reasons for this phenomenon.

B.   China

Nicholas Howson's contribution to this volume presents a general introduction to the current law and regulation of insider trading in the People's Republic of China, and the reality of enforcement against insider trading in China's domestic capital markets. His analysis focuses on the extremely broad scope of insider trading liability created under nonpublic "guidance" formulated by the Chinese securities regulator, which guidance departs significantly from the more narrowly drawn insider trading prohibition established in China's 2006 Securities Law. Although the statute establishes a combination of the classical/fiduciary duty plus misappropriation theories for liability, the agency guidance—both formally and in application—results in liability for those trading while merely in possession of inside information.

Hui Huang's chapter also provides an in-depth and updated analysis of insider trading regulation in China, looking at both the law "in the books" and "in action." Beginning in the early 1990s, China has gradually set up a regulatory regime for insider trading in line with international experiences. Twenty years on, Huang examines the effectiveness of China's insider trading regime. He critically examines the key elements of insider trading law, as well as its theoretical basis in light of recent cases, from a comparative perspective. He then reports the results of an empirical study of China's insider trading cases to provide insight into public and private enforcement of the law, and, based on the findings, makes relevant suggestions to improve the efficacy of insider trading regulation in China.

C.   Europe

Kern Alexander's chapter analyzes UK law governing insider trading and how it has evolved in recent years. Although the substantive law has generally remained the same, UK authorities are increasing investigations and enforcement to counter the reputation of the City of London as a rather "light touch" jurisdiction that has tolerated market misconduct. Insider dealing is a criminal offense defined under Part V of the Criminal Justice Act 1993. In contrast, market abuse is a civil offense as set forth in sections 118–123 of the Financial Services and Markets Act 2000. Alexander reviews the UK insider dealing law and analyzes some related issues concerning the difficulty and complexity of its application. He then discusses the UK market abuse offense and its development under the EU Directive on Insider Dealing and Market Manipulation. His final section discusses recent efforts by the UK Financial Services Authority to increase investigations and enforcement and to develop a more proactive posture in dealing with market misconduct in UK financial markets.

Katja Langenbucher's chapter provides an overview of EU insider trading law, which thus far consists of one core and two implementing directives, with proposals for a regulation and a directive pending. The European Court of Justice has heard three cases on insider trading law, while a fourth was pending at the time of writing. In discussing these laws and cases, Langenbucher argues that European law views insider trading as a form of market abuse that hinders prompt disclosure. This approach is reflected in the Directive's

technical setup, as the existence of inside information automatically triggers both a prohibition on insider trading and a disclosure requirement.

Matthijs Nelemans and Michael Schouten's chapter analyzes the European regulatory
framework with respect to insider trading in the context of takeover bids. They distinguish
between trading by the bidder, by the target, and by classical insiders such as officers and
employees, and where relevant compare EU law with US federal securities laws. First,
they address the issue of precisely when information about potential takeover bids qualifies as inside information. Secondly, they address the prohibition on selectively sharing
inside information with third parties, the prohibition on tipping, and the obligation to
make public disclosure. Thirdly, they analyze the extent to which bidders are permitted to
build a stake in the target prior to announcement of the offer. In connection therewith,
Nelemans and Schouten also discuss the prohibition of target companies and classical
insiders to trade on information regarding a pending offer. Finally, they discuss reporting obligations in respect of inside trades. Their analysis suggests that European insider
trading laws are insufficiently tailored for corporations, and that significant uncertainty
remains as to the precise scope of the prohibition on insider trading in the context of
takeover bids.

D.   Japan

Mark Ramseyer's contribution to this volume begins by explaining that, following World
War II, the US-controlled occupation authority imposed an American-style securities
statute on Japan. The US statute did not ban insider trading at the time, so neither did the
new Japanese law. When the US courts developed the prohibition of insider trading in the
1960s, Japanese regulators and courts did not follow their lead. As late as the mid-1980s,
Japan thus had left insider trading largely unregulated.

In 1988, the Japanese Diet adopted a statute that banned and criminalized insider
trading. Rather than use a vague rule like the US's Rule 10b-5, the Japanese law carefully specified which investors, which trades, and which contexts would trigger the ban.
In 2004, it added an administrative surcharge regime. Commentators in Japan ostensibly
urged the Diet to adopt the bill because they hoped to restore investor confidence in the
stock market. If the ban restored investor confidence, it did not show. Shortly after the
ban took effect, the Japanese stock market collapsed.

IV.   EMPIRICAL RESEARCH

In this volume, Laura Beny and Nejat Seyhun investigate whether the increase in enforcement actions against insider trading by the SEC and the Department of Justice in recent
years is a response to increased illegal insider trading activity. They examine the pricing
of common stocks and options around the announcement of tender offers to detect the
presence of illegal insider trading, so as to determine whether illegal insider trading occurs
before tender offers and whether illegal insider trading has become more rampant over
time. Their findings suggest that the pre-takeover announcement run-up in stock prices
has become larger over time. During the 2006–2011 sub-period, the pre-bid run-up was
50 percent higher than in the pre-2006 period. They also find that toehold investments by

bidders do not explain the time-series variation in stock price behavior around takeovers. In contrast, the increases in the implied volatility of the options on target stock they find are consistent with increasing illegal insider trading.

Laura Beny's solo chapter uses data from a cross-section of countries between 1980 and 1999 to find that a country's political system—not its legal or financial system—best explains its proclivity to regulate insider trading. Specifically, more democratic nations enacted and enforced insider trading laws earlier than less democratic nations, controlling for wealth, financial development, legal origin, and other factors. Furthermore, controlling for the same factors, left-leaning governments were latecomers to insider trading legislation and enforcement relative to right-leaning and centrist governments.

According to Beny, these results are generally consistent with the political theory of capital market development and inconsistent with the legal origins theory of capital market development. They also challenge theoretical claims that insider trading restrictions are market-inhibiting because the kinds of governments that appear more inclined to regulate insider trading are precisely the governments that are generally thought to pursue market-promoting policies.

Alexandre Padilla's chapter offers a critique of the broader empirical literature about the effects of insider trading laws on capital markets. He argues that while the literature shows that, statistically, insider trading laws positively affect capital market development, this correlation does not actually prove that insider trading is harmful to markets. In addition, he argues that many of the benefits of insider trading laws might translate in the long run into costs resulting in more shareholders' expropriation. Building on Hayek's work on understanding the role of the price system as a mechanism to economize on information and, more particularly, on local knowledge, he argues that allowing insider trading could under certain circumstances reduce shareholders' expropriation on the part of corporate management. Finally, Padilla suggests possible new lines of empirical research to address the questions raised in the chapter.

V.   THE POLICY DEBATE

Insider trading's modern normative jurisprudence began with the 1966 publication of Henry Manne's *Insider Trading And The Stock Market*. Manne contended that insider trading promotes market efficiency and creates efficient incentives for innovative corporate managers. In reply, defenders of an insider trading ban typically have relied either on fairness arguments or claims that insider trading has substantial economic costs.

A.   The Case for Deregulation

Manne identified two principal ways in which insider trading benefits society and/or the firm in whose stock the insider traded. First, he argued that insider trading causes the market price of the affected security to move towards the price that the security would command if the inside information were publicly available. If this is so, both society and the firm benefit through increased price accuracy. Secondly, he posited insider trading as an efficient way of compensating managers for having produced information. If this is so, the firm benefits directly (and society indirectly) because managers have a greater incentive to produce additional information of value to the firm.

1.   Insider trading and efficient pricing of securities

Although US securities laws purportedly encourage accurate pricing by requiring disclosure of corporate information, they do not require the disclosure of all material information. Where disclosure would interfere with legitimate business transactions, disclosure by the corporation is usually not required unless the firm is dealing in its own securities at the time. When a firm withholds material information, however, the market can no longer accurately price its securities.

Manne essentially argued that insider trading is an effective compromise between the need for preserving incentives to produce information and the need for maintaining accurate securities prices. Suppose a firm, the stock of which currently sells at fifty dollars per share, has discovered new information that, if publicly disclosed, would cause the stock to sell at sixty dollars. Absent insider trading or leaks, the stock's price will remain at fifty dollars until the information is publicly disclosed and then rapidly rise to the correct price of sixty dollars. If insiders trade on this information, however, the price of the stock will gradually rise towards the correct price. Thus, insider trading acts as a replacement for public disclosure of the information, preserving market gains of correct pricing while permitting the corporation to retain the benefits of nondisclosure.[54]

Despite the anecdotal support for Manne's position provided by *Texas Gulf Sulphur* and similar cases, empirical evidence on the point remains scanty. Early market studies indicated insider trading had an insignificant effect on price in most cases.[55] Subsequent studies suggested the market reacts fairly quickly when insiders buy securities, but the initial price effect is small when insiders sell.[56] These studies are problematic, however, because they relied principally (or solely) on the transactions reports corporate officers, directors, and 10 percent shareholders are required to file under Section 16(a). Because insiders are unlikely to report transactions that violate Rule 10b-5, and because much illegal insider trading activity is known to involve persons not subject to the § 16(a) reporting requirement, conclusions drawn from such studies may not tell us very much about the price and volume effects of illegal insider trading. Accordingly, it is significant that a study of SEC insider trading cases found that the defendants' insider trading led to quick price changes.[57] That result supports Manne's empirical claim, subject to the caveat that reliance on data obtained from SEC prosecutions arguably may not be conclusive as to the price effects of undetected insider trading due to selection bias, although the study in question admittedly made strenuous efforts to avoid any such bias.

Turning to theory, the anonymity of impersonal market transactions makes it far

---

[54]   Henry Manne, Insider Trading And The Stock Market 77–91 (1966).

[55]   See Roy A. Schotland, Unsafe at Any Price, 53 Va. L. Rev. 1425, 1443 (1967) (citing studies).

[56]   Dan Givoly & Dan Palmon, Insider Trading and the Exploitation of Inside Information: Some Empirical Evidence, 58 J. Bus. 69 (1985).

[57]   Lisa Meulbrock, An Empirical Analysis of Illegal Insider Trading, 47 J. Fin. 1661 (1992).

from obvious that insider trading will have any effect on prices. Suppose an insider buys stock on good news. The supply of stock remains constant (assuming the company is not in the midst of a stock offering or repurchase), but demand has increased, so a higher equilibrium price should result. Because a given security represents only a particular combination of expected return and systematic risk, for which there is a vast number of substitutes, the correct measure for the supply of securities thus is not simply the total of the firm's outstanding securities, but the vastly larger number of securities with a similar combination of risk and return. Accordingly, the supply/demand effect of a relatively small number of insider trades should not have a significant price effect. Over the portion of the curve observed by individual traders, the demand curve should be flat rather than downward sloping.

Instead, if insider trading is to affect the price of securities it is through the derivatively informed trading mechanism of market efficiency. Derivatively informed trading affects market prices through a two-step mechanism. First, those individuals possessing material nonpublic information begin trading. Their trading has only a small effect on price. Some uninformed traders become aware of the insider trading through leakage or tipping of information or through observation of insider trades. Other traders gain insight by following the price fluctuations of the securities. Finally, the market reacts to the insiders' trades and gradually moves towards the correct price. The problem is that while derivatively informed trading can affect price, it functions slowly and sporadically. Given the inefficiency of derivatively informed trading, many observers doubt whether market efficiency provides a robust justification for allowing insider trading.

Having said that, however, in this volume Alexandre Padilla offers a critique of the empirical literature on the effects insider trading laws have on capital markets. He argues that many of the purported benefits of regulating insider trading put forward by proponents of the prohibition are actually harmful for markets. His chapter argues that, although the literature shows that there is a statistically significant correlation between insider trading laws and capital market development, this correlation does not actually prove that insider trading is harmful to markets. In addition, he argues that regulation leads to unintended consequences that might be averted if insider trading was allowed or, at least, if the decision whether to allow or ban it was left to securities markets. Building on Hayek's work on understanding the role of local knowledge in enabling an efficient price system he provides a modern version of Manne's argument that allowing insider trading will enhance the price system.

2.   Insider trading as an efficient compensation scheme

Manne's other principal argument against the ban on insider trading rested on the claim that allowing insider trading was an effective means of compensating entrepreneurs in large corporations. Manne distinguished corporate entrepreneurs from mere corporate managers. The latter simply operate the firm according to predetermined guidelines. By contrast, an entrepreneur's contribution to the firm consists of producing new valuable information. The entrepreneur's compensation must have a reasonable relation to the value of his contribution to give him incentives to produce more information. Because it is rarely possible to ascertain information's value to the firm in advance, predetermined compensation, such as salary, is inappropriate for entrepreneurs. Instead, claimed Manne, insider trading is an effective way to compensate entrepreneurs for innovations. The increase in the price of the security following public disclosure provides an imperfect but comparatively accurate measure of the value of the innovation to the firm. The entrepreneur can recover the value of his discovery by purchasing the firm's securities prior to disclosure and selling them after the price rises.[58]

Manne argued salary and bonuses provide inadequate incentives for entrepreneurial inventiveness because they fail to accurately measure the value to the firm of innovations. Query, however, whether insider trading is any more accurate. Even assuming the change in stock price accurately measures the value of the innovation, the insider's compensation is limited by the number of shares he can purchase. This, in turn, is limited by his wealth. As such, the insider's trading returns are based, not on the value of his contribution, but on his wealth.

Another objection to the compensation argument is the difficulty of restricting trading to those who produced the information. Where information is concerned, production costs normally exceed distribution costs. As such, many firm agents may trade on the information without having contributed to its production.

A related criticism is the difficulty of limiting trading to instances in which the insider actually produced valuable information. In particular, why should insiders be permitted to trade on bad news? Allowing managers to profit from inside trading reduces the penalties associated with a project's failure because trading managers can profit whether the project succeeds or fails. If the project fails, the manager can sell his shares before that information becomes public and thus avoid an otherwise certain loss. The manager can go beyond mere loss avoidance into actual profit making by short selling the firm's stock. A final objection to the compensation thesis follows from the contingent nature of insider trading. Because the agent's trading returns cannot be measured in advance, neither can the true cost of his reward. As a result, selection of the most cost-effective compensation package is made more difficult. Moreover, the agent himself may prefer a less uncertain compensation package. If an agent is risk averse, he will prefer the certainty of a $100,000 salary to a salary of $50,000 and a 10 percent chance of a bonus of $500,000 from insider trading. Thus, the shareholders and the agent would gain by exchanging a guaranteed bonus for the agent's promise not to trade on inside information.

In this volume, we are honored to have Manne contribute a chapter in which he revisits and updates the compensation argument. Manne remains concerned with using compensation to properly incentivize entrepreneurs, especially in large, publicly held corporations, where he argues discovery and unpredictable innovation indisputably take place despite the literature's fascination with startups. The puzzling question is how such firms compensate entrepreneurs. Manne reviews developments in compensation practices in the years since he first broached the subject and concludes that none have solved the basic problem of optimizing entrepreneurial incentives. Instead, he argues, they serve as second best substitutes for allowing insiders to trade on the basis of information they develop. Despite the concerns raised above, Manne thus contends that the current compensation regime is equally flawed. No system can be perfect and

---

[58]   Manne, supra note 54, at 131–41.

insider trading offers many advantages as a way of creating firm-wide incentives to innovate.

B.   The Case for Regulation

1.   Fairness

There is a widely shared view that there is something inherently sleazy about insider trading. As a California court put it, insider trading is "a manifestation of undue greed among the already well-to-do, worthy of legislative intervention if for no other reason than to send a message of censure on behalf of the American people."[59]

Given the draconian penalties associated with insider trading, however, such vague and poorly articulated notions of fairness surely provide an insufficient justification for the prohibition. Fairness can be defined in various ways. Most of these definitions, however, collapse into the various efficiency-based rationales for prohibiting insider trading. We might define fairness as fidelity, for example, by which I mean the notion that an agent should not cheat her principal. But this argument only has traction if insider trading is in fact a form of cheating, which in turn depends on how we assign the property right to confidential corporate information. Alternatively, we might define fairness as equality of access to information, as many courts and scholars have done, but this definition must be rejected in light of *Chiarella*'s rejection of the *Texas Gulf Sulphur* equal access standard. Finally, we might define fairness as a prohibition of injuring another. But such a definition justifies an insider trading prohibition only if insider trading injures investors, which seems unlikely. Accordingly, fairness concerns do little to advance the case for banning insider trading.

2.   Injury to investors

An investor who trades in a security contemporaneously with insiders having access to material nonpublic information likely will allege injury in that he sold at the wrong price; i.e., a price that does not reflect the undisclosed information. If a firm's stock currently sells at $10 per share, but after disclosure of the new information will sell at $15, a shareholder who sells at the current price thus will claim a $5 loss.

The investor's claim, however, is fundamentally flawed. It is purely fortuitous that an insider was on the other side of the transaction. The gain corresponding to the shareholder's loss is reaped not just by inside traders, but by all contemporaneous purchasers whether they had access to the undisclosed information or not.[60]

Granted, the investor might not have sold if he had had the same information as the insider, but even so the rules governing insider trading are not the source of his problem. On an impersonal trading market, neither party knows the identity of the person with whom he is trading. Thus, the seller has made an independent decision to sell without

[59]   Friese v. Superior Court, 36 Cal.Rptr.3d 558, 566 (Cal. App. 2005).

[60]   Granted, insider trading results in outside investors as a class reaping a smaller share of the gains from new information. William Wang, Trading on Material Nonpublic Information on Impersonal Stock Markets: Who Is Harmed, and Who Can Sue Whom Under SEC Rule 10b-5?, 54 S. Cal. L. Rev. 1217 (1981) (positing the "law of conservation of securities").

knowing that the insider is buying; if the insider were not buying, the seller would still sell. It is thus the nondisclosure that causes the harm, rather than the mere fact of trading.[61]

The information asymmetry between insiders and public investors arises out of the mandatory disclosure rules allowing firms to keep some information confidential even if it is material to investor decision making. Unless immediate disclosure of material information is to be required, a step the law has been unwilling to take, there will always be winners and losers in this situation. Irrespective of whether insiders are permitted to inside trade or not, the investor will not have the same access to information as the insider. It makes little sense to claim that the shareholder is injured when his shares are bought by an insider, but not when an outsider buys them without access to information. To the extent the selling shareholder is injured, his injury thus is correctly attributed to the rules allowing corporate nondisclosure of material information, not to insider trading. A more sophisticated argument is that the price effects of insider trading induce shareholders to make poorly advised transactions. It is doubtful whether insider trading produces the sort of price effects necessary to induce shareholders to trade, however. As noted earlier, while derivatively informed trading can affect price, it functions slowly and sporadically. Given the inefficiency of derivatively informed trading, price or volume changes resulting from insider trading will only rarely be of sufficient magnitude to induce investors to trade.

Assuming for the sake of argument that insider trading produces noticeable price effects, however, and further assuming that those effects mislead some investors, the inducement argument remains flawed because many transactions would have taken place regardless of the price changes resulting from insider trading. Investors, who would have traded irrespective of the presence of insiders in the market, benefit from insider trading because they transacted at a price closer to the correct price; i.e., the price that would prevail if the information were disclosed. In any case, it is hard to tell how the inducement argument plays out when investors are examined as a class. For any given number who decide to sell because of a price rise, for example, another group of investors may decide to defer a planned sale in anticipation of further increases.

An argument closely related to the investor injury issue is the claim that insider trading undermines investor confidence in the securities market. In the absence of a credible investor injury story, it is difficult to see why insider trading should undermine investor confidence in the integrity of the securities markets.

In sum, neither investor protection nor maintenance of confidence have much traction as theoretical justifications for any prohibition of insider trading. Nor do they have much explanatory power with respect to the prohibition currently on the books. An investor's rights vary widely depending on the nature of the insider trading transaction, the identity of the trader, and the source of the information. Yet, if the goal is investor protection, why should these considerations be relevant?

Recall, for example, *United States v. Carpenter*.[62] R. Foster Winans wrote the Wall

---

[61]   On an impersonal exchange, moreover, the precise identity of the seller is purely fortuitous and it is difficult to argue that the seller who happened to be matched with the insider has been hurt more than any other contemporaneous seller whose sale was not so matched.

[62]   United States v. Carpenter, 791 F.2d 1024, 1026–27 (2d Cir. 1986), aff'd, 484 U.S. 19 (1987).

Street Journal's "Heard on the Street" column, a daily report on various stocks that is said to affect the price of the stocks discussed. Journal policy expressly treated the column's contents prior to publication as confidential information belonging to the newspaper. Despite that rule, Winans agreed to provide several co-conspirators with prepublication information as to the timing and contents of future columns. His fellow conspirators then traded in those stocks based on the expected impact of the column on the stocks' prices, sharing the profits. In affirming their convictions, the Second Circuit anticipated *O'Hagan* by holding that Winans's breach of his fiduciary duty to the Wall Street Journal satisfied the standards laid down in *Chiarella* and *Dirks*. From either an investor protection or confidence in the market perspective, however, this outcome seems bizarre at best. For example, any duties Winans owed in this situation ran to an entity that had neither issued the securities in question nor even participated in stock market transactions. What Winans's breach of his duties to the Wall Street Journal has to do with the federal securities laws, if anything, is not self-evident.

The incongruity of the misappropriation theory becomes even more apparent when one considers that its logic suggests that the Wall Street Journal could lawfully trade on the same information used by Winans. If we are really concerned with protecting investors and maintaining their confidence in the market's integrity, the inside trader's identity ought to be irrelevant. From the investors' point of view, insider trading is a matter of concern only because they have traded with someone who used their superior access to information to profit at the investors' expense. As such, it would not appear to matter whether it is Winans or the Journal on the opposite side of the transaction. Both have greater access to the relevant information than do investors.

The logic of the misappropriation theory also suggests that Winans would not have been liable if the Wall Street Journal had authorized his trades. In that instance, the Journal would not have been deceived, as *O'Hagan* requires. Winans' trades would not have constituted an improper conversion of nonpublic information, moreover, so that the essential breach of fiduciary duty would not be present. Again, however, from an investor's perspective, it would not seem to matter whether Winans's trades were authorized or not. Finally, conduct that should be lawful under the misappropriation theory is clearly proscribed by Rule 14e-3. A takeover bidder may not authorize others to trade on information about a pending tender offer, for example, even though such trading might aid the bidder by putting stock in friendly hands. If the acquisition is to take place by means other than a tender offer, however, neither Rule 14e-3 nor the misappropriation theory should apply. From an investor's perspective, however, the form of the acquisition seems just as irrelevant as the identity of the inside trader.

All of these anomalies, oddities, and incongruities have crept into the federal insider trading prohibition as a direct result of *Chiarella*'s imposition of a fiduciary duty requirement. None of them, however, are easily explicable from either an investor protection or a confidence in the market rationale.

3.   Injury to the issuer

Unlike many forms of tangible property, more than one person can use information without necessarily lowering its value. If a manager who has just negotiated a major contract for his employer then trades in his employer's stock, for example, there is no reason to believe that the manager's conduct necessarily lowers the value of the contract to the employer. But while insider trading will not always harm the employer, it may do so in some circumstances.

a.   Delay   If a manager discovers or obtains information (either beneficial or detrimental to the firm), she may delay disclosure of that information to other managers so as to assure herself sufficient time to trade on the basis of that information before the corporation acts upon it. Even if the period of delay by any one manager is brief, the net delay produced by successive trading managers may be substantial. Unnecessary delay of this sort harms the firm in several ways. The firm must monitor the manager's conduct to ensure timely carrying out of her duties. It becomes more likely that outsiders will become aware of the information through snooping or leaks. Some outsider may even independently discover and utilize the information before the corporation acts upon it. Although delay is a plausible source of harm to the issuer, its importance is easily exaggerated. The available empirical evidence scarcely rises above the anecdotal level, but does suggest that measurable delay attributable to insider trading is rare.[63] Given the rapidity with which securities transactions can be conducted in modern secondary trading markets, moreover, a manager need at most delay corporate action long enough for a five minute telephone conversation with her stockbroker. Delay (either in transmitting information or taking action) also often will be readily detectable by the employer. Finally, and perhaps most importantly, insider trading may create incentives to release information early just as often as it creates incentives to delay transmission and disclosure of information.

b.   Interference with corporate plans   Trading during the planning stage of an acquisition is a classic example of how insider trading might adversely interfere with corporate plans. If managers charged with overseeing an acquisition buy shares in the target, and their trading has a significant upward effect on the price of the target's stock, the takeover will be more expensive. If their trading causes significant price and volume changes, that also might tip off others to the secret, interfering with the bidder's plans, as by alerting the target to the need for defensive measures.

The risk of premature disclosure poses an even more serious threat to corporate plans. The issuer often has just as much interest in when information becomes public as it does in whether the information becomes public. Suppose Target, Inc., enters into merger negotiations with a potential acquirer. Target managers who inside trade on the basis of that information will rarely need to delay corporate action in order to effect their purchases. Having made their purchases, however, the managers now have an incentive to cause disclosure of Target's plans as soon as possible. Absent leaks or other forms of derivatively informed trading, the merger will have no price effect until it is disclosed to the market, at which time there usually is a strong positive effect. Once the information is disclosed, the trading managers will be able to reap substantial profits, but until disclosure takes place, they bear a variety of firm-specific and market risks. The deal, the stock market, or both may collapse at any time. Early disclosure enables the managers to minimize those risks by selling out as soon as the price jumps in response to the announcement.

---

[63]   Michael P. Dooley, Enforcement of Insider Trading Restrictions, 66 Va. L. Rev. 1, 34 (1980).

If disclosure is made too early, a variety of adverse consequences may result. If disclosure triggers competing bids, the initial bidder may withdraw from the bidding or demand protection in the form of costly lock-ups and other exclusivity provisions. Alternatively, if disclosure does not trigger competing bids, the initial bidder may conclude that it overbid and lower its offer accordingly. In addition, early disclosure brings the deal to the attention of regulators and plaintiffs' lawyers earlier than necessary. Although insider trading probably only rarely causes the firm to lose opportunities, it may create incentives for management to alter firm plans in less drastic ways to increase the likelihood and magnitude of trading profits. For example, trading managers can accelerate receipt of revenue, change depreciation strategy, or alter dividend payments in an attempt to affect share prices and insider returns. Alternatively, the insiders might structure corporate transactions to increase the opportunity for secret keeping. Both types of decision may adversely affect the firm and its shareholders. Moreover, this incentive may result in allocative inefficiency by encouraging over-investment in those industries or activities that generate opportunities for insider trading.

c. Injury to reputation   Insider trading by corporate managers supposedly casts a cloud on the corporation's name, injures stockholder relations, and undermines public regard for the corporation's securities.[64] Reputational injury of this sort could translate into a direct financial injury by raising the firm's cost of capital. Because shareholder injury is a critical underlying premise of the reputational injury story, however, this argument would appear to collapse at the starting gate. As we have seen, it is very hard to create a plausible shareholder injury story.

C.   A Public Choice Theory Analysis of Insider Trading Regulation

Some critics of the insider trading prohibition contend that the prohibition can be explained by a public choice-based model of regulation in which rules are sold by regulators and bought by the beneficiaries of the regulation.[65] On the supply side, the federal insider trading prohibition may be viewed as the culmination of two distinct trends in the securities laws. First, as do all government agencies, the SEC desired to enlarge its jurisdiction and enhance its prestige. Administrators can maximize their salaries, power, and reputation by maximizing the size of their agency's budget. A vigorous enforcement program directed at a highly visible and unpopular law violation is surely an effective means of attracting political support for larger budgets. Given the substantial media

---

[64]   Compare Diamond v. Oreamuno, 248 N.E.2d 910, 912 (N.Y. 1969) (discussing threat of reputational injury) with Freeman v. Decio, 584 F.2d 186, 194 (7th Cir. 1978) (arguing that injury to reputation is speculative).

[65]   This section focuses on slightly different, but wholly compatible, stories about insider trading told by Professor Michael Dooley and Professors David Haddock and Jonathan Macey. Dooley's version explains why the SEC wanted to sell insider trading regulation, while Haddock and Macey's explains to whom it has been sold. See MICHAEL P. DOOLEY, FUNDAMENTALS OF CORPORATION LAW 816–57 (1995); David D. Haddock and Jonathan R. Macey, *Regulation on Demand: A Private Interest Model, with an Application to Insider Trading*, 30 J.L. & Econ. 311 (1987); see also JONATHAN R. MACEY, INSIDER TRADING: ECONOMICS, POLITICS, AND POLICY (1991).

attention directed towards insider trading prosecutions, and the public taste for prohibiting insider trading, it provided a very attractive subject for such a program.

Secondly, during the prohibition's formative years, there was a major effort to federalize corporation law. In order to maintain its budgetary priority over competing agencies, the SEC wanted to play a major role in federalizing matters previously within the state domain. Insider trading was an ideal target for federalization. Rapid expansion of the federal insider trading prohibition purportedly demonstrated the superiority of federal securities law over state corporate law. Because the states had shown little interest in insider trading for years, federal regulation demonstrated the modernity, flexibility, and innovativeness of the securities laws. The SEC's prominent role in attacking insider trading thus placed it in the vanguard of the movement to federalize corporate law and ensured that the SEC would have a leading role in any system of federal corporations law.

The validity of this hypothesis is suggested by its ability to explain the SEC's devotion of significant enforcement resources to insider trading during the 1980s. During that decade, the SEC embarked upon a limited program of deregulating the securities markets. Among other things, the SEC adopted a safe harbor for projections and other soft data, the shelf registration rule, and the integrated disclosure system, and expanded the exemptions from registration under the Securities Act. At about the same time, however, it adopted a vigorous enforcement campaign against insider trading. Not only did the number of cases increase substantially, but the SEC adopted a "big bang" approach under which it focused on high visibility cases that would produce substantial publicity. In part this may have been due to an increase in the frequency of insider trading, but the public choice story nicely explains the SEC's interest in insider trading as motivated by a desire to preserve its budget during an era of deregulation and spending restraint.

The public choice story also explains the SEC's continuing attachment to the equal access approach to insider trading. The equal access policy generates an expansive prohibition, which federalizes a broad range of conduct otherwise left to state corporate law, while also warranting a highly active enforcement program. As such, the SEC's use of Rule 14e-3 and the misappropriation theory to evade *Chiarella* and *Dirks* makes perfect sense. By these devices, the SEC restored much of the prohibition's pre-*Chiarella* breadth and thereby ensured that its budget-justifying enforcement program would continue unimpeded.

Turning to the demand side, the insider trading prohibition appears to be supported and driven in large part by market professionals, a cohesive and politically powerful interest group, which the current legal regime effectively insulates from insider trading liability. Only insiders and quasi-insiders such as lawyers and investment bankers have greater access to material nonpublic information than do market professionals. By basing insider trading liability on breach of fiduciary duty, and positing that the requisite fiduciary duty exists with respect to insiders and quasi-insiders but not with respect to market professionals, the prohibition protects the latter's ability to profit from new information about a firm.

When an insider trades on an impersonal secondary market, the insider takes advantage of the fact that the market maker's or specialist's bid-ask prices do not reflect the value of the inside information. Because market makers and specialists cannot distinguish insiders from non-insiders, they cannot protect themselves from being taken advantage of in this way. When trading with insiders, the market maker or specialist thus will always be on the wrong side of the transaction. If insider trading is effectively prohibited, however, the market professionals are no longer exposed to this risk.

Professional securities traders likewise profit from the fiduciary duty-based insider trading prohibition. Because professional investors are often active traders, they are highly sensitive to the transaction costs of trading in securities. Prominent among these costs is the specialist's and market maker's bid-ask spread. If a ban on insider trading lowers the risks faced by specialists and market makers, some portion of the resulting gains should be passed on to professional traders in the form of narrower bid-ask spreads. Analysts and professional traders are further benefited by a prohibition on insider trading, because only insiders are likely to have systematic advantages over market professionals in the competition to be the first to act on new information. Market professionals specialize in acquiring and analyzing information. They profit by trading with less well-informed investors or by selling information to them. If insiders can freely trade on nonpublic information, however, some portion of the information's value will be impounded into the price before it is learned by market professionals, which will reduce their returns.

Circumstantial evidence for the demand-side hypothesis is provided by SEC enforcement patterns. In the years immediately prior to *Chiarella*, enforcement proceedings often targeted market professionals. The frequency of insider trading prosecutions rose dramatically after *Chiarella* held insider trading was unlawful only if the trader violated a fiduciary duty owed to the party with whom he trades. Yet, despite that increase in overall enforcement activity, there was a marked decline in the number of cases brought against market professionals.

In his contribution to this volume, Todd Henderson updates the public choice analysis recounted above. Henderson documents a significant change in the target of enforcement in civil and criminal cases, finding that over the past three decades the emphasis of enforcement has shifted more towards securities market professionals instead of corporate insiders. Is the enforcement of insider trading laws in the public interest? One approach to answering this question is to examine the pattern of enforcement to see if it is better explained by a public interest account or by the balance of private interests with a stake in the enforcement of these laws. As described above, David Haddock and Jonathan Macey took stock of insider trading laws in the early 1980s, and concluded that it was best explained by a private interest account. They observed the pattern of enforcement emphasized prosecuting corporate executives instead of securities trading professionals, but noted a more even treatment in cases involving corporate takeovers. This was best explained by the fact that at the time corporate insiders had little stake in insider trading enforcement in light of their paucity of trading activity, but were threatened by corporate takeovers. Henderson's chapter updates the Haddock and Macey account by tracking the changes to private interests since 1983 and seeing whether they explain the current pattern of enforcement. Securities professionals are much more likely to be prosecuted today, both in civil and criminal cases, and this can be explained by the fact that corporate insiders now trade in much greater amounts and the threat from trading as a takeover device is stronger. Henderson therefore concludes that the private interest account fits as well today as it did three decades ago.

D.   An Alternative Disclosure-Based Regime

Thomas Lambert's contribution to this volume begins by arguing that insider trading may create both social harms and social benefits. Attempts to regulate such "mixed bag" business practices may err in two directions. They may wrongly permit or encourage socially undesirable instances of the practice at issue. Alternatively, they may wrongly condemn or deter socially desirable instances. Attempts to avoid error in one direction or another (error costs) by heightening the liability inquiry will tend to increase the regulatory regime's administrative costs (decision costs). Decision theory therefore calls for regulating mixed bag practices under a regime that minimizes the sum of error and decision costs.

Adjudged under the decision-theoretic criterion, Lambert argues, both the current regime for regulating insider trading in the United States and the more restrictive approach apparently favored by enforcement agencies are failures. The "contractarian" approach favored by many law and economics scholars would represent an improvement over both approaches, but it, too, may be suboptimal.

Lambert therefore advocates an optional, disclosure-based regulatory regime. Such an approach would (1) enhance the market efficiency benefits of insider trading by facilitating "trade decoding," while (2) reducing potential costs stemming from deliberate mismanagement, disclosure delays, and infringement of informational property rights.

PART 1

US LAW AND POLICY

2. Launching the insider trading revolution: *SEC v. Capital Gains Research Bureau*
A.C. Pritchard

Securities and Exchange Commission v. Capital Gains Research Bureau, Inc.[1] marked the resurgence of the SEC in the Supreme Court, sparking a decade-long winning streak there. The *Capital Gains* decision, although turning on an interpretation of the Investment Advisers Act of 1940,[2] also gave the green light to the SEC to push the boundaries of its power in other areas. Moreover, *Capital Gains* suggested that the SEC could expand its power through agency and judicial interpretation of existing statutes and regulation, without resorting to the cumbersome rulemaking process under the Administrative Procedure Act, or, still more daunting, seeking legislation. After its victory in *Capital Gains*, the SEC would push an aggressive interpretation of § 10(b) of the Exchange Act in the lower courts, particularly the Second Circuit, to crack down on insider trading. This chapter uncovers the seeds of the SEC's insider trading crusade in *Capital Gains* and how that opinion influenced subsequent securities jurisprudence.

I proceed as follows. Section I provides background on the SEC and its relationship with the Supreme Court prior to *Capital Gains*. Section II follows the SEC's *Capital Gains* enforcement action as it made its way up through the district court and the Second Circuit. Section III explores how the case unfolded in the Supreme Court. Section IV then assesses *Capital Gains'* long-term impact. A brief Conclusion follows.

I. BACKGROUND

A generation before the *Capital Gains* decision, the fledgling SEC had put itself at the center of the nation's political discourse. A voting public weary of the deprivation and misery of the Great Depression cheered as the SEC went after the Wall Street fat cats. William O. Douglas catapulted to national prominence during the New Deal as chairman of the SEC by bringing the New York Stock Exchange to heel in the wake of the Richard Whitney scandal.[3] The SEC stayed in the headlines during its long fight to dismantle the giant public utility empires under the mandate of the Public Utility Holding Company Act ("PUHCA"). The agency enjoyed an enviable record of success in the high court, losing only two out of thirteen PUHCA cases decided;[4] overall, the agency lost only three

---

[1] 375 U.S. 180 (1963).
[2] 54 Stat. 847, as amended 15 U.S.C. § 80b-1 et seq.
[3] Bruce Allen Murphy, Wild Bill 136–154 (2003).
[4] SEC v. Chenery (Chenery I), 318 U.S. 80 (1943); American Power and Light Co. v. SEC, 325 U.S. 385 (1945). The *Chenery I* defeat was essentially undone by the Court four years later when

cases out of twenty-five between 1936 and 1955.[5] After the Supreme Court decided the last of that string of PUHCA cases, the SEC's involvement in cases at the Court went into a marked decline. The Court decided only three securities cases of any kind between 1956 and 1960; two of those were per curiam.[6]

That dearth of securities litigation reflected the SEC's diminished role.[7] By the 1950s, the public utilities had been brought low and the campaign to tame Wall Street was a rapidly fading memory. The SEC was no longer the prominent political actor that it had been in the 1930s under the leadership of Douglas. World War II, which saw government and business join hands in the effort to defeat the totalitarian threats of Germany and Japan, reduced the SEC to a political afterthought. The agency, deemed "non-essential" to the war effort, saw itself downsized and exiled to Philadelphia, not to return to Washington until 1948. The agency's return from exile did not signal a return to relevance. The Truman and Eisenhower administrations had other political priorities, and the SEC chairmen appointed by those presidents were not fueled by the ambition that had driven Douglas in that role a generation earlier.

The 1960s—and the election of John F. Kennedy—marked the beginning of a new era for the administrative agencies and a rejuvenated SEC. Kennedy called on James Landis—a New Deal SEC chairman—to draft a report outlining reforms for the administrative agencies.[8] Landis urged that more money be allocated to the SEC, but more generally, he called for rejuvenated leadership by "gradually restaffing [the agencies] with men who, because of their competence and their desire to fulfill the legislative mandates described in the basic statutes establishing these agencies, will inspire a sense of devotion to and pride in the public service by their many employees."[9] At the SEC, the new leadership called for by Landis came in the form of William Cary. The Columbia corporate law professor was Kennedy's second choice, called upon after Harvard's Louis Loss, the dean of securities scholars, had turned Kennedy down.[10] Despite being Kennedy's second choice, Cary had strong links to the SEC's New Deal glory days: Cary had been a student in one of Professor William O. Douglas's last corporate finance classes, and he later went to work for Chairman Douglas at the SEC.[11] Things were going to happen at the SEC on Cary's watch; Cary signaled his intent to push the agency in a more activist direction shortly after his arrival. Cary's opinion for the Commission in *Cady, Roberts & Co.*[12] announced in unmistakable fashion the agency's newfound commitment to interpreting

---

the case returned to the Court. SEC v. Chenery (Chenery II), 332 U.S. 194 (1947). Engineers Public Service v. SEC, 332 U.S. 788 (1947), was rendered moot by a settlement.

[5]   The SEC's additional loss was Jones v. SEC, 298 U.S. 1 (1936). This decision pre-dated Franklin Delano Roosevelt's New Deal transformation of the Court.

[6]   SEC v. La. Pub. Ser. Comm'n, 353 U.S. 368 (1957) (per curiam); SEC v. Variable Annuity Life Ins., 359 U.S. 65 (1959); Dyer v. SEC, 359 U.S. 499 (1959) (per curiam).

[7]   See generally Joel Seligman, The Transformation of Wall Street 241–289 (3rd Ed. 2003).

[8]   James M. Landis, Report on Regulatory Agencies to the President-Elect (December 1960).

[9]   Id. at 1. Of direct relevance to *Capital Gains*, Landis called for greater regulation of investment advisers, "many of whom have morals not exceeding those of tipsters at the race track." Id. at 33.

[10]   Seligman, supra note 7, at 291.

[11]   Id. at 293.

[12]   40 SEC 907 (1961).

broadly its statutory mandate. In *Cady, Roberts*, the Commission interpreted Rule 10b-5 of the Exchange Act to prohibit insider trading. The Commission had adopted Rule 10b-5 two decades earlier under its § 10(b) authority as a general anti-fraud prohibition, but the rule (and statute) makes no mention of insider trading. Notwithstanding this omission, the SEC found in *Cady, Roberts* that the partner of a brokerage firm had violated Rule 10b-5 when he traded on non-public information. The partner had learned, in his role as a director of a public company, that the company was planning to cut the size of its dividend. In concluding that the partner had violated Rule 10b-5, Cary set out a broad standard for the insider trading prohibition:

> The obligation rests on two principal elements; first, the existence of a relationship giving access, directly or indirectly, to information intended to be available only for a corporate purpose and not for the personal benefit of anyone, and second, the inherent unfairness involved where a party takes advantage of such information knowing it is unavailable to those with whom he is dealing.[13]

These elements are conspicuously absent from the text of either Rule 10b-5 or § 10(b). Cary gave notice that in interpreting "[the] elements [of § 10(b)] under the broad language of the anti-fraud provisions we are not to be circumscribed by fine distinctions and rigid classifications."[14] Thus, Cary announced the SEC's intent to root out information asymmetries in the secondary markets to protect "the buying public" "from the misuse of special information."[15] The securities laws would be interpreted as needed to achieve that goal; statutory literalism would not be an impediment. But Cary's broad vision of the SEC's authority had not yet been validated by a court. The respondents in *Cady, Roberts* did not seek review of the agency's order, so it remained to be seen whether Cary's novel interpretation of § 10(b) would withstand judicial scrutiny.

There were potential landmines waiting for the SEC's insider trading initiative. Just a month after the SEC handed down *Cady, Roberts* it argued before the Supreme Court in *Blau v. Lehman*.[16] *Blau* involved the interpretation of the "short-swing" profits rule of § 16(b) of the Exchange Act. Despite the focus on insider trading during the hearings that led to the adoption of the Exchange Act, § 16(b) is the only Exchange Act provision, as it was adopted by Congress in 1934, that deals explicitly with insider trading.

The facts of *Blau* bore some similarities to *Cady, Roberts*. At issue was whether the knowledge of a Lehman Brothers partner, Thomas, who was serving as a director of a public company, Tide Water, could be attributed to the investment bank.[17] If Lehman was charged with Thomas's knowledge, then the bank's profits from trading in Tide Water's stock would be subject to disgorgement. The district court found that Thomas had not shared his knowledge of Tide Water's affairs with his Lehman partners.[18] The Second Circuit affirmed the decision over the dissent of Judge Charles Clark.[19]

---

[13] Id. at 912 (footnote omitted).
[14] Id.
[15] Id. at 913.
[16] 368 U.S. 403 (1962).
[17] Id. at 404–406.
[18] Id. at 407.
[19] Blau v. Lehman, 286 F.2d 786 (2nd Cir. 1960), and id. at 793 (Clark, J., dissenting).

Clark plays a central role in our tale, and his background suggested that he would be predisposed to the SEC's arguments. Clark was the former dean of the Yale Law School, where he had been a colleague of William O. Douglas. Clark, like Douglas, was a committed New Dealer.[20] Moreover, he had worked for the SEC part time for a brief period at Douglas's behest.[21] The two remained friends[22] notwithstanding a falling out when Douglas persuaded Clark to endorse Roosevelt's Court-packing plan while Douglas remained silent.[23] In fact, Clark had hoped that Douglas would succeed him as dean at Yale, but that hope was dashed by Douglas's appointment to the Supreme Court.[24] Clark's judicial philosophy, like Douglas's, allowed plenty of room for judges to chart a novel course: "We need the unprincipled decision, *i.e.*, the unprecedented and novel decision . . . to mark judicial progress."[25]

Clark's *Blau* dissent stressed that the courts should defer to the SEC. When the case was initially decided, he fretted that the SEC's views were not solicited.[26] After the decision came down, the SEC petitioned for leave to participate as amicus and to file a petition for rehearing, and Clark lobbied hard to have the case heard.[27] When the petition was denied, Clark was nearly apoplectic. He complained that the majority's opinion "leaves this important area of the law almost ludicrously uncertain. . . . My own criticisms uttered in my dissent have remained unanswered and have now, as is apparent, the support of the S.E.C."[28] Worse yet, the Second Circuit's rule built "unfair discrimination" "into an important remedial statute—a discrimination substantially eliminating the great Wall Street trading firms from the statute's operations."[29]

Clark's populist tone evidently struck a chord with the Supreme Court, as seven justices

---

[20]   Clark was best known as the architect of the Federal Rules of Civil Procedure, which had been adopted in 1938 when Clark was serving as the head of the Federal Rules Advisory Committee. Charles E. Clark, The New Federal Rules of Civil Procedure: The Last Phase— Underlying Philosophy Embodied in Some of the Basic Provisions of the New Procedure, 23 A.B.A. J. 976 (1937).

[21]   Seligman, supra note 7, at 111.

[22]   William O. Douglas, Charles E. Clark, 73 Yale L.J. 3, 3 (1963).

[23]   Murphy, supra note 3, at 129.

[24]   Letter from Charles Clark to Arthur B. Darling (March 20, 1939), Charles E. Clark Papers, Series I, Box 1, Folder 2, Yale University Library, Manuscripts and Archives (hereinafter Clark Papers) ("There was one blow to my plans which came in today when Bill Douglas was named to the Supreme Court, for I had expected, as seemed rather likely, that he would succeed me as dean."). In this same letter, Clark was rather prescient in predicting that Douglas would chafe under the confines of the bench. Id. ("Douglas is one of the ablest and sincerest persons I know, and it is a grand thing to have so young and vigorous a person on the bench, unless indeed one believes that he could have done more elsewhere. . . . It is hard to think of so vigorous a personality as Douglas confined so young.")

[25]   Charles E. Clark, A Plea for the Unprincipled Decision, 49 Va. L. Rev. 660, 665 (1963).

[26]   *Blau*, 286 F.2d at 796 (Clark, J., dissenting) ("[I]t would seem to me that at least before we dispose of this vastly important issue we should ask the S.E.C. for its informed comments.")

[27]   Memo of Charles Clark to J.E.L., S.R.W., L.P.M., H.J.F., J.J.S. (Jan. 13,1961), Clark Papers, Series II, Box 45, Folder 186 ("May I suggest that, even if some of our colleagues do not want the real help the Commission can give here, I do feel some surprise and chagrin that they are willing to prevent those who do from receiving it.")

[28]   *Blau*, 286 F.2d at 799 (Clark, J., dissenting from denial of rehearing *in banc*).

[29]   Id.

voted to grant certiorari.[30] When *Blau* came to the Supreme Court, the SEC, alongside its allies in the plaintiffs' bar, urged that § 16(b) be read broadly "on policy grounds."[31] According to the SEC, Thomas's knowledge should be attributed to the partnership and Lehman Brothers "should be held liable even though it is neither a director, officer, nor a 10% stockholder."[32] The agency's argument was weakened, however, by its concession that "such an interpretation is not justified by the literal language of § 16(b)."[33] The Court noted the breadth of the SEC's argument: "The argument of . . . the Commission seems to go so far as to suggest that § 16(b)'s forfeiture of profits should be extended to include all persons realizing 'short swing' profits who either act on the basis of 'inside' information or have the possibility of 'inside' information."[34] Shades of *Cady, Roberts*? The SEC's preferred construction would have broadened § 16(b) to make it a general prohibition against insider trading.

The Court, while acknowledging the SEC's "persuasive policy arguments that the [Exchange] Act should be broadened in this way to prevent 'the unfair use of information' more effectively," declined the SEC's invitation to ignore § 16's language.[35] Amending the statute, according to the Court majority, was not its job: "Congress can and might amend § 16(b) if the Commission would present to it the policy arguments it has presented to us, but we think that Congress is the proper agency to change an interpretation of the Act unbroken since its passage, if the change is to be made."[36] In other words, lofty policy goals would not allow an end run around plain statutory text. The Court insisted on adherence to the statutory text despite an impassioned dissent from the Court's resident securities expert, Justice Douglas, who echoed Clark's moralistic tone. Douglas complained that the majority had "sanction[ed], as vested, a practice so notoriously unethical as profiting on inside information."[37] For the SEC, the *Blau* opinion offered scant hope that the Supreme Court would be receptive to the free-ranging method of statutory interpretation deployed by Chairman Cary in *Cady, Roberts*.

II.   THE LOWER COURT OPINIONS

The SEC had not yet launched its campaign against insider trading when it brought an enforcement action against Capital Gains Research Bureau, Inc. and its owner, Harry P. Schwarzmann.[38] The facts of the case placed it in the nebulous area between pure omissions and misleading half-truths. Capital Gains published a newsletter, "Capital Gains

---

[30]   Blau v. Lehman, No 66, Docket Sheet (April 21, 1961) ("Grant: All but Stewart and Black who voted to deny"), Earl Warren Collection, Box 375, Library of Congress.

[31]   *Blau*, 368 U.S. at 410.

[32]   Id. at 410–411.

[33]   Id. at 411.

[34]   Id.

[35]   Id.

[36]   Id. at 413.

[37]   Id. at 414 (Douglas, J., dissenting).

[38]   A detailed history of the enforcement action can be found in Arthur Laby, SEC v. Capital Gains Research Bureau and the Investment Advisers Act of 1940, 91 B. U. L. Rev. 1051, 1056–1059 (2011).

Report," which it distributed to approximately 5,000 subscribers. The newsletter high-lighted a number of stocks in each issue, generally predicting an increase in price.[39] The SEC alleged that on a number of occasions the defendants had purchased shares in the companies recommended in advance of the distribution of the newsletter.[40] The stocks increased in price and trading volume after the distribution of the newsletter and Capital Gains liquidated its positions within a week or two thereafter.[41] The SEC argued that the failure by Capital Gains to disclose its purchases and subsequent sales violated § 206 of the Investment Advisers Act, which makes it unlawful (1) "to employ any device, scheme or artifice to defraud any client or prospective client" or (2) "to engage in any transac-tion, practice, or course of business which operates as a fraud or deceit upon any client or prospective client."[42]

The district court denied the SEC's motion for a preliminary injunction, concluding that § 206(1) and (2) used "the words 'fraud' and 'deceit'. . . in their technical sense."[43] The trial court's use of the word "technical" would come to have important implications. What did the court mean by "technical"? Apparently, something close to common law notions of deceit. For § 206(2) to be satisfied, the SEC would have to show that Capital Gains' clients had lost money as a result of Capital Gains' sales. For § 206(1) to be satisfied, the SEC would have to show that Capital Gains intended to cause its clients loss.[44] The district court's discussion ignores the possibility that a fiduciary duty might give rise to a duty of disclosure, i.e., equitable notions of fraud like those found in the SEC's *Cady, Roberts* decision. Instead, the district court read § 206 as incorporating traditional common law notions of fraud involving material misrepresentations.

The SEC appealed to the Second Circuit. In a case in which the agency was pushing the boundaries of its authority, the panel it drew did not bode well. The panel consisted of two Eisenhower appointees, Leonard Moore and Sterry Waterman,[45] and, the lone bright spot for the SEC, Charles Clark, the dissenter in *Blau*.

Judge Moore wrote the opinion for the panel upholding the district court's denial of the injunction.[46] The SEC won a minor victory with the court's holding that the district court was wrong in requiring the SEC to show actual losses to investors, necessarily reject-ing the narrowest version of common law fraud in interpreting § 206. Nonetheless, the majority opinion appeared to require an affirmative misrepresentation by the defendant, not simply secret profits: "The test is not gain or loss. It is whether the recommendation was honest when made."[47] How could the court determine if the recommendation was honest? As Moore wrote to his colleagues, "the advice may be tainted with self-interest, but such a fact cannot be assumed or inferred. It must be established by proof such as

---

[39]   *Capital Gains*, 375 U.S. at 182–183.

[40]   SEC v. Capital Gains Research Bureau, Inc., 300 F.2d 745, 747 (2nd Cir. 1961). In one case, Capital Gains had sold short the shares of a company that received a negative recommendation.

[41]   Id.

[42]   15 U.S.C. § 80b-6(1) & (2).

[43]   SEC v. Capital Gains Research Bureau, Inc., 191 F. Supp. 897 (1961).

[44]   Id. at 899.

[45]   Federal Judicial Center, History of the Federal Judiciary, available at www.fjc.gov (last visited November 8, 2012).

[46]   *Capital Gains*, 300 F.2d at 746, 751.

[47]   Id. at 749.

deliberate misstatements of fact or belief that a stock had a dismal rather than bright future."[48] A dishonest recommendation would be actionable under § 206, but undisclosed actions would not be actionable, as long as those actions were not inconsistent with that recommendation.

Were Capital Gains' purchases and sales inconsistent with its recommendations? The SEC urged that "the failure to disclose to clients to whom purchase was recommended that they (defendants), too, had made purchases, constituted a scheme to defraud by failing to disclose a material fact."[49] What was the material fact? The SEC argued that Capital Gains' "advice to buy was dishonest and fraudulent" because it failed to disclose the advisers' intention to sell its stock in the near future.[50] This characterization of the SEC's allegation sounds in misleading omission; there is no mention of fiduciary duty here.

The nature of the SEC's allegations becomes murky, however, when the court concedes that there can be no "serious dispute that a relationship of trust and confidence should exist between the adviser and the advised."[51] Does the existence of a fiduciary duty alter when a misleading omission becomes actionable? Apparently not; a fiduciary duty would not necessarily carry a corresponding disclosure obligation. The duty of trust and confidence would be violated only by intentional acts of disloyalty, such as the investment adviser's "failure to disclose that he was being paid to tout a stock."[52] Moore distinguished the SEC's recent *Cady, Roberts* decision as involving a situation "where inside or so-called confidential information was possessed by one party to the transaction which was not disclosed to the other."[53] Why that relationship would give rise to an affirmative duty of disclosure, while the relationship of an investment adviser to client would not, is left unclear in Moore's opinion. Query why the presence of an affirmative statement should preclude a parallel fiduciary duty of disclosure.

Given the fragility of the distinctions drawn by Moore, his final rationale for the court's decision may have been the most telling: the need for rulemaking.

> [W]hat the SEC would have the court do here is to create a law which Congress has never enacted or a regulation which the SEC has never promulgated which, in effect, would prohibit investment advisers or their employees from purchasing or selling any of the many stocks covered by their services.[54]

The SEC would have disclaimed any inference that its preferred interpretation would sweep as broadly as Moore suggested. The uncertainty over the contours of the SEC's interpretation of § 206, however, only reinforced the need for the specificity that a formal rulemaking could provide. And rulemaking was certainly feasible; just three days after *Capital Gains* was argued before the appellate judges, the SEC announced a proposal to

---

[48]   Memorandum of LPM, SEC v. Capital Gains Research (Oct. 17, 1961), Clark Papers, Series II, Box 55, Folder 262.

[49]   *Capital Gains*, 300 F.2d at 747.

[50]   Id. at 748.

[51]   Id. at 749.

[52]   Id.

[53]   Id.

[54]   Id.

amend its rules under the Investment Advisers Act to require recordkeeping of securities transactions by investment advisers and their personnel.[55] If the SEC could require recordkeeping, it could require disclosure.

Judge Waterman also emphasized the need for rulemaking in his memo to his colleagues on the panel. That need was made more acute by Waterman's perception of prevailing industry practice:

> I know of no outfit that discloses what it proposes to do about the stock it or its officers may happen to own when it advises you and me what to do with our money. If the SEC wants to go into this field—and perhaps it should—it should get out some rules first.[56]

Despite his agreement with Moore on the need for rulemaking, Waterman concurred only in the result, offering no rationale for his separate position.

Judge Moore's opinion provoked a dissent from Clark that echoed his shrill tone in *Blau*. The majority had "endorse[d] and in effect validate[d] a distressingly low standard of business morality," a result that "top advisers . . . not only do not desire, but find rather shocking, in the doubt thus cast upon the good faith and loyalty of their profession."[57] Clark worried about a lemons problem; loyal advisers, argued Clark, needed to be safeguarded "against the stigma of unscrupulous tipsters and touts."[58] Unlike Moore, Clark placed considerable weight on the conclusion that an investment adviser was a fiduciary, whose "first duty . . . is loyalty to his beneficiary; if he is engaged in feathering his own nest, he cannot be giving his client that wholly disinterested advice which it is his stock in trade to provide."[59]

The SEC petitioned for rehearing en banc, which was met by dueling memos from Clark and Moore.[60] Moore's position was weakened, however, by the position of Waterman, who had only concurred in the original result, apparently because Moore had rejected a number of his suggestions.[61] That three-way split was sufficient to induce a majority in favor of rehearing en banc to clarify the situation.[62] Ultimately, only Moore voted to deny the petition.[63]

What followed was a heated debate among the judges of the Second Circuit on the role

---

[55]   SEC, Investment Advisers Act of 1940, Rel. No 120 (Oct. 16, 1961), Clark Papers, Series II, Box 55, Folder 262.

[56]   Memorandum of SRW, SEC v. Capital Gains Research (Oct. 19, 1961), Clark Papers, Series II, Box 55, Folder 262.

[57]   *Capital Gains*, 300 F.2d at 751 (Clark, J., dissenting).

[58]   Id. at 752.

[59]   Id.

[60]   Memorandum of CEC, SEC v. Capital Gains Research (Jan. 17, 1962) & Memorandum of LPM, SEC v. Capital Gains Research (Jan. 17, 1962), Clark Papers, Series II, Box 55, Folder 262.

[61]   Memorandum of SRW, SEC v. Capital Gains Research (Jan. 22, 1962), Clark Papers, Series II, Box 55, Folder 262.

[62]   Memorandum of I[rving] R. K[aufman], SEC v. Capital Gains Research (Jan. 22, 1962) & Memorandum of T[hurgood] M[arshall], SEC v. Capital Gains Research (Jan. 22, 1962), Clark Papers, Series II, Box 55, Folder 262 (both citing three-way result as reason for granting en banc review).

[63]   Order Granting Petition for Rehearing In Banc, SEC v. Capital Gains Research (Jan. 23, 1962), Clark Papers, Series II, Box 55, Folder 262.

of statutory interpretation in expanding the boundaries of the securities laws. At oral argument, Judge Henry Friendly pressed the SEC's counsel on the history of § 206. If § 206 was modeled on § 17(a) of the Securities Act, why had Congress omitted the second clause of § 17(a), which makes it an offense "to obtain money or property by means of any untrue statement of a material fact or any omission to state a material fact necessary in order to make statements made, in light of the circumstances under which they were made, not misleading"?[64] Judges Waterman and Lumbard wondered why the SEC had not adopted "simple rules" requiring disclosure of the trading alleged to be fraudulent, while Judge Moore complained of the unfairness of not providing the defendant with notice.[65]

Clark, seizing the initiative, launched the first memo to his colleagues just two days after oral argument.[66] He focused on Friendly's question about the omission from § 206 of the language from § 17(a)(2) of the Securities Act. The rationale for its exclusion, according to Clark, was that it was unnecessary. Investment advisers do not deal directly with their clients, so including a clause relating to obtaining money or property through misrepresentation or omission "would have been a waste of ink and effort."[67] Section 206 was not aimed at common law deceit of this sort, but rather "to impose fiduciary obligations on those who serve as investment advisers."[68] Clark also rejected the argument that the SEC should have promulgated a rule, as "quite frankly judicial legislation amending the statute, since the statute is directly prohibitory."[69] Clark urged deference:

> The SEC is indeed unfortunate in having to bring its regulatory processes before so conservative a court as ours; I wonder if any other federal appellate court would give the Commission a like run-around. I believe we should let it get on with its heavy tasks without the kind of judicial harassment it has here received.[70]

Clark retained his New Deal faith in the expertise of agencies.

Friendly, a prominent proponent of agency rulemaking,[71] was quick to respond.[72] He echoed Moore and Waterman's earlier arguments in urging that Congress's 1960 amendment of § 206 to add rulemaking authority in subsection (4) allowed "the SEC [to] accomplish everything it seeks."[73] In Friendly's view, both a "device, scheme or artifice to defraud" and a "transaction, practice or course of business which operates as a fraud or deceit" if "read in their ordinary sense" were lacking—the defendants did not believe

---

[64]   Clark Argument Notes (Feb. 21, 1962), Clark Papers, Series II, Box 55, Folder 262.

[65]   Id.

[66]   Supplemental Memo on Rehearing *in Banc*, CEC, SEC v. Capital Gains Research (Feb. 23, 1962), Clark Papers, Series II, Box 55, Folder 262.

[67]   Id. at 3.

[68]   Id. at 3–4.

[69]   Id. at 4. Clark contrasted § 10(b). Id. at 5. ("When Congress wanted to make a provision not self-executing, but dependent on the adoption of regulations, it knew how to do it expressly, as it did in § 10(b) of the Securities Exchange Act of 1934.")

[70]   Id. at 5.

[71]   Henry J. Friendly, The Federal Administrative Agencies: The Need for Better Definitions of Standards (1962).

[72]   Memorandum of HJF, SEC v. Capital Gains Research (Feb. 26, 1962), Clark Papers, Series II, Box 55, Folder 262.

[73]   Id. at 1.

that their sales would depress the price of the securities to the detriment of their customers.[74] Friendly, like Moore, was looking for badges of intentional fraud. Friendly invoked *Blau*—handed down by the Supreme Court just the month before—as a caution "against judicial expansion of provision of the securities laws to accomplish objectives believed to be salutary."[75] He also scoffed at "the liberal use of such terms as 'fiduciaries'—making people who sell an advisory service sound like trustees of an express trust."[76] Friendly urged that the differences between § 17(a) and § 206 must have had some purpose: "nothing could have been easier than to prohibit the giving of advice which contained 'any untrue statement of a material fact or any omission' etc."[77] Indeed, the SEC had included similar language when it adopted Rules 10b-5 and 15c 1-2.[78] Friendly then went on to present an extended history of Congress's amendment to § 206 in 1960, from which he concluded that the power the SEC sought in this case had previously been absent from § 206, but was now available to the agency through rulemaking pursuant to § 206(4).[79] For Friendly, Congress's omission of "omission" from § 206 had interpretive consequences, and labeling the investment adviser a fiduciary could not alter that conclusion.

The other Second Circuit judges quickly picked sides. Deference to regulatory agencies had clear ideological overtones and the judges on the Second Circuit were closely split—four of the judges (Lumbard, Waterman, Moore, and Friendly) had been appointed by President Dwight Eisenhower, one had been appointed by Roosevelt (Clark), who had recently been joined by three Kennedy appointees (Irving Kaufman, Paul Hays, and Thurgood Marshall). The remaining judge, John Smith, had been appointed to the district court by Roosevelt before being elevated to the appellate court by Eisenhower.[80]

Clark was quickly joined by Kaufman, Marshall, and Smith in voting to reverse. Kaufman was sharply critical of the notion that the SEC should be required to issue regulations in advance of enforcement:

> I cannot subscribe to any notion that the S.E.C. is in any way limited in its enforcement of Section 206 to the issuance of regulations prior to initiation of court action. It has been effectively pointed out that in the area of fraud and deception there can be no all-encompassing regulations. The S.E.C. should not be required to spell out the activities prohibited by the statutes any more than the courts have been made to lay down comprehensive definitions of fraud for common law purposes.[81]

Marshall's brief memo rejected the notion that "[r]egulative statutes [could be] circumscribed by common law principles."[82] Smith argued that Capital Gains' trading may have

---

[74]   Id. at 2.
[75]   Id.
[76]   Id.
[77]   Id. at 3.
[78]   Id. at 4.
[79]   Id. at 5–7. Friendly pointedly chided the SEC for its failure to research this legislative history "which the SEC has not 'had time' to do in the 15 months this case has been pending." Id. at 1.
[80]   Federal Judicial Center, History of the Federal Judiciary, supra note 45.
[81]   Memorandum of IRK, SEC v. Capital Gains Research, at 2 (Feb. 27, 1962), Clark Papers, Series II, Box 55, Folder 262.
[82]   Memorandum of TM, SEC v. Capital Gains Research (Feb. 28, 1962), Clark Papers, Series II, Box 55, Folder 262.

influenced the market price,[83] or at least that the court should defer to the SEC on this point. "That such purchases and sales had some effect upon the market price of the securities is vigorously asserted by the commission, an agency presumably possessed of some expertise in the area and whose views should consequently not lightly be brushed aside."[84]

Soon the tide turned, however, with the remaining judges siding with Friendly. Hays was swayed by Friendly's reading of the legislative history, which persuaded him that "Congress did not intend to include in the statute as originally enacted such subtleties as this failure to disclose an adverse interest."[85] Waterman wrote at length to explain his disagreement with Moore's original opinion and reasons for voting to affirm.[86] Waterman disagreed with Moore's original opinion because he thought "Capital Gains' advice might well affect the price of stock," but Moore declined to delete the opinion's discussion suggesting that a market effect was unlikely.[87] Waterman nonetheless voted to affirm, disagreeing with Clark on the ethical issues: "I think it inevitable that an honest man honestly advising someone who is paying him for the advice is also entitled to handle his own private affairs as he chooses."[88] He was also skeptical of the SEC's understanding of market customs. "The releases of no advisory services known to me, the SEC lawyer to the contrary notwithstanding, discloses in any way what the corporation or its officers or its directors intend to do about the stock they recommend, or what holdings are owned in that stock by it or them."[89] Capital Gains' trading was not fraudulent, in Waterman's view, "but instead, at the worst . . . a device by which Capital Gains could make a dollar for itself without costing its clients anything."[90] Waterman was not inclined to defer to the SEC on questions of practice in the securities industry. Given this "common practice," he concluded that "the stock transactions of the defendant were not clearly fraudulent

---

[83] Memorandum of JJS, SEC v. Capital Gains Research, at 2 (Feb. 28, 1962), Clark Papers, Series II, Box 55, Folder 262 ("[I]n each instance of trading by Capital Gains, there is the distinct possibility that the concealed purchase, by reducing the presently available shares, may have adversely affected the price paid by clients of the service. This is a hidden addition to the fee charged the client. In addition, it may well have been true that at least some of the shares sold by Capital Gains were purchased by subscribers or others acting upon the recommendation of Capital Gains. . . .")

[84] Id.

[85] Memorandum of PRH, SEC v. Capital Gains Research (March 1, 1962), Clark Papers, Series II, Box 55, Folder 262.

[86] Memorandum of SRW, SEC v. Capital Gains Research (March 1, 1962), Clark Papers, Series II, Box 55, Folder 262.

[87] Id. at 2.

[88] Id.

[89] Id. See also id. at 4. ("I think what the defendant did in this case is less odious than the acts committed by losing defendants in the earlier cases involving parallel sections of the security acts. One reason for my belief is that all large investment advisers as well as large brokers and dealers regularly trade in the securities about which they advise or in which they deal. Secondly, it seems to be the custom of the trade for even brokers merely to state they 'may or may not have a position in the securities which they recommend.'") Indeed, Waterman believed that purchasing ahead of the recommendation was validation that the recommendation was bona fide: "a purchaser of an advisory service would not think much of the advisory service or the person running it if the advisory service personnel would not buy if the recommendation was to buy." Id. at 3.

[90] Id. at 1.

or clearly a breach of trust by it to its subscribers."[91] Accordingly, "this proceeding . . . should not have been brought until after the promulgation of a rule."[92] The day after Waterman circulated his memo, Moore wrote tersely, "I vote to affirm."[93] With the court split 4–4, Lumbard, the chief judge weighed in, voting to affirm.[94]

Only after all the votes were in was the SEC heard from again. Judge Friendly had inquired of the SEC's counsel why there was no analogue to § 17(a)(2) of the Securities Act in § 206 of the Investment Advisers Act. The SEC's response to Friendly's question was essentially, "We don't know."[95] Oddly enough, this response failed to sway any of the judges in the majority. Nor did Clark's personal lobbying of Hays in an effort to bring him back to the side of the Democratic appointees.[96]

All that remained was the drafting of a new opinion. This was a somewhat delicate matter as Moore's initial effort had drawn little support from his colleagues. Moore returned to the drawing board with instructions from Lumbard to incorporate the views of Friendly in his opinion.[97] Moore cut the objectionable discussions relating to the standard for an injunction and the materiality of the alleged omissions.[98] He added Friendly's rendition of the legislative history,[99] as well as *Blau*'s caution "against the excessive judicial expansion of provisions of the securities laws to accomplish objectives believed to be salutary."[100]

Clark's new dissent praised the securities laws extravagantly: "this legislation was brilliantly successful in responding to a genuine social need. It is a prime demonstration of the capacity of a democratic government to meet a social crisis skillfully and positively."[101] The majority's opinion, however, "comes as a real shock" that would "scuttle the last of these highly useful statutes and leave it as but a shell."[102] The securities laws, urged Clark, should be "liberally construed to effectuate the broad remedial purpose of the acts."[103] Clark also criticized the majority's reliance on the 1960 amendments to § 206: "To determine the intention of Congress of 1940 we must look backwards from the date

---

[91]   Id. at 4.

[92]   Id. at 6.

[93]   Memorandum of LPM, SEC v. Capital Gains Research (March 1, 1962), Clark Papers, Series II, Box 55, Folder 262.

[94]   Memorandum of JEL, SEC v. Capital Gains Research (March 7, 1962), Clark Papers, Series II, Box 55, Folder 262.

[95]   Letter of David Ferber, Associate General Counsel of the SEC to the Second Circuit, SEC v. Capital Gains Research Bureau (March 6, 1962), Clark Papers, Series II, Box 55, Folder 262.

[96]   Note from Charles E. Clark to Paul Hays (March 28, 1962), Clark Papers, Series II, Box 55, Folder 262. ("Perhaps my greatest trouble is your reliance on H.J.F.'s memo—which I'm afraid I must hold the most specious of the lot. There is just nothing to rest on in his excursions into legisl. history—unfortunately a smoke screen.")

[97]   Memorandum of JEL, SEC v. Capital Gains Research (March 7, 1962), Clark Papers, Series II, Box 55, Folder 262.

[98]   SEC v. Capital Gains Research Bureau, Inc., 306 F.2d 606, 608 (2nd Cir. 1962) (en banc).

[99]   Id. at 609–611.

[100]   Id. at 609 (citing *Blau v. Lehman*, 368 U.S. 403 (1962)).

[101]   *Capital Gains*, 306 F.2d at 611–612 (Clark, J., dissenting).

[102]   Id. at 612.

[103]   Id. at 614.

of passage, not forwards."[104] And he rejected the suggestion that the SEC could reach the defendants' conduct through rulemaking: "the hope of regulation which will require Capital Gains to meet appropriate fiduciary standards not contained in the statute is illusory indeed."[105]

Clark forwarded the opinions to Louis Loss,[106] who was "literally appalled" by the majority opinion.[107] Loss could "hardly think of anything more low-down than a paid investment adviser's using his influence with his clients to feather his own nest."[108] Clark took comfort in Loss's endorsement of his position, but soon enough he would get an even more authoritative vote of confidence.[109]

III.   THE SUPREME COURT

After the knockdown, drag-out fight in the Second Circuit, the course of *Capital Gains* in the Supreme Court was surprisingly tame. Five justices voted to grant certiorari,[110] with Chief Justice Warren expressing concern that the Second Circuit "ha[d] gone overboard in its opinion and gives aid + comfort to sharp dealers."[111] The result was lopsided, with only Justice John Marshall Harlan voting to affirm.

Justice Arthur Goldberg was assigned the opinion. Goldberg's initial circulation did not emphasize the investment adviser's status as a fiduciary.[112] The language relating to fraud by fiduciaries was added in response to a letter from Justice Byron White, who suggested that:

> [T]he treatment might be stronger if the investment adviser may be looked upon as a fiduciary . . . and if the content of fraud and deceit as applied to a fiduciary is considered. . . . If the fiduciary has a settled duty to disclose and if his failure to do so is termed fraudulent, there was little need for Congress in dealing with the fiduciary in the Investment Advisers Act to speak

---

[104]   Id. at 615.

[105]   Id. at 619.

[106]   Letter of Charles E. Clark to Professor Louis Loss (July 31, 1962), Clark Papers, Series II, Box 55, Folder 262.

[107]   Letter of Louis Loss to Charles E. Clark (December 17, 1962), Clark Papers, Series II, Box 55, Folder 262.

[108]   Id.

[109]   *Capital Gains* was closely followed back in the Second Circuit, with District Court Judge William Timbers, formerly General Counsel at the SEC, providing Clark with updates on the case's progress in the Supreme Court. See Handwritten Note from William H. Timbers to Judge Clark (9/20/--) (advising Clark that SEC had authorized certiorari petition and was awaiting approval from the Solicitor General); Memo from WHT to CEC (12/3/1962) (advising Clark that SEC had filed certiorari petition); Letter from William H. Timbers to Hon. Charles E. Clark (1/21/1963) (advising Clark that certiorari had been granted), Charles E. Clark Papers, Series II, Box 55, Folder 262.

[110]   SEC v. Capital Gains Research Bureau, No 42, Docket Sheet (January 18, 1963) ("Grant: Goldberg, White, Douglas, Black, C.J."), Earl Warren Collection, Box 378, Library of Congress.

[111]   Handwritten Notes, Cert. Memo, SEC v. Capital Gains Research Bureau, No 42 (Undated), Earl Warren Collection, Box 247, Library of Congress.

[112]   SEC v. Capital Gains Research Bureau, First Circulation (Nov. 27, 1963), Arthur Goldberg Collection, Box 17, Folder 3, Northwestern University Library.

of anything but fraud in order to reach a failure to disclose a material fact or at the very least a conflict of interest.[113]

In other words, the Second Circuit majority had gotten the case wrong not because it restricted § 206 to common law fraud, but rather because material nondisclosure by a fiduciary was fraud per se. If the investment adviser was treated as a fiduciary, the common law (or at least equity) did not need to be stretched to treat nondisclosure as fraudulent.[114] No specific mention of omissions in § 206 would be required, nor would rulemaking.

Goldberg quickly latched on to White's suggestion, revising his opinion to emphasize the relation between fiduciary status and fraud:

> Nor is it necessary, in a suit against a fiduciary, which Congress recognized the investment adviser to be, to establish all the elements required in a suit against a party to an arms-length transaction. Courts have imposed on a fiduciary an affirmative duty of "utmost good faith, and full and fair disclosure of all material facts."[115]

Notable here is the lack of analysis underlying the conclusion that investment advisers are fiduciaries.[116] Notwithstanding Goldberg's breezy treatment of this issue, the holding here would become the germ of the insider trading prohibition that the Court would later recognize under § 10(b).

Having used equity to free § 206 from the common law constraints that the lower courts had imposed on it, Goldberg announced an interpretive canon that was surely music to William Cary's ears: "Congress intended the Investment Advisers Act of 1940 to be construed like other securities legislation enacted for the purpose of avoiding frauds, not technically and restrictively, but flexibly to effectuate its remedial purposes."[117] Having adopted this flexible/remedial interpretive canon from Clark's dissent, Goldberg brushed aside the differences between § 17(a) of the Securities Act and § 206 of the Investment Advisers Act: "Congress, in enacting [§ 206] . . . deemed a specific proscription against

---

[113]   Letter from Byron R. White to Arthur Goldberg, Re: No 42—SEC v. Capital Gains Research Bureau (December 2, 1963), Arthur Goldberg Collection, Box 17, Folder 3, Northwestern University Library.

White was relying upon the research of his law clerk, Rex Lee, as the basis for his suggestions. See REL, Memo, No 42 OT 1963, SEC v. Capital Gains Research Bureau, Concealment by a fiduciary as fraud, Byron R. White Collection, Box 35, Folder 6, Library of Congress ("Early cases in this Court . . . indicate by dictum that a fiduciary or one who occupies a special relation to another, commits fraud when he fails to disclose a material fact.") Lee would come to play a role again in the development of insider trading law, when as Solicitor General, he would urge the Supreme Court to reverse the SEC's broad view of tipper–tippee liability. See Dirks v. SEC, 463 U.S. 646, 648 (1983).

[114]   On the status of investment advisers as fiduciaries, see Laby, supra note 38, at 1066–1078.

[115]   SEC v. Capital Gains Research Bureau, Second Circulation, at 14 (Dec. 4, 1963), Arthur Goldberg Collection, Box 17, Folder 3, Northwestern University Library (citations omitted).

[116]   James R. Ukropina, The Investment Advisers Act and the Supreme Court's Interpretation of its Anti-Fraud Provisions, 37 S. Cal. L.Rev. 359, 362 (1964). ("A more relevant inquiry from the outset might have been to ask whether or not a subscriber to a market letter costing $18 a year should be considered to have entered into a fiduciary relationship when he pays his subscription price. Further discussion of this issue would seem warranted since disputes still exist in tort law as to the nature of many relationships and the consequential necessity for disclosure.")

[117]   *Capital Gains*, 375 U.S. at 195 (citations and quotations omitted).

nondisclosure surplusage."[118] Clark's ultimate victory over Friendly was secured; it seemed that statutory text could be overcome by the flexible/remedial interpretive canon. It remained to be seen whether that canon would be generally applied when interpreting the securities laws.

IV. THE INFLUENCE OF *CAPITAL GAINS*

Capital Gains' interpretive approach would find fertile ground in the Second Circuit. Clark was elated when he heard that his position had been vindicated by the Supreme Court.[119] He died only four days later,[120] but the other judges of the Second Circuit took up the SEC's cause. Four years later, in *SEC v. Texas Gulf Sulphur*, Judge Waterman would write for the majority of the Second Circuit validating the SEC's expansive reading of § 10(b) of the Exchange Act.[121] *Capital Gains* would be cited by the *Texas Gulf Sulphur* majority for the proposition that even negligent insider trading would be unlawful.[122] *Capital Gains* was cited not only for that particular proposition of law, but also for the flexible/remedial interpretive presumption: "the securities laws should be interpreted as an expansion of the common law . . . to effectuate the remedial design of Congress."[123] Friendly was forced by the precedential weight of *Capital Gains* to concede that negligence would suffice in an SEC suit seeking injunctive relief, but he fought a rearguard action (which he would eventually win) against allowing suits for money damages without a showing of scienter.[124] Lumbard and Moore found themselves in dissent, forced to give lip service to *Capital Gains*' flexible/remedial interpretive canon, but refusing to follow it to its logical conclusion.[125] Nonetheless, Chairman Cary's broad approach to insider trading in *Cady, Roberts* now had been validated by the most important circuit court for securities law.

The Supreme Court's first citation to *Capital Gains* was equally promising for the SEC. Justice Blackmun, writing for the Court in *Affiliated Ute Citizens v. United States*, cited *Capital Gains* for the proposition that "Congress intended securities legislation enacted for the purpose of avoiding frauds to be construed 'not technically and restrictively, but flexibly to effectuate its remedial purposes.'"[126] The flexible/remedial interpretation in *Affiliated Ute* allowed the Court to excuse proof of reliance under Rule 10b-5 in cases "involving primarily a failure to disclose."[127] Thus, the Supreme Court took another step toward validating an insider trading prohibition under the rubric of Rule 10b-5.

---

[118] Id. at 198–199.

[119] Email to author from Harry Reasoner, law clerk to Charles Clark (May 13, 2012).

[120] Federal Judicial Center, History of the Federal Judiciary, supra note 45.

[121] 401 F.2d 833 (2nd Cir. 1968) (en banc).

[122] Id. at 855.

[123] Id.

[124] *Texas Gulf Sulphur*, 401 F.2d at 864, 868 (Friendly, J., concurring).

[125] *Texas Gulf Sulphur*, 401 F.2d at 870 (Moore, J., dissenting, joined by Lumbard, C.J.).

[126] 406 U.S. 128, 151 (1972). Justice Douglas asserts the same proposition in *Superintendent of Insurance v. Bankers Life and Casualty Co.*, 404 U.S. 6, 12 (1971) ("Section 10(b) must be read flexibly, not technically and restrictively"), but he provides no citation.

[127] *Affiliated Ute*, 406 U.S. at 153.

Headwinds soon arose for the flexible/remedial principle, however, with the appointment of Lewis Powell to the Supreme Court.[128] The SEC cited *Capital Gains*' flexible/remedial principle in its brief in *United Housing Foundation, Inc. v. Forman*.[129] Powell ignored *Capital Gains* in drafting his majority opinion; it is cited by Justice Brennan in his dissent.[130] The case was cited again by the SEC the following term as supporting a negligence standard for § 10(b) of the Exchange Act.[131] Powell, again writing for the Court, rejected flexible interpretation of the securities laws in light of "the language of § 10(b), which so clearly connotes intentional misconduct."[132] Justice Blackmun, in dissent, cited *Capital Gains* and his own opinion in *Affiliated Ute* for the principle of flexible/remedial interpretation.[133]

A pattern was set. The SEC would cite *Capital Gains* in support of a broad interpretation of the securities laws, and the Supreme Court—under the influence of Justice Powell—would brush it aside, insisting that the language of the statute would not support the interpretation.[134] The conflict over this interpretive principle between the conservative and liberal blocs of the Court would come to a head in two cases from the October 1979 term.

The first case, *Chiarella v. United States*,[135] laid the groundwork for the Court's insider trading jurisprudence under § 10(b). Justice Powell, writing for the Court, construed *Cady, Roberts* and *Texas Gulf Sulphur* and its progeny in the Second Circuit narrowly, fitting those decisions into the common law framework that Powell favored.[136] More gallingly to Blackmun, Powell read *Affiliated Ute* as imposing "liability premised upon a duty to disclose arising from a relationship of trust and confidence between parties to a transaction."[137] After reading Powell's draft opinion, Blackmun wrote to his law clerk, "I think it advisable, also, to point out, if it is the case, that Justice Powell is giving a narrowing interpretation to *Affiliated Ute Citizens*. I wrote that opinion, and I certainly don't want it unduly narrowed."[138] In his first draft of his dissent, Blackmun wrote: "It seems to me that with its decision in this case the Court continues its emasculation of § 10(b) . . .

---

[128]   Powell was only recently appointed to the Court at the time *Affiliated Ute* was decided and he did not participate in the decision. Id. at 157. On Powell's resistance to the SEC's efforts to expand the boundaries of the securities law, see generally A.C. Pritchard, Justice Lewis F. Powell, Jr. and the Counter-Revolution in the Federal Securities Laws, 52 Duke L. J. 841 (2003).

[129]   Brief for the Securities and Exchange Commission as Amicus Curiae, United Housing Foundation, Inc. v. Forman, Nos. 74-157 and 74-647, at 10–11.

[130]   United Housing Foundation, Inc. v. Forman, 421 U.S. 837, 867–868 (1975) (Brennan, J., dissenting).

[131]   Ernst & Ernst v. Hochfelder, 425 U.S. 185, 200 (1976).

[132]   Id. at 201.

[133]   Id. at 217. Blackmun had also cited *Capital Gains* the previous term in dissent. See Blue Chip Stamps v. Manor Drug Stores, 421 U.S. 723, 762 (1975) (Blackmun, J., dissenting).

[134]   See, e.g., Santa Fe Industries, Inc. v. Green, 430 U.S. 462, 475 & n. 15 (1977) (distinguishing *Capital Gains* on the ground that the case involved deceptive nondisclosure).

[135]   445 US 222 (1980).

[136]   A.C. Pritchard, United States v. O'Hagan: Agency Law and Justice Powell's Legacy for the Law of Insider Trading, 78 B.U. L.Rev. 13 (1998).

[137]   *Chiarella*, 445 U.S. at 230.

[138]   Memo from HAB to Mark, No 78-1202—Chiarella v. United States (2/4/80), Harry Blackmun Papers, Library of Congress.

I, of course, have been unsuccessful in my attempts to stop this trend."[139] This defeatist language did not make it into the final version of Blackmun's dissent, but the published version did little to disguise his bitterness:

> The Court continues to pursue a course, charted in certain recent decisions, designed to transform § 10(b) from an intentionally elastic "catchall" provision to one that catches relatively little of the misbehavior that all too often makes investment in securities a needlessly risky business for the uninitiated investor. . . . [T]he Court fails even to attempt a justification of its ruling in terms of the purposes of the securities laws, or to square that ruling with the long-standing but now much abused principle that the federal securities laws are to be construed flexibly rather than with narrow technicality.[140]

Blackmun argued that his *Affiliated Ute* opinion gave "strong support to the principle that a structural disparity in access to material information is a critical factor under Rule 10b-5 in establishing a duty either to disclose the information or to abstain from trading."[141] This is the parity of information theory that the SEC had been pushing—successfully—in the Second Circuit. Under *Capital Gains'* flexible interpretive approach, *Affiliated Ute* probably would have been read as Blackmun favored. The Supreme Court, however, was now under the sway of Justice Powell in the field of securities law. Powell favored the technical and restrictive interpretation rejected by *Capital Gains*, notwithstanding the concessions he made to *Capital Gains'* equitable notions of fraud in framing the more limited insider trading prohibition under § 10(b) in *Chiarella*.

The second securities case of the term, *Aaron v. SEC*,[142] rejected *Capital Gains'* interpretive principle even more emphatically. *Aaron* raised the question of the state of mind required under § 10(b) in an SEC enforcement action seeking injunctive relief. Again the SEC urged the Court to follow *Capital Gains* and not require a showing of intent.[143] The Court demurred, distinguishing *Capital Gains* on the grounds that § 206's language and legislative history differed from § 10(b)'s.[144] Moreover, the *Aaron* Court was explicit in rejecting *Capital Gains'* flexible/remedial interpretive principle: "generalized references to the remedial purposes of the securities laws will not justify reading a provision more broadly than its language and the statutory scheme reasonably permit."[145] Blackmun was again in dissent, unpersuaded by the Court's attempt to distinguish *Capital Gains*.[146]

Not much was left of *Capital Gains* at this point, but Powell wanted to go further, completely purging it from the judicial lexicon. The following term, in a case involving the definition of a sale under the Securities Act,[147] Powell offered to join Chief Justice Burger's opinion for the majority if the Chief would refrain from citing:

---

[139]   Id.
[140]   *Chiarella*, 445 U.S. at 246–247 (Blackmun, J., dissenting) (citations omitted).
[141]   Id. at 251.
[142]   446 U.S. 680 (1980).
[143]   Id. at 693.
[144]   Id. at 694.
[145]   Id. at 695.
[146]   Id. at 703, 705–710 (Blackmun, J., dissenting).
[147]   Rubin v. United States, 449 U.S. 424 (1981).

[T]he 1963 case of *SEC v. Capital Gains Research Bureau*, quoting language to the effect that federal security laws must be construed "not technically and restrictively but flexibly to effectuate [their] remedial purposes."

A number of more recent decisions, for example, *Hochfelder* relied on by your opinion, have looked primarily to the plain language of the securities acts. These are highly technical and well drawn statutes, and as you make clear by the remainder of your opinion this case falls within the explicit language of §§2(3) and 17(a). Thus, the quote from *Capital Gains Research Bureau* is unnecessary and perhaps could be viewed as undercutting to some extent your reliance on the statutory language itself.[148]

Chief Justice Burger excised the offensive language from *Capital Gains*.[149]

Powell had won a minor victory, but he had not yet put a stake through the heart of *Capital Gains'* flexible/remedial principle. Two terms later, in a case in which Powell did not participate, Justice Thurgood Marshall cited *Capital Gains*.[150] And the term after Powell retired, Blackmun referred to the flexible/remedial principle in interpreting § 12(a)(1) of the Securities Act.[151] Blackmun went on, however, to ground the decision in the statutory language, rejecting the broader interpretation adopted by the court of appeals. After that passing reference, nearly fifteen years would go by before Justice Stevens would cite *Capital Gains* for the flexible/remedial interpretive principle, in a case involving insider trading.[152] Stevens's invocation did not mark a revival; *Capital Gains* has not been cited by the Supreme Court since.

V.   CONCLUSION

Capital Gains made two important innovations in the Supreme Court's securities jurisprudence. The first was that a statutory anti-fraud provision could incorporate, without specific reference, duties of disclosure owed by fiduciaries to their beneficiaries. The second was the interpretive principle that the securities laws are to be flexibly construed to achieve their remedial objectives. The first contribution has survived as part of insider trading law, accepted unreservedly by Justice Blackmun in *Affiliated Ute* and more grudgingly by Justice Powell in *Chiarella*. The second contribution has not fared as well despite Justice Blackmun's adoption of it in *Affiliated Ute*. Interpretation of the securities laws was cabined by the Supreme Court, primarily Justice Powell, as the Court resisted the efforts of the SEC and private plaintiffs to expand their reach. Powell's successors on the Court have been no more generous with their interpretation. The flexible/remedial principle survives—if it does survive—only as a ritual incantation before proceeding to parse precisely the terms of the statute at issue.

Why has the flexible/remedial principle fared so poorly of late? The easy answer is that

---

[148]   Letter from Justice Lewis F. Powell, Jr., to Chief Justice Warren E. Burger (Jan. 8, 1981), Powell Archives, Washington & Lee Law Library.

[149]   Letter from Chief Justice Warren E. Burger to Justice Lewis F. Powell, Jr. (Jan. 8, 1981), Powell Archives, Washington & Lee Law Library.

[150]   Herman & MacLean v. Huddleston, 459 U.S. 375, 389 (citing *Capital Gains*) and id. at 391 (Powell not participating).

[151]   Pinter v. Dahl, 486 U.S. 622, 653 (1988).

[152]   SEC v. Zandford, 535 U.S. 813, 819 (2002).

the Supreme Court has become more conservative since its heady Warren Court days. A more critical answer is that the principle lacks analytical content. The principle could be rephrased simply as "SEC wins" and it would be just as useful. It does not provide a court with any guidance in attempting to discern the outer boundaries of the SEC's authority. Unless a court is willing to cede the SEC unlimited authority, "flexible" interpretation offers no help in deciding concrete cases.

Statutory language, the "technical" tool of choice for Justice Powell and his successors, offers something tangible, something *judicial*, for a judge to work with. To be sure, policy preferences may be lurking just below the surface. That preference for grounding results in statutory text may be unsatisfying for those dissatisfied with the reluctance of Congress to provide meaningful guidance in controversial areas such as insider trading. And it would surely be unsatisfying for New Dealers like Charles Clark and William O. Douglas, who put their faith in the expertise of administrative agencies like the SEC. For the foreseeable future, however, do not expect the Supreme Court to revive *Capital Gains* as a substitute for legislation and rulemaking in the field of securities law.

3. What were they thinking? Insider trading and the scienter requirement

Donald C. Langevoort

On its face, the connection between insider trading regulation and the state of mind of the trader or tipper seems fairly intuitive. Insider trading is a form of market abuse: taking advantage of a material, nonpublic secret to which one is not entitled, generally in breach of some kind of fiduciary-like duty. It is an exploitation of status or access, typically coupled with some form of faithlessness. Certainly the extraordinary public attention that insider trading enforcement and prosecutions command reflects the idea that the essence of unlawful insider trading is cheating. These prosecutions are main-stage morality plays, with greed as the story line.[1] The Securities and Exchange Commission (SEC) in particular seems to sense that it garners public political support by casting itself in the role of tormentor of the greedy.

If this is right, then what the legal system should be looking to proscribe is deliberate exploitation—trading on the basis of information in order to gain an unfair, unlawful advantage over others in the marketplace. That involves a fairly tight causal connection between knowledge of the information and the decision to buy or sell.

This chapter will examine both the law and the psychology associated with this pursuit. The US law of insider trading is actually much more conflicted and confusing as to the necessary state of mind for either trading or tipping.[2] Mostly, this is a product of conceptual confusion in how we define unlawful insider trading—the quixotic effort to build a coherent theory of insider trading by reference to the law of fraud, rather than a more expansive market abuse standard. It is familiar enough that the courts (at the SEC's urging) have taken dominion of the law of insider trading by deeming it a species of fraud. That is intellectually awkward because there is relatively little about unlawful insider trading that can fairly be considered deceptive, yet deception is the essence of fraud. The result is a crazy-quilt of made-up doctrinal innovations to declare abusive trading fraudulent, either vis-à-vis other marketplace traders (the affirmative duty to disclose when there is a pre-existing duty of trust) or the source of the information (misappropriation by feigning loyalty to the entrustor). Another layer of complication ensues when the subject of the prosecution did not trade but instead gave the information to someone else, so that we have to ask why this communication occurred. Given this patchwork, it

---

[1] See Donald C. Langevoort, Rereading Cady Roberts: The Ideology and Practice of Insider Trading Regulation, 99 Colum. L. Rev. 1319 (1999).

[2] This issue is well explored in the literature. See, e.g., Allan Horwich, Possession versus Use: Is there a Causation Element in the Prohibition on Insider Trading?, 52 Bus. Law. 1235 (1997); Donna M. Nagy, The Possession versus Use Debate in the Context of Trading by Traditional Insiders: Why Silence Can Never be Golden, 67 U. Cinn. L. Rev. 1129 (2009). For a lengthier exposition of the doctrinal issues discussed here, see Donald C. Langevoort, Insider Trading: Regulation, Enforcement and Prevention 3:13–3:14 (2012 ed.).

actually becomes very difficult to describe the legally required state of mind for insider trading prosecutions.

But there is also an interesting psychological question. What actually is going through the mind of the alleged trader or tipper? Is it always simple greed? Or can there be an element of unconscious perception—or rationalization—at work? Given the complexity and occasional arbitrariness of the law, what role might this indeterminacy play in trading decisions? My sense is that the motivations and causal explanations for what is charged as insider trading are often quite murky and not easily explained by pure greed. The poster example for the "what were they thinking" question is Martha Stewart, an extraordinarily savvy and successful businesswoman who went to jail for a cover-up after being accused of selling stock to avoid a loss of less than $50,000, a tiny fraction of her net wealth.[3] This chapter will try to connect the law of insider trading to a more sophisticated approach to state of mind, motivation, and causation.

I.   THE SURPRISINGLY HARD DOCTRINAL ISSUES IN ASSESSING STATE OF MIND FOR INSIDER TRADING

One of the necessary consequences of treating insider trading as fraud is a requirement of scienter. The Supreme Court has insisted that the statutory authorization for the main antifraud prohibition in the securities laws—§ 10(b) of the Securities Exchange Act and Rule 10b-5 thereunder—requires intentionality, something more than negligence.[4] But what intentionality means generally remains contested, with the main question being whether some form of recklessness can suffice. The prevailing view in the lower courts is yes, though most insist that the recklessness must have a subjective dimension to it, something akin to conscious or deliberate avoidance of the truth.[5]

Mapping this onto the law of insider trading has been difficult. As noted at the outset of this chapter, the intuitive characterization with respect to trading (putting aside tipping for the moment) is that scienter means that the insider must have deliberately taken advantage of—i.e., *used*—the information for personal gain. Use implies a causal connection between the information and the trade, which if broken negates the intentionality of the allegedly bad act. By and large, the case law invokes the use locution, often referring to the essence of insider trading intentionality as trading "on the basis of" the information in question.[6]

Hence it is not surprising that cases have arisen where the defendant concedes (at least *arguendo*) that he came into possession of information that can be characterized as both material and nonpublic but that this was not the reason that he bought or sold. Rather,

---

[3]   See infra notes 43–44 and accompanying text.

[4]   Ernst & Ernst v. Hochfelder, 425 U.S. 185 (1976). Although such a requirement might not be evident from the text of Rule 10b-5, the Supreme Court considered it implicit in the underlying statutory authorization in § 10(b).

[5]   For a discussion of the case law, see James D. Cox et al., Securities Regulation: Cases and Materials 671–674 (6th ed. 2009).

[6]   E.g., Dirks v. SEC, 463 U.S. 646 (1983). *Dirks* read into the law a personal benefit requirement for purposes of the law of "tipping," which strongly implies misuse. Id. at 662–664.

there was an entirely independent causal explanation for the trade, i.e., that he would have traded anyway, at the same time and in the same amount, even without access to the information. Perhaps the best known example of this in the case law is a director-defendant who sold a sizable amount of his company's stock after receiving disappointing news about the company's financial condition during a board meeting.[7] His defense was that he had already made plans to sell that stock in order to buy a large truck for his son, who was going into the transport business, so that there was no causal connection between what he might have learned at the meeting and the subsequent sale.

Following from the intuition that insider trading is about the misuse of information, the court agreed that such a defense can properly be raised. To be sure, the court was extremely skeptical of the defense as a factual matter, and so held that a presumption of misuse was warranted that the defendant would then have the burden of rebutting. Some other cases, particularly criminal prosecutions, have articulated the same causation standard without any such presumption, thus apparently allocating to the prosecution the burden of proving causation.[8]

That gets us into the mind of the alleged insider trader, which is inevitably very difficult. Some of the practical burden, however, is ameliorated by the fact that this form of subjective intent can be proven circumstantially—fact-finders are entitled to draw inferences about causation from the surrounding facts. As we shall see later on, this introduces a great deal of creative freedom for judges or juries to tell a story of their own making in characterizing the defendant's state of mind. So, we shouldn't overstate any burden that this way of reading the law puts on prosecutors or the SEC, so long as they can persuade the fact-finder of the defendant's greedy character or disposition.[9]

But this approach to scienter in insider trading cases has been contested, and by no means represents a clear statement of prevailing law. The SEC has long rejected the view that causation has any proper role to play: that all that is necessary is that the trader was aware of the information in question, which is often referred to as a "possession" test.[10] Hence the split among the courts is referred to as the "possession versus use" debate, and is controversial in discussions about insider trading law outside the United States as well.[11]

There are numerous arguments in favor of a possession standard. Some are simply pragmatic—that searching for causation inside the mind of the trader is subject to too much confusion and potential error, and so not worth the effort. The leading court favoring a possession standard has said, in dicta:

---

[7]   See SEC v. Adler, 137 F.3d 1325 (11th Cir. 1998).

[8]   See United States v. Smith, 155 F.3d 1051 (9th Cir. 1998); SEC v. Talbot, 430 F. Supp.2d 1029 (C.D. Cal. 2006).

[9]   Most cases articulating a "use" requirement end up finding the standard met. E.g., United States v. Henke, 222 F.3d 633 (9th Cir. 2000).

[10]   In re Sterling Drug Inc., 14 S.E.C. Docket 824 (1978). This was not always so: see In re Investors Mgt. Co., 44 S.E.C. 633 (1971). *Investors Management* involved a possession versus use issue beyond the scope of this chapter: how the scienter standard applies to institutional trading, where there might be a separation of personnel between those who might know a fact, and those who determine purchases and sales.

[11]   See Hui Huang, The Insider Trading "Possession versus Use" Debate: An International Analysis, 34 Sec. Reg. L.J. 130 (2006).

Because the advantage is in the form of information, it exists only in the mind of the trader. Unlike a loaded weapon, which may stand ready but unused, information cannot lay idle in the human brain. The individual with such information may decide to trade upon that information, to alter a previously decided-upon transaction, to continue with a previously planned transaction even though publicly available information would now suggest otherwise, or simply do nothing. . . . As a matter of policy, then, a requirement of a causal connection between the information and a trade could frustrate attempts to distinguish between legitimate trades and those conducted in connection with insider trading.[12]

On a more conceptual level, there is also the point that causation is about motivation, which is generally said not to be crucial to a scienter inquiry in Rule 10b-5 cases. It usually doesn't matter why the defendant lied (indeed, there may be good reasons to do so) but simply that he was aware of the truth at the time he uttered the falsity. Moreover, the idea that recklessness suffices for scienter strongly suggests that knowingly taking advantage of the information is not the only way to satisfy the state of mind requirement— recklessness comports better with possession than use. Finally, there is a fiduciary duty-based justification—fiduciaries are obliged to reveal material information known to be in their possession without any requirement that they be trying to gain from it. That latter point, however, may once again mainly show the awkwardness of trying to import so much prophylactic fiduciary duty thinking into a deception-oriented antifraud regime.

The SEC did not stay idle as this split among the courts became clear. In 2000, the Commission sought to resolve the dispute by adopting Rule 10b5-1, which articulates the law of insider trading in terms of a prohibition on trading "on the basis of" inside information, but then defines "on the basis of" as simple awareness as per the possession test. The SEC described awareness in familiar terms—"having knowledge; conscious; cognizant."[13] Somewhat surprisingly, this attempted codification of the possession standard has not been entirely effective. While some courts have taken it into account as authoritative, others seem to ignore Rule 10b5-1 and stick to the idea that causation remains the controlling requirement, albeit perhaps with a presumption of use.[14] Possibly, this is based on the sense that scienter is embedded in the statutory rulemaking authorization in § 10(b), over which the Commission has limited power of modification. Indeed, there have been serious claims that Rule 10b5-1, in this one respect, was beyond the SEC's rulemaking authority.[15]

Again, we should not overstate the practical importance of all this, given the permissibility (indeed inevitability) of circumstantial proof of misuse. In fact, there is often a reversal of direction in circumstantial proof when the defendant denies any knowledge of the information whatsoever. Under those circumstances, courts generally permit the SEC or prosecutor to try to show possession circumstantially by offering evidence of misuse

---

[12]   United States v. Teicher, 987 F.2d 112 (2d Cir. 1993). For a more recent decision, see United States v. Royer, 549 F.3d 886 (2d Cir. 2008).

[13]   See Securities Act Release 7881, Aug. 15, 2000.

[14]   E.g., United States v. Anderson, 533 F.3d 623 (8th Cir. 2008); SEC v. Bauer, 2011 WL 2115924 (E.D. Wis. 2011).

[15]   See United States v. Nacchio, 519 F.3d 1140, 1167–1169 (10th Cir. 2008); see also Carol Swanson, Insider Trading Madness: Rule 10b5-1 and the Death of Scienter, 52 U. Kan. L. Rev. 147 (2003).

(e.g., patterns of behavior that are explainable only in terms of an effort by the defendant to take advantage of the information, such as the very short time between learning it and trading, or trading in particularly large amounts vis-à-vis normal investing patterns).[16]

So this is one place in the law where we seek to inquire into the "why" behind the choice to buy or sell when there is an allegation of insider trading. There are other places, however. One—which has not received as much judicial or academic commentary as it should—has to do with what we mean by awareness when there are doubts about either the materiality or public nature of the information.[17] In other words, is it important (or essential) that the defendant appreciate that what is in his possession would be significant to other investors, or is unavailable to them? Materiality is one of the hardest fact determinations in the securities laws, an effort to distinguish the unimportant from the significant. Implicitly, the "use" test takes care of this by assuring that the information at least motivated the defendant's trade; the "possession" test does not so insist, and so raises the possibility that information might objectively be material—or at least so judged by the fact-finder—without the defendant actually realizing that it was significant. The same could occur where the defendant did not fully appreciate the secrecy of the information. That is entirely plausible in cases where information may have found its way into the public domain, by leaks or other informal means, even though there has been no public announcement. Here, too, the law can be quite murky. Some courts say that broad general dissemination is necessary before information becomes public, while others suggest that enough leakage will suffice.[18]

The final place where state of mind questions become challenging is in the law of tipping. The Supreme Court has allowed insider trading cases to go forward against an insider who does not trade but instead passes on the information to someone else.[19] But to restrain liability for otherwise legitimate communications, the Court—at least for classical insider trading cases—insisted on proof that the insider was breaching a fiduciary duty for personal benefit by passing on the information, and that the recipient knew or had reason to know of the self-serving breach. That once again takes us inside the mind of the insider, this time to check for selfish motivation. This is made partly easier by the extraordinarily capacious definition of personal benefit offered by the Court. The requisite personal benefit need not be pecuniary (e.g., a kick-back from the recipient), but can consist of a reputational gain or even the warm glow from making a gift of the information to a family member or friend. We have to check the mind of the recipient as well, to see if there was enough awareness or suspicion that selfishness was at work in motivating the insider's tip. Many cases offer particularly vexing problems here, especially when there is a chain of tippers and tippees—the situation where the insider tells a friend, who tells some other acquaintances, and so on.[20]

As with the other state of mind subjects we have surveyed, there is some doctrinal inconsistency here, too. Insider trading cases take one of two basic forms, classical or

---

[16]   E.g., SEC v. Roszak, 495 F. Supp.2d 875, 890 (N.D. Ill. 2007).

[17]   See Langevoort, supra note 2, at 5:5; Allan Horwich, The Neglected Relationship of Materiality and Recklessness in Actions Under Rule 10b-5, 55 Bus. Law. 1023 (2000).

[18]   See Langevoort, supra note 2, at 5:4.

[19]   See Dirks v. SEC, 463 U.S. 646 (1983).

[20]   See Langevoort, supra note 2, at 4:10–4:11.

"misappropriation." The test just described clearly applies in classical cases, but not necessarily when the allegation is that the insider-tipper defrauded the source of the information by giving it to someone else. While most of the time the selfish (broadly defined) motivation for the tip is obvious enough, the SEC and a few courts have said that it is not essential as part of the prosecution.[21] The point seems to be that it is possible to have a purely reckless tip, where the tipper supposedly misappropriates by passing on the information to someone who trades not to facilitate that trading, but with indifference to the likelihood that that would happen.

What characterizes each of these doctrinal questions is the necessity for the fact-finder to enter the mind of the accused insider trader or tipper to draw some kind of inference about causation and/or motivation. As we shall see in the next part of this chapter, that is laden with difficulty. Separately, note the doctrinal confusion in and of itself—often it is impossible to say with any degree of confidence whether a particular instance of trading is lawful or not. That indeterminacy has its own psychological consequences, as we shall also see.

II. EXPLAINING INSIDER TRADING

The aim of this second section is to offer a taxonomy of "state of mind" explanations for allegedly illegal insider trading, beyond the one possibility already discussed (trading for a reason other than the inside information). This is meant solely as a descriptive exercise; later on, the conclusion will try to link this back to the various legal muddles. Here we will be content to grapple with the "what were they thinking" question.

A. Rational Choice: Risks and Benefits

The first explanation is the simplest, and probably the most robust. Along the lines of the orthodox approach to the economics of criminality, we can simply say that to the person faced with an opportunity for insider trading, the benefits in terms of gains exceed the risk. Famously, James O'Hagan, the subject of the Supreme Court's misappropriation theory decision, was apparently motivated by the need to avoid detection of his own embezzlement of client funds from the law firm's accounts, which he was going to replace with the proceeds of the insider trading.[22] The benefits, presumably, are mainly monetary, though we could easily add other forms of utility such as thrill-seeking satisfaction, status enhancement, ego gratification, and the like.

The risks are impossible to assess with rigor. One can predict that, if one is caught, the SEC will seek monetary recovery in the order of three times the gains from the trading,[23] which would set up a fairly concrete decision structure. But there is also a real risk of criminal prosecution, with significant jail time upon conviction. In addition, there is

---

[21] For a discussion of the issue, see SEC v. Sargent, 229 F.3d 68 (1st Cir. 2000).

[22] See United States v. O'Hagan, 139 F.3d 631 (8th Cir. 1996) (on remand, noting evidence of theft from law firm client accounts).

[23] See Langevoort, supra note 2, at 8:4, 8:9.

ample collateral damage even from simple civil enforcement, including attorneys' fees that may not be covered by indemnification or insurance, career loss and other reputational sanctions, and so forth. Even more difficult to assess is the risk of detection. It seems to be common wisdom that the risk of detection is quite low, but it is hard for anyone to know for sure. There is ample evidence of price run-ups in advance of public announcements of major corporate events like M&A transactions, but it is impossible to assess how much of this is illegal trading as opposed to information leakage, which (especially given the murky state of the law) may be lawful.[24] The number of insider cases brought by the SEC in any given year is between fifty and seventy, plus a handful of criminal cases outside the Commission. One could reasonably conclude that the odds are strongly against detection.

A recent paper by Battacharaya and Marshall seeks to address the rational choice structure of insider trading enforcement by looking at a set of high-ranking officers of public companies who have been found liable for insider trading.[25] Their hypothesis is that "poorer" managers should be more heavily represented in the sample than "richer" managers, because the former have less to lose, career-wise, if their unlawful trading is detected. The data, however, reject that hypothesis, leading the authors to suggest that insider trading may not be an entirely rational choice calculation.

B.   Risk Mis-estimation

Because the risk estimation associated with an insider trading decision is so speculative, it is hard to assess its rationality. Later on, we will come back to how emotional impulses and other cognitive factors might bias this estimation. But before getting there, we should probably consider the possibility that people systematically underestimate the risk of detection, even if the risk is relatively low. In other words, do they perceive the risk to be even lower than it really is?

We can only speculate. The SEC and prosecutors bring publicity to bear on their cases in an effort to make it seem like detection is commonplace, and we cannot rule out that this campaign works to inflate the perception of likelihood of detection. On the other hand, it is likely that insider trading opportunities arise in settings (like M&A work at an investment banking firm or law firm) where there are direct or indirect observations of likely illegal trading, which if not detected by the authorities will probably bias the judgment as to likelihood downward (as well as increase the ego and status pressures to conform). In this sense, insider trading is likely to be viral, and if the probability of detection is indeed low as a statistical matter, the perception that people are getting away with it will seem especially high until an enforcement action hits close to home.

In any event, public knowledge of how insider traders are caught is relatively sparse

---

[24]   See Lisa Muelbroek, An Empirical Analysis of Illegal Insider Trading, 47 J. Fin. 1661 (1992).

[25]   See Utpal Bhattacharaya & Cassandra Marshall, Do They Do It for the Money?, 18 J. Corp. Fin. 92 (2012). A study of a sample of students indicates that they believe, on average, that severity of penalties for insider trading is the primary deterrence factor. Joseph D. Beams et al., A Test of Deterrents to Insider Trading Using Importance Ratings, 8 Acct'g & Pub. Int. 94 (2008).

(though maybe not in elite social and economic circles). Recent publicity about wiretaps and other criminal detection devices notwithstanding, most cases arise from backward induction from evidence of unusual stock price moves, although tips are another source.[26] Thus it would not be foolish to assume that if one's trading was limited enough or disguised enough not to affect price, it could scarcely be detected, assuming reasonable cover-up efforts like trading through someone else's account. The flaw in this thinking is in assuming that no one else is trading contemporaneously on the same information. But if there are other insiders, tippees or followers, the warning bells at the regulators may ring even if the person's own trading is fairly limited. And the data exist to find out who was trading in the right direction in the days or weeks before an announcement, with very sophisticated software that can identify clusters of trading or other factors to suggest connections among traders. From that it is just detective work, typically aided by "flipping" certain subjects of the investigation in order to have them reveal their sources, from which other contacts with that same source can then readily be identified.

C. Cultural Influences

One of the standard critiques of the rational choice approach to criminality is that it underestimates the degree to which people will behave "appropriately" even in the absence of optimal sanctions because of an innate or socially constructed sense of what is right and wrong. In the social psychology literature, there are ample claims that at low levels of probability of detection (and assuming no truly draconian penalties) most people conform to expectations as to appropriate standards of what constitutes legitimate behavior.[27] That is not the same as lawful behavior—some forms of unlawfulness (e.g., moderate speeding on open highways) are deemed legitimate. In addition, some legal rules do not have much social legitimacy, and so will carry little power in the absence of strong threats of punishment. Obviously, legitimacy varies in both larger and smaller cultures. Given the vigorous debates about whether insider trading is good or bad, one could reasonably predict that cynically viewing insider trading regulation as foolish or the product of special interest pressure would make it more likely that one would engage in unlawful trading.[28]

There is an interesting literature emerging that seeks to test the cultural legitimacy of insider trading restrictions on a society-wide basis. Survey evidence by Statman asked various university students and finance professionals around the world to react to a fact situation based on the *O'Hagan* case, mentioned earlier, in terms of whether his behavior was fair or acceptable.[29] That it was not acceptable was the overwhelmingly commonplace judgment in the USA and the Netherlands, with only slightly more ambivalence in Australia and Israel. By contrast, in countries like India, Turkey, and Italy, roughly half

---

[26] See Langevoort, supra note 2, at 1:13–1:15.

[27] See Mohammad Abdolmonhammadi & Jahangir Sultan, Ethical Reasoning and the Use of Insider Information in Stock Trading, 37 J. Bus. Ethics 165 (2002).

[28] See Joseph D. Beams et al., An Experiment Testing the Determinants of Non-compliance with Insider Trading Laws, 45 J. Bus. Ethics 309 (2003).

[29] See Meir Statman, Perspectives: Local Ethics in a Global World, 63 Fin. Analysts J. 32 (May–June 2007); Meir Statman, The Cultures of Insider Trading, 89 J. Bus. Ethics 51 (2009).

the respondents rated the behavior as completely acceptable. (Some evidence also ties the incidence of insider trading to cultural variations as to risk tolerance.[30])

This suggests that there could easily be cultural patterns to insider trading behavior at low levels of detection risk, simply because of differing views as to the legitimacy of the legal restraints. And of course broad social or cultural forces can easily be trumped by local ones, in certain markets, firms, or lines of business. Cultural perception, say, at an investment banking firm that insider trading is harmless and a sign of economic connectedness could easily blunt the perception of wrongfulness that otherwise might exist widely in a country like the USA among the more general population.[31]

D.   Failure to Understand (or Properly Apply) the Law

To me, one of the most likely explanations for instances of insider trading is a failure by the trader or tipper to properly appreciate what the law is, or to apply the law to the facts accurately. The issues here fall into two related categories.

We have already seen some of the issues on which courts still have not agreed: the possession versus use disagreement, the precise meaning of "nonpublic," and the role of personal benefit in misappropriation cases, for example. The law of insider trading has evolved in a common law style, so that even a well-trained lawyer could not always give a confident answer as to what the prevailing legal standard is.

But that problem is dwarfed by the relative indeterminacy of so many of the legal standards that are well established. The most obvious example is materiality, a subject that Joan Heminway has explored in some depth.[32] Materiality refers to likely importance; in insider trading, it is a proxy for that which is important enough that a reasonable person would expect the market price to move upon discovery of the information, thereby creating a pre-discovery profit opportunity to exploit. To the insider or tipper, of course, that is only a prediction: the market reaction is observed only after the allegedly unlawful activity. Much of the time, the information in the insider's possession only suggests that there might be a significant event, without one yet having ripened into concrete reality. This is material if, looking jointly at the probability of occurrence and the magnitude of the impact, the expected value of the event is significant enough.[33] By all accounts, these are hard calculations to make prior to the event (and, as discussed below, are subject to a very different perspective when judged in hindsight).

Quite possibly, some insiders have no sound intuition of this, but rather assume that insider trading is about risk-free profits, which assumes something akin to certainty embedded in the secret. Even if not, insiders will often confront factual ambiguity that is not easy to assess. A recent SEC enforcement action targeted mid-level managers at a

---

[30]   See Bart Frijns et al., *A Proclivity to Cheat: How Culture Influences Illegal Insider Trading*, available at http://papers.ssrn.com/sol3/papers.cfm?abstract_id=1972585 (last visited Nov. 8, 2012).

[31]   See Donald C. Langevoort, *Chasing the Greased Pig Down Wall Street: A Gatekeeper's Guide to the Psychology, Culture and Ethics of Financial Risk Taking*, 96 Cornell L. Rev. 1209, 1215 (2011).

[32]   See Joan Heminway, *Materiality Guidance in the Context of Insider Trading: A Call for Action*, 52 Am. U. L. Rev. 1131 (2003).

[33]   See *Basic Inc. v. Levinson*, 485 U.S. 224 (1988).

railway company that was being sold. They were not privy to information about the sale, but gleaned the possibility from a variety of facts, including well-dressed people inspecting railway assets, unusual assignments to provide lists of such assets, and the like. The district court let the case go forward on materiality, while expressing some discomfort as to the softness of the "facts" in defendants' possession.[34]

There are many other areas where similarly difficult or counter-intuitive issues lurk. When information is sufficiently "out there" to be public is hard to assess—quite a number of insiders have been the subject of enforcement proceedings even though information about the event was already in the newspapers at the time of their trading, because the SEC contends that what they knew was more certain that what the media were reporting.[35] The issue of duty is also murky. How many people not deeply familiar with the law in this area would realize that it *is* permissible to trade on most kinds of information that one overhears some executives talking about at a restaurant, but that it is *not* lawful to trade on similar information heard coming from an executive at, say, an Alcoholics Anonymous meeting?[36]

Without at this point passing judgment on insiders' excuses as to ignorance of the law, the murkiness of the inferences necessary to determine legality or not connects back to our discussion of perceptions of legitimacy as strong indicators of behavior when likelihood of detection is low. Where there are competing factual inferences—i.e., the trader can say that he is simply being smart, not cheating—the ability to construe the trading opportunity as legitimate goes up.

E.   Psychological Bias and Insider Trading

To this point, by and large, we have been assuming that the decision to trade or tip is a matter of conscious deliberation, with all these factors—anticipated gain, risk of detection, cultural or moral legitimacy, and legal indeterminacy—competing to determine the judgment about how to act. But to most research psychologists, that would be grossly simplistic.

Contemporary research on judgment and decision making strongly suggests that the conscious portion of choice is just the proverbial tip of the iceberg; that what we are aware of in making a decision is often a poor representation of how or why the choice was made. The research is still evolving as to precisely how, when, and why various factors (neurochemical, dispositional, situational) might dominate, but insights from cognitive neuroscience are increasing rapidly, including from a research subspecialty specifically devoted to economic and investment choice.[37]

At the risk of oversimplification, the main idea here is that impulses like fear and greed will influence how a situation is perceived, greasing the pathway by which conscious

---

[34]   See SEC v. Steffes, 2012 WL 3418305 (N. D. Ill. 2012).

[35]   See SEC v. Mayhew, 121 F.3d 44 (2d Cir. 1997).

[36]   Compare SEC v. Switzer, 590 F. Supp. 756 (W.D. Okla. 1984) with SEC v. McGee, Litig. Release 22288, March 14, 2012.

[37]   E.g., Andrew W. Lo, Fear, Greed and Financial Crisis: A Cognitive Neuroscience Perspective, in J.P. Fouque & J. Langsam, eds., Handbook on Systemic Risk, forthcoming.

deliberation follows the desire. In an interesting survey of the research for portfolio managers, William Bernstein writes:

> Being evolutionarily ancient, the human limbic system does not look very different from that of frogs or reptiles. Located in the limbic system's front part, just behind each eye, is a pair of structures called the *nuclei accumbens*. Neuroscientists have determined that these tiny paired structures respond most intensely to the anticipation of reward (be it culinary, sexual, social or monetary) as opposed to the reward itself, and that this anticipation response can be rapidly conditioned by just a few preceding rewards. To label the *nuclei accumbens* our "greed center" is not too much of an exaggeration. They activate each time an investor turns on CNBC television at 9:20 a.m. during a bull market and connects Maria Bartiromo's smiling, winsome visage with his or her escalating net worth, or when a banker contemplates a risky but potentially profitable loan transaction.[38]

Such activation influences both what is paid attention to, and how situational variables are interpreted. In that sense, this process of "motivated reasoning" readily links back to each of the explanations for insider trading that we have considered thus far.[39] As to risk perception, for example, even without motivation, we can misconstrue baseline risk simply because of the paucity of information about enforcement. But motivation can then build on this, turning the sense in which colleagues have (or seem to have) taken advantage of inside information into an artificial feeling of almost no risk. At the same time, of course, that same observation may increase the desire as well: as Charles Kindleberger perceptively wrote, nothing disturbs a person's judgment and well-being more than watching a friend get rich.[40] We can also see easily enough how desire will also influence the perception of legitimacy. What is fair is very much in the mind of the beholder, and can represent little more than the rationalization of wants.[41]

But it is the indeterminacy of the law, and factual inferences relating thereto, where particularly powerful greasing can take place. The mind will try to find ways to construe the situation so as to invoke real or imagined excuses and safe harbors. A director learning bad news about his or her company may come to think that a decision to sell was actually made some time ago based on other circumstances, but just delayed—the inside information is not really being "used." Uncertainty might be inflated to diminish the perception of materiality; imagining that others must know (and be acting) on the information will blunt the inference of non-publicness.

These are just inferences from the psychological research, of course. We cannot study the mind of the insider trader directly.[42] But we have some anecdotal glimpses to draw from, the most celebrated of which is the story of Martha Stewart's troubles stemming

---

[38]   William Bernstein, Of Laws, Lending and Limbic Systems, 66 Fin. Analysts J. 17, 19 (Jan.– Feb. 2010).

[39]   E.g., David M. Bershoff, Why Good People Sometimes Do Bad Things: Motivated Reasoning and Unethical Behavior, 25 Personality & Soc. Psych. Bull. 28 (1999).

[40]   Charles Kindleberger, Manias, Crashes and Panics 15 (4th ed. 2000).

[41]   For a book-length treatment of these kinds of processes generally see Max H. Bazerman & Ann E. Tenbrunsel, Blind Spots: Why We Fail to Do What's Right and What to Do About It (2011).

[42]   There are occasional "mea culpas" from convicted insider traders, trying to explain their thinking—often by reference to pervasive rationalizations or stupidity.

from her sales of stock in ImClone in December 2001. Stewart was a friend and acquaintance of Sam Waksal, the founder of ImClone, and they shared the same stockbroker (Bacanovic) at Merrill Lynch. They all knew that ImClone was soon to receive a highly significant ruling from the Food and Drug Administration (FDA) about an important drug under development. On December 27, Stewart received a call from Bacanovic's assistant while on a holiday flight, telling her essentially that ImClone was trading down and the Waksals were selling their stock. She immediately told the broker's assistant to sell her stock as well, and avoided a loss of approximately $45,000 from so doing.

On its face, this was at least a reckless decision. Stewart sold the stock in a highly visible account at a well-known broker-dealer as a result of information at least closely connected to the top levels of management at ImClone. She was reasonably familiar with the prohibition against insider trading, though perhaps not all its nuances. Even conceding some difficult legal issues as to whether she could take advantage of this information or not, the risk should have been palpable. So what was she thinking?

This takes us to Stewart's thought-process that day, and here we can draw on some background facts provided by behavioral finance scholar Meir Statman.[43] Stewart was not a very successful investor. She had a portfolio loaded with technology stocks (ImClone, in the biotech field, was one), and was badly hurt by the technology sector sell-off that occurred in 2000 and 2001. Her portfolio value (excluding her own company's stock) declined from $4,530,730 in June 2000 to $2,510,973 in December 2001.

What was most notable is how reluctant she was to sell her stocks, which may connect to a tendency often noted in the behavioral finance literature. Stewart was regularly favored with initial public offering allocations, meaning that she was able to buy the stocks at a deep discount to likely near-term market values. Whether or not they "flip" immediately, many investors take their profit in the near term. Stewart did not, holding the shares through expectedly dramatic price increases and then, later on, through the bursting of the tech stock bubble. She thus managed to lose money even having started in such an extraordinarily favorable position. Whose fault this was is not clear; Stewart apparently blamed Bacanovic and Merrill. In any event, Bacanovic met with Stewart in mid-December to urge her to sell her "loss" stocks before the end of the year to offset against taxable income. They discussed each of the holdings, including ImClone, and Stewart finally sold off all twenty-two of her loss stocks on December 21 and 24 for a combined loss of $1,037,874. Because ImClone was one of her few profitable stocks (and by far her most profitable), she held onto it. She had bought ImClone at $16, and as of mid-December had a gain of some $186,000. Crucially, Stewart said that this selling "made her stomach turn," an interesting psychological point. In fact, the tax losses were quite valuable given Stewart's other income. However, having to finally admit defeat and take

---

[43]   The specific facts recounted here are drawn from Meir Statman, Martha Stewart's Lessons in Behavioral Finance, 7 J. Inv. Consulting 1 (2005). For an elaboration, from which much of the following analysis is taken, see Donald C. Langevoort, Reflections on Scienter (and the Securities Fraud Case Against Martha Stewart that Never Happened), 10 Lewis & Clark L. Rev. 1 (2006). Interesting commentary on Stewart's trial is found in Jeffrey Toobin, A Bad Thing: Why Did Martha Stewart Lose?, The New Yorker, March 22, 2004, at 61, and Jeanne L. Schroeder, Envy and Outsider Trading: The Case of Martha Stewart, 26 Cardozo L. Rev. 2023 (2005). For a book containing various perspectives on the case, see Joan MacLeod Heminway, Martha Stewart's Legal Troubles (2007).

the losses—notwithstanding such potential for gain a year or two earlier—was devastating to Stewart's ego, and generated a good deal of anger and regret. So far as her investments were concerned, Stewart was in late December in an emotionally depressed state.

Then, on December 27, just three days after the stomach-turning sales were done, she got the phone call from Bacanovic's assistant indicating that her only remaining winner, ImClone, was also about to implode. One can at least appreciate what was no doubt a very emotional response—*not this one, too.* If she had a chance to avoid this loss by selling before the market adjusted, such risky behavior can at least be placed in context,[44] though it certainly would not be a defense to insider trading.

But what about the legal risk? Consider what Stewart learned from Bacanovic's assistant. Initially, there were two bits of information in the phone message—that the Waksals were selling and that Bacanovic expected the price to decline. She called the broker's assistant and learned one more fact—that the price had already fallen a good bit. My suspicion is that (especially in an angry and emotional state) she could easily construe this to mean that adverse information had already reached the market, and the big institutions were starting to bail out. She did not want to be left behind, again.

As to the Waksals selling, I suspect that she construed this as the Waksals and much of Wall Street. In fact, it is hard to imagine (especially to a former stockbroker) that she would assume that she was being told that the Waksals were selling illegally—which would be the case if the information had not yet made it to the market. Illegal sales by senior executives do not usually occur in an unconcealed fashion through a reputable broker. Again, the more likely inference is that word about Erbitux had become public and that the Waksals were joining the crowd. Whether this is a successful defense as a matter of law is a bit murky. As Rule 10b5-1 shows, the SEC prefers a simplified state of mind inquiry, and could claim that even if the foregoing were true: (1) Stewart still had one piece of information that the rest of the world did not, received from a private source in arguable breach of fiduciary duty; (2) under these circumstances, she recklessly failed to ascertain the state of public knowledge before selling; and (3) that information does not become public until it is fully internalized by the market (i.e., trading by the smart money is not enough if the price is still adjusting).

But I doubt that under the emotional pressure prompting so many psychologically potent forces—loss aversion, regret, and stomach-turning shame—she would have construed the situation with such acuity. Her mind wanted to sell that stock, and the construal gave her permission to do so. Others were selling, so she could, too. Bad judgment, perhaps, but not all that surprising psychologically. Like so many bad judgments by those with high ego and self-esteem, it generated a poorly executed cover-up, which is what actually landed Martha Stewart in jail.

III.   CONNECTING THE EXPLANATIONS AND THE LAW

Our remaining task in this chapter is to connect these explanations to the legal conundrums discussed in the first section. Obviously, when insider trading is a deliberate

---

[44]   See Statman, *supra* note 43.

choice to assume the risk of detection because of the expected utility in terms of money, thrill, ego, or whatever, the explanations add little. The penalty structure of US insider trading law is built on the implicit assumption that these cases are about greed, and can be deterred by getting the right mix of sanctions and detection resources. We might not have the optimal mix, but it would not be because we misunderstand what is happening. If anything, stopping here underscores the idea that "misuse" of inside information is what we are trying to reach, so that courts that prefer that formulation of the law have it right.

That there might well be individual or cultural legitimation of insider trading at work when someone chooses this same risk might alter the characterization of what is going on—there is a rejection rather than an appreciation of wrongdoing—but that is not a particularly troubling legal issue, either. Similarly, misconstrual of the law generally is met with the response that ignorance is no excuse. It does get harder, however, when misconstruals go to facts (like materiality or non-publicness) rather than law (duty). Scienter does suggest that there must be some contemporaneous appreciation of both significance and secrecy to which eyes are being shut. As suggested in our discussion of the Martha Stewart case, I think there was a plausible argument that she thought—too hastily, perhaps, but without conscious doubt—that word of the FDA action had become public knowledge at least within sophisticated trading markets, which could be a defense to liability. Here the stress turns to recklessness, and the difficulties in drawing the line between deliberate indifference to a known risk and conduct that, in hindsight at least, is hard to explain. That said, if insider trading law is meant to address deliberate exploitation of entrusted information, extending liability too far in the direction of recklessness is unnecessary to carry out the law's expressive function.

Indeed, one of the least understood issues in insider trading law today is the role of recklessness. What do we mean by reckless insider trading? One can readily imagine a case where an executive suspects good or bad news at the time he directs a trade without being sure and proceeds to buy or sell anyway, but this type of case need not reach for recklessness because the very set of facts that made him aware of the risk would probably be material nonpublic information. A possession rather than use standard would no doubt be helpful to the enforcers in a case such as this, but that is simply a practical advantage in dealing with uncertainty, one of the standard arguments for a possession test.

When we turn to tipping, however, we see more room for argument. Suppose a person passes on information to another without actually intending to make a tip (much less for personal benefit), but under circumstances where there is a cognizable risk that trading will result. The personal benefit test makes enforcement under the classical theory hard here, but—under substantial SEC prodding, as we saw earlier—a number of courts say that test does not apply in misappropriation cases. Probably, the main effect of this line of authority is to open up the possibility of reckless tipping. There are a number of cases that might fit this category, most notably those involving employees of magazine printers who sold advance copies of magazines (e.g., *Business Week*) to persons who wanted to know what companies would be mentioned favorably in order to profit from the anticipated market rise.[45] It was not clear that the employees necessarily knew of this intent, and there

---

[45]   See United States v. Falcone, 257 F.3d 226 (2d Cir. 2001).

were other reasons the purchasers might have wanted advance copies besides the intent to trade. Here, however, we still have a solid "greed" story.

As we turn to the possible psychological explanations for trading or tipping, the law's standards seem more naive. For example, a standard that requires a fact-finder to determine that the receipt of the inside information "caused" the trade assumes an overly simple model of decision making. Insiders can easily come to believe that they really did have other reasons for trading, and apart from rough assessments of credibility, fact-finders have little to guide them in determining if this is right. The Second Circuit, quoted earlier, was reasonably sophisticated in its skeptical assessment of this task.[46]

On the other hand, a standard of "awareness" fares poorly from a psychological standpoint, too. If there is a punch line to the research we have described, it is that much of what is crucial to behavior occurs outside of awareness, with awareness generating something of a false consciousness. That is to say, some subset of what we treat as insider trading—some, but by no means all—probably is not experienced by the individual in question as awareness that any material nonpublic information is being exploited. A hard question in the law of insider trading is how to characterize the behavior of someone who we think should have known better but may have lacked the contemporaneous appreciation ordinarily associated with scienter. Once again, this is work usually done by invoking recklessness, which is not a particularly good fit with what we mean by insider trading.

However, we should not obsess too much on all this. All these scienter labels are attached by judges and jurors acting outside the mind of the defendant, in hindsight.[47] The uncertainties and ambiguities that might have clouded the mind of the defendant at the time will not be at work in their own minds as they pass judgment. The certainty of the money made by the defendant will be particularly salient, and the tendency to explain behavior in terms of individual disposition—referred to by psychologists as the fundamental attribution bias—means that the fact-finder will interpret the story more readily in terms of intentionality.

None of this is necessarily unique to the law of insider trading—all forms of law that depend on relatively exacting state of mind standards suffer if they ask fact-finders to determine liability through simplistic labels like intent or recklessness. But insider trading is somewhat unique because, for better or worse, we have made a level of evil disproportionate to its actual economic impact. If insider trading prosecutions are intended as little morality plays in the name of promoting a brand that is about fair play in the securities markets, as I suggested at the outset, we should worry at least a little about what really was in the mind of the trader or tipper unless we are just making examples of them for public consumption.

---

[46]   See U.S. v. Teicher, 987 F.2d 112 (2d Cir. 1993).
[47]   See Mitu Gulati et al., Fraud by Hindsight, 98 Nw. U. L. Rev. 773 (2004).

4. Entrepreneurship, compensation, and the corporation*

Henry G. Manne

Much of the economics literature on the compensation of various personnel involved with large, publicly held companies has failed to come to grips explicitly with three important economic realities. The first is that there is no single model of corporate organization that will turn up valid answers for all occasions.[1] The corporate entity is a many-splendored thing, ranging from the elemental, one-person shop to the giant behemoth with millions of shareholders no one of whom has anything like a controlling influence on corporate affairs. In between these two lie every conceivable combination and permutation of ownership form and distribution, voting rights, contractual provisions (charters and by-laws included) relating to managerial authority and compensation, dividend policies, organizational culture, norms, and applicable laws.

The second reality is that there are numerous economic functions involved in every corporation, although these intellectually distinguishable functions are rarely isolated for cogent analysis. Shortage of a rich vocabulary may be part of the problem, but chances are that analytical lethargy plays a larger role. For example, we frequently use the word "entrepreneurship" to describe the organizational—and sometimes purely managerial or administrative—task of founding a business, as though that were the sole role of the entrepreneur. Manifestly, it is important but, just as clearly, entrepreneurial innovation does not cease with the formation of a business firm. Innovation and discovery may and do regularly occur in all phases of a business enterprise, from production to finance to human resources to marketing and so on, even though these areas of potential innovation are rarely seen as quintessential venues of the entrepreneurial function in large, publicly-held companies. Furthermore, as is well known, technological developments within such corporations may on occasion be nothing more than the product of the exercise of a routine managerial function, although they will be popularly referred to as "innovations."

The risk-taking function too is often confounded with the entrepreneurship function, even though each of these functions may exist exclusively, with no trace of the other. For example, economic risk can obviously be transferred by contract to someone who bears no entrepreneurial responsibility. Successful innovation comes in many forms and in many areas of business, far too many, as we shall discuss below, to allow us either to

---

*   This chapter was originally published in The Quarterly Journal of Austrian Economics, Vol. 14, No.1 (Spring 2011), pp. 3–24.
[1]   The definition of "corporation" in this chapter is broadened to include corporation-like business associations, some of which have publicly traded equity securities. For a discussion of the importance of non-corporate forms and the "uncorporation," see Larry E. Ribstein, The Rise of the Uncorporation (2009); Larry E. Ribstein, Partnership Governance of Large Firms, 76 U. Chi. L. Rev. 289 (2009); Larry E. Ribstein, The Uncorporation and Corporate Indeterminacy, 2009 U. Ill. L. Rev. 131.

simplify it as one form of economic function or to plan meaningfully to compensate for specific cases as they appear.

The third source of fuzzy analysis of corporate affairs arises with the failure to be clear about what is meant by "compensation." In common parlance, we generally mean this term to cover salaries, bonuses, stock options, and various perks of office transferred, pursuant to an employment contract, to an employee in exchange for the performance of a specified amount and quality of effort. Here things begin to get complicated, for surely real compensation, in an economic and non-legal sense of the term, is every benefit or positive utility (including discounted future opportunities) offered up on one side of the employment contract. These benefits are very rarely contemplated in discussions of corporate employee compensation. They may include, for example, working conditions, access to exogenously valuable knowledge, interpersonal relationships, potential for promotion, reputational gains, and lax monitoring. These may show up explicitly on occasion in employment contracts, but, at the margin, each of these may be a very important part of the total compensation picture.

When we put these three complexities into one mix, we begin to see the difficulty of making sense of the entrepreneurial compensation quagmire. We rarely even know when the entrepreneurial function is being rewarded in corporate development (apart, perhaps, from the case of stock granted to a promoter on the formation of a firm), as there are too many confounding circumstances to allow discrete measurement. A corporate founder may also be the inventor of a product to be marketed by a company formed by assembling his or her own personal capital and labor and that of other contributors. The founder may own shares and, at the same time, draw a salary and other compensation, compete in the market for corporate managers, retire early, trade profitably in the stock market, and enjoy the regard of his or her community. Which of these is the entrepreneurial compensation, which is the return to capital, which is the managerial compensation, and which is just plain luck? No amount of regressing can give us a clear answer to this question.

To complicate matters further, we do not even have general agreement on exactly how to define the entrepreneurial function. Representatives of the Austrian School of Economics, particularly Israel Kirzner, have offered the most integrated, robust, and consistent theory of the entrepreneur[2] and distinguished various entrepreneurial and non-entrepreneurial functions,[3] although that approach is still handled at arm's length

---

[2] See Israel M. Kirzner, Competition and Entrepreneurship (1973); Israel M. Kirzner, Perception, Opportunity, and Profit: Studies in the Theory of Entrepreneurship (1979); Israel M. Kirzner, Uncertainty, Discovery, and Human Action: A Study of the Entrepreneurial Profile in the Misean System, in Method, Process, and Austrian Economics: Essays in Honor of Ludwig von Mises 139 (Israel M. Kirzner ed., 1982); Israel M. Kirzner, Entrepreneurial Discovery and the Competitive Market Process: An Austrian Approach, 35 J. Econ. Lit. 65 (1997). For additional sources discussing the Austrian concept of entrepreneurship, see Austrian Economic and Entrepreneurial Studies (Roger Koppl ed., 2003); Roger Koppl & Maria Minniti, Market Processes and Entrepreneurial Studies, in Handbook of Entrepreneurship Research: An Interdisciplinary Survey and Introduction 81 (Zoltan J. Acs & David B. Audretsch eds., 2003).

[3] For an Austrian analysis of various functions performed by entrepreneurs, capitalists, and managers, as well as possible overlaps among these categories, in the context of corporate governance, see Peter G. Klein, Entrepreneurship and Corporate Governance, 2 Q.J. Austrian Econ. 19 (1999). For a description of the development of the entrepreneur–capitalist–manager taxonomy

by most mainstream economists.[4] The Austrian theory has the entrepreneur as the "discoverer" of new combinations of resources, new ways of doing things, new products or innovations in marketing, new organizational forms, or, more succinctly, whatever shakes up the allocational status quo. But the closely related approach followed here, with more emphasis on a kind of Knightian uncertainty[5] about what an entrepreneur will produce, confounds the compensation issue even more, since the output (substance and value) of the entrepreneurial function can never be anticipated or known in advance. If the innovation were predictable, it would no longer be entrepreneurial, and, as we have seen, even when its presence is sensed after the fact, it is generally too difficult to separate from other functions to allow precise measurement for reward purposes. This "loop" presents a great anomaly. We know that an entrepreneurial function exists because there could be no real economic progress, which we witness every day, without this function. Joseph Schumpeter pointed out long ago that entrepreneurship is the factor that lets us avoid a perfectly static equilibrium, the famous circular system with no progress or growth.[6]

So there is a howdy-do, an economic function necessary to the very existence of progress but with no obvious way of specifically identifying it or compensating for it. But the operative term there is "obvious," since we can surmise that, in one way or another, the function is being provided and, if it is being provided, then it is most likely being compensated for. Frank Knight's hunch that entrepreneurship in aggregate was provided freely in a market economy because of the truly "residual" nature of compensation for such services[7] may be correct, and there is some corroborating evidence for the proposition.[8] But Knight's claim was made before anyone even recognized the problem of entrepreneurship in large, publicly held companies, and it seems more likely that this function is now being provided on a more or less conventional market basis. That is, it is being paid for, and more pay elicits more of this activity. However, in all fairness, we should note that Knight did not claim that more compensation would not elicit more entrepreneurial services, only that society had received more entrepreneurial services than were paid for.

Schumpeter famously predicted that the large corporation would ultimately disappear into a bureaucratic black hole without innovation.[9] One of the implicit rationales for this prediction is that such entities could provide no way to compensate the entrepreneurial

---

in economic theory, including the contributions of the Austrian School of Economics, see Robert L. Formaini, The Engine of Capitalist Process: Entrepreneurs in Economic Theory, Econ. & Fin. Rev., 4th Q. 2001, at 2.

4   See William J. Baumol, On Austrian Analysis of Entrepreneurship and My Own, in Austrian Economic and Entrepreneurial Studies, supra note 2, at 57 (stating that "what the literature [on entrepreneurship] has produced is largely attributable to the Austrian economists . . . But in standard microtheory [entrepreneurs] are completely invisible.").

5   Uncertainty is an unpredictability so great that we cannot even assign an approximate risk of its happening. See Frank H. Knight, Risk, Uncertainty and Profit ch. 7 (1921).

6   Joseph A. Schumpeter, The Theory of Economic Development: An Inquiry into Profits, Capital, Credit, Interest, and the Business Cycle ch. 2 (Redvers Opie trans., Harvard Univ. Press 1934) (1911).

7   See Knight, supra note 5, chs. 10–11; Frank H. Knight, Profit and Entrepreneurial Functions, 2 J. Econ. Hist. (Supp.) 126 (1942).

8   See, e.g., Barton H. Hamilton, Does Entrepreneurship Pay? An Empirical Analysis of the Returns to Self-Employment, 108 J. Pol. Econ. 604 (2000).

9   Joseph A. Schumpeter, Capitalism, Socialism and Democracy pt. 2, chs. 12, 14 (1942).

function. But large corporations are still here, even larger than when Schumpeter wrote, and we still do not live in this Schumpeterian static corporate world. Entrepreneurship in the sense of discovery and unpredictable innovation is indisputably going on even in very large corporations, and it is by no means fully routinized. Certainly, it is more likely that the entrepreneurial function is being compensated for, albeit not in a fashion captured in simple supply and demand models,[10] taught in business school theories of executive compensation, or implicitly envisioned in corporation-law casebooks. The mere fact that we cannot account for this exchange in our standard double-entry bookkeeping or even with our advanced econometric techniques does not make the likelihood of some form of compensation any less real.

The problem is not so critical if one thinks of the entrepreneurial services produced by an Edison or a Ford or a Gates. They were, in addition to being entrepreneurs under anyone's definition, capitalists, managers, inventors, risk takers, and employees of the companies they founded. Whether they became enormously wealthy because of their exercise of the entrepreneurial function—or of the capitalist or managerial one—is hardly of great social moment. But for myriad individuals otherwise connected with large, publicly held companies, the problem can become acute. Indeed, a good deal of the modern discussion about designing compensation plans to coordinate the interests of owners and managers is, in effect, a discussion of how to motivate or reward entrepreneurial services, even though we rarely recognize it as such.[11]

Business improvement and innovation may often be indistinguishable from normal good management, and yet they are separate and distinct functions, one relating to the performance of a known and describable function and the other to the development of something totally unpredictable. Furthermore, entrepreneurial contributions may be made by people both inside and outside the organization, which is, by definition, not possible for managerial functions. In addition, perhaps most important to this discussion, often we cannot even recognize an entrepreneurial contribution—or its value—until long after it has occurred.

While we tend to think of entrepreneurial contributions as the large, creative-destruction type of changes, the truth is commonly very different. It may be the case that

---

[10]   See Edith Penrose, The Theory of the Growth of the Firm 75 (3d ed. 1995). ("There is no supply curve or production function into which such services can be fitted, but they are nevertheless inputs in production.")

[11]   Indeed, it is safe to say that the vast amount of discussion of faulty compensation plans for executives caught up in the recent financial chaos misses the mark widely. Their contracts may well have encouraged too much risk taking, i.e., more than the shareholders would have wanted ex ante, as has been widely alleged. See, e.g., Compensation Structure and Systemic Risk: Hearing Before the H. Comm. on Financial Services, 111th Cong. (2009); Richard A. Posner, A Failure of Capitalism: The Crisis of '08 and the Descent into Depression 99–100, 257, 297–99 (2009); Steven L. Schwarcz, Conflicts and Financial Collapse: The Problem of Secondary-Management Agency Costs, 26 Yale J. on Reg. 457 (2009); Michael Lewis, The End, Portfolio, Dec. 2008, at 114. But the risk-taking function is not the same as the entrepreneurial one, and there is simply no way, even ex ante, to determine that employees were motivated to produce too much entrepreneurial innovation. Buying ever greater amounts of subprime mortgage-backed securities according to a computerized algorithm is the essence of an administrative function which bears no relation to anything that might appropriately be termed entrepreneurial. Inventing the algorithm, however, is a different story.

individual, discrete examples of entrepreneurship occur with enormous frequency, albeit in small or even barely noticeable increments.[12] Discovering the incandescent lamp is one thing, but finding a new way to feed in the inputs on an assembly line, clearly a possible candidate for being called entrepreneurial, will usually not receive that same degree of attention or acclaim, at least until it shows up on the proverbial bottom line. Even then, the real source of the revenue gain may be difficult to specify. Also, it may take years for the books of the company to register the new value created.[13] The stock market may be "efficient" in the sense of processing available information, but it must have information inputs to do its job.

We do sometimes recognize the innovations of employees—but never of outsiders— with such compensation forms as bonuses, new grants of stock or stock options, or increased salary.[14] Equity-based compensation, such as stock or stock options, may also include a component for entrepreneurial actions to the extent that such compensation has an ex ante motivating force for innovation. But it is unlikely that these forms of compensation, without perhaps reaching enormous size, as we sometimes do see, can ever motivate a desirable or efficient level of entrepreneurial activity.[15] Suffice it to say for now that they were never designed expressly with compensation for entrepreneurial services in

---

[12]   Schumpeter himself noted that "the entrepreneurial element may be present to a very small extent even in very humble cases and in these the entrepreneurial function may be all but drowned in other activities." Joseph A. Schumpeter, Economic Theory and Entrepreneurial History, in Change and the Entrepreneur: Postulates and Patterns for Entrepreneurial History 63, 70 (Research Ctr. in Entrepreneurial History, Harvard Univ. ed., 1949). This piece, written shortly before Schumpeter died and probably not in its absolutely final form, represents the author's major sally into an explanation of the entrepreneurial function in connection with large corporations. Unfortunately, he never noted the ongoing problem of compensation for this function.

[13]   This example is merely one of many reasons it would be better public policy to encourage early utilization of new information in the stock market instead of hindering, delaying, and distorting it, as our regulatory scheme now does: "The new approach would suggest that it is undesirable to have laws discouraging stock trading by anyone who has any knowledge relevant to the valuation of a security. Thus, assembly-line workers, administrative assistants, office boys, accountants, lawyers, salespeople, competitors, financial analysts and, of course, corporate executives (government officials are another story) should all be encouraged to buy or sell stocks based on any new information they might have. Only those privately enjoined by contract or other legal duty from trading should be excluded." Henry G. Manne, The Welfare of American Investors, Wall St. J., June 13, 2006, at A16.

[14]   In an otherwise superb discussion of the role of the entrepreneur in large firms, Frederic E. Sautet, An Entrepreneurial Theory of the Firm 101–04 (2000), there is still an inadequate discussion of these forms of entrepreneurial compensation.

[15]   We might debate what the efficient or optimal level of entrepreneurial services is, since the function does not neatly fit into traditional economic analytics of efficient output. We can conceive of not having enough entrepreneurship, as is the case with many underdeveloped countries, but it is difficult to make sense of any concept of over-production of entrepreneurship. However, for the view that there is an optimal level of ignorance, see Joseph E. Stiglitz, Whither Socialism? 52–53 (1994). Perhaps the statement in the text should refer to motivating entrepreneurial activity without reference to the amount as being efficient, and it might be one case in which the efficient level is also the maximum level. In the scheme of using insider trading to compensate entrepreneurial activity, as is being proposed in this chapter, there could never be such a thing as "too much" incentive. In other words, if the development is not worthy, it will not be reflected in a higher stock price and, therefore, cannot reward the developer.

mind. On that Schumpeter was perhaps inadvertently correct when he said that "the fact that personal gain, beyond salary and bonus cannot, in corporate business, be reaped by executives except by illegal or semi-illegal practices shows precisely that the structural idea of the corporation is averse to it."[16]

There are fundamental problems with each of these as forms of compensation to the corporate entrepreneur, but Schumpeter was undoubtedly too hasty in proclaiming the large corporation as incompatible with innovation.[17] For the most part, the problem is that the settling up with bonuses or additional compensation is always done post hoc and, therefore, is subject to great disagreement about such matters as the appropriate amount, the proper identity of the recipients of the extra compensation, and the correct evaluation of each individual's contribution and whether any reward is appropriate at all. This problem becomes especially acute when we consider the special psychological characteristics of great entrepreneurs, most notably optimism, which Knight so insightfully noted.[18]

Certain parts of the discussion I tried to initiate on this subject many years ago are perhaps even more relevant today than they were then. To be consistent with the idea of the entrepreneur as a creator of new combinations and the discoverer of new ideas, information, or opportunities, a system of compensation is required that can more accurately and more quickly assess the true present value of these contributions than can a compensation committee, even if the allocational question remains open. A pre-existing equity stake in the company (even assuming that the stock market will accurately measure the value of the innovation) can never perform the appropriate reward function, since the value of the reward is shared equally, per share, with all other shareholders. That reflects the capitalist's or risk taker's function, not the entrepreneur's. Furthermore, the amount of stock held by the entrepreneur would have been determined long before the innovation occurs and for reasons generally unrelated to the contribution. Only if the entrepreneur is also the owner of all or the bulk of the company's shares (thus combining two economic functions in one person) can this form of reward be considered an appropriate form of compensation for the entrepreneur. But then we are talking about the likes of the early Ford or Edison examples and not about lesser mortals in modern large, publicly held companies.

Furthermore, the idea of entrepreneurs receiving their reward via stock ownership misses another salient feature of true entrepreneurship. Stock ownership entails risk, which is not necessarily or peculiarly a part of the entrepreneurial function. While the

---

[16]   Schumpeter, supra note 9, at 156 n.1. But, as we shall see, the system does allow an appropriate form of compensation, insider trading, although Schumpeter may have included that among the illegal or semi-illegal forms of compensation. His failure to clarify this point, as well as his omission of stock and stock options from this list, has always been a mystery. In his equally puzzling description of "the modern businessman, whether entrepreneur or mere managing administrator," Schumpeter remarked that, "[w]hether a stockholder or not, his will to fight and to hold on is not and cannot be what it was with the man who knew ownership and its responsibilities in the fullblooded sense of those words." Id. at 156.

[17]   I dealt with this topic some years ago and will not repeat that discussion here. See Henry G. Manne, Insider Trading and the Stock Market ch. 9 (1966); Henry G. Manne, In Defense of Insider Trading, Harv. Bus. Rev., Nov.–Dec. 1966, at 113.

[18]   Knight, supra note 5, at 283–86.

stock price will more accurately than any other mechanism evaluate and price the contribution of the corporate entrepreneur, full exploitation (in the sense of being rewarded for) of new information developed by the entrepreneur can be achieved only by trading in the stock and not simply by owning it. We should anticipate that share trading rather than share holding would be the hallmark of the corporate entrepreneur in large, publicly held companies.[19]

Thus, if the United States government had not progressively outlawed insider trading since 1961,[20] we should expect to find that the wealth of many individuals connected with large corporations, particularly but by no means exclusively those responsible for the progress and development of the business, is explained as much or more by share trading than by share ownership.[21] Yet, as insider trading has been increasingly demonized and criminalized, other forms of compensation have had to be substituted for this one. The amounts required of these other forms of compensation, as discussed in more detail below, are apt to appear scandalously high if they are to approximate appropriate compensation for entrepreneurs, another good example of the unintended and unforeseen consequences of regulation.

This analysis may also help explain a persistent conundrum in modern corporate economics: why are larger corporations, generally speaking, less entrepreneurial than smaller ones? Surely Schumpeter's pop-sociological theory that bureaucratic, risk-averse types will dominate—or rather be created by—large corporations[22] is not a robust explanation. We see too many examples to the contrary. A more cogent answer flows directly from our assumptions regarding entrepreneurial personality, compensation, and a little arithmetic.

As a corporation grows in absolute size, the effect of any given development on share price becomes less and less in absolute terms. That is, a billion dollar development in a publicly held company with a market capitalization of 50 billion dollars will have half the per share price consequence of the same development in a company with a 25 billion dollar capitalization. Thus, if entrepreneurs want large gains and small risk,[23] we should expect persons with true entrepreneurial personalities, i.e., with high confidence levels

---

[19] To the extent that this observation is correct, it demonstrates how very misguided a great deal of the criticism of insider trading has been, beginning with the complaint, which was articulated in a pivotal book, about corporate managers owning too few shares. Adolf A. Berle, Jr. & Gardiner C. Means, The Modern Corporation and Private Property (1932).

[20] Cady, Roberts & Co., 40 S.E.C. 907 (1961), is considered to be the starting point of modern insider trading regulation, but it was many more years before anything that could be termed significant enforcement began. For sources analyzing different perspectives on the emergence of this phenomenon, see Stanislav Dolgopolov, Insider Trading, Chinese Walls, and Brokerage Commissions: The Origins of Modern Regulation of Information Flows in Securities Markets, 4 J.L. Econ. & Pol'y 311 (2008); Michael P. Dooley, Enforcement of Insider Trading Restrictions, 66 Va. L. Rev. 1 (1988); David D. Haddock & Jonathan R. Macey, Regulation on Demand: A Private Interest Model, with an Application to Insider Trading Regulation, 30 J.L. & Econ. 311 (1987); Thomas W. Joo, Legislation and Legitimation: Congress and Insider Trading in the 1980s, 82 Ind. L.J. 575 (2007).

[21] The same is very likely true for pre-1961 companies, although no one to my knowledge has analyzed this issue.

[22] Schumpeter, supra note 9, at 141, 156.

[23] This notion is derived from both Knight's and Kirzner's view of the entrepreneur. For a general discussion of these views, see Sautet, supra note 14.

in Knight's terms, to be attracted to smaller corporations, where they can realize greater trading profits from the same level of contribution.

This theory does not preclude innovation and entrepreneurship in larger corporations; it merely suggests that smaller publicly held firms would, in the absence of rules against insider trading, have a comparative advantage in attracting employees with a more entrepreneurial bent. Thus, another unnoticed and unintended consequence of insider trading regulation has been to discriminate against smaller publicly held companies in relative favor of larger ones. The regulatory framework, to the extent that it is effectively enforced, removes one of the most significant competitive advantages smaller companies have. This analysis could help explain why there was no great hue and cry from America's top businesses when the Securities and Exchange Commission (SEC) high-handedly wrote new law on insider trading in 1961.[24]

But even without the implicit subsidy from insider trading regulation, the larger firms still have means to compete for entrepreneurial employees. To compete effectively in the market for entrepreneurial talent with the smaller publicly held companies, the larger companies would have to—and do—offer higher salaries and other perks than would the smaller ones. Thus we have a new explanation for the correlation often found between the relative size of a company and the compensation levels of its executives. We may also have found a new and cogent, if partial, explanation for the apparently scandalously high salaries and other perks in large, publicly held companies that have come to public attention in recent years. It takes a lot of straight salary to compensate an executive for the loss of the right to trade on new information. As Michael Jensen and Kevin Murphy argued many years ago, the form of compensation may count for more than the level, although they did not consider insider trading in the mix.[25]

For these reasons and perhaps others, specific amounts of salary or stock will probably never capture the essential requirement of effective entrepreneurial compensation. The incentive system must appeal to the confident nature of the entrepreneur as well as to the entrepreneurial instinct to "cash in big" from new contributions.[26] Facing a compensation committee's ex post evaluation of an invention will hardly appeal to this type of personality. As we have seen, all conventional compensation devices suffer from the twin problems of valuing innovations and determining the person directly responsible for a new development who deserves to be rewarded, matters about which the innovator and his or her employer will almost certainly disagree.[27]

---

[24]   For other possible explanations of why this development was met with silence, see Henry G. Manne, Insider Trading: Hayek, Virtual Markets, and the Dog that Did Not Bark, 31 J. Corp. L. 167 (2005).

[25]   See Michael C. Jensen & Kevin J. Murphy, CEO Incentives: It's Not How Much You Pay, but How, Harv. Bus. Rev., May–June 1990, at 138, 138. ("On average, corporate America pays its most important leaders like bureaucrats. Is it any wonder then that so many CEOs act like bureaucrats rather than the value-maximizing entrepreneurs companies need to enhance their standing in world markets?")

[26]   In this context, the stock option fails for the same reason as prior stock ownership does.

[27]   As well they should. These matters involve inherent uncertainty, and it can be safely predicted that mistakes, judged ex post, will occur. The insider trading compensation device does not entirely dispense with these errors, but it does generally compensate for entrepreneurial activity while doing away with the disagreements and personal involvements in compensation decisions.

The incentive to act entrepreneurially must exist in advance of the contribution and with an understanding that in fact nothing of value may be developed, another reason why it is so difficult to design an ex ante compensation system for entrepreneurial developments in a large corporation. In this sense, consider the research scientist who is hired to invent or develop something with an inherently uncertain outcome, such as a cure for cancer. There obviously can be no guarantee of the results of such research, and yet the compensation and its form must be appropriate to entice this person to do the work in the hopes of cashing in big. A salary combined with the right to trade in the stock market on any new information produced will generally satisfy the requirements of a compensation system to elicit the desired kind of effort exerted by such a scientist. Furthermore, the incentive should ideally be able to go to any individual in the corporate organization who might, whether predicted to or not, make an entrepreneurial contribution. In a real sense, it is a particular personality trait that the employer wants and not necessarily or exclusively an individual of known skills and propensities, although that too may occur. Allowing trading on new information produced again appears perfectly consistent with this requirement.[28]

So an entrepreneurial compensation system must possess some unusual characteristics if it is to successfully attract the sought-after services. It must appeal to the personality of the entrepreneurial type; it must avoid valuation and attribution issues post hoc; and it must ideally motivate any prospective employee—and possibly even outsiders—to act as an entrepreneur. It is hard even to imagine a system that will meet all these requirements other than the right of corporate employees with valuable new information to trade on that news in advance of public disclosure.

Insider trading as a form of compensation also has some peculiar characteristics that will distinguish it analytically from other forms of compensation. The most obvious difference is that the value of individual transactions to be made in the future cannot by their nature be determined in advance, even though, as noted earlier, a real market value must be attached at least implicitly to a general right to engage in insider trading. It cannot be assumed, even with the most efficient stock market, that the profits from trading on inside information will correctly and precisely measure or evaluate a corporate entrepreneur's contributions, even though in some cases, perhaps merely coincidentally, this correct allocation of trading profits may happen. Obviously, the amount of stock or other securities the insider is willing to purchase on the information that he or she created or learned about will vary with a number of exogenous

---

Furthermore, it does no significant harm and entails some other very real benefits in the process. See Manne, supra note 17.

[28] As noted earlier, Schumpeter never explicitly addressed the problem of compensation for entrepreneurial services in large, publicly held companies. He does, however, have one passage that sounds surprisingly consistent with the argument being made in this chapter: "If a man sets up a new industrial organization . . . the value of the assets that enter into this organization increases. This increase no doubt embodies, at least ideally, a discounted value of the expected surplus returns. But it is in this increase in asset returns itself rather than the [expected surplus] returns that constitute the entrepreneurial gain, and it is in this way that industrial fortunes are typically created."

Schumpeter, supra note 12, at 71. If this notion were to be transformed into the entrepreneurial compensation problem in large, publicly held companies, it would seem to describe the process of profiting from insider trading.

circumstances, including the availability of credit to the employee[29] and the certainty of the information's estimated value. Furthermore, stock prices at any given moment reflect a variety of other information or misinformation inputs, so that it will frequently be difficult to isolate and measure the value of one particular entrepreneurial development. Similarly, trading quickly, i.e., buying and then selling right after the disclosure (or vice versa), reduces the risk of holding corporate securities, but it does not remove it entirely.

Insider trading remains the system par excellence of compensating entrepreneurs in large, publicly held companies, and it does not matter one whit that the amount the employee realizes by his or her trading may be more or less than the marginal value of the contribution, that the wrong person may be rewarded with this right, that profit can be made from bad news as well as good news, or that the system might seem unfair to economics-challenged regulators and moralists.[30] The system and not the payment, as we shall explain below, is the critical factor. Of course, there are myriad other considerations in the insider trading debate. The present discussion is limited to the appropriateness of insider trading as a form of entrepreneurial compensation in large, publicly held companies.[31] Unfortunately, only a handful of sources have paid proper attention to the entrepreneurial compensation argument which I offered substantially in these terms over forty years ago,[32] although several commentators have recognized the value of the right to trade on inside information as a form of compensation, another way of acknowledging that this right does have a market value and thus could perform as a form of compensation.[33]

It should be emphasized here that the use of insider trading rights as a form of com-

---

[29]   This point implicates the discussion in my 1966 book of investment bankers performing some sort of clearinghouse function for new information, thus allowing corporate entrepreneurs to virtually trade information with other corporate entrepreneurs through time and to trade knowledgably in securities of various companies for the purpose of diversification instead of going heavily into debt in order to fully exploit one significant piece of information. See Manne, supra note 17, at 69–71.

[30]   There are after all other advantages to this system too, but they are not being discussed here. See generally id.

[31]   The clarification I entered in my 2005 article, Manne, supra note 24, at 170–74, referred only to the problem of trying to design ex ante an explicit executive compensation plan that would utilize the right to trade on inside information as an explicit part of the package. I certainly did not intend to retract the idea that a general rule of allowing insider trading was the best device we could imagine for appropriately rewarding entrepreneurial services in large, publicly held companies.

[32]   See, e.g., Antonio E. Bernardo, Contractual Restrictions on Insider Trading: A Welfare Analysis, 18 Econ. Theory 7 (2001); Frank H. Easterbrook, Insider Trading as an Agency Problem, in Principals and Agents: The Structure of Business 81 (John W. Pratt & Richard J. Zeckhauser eds., 1985); Robert J. Haft, The Effect of Insider Trading Rules on the Internal Efficiency of the Large Corporation, 80 Mich. L. Rev. 1051 (1982). For a succinct summary of the compensation debate, see Stephen M. Bainbridge, Insider Trading, in 3 Encyclopedia of Law and Economics 772, 780–82 (Boudewijn Bouckaert & Gerrit De Geest eds., 2000).

[33]   See, e.g., Lucian Arye Bebchuk & Chaim Fershtman, The Effects of Insider Trading on Insiders' Effort in Good and Bad Times, 9 Eur. J. Pol. Econ. 469 (1993); Dennis W. Carlton & Daniel R. Fischel, The Regulation of Insider Trading, 35 Stan. L. Rev. 857 (1983); Ronald A. Dye, Insider Trading and Incentives, 57 J. Bus. 295 (1984); Jie Hu & Thomas H. Noe, Insider Trading and Managerial Incentives, 25 J. Banking & Fin. 681 (2001). These sources suggest that, under certain conditions, insider trading could serve as an efficient compensation mechanism,

pensation has the double advantage of applying to people both within and outside the company, since the incentive will have a generalized effect on all employees and related outsiders. This system will influence the general corporate culture and will provide incentives for innovation for everyone, not merely those who might somehow be explicitly described as entrepreneurs.[34] In that sense, it is perhaps misleading to refer to insider trading as a form of compensation for any specific individual. It is an incentive device available to anyone, especially employees, who chooses to take advantage of it, and this device will go a long way towards generating a pervasive corporate culture of innovation. That, after all, is what is wanted, not some new provision to add to the standard form employment contract. While such a corporate culture may willy-nilly result in considerable employee attention to the stock market, as has been complained about in connection with insider trading,[35] that actually should be seen primarily as a part of the solution and not significantly as a part of the problem.

Today, with the regulation, criminalization, and vilification of insider trading, many, probably most, corporate employees—particularly the entrepreneurial ones who would be the easiest for regulators to spot—would not try to profit from an innovation by trading in their companies' securities before the innovation's value is reflected in the stock price as a result of public disclosure. But along with that hesitation to trade undoubtedly goes a loss of incentive for developing new ideas and certainly the loss of a culture that could encourage entrepreneurship. It is highly doubtful that the outlawing of insider trading in the United States has not had a significant deleterious effect on the long-term performance of our publicly held companies.[36]

Two factors have prevented this bit of "fairness" regulation from totally, or at least

---

but none of them makes a distinction between entrepreneurs and managers as the appropriate recipients.

[34] Again Schumpeter seems to have understood the point: "[T]he entrepreneurial function need not be embodied in a physical person and in particular a single physical person. Every social environment has its own ways of filling the entrepreneurial function. . . . [T]he entrepreneurial function may be and often is filled co-operatively. With the development of the largest-scale corporations this has evidently become of major importance: aptitudes that no single individual combines can thus be . . . built into a corporate personality; on the other hand, the constituent physical personalities must inevitably to some extent, and very often to a serious extent, interfere with each other. In many cases, therefore, it is difficult or even impossible to name an individual that acts as 'the entrepreneur' in a concern. The leading people in particular, those who carry the titles of president or chairman of the board, may be mere co-ordinators or even figure-heads . . .." Schumpeter, supra note 12, at 71–72.

[35] See, e.g., James D. Cox, Insider Trading and Contracting: A Critical Response to the "Chicago School", 1986 Duke L. J. 628, 646 (voicing a concern about "the manager's use of personal resources and time to trade in his firm's stock"); Haft, supra note 32, at 1063 (arguing that "[c]ompetition [for inside information] might . . . turn management information systems designed for corporate purposes into stock market ticker tapes").

[36] Ironically—and somewhat inartfully—the potential impact of insider trading regulation on corporate entrepreneurship was perhaps recognized at the very dawn of federal securities regulation by a member of FDR's inner circle: "[T]o make sure that management shall be limited in its profits motive to long-term periods, the authors [of the bill that ultimately became the Securities Exchange Act of 1934] . . . convert management into a mere salariat and bureaucracy which cannot, excepting through increased salary and 'lock-in' investments share in entrepreneurial profits through exercising options as extra reward or making judicious investment even for cash in

in good measure from seriously, injuring large, publicly held companies in the fashion Schumpeter predicted. The first is that, at least until recently, we did not consider controlling the level of other forms of compensation that might substitute for insider trading as an incentive system for entrepreneurial services,[37] and this trade-off might become even more important because of different post-crisis proposals to limit explicit forms of executive compensation.[38] The other factor is the near impossibility of effective enforcement of laws against insider trading.[39] While the publicity-motivated prosecutions and the hyped-up propaganda that have long characterized the SEC's campaign against insider trading deter some people from engaging in the practice, all indications are that it still

---

their own companies with the expectations of selling out when occasion arises regardless of any fixed period."

Alexander Sachs, Lehman Corp., Memorandum on Obstacles in the Securities Exchange Act to Efficient Investment and Enterprising Management II-1–II-2 (Feb. 1934) (on file with author).

[37]   On the other hand, several empirical studies attempted to test whether potential trading gains are reflected via a decrease in the cash portion of compensation packages, although they yielded mixed results. Compare Kevin J. Hebner & Takao Kato, Insider Trading and Executive Compensation: Evidence from the U.S. and Japan, 6 Int'l Rev. Econ. & Fin. 223 (1997) (reflected), Darren T. Roulstone, The Relation Between Insider-Trading Restrictions and Executive Compensation, 41 J. Acct. Res. 525 (2003) (same), and M. Todd Henderson, Implicit Compensation (Univ. of Chicago Law Sch., John M. Olin Law & Econ. Working Paper No 521 (2d ser.)), available at http://ssrn.com/abstract=1605170 (accessed 20 Nov., 2012) (same), with Steffen Brenner, On the Irrelevance of Insider Trading for Managerial Compensation, Eur. Econ. Rev. (forthcoming) (not reflected), and Teresa Diane Trapani Teeuwen, An Investigation of the Relationship Between CEO Compensation and CEO Trading Profits (May 1991) (unpublished Ph.D. dissertation, University of Kansas) (on file with author) (same). See also George-Levi Gayle & Robert A. Miller, Insider Information and Performance Pay, 55 CESifo Econ. Stud. 515, 519, 527–28 (2009) (considering the proposition that, "[r]ather than discourage managers from benefitting from their insider knowledge, the board might optimally sanction it" and offering empirical evidence that "supports the hypothesis that rather than simply benefiting from their private information by structuring their compensation package in an advantageous way, managers are also motivated, through their work choices, to raise the mean of unanticipated abnormal returns"); Wei Zhang et al., Insider Trading and Pay–Performance Sensitivity: An Empirical Analysis, 32 J. Bus. Fin & Acct. 1887 (2005) (presenting empirical evidence to suggest that, "in the presence of more aggressive insider trading, shareholders and the managers negotiate compensation contracts that are less sensitive to performance").

[38]   See Michael V. Seitzinger, Cong. Research Serv., No RS22583, Executive Compensation: SEC Regulations and Congressional Proposals (2009), available at http://waxman.house.gov/sites/waxman.house.gov/files/documents/UploadedFiles/Exec_Compensation.pdf (accessed 20 Nov., 2012).

[39]   This difficulty was analyzed in Dooley, supra note 20. Among other reasons for this difficulty of enforcement is the fact that, under the right circumstances, as much gain can be had from knowing when not to sell or not to buy as from the obverse. But, since there is no "transaction," this behavior is not generally a violation of Rule 10b-5, 17 C.F.R. 240.10b-5 (2007). Results in recent empirical studies relating to enforcement, however, have been a mixed bag, which probably reflects severe methodological problems. See, e.g., Arturo Bris, Do Insider Trading Laws Work?, 11 Eur. Fin. Mgmt. 267 (2005); Aaron Gilbert et al., Insiders and the Law: The Impact of Regulatory Change on Insider Trading, 47 Mgmt. Int'l Rev. 745 (2007); Bart Frijns et al., Elements of Effective Insider Trading Laws (n.d.) (unpublished manuscript, on file with author), available at http://ssrn.com/abstract=1443597 (accessed 20 Nov., 2012).

flourishes, perhaps even done by the right people sometimes.[40] Commonly, even today, a major news story about a corporation is preceded by a movement of the stock price in the direction indicated by the news. Traders are cashing in on the development; it would certainly be desirable if they were the same people who in some sense and in some measure were responsible for positive developments.

---

[40]   See, e.g., Illegal Insider Trading: How Widespread Is the Problem and Is There Adequate Criminal Enforcement?: Hearings Before the S. Comm. on the Judiciary, 109th Cong. (2006); Brent Shearer, Forbidden Fruit, Mergers & Acquisitions, Oct. 2007, at 66; Jenny Strasburg & Chad Bray, Six Charged in Vast Insider-Trading Ring, Wall St. J., Oct. 17, 2009, at A1.

5. Regulating insider trading in the post-fiduciary duty era: equal access or property rights?
Stephen M. Bainbridge

I. INTRODUCTION

Why do we regulate insider trading? In *Texas Gulf Sulphur*,[1] the US Second Circuit Court of Appeals opined that "all investors trading on impersonal exchanges" should have "relatively equal access to material information"[2] and "be subject to identical market risks."[3] This rationale presented a number of doctrinal and policy problems, but at least was linked to a core problem of securities regulation; namely, controlling flows of information to the capital markets.

In his *Chiarella*[4] and *Dirks*[5] opinions, US Supreme Court Justice Lewis Powell led the Court in rejecting the equal access rationale in favor of a new focus on disclosure obligations arising out of fiduciary relationships. In doing so, Powell solved some of the problems created by the equal access rationale, but created a new set of doctrinal and policy issues. In particular, Powell's rationale largely severed the link between the insider trading prohibition and the core concerns of securities law.

Powell's fiduciary duty rationale met substantial resistance from the US Securities and Exchange Commission (SEC) and the lower courts. Through both regulatory actions and judicial opinions, the SEC and the courts gradually chipped away at the fiduciary duty rationale.[6] In recent years, the trend has accelerated, with several developments having substantially eviscerated the fiduciary duty requirement.

The current unsettled state of insider trading jurisprudence necessitates rethinking the foundational premises of that jurisprudence from first principles. This chapter argues that the correct rationale for regulation of insider trading is protecting property rights in information. Although that rationale obviously has little to do with the traditional concerns of securities regulation, this chapter further argues that the SEC has a sufficiently substantial advantage in detecting and prosecuting insider trading that it should retain jurisdiction over the offense.

---

[1] SEC v. Texas Gulf Sulphur Co., 401 F.2d 833 (2d Cir.), cert. denied, 394 U.S. 976 (1968).
[2] Id. at 847.
[3] Id. at 852.
[4] Chiarella v. US, 445 U.S. 222 (1980).
[5] Dirks v. SEC, 463 U.S. 646 (1983).
[6] In an important article, Professor Donna Nagy first brought attention to this trend. Donna M. Nagy, Insider Trading and the Gradual Demise of Fiduciary Principles, 94 Iowa L. Rev. 1315 (2009).

II. FROM EQUAL ACCESS TO FIDUCIARY DUTY

Because neither the text nor the legislative history of the Exchange Act § 10(b) or Rule 10b-5 defines insider trading—or even expressly proscribes it—it was left to the courts to develop not just the relevant legal rules but also the very justification for prohibiting insider trading. In *SEC v. Texas Gulf Sulphur Co.*,[7] the Second Circuit held that an insider in possession of material nonpublic information must either disclose such information before trading or abstain from trading until the information becomes public. *Texas Gulf Sulphur* thus brought insider trading into the domain of securities law and, accordingly, within the SEC's regulatory jurisdiction.

There was, however, nothing inevitable about that outcome. State corporate law had regulated insider trading for decades before *Texas Gulf Sulphur* was decided. Well-established state precedents treated the problem as one implicating not concepts of deceit or manipulation, but rather the fiduciary duties of corporate officers and directors.[8] Accordingly, the Second Circuit could have held that insider trading simply was not within Rule 10b-5's regulatory purview.

In order to link insider trading to the goals of the federal securities laws, the Second Circuit claimed Congress intended those laws to ensure that "all investors trading on impersonal exchanges have relatively equal access to material information"[9] and "be subject to identical market risks."[10] As a rationale for regulating insider trading, equality of access has some appeal. Disclosure, after all, is a basic principle of securities regulation. Equal access also addresses the purported unfairness inherent when insiders trade with less well-informed outsiders.

The *Texas Gulf Sulphur* court cited no legislative history or statutory text supporting the equal access principle, however, relying instead on one SEC administrative proceeding. As Michael Dooley argued, moreover, "insider trading in no way resembles deceit. No representation is made, nor is there any reliance, change of position, or causal connection between the defendant's act and the plaintiff's losses."[11] Equal access thus was not an inherent feature of the securities laws scheme as contemplated by Congress but rather simply the product of judicial fiat.

Equal access also implied a prohibition that swept far too broadly. In *Chiarella*, for example, Justice Powell noted that a broad equal access rule might "prohibit a tender offeror's purchases of target corporation stock before public announcement of the offer," a step Congress clearly had declined to take when it adopted the Williams Act to regulate tender offers.[12] In *Dirks*, Justice Powell further explained that such a broad policy basis for regulating insider trading implied a ban that "could have an inhibiting influence on the

---

[7]   401 F.2d 833 (2d Cir.), cert. denied, 394 U.S. 976 (1968).

[8]   Stephen M. Bainbridge, Incorporating State Law Fiduciary Duties into the Federal Insider Trading Prohibition, 52 Wash. & Lee L. Rev. 1189, 1218–27 (1995).

[9]   *Texas Gulf Sulphur*, 401 F.2d at 847.

[10]   Id. at 852.

[11]   Michael P. Dooley, Enforcement of Insider Trading Restrictions, 66 Va. L. Rev. 1, 59 (1980).

[12]   *Chiarella*, 445 U.S. at 233.

role of market analysts, which the SEC itself recognizes is necessary to the preservation of a healthy market."[13]

> It is commonplace for analysts to "ferret out and analyze information," and this often is done by meeting with and questioning corporate officers and others who are insiders. And information that the analysts obtain normally may be the basis for judgments as to the market worth of a corporation's securities. The analyst's judgment in this respect is made available in market letters or otherwise to clients of the firm. It is the nature of this type of information, and indeed of the markets themselves, that such information cannot be made simultaneously available to all of the corporation's stockholders or the public generally.[14]

It was in order to avoid chilling such legitimate activity that Powell sought out a policy rationale that would sweep far less broadly. He found it in the principle that the duty to disclose or abstain "arises from a specific relationship between two parties."[15] Accordingly, "there can be no duty to disclose where the person who has traded on inside information 'was not [the corporation's] agent, . . . was not a fiduciary, [or] was not a person in whom the sellers [of the securities] had placed their trust and confidence.'"[16]

Just as there had been nothing historically or economically inevitable about *Texas Gulf Sulphur*'s imposition of the equal access standard, there equally was nothing inevitable about the Supreme Court's rejection of that standard. The equal access standard was consistent with a trend towards affirmative disclosure obligations and away from *caveat emptor* that was sweeping across a broad swath of the common law.[17] In rejecting this trend, Justice Powell arguably shifted the focus of insider trading liability from deceit to agency, a point that becomes especially significant later in our analysis.[18] Nothing in the text of the statute or the rule explicitly mandated that shift; nor did the relevant precedents require it. To the contrary, Justice Powell's use of precedent in *Chiarella* and *Dirks* was highly suspect. In *Dirks*, for example, he opined:

> In the seminal case of *In re Cady, Roberts & Co.*, the SEC recognized that the common law in some jurisdictions imposes on "corporate 'insiders,' particularly officers, directors, or controlling shareholders" an "affirmative duty of disclosure . . . when dealing in securities." The SEC found that . . . breach of this common law duty also establish[ed] the elements of a Rule 10b-5 violation . . . ."[19]

Although he acknowledged that the common law duty upon which *Cady, Roberts* purportedly rested existed only in "some jurisdictions," he failed to acknowledge that that duty was essentially limited to face-to-face transactions between the issuer's offic-

---

[13]   *Dirks*, 463 U.S. at 658.
[14]   Id. at 658–59 (citations and footnotes omitted).
[15]   *Chiarella*, 445 U.S. at 233.
[16]   *Dirks*, 463 U.S. at 654 (quoting *Chiarella*, 445 U.S. at 232).
[17]   Donald C. Langevoort, Words From on High About Rule 10b-5: Chiarella's History, Central Bank's Future, 20 Del. J. Corp. L. 865, 870–71 (1995).
[18]   A.C. Pritchard, United States v. O'Hagan: Agency Law and Justice Powell's Legacy for the Law of Insider Trading, 78 Bos. Univ. L. Rev. 13 (1998).
[19]   *Dirks*, 463 U.S. at 653.

ers or directors and the issuer's current shareholders. With no analysis or citation of authority, moreover, Powell extrapolated from this limited state common law duty the all-encompassing federal rule that all "insiders [are] forbidden by their fiduciary relationship from personally using undisclosed corporate information to their advantage."[20]

Powell also failed to reconcile his fiduciary duty-based framework with a central principle of Rule 10b-5 jurisprudence; namely, that there is no such thing as a "federal fiduciary principle."[21] In *Santa Fe*, the Supreme Court had held that Rule 10b-5 did not reach claims "in which the essence of the complaint is that shareholders were treated unfairly by a fiduciary."[22] This is, of course, the very essence of the complaint made in insider trading cases. The Court also expressed reluctance "to federalize the substantial portion of the law of corporations that deals with transactions in securities, particularly where established state policies of corporate regulation would be overridden,"[23] which is precisely what the federal insider trading prohibition did.

Powell's reframing of insider trading law thus was no less problematic than the equal access principle it replaced. Like equal access, the fiduciary duty approach lacked any basis in the text or legislative history of the statute and rule. Like equal access, precedent weakly supported Powell's approach. Instead, like equal access, basing insider trading liability on a fiduciary duty to disclose was essentially a matter of judicial fiat. It was the deference his colleagues paid Powell on securities law matters that turned it into law, rather than its intrinsic merits.[24] Unlike equal access, however, Powell's approach lacked any obvious link to the purposes of the securities laws and, moreover, created a clear conflict with the federalism-based limits on those laws.

III.   THE SEC STRIKES BACK

The SEC has powerful institutional reasons for favoring a broad insider trading prohibition. A vigorous enforcement program directed at a highly visible and unpopular law violation such as insider trading is an effective means of attracting political support for larger budgets. The SEC's prominent role in attacking insider trading also placed it in the vanguard of the movement to federalize corporate law and ensured that the Commission would have a leading role in any system of federal corporations law.[25]

It is thus not surprising that the SEC responded to the substantial narrowing of the insider trading prohibition effected by *Chiarella* and *Dirks* by developing new theories of liability that would recapture as much of the lost ground as possible. The process began with development of the so-called misappropriation theory. It bans the use of

---

[20]   Id. at 659.

[21]   See Santa Fe Indus. v. Green, 430 U.S. 462, 479 (1977).

[22]   Id. at 477.

[23]   Id. at 479.

[24]   See generally Stephen M. Bainbridge & G. Mitu Gulati, How Do Judges Maximize? (The Same Way Everybody Else Does—Boundedly): Rules of Thumb in Securities Fraud Opinions, 51 Emory L. J. 83 (2002).

[25]   See Bainbridge, supra note 8, at 1247–48.

"confidential information for securities trading purposes, in breach of a duty owed to the source of the information,"[26] even if the inside trader owed no duties to the persons with whom he traded or the issuer of the securities in which he traded. Someone thus can be held liable under this theory only where they have deceived the source of the information by failing to disclose to the source their intent to trade on the basis of the information learned from the source.[27]

The misappropriation theory perhaps complied with the letter of the *Chiarella/Dirks* fiduciary relationship-based framework, but it clearly evaded the spirit of Powell's intent. The misappropriation theory first reached the Supreme Court in *US v. Carpenter*.[28] After the court initially voted to deny certiorari, Justice Powell prepared a draft dissent arguing that the misappropriation theory was inconsistent with *Chiarella* and *Dirks*. In Powell's view, Rule 10b-5 had incorporated the common law principle that silence is fraudulent solely where one party to the transaction owes a fiduciary duty of disclosure to the other.[29] Breach of a duty owed to someone else, such as the source of the information, thus did not violate Rule 10b-5.

Powell's draft dissent was never published. The Supreme Court decided to grant certiorari in the *Carpenter* case. While the case was pending, however, Powell retired from the Court. The Court thereafter affirmed the defendant's misappropriation theory-based convictions by a 4–4 vote without opinion. Because *Carpenter* thus set no precedent, the way was left open for the misappropriation theory to continue chipping away at the *Chiarella/Dirks* framework.

When the Supreme Court finally ruled on the misappropriation theory in *O'Hagan*, Justice Ginsburg's opinion validating the theory confirmed that a far more sweeping prohibition had displaced Powell's approach to insider trading. In particular, Ginsburg expressly rejected "the notion that *Chiarella* required that the fraud be between parties to the securities transaction."[30] The misappropriation theory thereby significantly expanded the categories of persons covered by the insider trading prohibition. While the resulting prohibition perhaps was not quite as sweeping as equal access had been, the prospect of liability had been resurrected with respect to most of the significant categories of potential defendants freed from that prospect by *Chiarella*.

As noted above, Powell's claim that liability required a duty of disclosure arising out of a relationship between the parties to the transaction was not obviously required by the securities laws; it was mere judicial fiat. The same was true of Justice Ginsburg's claim that liability could be premised on a duty of disclosure owed to the source of the information.[31]

As was the case with both equal access and Powell's approach, moreover, Ginsburg's version of the misappropriation theory was difficult to square with the basic premises

---

[26]   U.S. v. O'Hagan, 521 U.S. 642, 652 (1997).

[27]   Id. at 2208.

[28]   484 U.S. 19 (1987).

[29]   A.C. Pritchard, Justice Lewis F. Powell, Jr. and the Counter-Revolution in the Federal Securities Laws, 52 Duke L. J. 841, 944 (2003).

[30]   Pritchard, supra note 18, at 42.

[31]   See Nagy, supra note 6, at 1335. ("Unfortunately, the Court in *O'Hagan* never came to terms with why its misappropriation theory 'was limited to those who breached a recognized duty' and why 'feigning fidelity' to the information's source was essential.")

of securities regulation. Securities laws seek to protect investors and preserve investor confidence in the integrity of the securities markets.[32] As formulated by Justice Ginsburg, however, the misappropriation theory seems largely detached from those goals.

In *US v. Carpenter*,[33] for example, the key defendant was R. Foster Winans, who wrote the Wall Street Journal's "Heard on the Street" column, which was (and is) a daily report on various stocks that is said to affect the price of the stocks discussed. Journal policy expressly treated the column's contents prior to publication as confidential information belonging to the newspaper. Despite that rule, Winans provided several co-conspirators with prepublication information as to the timing and contents of future columns. His fellow conspirators then traded in those stocks based on the expected impact of the column on the stocks' prices, sharing the profits.

Any duties Winans owed in this situation ran to an entity that had neither issued the securities in question nor even participated in stock market transactions. What Winans's breach of his duties to the Wall Street Journal has to do with the federal securities laws is not immediately apparent.

The incongruity of the misappropriation theory becomes even more apparent when one considers that its logic suggests that the Wall Street Journal could lawfully trade on the same information used by Winans. If we are really concerned with protecting investors and maintaining their confidence in the market's integrity, the inside trader's identity ought to be irrelevant. As *Texas Gulf Sulphur* recognized, from the investors' point of view, insider trading is a matter of concern because they have traded with someone with superior access to information. From the investor's perspective, it does not matter whether it is Winans or the Journal on the opposite side of the transaction. Both have greater access to the relevant information than do investors.

The logic of the misappropriation theory also suggests that Winans would not have been liable if the Wall Street Journal had authorized his trades. In that instance, his trades would not have constituted an improper conversion of nonpublic information and the essential breach of fiduciary duty would not be present. Again, however, from an investor's perspective, it would not seem to matter whether Winans's trades were authorized or not.

Turning to other examples, because it is premised on a fiduciary duty of disclosure owed to the source of the information, the misappropriation theory has no application to "securities trading by a stranger who had stolen confidential information from its source."[34] It is equally inapplicable to fiduciaries that "brazenly shared with their principal their intention to trade."[35] Once again, however, such trades seem just as likely to shake investor confidence as any of the trades proscribed by *O'Hagan*.

---

[32]   See, e.g., Central Bank of Denver, N.A. v. First Interstate Bank of Denver, N.A., 511 U.S. 164, 173 (1994) ("the broad congressional purposes behind the [securities laws are] to protect investors from false and misleading practices that might injure them").

[33]   791 F.2d 1024 (2d Cir. 1986), aff'd, 484 U.S. 19 (1987).

[34]   Nagy, supra note 6, at 1334.

[35]   Id. at 1335.

IV.   FROM FIDUCIARY DUTY BACK TO EQUAL ACCESS

In a rare moment of candor, a former SEC Commissioner admitted that the Commission's development of the misappropriation theory served "merely a pretext for enforcing equal opportunity in information."[36] Yet, so long as the ban on insider trading remained tethered to fiduciary relationships, it could not recapture all of the ground lost in *Chiarella*. It is thus not surprising that the SEC has repeatedly advanced new theories of liability that push the boundaries of fiduciary relationships to the breaking beyond and, especially in recent years, outright abandon the fiduciary duty-based framework.

A.   Stretching Fiduciary Duty to the Breaking Point

In *Chiarella*, Justice Powell had premised liability on "a fiduciary or other similar relation of trust and confidence between" the parties to the transaction.[37] This formulation posed two avenues for expanding the scope of the insider trading liability. First, as Professor Nagy observed, the *Chiarella*, *Dirks*, and *O'Hagan* trilogy demonstrated that the Supreme Court was "willing to stretch fiduciary principles to no small degree, when doing so facilitates a desirable policy outcome."[38] In turn, this "emboldened lower courts to approach new issues with similar results-oriented reasoning" stretching the concept of a fiduciary relation to breaking point.[39]

Secondly, the reference to a "similar relation of trust and confidence" suggested another avenue for policy-driven outcomes. If a court wished to impose liability, it simply needed to conclude that the relationship in question involves trust and confidence, even though the relationship bears no resemblance to those in which fiduciary-like duties are normally imposed. In *US v. Chestman*,[40] the Second Circuit tried to prevent such outcomes by holding that a relationship of trust and confidence must be "the functional equivalent of a fiduciary relationship" before liability can be imposed.[41] In the case at bar, the relationship in question was a marital one between spouses. The Court held that that relationship lacked the "discretionary authority and dependency" inherent in fiduciary relationships.[42] In addition, the Court emphasized that "entrusting confidential information to another does not, without more, create the necessary relationship and its correlative duty to maintain the confidence."[43]

In 2000, however, the SEC eviscerated *Chestman* by adopting Rule 10b5-2. It provides "a nonexclusive list of three situations in which a person has a duty of trust or confidence for purposes of the 'misappropriation' theory."[44] First, such a duty exists whenever someone

---

[36]   Charles C. Cox & Kevin S. Fogarty, Bases of Insider Trading Law, 49 Ohio St. L. J. 353, 366 (1988).

[37]   *Chiarella*, 445 U.S. at 228.

[38]   Nagy, supra note 6, at 1339–40.

[39]   Id.

[40]   947 F.2d 551 (2d Cir.1991) (citations omitted), cert. denied, 503 U.S. 1004 (1992).

[41]   Id. at 568.

[42]   Id. at 569.

[43]   Id. at 568.

[44]   Exchange Act Rel. No 43,154 (Aug. 15, 2000).

agrees to maintain information in confidence. Secondly, such a duty exists between two people who have a pattern or practice of sharing confidences such that the recipient of the information knows or reasonably should know that the speaker expects the recipient to maintain the information's confidentiality. Thirdly, such a duty exists when someone receives or obtains material nonpublic information from a spouse, parent, child, or sibling.

In adopting the rule, the SEC made a subtle move by turning the Supreme Court's conjunctive phrase "trust and confidence" into the disjunctive form "trust or confidence." As Professor Nagy explains:

> This change from the conjunctive to the disjunctive extends the scope of the misappropriation theory considerably. To be sure, the terms "trust" and "confidence" are often used synonymously to describe reliance on the character or ability of someone to act in a right and proper way. But as used in Rule 10b5-2, the term "confidence" may align more with an obligation of "confidentiality" than with obligations predicated on trust and loyalty.[45]

The potential significance of this move is illustrated by *SEC v. Cuban*.[46] Defendant Mark Cuban was a large shareholder in a firm called Mamma.com Inc. Cuban was informed by Mama.com's CEO that the company planned a private investment in public equity (PIPE) offering that would result in significant dilution of outstanding shares and concomitant drop in stock price. Cuban sold his shares before the PIPE offering was made public and thereby avoided a substantial loss. The SEC then brought suit, arguing that Cuban breached a "duty created by his agreement to keep confidential the information that Mamma.com's CEO provided him about the impending PIPE offering."[47] The district court partially rejected the SEC's position. Despite Rule 10b5-2, the court held that the relevant Supreme Court precedents contemplated liability based on breach of a contractual obligation but only if the contract imposed a duty of confidentiality and a duty of non-use. On appeal, the Fifth Circuit vacated the district court opinion and remanded for trial without reaching the issue of Rule 10b5-2's validity.

Even assuming the district court's restriction on 10b5-2 is eventually upheld, Rule 10b5-2 will still violate the *Chiarella/Dirks* framework. As the *Chestman* opinion correctly explained, those cases clearly require something more than a mere contract. They require a fiduciary relationship. If Rule 10b5-2 is valid, however, that requirement has been stretched to its breaking point.[48]

B. Insider Trading Liability Without a Fiduciary Relationship

1. Rule 14e-3
The SEC adopted Rule 14e-3 in response to the wave of insider trading activity associated with the increase in merger and acquisition activity during the 1980s. The rule prohibits

---

[45] Nagy, supra note 6, at 1360.
[46] 634 F.Supp.2d 713 (N.D. Tex. 2009), vacated and remanded, 620 F.3d 551 (5th Cir. 2010). Along with several other insider trading scholars, the author signed amicus briefs in both the district and circuit court proceedings in support of defendant Cuban's interpretation of Rule 10b5-2.
[47] Id. at 721.
[48] For an argument that Rule 10b5-1 similarly eviscerates the fiduciary relationship requirement, see Nagy, supra note 6, at 1353–57.

insiders of the bidder and target from divulging confidential information about a tender offer to persons that are likely to violate the rule by trading on the basis of that information. Rule 14e-3 also, with certain narrow and well-defined exceptions, prohibits any person that possesses material information relating to a tender offer by another person from trading in target company securities if the bidder has commenced or has taken substantial steps towards commencement of the bid.

Unlike both the disclose or abstain rule and the misappropriation theory under Rule 10b-5, Rule 14e-3 liability is not premised on breach of a fiduciary duty. There is no need for a showing that the trading party or tipper was subject to any duty of confidentiality, and no need to show that a tipper personally benefited from the tip. In light of the well-established fiduciary duty requirement under Rule 10b-5, however, the rule should have run afoul of *Schreiber v. Burlington Northern, Inc.*[49] In that case, the Supreme Court held that § 14(e) was modeled on § 10(b) and, like that section, requires a showing of misrepresentation or nondisclosure. As such, the two sections are to be interpreted *in pari materia*. Because § 10(b) requires a showing of a breach of a disclosure duty arising out of a fiduciary relationship, Rule 14e-3 appeared to exceed the SEC's statutory authority.

In *O'Hagan*, however, the Supreme Court upheld Rule 14e-3 as a valid exercise of the SEC's rulemaking authority despite the absence of a fiduciary duty element.[50] It thus set the stage for subsequent developments abandoning the fiduciary duty element.

2.   Hackers and other non-fiduciary thieves

SEC v. Dorozhko[51] dealt with a question left open by *O'Hagan*; namely, the liability of persons who steal inside information but have no fiduciary duty to either the source of the information or the issuer of the securities in which the thief trades. In *Dorozhko*, the SEC alleged that a computer hacker broke into a health information company's computer system and stole confidential information about an undisclosed earnings decline. The hacker then made a substantial profit by selling the company's stock short. The Second Circuit tried to finesse the fiduciary duty requirement by arguing that "the SEC's claim against the defendant—a corporate outsider who owed no fiduciary duties to the source of the information—is not based on either of the two generally accepted theories of insider trading."[52] The problem is that the only hole into which this case fits is the one designed for an insider trading peg.

An affirmative misappropriation can be actionable under Section 10(b) and Rule 10b-5 if it is committed in connection with the purchase or sale of a security. In order to find that the hacker committed an affirmative misrepresentation, a court first must find a lie. Calling computer hacking a lie is a rather considerable stretch. At most, the hacker "lies" to a computer network, not a person. Hacking is theft; it is not fraud.

Even if hacking is fraudulent in the sense of an affirmative misrepresentation, the requisite misrepresentation must be made in connection with a purchase or sale of a security to be insider trading. In *SEC v. Zandford*,[53] the Supreme Court emphasized that

---

[49]   472 U.S. 1 (1985).
[50]   521 U.S. at 667–77.
[51]   574 F.3d 42 (2d Cir. 2009).
[52]   Id. at 45.
[53]   535 U.S. 813 (2002).

"the statute must not be construed so broadly as to convert every common-law fraud that happens to involve securities into a violation of § 10(b)."[54] Accordingly, the district court in *Dorozhko* correctly "found it 'noteworthy' that in the over seventy years since the enactment of the Securities Exchange Act of 1934, 'no federal court has ever held that those who steal material nonpublic information and then trade on it violate § 10(b),' even though 'traditional theft (e.g. breaking into an investment bank and stealing documents) is hardly a new phenomenon, and involves similar elements for purposes of our analysis here.'"[55]

"Traditional theft" has not given rise to insider trading liability because, the district court correctly noted, "the Supreme Court has in a number of opinions carefully established that the essential component of a § 10(b) violation is a breach of a fiduciary duty to disclose or abstain that coincides with a securities transaction."[56] *Dorozhko* thus is properly understood to be an end run by the SEC—aided and abetted by the Second Circuit—around that carefully established requirement. As such, it establishes an important precedent for the SEC and courts to collaborate on future inventive means of end-running the Supreme Court's clear insider trading jurisprudence.

3.   SOX § 807

Section 807 of the Sarbanes–Oxley Act (SOX) added a new § 1348 to the US Criminal Code, which provides that:

> Whoever knowingly executes, or attempts to execute, a scheme or artifice—
>   (1) to defraud any person in connection with any security of an issuer with a class of securities registered under section 12 of the Securities Exchange Act of 1934 or that is required to file reports under section 15(d) of the Securities Exchange Act of 1934; or
>   (2) to obtain, by means of false or fraudulent pretenses, representations, or promises, any money or property in connection with the purchase or sale of any security of an issuer with a class of securities registered under section 12 of the Securities Exchange Act of 1934 or that is required to file reports under section 15(d) of the Securities Exchange Act of 1934 shall be fined under this title, or imprisoned not more than 25 years, or both.[57]

Neither the text nor its sparse legislative history shed much light on what Congress intended it to do. About all one can say for sure is that Congress intended to significantly increase the penalties in securities fraud cases and to make it easier for prosecutors to prove such cases by eliminating the so-called "technical elements" of existing provisions such as § 10(b) and Rule 10b-5.[58] Is Powell's fiduciary duty requirement such a technical element?

In *US v. Mahaffy*,[59] defendant stockbrokers tipped nonpublic information to defendant day traders in return for cash. The case could and should have been prosecuted under the misappropriation theory. In *Mahaffy*, however, the prosecutors charged the defendants with violation § 1348. In upholding the charge as a proper one, the district court did

---

[54]   Id. at 820.
[55]   SEC v. Dorozhko, 606 F. Supp. 2d 321, 339 (SDNY 2008).
[56]   Id. at 323.
[57]   Sarbanes–Oxley Act of 2002 § 807, Pub. L. No 107-204, 116 Stat. 745 (2002) (to be codified at 18 USC § 1348) (citation omitted).
[58]   Kenneth M. Breen & Keith W. Miller, Securities Fraud, 32 Champion 49 (2009).
[59]   2006 WL 2224518 (E.D.N.Y. 2006).

not require the prosecution to prove that the tippers had breached a duty of confidence arising out of a fiduciary relationship owed either to the source of the relationship or to the persons with whom the tippees traded. Indeed, of the Supreme Court trilogy, the district court mentioned only *O'Hagan* and only in passing.[60]

"The *Mahaffy* decision [thus] reflects the first step of a potential sea change in the elements required of the government to prove a criminal insider trading violation."[61] It casts aside, albeit *sub silentio*, the need for the prosecution to show a breach of a duty to disclose arising out of a fiduciary relationship or similar relationship of trust and confidence. Instead, by analogizing "§ 1348 to an honest services fraud case," *Mahaffy* "requires only a material misrepresentation, not a violation of confidence."[62] Although the SEC will be unable to avail itself of § 1348 potentially significant gutting of the fiduciary duty requirement, since the SEC lacks power to bring criminal cases, § 1348 thus must nevertheless be counted as having knocked one more brick out of the wall.

V.   FROM EQUAL ACCESS TO PROPERTY RIGHTS IN INFORMATION

Justice Powell's vision of an insider trading prohibition based on and constrained by a fiduciary relationship between the parties to the transaction is fast fading. As we have seen, new theories that stretch the fiduciary duty requirement to the breaking point have found acceptance. Perhaps emboldened by those successes, the SEC and lower courts have even developed several theories under which liability can be imposed without reference to fiduciary duties.[63]

Setting aside *stare decisis*, there is no obvious reason why courts should cling to the fiduciary duty requirement. The late Chief Justice Rehnquist famously remarked that Rule 10b-5 is "a judicial oak which has grown from little more than a legislative acorn."[64] We are dealing here with a species of federal common law, in which courts have relied more on policy and prudential considerations than either the text or the statute.[65] The courts created the fiduciary duty requirement by judicial fiat, with no substantial basis in either precedent or statute, so if policy and prudence argue for a different approach, they should be free to adopt one.

At present, however, we are stuck in an odd sort of halfway house. Without clear

---

[60]   Id. at *12.

[61]   Breen & Miller, supra note 58.

[62]   Id.

[63]   One of the more puzzling features of the federal insider trading prohibition is the willingness of courts to aid and abet the Commission's efforts. Although the SEC's incentive to erect a broad insider trading prohibition seems easily explicable, it is far less clear why courts would be willing to go along. Yet they have consistently done so. For an explanation of this phenomenon, see Stephen M. Bainbridge, Insider Trading Regulation: The Path Dependent Choice between Property Rights and Securities Fraud, 52 SMU L. Rev. 1589 (1999).

[64]   Blue Chip Stamps v. Manor Drug Stores, 421 U.S. 723, 737 (1975).

[65]   Paul Gonson & David E. Butler, In Wake of "Dirks," Courts Debate Definition of "Insider," Leg. Times, Apr. 2, 1984, at 16. ("Modern development of the law of insider trading is a classic example of common law in the federal courts.")

guidance from the Supreme Court, the lower courts understandably have felt compelled to at least pay lip service to Powell's vision. At the same time, however, there has been enough erosion of that vision to move us substantially back towards an equal access test. Indeed, it seems fair to say that the developments reviewed above all point towards a gradual return to equal access as the foundational rationale for regulating insider trading.

Reviving the old equal access standard, however, makes no policy sense. As we have seen, equal access is no more compelled by the statute than was Powell's vision. Instead, like Powell's vision, it was the product of judicial fiat rather than Congressional intent. In addition, as Powell correctly complained, equality of access results in standards that inevitably chill important functions by market makers and analysts that contribute significantly to the efficiency of the capital markets. Taken to its logical extreme, moreover, equal access would forbid traders from trading on the basis of their own intentions. Under current law, for example, a prospective takeover bidder can buy up to 5 percent of an issuer's equity securities before having to disclose its intentions. Under an equal access standard, however, a prospective takeover bidder would face liability because it failed to disclose information it possessed that was unavailable to others.

If one steps back and evaluates insider trading from first principles, what immediately jumps out at one is that we are really dealing with property rights in information. There are essentially two ways of creating property rights in information. First, the law may allow the owner to enter into transactions without disclosing the information. Secondly, the law may prohibit others from using the information. In effect, the federal insider trading prohibition vests a property right of the latter type in the party to whom the insider trader owes a fiduciary duty to refrain from self-dealing in confidential information.

Granted, the insider trading prohibition does not look very much like most property rights. Enforcement of the insider trading prohibition admittedly differs rather dramatically from enforcement of, say, trespassing laws. The existence of property rights in a variety of intangibles, including information, however, is well established. Trademarks, copyrights, and patents are but a few of the better-known examples of this phenomenon. There are striking doctrinal parallels, moreover, between insider trading and these other types of property rights in information. Using another's trade secret, for example, is actionable only if taking the trade secret involved a breach of fiduciary duty, misrepresentation, or theft.

In context, moreover, even the insider trading prohibition's enforcement mechanisms are not inconsistent with a property rights analysis. Where public policy argues for giving someone a property right, but the costs of enforcing such a right would be excessive, the state often uses its regulatory powers as a substitute for creating private property rights. Insider trading poses just such a situation. Private enforcement of the insider trading laws is rare and usually parasitic on public enforcement proceedings. Indeed, the very nature of insider trading arguably makes public regulation essential precisely because private enforcement is almost impossible. The insider trading prohibition's regulatory nature thus need not preclude a property rights-based analysis.

The rationale for prohibiting insider trading is the same as that for prohibiting patent infringement or theft of trade secrets: protecting the economic incentive to produce socially valuable information. As the theory goes, the readily appropriable nature of information makes it difficult for the developer of a new idea to recoup the sunk costs incurred to develop it. If an inventor develops a better mousetrap, for example, he cannot profit on that invention without selling mousetraps and thereby making the new design available to potential competitors. Assuming both the inventor and his competitors incur roughly equivalent marginal costs to produce and market the trap, the competitors will be able to set a market price at which the inventor likely will be unable to earn a return on his sunk costs. *Ex post*, the rational inventor should ignore his sunk costs and go on producing the improved mousetrap. *Ex ante*, however, the inventor will anticipate that he will be unable to generate positive returns on his up-front costs and therefore will be deterred from developing socially valuable information. Accordingly, society provides incentives for inventive activity by using the patent system to give inventors a property right in new ideas. By preventing competitors from appropriating the idea, the patent allows the inventor to charge monopolistic prices for the improved mousetrap, thereby recouping his sunk costs. Trademark, copyright, and trade secret law all are justified on similar grounds.

In many cases, of course, more than one person can use information without necessarily lowering its value. If a manager who has just negotiated a major contract for his employer then trades in his employer's stock, for example, there is no reason to believe that the manager's conduct necessarily lowers the value of the contract to the employer. But while insider trading will not always harm the employer, it may do so in some circumstances.

First, insider trading could injure the firm if it creates incentives for managers to delay the transmission of information to superiors. Decision making in any entity requires accurate, timely information. In large, hierarchical organizations, such as publicly traded corporations, information must pass through many levels before reaching senior managers, which increases the risk of distortion or delay.[66] This risk can be reduced by downward delegation of decision-making authority but not eliminated. Managers who discover or obtain information (either beneficial or detrimental to the firm) may delay disclosure of that information to other managers so as to assure themselves sufficient time to trade on the basis of that information before the corporation acts upon it. Even if the period of delay by any one manager is brief, the net delay produced by successive trading managers may be substantial. Conversely, insider trading may create incentives to release information early just as often as it creates incentives to delay transmission and disclosure of information.

Secondly, insider trading might adversely interfere with corporate plans. If managers charged with overseeing an acquisition buy shares in the target, and their trading has a significant upward effect on the price of the target's stock, the takeover will be more expensive. If their trading causes significant price and volume changes, that also might tip off others to the secret, interfering with the bidder's plans, as by alerting the target to the need for defensive measures.

The risk of premature disclosure poses an even more serious threat to corporate plans. The issuer often has just as much interest in when information becomes public as it does in whether the information becomes public. Suppose Target, Inc., enters into merger negotiations with a potential acquirer. Target managers who inside trade on the basis of that information will rarely need to delay corporate action in order to effect their purchases. Having made their purchases, however, the managers now have an incentive to cause dis-

---

[66]   See generally Robert J. Haft, The Effect of Insider Trading Rules on the Internal Efficiency of the Large Corporation, 80 Mich. L. Rev. 1051 (1982).

closure of Target's plans as soon as possible. Absent leaks or other forms of derivatively informed trading, the merger will have no price effect until it is disclosed to the market, at which time there usually is a strong positive effect. Once the information is disclosed, the trading managers will be able to reap substantial profits, but until disclosure takes place, they bear a variety of firm-specific and market risks. The deal, the stock market, or both may collapse at any time. Early disclosure enables the managers to minimize those risks by selling out as soon as the price jumps in response to the announcement.

If disclosure is made too early, a variety of adverse consequences may result. If disclosure triggers competing bids, the initial bidder may withdraw from the bidding or demand protection in the form of costly lock-ups and other exclusivity provisions. Alternatively, if disclosure does not trigger competing bids, the initial bidder may conclude that it overbid and lower its offer accordingly. In addition, early disclosure brings the deal to the attention of regulators and plaintiffs' lawyers earlier than necessary.

Although insider trading probably only rarely causes the firm to lose opportunities, it may create incentives for management to alter firm plans in less drastic ways to increase the likelihood and magnitude of trading profits. For example, trading managers can accelerate receipt of revenue, change depreciation strategy, or alter dividend payments in an attempt to affect share prices and insider returns. Alternatively, the insiders might structure corporate transactions to increase the opportunity for secret keeping. Both types of decision may adversely affect the firm and its shareholders. Moreover, this incentive may result in allocative inefficiency by encouraging over-investment in those industries or activities that generate opportunities for insider trading.

Thirdly, managers may elect to follow policies that increase fluctuations in the price of the firm's stock.[67] They may select riskier projects than the shareholders would prefer, because, if the risks pay off, they can capture a portion of the gains in insider trading and, if the project flops, the shareholders bear the loss. Indeed, insider trading may even encourage management to select negative net present value investments, not only because shareholders bear the full risk of failure, but also because failure presents management with an opportunity for profit through short selling. As a result, shareholders might prefer other incentive schemes.

Fourthly, corporations have significant liability exposure when their agents inside trade. Section 20(a) of the Securities Exchange Act provides that:

> Every person who, directly or indirectly, controls any person liable under any provision of this chapter or of any rule or regulation thereunder shall also be liable jointly and severally with and to the same extent as such controlled person to any person to whom such controlled person is liable, unless the controlling person acted in good faith and did not directly or indirectly induce the act or acts constituting the violation or cause of action.

Because the corporate employer doubtless controls its employees for this purpose, the corporation faces potential controlling person liability when insiders violate the federal securities laws by, inter alia, insider trading.

The potential for control person liability was expanded by the Insider Trading and

---

[67] Frank H. Easterbrook, Insider Trading, Secret Agents, Evidentiary Privileges, and the Production of Information, 1981 Sup. Ct. Rev. 309, 332.

Securities Fraud Enforcement Act of 1988, which created an additional controlling person liability regime specifically applicable to insider trading by controlled persons. Under the Securities Exchange Act § 21A(b), the SEC must prove that the controlling person "knew or recklessly disregarded" the fact that one of its employees or other controlled persons was "likely to engage" in illegal insider trading. In addition, the SEC must show that the control person "failed to take appropriate steps" to prevent such trading. If the SEC makes that showing, the control person may be held liable for the greater of $1.1 million or three times the amount of profit gained or loss avoided by the inside trader.

Finally, evidence of insider transactions is highly relevant to private securities litigation. Conventional wisdom posits that public corporations, especially in technology sectors, have become highly vulnerable to such litigation. As the story usually goes, a technology corporation that fails to meet its quarterly earnings projection will experience a drop in its stock price when that news is announced, and will shortly thereafter be sued for fraud under Rule 10b-5.

In 1995, Congress adopted the Private Securities Litigation Reform Act (PSLRA) to curtail what it believed was a widespread problem of merit-less strike suits. Of particular relevance to insider trading compliance programs, one of the PSLRA's provisions established a new (and arguably higher) pleading standard with respect to the scienter element of Rule 10b-5, requiring that a complaint detail facts giving rise to a "strong inference" of scienter.

Post-PSLRA, plaintiffs' securities lawyers have often sought to satisfy the scienter pleading standard by alleging that insiders sold shares in suspicious amounts and/or at suspicious times. Insider sales supposedly provide inferential evidence that senior management knew that earnings forecasts would not be met and sold to avoid the price drop that follows from announcements of lower than expected earnings. According to one report, 57 percent of "post-PSLRA cases, and 73% of those involving high technology, include allegations of insider sales, whereas only 21% of pre-act cases contained such allegations."[68]

Even taken together, the various risks posed by insider trading of injury to the issuer perhaps do not provide as compelling a justification for the insider trading prohibition as the risk of injury by infringement does for the patent system. The property rights approach nevertheless has considerable power. Consider the prototypical insider trading transaction, in which an insider trades in his employer's stock on the basis of information learned solely because of his position with the firm. There is no avoiding the necessity of assigning a property interest in the information to either the corporation or the insider. A rule allowing insider trading assigns a property interest to the insider, while a rule prohibiting insider trading assigns it to the corporation.

In any event, whether insider trading harms the corporation is not dispositive. Creation of a property right with respect to a particular asset typically is not dependent upon there being a measurable loss of value resulting from the asset's use by someone else. Indeed, creation of a property right is appropriate even if any loss in value is entirely subjective, both because subjective valuations are difficult to measure for purposes of awarding

---

[68]   John L. Latham & Todd R. David, Compliance Programs Curb Risk of Insider Trading, Nat'l L. J., June 28, 1999, at B8.

damages and because the possible loss of subjective values presumably would affect the corporation's incentives to cause its agents to develop new information. As with other property rights, the law therefore should simply assume (although the assumption will sometimes be wrong) that assigning the property right to agent-produced information to the firm maximizes the social incentives for the production of valuable new information.

Because the relative rarity of cases in which harm occurs to the corporation weakens the argument for assigning it the property right, however, the critical issue may be whether one can justify assigning the property right to the insider. On close examination, the argument for assigning the property right to the insider is considerably weaker than the argument for assigning it to the corporation. The only plausible justification for doing so is the argument that legalized insider trading would be an appropriate compensation scheme. In other words, society might allow insiders to inside trade in order to give them greater incentives to develop new information.

Henry Manne in fact famously argued that insider trading is an effective means of compensating entrepreneurs in large corporations.[69] Manne distinguished corporate entrepreneurs from mere corporate managers. The latter simply operate the firm according to predetermined guidelines. By contrast, an entrepreneur's contribution to the firm consists of producing new valuable information. The entrepreneur's compensation must have a reasonable relation to the value of his contribution to give him incentives to produce more information. Because it is rarely possible to ascertain information's value to the firm in advance, predetermined compensation, such as salary, is inappropriate for entrepreneurs. Instead, claimed Manne, insider trading is an effective way to compensate entrepreneurs for innovations. The increase in the price of the security following public disclosure provides an imperfect but comparatively accurate measure of the value of the innovation to the firm. The entrepreneur can recover the value of his discovery by purchasing the firm's securities prior to disclosure and selling them after the price rises.

Manne argued that salary and bonuses provide inadequate incentives for entrepreneurial inventiveness because they fail to accurately measure the value to the firm of innovations. Query, however, whether insider trading is any more accurate. Even assuming the change in stock price accurately measures the value of the innovation, the insider's compensation is limited by the number of shares he can purchase. This, in turn, is limited by his wealth. As such, the insider's trading returns are based, not on the value of his contribution, but on his wealth.

Another objection to Manne's argument is the difficulty of restricting trading to those who produced the information. Where information is concerned, production costs normally exceed distribution costs. As such, many firm agents may trade on the information without having contributed to its production.

A related criticism is the difficulty of limiting trading to instances in which the insider actually produced valuable information. In particular, why should insiders be permitted to trade on bad news? Allowing managers to profit from inside trading reduces the penalties associated with a project's failure because trading managers can profit whether the project succeeds or fails. If the project fails, the manager can sell his shares before that

---

[69]   Henry Manne, Insider Trading and the Stock Market (1966).

information becomes public and thus avoid an otherwise certain loss. The manager can go beyond mere loss avoidance into actual profit making by short selling the firm's stock.

A final objection follows from the contingent nature of insider trading. Because the agent's trading returns cannot be measured in advance, neither can the true cost of his reward. As a result, selection of the most cost-effective compensation package is made more difficult. Moreover, the agent himself may prefer a less uncertain compensation package. If an agent is risk averse, he will prefer the certainty of a $100,000 salary to a salary of $50,000 and a ten percent chance of a bonus of $500,000 from insider trading. Thus, the shareholders and the agent would gain by exchanging a guaranteed bonus for the agent's promise not to trade on inside information.

Because insider trading thus is an inefficient compensation scheme, there is no rationale for assigning the property right to insiders rather than to the corporation. Because there is no avoiding the necessity of assigning the property right to the information in question to one of the relevant parties, the argument for assigning it to the corporation therefore should prevail.

If accepted, the property rights rationale actually explains many aspects of the insider trading prohibition far better than do any of the more traditional securities fraud-based justifications.[70] The basic function of a securities fraud regime is to ensure timely disclosure of accurate information to investors. Yet, it seems indisputable that the insider trading prohibition does not lead to increased disclosure. Instead, the disclose or abstain rule typically collapses into a rule of abstention.

Consider also the apparent incongruity that Winans (the defendant in *Carpenter*) could be held liable for trading on information about the Wall Street Journal's "Heard on the Street," but the Journal could have lawfully traded on the same information. This result makes no sense from a traditional securities law perspective. From a property rights perspective, however, the result in *Carpenter* makes perfect sense. Because the information belonged to the Journal, it should have been free to use the information as it saw fit, while Winans' use of the same information amounted to a theft of property owned by the Journal.

A property rights-based approach also helps make sense of a couple of aspects of *Dirks* that are quite puzzling when approached from a securities fraud-based perspective. One is the Court's solicitude for market professionals. After *Dirks*, market analysts were essentially exempt from insider trading liability with respect to nonpublic information they develop because they usually owe no fiduciary duty to the firms they research. *Dirks* thus essentially assigned the property right to such information to the market analyst rather than to the affected corporation. From a disclosure-oriented perspective, this is puzzling; the analyst and/or his clients will trade on the basis of information other investors lack.

---

[70]   To be sure, not all aspects of the federal prohibition can be so explained. For example, because property rights generally include some element of transferability, it may seem curious that federal law, at least in some circumstances, does not allow the owner of nonpublic information to authorize others to use it for their own personal gain. See, e.g., 17 C.F.R. 240.14e-3(d) (a tender offeror may not divulge its takeover plans to anyone likely to trade in target stock). This does not undermine the general validity of the property rights justification. Rather, if protection of property rights is taken as a valid public-regarding policy basis for the prohibition, it gives us a basis for criticizing departures from that norm.

From a property perspective, however, the rule is justifiable because it encourages market analysts to expend resources to develop socially valuable information about firms and thereby promote market efficiency.

The property rights rationale also supports the view that the fiduciary duty at issue in *Chiarella* and *Dirks* is the duty against self-dealing. From a disclosure-oriented approach, in which maximizing disclosure is the principal policy goal, reliance on a self-dealing duty makes no sense because requiring such a breach limits the class of cases in which disclosure is made. In contrast, from a property rights perspective, an emphasis on self-dealing makes perfect sense, because it focuses attention on the basic issue of whether the insider converted information belonging to the corporation.

VI.   WHY MAKE A FEDERAL CASE OUT OF IT?

While it seems clear that society needs some regulation of insider trading to protect property rights in corporate information, it is not at all clear that securities fraud is the right vehicle for doing so. Prudential considerations, however, suggest that the SEC has a comparative advantage vis-à-vis private actors in enforcing insider trading restrictions. Virtually all private party insider trading lawsuits are parasitic on SEC enforcement efforts, which is to say that the private party suit was brought only after the SEC's proceeding became publicly known. This condition holds because the police powers available to the SEC, but not to private parties, are essential to detecting insider trading. Informants, computer monitoring of stock transactions, and reporting of unusual activity by self-regulatory organizations and/or market professionals are the usual ways in which insider trading cases come to light. As a practical matter, these techniques are available only to public law enforcement agencies. In particular, they are most readily available to the SEC.

Unlike private parties, who cannot compel discovery until a nonfrivolous case has been filed, the SEC can impound trading records and compel testimony simply because its suspicions are aroused. As the agency charged with regulating broker-dealers and self-regulatory organizations, the SEC is also uniquely positioned to extract cooperation from securities professionals in conducting investigations. Finally, the SEC is statutorily authorized to pay bounties to informants, which is particularly important in light of the key role informants played in breaking most of the big insider trading cases of the 1980s.

Internationalization of the securities markets is yet another reason for believing the SEC has a comparative advantage in detecting and prosecuting insider trading.[71] Sophisticated insider trading schemes often make use of offshore entities or even offshore markets. The difficulties inherent in extraterritorial investigations and litigation, especially in countries with strong bank secrecy laws, probably would preclude private parties from dealing effectively with insider trading involving offshore activities. In contrast, the SEC has developed

---

[71]   On the relationship between globalization of capital markets and insider trading regulation, see generally Merritt B. Fox, Insider Trading in a Globalizing Market: Who Should Regulate What?, 55 L. & Contemp. Prob. 263–302 (1992); Donald C. Langevoort, Fraud and Insider Trading in American Securities Regulation: Its Scope and Philosophy in a Global Marketplace, 16 Hastings Int'l & Comp. L. Rev. 175 (1993); Steven R. Salbu, Regulation of Insider Trading in a Global Market Place: A Uniform Statutory Approach, 66 Tulane L. Rev. 837 (1992).

memoranda of understanding with a number of key foreign nations, which provide for reciprocal assistance in prosecuting insider trading and other securities law violations. The SEC's ability to investigate international insider trading cases was further enhanced by the 1988 Act, which included provisions designed to encourage foreign governments to cooperate with SEC investigations.

VII. CONCLUSION

In *O'Hagan*, the Supreme Court could have treated the insider trading prohibition's location in the federal securities laws as a historical accident, which has some continuing justification in the SEC's comparative advantage in detecting and prosecuting insider trading on stock markets. The Court should have then focused on the problem as one of implicating fiduciary duties with respect to property rights in information, rather than one of deceit or manipulation. Unfortunately, the majority chose not to do so. Instead, the Court chose to perpetuate the fiction started in *Cady, Roberts* and *Texas Gulf Sulphur* that insider trading is securities fraud.

None of the choices made by the courts throughout this process were inevitable or even necessary consequences of statute or precedent. To the contrary, the courts all along have been creating a federal common law of insider trading. The courts should acknowledge that simple fact. After doing so, the rules they pronounce should be based on protection of property rights, not on inapt securities fraud concepts.

6. The Facebook effect: secondary markets and insider trading in today's startup environment
Stephen F. Diamond

I. INTRODUCTION

The ubiquitous social networking company Facebook made headlines in the spring of 2011 when it fired a widely respected senior manager because he violated the firm's insider trading policy.[1] The dismissal was controversial not only because it surprised Silicon Valley and led many there to rush to the executive's defense, but also because it opened up a new chapter in a long-running policy debate about the nature of insider trading. The debate revealed a good deal of confusion about the legality and significance of insider transactions. One leading technology sector blog even went so far as to quote unnamed sources in a post on the matter stating—inaccurately—that insider trading was legal as long as it took place in the shares of a private company.[2]

Beyond the issue of insider trading, however, the incident raised concerns about the emergence of new private capital markets such as SharesPost and SecondMarket, where prior to their initial public offerings (IPOs) the securities of high-flying companies such as Facebook, Yelp, Zynga, and Groupon could be bought and sold with relative ease without the need to make the kinds of disclosure required of publicly traded companies. The trades that the Facebook executive made were allegedly carried out on such a private trading platform.

If the numbers reported in the wake of these trades can be believed, valuations of some private companies can reach stratospheric levels. Based on a pre-IPO trade in Facebook stock made through its service, SharesPost valued the social networking company at nearly $103 billion in 2012, up from $17 billion in the spring of 2010.[3] These kinds of numbers drive up the demand for shares in private companies. Because corporate insiders are one of the few sources of supply of such shares, skyrocketing valuations may tempt insiders to engage in trades with investors outside the company. The temptation to trade may be exacerbated when, as in the current economic crisis,

---

[1] Miguel Helft, Facebook Fires Employee for Insider Trading, N.Y. Times Blogs (Bits) (Apr. 1, 2011, 3:40 PM, updated 4:53 PM), http://bits.blogs.nytimes.com/2011/04/01/facebook-fires-employee-for-insider-trading/ (last visited Nov. 20, 2012).

[2] Michael Arrington, Facebook Terminated Corporate Development Employee Over Insider Trading Scandal, TechCrunch (Mar. 31, 2011), http://techcrunch.com/2011/03/31/facebook-terminated-corporate-development-employee-over-insider-trading-scandal/ (last visited Nov. 20, 2012).

[3] Brian Womack, Facebook Valued At $102.8 Billion In Final Auction On SharesPost, Bloomberg, Mar. 30, 2012, http://www.bloomberg.com/news/2012-03-30/facebook-valued-at-102-8-billion-in-final-sharespost-auction.html (last visited Nov. 20, 2012).

startups have long delayed expected public offerings of their stock.[4] Not all private trades by insiders are illegal, of course, but the Facebook incident highlights why it is important for lawyers engaged in representing startup companies or investors in such companies to consider carefully the impact of federal and state securities laws on insider transactions.

II.   BUSINESS LAWYERS ARE "SECURITIES LAWYERS"

Many law students avoid taking securities law in law school, yet it becomes clear in practice that almost any lawyer advising a business will encounter securities law issues. Thus, it is helpful to recall that the Securities and Exchange Commission (SEC) paints with a broad brush the definition of who is or is not practicing securities law. Although the SEC imposes no registration requirement or other formal oversight of attorneys, Section 307 of the Sarbanes Oxley Act of 2002[5] (SOX) mandated that the SEC establish "minimum standards of professional conduct for lawyers appearing and practicing before the Commission."[6] The SEC implemented a final rule with respect to these standards in January 2003.[7]

In light of the broad approach long taken by the Commission to the phrase "appearing and practicing," which has its origins in the longstanding rules of practice on which the new rule[8] implementing this SOX provision is based, a lawyer who provides what seems to be the simplest form of advice to a new business entity may, in fact, be considered to be practicing securities law. The SOX provision, for example, includes the following as a form of "appearing and practicing" before the Commission:

> (iv) Advising an issuer as to whether information or a statement, opinion, or other writing is required under the United States securities laws or the Commission's rules or regulations thereunder to be filed with or submitted to, or incorporated into any document that will be filed with or submitted to, the Commission.[9]

Even at the earliest stage of the incorporation of a business, decisions need to be made with respect to the basic capital structure of the new entity. How much and what classes of stock will be authorized and issued? On what terms and conditions will they be issued? At what price per share will they be valued? To whom will the securities be issued? And, of course, will it be necessary to register the issuance of these securities with the SEC or,

---

[4]   IPO Task Force, Rebuilding the IPO On-Ramp 6 (2011). ("The average age at IPO of companies going public between 1997 and 2001 was approximately five and a half years, compared with more than nine years for companies going public between 2006 and 2011.")

[5]   Sarbanes Oxley Act of 2002, 15 U.S.C. §§ 7201–7266 (2002).

[6]   Id. § 7245.

[7]   Standards of Professional Conduct for Attorneys Appearing and Practicing Before the Commission in the Representation of an Issuer, 17 C.F.R. § 205 (2012). See also Standards of Professional Conduct for Attorneys, Securities Act Release No 33,8185, Exchange Act Release No 34,47276, 68 Fed. Reg. 6296 (Feb. 6, 2003).

[8]   17 C.F.R. § 205.2(a) (2012).

[9]   17 C.F.R. § 205.2(a)(1)(iv) (2012).

in the case of Silicon Valley startups, qualify them with the California Department of Corporations? Or is there an exemption from registration and qualification available?[10] The last of these questions falls squarely under the Commission's definition because a lawyer representing a newly formed corporation must help the founders decide whether they need to make a filing with the SEC in connection with the issuance of the company's securities.

The potential penalties for violating state and federal securities laws are severe. Willful violations of the California securities law are punishable by a fine of up to $1 million or imprisonment for up to one year, or both.[11] Willful violations of the 1933 Act are punishable by a fine of up to $10,000 or imprisonment for up to five years, or both.[12] Although criminal convictions under these statutes are relatively rare, prosecutions for charges under insider trading laws are increasing in frequency. Most visibly, in 2011 hedge fund billionaire Raj Rajaratnam was convicted of 14 counts of conspiracy and securities fraud and sentenced to 11 years in federal prison in connection with a widespread insider trading operation that he masterminded.[13] In 2012, Rajat Gupta, a former managing partner of McKinsey & Co. and board member of Goldman Sachs, was also found guilty of passing inside information to Rajaratnam and faces the possibility of decades in prison.[14] Thirteen other figures involved in the Rajaratnam scandal have each received, on average, a sentence of three years in prison.[15]

III. "FOLLOW THE MONEY"

The clearest way to understand the potential effect of the securities laws on a startup company is to track the creation, distribution, and resale of securities issued by the company. Numerous issues related to both securities and corporate law emerge in the startup company process, most of which are beyond the scope of this chapter.[16] However, the process can be tracked to better understand the impact of both the insider trading laws and the issues triggered by the emergence of new trading platforms such as SharesPost and SecondMarket.

Once a startup company is incorporated, it typically issues shares of common stock to founders and early stage employees. Later, as the firm expands, it may issue preferred stock to angel investors or venture capitalists. The fundamental question that must

---

[10] See generally Securities Act of 1933, as amended, 15 U.S.C. §§ 77a–77aa (2012) (1933 Act); California Corporate Securities Law of 1968, Corp. C. §§ 25000–25707 (2012).

[11] See Corp. C. § 25540 (2012).

[12] See 15 U.S.C. § 77x (2012).

[13] Peter Lattman, Galleon Chief Sentenced to 11-Year Term in Insider Case, N. Y. Times, Oct. 30, 2011, http://dealbook.nytimes.com/2011/10/13/rajaratnam-is-sentenced-to-11-years/ (last visited Nov. 20, 2012).

[14] Patricia Hurtado, et al., Rajat Gupta Convicted Of Insider Trading, Bloomberg, Jun. 16, 2012, http://www.bloomberg.com/news/2012-06-15/rajat-gupta-convicted-of-insider-trading-by-u-s-jury.html (last visited Nov. 20, 2012).

[15] Lattman, supra note 13.

[16] See generally California Continuing Education of the Bar, Financing and Protecting California Businesses (2006, updated Mar. 2012).

be asked when a company contemplates an issuance of securities such as common or preferred stock is whether the issuance will require registration with the SEC or qualification by the California Department of Corporations. If registration and qualification are required the company will have to undertake the expensive and time-consuming preparation of an information package that must be reviewed and approved by regulators and then provided to potential investors.

The central principle animating the federal registration requirement is whether the individuals receiving or purchasing the securities can "fend for themselves,"[17] *i.e.*, whether they have sufficient information and sophistication to decide whether the investment decision they are being asked by the issuer to make is a reasonable one. If they can fend for themselves, then the transaction in those securities will not be a public offering and thus will be exempt from registration.[18] Because this standard can be challenging to meet, the SEC has, over the years, used its rule-making authority to establish safe harbors from registration that allow a transaction to proceed with certainty that registration is not required. If an issuer or seller of a security is not confident that the sale will be exempt or that it meets the strict requirements of a safe harbor, then the transaction must be registered with the SEC and likely also qualified by the California Department of Corporations.

The California securities law is a so-called "merit statute" that applies a "fair, just and equitable" standard to proposed offers or sales of securities in California.[19] Just as federal law does, California law offers a set of exemptions from its qualification requirements.[20] In some instances, federal law pre-empts the California requirement to qualify the offer and sale of securities under California law.[21]

The legal framework described above implements what one might call the "prime directive" of securities law, namely that the offer and sale of any security must be registered (with the SEC) and/or qualified (by the California Department of Corporations) or both, unless an applicable exemption is available. It should not come as a surprise that securities regulators take a very broad view of what constitutes a "security." Parsing out the elements of that definition is beyond the scope of this chapter, but almost any financial instrument issued by a startup to investors, such as preferred stock, common stock, or options to purchase either of those, will fall within that definition.[22]

Because the registration and qualification process is costly, complex, and time consuming, federal and state regulators have established several safe harbors that make capital formation simpler and cheaper for issuers. Thus, in most instances, it is fairly straightforward for firms to issue securities to founders as well as early stage employees and investors without incurring the cost of registration and qualification.[23] As the company grows in size, it may wish to raise additional rounds of capital by engaging in similar private placements (*i.e.*, sales of securities made without registration or qualification) with investors,

---

[17]   SEC v. Ralston Purina Co., 346 U.S. 119, 125 (1953).
[18]   See id.
[19]   See Corp. C. § 25140(a) (2012).
[20]   See Corp. C. §§ 25102, 25102.1, 25102.5, 25103–25104 (2012).
[21]   See 15 U.S.C. § 77r(b) (2012).
[22]   See 15 U.S.C. § 77b(a)(1) (2012); Corp. C. § 25019 (2012).
[23]   See, e.g., Rule 701, 17 C.F.R. § 230.701 (2012); Corp. C. § 25102(f) (2012).

as well as to issue additional shares to employees or consultants. Each such issuance will require its own exemption or safe harbor.

Whether a company's securities are sold through a public offering or a private placement, the company is required in most cases to make available to potential purchasers a basic information package that helps level the playing field between the issuer and the purchaser. In a public offering (*i.e.*, a securities offering that is registered with the SEC), the package will include a prospectus that is reviewed and commented on by the SEC staff itself before actual sales of securities can take place. In a private placement, the issuer may provide potential investors with direct access to business records (*e.g.*, if the investors are senior officers of the issuer or early stage angel investors) or prepare an offering memorandum or private placement memorandum that summarizes key business and financial information. It is in the issuer's interest to provide enough information to enable investors to make a reasonable decision regarding whether to enter into the transaction. The issuer's motivation to disclose material information is reinforced by the fact that the anti-fraud rules apply to all securities transactions, including transactions exempt from registration.[24]

IV.   THE SECONDARY MARKET FOR SECURITIES

The initial issuance and sale of securities by a startup company represents the first stage in creating a market for a company's securities. Once the shares or other securities are in the hands of those initial purchasers, they can be resold to other investors, thus providing liquidity for the original purchaser. In this secondary "resale" market, of course, no cash is generated for the issuer, only for the seller. Nonetheless, the seller must still comply with federal and state securities laws—the "prime directive" still applies.[25] Thus, unless an exemption is available, a seller must provide sufficient information to a potential purchaser to enable him or her to make a reasonable decision regarding whether to buy the securities offered. The purchaser normally must have the sophistication to analyze the information provided, thus meeting the "fend for themselves" standard discussed above.

Unless the seller has negotiated with the original issuer (*e.g.*, in a registration rights agreement) to make the information available, the information requirement will be a difficult burden to meet. Moreover, even if an exemption from registration or qualification is available, the anti-fraud rules still apply.

There are readily available safe harbors that exempt most secondary sales of common stock in public corporations.[26] A much greater challenge is presented to the shareholder of a private company such as a typical startup. Because very little information is available publicly about such a company, a shareholder may find his or her investment in the company "locked in," awaiting the registration of his or her shares through an IPO. The shareholder may have received sufficient information from the company to purchase

---

[24]   See 15 U.S.C. § 78j(b) (2012); 17 C.F.R. § 240.10b-5 (2012). See also Preliminary Notes, 17 C.F.R. § 230.701 (2012).

[25]   See 15 U.S.C. § 77d(1)–(2) (2012); Corp. C. § 25130 (2012).

[26]   See 15 U.S.C. § 77d(1) (2012); Corp. C. § 25111 (2012).

the securities initially from the firm. When he or she wishes to resell the shares, however, there may not be sufficient current information available to enable a prospective purchaser to make a reasonable decision regarding whether to purchase the shares in the resale (secondary) transaction.

Although all private companies face this problem, it has been exacerbated by recent difficult macroeconomic conditions. Since the dot.com crash in 2000–01, the length of time required for a startup to reach the IPO stage has increased significantly.[27] The volatile market conditions that emerged in the wake of the 2008 credit crisis have made the problem more severe. Although it was formerly possible for companies to conduct relatively small IPOs, that is no longer the case. For example, when Intel first went public in 1971, it raised only $7.2 million.[28] Today, however, a company must often be large enough to raise at least $100 million for an investment bank to be willing to expend the effort needed for a successful transaction.[29] In late 2011, there were more than 200 companies waiting to complete their IPOs because market volatility caused a number of prospective new public companies to withdraw from the registration process.[30] In September 2011, for the first time in 29 months, no IPOs whatsoever were conducted.[31] As a result, an unknown number of investors in private companies have been left holding shares in companies that they would likely wish to sell but cannot because there is inadequate information available for prospective purchasers.

In light of these rough waters, new ways of providing liquidity to investors in early stage companies have emerged. Trading platforms such as SharesPost and SecondMarket offer shareholders in private companies an opportunity to connect with willing purchasers of their shares. As SecondMarket stated on its website, "SecondMarket specializes in designing and implementing fully-customized liquidity programs for private companies. Through these liquidity programs, private company shareholders can sell stock to company-approved investors in a company-controlled process."[32] Approximately $4.6 billion worth of securities of private companies traded hands in 2010, although most of those transactions were done between buyers and sellers directly without participation of the new trading platforms.[33] For both sellers and buyers of securities on the new trading

---

[27]   IPO Task Force, supra note 4.

[28]   Bruce C.N. Greenwald, et al., Value Investing 111 (2004).

[29]   Sandy Robertson, Remarks at the Executive Forum on Market Issues and Opportunities for Private Companies (May 10, 2011).

[30]   Rebecca Lipman, IPO Drought: For the First Time in 29 Months, Not a Single IPO, Kapitall Wire, Oct. 7, 2011, http://wire.kapitall.com/investment-idea/ipo-drought-for-the-first-time-in-29-months-not-a-single-ipo/ (last visited Nov. 20, 2012).

[31]   Id.

[32]   SecondMarket at https://www.secondmarket.com/private-company?t=fl (last visited Nov. 15, 2011).

[33]   Jean Eaglesham, Guidance Is Sought on Private Trading of Closely Held Companies, Wall St. J., May 9, 2011, http://professional.wsj.com/article/SB10001424052748704810504576310262093052504.html#articleTabs%3Darticle (last visited Nov. 20, 2012). So-called "tertiary trades"— where an investor who bought from an individual who received shares in a distribution wishes to resell those shares to another third-party investor—reportedly only rarely take place on the new trading platforms. Moreover, issuers do not generally engage in initial capital-raising offerings on these platforms. The platforms are thus distinguishable from stock exchanges such as the NASDAQ and NYSE.

sites, the rules applicable to secondary securities transactions represent a complex legal minefield. Those rules ensure that the liquidity provided by secondary securities markets does not come at the cost of the core investor protections found in the federal and state securities laws.

The supply of securities for the new secondary trading platforms comes from several sources, each of which is seeking liquidity in startups that have not yet accessed the public markets or found another exit opportunity such as an acquisition. These sources include current and former employees whose stock options have vested, consultants or other service providers who may have earned shares as part of their short-term contributions to a business, and, finally, current investors in the startup. These security holders own so-called "restricted securities," *i.e.*, shares issued without registration. To resell the securities to third parties, the security holder must find either a new exemption or a safe harbor from registration with the SEC and qualification with the California Department of Corporations.[34]

The federal securities laws do not provide an explicit exemption for the resale of restricted securities. Instead, a doctrine has been crafted over time in a series of decisions by courts, the SEC, and market participants that allows for valid resales of restricted securities. This doctrine combined language found in one section of the 1933 Act[35] with definitional information found in another[36] to form a new informal rule known as "Rule 4(1½)." Later, the SEC issued Rules 144[37] and 144A[38] that created "safe harbors" for resales, thus providing buyers and sellers greater certainty that such transactions comply with the securities laws.

Ensuring that a resale complies with the securities laws is important for all three concerned parties—the seller, the buyer, and the issuer. The seller wants to avoid the costly and time-consuming obligation to draft a prospectus, which of course would require the issuer's cooperation. A buyer wants to make sure that the transaction complies so that the buyer can look forward to a further resale later on. The issuer has an important residual concern: if a resale without registration is not handled properly, the SEC could find that the seller was, in fact, acting as a statutory "underwriter" facilitating the distribution of the securities.[39] If so, the two-part sale—the initial placement of the securities by the issuer with the seller and the later attempted resale by the seller to the buyer—would be collapsed into one transaction in which the issuer, as well as the seller-underwriter, would have joint responsibility for providing full prospectus-like disclosure to the buyer.

To ensure that buyers and sellers do not run afoul of these rules, the websites of the new trading firms explain that they screen potential investors so that they qualify for securities law exemptions or safe harbors.[40] Thus, potential purchasers of the stock of private companies must qualify as "accredited investors" in order to participate in auctions for their

---

[34]   See 15 U.S.C. § 77d(1)–(2) (2012); Corp. C. § 25130 (2012).

[35]   Id. § 77d(1).

[36]   Id. § 77d(2).

[37]   Rule 144, 17 C.F.R. § 230.144 (2012).

[38]   Rule 144A, 17 C.F.R. § 230.144A (2012).

[39]   See 15 U.S.C. § 77b(a)(11) (2012).

[40]   See, e.g., SharesPost, Compliance with Securities Laws at https://www.sharespost.com/pages/legal#securities_laws_section (last visited Jul. 10, 2012).

securities. Accredited investors are generally thought to be able to "fend for themselves" when it comes to deciding whether to purchase shares in a private transaction. The federal securities laws define an "accredited investor" to include a range of financial or business institutions as well as natural persons who meet certain qualifications.[41]

In addition, the secondary market sites state that they only allow sellers who have held their shares for more than one year (the holding period required by the Rule 144 safe harbor[42]) to resell their shares to other investors. The holding period helps to ensure that the original sale by the issuer (or its affiliate) to that seller was in fact an investment and not a distribution that would trigger a registration requirement. Finally, buyers on both SharesPost and SecondMarket must certify that they are qualified to participate in a private securities transaction.

V. BACK TO INSIDER TRADING

The growing concern about insider trading in the purchase and sale of the securities of private companies is founded on the laws governing the securities transactions discussed above. The primary policy motivation underpinning the regulation of trading by insiders (whether buying or selling) is the potential information asymmetry between the insider and his or her counter-party in the transaction. Inevitably, the insider will have more information about the fundamentals of a business than an outsider. Federal and state securities laws are intended, in part, to "level the playing field" among buyers and sellers by mandating disclosure of material information about a security as well as prohibiting fraud in securities transactions.[43]

The strongest view of insider trading thus argues for an absolute "disclose or abstain" approach[44] to achieve what the Second Circuit called "relatively equal access" to material information among all market participants.[45] As discussed below, this approach is now limited by the requirement that the insider be in breach of a fiduciary obligation when he or she trades or provides information to others who trade. Nonetheless, this approach remains perhaps the most useful starting point for anyone in possession of material non-public information about a company's security, particularly employees or other potential insiders. In other words, if one party is in possession of material nonpublic information it is important for that party to stop before trading and ask whether he or she has an obligation here to "disclose or abstain." If so, that party must either provide the potential counter-party with the same material information that the first party has about the issuer, or else abstain entirely from entering into the transaction.

It is perfectly permissible, of course, for insiders to buy or sell the securities of the company of which they are considered insiders if there is in fact a level playing field

---

41   See 17 C.F.R. § 230.501(a)(1)–(5) (2012).
42   See 17 C.F.R. § 230.144(d)(1)(ii) (2012).
43   SEC, SEC Enforcement Actions—Insider Trading Cases (2012), http://www.sec.gov/spot light/insidertrading/cases.shtml (last visited Nov. 20, 2012) (insider trading "undermin[es] the level playing field that is fundamental to the integrity and fair functioning of the capital markets").
44   See U.S. v. O'Hagan, 521 U.S. 642, 661 (1997).
45   SEC v. Texas Gulf Sulphur, 401 F.2d 833, 848 (2d Cir. 1968), cert. denied, 394 U.S. 976 (1969).

between the insider and the counter-party on the other side of the transaction. Even if there is not equal access to the same information, absent a fiduciary duty, an insider may also be able to trade.[46] Thus, insider trading per se is not always illegal. But it does not matter if the company is public or private, as was suggested by some in the wake of the controversy over Facebook's dismissal of the executive who engaged in the purchase of Facebook shares on a secondary market platform.[47] All securities transactions are subject to the insider trading laws and rules. More importantly, it will often be difficult for individual insiders—who are not typically securities lawyers—to determine when they are free to trade.

The prohibition on insider trading is based largely on the SEC's and the federal courts' interpretation of the Securities Exchange Act of 1934 (1934 Act) rather than on an explicit statutory ban on the practice.[48] The 1934 Act was passed in the wake of the stock market crash of 1929 during a period when it was widely believed that those "in the know" had benefitted at the expense of the wider investing public through a variety of manipulative investment practices. A Congressional investigation was concerned about this issue, stating in an oft-cited passage:

> Among the most vicious practices unearthed at the hearings . . . was the flagrant betrayal of their fiduciary duties by directors and officers of corporations who used their positions of trust and the confidential information which came to them in such positions, to aid them in their market activities. Closely allied to this type of abuse was the unscrupulous employment of inside information by large stockholders. . . .[49]

Thus, § 10(b) of the 1934 Act[50] states:

> It shall be unlawful for any person, directly or indirectly, by the use of any means or instrumentality of interstate commerce or of the mails, or of any facility of any national securities exchange—. . .
>
> b. To use or employ, in connection with the purchase or sale of any security registered on a national securities exchange or any security not so registered . . . , any manipulative or deceptive device or contrivance in contravention of such rules and regulations as the Commission may prescribe as necessary or appropriate in the public interest or for the protection of investors.

The SEC followed the passage of the 1934 Act by promulgating Rule 10b-5 in 1942. Rule 10b-5 makes it unlawful "in connection with the purchase or sale of any security":[51]

---

[46]   See, e.g., Dirks v. SEC, 463 U.S. 646 (1983).

[47]   Arrington supra n. 2.

[48]   The 1934 Act does contain one explicit prohibition on insider trading in § 16(b). See 15 U.S.C. § 78p(b) (2012). However, this is a limited remedy. In addition to directors and officers, only holders of more than 10 percent of the company's stock are subject to the § 16(b) prohibition. There is no tipper–tippee liability (discussed below) in the statutory language. Section 16(b) requires persons covered to return to the company any profits on purchases and sales that take place within six months of each other—the so-called "short swing" trading window. The broadly worded prohibition forces many trades to unwind that are not affected by inside information and can miss many that are so affected.

[49]   S. Rep. No 1455 at 55 (1934).

[50]   15 U.S.C. § 78j(b) (2012).

[51]   17 C.F.R. § 240.10b-5 (2012).

(a) To employ any device, scheme, or artifice to defraud,
(b) To make any untrue statement of a material fact or to omit to state a material fact necessary in order to make the statements made, in the light of the circumstances under which they were made, not misleading, or
(c) To engage in any act, practice, or course of business which operates or would operate as a fraud or deceit upon any person.

Today, the insider trading prohibition is grounded on a narrower basis than the "level playing field" approach. In most instances, only where the insider owes a fiduciary duty to a less well-informed counter-party with respect to the information about the securities that he or she intends to trade would a purchase or sale to that counter-party be prohibited by law. The courts recognized this duty before modern statutory securities law and it was set forth as early as the U.S. Supreme Court's 1909 opinion in *Strong v. Repide*.[52] In that case, the Court held that even though a director may not be under a fiduciary duty to disclose to a shareholder his or her knowledge affecting the value of the shares, a disclosure obligation might exist in special cases. This declaration of a "special circumstances" test began the process of dissolving the prevailing older rule that corporate directors and officers were free to take advantage of their inside knowledge when dealing with corporate shareholders.

Over time, as both the SEC and the courts began to interpret § 10(b) and Rule 10b-5, the "special circumstances" approach broadened into the "classical theory" of insider trading. This theory covers both "permanent insiders" and those who become "temporary insiders" due to their access to material nonpublic information. The latter can include underwriters, lawyers, accountants, and consultants.[53] Neither type of insider can legally trade in the securities of the entity to which they owe a fiduciary obligation while material nonpublic information remains undisclosed to the wider market. As the Supreme Court stated in *United States v. O'Hagan* (citations omitted):

> [T]rading on such information qualifies as a "deceptive device" under § 10(b), . . . because "a relationship of trust and confidence [exists] between the shareholders of a corporation and those insiders who have obtained confidential information by reason of their position with that corporation.". . . That relationship . . . "gives rise to a duty to disclose [or to abstain from trading] because of the 'necessity of preventing a corporate insider from . . . tak[ing] unfair advantage of . . . uninformed . . . stockholders.'"[54]

In theory, the prohibition applies not only to actual insiders but also to persons who have been tipped off by those insiders. This is known as "tipper–tippee liability." The extension of liability to tippers and tippees enabled securities regulators to close a potential loophole that might have allowed insiders to pass on information to a friendly third party to trade, thus avoiding direct liability. There are two elements that must be met to impose liability on the tipper: (1) he or she must have had a duty that was violated by the disclosure of insider information to the tippee; and (2) he or she must have received some form of personal benefit from the disclosure.[55] Tippee liability is predicated on the exist-

---

[52] 213 U.S. 419 (1909).
[53] See U.S. v. O'Hagan, 521 U.S. 642, 652 (1997).
[54] Id. at 651–652.
[55] See Dirks v. SEC, 463 U.S. 646, 662 (1983); SEC v. Yun, 327 F.3d 1263, 1269 (11th Cir. 2003).

ence of the tipper's duty as well as awareness by the tippee that the duty was breached.[56] The ongoing Galleon hedge fund scandal involves examples of both tipper and tippee liability and demonstrates the aggressive posture the SEC takes towards this form of insider trading.

In *O'Hagan*, the Court broadened the scope of those covered by the insider trading prohibition with an endorsement of the "misappropriation theory" of insider trading. In that case, a lawyer working at a law firm representing the acquirer of a target company bought securities in the target before the takeover announcement. The Court held that the lawyer violated § 10(b) and Rule 10b-5 "when he misappropriate[d] confidential information for securities trading purposes, in breach of a duty owed to the source of the information," namely his own law firm and its client, the acquiring firm.[57] Thus, the misappropriation theory complements the classical theory of insider trading with a ban on trading by outsiders who trade on "confidential information that will affect the corporation's security price when revealed, but who owe no fiduciary or other duty to that corporation's shareholders."[58]

VI.   INSIDER TRADING POLICIES

Determining whether a duty of nondisclosure is present and providing the kind of information that truly levels the playing field can be difficult, particularly in the context of startup companies. As a consequence, a directive to "disclose or abstain" will result in an abstention from trading, absent exceptional circumstances. Only the startup firm itself can effectively make available to counter-parties the kind of information that would ensure that a sale or purchase does not run afoul of the prohibition on insider trading. It is therefore prudent for the company itself to set the terms under which its employees, consultants, and advisors can trade in its securities.

Some startup companies have established an insider trading policy (IT Policy) in order to minimize the potential for problems.[59] In fact, it was his violation of such a policy that triggered the dismissal of the Facebook employee discussed above.[60] An IT Policy was previously thought necessary only for companies whose securities already trade or are about to begin trading on the public capital markets. With the emergence of significant opportunities for insiders to trade on secondary markets such as SharesPost and SecondMarket, however, it is now important for many startup companies to consider implementing such policies.

Prepared by outside securities counsel, an IT Policy should make clear to all company

---

[56]   See Dirks, 463 U.S. at 661.

[57]   U.S. v. O'Hagan, 521 U.S. at 652.

[58]   Id. at 653 (citation omitted).

[59]   Amy Miller, Startup Companies Get Stock Transfer Advice, The Recorder, May 8, 2012, http://www.law.com/jsp/cc/PubArticleCC.jsp?id=1336331727848 (last visited Nov. 20, 2012). ("Long before filing to go public, both Facebook and Zynga Inc. instituted insider trading policies prohibiting current employees from selling their shares in the companies on secondary markets, except during periods when the companies opened trading windows.")

[60]   Helft, supra note 1.

employees that trading by insiders may in certain circumstances be illegal under federal securities laws and carry severe penalties, including the possibility of imprisonment. Employees are more likely to take notice of their responsibilities under federal law when they are reminded that § 32(a) of the Exchange Act[61] authorizes a judge to impose up to a $5 million fine and a 20-year prison sentence on those convicted of a § 10(b) violation.[62] Section 32(a) also allows for criminal prosecutions against the issuing company if it is held responsible as a controlling person with respect to the illegal trading activity of its employees.[63] Congress further raised the stakes for illegal insider trading with the passage of the Insider Trading Sanctions Act of 1984,[64] which allows the SEC to secure treble damages against violators.[65] Finally, in 1988, Congress created a private right of action to allow those who traded contemporaneously with insiders to sue for damages.[66]

The IT Policy should establish a general principle that no employee should trade or cause someone else to trade the company's securities while in possession of material nonpublic information. The company may wish to condition the issuance of stock to employees on an agreement not to trade in those securities until an agreed-on exit, such as a public offering. Some companies have gone further, replacing traditional stock options with various forms of restricted stock units (RSUs) that cannot be sold and for which there is no secondary market. The recipients of RSUs do not receive actual stock in the issuing firm until a public offering is conducted.[67]

The IT Policy itself should help educate rank and file employees, who are very likely not to have any familiarity with securities law, by providing clear examples of what material information means. Material information includes anything that might be considered reasonably important to the counter-party when making a decision concerning whether to engage in the purchase or sale of a security. This could include financial information such as revenues, operating margins, or net income; risk factors such as potential environmental liabilities; and background information on key executives. A leading U.S. Supreme Court opinion defined materiality as including anything that could significantly alter the "total mix" of information available about a particular company.[68] Given the vagueness of this formulation, an IT policy should err on the side of over-inclusiveness when it defines materiality. A good example of such a policy, although it was prepared for a public company, can be found on the website of the Practical Law Company.[69]

---

[61]   15 U.S.C. § 78ff(a) (2012).

[62]   15 U.S.C. § 78j(b) (2012).

[63]   One of the benefits of implementing an IT Policy is not only that it can lead to fewer instances of illegal trading by insiders but also that it can lead to mitigated sentences for a company under the Federal Sentencing Guidelines and provide a defense for the company to the imposition of controlling person liability. See United States Sentencing Commission, 2011 Federal Sentencing Guidelines Manual (2011), http://www.ussc.gov/Guidelines/2011_Guidelines/Manual_HTML/index.cfm (last visited Nov. 20, 2012).

[64]   Pub. L. No 98-376, 98 Stat. 1264 (1984).

[65]   See 15 U.S.C. § 78u-1(a)(2)—(3) (2012).

[66]   See Insider Trading and Securities Fraud Enforcement Act, 15 U.S.C. § 78u-1 (2012).

[67]   See Zynga, Inc., SEC No-Action Letter, 2011 SEC No-Act. LEXIS 415 (Jun. 17, 2011).

[68]   See TSC Indus., Inc. v. Northway, Inc., 426 U.S. 438, 449 (1976).

[69]   Alan J. Berkeley, Sample Corporate Policy on Insider Trading, at http://us.practicallaw.com/7-502-0160?q=insider%20trading%20policy (last visited Nov. 20, 2012).

VII.   CONCLUSION

Although the founders of, and investors in, early stage companies may chafe at the restrictions that an IT Policy places on liquidity, it is important that their counsel remind them of the far more catastrophic risk of facing liability for insider trading. In the intensely competitive environment of the startup world, reputational capital is likely the most precious asset that a young company owns. To risk that capital for short-term financial gain at the expense of outsiders makes no sense.

7. Regulation FD: an alternative approach to addressing information asymmetry

Jill Fisch

Although commentators have identified various reasons to regulate insider trading,[1] one rationale is to reduce the existence of information asymmetries in the securities markets. In its litigations in *Chiarella* and *Dirks*, the government attempted to use fraud-based theories of liability to address information asymmetries. The Supreme Court limited the effectiveness of this approach by requiring a predicate breach of duty for a violation of Rule 10b-5.[2]

The Securities and Exchange Commission (SEC) responded in August 2000, by adopting Regulation Fair Disclosure.[3] Regulation FD took an alternative approach to information asymmetry that was not grounded in theories of fraud but, instead, in issuer disclosure obligations.[4] Specifically the Rule focused on corporate issuers and corporate officials as the sources of such asymmetries, reasoning that if selective disclosures by corporate insiders could be prevented at the source, regulators would have less need to address trading by the recipients of that information.[5]

Although critics originally raised concerns that Regulation FD would chill information flow to the market, empirical studies suggest that changes in corporate policies did not meaningfully reduce disclosure. At the same time, the effects of Regulation FD remain unclear. After an initial series of enforcement actions, the SEC faced a stunning defeat in the *Siebel Systems* case and virtually ceased to use Regulation FD for several years.[6] Private meetings and similar opportunities for selective disclosure continue to present the potential for information asymmetries, however,[7] and the SEC has responded by showing

---

[1] See, e.g., Stephen M. Bainbridge, Insider Trading, in 5650 Encyclopedia of Law and Economics 772 (Boudewijhn Bouckaert & Gerrit De Geest, eds. 2000), available at http://encyclo.findlaw.com/5650book.pdf (last visited Nov. 14, 2012).

[2] See id. at 773–774 (describing the Supreme Court's decisions in *Chiarella* and *Dirks* as requiring an insider's breach of a fiduciary duty as a predicate to insider trading liability).

[3] SEC Regulation FD, 17 C.F.R. § 243.100 (2000).

[4] See Proposed Rule: Selective Disclosure and Insider Trading, SEC Release Nos. 33-7787, 34-42259, IC-24209 (Dec. 20, 1999), 64 Fed. Reg. 72590-01 (Dec. 28, 1999) [hereinafter Proposing Release]. ("The approach we propose does not treat selective disclosure as a type of fraudulent conduct or revisit the insider trading issues addressed in Dirks.")

[5] Id. at 72574 ("we propose to use our authority to require full and fair disclosure from issuers. . . . We believe this approach would further the full and fair public disclosure of material information, and thereby promote fair dealing in the securities of covered issuers.").

[6] SEC v. Siebel Systems, Inc., 384 F.Supp.2d 694 (S.D.N.Y. 2005).

[7] See David Enrich & Dana Cimilluca, Banks Woo Funds With Private Peeks, Wall St. J., May 16, 2011, available at http://online.wsj.com/article/SB10001424052748703841904576256520217477678.html (last visited Nov. 14, 2012).

renewed attention to enforcement of Regulation FD. The SEC's most recent approach reflects an effort to provide ongoing guidance to issuers about its key concerns in this area.

I.   THE SEC'S ADOPTION OF REGULATION FD

The SEC has traditionally expressed concern about insider trading and the effect of that trading on the fairness and integrity of the securities markets.[8] One focus of this concern has been selective disclosure—the practice by issuers and corporate officials, in some cases, of disclosing corporate information to select analysts, institutional investors or other market participants, prior to disclosing that information to the general public. The ability of issuers to control the manner and timing of information disclosures, in the view of the SEC, offered corporate officials the opportunity to treat information as a commodity to curry favor with particular market participants, create analyst conflicts of interest, or engage in self-dealing. More generally, the SEC viewed selective disclosure, like other insider trading, as a threat to market integrity and investor confidence.[9]

As the SEC explained in its proposing release, it had previously addressed selective disclosure through the general antifraud provision—SEC Rule 10b-5.[10] The SEC's ability to treat selective disclosure as securities fraud was compromised, however, by the Supreme Court's decisions in *Chiarella*[11] and *Dirks*.[12] In particular, these decisions imposed a requirement, for insider trading to be fraudulent, that the trader has received the information as the result of a breach of duty.[13] This legal standard created particular difficulties of application in connection with research analysts. The SEC found that public companies were "disclosing important nonpublic information, such as advance warnings of earnings results, to securities analysts or selected institutional investors or both, before making full disclosure of the same information to the general public."[14] Nonetheless, the evidence in most cases of selective disclosure did not seem to support the "personal benefit" required under *Dirks*.[15]

Consequently, in October 2000, the SEC adopted Regulation FD.[16] Regulation FD

---

[8]   See, e.g., Cady, Roberts & Co., Release No 34-6668, 40 SEC 907 (1961) (opinion of Chairman Cary) (explaining importance of insider trading liability in protecting the securities markets from abuses, "including specifically improper transactions by officers, directors, and principal stockholders").

[9]   See Panel Discussion: The SEC's Regulation FD, 6 Fordham J. Corp. & Fin. L. 273, 278 (2001) (remarks of Professor Harvey J. Goldschmid) (explaining that the same policy rationale applied to regulating selective disclosure as for insider trading).

[10]   17 C.F.R. § 240.10b-5 (2011). See Proposing Release, supra note 4; Final Rule: Selective Disclosure and Insider Trading, SEC Release Nos. 33-7881, 34-43154, IC-24599, 65 Fed. Reg. 51716 (Aug. 24, 2000) [hereinafter Adopting Release].

[11]   Chiarella v. United States, 445 U.S. 222 (1980).

[12]   Dirks v. SEC, 463 U.S. 646 (1983).

[13]   See discussion in the Introduction to this volume.

[14]   Adopting Release, supra note 10, at 51716.

[15]   See Dirks v. SEC, 463 U.S. at 662 (requiring a personal benefit to the tipper for tipper/tippee liability).

[16]   See Regulation Fair Disclosure, 17 C.F.R. § 243.100 (2000); Adopting Release, supra note 10.

was promulgated as an "issuer disclosure rule."[17] Rather than being addressed to insider trading or fraudulent conduct, Regulation FD was, in the SEC's words, "similar to existing Commission rules under Exchange Act Sections 13(a) and 15(d)."[18] Nonetheless, the SEC explicitly explained that the Rule targeted conduct that had been the subject of insider trading enforcement actions prior to *Dirks* and *Chiarella*.[19]

The structure of Regulation FD is straightforward. Regulation FD addresses the disclosure of information rather than its subsequent use, and is expressly directed to the sources of the information: issuers and corporate officials.[20] The Rule applies only to disclosures to four categories of recipients: "(1) brokers and dealers; (2) investment advisors and certain institutional investment managers; (3) investment companies and hedge funds; and (4) holders of the issuer's securities in circumstances in which it is reasonably foreseeable that the holder will purchase or sell the issuer's securities on the basis of the information."[21] Thus the Rule focuses on investor and capital market disclosures rather than ordinary business communications with a firm's customers, suppliers, and the like. The Rule also exempts communications to recipients who owe a duty of confidentiality to the issuer, including lawyers, accountants, and, at the time of its adoption, credit-rating agencies.[22] In conjunction with the passage of Dodd–Frank, the exemption for communications to credit-rating agencies was eliminated.[23]

Rather than explicitly prohibiting selective disclosure, Regulation FD takes the form of a disclosure mandate, requiring public disclosure of all material information that is disclosed by the issuer or its agents to someone within the enumerated categories of recipients. If the issuer intentionally discloses material non-public information to such a recipient, it is required to disclose that information, simultaneously, to the public. If the initial disclosure of the information is inadvertent, the issuer must publicly disclose the information "promptly," which the Rule defines to mean "as soon as reasonably practicable (but in no event after the later of 24 hours or the commencement of the next day's trading on the New York Stock Exchange)." The Rule allows the issuer to make public disclosure by filing a Form 8-K or through another means of disclosure that is "reasonably designed to provide broad, non-exclusionary distribution of the information to the public."

Regulation FD incorporates the materiality standard of federal securities fraud. Nonetheless, the Rule does not involve a fraud-based conception of liability. In addition,

---

[17]   Adopting Release, supra note 10, at 51716.

[18]   Proposing Release, supra note 4, at 72594.

[19]   Id. at 72593. Similarly, the Rule was adopted in conjunction with two other Rules designed to clarify the application of Rule 10b-5 to certain types of insider trading. Id. at 72591.

[20]   The Rule applies to disclosures by issuers and their agents. The term "person acting on behalf of an issuer" is defined to include senior management, investor relations personnel, and people who communicate regularly with market participants, but not all corporate employees. 17 C.F.R. § 243.101(c) (2011).

[21]   SEC Regulation FD, 17 C.F.R. § 243.100(a)-(b)(1) (2011).

[22]   17 C.F.R. § 243.101(b)(2)(i) (2011).

[23]   Dodd–Frank § 939B removes the credit-rating agency exemption from Regulation FD. The SEC has implemented section 939B through formal rule making. See Removal from Regulation FD of the Exemption for Credit Rating Agencies, Securities Act Release No 33-9146, 75 Fed. Reg. 61050, 61050 (Oct. 4, 2010) (to be codified at 17 C.F.R. pt. 243).

Regulation FD specifically provides that its violation does not constitute a violation of SEC Rule 10b-5.[24]

Many comments submitted in response to the proposed Rule reflected a concern about identifying when "material" information had been disclosed and would require corrective public disclosure. In response, the Adopting Release included seven categories of information that the Commission indicated were likely to be considered material.[25] These categories included: (1) earnings information; (2) mergers and acquisitions; (3) new products or discoveries; (4) change in control or management; (5) change in auditors; (6) events regarding the issuer's securities, such as a default or stock split; and (7) bankruptcies or receiverships.[26]

The SEC also announced, in the Adopting Release, its intention to retain the so-called "mosaic theory" in its analysis of materiality under Regulation FD.[27] The mosaic theory posits that information does not become material merely because it can "assume heightened significance when woven by the skilled analyst into the matrix of knowledge obtained elsewhere."[28] As the SEC explained, "an issuer is not prohibited from disclosing a non-material piece of information to an analyst, even if, unbeknownst to the issuer, that piece helps the analyst complete a 'mosaic' of information that, taken together, is material."[29]

II. INITIAL EXPERIENCE UNDER REGULATION FD

Early reactions to the Rule were highly critical. In particular, the business community expressed concern that Regulation FD would chill disclosure.[30] Commentators warned

---

[24] 17 C.F.R. § 243.102 (2011).

[25] See Adopting Release, supra note 10, at 51721.

[26] Id.

[27] The mosaic theory is not a creation of the SEC, but a judicially imposed limitation on the scope of materiality for purposes of insider trading analysis. *See* SEC v. Bausch & Lomb, Inc., 565 F.2d 8, 14 (2d Cir. 1977) (holding that "corporate management may reveal to securities analysts or other inquirers non-public information that merely fills 'interstices in analysis,' or tests 'the meaning of public information.'").

[28] Id. at 9; see also Elkind v. Liggett & Myers, Inc., 635 F.2d 156, 165–66 (2d Cir. 1980) (warning that the assessment of materiality in the context of the mosaic theory must be evaluated on a case-by-case basis).

[29] See Adopting Release, supra note 10, at 51722. The SEC has only explicitly recognized the mosaic theory in the context of Regulation FD, but defendants in recent insider trading cases have argued that their actions analogously constituted the mere "piecing together" of "multiple tidbits of non-public information." See Andrew Ross Sorkin, Just Tidbits, or Material Facts for Insider Trading?, N.Y. Times, Dec. 29, 2010, available at http://dealbook.nytimes.com/2010/11/29/just-tidbits-or-material-facts-for-insider-trading/ (last visited Nov. 14, 2012).

[30] See, e.g., Adopting Release, supra note 10, at 51718; Scott Russell, Regulation Fair Disclosure: The Death of the Efficient Capital Market Hypothesis and the Birth of Herd Behavior, 82 B.U.L. Rev. 527, 545 (2002) (summarizing concerns articulated by commentators about "inappropriate liability and the chilling effect on issuer disclosures"); Michael Schroeder, Raytheon's Disclosure to Analysts Is Investigated, Wall St. J., Mar. 15, 2001, at A3 (quoting SEC Commissioner Laura Unger reporting complaints about Regulation FD and concerns about the effect on corporate

that issuer fears about potential liability would reduce or eliminate their informal communications with the market.[31]

In the months after the SEC adopted Regulation FD, however, predictions of widespread market disruptions were not borne out.[32] Although issuers reported changing their disclosure policies and practices in response to the Rule, the market did not experience dramatic reductions in the dissemination of information[33] or substantial increases in price volatility.[34] Instead, issuers adapted their disclosure practices in response to the adoption of Regulation FD. For the most part, these adaptations resulted in increased public access to issuer information. Issuers began to open their earnings conference calls to the general public and to broadcast their analyst meetings on their websites.[35] An early report indicated that, following adoption of the Rule, issuer use of webcasts quadrupled.[36] Issuers began to develop best practices under Regulation FD that included, in addition to granting the general public access to information sessions that had previously been open only to invited participants, more frequent updating of their public disclosures.[37] These practices were enhanced by contemporaneous advances in technology that permitted greater use of the internet and corporate websites by virtually all investors.

Researchers rapidly sought to evaluate the effects of Regulation FD, and early studies reported conflicting results.[38] One survey by PricewaterhouseCoopers, conducted a year after Regulation FD was adopted, found that top executives were largely supportive of the

---

communications); see also Peter Talosig III, Regulation FD—Fairly Disruptive? An Increase in Capital Market Inefficiency, 9 Fordham J. Corp. & Fin. L. 637 (2004).

[31]   See Adopting Release, supra note 10, at 51726 ("Several [commentators] suggested, however, that the language in the Proposing Release offered insufficient protection from private lawsuits"); Talosig, supra note 30.

[32]   See Panel Discussion, supra note 9, at 291–92 (remarks of Richard Anderson, Senior Vice President, Thomson Financial/Carson Global Consulting).

[33]   See, e.g., Jeff D. Opdyke, How Much Are Stocks Hurting From Recent Rash of Profit Preannouncements Tied to New Rule, Wall St. J., Mar. 2, 2001, at C1 ("First Call/Thompson Financial statistics show that through the end of February, 551 companies have offered up earnings guidance for the current quarter. That is nearly five times the volume of the year-earlier period.")

[34]   Id.

[35]   See Panel Discussion, supra note 9, at 292 (remarks of Richard Anderson, Senior Vice President, Thomson Financial/Carson Global Consulting).

[36]   See SEC, Commissioner Laura S. Unger, Special Study: Regulation Fair Disclosure Revisited (2001), available at http://www.sec.gov/news/studies/regfdstudy.htm (last visited Nov. 14, 2012) [hereinafter Unger Special Study] ("between October 1, 2000 and April 23, 2001, the number of corporate webcasts on its service nearly quadrupled from the same period twelve months earlier (3,000 to 11,000)").

[37]   See, e.g., Stanley Keller, SEC Regulation FD—The Selective Disclosure Rules, ALI-ABA Course of Study Materials, Postgraduate Course in Federal Securities Law (July 2002) (describing evolving best practices for corporate compliance with Regulation FD).

[38]   See Richard Walker, Director, Division of Enforcement, Remarks Before the Rocky Mountain Securities Conference (May 18, 2001), available at http://www.sec.gov/news/speech/spch492.htm (last visited Nov. 14, 2012) (describing multiple studies reporting effects of Regulation FD on information disclosure, issuer compliance costs and stock price volatility); see also Unger Special Study, supra note 36 (summarizing the findings of eight surveys about Regulation FD conducted in 2001).

Rule. Nearly 90 percent of the executives surveyed supported the Rule, 75 percent reported that it had not impacted their company's stock price, and roughly half of respondents reported no increase in compliance costs while those who reported an increase described it as "low to moderate."[39]

At the same time, market participants expressed concern that, in making their disclosures more widely available, issuers were decreasing the quality of the information that they released. A survey by the Association for Investment Management and Research conducted in 2001 revealed that market professionals—analysts and portfolio managers—reported receiving less information and lower quality information from issuers.[40] The survey suggested that research analysts and other securities professionals were responding by conducting more independent research rather than relying primarily on issuer disclosures.[41]

The first formal empirical study of the impact of the Rule was conducted by academics at the business schools at University of Southern California and Purdue University.[42] The study, which examined more than 2000 firms immediately after the adoption of Regulation FD, found "no evidence that Regulation FD impaired the quality and quantity of investors' information."[43] The study found an increase in the informational efficiency of stock prices and "a marked increase in firms' voluntary disclosure frequency."[44]

SEC Commissioner Unger released a study examining Regulation FD one year after its effective date.[45] The study summarized the testimony at an April 2001 SEC Roundtable and identified various issues of concern, including a need for further guidance on materiality, the incorporation of technological developments to facilitate public disclosure, and the effect of the Rule on the quality of disclosure, particularly with respect to forward-looking information. The study's primary recommendation called for the SEC to continue to evaluate corporate disclosure post-FD to determine if modifications to the Regulation were necessary.

III.   EARLY ENFORCEMENT ACTIONS

In conjunction with its adoption of Regulation FD, the SEC announced that it would attempt to enforce the Rule in a way that minimized its chilling effect on issuer

---

[39]   See PricewaterhouseCoopers, Regulation FD Significantly Improves Disclosure, PricewaterhouseCoopers Survey Finds (Oct. 17, 2001), available at http://www.barometersurveys. com/vwAllNewsByDocID/EC0DF4912CF1BFFD45256B8E00013366/index.html (last visited Nov. 14, 2012).
[40]   See The CPA Journal, Research Studies Show Differing Views on Regulation FD (Dec. 2001), available at http://www.nysscpa.org/cpajournal/2001/1200/nv/nv2.htm (last visited Nov. 14, 2012).
[41]   Id.
[42]   Frank Heflin, K.R. Subramanyam & Yuan Zhang, Regulation FD and the Financial Information Environment: Early Evidence, 78 Acct'g Rev. 1 (2003).
[43]   Id. at 4.
[44]   Id.
[45]   See Unger Special Study, supra note 36.

communications with the market.[46] Nonetheless, the Commission rapidly brought a number of enforcement actions.[47] From 2002 to 2005, the SEC brought seven enforcement actions against issuers and corporate officials and published one report of investigation.[48] Most of these actions concerned private communications about corporate earnings[49] and all but one, *Siebel Systems*, were settled and not contested.

The actions demonstrated the scope of the SEC's commitment to the new Rule and its intention, through its selection of cases, to provide broader guidance to issuers and the market about the scope of communications that it viewed as problematic. The SEC's cases, in particular, revealed the Commission's intention not to limit its application of the Rule to cases involving literal factual inconsistencies between private communications and public disclosures.[50] Instead, the SEC's actions targeted more subtle methods— winks and nods—for providing selected recipients with informational advantages. These methods included, for example, a corporate official's reaffirmation of earnings estimates that had previously been publicly released (*Flowserve*);[51] reviewing and correcting drafts of analyst reports (*Senetek*);[52] disclosure made through a combination of statements and a corporate official's conduct, tone, and demeanor (*Schering-Plough*);[53] and the use of code words in public statements that were subsequently clarified through private con-

---

[46]   See, e.g., Letter from then-SEC Chairman designee Harvey L. Pitt to the Chief Clerk, United States Senate, Committee on Banking, Housing & Urban Affairs, July 23, 2001 ("The Commission's Enforcement Staff has stated that it will not attempt to second-guess reasonable, good faith judgments by persons who honestly attempt to comply with Regulation FD. I agree with that approach"); Speech of then-Enforcement Director Richard H. Walker, "Regulation FD: An Enforcement Perspective," before the Compliance and Legal Division of the Securities Industry Association, New York, Nov. 1, 2000 (stating that, at least in the early stages, the Enforcement Division will focus its efforts on "egregious violations" and that the division is "not looking to frustrate the purpose of the rule—which is to promote broader and fairer disclosure of information to investors—by second-guessing reasonable disclosure decisions made in good faith, even if we don't agree with them.").

[47]   See SEC Brings First Regulation FD Enforcement Actions, No 2002-169 (Nov. 25, 2002), available at http://www.sec.gov/news/press/2002-169.htm (last visited Nov. 14, 2012) (announcing the first four enforcement actions brought under Regulation FD).

[48]   See Marc H. Folladori, Interlude for Regulation FD, Practicing Law Institute Course Handbook, October 2008.

[49]   The SEC had previously stated, in its Adopting Release, that a corporate official that provides earnings guidance during private meetings with analysts "takes on a high degree of risk under Regulation FD." Adopting Release, supra note 10, at 51,721.

[50]   See William S. Lamb et al., SEC Continues to Define Regulation FD Parameters Through Enforcement Actions: Reaffirmation of Guidance Can Constitute Violation, 24 No 5 Banking & Fin. Serv. Pol'y Rep. 3, 4 (2005).

[51]   See Order Instituting Cease-and-Desist Proceedings, In the Matter of Flowserve Corp., Release No 51427, Admin. Proceeding File No 3-11872, at 3 (Mar. 24, 2005).

[52]   See Order Instituting Cease-and-Desist Proceedings, In the Matter of Senetek P.L.C., Release No 50400, Admin. Proceeding File No 3-11668, at 2 (Sept. 16, 2004).

[53]   See Order Instituting Cease-and-Desist Proceedings, In the Matter of Schering-Plough Corp., Exchange Act Release No 48,461, Admin. Proceeding File No 3-11,249, at 3–7 (Sept. 9, 2003); SEC Files Settled Regulation FD Charged Against Schering-Plough Corp. and its Former Chief Executive, Litigation Release No 18,330, Case No 1:03CV01880 (D.D.C.) (CKK) (Sept. 9, 2003); Jon Jordan, Corporate Issuers Beware: Schering-Plough and Recent SEC Enforcement Actions Signal Vigorous Enforcement of Regulation FD, 58 U. Miami L. Rev. 751 (2004).

versations (*Motorola*).[54] The SEC's choice of enforcement actions reflected its view that officials could violate Regulation FD not just by what they said, but by how they said it.[55]

IV.   *SIEBEL SYSTEMS*

The SEC faced a critical juncture in its enforcement of Regulation FD with the federal court litigation in the *Siebel Systems* case. Siebel was actually a repeat offender. In November 2001, Siebel's CEO made optimistic statements at a private technology conference that, according to the SEC, differed materially from the statements made by the CEO on a public conference call. Following the optimistic private statements, Siebel's trading volume doubled and its stock price increased by 16.5 percent. The SEC brought an enforcement action (*Siebel I*) that Siebel settled by agreeing to a cease and desist order and paying a $250,000 penalty.

Only six months after the cease and desist order was entered, in April 2003, Siebel engaged in conduct that the SEC viewed as similar to its prior Regulation FD violation.[56] Siebel communicated a negative outlook for the company in early April 2003 through a series of public disclosures. Following those communications, on April 30, 2003, Siebel's Chief Financial Officer and Investor Relations Director met privately with several institutional investors. At the private meetings, which were organized by Morgan Stanley, Siebel's CFO, Kenneth Goldman, characterized Siebel's business activity levels as "good" and "better" and disclosed that new deals were coming into the company's pipeline. According to the SEC's complaint, which carefully parsed these statements against the company's prior disclosures, these descriptions of Siebel's business were inconsistent with and affirmatively more positive than the prior public statements.[57]

Morgan Stanley subsequently communicated Goldman's remarks from the meetings to its other institutional clients. Morgan Stanley personnel characterized the tenor of the communications as "the body language was positive."[58] The SEC's complaint documented that the investors that attended the meetings and other institutional

---

[54]   Motorola, Inc., Exchange Act Release No 46,898, 2002 WL 31650174 (Nov. 25, 2002).

[55]   See Pepper Hamilton, Regulation FD Compliance after Schering-Plough—Mind Your Mannerisms (Nov. 10, 2003), available at http://www.pepperlaw.com/publications_article. aspx?ArticleKey=250 (last visited Nov. 14, 2012) ("the SEC also chose this set of facts to reinforce its views about the role non-verbal cues and signals can play in a Regulation FD violation").

[56]   Complaint at ¶ 4, SEC v. Siebel Systems, Inc., 384 F. Supp. 2d (No 04 CV 5130) (2004), available at http://www.sec.gov/litigation/complaints/comp18766.pdf (last visited Nov. 14, 2012).

[57]   Id. at ¶ 49 ("These statements materially contrasted with the public statements that Thomas Siebel had made during the April 4 and 23 conference calls and at the Deutsche Bank conference on April 28. For example, in contrast to the apocalyptic economic environment that Thomas Siebel described at the Deutsche Bank conference, Goldman's disclosures at the April 30 Alliance meeting and Morgan Stanley dinner were significantly more positive and upbeat"); see also SEC's opposition to Siebel's motion to dismiss at 8 (stating that Siebel's private statements "materially contrasted with the Company's prior public statements").

[58]   Id. at ¶ 52.

investors responded by purchasing Siebel stock.[59] The day after the meetings, Siebel's stock price increased by 8 percent and its trading volume doubled.[60]

When the SEC brought a second enforcement action against Siebel and its officials, the defendants filed a motion to dismiss the complaint. Although the defendants raised a variety of arguments, the court did not reach most of them because it concluded that the defendants' private statements did not differ materially from information that had been publicly released.[61] As a result, the court held that the SEC's complaint failed to state a claim.[62]

In arguing that Goldman's private statements were material, the SEC emphasized the reaction by investors to those statements. As the SEC stated, "[t]he materiality of the information is confirmed by the actions of those who attended the private meetings."[63] Thus Siebel presented the issue of the extent to which stock price movements and investor trading reactions to the information could be used to establish materiality as opposed to a comparison of the precise wording used by corporate officials in different contexts. The issue was important because of the potential for corporate officials to convey information indirectly—through winks, nods, and body language.[64]

With respect to this important aspect of Regulation FD, the court's decision dealt the SEC a substantial blow. Although the court stated that stock price movement and investor reactions to information could be considered relevant factors in determining the materiality of Siebel's statements, it stated that they were not sufficient.[65] Instead, the court engaged in a precise comparison of Siebel's public and private statements and concluded that the SEC had been too demanding, requiring in essence that companies examine their statements with the precision of a "lexicologist."[66] Because the court concluded that Siebel's private statements were "equivalent in substance to the information publicly disclosed [by the company]," it found no violation.[67]

More problematic was the freedom created by the *Siebel* opinion for corporate officials to engage in subjective characterizations that were not disclosed to the public even if investors viewed those characterizations as altering the total mix of information available to the market.[68] The court stated that "[t]he regulation does not prohibit

---

[59] Id. at ¶ 53.

[60] Id. at ¶ 54.

[61] SEC v. Siebel Systems, Inc., 384 F. Supp. 2d 694, 709 (S.D.N.Y. 2005).

[62] Id. at 710.

[63] Plaintiff's Brief in Opposition to Motion to Dismiss, at 2, SEC v. Siebel Systems, Inc., 384 F. Supp. 2d (2005) (No 04 CV 5130), 2004 WL 3142263.

[64] See Adopting Release, supra note 10, at 51721 (noting that corporate officials can violate Regulation FD "whether the information about earnings is communicated expressly or through indirect 'guidance,' the meaning of which is apparent though implied.").

[65] See SEC v. Siebel Systems, Inc., 384 F. Supp. 2d 694, 707 (S.D.N.Y. 2005) (noting that "although stock movement is a relevant factor to be considered in making the determination as to materiality, it is not, however, a sufficient factor alone to establish materiality.").

[66] Id. at 705.

[67] Id.

[68] As one review characterized the decision, "The fact that nonpublic subjective general impressions may cause movement in stock price or trading volume does not, in and of itself, create a presumption that material information was disclosed and Regulation FD was violated." Robert F. Carangelo & Jaclyn G. Braunstein, Weil Gotshal, Siebel Systems: A Speed Bump for the SEC

persons speaking on behalf of an issuer, from providing mere positive or negative characterizations, or their optimistic or pessimistic subjective general impressions, based upon or drawn from the material information available to the public."[69] This analysis seemed directly in tension with the Supreme Court's guidance in *Virginia Bankshares*, that expressions by corporate officials of their reasons, opinions, or beliefs were likely to be particularly important to investors in light of the "knowledge and expertness" of those officials.[70]

V. AFTER *SIEBEL SYSTEMS*

The SEC's immediate response to *Siebel Systems* was to cease bringing enforcement actions based on Regulation FD. Following the decision, the SEC did not bring another Regulation FD enforcement action for more than four years.[71] This reluctance can be seen as a reaction not just to the loss, but to the nature of the *Siebel* court's opinion which commentators described as a "public scolding."[72]

Following this hiatus, the SEC resumed its efforts to use Regulation FD, but cautiously.[73] Although the SEC has not formally retreated from its concern about implicit disclosures, it resumed its enforcement efforts with a case involving private statements that were directly inconsistent with the issuer's public disclosures. In addition, the SEC issued several compliance and disclosure interpretations to provide guidance concerning

---

on the Road to Regulation FD Enforcement?, at 11 (Dec. 2005), available at http://www.weil.com/news/pubdetail.aspx?pub=8086 (last visited Nov. 14, 2012).

[69]   *Siebel Systems*, 384 F. Supp. 2d at 707.

[70]   Virginia Bankshares, Inc. v. Sandberg, 501 U.S. 1083, 1090–91 (1991).

[71]   See Kit Addleman & Tracy G. Smith, Haynes and Boone LLP, SEC's Regulation FD Enforcement Actions Bring Compliance Lessons to Light, Bloomberg Law Reports: Federal Securities Law. The SEC did bring a cease and desist action, in 2007, against Electronic Data Systems (EDS); Order Instituting Cease-and-Desist Proceedings, In the Matter of Electronic Data Systems Corp., Release No 56519, Admin. Proceeding File No 3-12825 (Sept. 25, 2007), available at www.sec.gov/litigation/admin/2007/34-56519.pdf (last visited Nov. 14, 2012). The *EDS* case was brought as an administrative proceeding, however, rather than an enforcement action, thereby avoiding the risk for the SEC of litigating in federal court if the defendants did not agree to settle the charges. See Gibson Dunn, 2011 Mid-Year Securities Enforcement Update, at 11 (July 18, 2011), available at http://www.gibsondunn.com/publications/pages/2011Mid-YearSecuritiesEnforcementUpdate.aspx (last visited Nov. 14, 2012) (explaining, in the context of insider trading charges filed against Rajat Gupta, why "[a]n administrative proceeding is generally viewed as a more favorable venue for the Enforcement Division").

[72]   Kristen A. Truver, Note, Cutting the Party Line: How the SEC Can Silence Persisting Phone Call Tips, 39 Hofstra L. Rev. 447, 470 (2010).

[73]   See id. (describing SEC as "hesitant and conservative in pleading Regulation FD in actions through 2009"). Commentators have also suggested that, in some cases, the SEC failed to bring allegations of an FD violation, even when supported by the facts, in favor of relying on other provisions of the federal securities laws. See id. at 471 (offering, as an example of the SEC's reluctance to use Regulation FD, 2010 enforcement action against State Street); id. at 481 (describing cases in which, according to the author, the SEC should have used Regulation FD, but did not).

the SEC's policies. The releases focused, in particular, on the extent to which informal communications with analysts create potential problems under Regulation FD.[74]

In 2009, the SEC filed its first Regulation FD enforcement action since the *Siebel Systems* decision against Christopher Black, the former CFO of American Commercial Airlines (ACL). According to the SEC's litigation release, Black sent private e-mails to eight sell-side analysts from his home, on a weekend, disclosing that earnings would be lower than the guidance that had been issued by the company just days before. In contrast to the *Siebel* case, Black's comments were both written and clearly inconsistent with the company's public statements.

Notably as well, the SEC did not bring an enforcement action against ACL. According to the SEC, ACL had maintained compliance systems reasonably designed to educate corporate employees and to prevent Regulation FD violations.[75] Unlike Siebel, ACL filed an 8-K on the first trading day after it learned of Black's disclosures. ACL also self-reported the violation to the SEC and cooperated with the SEC's investigation. In addition, ACL took remedial measures to prevent future violations. The SEC's decision can be understood as a message to corporate issuers as to the value of adopting compliance procedures, cooperating with any SEC investigation and remedying any potential selective disclosures promptly.

In March 2010, the SEC brought an enforcement action against Presstek, Inc. and its former CEO, Edward Marino.[76] Marino, according to the SEC, selectively disclosed negative financial information to a registered investment adviser two days before the end of the quarter and one day before Presstek publicly announced that its earnings would be below prior estimates. Like the *Black* case, *Presstek* involved what might be considered an egregious or a clearly material selective disclosure—tipping investors or analysts right before the public disclosure of an earnings surprise is precisely the type of disclosure to which Regulation FD was addressed. Unlike the *Black* case, the SEC did sanction Presstek despite the existence at the company of FD disclosure policies. Although the SEC's rationale for proceeding against the issuer was not clear, it may have been concerned about sending a message that the mere existence of a compliance program would not insulate an issuer from liability.[77]

Office Depot was the third Regulation FD enforcement action within a period of

---

[74]   See SEC Compliance and Disclosure Interpretations: Regulation FD, June 4, 2010, available at http://www.sec.gov/divisions/corpfin/guidance/regfd-interp.htm (last visited Nov. 14, 2012). In particular, the SEC noted that issuer confirmation of prior forecasts may trigger an FD reporting obligation depending on the amount of time that had passed since the prior forecast and the extent to which intervening events had occurred. The SEC also noted that issuers may comment on analyst models, including correcting historical facts and sharing inconsequential data, without triggering obligations under Regulation FD.

[75]   See Litigation Release, SEC v. Christopher A. Black, Lit. Rel. No 21222 (Sept. 24, 2009, available at http://www.sec.gov/litigation/litreleases/2009/lr21222.htm (last visited Nov. 14, 2012). The SEC stated that ACL "cultivated an environment of compliance." Id.

[76]   See Litigation Release, SEC v. Presstek, Inc., Lit. Release 21443 (Mar. 9, 2010), available at http://www.sec.gov/litigation/litreleases/2010/lr21443.htm (last visited Nov. 14, 2012).

[77]   See, e.g., Kimberley D. Krawiec, Cosmetic Compliance and the Failure of Negotiated Governance, 81 Wash. U. L.Q. 487 (2001) (warning of the potential for ineffective compliance programs).

slightly more than a year.[78] *Office Depot* reflected a somewhat more aggressive enforcement decision by the SEC. Faced with the concern that the company would not meet
analysts' earnings estimates, Office Depot's CEO and CFO coordinated a strategy for
privately contacting 18 analysts in order to lower the analysts' expectations. The strategy
included the preparation of talking points that referenced comparable companies' lower
than expected performance and weakening economic conditions.[79] Six days later, the
company publicly announced that earnings would be "negatively impacted due to continued soft economic conditions."[80]

Notably, *Office Depot* involved issuer signaling rather than issuer statements that
directly contradicted public disclosures. The specific statements contained in Office
Depot's talking points and communicated privately to the analysts were reminders
about negative information contained in the company's prior public statements or references to other issuers whose earnings were negatively affected by economic downturn.
Accordingly, although the company engaged in a deliberate campaign to persuade analysts to lower their earnings estimates through private communications, it is unclear how a
court would have analyzed the SEC's claims under *Siebel*.[81] The case is also notable in that
the SEC brought its enforcement action against the CEO and CFO although the selective
disclosures were made by their subordinates.[82]

One of the SEC's most recent enforcement actions involved an unusual fact pattern.[83] In *First Third Bancorp*, the defendant decided to redeem certain trust preferred
securities on the basis that a provision of Dodd–Frank had created a "capital treatment
event."[84] First Third instructed the trustee to redeem the securities and to provide "all

---

[78]   See Order Instituting Cease-and-Desist Proceedings, In the Matter of Office Depot, Inc.,
Release No 63152, Admin. Proceeding File No 3-14094 (Oct. 21, 2010), available at www.sec.gov/
litigation/admin/2010/34-63152.pdf (last visited Nov. 14, 2012).
[79]   Id. at 3–4.
[80]   Id. at 5.
[81]   Both executives settled with the SEC and agreed to pay civil penalties of $50,000. Office
Depot agreed to pay a $1 million penalty. In imposing the latter penalty, the SEC observed that
Office Depot had no formal written Regulation FD policies or procedures and had conducted no
formal employee training on Regulation FD. The statement implied that the existence of such policies might have reduced the size of the penalty.
[82]   Of course the CEO and CFO were the ones who developed the plan and created the talking
points communicated by their subordinates.
[83]   The SEC's enforcement action in *China Voice* also differs markedly from prior cases.
See SEC, Court Enters Final Judgments Against China Voice Holding Corp. and its Former
CFO, David Ronald Allen, Litig. Rel. No 22178, Dec. 5, 2011, http://www.sec.gov/litigation/litre
leases/2011/lr22178.htm (last visited Jan. 10, 2013). *China Voice* involved a Ponzi scheme, and
the SEC's complaint alleged a massive fraud in which the defendants raised money through false
statements and used the proceeds to repay prior investors. The FD claims involved allegations
that corporate officials selectively disclosed non-public information to a China Voice shareholder
who was himself a participant in the fraud. The complaint does not reveal the SEC's rationale for
including Regulation FD among the claims, and the implications of the case with respect to future
enforcement actions are unclear. See Complaint, SEC v. David Ronald Allen, No 11CV00882, 2011
WL 1599661 (N.D. Tex.), Apr. 28, 2011.
[84]   See Order Instituting Cease-and-Desist Proceedings, In the Matter of First Third Bancorp,
Release No 63152, Admin. Proceeding File No 3-14639 (Nov. 22, 2010), available at http://www.sec.
gov/litigation/admin/2011/34-65808.pdf (last visited Jan. 10, 2013).

appropriate" notices of redemption. In accordance with the governing trust documents, the trustee provided such a notice to the Depository Trust Company, the only registered holder of record. DTC then posted the notice of redemption on its website which was password protected and available only to subscribers. When First Third became aware of unusual trading volume in the securities, it filed an 8-K. The SEC's settlement with First Third included only a cease and desist order and no civil penalty, and noted the defendant's cooperation and remedial actions once it became aware of the significance of the selective disclosure. It is likely that the SEC's decision to bring the action was motivated, in part, by a desire to call attention to the potential for selective disclosures even when information is disclosed over the internet or through a website. These concerns are considered in more detail in the SEC's release on internet disclosures discussed below.

As this book goes to press, the SEC's most recent Regulation FD investigation appears to involve Avon. In October 2011, Avon disclosed in its quarterly report that it had received an SEC subpoena relating to an investigation of possible violations of Regulation FD.[85] Media reports state that the focus of the investigation is a private meeting between Avon's CFO and a Citigroup research analyst.[86] The analyst's report referred to information supplied by the CFO at that meeting. The Avon investigation reflects the SEC's ongoing suspicion over private meetings between corporate officials and analysts or investors. Although the facts of the case remain unclear, the information available should suggest to issuers that such meetings are likely to trigger scrutiny. This message is reinforced by remarks made by SEC official David Rosenfeld, at a conference in February 2012.[87] According to media reports, Rosenfeld expressed concern as to whether issuers can participate in the common practice of private meetings and calls consistent with their obligations under Regulation FD.

Despite regulatory concerns, private meetings continue to be a mainstay of Wall Street practice.[88] Brokerage firms compete for valued commission revenues through their ability to arrange private meetings for their institutional investor clients.[89] Banks and brokers deny that such meetings are being used to convey material non-public information, claiming that they serve legitimate business purposes, and tout their ability to provide "access" as a means of differentiating themselves from their competitors.[90]

---

[85]   See Avon Faces SEC Probe, Looking at New Strategy, Reuters, Oct. 27, 2011, available at http://www.foxbusiness.com/markets/2011/10/27/avon-faces-sec-probe-looking-at-new-strategy/ (last visited Nov. 14, 2012).

[86]   See Avon's Cramb Gave Citi Bribery Probe Info, Reuters, Nov. 2, 2011, available at http://www.reuters.com/article/2011/11/02/avon-idUSN1E7A021U20111102 (last visited Nov. 14, 2012).

[87]   See Charlie Gasparino, Regulators May Expand Definition of Insider Trading, Fox Business, Feb. 15, 2012, available at http://www.foxbusiness.com/industries/2012/02/15/regulators-may-expand-definition-insider-trading/ (last visited Nov. 14, 2012).

[88]   See Enrich & Cimilluca, supra note 7 (describing "longstanding" practice by investment banks of arranging private issuer meetings for their hedge fund clients).

[89]   See Dominic Jones, Despite Reg FD, Study Finds Traders Profit From Private CEO Meetings, IR Web Report, Aug. 23, 2011, available at http://irwebreport.com/20110823/selective-access-profitable-study/ (last visited Nov. 14, 2012) (stating that US investors allocate $1.4 billion in trading revenues in exchange for private access).

[90]   See Enrich & Cimilluca, supra note 7.

VI.   THE EFFECTS OF REGULATION FD

When Regulation FD was first adopted, commentators widely agreed that it was difficult to predict its long-term effects. Scholars have drawn upon the prior ten years of experience with the Rule to produce an extensive body of empirical research. The mixed results of this research make it difficult, however, to draw definitive conclusions about the effects of the Regulation.

There is substantial evidence that Regulation FD reduced selective disclosure and information asymmetries.[91] A study by Bei Dong and others, for example, focuses on leakage of earnings information. The study concludes that, after the Rule's adoption, information leakages were reduced prior to earnings disclosures and that price volatility increased after the adoption, suggesting that the public disclosures revealed information not previously available to traders.[92] Importantly, the study also suggests that the reduction of these asymmetries is beneficial to the market. It finds that Regulation FD reduced bid-ask spreads, reflecting reduced concern by market participants over the potential information advantages possessed by their trading counterparties. Sinha and Gadarowski report similar results, finding that information leakage around voluntary management disclosures was reduced after Regulation FD.[93] Another study reports that the ability of analysts to exploit social ties to gain informational advantages virtually disappeared in the post-FD era.[94]

Critics had predicted that Regulation FD would reduce information flow as issuers, unwilling to disclose publicly, would reduce the overall amount of their disclosure. The studies of this issue are mixed.[95] At least some studies have found reduced overall disclosure, especially by smaller firms.[96] Scholars also report that Regulation FD delays the disclosure of information, at least in some cases.[97] On the other hand, studies have found

---

[91]   See, e.g., William J. Kross & Inho Suk, Does Regulation FD Work? Evidence from Analysts' Reliance on Public Disclosure, 53 J. of Acct. & Econ. 225 (Feb.–Apr., 2012) (concluding that Regulation FD "levels the playing field between analysts and individual investors").

[92]   See Bei Dong et al., The Effects of Regulation FD on Informal and Institutionalized Leakages of Information in Earnings Press Releases (unpublished manuscript) (on file with the Darden School of Business, University of Virginia) (Jan. 3, 2012), available at http://www.darden.virginia.edu/web/uploadedFiles/Paper%20for%20K%20Ramesh%20-%20DLRS%20December%202011.pdf (last visited Nov. 14, 2012).

[93]   See Praveen Sinha & Christopher Gadarowski, The Efficacy of Regulation FD, 45 Fin. Rev. 331 (May 2010). Another study finds that FD reduced analysts' ability to predict earnings surprises. Dan Palmon & Ari Yezegel, Analysts' Recommendation Revisions and Subsequent Earnings Surprises: Pre-and-Post Regulation FD, 26 J. Acct. Auditing & Fin. No 3 (2011).

[94]   See Andrea Frazzini, Christopher J. Malloy & Lauren Cohen, Sell Side School Ties (Harvard Bus. Sch. Fin., Working Paper No. 08-074, Feb. 20, 2008).

[95]   See Brian J. Bushee et al., Do Investors Benefit from Selective Access to Management? (Dec. 23, 2011), available at http://ssrn.com/abstract=1880149 (last visited Nov. 14, 2012) (finding that Regulation FD did not substantially reduce information disclosures by firms in conference calls; see also Sinha & Gadarowski, supra note 93 (describing mixed results of studies of disclosure quality and quantity post-Regulation FD).

[96]   See Edward R. Lawrence et al., Effect of Regulation FD on Disclosures of Information by Firms, 21 Applied Fin. Econ. 979 (2011).

[97]   See Paul A. Griffin et al., Enforcement and Disclosure under Regulation Fair Disclosure: An Empirical Analysis, 51 Acct. & Fin. 947 (2011).

increased reliance by analysts on public disclosures, and an increasing use by issuers of earnings guidance as a substitute for selective disclosures.[98]

Some of the Regulation FD studies indicate that Regulation FD reduced information quality.[99] Lawrence et al., for example, find that firms release less negative information subsequent to the adoption of Regulation FD.[100] Agrawal et al. find a reduction in analysts' forecast accuracy.[101] Another study finds that institutional investors are less able to identify mis-priced public offerings post-Regulation FD.[102]

Perhaps most troublingly, there is evidence that information asymmetries persist after the adoption of Regulation FD and that selective access to management continues to provide investors with trading advantages.[103] For example, one recent study finds that investor trade sizes increase after investors obtain private meetings with corporate officials—and that those sizes further increase if the official involved is the CEO.[104] To the extent that, as the SEC argued in *Siebel*, trading behavior is evidence that the investor has received material information, these data raise the concern that such information continues to be communicated selectively. Moreover, this research supports the SEC's continued focus on private meetings as potential sources for the communication of non-public information.

VII.   TECHNOLOGICAL DEVELOPMENTS AND REGULATION FD

Issuers have adapted their disclosure practices to reflect the selective disclosure concerns reflected in Regulation FD. The world of information and disclosure continues to evolve, however. Some of the most challenging changes that have occurred and are yet to come concern the effect of technological developments on an issuer's ability to make public disclosures.

A.   Issuer Websites

The SEC adopted Regulation FD in the middle of a technology revolution. In the years following the Rule's adoption, the SEC noted dramatic increases in investor access to

---

[98]   See Anchada Charoenrook & Craig M. Lewis, Information, Selective Disclosure, and Analyst Behavior (Fin. Mkts. Rsch. Center, Working Paper, No. 04-14 Sept. 2007); see also id. at note 3 (describing studies finding increased issuer disclosures of earnings guidance).

[99]   Id.

[100]   See Lawrence et al., supra note 96.

[101]   See Anup Agrawal et al., Who Is Afraid of Reg FD? The Behavior and Performance of Sell-Side Analysts Following the SEC's Fair Disclosure Rules, 79 J. Bus. 2811 (Nov. 2006).

[102]   See Douglas O. Cook & Tian Tang, The Impact of Regulation FD on Institutional Investor Informativeness, 39 Fin. Mgmt. 1273 (2010).

[103]   See also David Solomon & Eugene Soltes, What Are We Meeting For? The Consequences of Private Meetings with Investors, Sep. 2012, available at http://www-bcf.usc.edu/~dhsolomo/meet.pdf (last visited Nov. 14, 2012) (describing the use of private meetings by different types of investors and the effect of these meetings on trading).

[104]   See Bushee et al., supra note 95.

the internet.[105] The SEC also noted that issuers were increasingly likely both to maintain a corporate website and to include links on that website to their SEC filings and other investor-oriented information. The internet offered the potential for issuers to provide broad-based dissemination of information quickly and inexpensively, and some commentators criticized the SEC for failing to incorporate internet-based disclosure into its requirements under Regulation FD.[106]

In 2008, the SEC responded. The Commission issued an interpretive release concerning company websites that included, in particular, guidance concerning the circumstances under which a website posting could satisfy the public dissemination requirement under Regulation FD.[107] The very recognition that a website posting could be sufficient to comply with the Rule reflected a change from the position adopted by the SEC in 2000. The release went on to provide guidance concerning the evaluation of whether a website posting constituted the necessary public disclosure required by the Rule. According to the SEC, the primary considerations in determining whether posting information on a company website constituted public disclosure for purposes of Regulation FD were: (1) whether the company website was "a recognized channel of distribution;" (2) whether the website posting made the information available to the general marketplace; and (3) whether there was a reasonable waiting period for investors and the market to react to the posted information.[108]

The SEC explicitly provided, in contrast to its earlier position, that "for some companies in certain circumstances, posting of the information on the company's web site, in and of itself, may be a sufficient method of public disclosure under Rule 101(e) of Regulation FD."[109] The SEC noted that the analysis was issuer-specific and would depend on an evaluation of the particular circumstances. The SEC further noted that the manner and accessibility of information on an issuer's website were critical factors in evaluating whether a website posting constituted a public disclosure. It is likely that the SEC's decision to bring an enforcement action in the *First Third* case was motivated, in part, by a desire to demonstrate to issuers the potential for selective disclosure in cases in which access to a website posting is limited.

---

[105] Compare Robert A. Prentice, The Internet and Its Challenges for the Future of Insider Trading Regulation, 12 Harv. J. L. & T. 263, 286 (1999) (stating in 1999 that a strong argument can be made that "information available only on a corporate website is not 'public'") with Commission Guidance on the Use of Company Websites, Release Nos. 34-58288, IC-28351, 17 C.F.R. 241, 271 (2008), available at http://www.sec.gov/rules/interp/2008/34-58288.pdf (describing growing investor access to the internet) (last visited Nov. 14, 2012).

[106] See Thomas Ishmael, Securities and Exchange Commission Regulation Fair Disclosure—A Modern Law with Outmoded Methods: An Appeal for Dissemination of Material Information on Corporate Websites, 33 Okla. City U. L. Rev. 629 (2009).

[107] See Commission Guidance on the Use of Company Websites, supra note 105; see also Lawrence J. Trautman, The SEC & The Internet: Regulating the Web of Deceit, 65 Consumer Fin. L. Q. Rep. (2011) (discussing the SEC's release and guidance).

[108] Commission Guidance on the Use of Company Websites, supra note 105. The release provided a list of factors to guide issuers in evaluating these considerations. The SEC also explained that the considerations were designed to determine whether website postings were "reasonably designed to provide broad, non-exclusionary distribution of the information to the public." Id. at 24.

[109] Id. at 25.

B. Social Media

Social media present still another challenge. Corporate executives increasingly discuss their companies using social media tools such as Facebook and Twitter. These methods of disclosure raise challenges over the traditional regulatory categories in that the communications are not typically made to a favored few, as in the case of private analyst meetings. Neither, however, are they open to the general public in the same way as a press release or Form 8-K would be. Informal and unstructured social media communications also stretch the concept of materiality.

One corporate executive has taken the use of social media communications to a new level. WebMediaBrands CEO Alan Meckler has made a practice of communicating corporate information to investors on a real time basis, using Twitter and his blog.[110] In December 2010, the SEC staff sent WebMediaBrands a comment letter questioning the company about Meckler's social media postings of company information.[111] The company defended Meckler's practices on the grounds that the particular tweet and blogged information at issue did not involve material, non-public information. The company also argued that Meckler's tweets and blog posts were equivalent to public distribution and, therefore, were Regulation FD compliant as a "recognized channel" of public distribution, at least for this company and this CEO.[112] To date, Meckler has not stopped his use of social media, and the SEC has not brought an enforcement action against him.[113]

To date, SEC investigations involving social media postings appear to be uncommon, and it is unclear how the SEC viewed WebMediaBrands' argument that the postings were public rather than selective disclosure. Nonetheless, issuers are beginning to consider such postings in their Regulation FD compliance and education programs. IBM, for example, provides guidelines on social computing to its employees.[114] Among these guidelines, IBM warns its employees not to blog or twitter about confidential company information, including the company's future performance and business plans. It is likely that attention to the implications of Regulation FD for social media will rapidly become a component of best practices for issuer compliance.

---

[110]   See Dominic Jones, CEO pushes Reg FD Limits on Twitter, IR Web Report, Sept. 15, 2011, available at http://irwebreport.com/20110915/ceo-pushes-reg-fd-limits-on-twitter/ (last visited Nov. 14, 2012).

[111]   See Letter from H. Christopher Owings, Asst. Dir. SEC, to Alan M. Meckler, Chairman & CEO, WebMediaBrands Inc. Dec. 9, 2010, at 1, available at http://www.sec.gov/Archives/edgar/data/1083712/000000000010074073/filename1.pdf (last visited Nov. 14, 2012) (asking issuer to explain whether CEO's blog postings providing updates "on future acquisitions, stock option purchases and new services . . . conveyed information in compliance with Regulation FD and other Commission rules and regulations").

[112]   See Letter from Donald R. Reynolds, attorney for WebMediaBrands Inc., to the SEC, at 4 (Jan. 7, 2011), available at http://www.sec.gov/Archives/edgar/data/1083712/000101968711000062/filename1.htm (last visited Nov. 14, 2012).

[113]   See Reese Darragh, CEO's Tweets Raise Reg FD Questions, Compliance Week, Nov. 8, 2011 (last visited Nov. 14, 2012).

[114]   IBM Social Computing Guidelines, http://www.ibm.com/blogs/zz/en/guidelines.html (last visited Mar. 20, 2012).

VIII.   CONCLUSION

Despite the apparent setback of the *Siebel Systems* decision, the SEC's efforts to address selective disclosure through the promulgation and enforcement of Regulation FD should be understood as successful. Issuers take seriously the applicable regulatory restrictions in engaging in private communications with investors and analysts and have structured compliance and education systems designed to reduce both intentional and unintentional selective disclosures. Although the SEC has brought a limited number of cases enforcing the Rule, its selections appear designed less to punish wrongdoers than to announce generally applicable standards of conduct and to expose areas of ongoing regulatory concern.

Several areas are likely to continue to raise SEC concerns. Private meetings are a problematic area. The Commission continues to be suspicious of the claim that private meetings between corporate executives and analysts and investors do not involve selective disclosures. The SEC's concerns are supported by recent empirical studies suggesting that private meetings confer trading benefits on their attendees. Nonetheless, the disclosure-based structure of Regulation FD appears better suited to balancing competing policy considerations in this area than the blunt force of antifraud liability. Similarly, the SEC will need to continue to refine its enforcement of Regulation FD to incorporate technological developments, including growing information transmission through the internet and social media. Responding to these developments requires a delicate balance in that technology offers the potential to level the informational playing field at the same time that it presents new mechanisms for abuse.

8. Decision theory and the case for an optional disclosure-based regime for regulating insider trading
Thomas A. Lambert

This chapter is being drafted amid what the *Wall Street Journal* has dubbed "an unprecedented era of insider trading prosecutions."[1] In just over two years, the U.S. government has secured 56 guilty pleas or convictions out of 63 individuals charged with insider trading.[2] Given the extensive enforcement resources currently allocated toward insider trading prosecutions, one might infer that stock trading on the basis of material, nonpublic information is an unmitigated "bad."

But that is most certainly not the case. As Stephen Bainbridge details in the Introduction to this *Handbook*, stock trading on the basis of material, nonpublic information may create social benefits as well as harms. Moreover, particular instances of insider trading will differ in terms of the amount of social harm or benefit they occasion: some instances will be, on net, harmful; others will create a net social benefit. Insider trading is, in short, a "mixed bag" type of economic activity.

Regulating mixed bag behavior is a tricky business. Liability rules may err in two directions: they may condemn or discourage good instances of the behavior (i.e., produce "Type I errors"), or they may acquit or encourage bad instances (i.e., produce "Type II errors"). In either case, social welfare suffers. Accordingly, the optimal regulatory regime would seek to minimize the sum of losses from improper condemnations and improper acquittals (total error costs), while keeping the cost of administering the liability rule (decision costs) in check.

Judged according to this criterion (i.e., does the liability rule minimize the sum of error and decision costs?), the USA's current regime for regulating insider trading fails. It is hard to administer, and it deters many instances of socially desirable informed trading. The more restrictive approach seemingly favored by U.S. enforcement agencies fares even worse. While a proposed laissez-faire or "contractarian" approach would likely represent an improvement over both the legal status quo and the approach favored by the enforcement agencies, that approach, too, may be suboptimal. A better approach would be to allow corporations and sources of material, nonpublic information to choose between the legal status quo and a disclosure-based regulatory regime. This chapter sets forth such an optional, disclosure-based approach and explains why it would be superior to the legal status quo and the leading proposed alternatives.

---

[1] See Jenny Strasburg, Michael Rothfeld & Susan Pulliam, FBI Sweep Targets Big Funds, Wall St. J. A1 (Jan. 19, 2012).
[2] Id.

This chapter proceeds as follows: Section I supplements the introduction's discussion of the pros and cons of stock trading on the basis of material, nonpublic information, explaining why insider trading is a mixed bag practice. Section II describes the "decision-theoretic" criterion for regulating mixed bag practices and evaluates the legal status quo and the leading proposed alternative regulatory systems according to that criterion. Section III sets forth an optional, disclosure-based approach, explains why it would be superior to the status quo and the leading alternative proposals, and evaluates potential drawbacks. Section IV concludes.

I. INSIDER TRADING AS A MIXED BAG BUSINESS PRACTICE

A. A Tale of Four Informed Traders

The mixed bag nature of insider trading can be seen by comparing four well-known instances of stock trading on the basis of material, nonpublic information.

1. *Texas Gulf Sulphur* officials[3]

In 1959, agents of the Texas Gulf Sulphur Company (TGS) discovered a major deposit of copper and zinc ore near Timmins, Ontario. Hoping to acquire nearby land and mineral rights at a favorable price, TGS's president ordered knowledgeable TGS agents to keep the discovery a secret so as not to tip off neighboring landowners. Disregarding that instruction, a number of TGS officials purchased TGS stock and call options (options to buy), causing the company's stock price to rise from $20\frac{7}{8}$ when chemical assay results confirmed the discovery to around $37 when the discovery was publicly announced. That suspicious 77 percent stock price increase over a few months might well have signaled to neighboring property owners that the company possessed undisclosed good news. So signaled, the neighbors might have demanded higher prices for their land and mineral rights, squandering TGS's opportunity to exploit its informational advantage.

2. *Ivan Boesky*[4]

Managers of FMC Corporation, which was generating large amounts of cash, sought to recapitalize the company in order to make it less attractive as a takeover target. They concocted a plan to borrow money, exchange non-manager shareholders' stock for cash plus a reduced equity stake, and exchange incumbent managers' stock for greater equity stakes. This plan would reduce a takeover threat because it would result in a more heavily leveraged company whose stock was held to a greater degree by incumbent managers. Arbitrageur Ivan Boesky, who had entered an information-sharing agreement with a number of individuals in the finance industry (including a Goldman Sachs partner

---

[3] The account of insider trading by Texas Gulf Sulphur officials is set forth in SEC v. Texas Gulf Sulphur, 401 F.2d 833 (2nd Cir. 1968).

[4] Boesky's insider trading is described in FMC Corp. v. Boesky, 852 F.2d 981 (7th Cir. 1988).

working on the FMC recapitalization), learned of the recapitalization plan. Boesky then made large purchases of FMC stock, causing the stock price to rise. This increased the amount the corporation had to pay to acquire non-managers' equity, effectively raising the cost of the recapitalization.

3.   Raymond Secrist and Ronald Dirks[5]

Raymond Secrist, a disgruntled former officer of Equity Funding of America (EFA), sought to disclose massive accounting fraud at his former company. He first conveyed information about the fraud to a number of regulatory agencies, including the U.S. Securities and Exchange Commission (SEC) and the state securities commissioners of California and Illinois. When none of the regulatory agencies followed up on his accusations, Secrist conveyed information about the fraud to Raymond Dirks, a securities analyst at the investment bank Hawkins Delafield. Urged by Secrist to expose the fraud, Dirks passed the information to the *Wall Street Journal*'s Los Angeles bureau chief and, in the words of the Court of Appeals, "badgered him to write a story for the *Journal* on the allegations of fraud at Equity Funding."[6] The bureau chief, however, doubted that such a massive fraud could have gone on undetected and therefore refused to report the allegations. Dirks then passed the information to a number of his institutional investor clients who traded on the basis of the information, causing EFA's stock price to plummet. The falling stock price led to exposure of the massive accounting fraud and, somewhat ironically, to Dirks's prosecution for insider trading.

4.   Ted Beatty[7]

Ted Beatty, a management trainee at energy trader Dynegy, Inc., became suspicious that his employer was exaggerating trading activity. When he looked further into Dynegy's operations, he discovered "Project Alpha," an Enron-like arrangement that "exaggerated cash flow from operations and cut taxes but was all but impossible for outsiders to fathom from Dynegy's public reports."[8] When Dynegy failed to give him the promotion he felt he deserved, Beatty resigned, planning to expose Dynegy's wrongdoing. He shared the information about Dynegy's misconduct with the New York investment fund Steadfast Capital and purchased his own put options (options to sell) on Dynegy. Concerned about potential insider trading liability, Beatty sold his puts at a loss after a few days, hoping instead to receive compensation as a consultant to Steadfast or as an informant to the *Wall Street Journal*, with whom he also shared the information. After the *Journal* published an article on Dynegy's questionable accounting, the SEC began an informal inquiry into Dynegy's finances, and the company's stock price plunged. Despite his effort to expose Dynegy's fraud, Beatty never received any compensation from Steadfast, the *Wall Street Journal*, or the SEC.

---

[5]   Secrist's effort to expose fraud and Dirks's sharing of inside information are described in Dirks v. SEC, 463 U.S. 646 (1983).

[6]   Dirks v. SEC, 681 F.2d 824, 831 (2nd Cir. 1982).

[7]   The story of Beatty's effort to ferret out fraud at Dynegy is related in Jathon Sapsford & Paul Beckett, Informer's Odyssey: The Complex Goals and Unseen Costs of Whistleblowing, Wall St. J. A1 (Nov. 25, 2002).

[8]   Id.

B.   A Brief Summary of Insider Trading's Pros and Cons

The foregoing examples illustrate one major "con" and a key "pro" of insider trading. The con, illustrated by *Texas Gulf Sulphur* and *Boesky*, is that such trading may result in effective theft of the corporation's valuable information, precluding the corporation from exploiting its information to procure a valuable corporate opportunity (e.g., cheap land purchases in *Texas Gulf Sulphur*, favorable recapitalization terms in *Boesky*).[9] If corporations cannot protect their valuable information by maintaining the exclusive right to use it, they will be less inclined to produce it in the first place. The pro, illustrated by *Dirks* and (to a lesser extent) the Beatty affair, is that insider trading may reveal fraud-induced stock mispricing.[10] If insider trading is likely to thwart attempts to inflate stock prices through accounting tricks and earnings manipulation, managers are less likely to engage in such chicanery in the first place. The four cases discussed above, then, are sufficient to establish the mixed bag nature of insider trading.

But there is much more.[11] On the con side, defenders of insider trading restrictions insist that it is fundamentally unfair for some traders to have an informational advantage over others, particularly when the advantaged traders are corporate insiders who are supposed agents of those who lack the informational advantage.[12] They further contend that insider trading causes efficiency losses by: (1) discouraging investment in a "rigged" stock market, thereby reducing the liquidity of capital markets;[13] (2) encouraging insiders to delay disclosures[14] or to make management decisions that increase potential trading profits but reduce firm value;[15] (3) infringing upon a corporation's informational property rights and thereby reducing its incentive to create valuable information, as illustrated

---

[9]   See generally Stephen M. Bainbridge, Corporation Law and Economics 598–607 (2002).

[10]   See generally Jonathan Macey, Corporate Governance: Promises Kept, Promises Broken 172–81 (2008); Robert Wagner, Gordon Gekko to the Rescue?: Insider Trading as a Tool to Combat Accounting Fraud, 79 U. Cin. L. Rev. 973 (2011).

[11]   Stephen Bainbridge's Introduction to this *Handbook* summarizes the voluminous literature on the costs and benefits of insider trading, so only a brief recap is required here.

[12]   See, e.g., Roy A. Schotland, Unsafe at Any Price: A Reply to Manne, Insider Trading and the Stock Market, 53 Va. L. Rev. 1425, 1439 (1967) ("Even if we found that unfettered insider trading would bring an economic gain, we might still forego that gain in order to secure a stock market and intracorporate relationships that satisfy such noneconomic goals as fairness, just rewards and integrity").

[13]   See, e.g., Jeffrey M. Laderman, et al., The Epidemic of Insider Trading, Bus. Wk., Apr. 29, 1985, at 78 (quoting then American Stock Exchange chairman and future SEC chairman, Arthur Levitt, Jr., as stating, "[i]f the investor thinks he's not getting a fair shake, he is not going to invest, and that is going to hurt capital investment in the long run").

[14]   See Robert J. Haft, The Effect of Insider Trading Rules on the Internal Efficiency of the Large Corporation, 80 Mich. L. Rev. 1051, 1054–55 (1982) (arguing that, if insider trading were permitted, "subordinates would stall the upward flow of critical information to maximize their opportunities for financial gain," resulting in an "impair[ment] [of] corporate decision-making at all hierarchical levels").

[15]   See, e.g., Saul Levmore, Securities and Secrets: Insider Trading and the Law of Contracts, 68 Va. L. Rev. 117, 149 (1982) (noting that if insider trading is permitted "an insider can profit from a decrease in the firm's stock price as well as an increase; the temptation of profit might actually encourage an insider to act against the corporation's interest").

by *Texas Gulf Sulphur* and *Boesky*;[16] and (4) reducing trading efficiency by increasing the "bid–ask" spread of stock specialists who systematically lose on trades with insiders (whom they cannot identify *ex ante*) and therefore tend to "insure" against such losses by charging a small premium on each trade.[17]

Proponents of legalizing insider trading discount these purported harms. With respect to the fairness argument, they contend that insider trading cannot be "unfair" to investors who know in advance that it might occur and nonetheless choose to trade.[18] They further maintain that the purported efficiency losses occasioned by insider trading are overblown. There is little evidence, they say, that insider trading reduces liquidity by discouraging individuals from investing in the stock market,[19] and it might actually increase such liquidity by providing benefits to investors in equities.[20] With respect to the claim that insider trading creates incentives for delayed disclosures and value-reducing management decisions, advocates of deregulation claim that such mismanagement is unlikely for several reasons. First, managers face reputational constraints that will discourage such misbehavior.[21] In addition, managers, who generally work in teams, cannot engage in value-destroying mismanagement without persuading their colleagues to go along with the strategy, and any particular employee's ability to engage in mismanagement will therefore be constrained by her colleagues' attempts to maximize firm value or to gain personally by exposing proposed mismanagement.[22] With respect to the property rights argument proponents of insider trading restrictions have asserted, deregulation proponents contend that, even if material nonpublic information is worthy of property protection, the property right need not be a non-transferable interest granted to the corporation; efficiency considerations may call for the right to be transferable and/or initially allocated to a dif-

---

[16]   See Bainbridge, supra note 9, at 598–607.

[17]   See, e.g., John C. Coffee, Jr., Is Selective Disclosure Now Lawful?, N.Y. L.J., July 31, 1997, at 5 ("[T]he more that the law successfully prohibits the use of nonpublic information, the more that the market maker can (and will be forced by competitive pressure to) narrow the bid/ask spread").

[18]   Kenneth Scott, Insider Trading: Rule 10b-5, Disclosure and Corporate Privacy, 9 J. Legal Stud. 801, 807–09 (1980) (observing that if the existence of insider trading is known, outsiders will not be disadvantaged because the price they pay will reflect the risk of insider trading); Frank H. Easterbrook, Insider Trading, Secret Agents, Evidentiary Privileges, and the Production of Information, 1981 Sup. Ct. Rev. 309, 323–30 (discussing and refuting fairness arguments).

[19]   See Dennis W. Carlton & Daniel R. Fischel, The Regulation of Insider Trading, 35 Stan. L. Rev. 857, 880, n. 76 (1983) ("[T]he notion that exchanges are harmed by insider trading is hard to square with the following facts: (1) the stock market was successful pre-1933 (before insider trading laws); (2) the stock market was successful pre-1960s (before judicial extension of insider trading laws); (3) the stock market is currently successful despite the existence of legal and perhaps illegal insider trading").

[20]   Cf. id. at 881 ("Compensating managers [by permitting insider trading] increases the size of the pie, and thus outsiders as well as insiders profit from the incentives managers are given to increase the value of the firm").

[21]   See id. at 884 (observing that a manager will be motivated, at least in part, by "his long run interest in his human capital").

[22]   See id. at 873–74 ("Managers often work in teams and thus must first persuade one another that the firm should undertake a particular strategy. . . . [T]he ability of any one manager to pursue bad opportunities will be constrained because other managers and employees will attempt to maximize the firm's value").

ferent party (e.g., to insiders).[23] Finally, legalization proponents observe that there is little empirical evidence to support the concern that insider trading increases bid–ask spreads.[24]

Turning to their affirmative case, proponents of insider trading legalization primarily emphasize two potential benefits of the practice. First, they observe that insider trading increases stock market efficiency[25] (i.e., the degree to which stock prices reflect true value), which in turn facilitates efficient resource allocation among capital providers and enhances managerial decision making by reducing agency costs resulting from overvalued equity.[26] In addition, legalization proponents contend, the right to engage in insider trading may constitute an efficient form of managerial compensation.[27]

Not surprisingly, proponents of insider trading restrictions have taken issue with both of these purported benefits. With respect to the argument that insider trading leads to more efficient securities prices, ban proponents retort that trading by insiders conveys information only to the extent it is revealed, and even then the message it conveys is "noisy" or ambiguous, given that insiders may trade for a variety of reasons, many of which are unrelated to their possession of inside information.[28] Defenders of restrictions further maintain that insider trading is an inefficient, clumsy, and possibly perverse compensation mechanism.[29]

---

[23] See id. at 878 (noting that the contention that inside information is property "does not address the key question of why the firm and not the managers always should be allocated the property right in information"); Easterbrook, supra note 18, at 331 (approving property rights approach but noting that "insider trading should be permitted to the extent the firm that created the information desires (or tolerates) such trading. The firm extracts value through exploiting the knowledge itself or reducing the salary of those who exploit it").

[24] See Stanislav Dolgopolov, Insider Trading and the Bid–Ask Spread: A Critical Evaluation of Adverse Selection in Market Making, 33 Cap. U. L. Rev. 83 (2004) (surveying empirical evidence regarding insider trading's effect on bid–ask spread and liquidity).

[25] See, e.g., Henry G. Manne, Insider Trading: Hayek, Virtual Markets, and the Dog that Did Not Bark, 31 J. Corp. L. 167, 169 (2005) (citing empirical evidence and observing that "[t]here is almost no disagreement that insider trading does always push the price of a stock in the correct direction").

[26] See Thomas A. Lambert, Overvalued Equity and the Case for an Asymmetric Insider Trading Regime, 41 Wake Forest L. Rev. 1045 (2006). For a description of the value-destruction occasioned by overpriced stock, see Michael C. Jensen, Agency Costs of Overvalued Equity, 34 Fin. Mgmt. 5 (2005).

[27] See Henry G. Manne, Insider Trading and the Stock Market 116–19 (1966); M. Todd Henderson, Insider Trading and CEO Pay, 64 Vand. L. Rev. 505 (2011) (presenting empirical evidence that boards of directors bargain with executives about the profits they expect to make from informed trades in firm stock); Carlton & Fischel, supra note 19, at 869–71.

[28] See Ronald J. Gilson & Reinier H. Kraakman, The Mechanisms of Market Efficiency, 70 Va. L. Rev. 549, 574 (1984) (discussing the limits of efforts to "decode" insider transactions).

[29] See, e.g., Bainbridge, supra note 9, at 591–92 (detailing limitations of insider trading as compensation mechanism); Easterbrook, supra note 18, at 332.

II.   A DECISION-THEORETIC ANALYSIS OF ACTUAL AND PROPOSED REGIMES FOR REGULATING INSIDER TRADING

A.   The Decision-Theoretic Approach

In light of the mixed bag nature of stock trading on the basis of material, nonpublic information, crafting a rule to govern the practice is somewhat difficult. A broad liability rule would properly condemn bad instances of insider trading, such as those involving effective theft of information that the corporation has a legitimate interest in protecting, but might also condemn or discourage good instances, such as trading that would reduce or prevent overvaluation, identify instances of fraud, etc. On the other hand, a narrow rule that rarely assigns liability would appropriately exculpate fraud-revealing and other socially desirable instances of insider trading but might also encourage misuse of a corporation's proprietary information or mismanagement aimed at generating trading profits. A nuanced rule that forbade or permitted instances of insider trading in light of the likely effect of the trading could be difficult for business planners to apply *ex ante* and for agencies and courts to enforce *ex post*. Thus, any liability rule will entail costs from improper convictions or acquittals (error costs) and from administering the rule in planning and/or adjudication (decision costs). The optimal regulatory strategy—the "decision-theoretic" approach—would seek to minimize the sum of error and decision costs.[30] The remainder of this section evaluates proposed and actual approaches to insider trading regulation according to this decision-theoretic criterion.

B.   Evaluation of Proposed and Actual Approaches

Over the past half-century, regulators and commentators have proposed alternative approaches to regulating insider trading, ranging from a rule that would prohibit stock trading in the face of any informational advantage to one that would recognize only contractual limits on insider trading. As Figure 8.1 shows, the currently prevailing regulatory regime falls somewhere between these extremes (albeit closer to the restrictive end of the regulatory spectrum). Each approach, we will see, raises concerns when evaluated according to the decision-theoretic criterion.

1.   Most restrictive: no trading by anyone in possession of material, nonpublic information

The most restrictive approach to regulating insider trading would simply prohibit a trader from buying or selling stock whenever she possesses material, nonpublic information about the underlying company. The SEC traditionally favored this restrictive approach on the ground that it would alleviate unfairness in equities trading by eliminating the

---

[30]   See Thomas A. Lambert, The Roberts Court and the Limits of Antitrust, 52 B. C. L. Rev. 871, 877–79 (2011) (setting forth decision-theoretic criterion in antitrust context); C. Frederick Beckner, III & Steven C. Salop, Decision Theory and Antitrust Rules, 67 Antitrust L. J. 41 (1999) (same).

Most Restrictive   *Least Restrictive*

| **Enforcers' Preferred Approach:** All stock trading on the basis of material, nonpublic information is forbidden. | **Legal Status Quo:** Stock trading on the basis of material, nonpublic information is prohibited if the trader owed (or inherited) a duty of confidence to either her trading partner or the source of her information. | **Contractarian Approach:** No governmental restrictions on stock trading on the basis of material, nonpublic information. Such trading is forbidden, if at all, by contract only. |

Figure 8.1   The spectrum of options for regulating stock trading on the basis of material, nonpublic information

informational advantage some traders have over others.[31] In *Texas Gulf Sulphur*, the Commission persuaded the U.S. Court of Appeals for the Second Circuit to endorse its approach. Relying on the Commission's *Cady, Roberts* enforcement decision,[32] the Second Circuit held that "all transactions in [*Texas Gulf Sulphur*] stock or calls by individuals apprised of the drilling results were made in violation of Rule 10b-5."[33] Stating its ruling more generally, the court explained that:

> [A]nyone in possession of material inside information must either disclose it to the investing public, or, if he is disabled from disclosing it in order to protect a corporate confidence, or he chooses not to do so, must abstain from trading in or recommending the securities concerned while such inside information remains undisclosed.[34]

That "disclose or abstain" duty, the court reasoned, arises from an implicit policy in Rule 10b-5 that all stock investors be placed on a "level playing field."[35]

Recent statements by enforcement authorities suggest that the agencies still favor the use of insider trading rules to eliminate informational advantages. Consider, for example, *Time* Magazine's February 2012 cover story on U.S. Attorney Preet Bharara, who is largely responsible for the current crackdown on insider trading:

> To hear him tell it, Bharara is after something bigger than just arrests. In his insider-trading cases, Bharara says he is not targeting hedge funds but rather leveling the playing field for all

---

[31]   See Stephen M. Bainbridge, Insider Trading Regulation: The Path Dependent Choice Between Property Rights and Securities Fraud, 52 SMU L. Rev. 1589, 1594–1601 (1999) (describing the SEC's attempt to base insider trading liability on stock trading while in possession of material, nonpublic information).

[32]   In re Cady, Roberts & Co., 40 SEC 907, 912 (1961).

[33]   SEC v. Texas Gulf Sulphur, 401 F.2d 833, 852 (2nd Cir. 1968).

[34]   Id. at 848.

[35]   Id. ("Rule 10b-5 . . . is based in policy on the justifiable expectation of the securities marketplace that all investors trading on impersonal exchanges have relatively equal access to material information"); id. at 851–52 ("The core of Rule 10b-5 is the implementation of the Congressional purpose that all investors should have equal access to the rewards of participation in securities transactions. It was the intent of Congress that all members of the investing public should be subject to identical market risks . . .").

investors at a time when fairness is vitally important. "Insider trading tells everybody at precisely the wrong time that everything is rigged," he says, "and only people who have a billion dollars and have access to and are best friends with people who are on boards of directors of major companies—they're the only ones who can make a true buck."[36]

Despite its intuitive appeal, a rule seeking to level the playing field among investors by banning all stock trading on the basis of material, nonpublic information would impair social welfare by imposing massive error costs. While the rule would properly convict the sort of opportunity-squandering trading at issue in *Texas Gulf Sulphur* and *Boesky* and would discourage corporate mismanagement aimed at generating trading profits, it would err by condemning the fraud-revealing trading (and tipping) at issue in *Dirks* and the Beatty affair. More importantly, it would largely disable securities analysts, who make money by ferreting out valuable information on publicly traded companies and recommending trades on the basis of their findings.[37] Because analysts' efforts play a key role in assuring that stock prices really reflect future earnings prospects, an insider trading rule that hobbled analysts by preventing them from exploiting the nonpublic information they discover would harm investors in the long run. A rule forbidding all trading on the basis of material, nonpublic information, then, fares poorly under the decision-theoretic criterion.

2.   Status quo: no "fraudulent" trading on the basis of material, nonpublic information
As the Introduction to this *Handbook* explains, prevailing insider trading doctrine does not create liability anytime one trades a stock while in possession of material, nonpublic information about the underlying company.[38] Because the primary statutory basis for the federal insider trading prohibition is an anti-fraud provision of the securities laws, insider trading is normally illegal only when it amounts to fraud.[39] Fraud, in turn, requires either an affirmative misrepresentation or a failure to speak in the face of a duty to do so. Since instances of insider trading do not typically involve affirmative statements by the traders, liability is generally premised on an actionable omission and thus requires that the trader owe, and fail to discharge, some "duty to speak" in connection with her trading.

The Supreme Court has recognized the existence of such a duty in two contexts. When the trader is trading in *her own* company's stock, her duty to speak arises from the fiduciary relationship that exists between her and her trading partner, a shareholder (or soon-to-be shareholder, in the case of an insider sale to a non-incumbent shareholder) of the corporation of which she is an agent.[40] Her fiduciary duty to her trading partner

---

[36]   Bill Saporito & Massimo Calabresi, The Street Fighter, Time 14, 16 (Feb. 13, 2012).

[37]   See Dirks v. SEC, 463 U.S. 646, 658 (1983) ("Imposing a duty to disclose or abstain solely because a person knowingly receives material nonpublic information from an insider and trades on it could have an inhibiting influence on the role of market analysts, which the SEC itself recognizes is necessary to the preservation of a healthy market").

[38]   See Chiarella v. U.S., 445 U.S. 222 (1980) (rejecting imposition of disclosure duty based on mere possession of material, nonpublic information).

[39]   There are some narrowly tailored insider trading prohibitions that do not require fraud by the trader, but their scope is limited. See, e.g., Exchange Act Rule 14e-3, 17 C.F.R. § 240.14e-3(a) (forbidding certain trading while in possession of nonpublic information about a forthcoming tender offer).

[40]   Chiarella, 445 U.S. at 227–30.

saddles the trader with a duty to disclose her material, nonpublic information before trading (or else refrain from trading). This is the "classical" theory of insider trading liability. When the trader is trading stock other than that of the company of which she is an insider, she normally owes no duty to her trading partner and thus cannot be liable for classical insider trading. She may, though, owe a duty to make a pre-trading disclosure to *the source* of her material, nonpublic information. If she is in a relationship of trust or confidence with that source and fails, prior to trading, to inform the trader of her intention to trade, she "feign[s] fidelity to the source of [her] information" and thereby commits fraud.[41] This is the "misappropriation" theory of insider trading liability.[42]

The Supreme Court has further held that a trader who does not owe a *personal* duty to speak to her trading partner or information source prior to trading may acquire such a duty if she received the material, nonpublic information through a "tip" from someone who does owe such a duty. The tippee-trader inherits her tipper's duty to speak if: (1) the tipper breached a duty of loyalty in sharing the information with the tippee; and (2) the tippee knew or should have known of the breach.[43]

Evaluated under decision theory's directive to craft rules that minimize the sum of error and decision costs, this complex set of rules fares better than the more restrictive approach favored by enforcement authorities. Like the latter approach, the legal status quo properly prohibits the sort of opportunity-squandering trading at issue in *Texas Gulf Sulphur* and *Boesky* and discourages corporate mismanagement aimed at generating trading profits. But unlike a rule banning stock trading (or tipping) by anyone possessing material, nonpublic information about the underlying company, the legal status quo would not disable the entire securities analysis industry. Stock analysts who: (1) are not insiders of the corporations they follow; (2) owe no duty of trust or confidence to their information sources; and (3) do not knowingly (or with constructive knowledge) receive material, nonpublic information from someone who is breaching his duty of loyalty in sharing the information, are free to trade and recommend trades on the valuable information they discover. By preserving analysts' incentive to engage in activity that is crucial to market efficiency and the protection of investors, the prevailing regime avoids the largest error costs threatened by the enforcement authorities' preferred approach.

But the legal status quo creates other significant error costs. First, it precludes corporations from authorizing insider trading as a form of managerial compensation, an alternative to potentially costlier methods of paying managers. Recent research by M. Todd Henderson has suggested that corporate managers do bargain over the right to trade their own companies' stock, reducing their demands for other forms of compensation in response to trading liberalization.[44] Were corporations allowed to authorize managerial trading on the basis of material, nonpublic information, they could likely reduce their cash and stock outlays to executives, leaving greater value for shareholders.

More importantly, perhaps, the legal status quo errs in prohibiting insider trading

---

[41]   U.S. v. O'Hagan, 521 U.S. 642, 655 (1997).

[42]   See generally id. at 651–53 (describing and distinguishing classical and misappropriation theories).

[43]   Dirks, 463 U.S. at 660.

[44]   Henderson, supra note 27.

that would reveal both fraud[45] and the sort of stock overvaluation that encourages value-destructive managerial decisions.[46] Recall that Raymond Dirks, the analyst whose tipping was largely responsible for revealing the massive fraud at Equity Funding, was prosecuted for his socially beneficial conduct. He managed to escape liability only because his tipper, Secrist, received no personal benefit in exchange for sharing information about the fraud at the company. Had Secrist received such a benefit (to Dirks's knowledge), Dirks's fraud-revealing efforts would have been illegal. Consider also that whistleblower Ted Beatty quickly reversed his decision to engage in the sort of trading that could have revealed the fraud at Dynegy because he was concerned about insider trading liability. Had Beatty been allowed to trade and recommend trades on the basis of his information about Dynegy management's misdeeds, the Enron-like fraud at Dynegy could have been discovered earlier.[47] Apart from these fraud-revealing benefits, insider trading may reveal and thereby reduce overvaluation that is not the result of fraud but nonetheless tends to encourage value-reducing managerial decisions.[48] The error costs resulting from the legal status quo are therefore substantial.

The complexity of the legal status quo also results in sizeable decision costs. Courts assessing the legality of stock trades by individuals possessing nonpublic information must determine: (1) whether the trader owed the requisite fiduciary duty (an easy matter for classical insider trading but often a difficult inquiry in the misappropriation context, where the potential duty is to an information source); (2) if the trader did not owe such a duty personally, whether she "inherited" one under *Dirks's* two-pronged tipping test; and (3) whether the trading was "on the basis" of the information at issue.[49] Business planners assessing liability risk must predict *ex ante* how reviewing courts would resolve those questions *ex post*.

The sum of error and decision costs stemming from the legal status quo, then, is substantial.

3. Least restrictive: allow contractual assignment of property right to material nonpublic information

At the laissez-faire end of the regulatory spectrum lies a proposed approach that would jettison top-down regulation and would instead permit corporations and sources of nonpublic information to establish and enforce their own insider trading policies. This approach springs from the insight that information shedding light on a company's future prospects is, at the end of the day, a valuable piece of property. Every insider trading case,

---

[45]   See Macey, supra note 10, at 172–81.

[46]   See Lambert, supra note 26.

[47]   See Macey, supra note 10, at 177 (discussing Beatty affair as example of insider trading's ability to reveal and deter fraud).

[48]   See Jensen, supra note 26 (describing value-destruction that tends to result from overvalued equity); Lambert, supra note 26 (explaining how insider trading could reduce agency costs of overvalued equity).

[49]   See SEC v. Adler, 137 F.3d 1325 (11th Cir. 1998) (holding that trading while in possession of material, nonpublic information creates presumption that the insider used the information in trading, but presumption is rebuttable); Exchange Act Rel. No 43,154 (Aug. 15, 2000) (positing rule (Rule 10b5-1) that trading while in possession of information is trading on the basis of such information, but recognizing exceptions).

then, involves a property rights dispute: in the context of classical insider trading, the trader battles with her own corporation over ownership of the nonpublic information; in the misappropriation context, she vies with the source of her information. Social welfare is maximized when title to this valuable property right is assigned to the party who can wring the most value from it. If the right is enforceable and transferable, and transaction costs are not prohibitive, the initial allocation of the right matters little; the parties will bargain for an allocation to whichever party can maximize the right's value.[50] The law, then, ought simply to define, enforce, and provide an initial allocation of the right to information about a firm's future prospects, permitting the parties to reallocate that right in accordance with their judgments about who values it most.[51]

The law might, for example, initially allocate to the corporation the right to undisclosed news about firm prospects but permit the firm to reallocate the right to insiders (or a select group of insiders) by licensing them to engage in stock trading on the basis of the information. In deciding whether to reallocate in this manner, firm managers would have to take account of pressures from both the labor and capital markets. On the one hand, the market for managerial labor may reward liberal insider trading policies, for the right to make money through insider trading is valuable to potential managers. On the other hand, capital market pressures will prevent corporations from adopting insider trading policies that are, on balance, harmful to investors. Because granting managers the right to engage in insider trading lowers their salary requirements, creates an incentive for them to create "good news" for the corporation, and lowers the likelihood of overvalued equity and its accompanying agency costs, the capital markets might reward firms with liberal insider trading policies. But, to the extent insider trading causes investor harm in excess of these benefits (e.g., by encouraging mismanagement aimed at generating trading profits), it will be disfavored by investors, who will price the firm's securities accordingly. Thus, advocates of the laissez-faire approach contend, market pressures will assure that corporations (and, in the misappropriation context, sources of material nonpublic information) will adopt insider trading policies that are, on the whole, value maximizing.

Because it eschews a one-size-fits-all approach and allows for firms, sources of nonpublic information, and potential traders to craft individualized policies that account for the potential value-enhancing and value-reducing effects of insider trading, the laissez-faire approach would likely impose lower error costs than either the legal status quo or enforcement authorities' preferred restrictive approach. For example, a cash-strapped firm might decide to authorize insider trading for some set of senior executives (in order to reduce the cash compensation it must pay them), while setting up a monitoring system to ensure that the executives are not making management decisions aimed at generating trading profits. Or a firm might permit mid-level, but not senior, managers to engage in insider trading in an effort to ferret out fraud or other sources of destructive overvaluation. Such tailored policies could allow firms to secure value-enhancing benefits of insider trading while avoiding value-destructive costs, reducing the overall error costs associated with inflexible

---

[50] See generally R.H. Coase, The Problem of Social Cost, 3 J. L. & Econ. 1 (1960).

[51] See, e.g., David D. Haddock & Jonathan R. Macey, A Coasian Model of Insider Trading, 80 Nw. U. L. Rev. 1449 (1986); Carlton & Fischel, supra note 19, at 878; Easterbrook, supra note 18, at 331.

regulation. Decision costs, too, may be lower under a contractarian approach, for courts and business planners could easily consult the contractual restrictions when assessing an instance of actual or contemplated stock trading. It is likely, then, that a laissez-faire approach, when evaluated according to the decision-theoretic criterion, fares better than both the legal status quo and enforcers' preferred approach.

The approach may not be optimal, however. The chief virtue of the approach is that it allows the rules on insider trading to be set by parties who: (1) are "close to the action" (knowledgeable of firm-specific considerations like the value of nontraditional executive compensation schemes, concerns about accounting fraud or equity overvaluation, etc.); and (2) have an interest in maximizing the value of information about firm prospects. Policies that are established in such a fashion are more likely to strike an appropriate balance between the pros and cons of insider trading, permitting such trading when it is likely to create greater benefit than cost and forbidding it when the balance tips in the opposite direction. The approach does nothing, though, to enhance the expected benefits or mitigate the expected costs of instances of insider trading. The following section proposes a regulatory approach that would do both.

III.   AN OPTIONAL, DISCLOSURE-BASED APPROACH

Critics of the contractarian, laissez-faire approach to insider trading have long contended that advocates of the approach overstate a key benefit of insider trading—its role in promoting informational efficiency[52]—and understate a key cost—its tendency to encourage mismanagement (or disclosure delays) aimed solely at creating trading profits.[53] If those critics are right, then the case for replacing the legal status quo with a contractarian approach is weakened. But that does not imply that the legal status quo is optimal; there is much unexplored territory between the legal status quo and the land of laissez-faire.

Within that territory lies an approach that would permit corporations and sources of material, nonpublic information to select between the legal status quo and a regime permitting *disclosed* trading on the basis of material, nonpublic information (see Figure 8.2). An optional, disclosure-based trading regime would differ from other disclosure-based proposals for regulating insider trading, such as Jesse Fried's 1998 proposal to mandate pre-trading disclosure,[54] in that it would require near contemporaneous—not pre-trading—disclosure of insider trading, and its goal would not be to discourage insider trading by reducing expected trading profits. Rather, it would aim to enhance the potential value-creating effects of instances of insider trading while diminishing potential value-destructive harms.

Subsection A sets forth the rationale for an optional, disclosure-based approach to regulating insider trading. Subsection B then fleshes out the contours of such an approach and explains why it would prevail over the status quo and the leading proposed

---

[52]   See supra note 28 and accompanying text.
[53]   See supra notes 14–15 and accompanying text.
[54]   See Jesse M. Fried, Reducing the Profitability of Corporate Insider Trading Through Pretrading Disclosure, 71 S. Cal. L. Rev. 303 (1998).

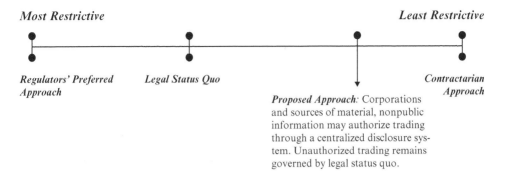

Figure 8.2   The regulatory spectrum, including the proposed approach

approaches when evaluated in light of the decision-theoretic criterion. Subsection C addresses potential drawbacks to the approach.

A.   The Rationale for an Optional, Disclosure-based Regime

Advocates of a contractarian, laissez-faire approach to insider trading regulation have long touted informed trading's ability to drive stock prices toward their fundamental value.[55] Insider trading has this price-corrective effect, liberalization advocates contend, because it conveys a valuable piece of information: that those closest to the company and most informed about its operations are willing to wager their own money on their belief that the company is mispriced (undervalued in the case of insider purchases of stock or call options; overvalued in the case of insider sales, short sales, or purchases of puts). Investors who are not privy to the actual facts motivating insider transactions will nonetheless follow the lead of trading insiders by buying or selling the stock or adjusting their reservation prices (the amount they would be willing to pay to obtain the stock or would require to give it up). As this process plays out, liberalization advocates assert, the market price of the stock will change to reflect the information conveyed by insider trades and, because insiders are the individuals best informed about the company's true prospects, will become more accurate.

This assumes, though, that insider trading does actually signal, or "derivatively inform," investors that there are insiders who are betting that their company's stock is mispriced. As Ronald Gilson and Reinier Kraakman famously explained, there are two mechanisms by which insider trading may signal mispricing.[56] "Price decoding" may occur if uninformed traders observe a price change occasioned by a sufficient volume of informed trading, assess the price change in light of the public information concerning the firm's prospects, and then infer what possible new information could explain the observed price change.[57] "Trade decoding" may occur if uninformed traders infer binary information regarding a firm's prospects (i.e., whether they are improving or worsening) from informed traders'

---

[55]   See supra note 25 and accompanying text.

[56]   Gilson & Kraakman, supra note 28, at 572–79 (describing derivatively informed trading).

[57]   Id. at 575.

transactions.[58] While price decoding provides richer information about the underlying company (*why*, as well as whether, the company's prospects are improving or worsening), it is unlikely to occur often because it requires trading of a quantity sufficient to cause some sort of change in price. Given the myriad substitutes (from the investor's standpoint) for any single corporation's stock, the demand curve for most corporations' stock is flat or nearly flat, and insider trading in a volume sufficient to change a company's stock price is rare.[59] The primary mechanism by which insider trading derivatively informs uninformed traders of stock mispricing, then, is trade decoding. Trade decoding, though, requires that uninformed traders identify instances of informed trading, and there are few mechanisms by which they may do so. Thus, conclude defenders of insider trading restrictions, advocates of liberalization have overstated insider trading's salutary effect on informational efficiency.

The disclosure-based approach proposed herein would remedy this problem by facilitating trade decoding. If an individual trading on the basis of material, nonpublic information publicly and contemporaneously disclosed both the basic details of her trade and the fact that she was making the trade while in possession of inside information, then uninformed traders could easily draw inferences about her perceptions of the firm's future prospects. If she also disclosed her identity and either her position in the company, in the case of classical insider trading, or the position of her information source, in the case of "outsider" trading policed under the misappropriation doctrine, uninformed traders could assess the "quality" of her signal. The proposed disclosure-based approach would therefore enhance one of insider trading's primary social benefits—its tendency to push stock prices in the right direction.

A disclosure-based approach would also constrain one of the potential harms from liberalizing insider trading: mismanagement aimed at creating trading profits. If corporate managers are permitted to trade on material, nonpublic information, they may benefit from bad news as well as good news. Liberalization may therefore perversely encourage managers to "create" bad news in order to earn a personal trading profit. It may also encourage them to put off disclosing information about the firm's prospects until they have had an opportunity to trade on the basis of the information. Of course, deliberately mismanaging the firm or delaying disclosures to earn trading profits would violate a manager's fiduciary duty of loyalty and could give rise to both shareholder derivative suits and adverse consequences in the labor market (i.e., the faithless manager could be dismissed and might have a hard time procuring a position in another firm). But if a manager's trades are conducted in secret,[60] injured shareholders may not suspect that mismanagement was deliberate or that disclosures were delayed, and employers (current and future) may have no reason to doubt the manager's fidelity. If managers' trades were immediately disclosed, shareholders and employers could tell if a manager earned a trading profit on

---

[58]   Id. at 573–74.

[59]   See R.A. Brealey, An Introduction to Risk and Return from Common Stocks 35–44 (2d ed. 1983); West v. Prudential Secs., Inc., 282 F.3d 935, 939 (7th Cir. 2002) (Easterbrook, J.) ("There are so many substitutes for any one firm's stock that the effective demand curve is horizontal").

[60]   Under current law, only directors, officers, and owners of at least 10 percent of a firm's voting securities must disclose trades of their own companies' stock, and the disclosure need not occur contemporaneously with the trading. See Exchange Act Rule 16(a), 17 C.F.R. § 240.16a-2 (2011).

bad news she helped create or if she apparently delayed a disclosure in order to exploit a trading advantage. A disclosure-based approach would therefore augment the discipline provided by shareholder suits and labor market pressures by making it easier to detect when a manager had engaged in deliberate mismanagement or disclosure delay.

A disclosure-based approach would also permit corporations and sources of material, nonpublic information to detect when a trader had effectively infringed their property rights. Such infringement would obviously occur when a trader violated a trading prohibition imposed by the corporation or information source. But even in the absence of an express trading prohibition, any trading that threatened to usurp a corporate opportunity—e.g., the trading in *Texas Gulf Sulphur* and *Boesky*—would amount to a species of "theft" that could be actionable under the corporate opportunity doctrine or some other breach of fiduciary duty theory. If instances of insider trading are immediately disclosed, corporations and sources of material, nonpublic information will find it easier to enforce their informational property rights, and insiders and recipients of nonpublic information will be less inclined to violate those rights.

B.   Description and Evaluation of the Proposed Approach

Until recently, contemporaneous public disclosure of stock trading on the basis of material, nonpublic information was impracticable. Even if a trader immediately disclosed her trade to the SEC and management of the company whose stock she traded, there was no practicable means of immediately informing millions of market participants that the trade had occurred. Because financial newswires traditionally disseminated market-moving news one story at a time, it would have been infeasible to publish insider trading reports for a large number of trades each day; the volume of data would have overwhelmed the system. Moreover, analysts following specific companies would have had no way to sift the newswire data to focus exclusively on the companies they were following. Insider trades could have been reported via telephone, wire, or fax and then disseminated in comprehensive daily reports, but such an operation would have been exceedingly costly, and any information would have been somewhat stale by the time it reached investors.

Today, by contrast, it would be a simple matter to set up a centralized reporting system for stock trading on the basis of material, nonpublic information. The SEC could host a centralized "Informed Trading Database" and make it searchable by company, so that any investor could learn of an instance of informed trading as soon as it occurred. The system could even be designed to permit analysts or investors to subscribe to reports on selected companies, where subscribers would be immediately notified via email or text message (SMS) the moment a new insider trading report is filed on a selected company.

In the optional, disclosure-based regulatory regime envisioned here, corporations and sources of material, nonpublic information could elect to avoid the legal status quo and authorize instances of insider trading that are disclosed through the system just described. For any instance of authorized trading,[61] the trader would have a defense to liability if she established that she traded after submitting an "Informed Trading Report" to the SEC's

---

[61]   An instance of authorized trading would be one in which the trader's corporation, in the context of the classical insider trading, or the source of the trader's nonpublic information, in the

Informed Trading Database. Instances of unauthorized trading[62] would continue to be governed by currently prevailing rules.

The details of the Informed Trading Report would differ slightly, depending on whether the trader was an insider trading in her own company's stock or an outsider trading on the basis of information received from a source to whom she owed a duty of trust or confidence. An insider trading in her own company's stock would first have to submit an electronic "Informed Insider Report." That short report would disclose: (1) her identity; (2) the position she occupies as an insider of the company whose stock she is trading (including any constructive insider position[63]); (3) the fact that she possesses material, nonpublic information; and (4) the nature of her transaction (e.g., a purchase of 200 shares of common stock). One trading on the basis of material, nonpublic information in the stock of a company of which she is not an insider would first have to file an "Informed Outsider Report," which would disclose: (1) the trader's identity; (2) the identity of the source of her material, nonpublic information; (3) the fact that she possesses such information; and (4) the nature of her transaction. As soon as the appropriate Informed Trading Report appeared in the searchable electronic reporting system—seconds after its submission—the trader could legally execute her trade.

Evaluated according to the decision-theoretic criterion, a regime permitting disclosed informed trading would fare better than any of the aforementioned regulatory approaches. Unlike the more restrictive approaches, the disclosure-based approach would permit corporations to achieve the value-enhancing benefits of insider trading: reduced managerial compensation costs, reduced agency costs from overvalued equity, fraud prevention, and a more "trustworthy" (accurate) stock price that would appeal to value investors. A disclosure-based regime would also enhance one social benefit and reduce two costs associated with the laissez-faire approach: contemporaneous reporting of informed trades would enhance overall market efficiency by facilitating trade decoding, would reduce trading-induced agency costs by permitting shareholders and employers to monitor managers for mismanagement aimed at creating trading profits, and would reduce concerns about the infringement of informational property rights by enabling corporations and sources of nonpublic information to detect infringement of such rights. A disclosure-based regime would thus impose less error cost than any of the aforementioned regulatory approaches. It would also entail lower decision costs than the legal status quo. For any instance of authorized informed trading, courts would not need to answer the many complex questions required for analysis under the prevailing liability regime; they could simply check to see whether the appropriate disclosure was made.

Finally, it is worth noting that adoption of an optional, disclosure-based approach could likely be achieved without any change in the statutory regime. If an insider's cor-

---

context of "outsider" trading policed under the misappropriation doctrine, had elected—for that trader—to forego the legal status quo in favor of the disclosure-based option.

[62]   An instance of unauthorized trading would be one in which the trader's corporation, in the context of the classical insider trading, or the source of the trader's nonpublic information, in the context of "outsider" trading policed under the misappropriation doctrine, had not elected to forego—for that trader—the legal status quo in favor of the disclosure-based option.

[63]   See Dirks v. SEC, 463 U.S. 646, 655 n.14 (1983) (recognizing that some outsiders "working for the corporation . . . may become fiduciaries of the shareholders").

poration has opted to permit disclosed insider trading (say, to reduce its compensation expenses or enhance the accuracy of its share price), then the fiduciary duty an inside trader owes her trading partner would not seem to entail the traditional duty to disclose the insider's material, nonpublic information and allow for its public dissemination before trading. By engaging in disclosed trading on nonpublic information, the insider would actually be furthering corporate objectives, and the insider's trading partner would be on notice that he might be trading with an informed insider. Under such circumstances, it would make scant sense to impose a duty on the trader to disclose her material, nonpublic information before trading, and absent any such duty, her failure to speak could not constitute the sort of actionable omission required for classical insider trading liability.

The legality of authorized and disclosed outsider trading is even clearer. If the source of the material, nonpublic information has elected to permit disclosed trading, then such trading does not involve "feigning fidelity to the source" of the information and therefore could not be fraudulent.[64] (Indeed, disclosed trading arguably would not involve fraud even if the source of material, nonpublic information had *not* authorized such trading; by disclosing the trade through the centralized disclosure system, the trader would seem to avoid feigning fidelity to the source.[65])

While statutory change may not be required to permit the sort of optional, disclosure-based regime proposed herein, regulatory action may be needed as a practical matter. The SEC itself is best positioned to host the sort of searchable Informed Trading Database required for the approach to work. And, of course, corporations and sources of material, nonpublic information are unlikely to authorize any sort of disclosed inside trading regime absent some sort of regulatory imprimatur affirming the legality of disclosed authorized trading.

C. Potential Concerns

Defenders of the prevailing legal regime are likely to raise a number of concerns about the proposal set forth above. We consider three here.

1. Would anyone do it?
An initial question is whether corporations and sources of material, nonpublic information would, in fact, authorize informed but disclosed trading. The short answer to the question is, "we don't know." That, however, is no reason to forbid experimentation. If, for example, a handful of corporations authorize informed but disclosed trading for some or all of their insiders and find that the capital markets reward their experimentation, one would expect other corporations to follow suit. There is, though, a first-mover problem: in an age of 24-hour news cycles, sensationalist journalism, and widespread financial and economic illiteracy among the press corps, what corporation wants to be reported as the first to "permit insider trading"?

One way to address such inertia would be to adjust the default rule. The SEC could announce that informed but disclosed trading will be legally permissible *unless*

---

[64] See U.S. v. O'Hagan, 521 U.S. 642, 655 (1997).

[65] Cf. id. at 659, n. 9.

prohibited by an insider's corporation or the source of an outside trader's material, nonpublic information, in which case the prevailing legal regime will govern. In other words, the proposal could be implemented on an "opt-out" basis. As a practical matter, an opt-out approach would likely authorize few instances of outside trading currently policed by the misappropriation doctrine; confidential sources of material, nonpublic information—law and accounting firms, investment banks, buyout firms, etc.—generally have already "opted out" by adopting policies that forbid their agents from sharing or trading on confidential information. Corporations, by contrast, often have no express policy forbidding insider trading, and those that elected not to adopt one immediately could serve as guinea pigs for the informed but disclosed regime. As a practical matter, then, an opt-out approach would initially permit many instances of disclosed classical insider trading while prohibiting most instances of outsider trading—a sensible result, given that the net benefits of informed trading are likely higher when a true insider is trading.

2.   Would traders routinely file Informed Trading Reports as a safety measure?

Under the proposed approach, the filing of an Informed Trading Report insulates authorized traders from insider trading liability. A potential concern, then, is that corporate insiders and traders who have contact with sources of material, nonpublic information may begin filing such reports routinely, even when they are not trading on the basis of material, nonpublic information. Should this occur, Informed Trading Reports could lose their value as signaling devices.

Prevailing securities regulations, however, could police such dilutive "wolf-crying." The Informed Trading Report requires a trader to attest that she is in possession of material, nonpublic information at the time of trading. Anyone who falsely claims to possess such information makes a material misstatement in connection with the sale or purchase of a security and thereby runs afoul of Exchange Act Section 10(b)[66] and Rule 10b-5 thereunder.[67] Because it would be a fairly simple matter to test whether traders were lying when they claimed to possess material, nonpublic information at the time of trading, the SEC could dissuade prophylactic filing of Informed Trading Reports by prosecuting a handful of apparent over-filers.

3.   What about tippee liability?

The proposed approach prescribes Informed Trading Reports for insiders (who would otherwise be susceptible to classical insider trading liability) and for outsiders who receive material, nonpublic information from a confidential source (and would otherwise be susceptible to liability under the misappropriation doctrine). But what about tippees— i.e., those who are not themselves insiders or confidants of information sources but who receive their nonpublic information from such insiders or confidants? The prevailing legal regime deems such a person to have "inherited" her information source's fiduciary duty if: (1) the source breached a fiduciary duty in receiving a personal benefit for sharing the

---

[66]   15 U.S.C. § 78(j)(b) (2011).
[67]   17 C.F.R. § 240.10b-5 (2011).

information; and (2) the tippee knew or should have known of that breach.[68] Under such circumstances, the tippee is an "accomplice" of her information source and essentially steps into that source's shoes.

There is no reason this tipping regime should not apply to the proposed disclosure-based approach. If the two-pronged *Dirks* test is satisfied, then the recipient of nonpublic information effectively steps into the shoes of her information source. If the information source could avoid liability only by filing an Informed Insider Report or an Informed Outsider Report, then the tippee would similarly have an obligation to file the appropriate report.

IV.   CONCLUSION

Crooner Johnny Mercer famously exhorted listeners to "accentuate the positive, eliminate the negative."[69] Mercer's advice may be especially useful to regulators addressing business conduct—like insider trading—that tends to have both positive and negative effects. A regulatory approach that enhances the positive effects of such a mixed bag practice while reducing its negative consequences will enhance social welfare by reducing the overall error costs associated with the regulatory regime.

This chapter has demonstrated how an optional, disclosure-based regulatory regime could accentuate a key social benefit of informed trading—its tendency to enhance informational efficiency—while simultaneously constraining its potential costs—most notably, agency costs and losses resulting from insecure property rights in market-moving information. Securities regulators would do well to consider this middle ground position between the legal status quo and a purely contractarian, laissez-faire approach.

---

68   Dirks v. S.E.C., 463 U.S. 646, 660 (1983).
69   Ac-Cent-Tchu-Ate the Positive, Johnny Mercer (lyrics) and Harold Arlen (music), 1944.

PART 2

STUDIES OF SPECIFIC DEFENDANTS

9. Applying insider trading law to congressmen, government officials, and the political intelligence industry
J.W. Verret

I. INTRODUCTION

This chapter considers the Stop Trading on Congressional Knowledge Act, or STOCK Act, passed by Congress by overwhelming margins in 2012 and signed by the President. The STOCK Act's goal was to apply insider trading prohibitions contained in the Securities Exchange Act to members of Congress, their staffs, and the executive and judicial branches.

The STOCK Act and congressional insider trading accusations were a hot topic in 2011 and 2012 after an exposé on 60 Minutes and a commercial by a Presidential candidate accused members of Congress of engaging in insider trading.[1] In addition to questions about the propriety of excluding members of Congress and government officials from the insider trading laws, the hearings and initial drafts of the law sought also to prohibit trading by outsiders who receive information from members of Congress. This would apply in part to what has come to be known as the political intelligence industry, though application of earlier versions of the law would have also encompassed investment analysts far removed from Washington.

Earlier versions of the STOCK Act included an outright prohibition on anyone outside of Congress trading on the basis of nonpublic information obtained from within Congress or the executive branch.[2] The final version of the STOCK Act that went into law did not explicitly cover the political intelligence industry however, but merely mandated a study by the Government Accountability Office about the industry.

Though political intelligence traders were not explicitly covered under these requirements, it is unclear whether or not they are nevertheless subject to insider trading laws under the misappropriation theory, the classical theory of insider trading as temporary insiders, and under tipper–tippee liability as a secondary result of the STOCK Act. This chapter will sketch the boundaries of application for the new STOCK Act, both with respect to government employees and to outside traders on political intelligence, and will explore some of the uncertainties all of these parties face in the wake of the STOCK Act.

In his article Professor Stephen Bainbridge summarized the policy debate over the

---

[1] See Rebecca Kaplan, Perry: Congressional Insider Trading Should be Illegal, November 14, 2011, CBSNews.com, available at http://www.cbsnews.com/8301-503544_162-57324577-503544/perry-congressional-insider-trading-should-be-illegal/ (last visited November 1, 2012).

[2] See Stephen M. Bainbridge, Insider Trading inside the Beltway, 36 J. Corp. L. 281, 295 (2011).

problems with members of Congress or government employees engaging in insider trading, and reminded us that Henry Manne's 1966 book on insider trading actually predicted the issue by warning of the dangers of government insider trading (though Manne otherwise opposed insider trading prohibitions).[3]

The emphasis of this chapter will not be that debate, but will rather consider two questions. First, what unforeseen doctrinal challenges will be presented by the STOCK Act's application of insider trading principles to members of Congress and government employees? Secondly, does the STOCK Act indirectly extend insider trading liability to outsiders trading on the basis of information that is obtained from members of Congress or government employees, and if not should the Securities and Exchange Commission (SEC) extend application to them? The two questions are interrelated, since many of the avenues for application to outside traders derive from the duties owed by individuals directly covered by the STOCK Act.

The arguments against insider trading by elected officials and government employees are compelling. Manne emphasized the perverted incentives it would give members of Congress to alter their focus in lawmaking.[4] Bainbridge argues that, in addition to Manne's focus, it also presents equity and fairness concerns when members of Congress exempt themselves from laws that apply to private citizens without justification.[5] Ribstein urged that the depth of government involvement in the economy post-2008 through regulation and government ownership further strengthens the case against insider trading by members of Congress and government employees.[6] The combined views of these leaders in the insider trading literature offer strong support to the general goals of the STOCK Act.

That is not the end of the analysis however. Stopping insider trading by elected officials and government employees may be a good thing. The doctrinal challenges that lie ahead, in applying a law developed in the corporate and contractual sphere to an entirely different relationship between elected officials, remain daunting. And it also leaves open a debate over the wisdom of applying the same rules to outsiders who trade on information obtained from government officials and further leaves open a measure of uncertainty and indeterminacy into just how far the STOCK Act actually applies to those outsiders.

II.   THE STOCK ACT

The STOCK Act provision that directly creates a new fiduciary duty on the part of members of Congress and their employees reads in pertinent part:[7]

---

[3]   See id. at 298.

[4]   See Henry Manne, Insider Trading and the Stock Market (1966).

[5]   Stephen M. Bainbridge, Insider Trading Inside the Beltway, 36 Journal of Corporation Law 281, 293–296 (2011).

[6]   See Larry E. Ribstein, Congressmen As Securities Traders, 14 Green Bag 269 (2011).

[7]   The STOCK Act was not available in the Federal Register at the time of writing, but is available at http://www.gpo.gov/fdsys/pkg/BILLS-112s2038enr/pdf/BILLS-112s2038enr.pdf (last visited November 1, 2012).

SEC. 4. PROHIBITION OF INSIDER TRADING.

(a) Affirmation of Nonexemption— Members of Congress and employees of Congress are not exempt from the insider trading prohibitions arising under the securities laws, including section 10(b) of the Securities Exchange Act of 1934 and Rule 10b-5 thereunder.

(b) Duty—

. . .

(2) AMENDMENT— Section 21A of the Securities Exchange Act of 1934 (15 U.S.C. 78u-1) is amended by adding at the end the following:

"(g) Duty of Members and Employees of Congress—

'(1) IN GENERAL— Subject to the rule of construction under section 10 of the STOCK Act and solely for purposes of the insider trading prohibitions arising under this Act, including section 10(b) and Rule 10b-5 thereunder, each Member of Congress or employee of Congress owes a duty arising from a relationship of trust and confidence to the Congress, the United States Government, and the citizens of the United States with respect to material, non-public information derived from such person's position as a Member of Congress or employee of Congress or gained from the performance of such person's official responsibilities. . . . Nothing in this subsection shall be construed to impair or limit the construction of the existing antifraud provisions of the securities laws or the authority of the Commission under those provisions.'"

The STOCK Act also includes companion provisions amending the Commodity Exchange Act to include trading by members and staff within the prohibition on insider trading. The statute also issues a similar prohibition against insider trading by creating a similar fiduciary obligation for judicial and executive branch employees. The STOCK Act further requires the Senate Select Committee on Ethics and the House Committee on Ethics to draft new implementing language as a companion measure to the statute's amendments to the Securities Exchange Act of 1934.

The STOCK Act enhances the reporting requirements for trading by members and staff and by the executive branch. It requires the Government Accountability Office and the Congressional Research Service to issue a report on the political intelligence industry. The statute further increases the online availability of trading reports filed by members and their staff and executive branch employees.

A provision was included in the Senate Bill to require that political intelligence industry professionals register as lobbyists, but that provision was removed before passage of the final legislation. The central debate over the STOCK Act focused on members of Congress, but it also included a side discussion over the role of political intelligence industry professionals, advisors to investors, who trade on information obtained from members of Congress, their staff, and executive agency officials.

One of the most interesting questions that will arise is the extent to which the STOCK Act will actually impede upon the political intelligence industry's operations by extending the reach of the insider trading prohibition for congressmen and their employees to outside "tippees" under the theory of insider trading developed in *Dirks v. SEC*.[8] This chapter will explore whether that is the case, and in order to do so will first explore the boundaries of the congressional duties created by the STOCK Act. Before that analysis commences, some background to the political intelligence industry is in order.

---

[8]   463 U.S. 646 (1983).

III.   THE POLITICAL INTELLIGENCE INDUSTRY

The political intelligence industry has become an active growth area in Washington, D.C. Though information about developments in legislation and regulation has always been valuable to companies and investors, recent developments like the bailout of 2008 and the passage of the Dodd–Frank Wall Street Reform Act have exponentially expanded the reach of government decisions into the profitability of entire sectors of the economy and made the services of political intelligence firms even more valuable. By one estimate the political intelligence industry has annual revenues of $100 million.[9]

The industry has a few different types of players. Registered lobbyists might, in addition to their representation, sell to clients any information they might obtain during the course of their work. Some consulting firms specialize in giving regular reports to institutional clients, including large investment funds that do not specialize in trading on political developments but may want to stay aware of major developments.

Still other investors may manage funds that directly specialize in political intelligence trading and have teams of in-house advisors with access to elected officials and regulators. Many members of the industry are former congressional staff aides, some who might register as lobbyists and some who might not, who regularly communicate with members of Congress and their staff. Political intelligence analysts may also actively donate to congressional campaigns.

Political intelligence analysts might advise on the likelihood that a particular provision will be inserted into a Bill; the likelihood the Bill will be reported out of a committee; the likelihood it will pass either chamber; any expected compromises when different Bills are merged under compromises in a conference committee; odds of passage; and the odds of a Presidential veto; and ultimately add useful information about how the rules and regulations implementing the legislation are likely to look to any executive or independent agencies tasked with enforcing the law and writing and implementing rules. They might also be in a position to advise about the likelihood and expected outcome of legal challenges to the final rule or regulation.

IV.   THE CONFLUX OF CORPORATE INSIDER TRADING THEORIES AND THE STOCK ACT

The STOCK Act makes reference to the existing prohibition on insider trading under Section 10 of the Securities Exchange Act and Rule 10 promulgated thereunder. As such, we will need to consider the three theories of insider trading that existed prior to the STOCK Act to define the contours of its application. This will include the classical theory of insider trading originating in the *Chiarella v. U.S.*[10] case, its extension to tippees

---

[9]   See Brody Mullins and Susan Pulliam, Hedge Funds Pay Top Dollar for Washington Intelligence, Wall Street Journal, October 4, 2011, available at: http://online.wsj.com/article/SB100 0142405311190407060457651479159131 9306.html (last visited November 1, 2012).
[10]   Chiarella v. U. S., 445 U.S. 222 (1980).

as defined in the *Dirks* case, and the misappropriation theory as developed in the *U.S. v. O'Hagan*[11] case.

A.   The Classical Theory of Insider Trading and its Extension to Tippees

The *Chiarella* case sets out the pre-requisite duty that forms the basis for the classical insider trading claim. It rests in some form of duty of trust and confidence, whether that is a state law fiduciary duty for corporate directors and officers or some other duty of trust and confidence originating in a special contractual relationship for which such a duty is a component.

> First not every instance of financial unfairness constitutes fraudulent activity under § 10(b). Second, the element required to make silence fraudulent—a duty to disclose—is absent in this case. No duty could arise from petitioner's relationship with the sellers of the target company's securities, for petitioner had no prior dealings with them. He was not their agent, he was not a fiduciary, he was not a person in whom the sellers had placed their trust and confidence.[12]

The language in the STOCK Act referencing a relationship of trust and confidence is clearly referring to this phrasing in *Chiarella* regarding a relationship arising from trust and confidence. The STOCK Act describes a relationship of trust and confidence between members and staffers of Congress and "The Congress, the United States Government, and the Citizens of the United States."

This grafts the classical theory of insider trading, originating in the fiduciary relationship between shareholders and the board of directors, into the relationship between congressmen and essentially the U.S. government and its citizens. As those relationships are markedly different, it should be no surprise that some fairly odd and unexpected complications could arise. For example, if the STOCK Act implements a classical insider trading duty to congressmen, then the existing interpretation of the duty (and the statute makes clear that existing interpretations of Section 10 and Rule 10b-5 apply) means that if members of Congress trade with foreigners, then they seemingly do not actually violate the insider trading prohibition in the STOCK Act.

Under the classical theory of insider trading, a failure to disclose inside information is premised on a failure to disclose to an existing shareholder selling securities to whom one owes a duty, or a failure to disclose the possession of inside information to a purchasing shareholder to whom one owes a duty once they become shareholders as a result of the sale.

If the duty is owed to the taxpayer, to the United States, or to Congress then if a person covered by the STOCK Act engaged in insider trading the counterparty to the transaction would not be or become someone to whom the insider owes any duty. Therefore it would seem that trading with individuals who are not citizens, Congress, or the U.S. government would not count as insider trading under the STOCK Act.

There will doubtless be other unforeseeable complications in using the classical

---

[11]   U.S. v. O'Hagan, 521 U.S. 642 (1997).
[12]   *Chiarella*, 445 U.S. at 232–233 (citation omitted).

theory of insider trading to define the contours of the STOCK Act's application of insider trading to congressmen and other government officials. The classical theory of insider trading essentially grafts the state law fiduciary duties of corporate officers and directors into federal securities laws. To offer a taste of how state law defines the duty in this context, the applicable law for Delaware incorporated entities, *Brophy v. Cities Service Co.*[13] and *Kahn v. Kohlberg Kravis Roberts & Co., L.P.*,[14] holds that the appropriation of confidential company information and trading based on the substance of that information constitutes a violation of the duty of loyalty owed by corporate fiduciaries. It is designed as a species of the corporate opportunity doctrine, which similarly limits the ability of executives to profit from opportunities that are discovered while serving as a fiduciary or employee, and from which the company might profit.

In this context one can look to the relevant law to determine what constitutes corporate information and what does not, and as a result one can determine circumstances under which a fiduciary would be able to obtain a permission from their beneficiary to use the information, determine what information counts as corporate information, and otherwise obtain some assurance of whether any trading might run the risk of violating a fiduciary duty to the corporation and its shareholders, and therefore also run the risk of violating the federal securities laws.

Ribstein argued against the broad application of fiduciary duty principles in instances where their potential ambiguity might harm transactional relationships.[15] He argued in favor of their application only in discrete instances in which an entrustment of property or power was present and in which the management of property is delegated to a manager but economic rights are attenuated. Ribstein premised his concept of a fiduciary duty on contractual relationships, which would certainly not apply in instances of congressional/voter relationships.

One must ask how the parallel duties might differ between the two groups. We know that using nonpublic information is considered to be a breach of one's fiduciary duty to the company and its stockholders. It does not arise from fraud to one's counterparty, as indeed trading on information in another firm is not considered to breach that duty. In this instance, the breach arises from a duty owed to a less readily definable set of individuals: the Congress, the government, and the citizens of the United States.

There are several unique attributes in the corporate insider trading and the political insider trading context that may not carry over between the two worlds. First, the relationship of trust and confidence in the corporate context is grounded in an existing state law fiduciary duty that can reference prior law, which builds a framework for understanding that duty. In the political context, the rights of taxpayers or citizens to sue members of Congress are quite limited, as are binding interpretations of congressional ethics rules, and so there is no corresponding set of case law to build an interpretation of the duty to taxpayers and the U.S. government. In the former case, one might conceivably obtain permission to trade on inside information by way of a shareholder approved charter

---

[13]   70 A. 2d 5 (1949).
[14]   23 A. 3d 831 (2011).
[15]   See Larry Ribstein, Fencing Fiduciary Duties, 91 Boston L. Rev. 857, 859 (2011).

amendment, but in the latter case it would only be achieved by way of a full repeal of the STOCK Act.

The implementing legislation also calls on the congressional ethics committee to adopt new changes to congressional ethics rules to cover this conduct. Any implementing language might bear on whether the misappropriation theory of insider trading applies, and/or might be deemed to serve as the underlying body of law interpreting a congressional member's fiduciary duties under the classical theory of insider trading in this regard. A lack of harmonization between congressional ethics rules, congressional employee ethics rules, and executive agency rules may nevertheless lead to further uncertainty and indeterminacy in the interaction of outside information analysts and government employees. Another seemingly open question is whether the application of the law would be altered by the findings of a House or Senate ethics committee that may exonerate a congressman from liability. Would it work to exonerate any potential tippees from liability?

The level of predictability that the foundational state case law provides will be important in determining whether tipper/tippee liability will apply. Tippees must either know or should know that their obtaining information will result in a violation of a tipper's fiduciary duty. But if the contours of a congressman's duty of trust and confidence to the taxpayer are nebulous or unclear, then it may prove difficult for the recipients of information to know when they can and when they cannot trade on the basis of that information or while in possession of that information.

Dirks holds that a tippee of information from a corporate insider can be held liable for insider trading where he knows or should have known that the tipper breached their fiduciary duty to the corporation by sharing the information, which will be the case where the insider sought to obtain a benefit from the disclosure to the tippee.[16] The benefit involved could be an outright monetary gain, a reputational benefit that might translate into earnings in the future, or a gift of profitable information to a friend.

One relevant question will be to what extent members of Congress or their staffs might become subject to the STOCK Act when they share nonpublic information with someone who has donated to a member of Congress's campaign where it is not clear that the information was given in exchange for the donation. Or, whether it would apply in the context of a member of Congress who might address someone who donated to the broader party of which that congressman or their staffer was a member. In this context political operatives regularly donate, and members or their staff might be regularly in contact, as a matter of course and not expect any direct benefit as a result.

The court also notes that attorneys, consultants, and others can become temporary fiduciaries of a corporation and be similarly held liable under a temporary fiduciary application of the classical theory of insider trading.[17] Still another important question will be whether anyone working with the government might be deemed a temporary fiduciary for purposes of these rules. A government contractor might seem a ready candidate for application of the temporary insider definition.

---

[16]   Dirks v. SEC, 463 U.S. 646, 660 (1983).
[17]   See id.

B.   The Misappropriation Doctrine

The misappropriation theory of insider trading applies when someone with confidential information breaches a duty to the source of the information, even though that source is outside of a corporation, and thereby cheats the source of the information by infringing on their ability to use it exclusively.[18]

Bainbridge notes that executive agency ethics rules pre-dating the STOCK Act would apply misappropriation doctrine insider trading liability to executive agency employees and congressional employees but not to members of Congress.[19] As such it would seem that the misappropriation doctrine would potentially apply where congressional staff, but not members of Congress, are involved, and if Bainbridge is correct that duty actually pre-dates the STOCK Act.

The STOCK Act established a relationship of trust and confidence between members of Congress, taxpayers, and the U.S. government and Congress. It does not however affirmatively require that members of Congress or their staffs maintain the confidentiality of information, and indeed if congressmen were required to maintain all information they learn on the job in confidence it might be impossible for them to represent their constituents. So it does not seem that the misappropriation doctrine will be of much use in interpreting the STOCK Act. It may be of use, however, any time members of Congress voluntarily agree to maintain the confidentiality of information as a part of their official duties.

This chapter has already noted that members of Congress may be exempt from the new STOCK Act if they trade with foreign citizens. If a member of Congress, for example, learned that the U.S. government was unlikely to approve a sale of arms to a foreign country, which would pave the way for a European company traded only in Europe to obtain the contract to sell those arms, it would seem that members of Congress and their employees would not be prohibited by the STOCK Act from trading on that information as long as they were aware that their counterparty on the trade was not an American citizen. It might be the case, though, that the misappropriation doctrine would cover the transaction if the congressman learned of the information through access to classified information which they agreed to keep confidential.

For example, members of the Intelligence or Armed Services Committees who obtain classified information may be covered under the misappropriation doctrine. This would have been true prior to passage of the STOCK Act and would be unaltered by the STOCK Act. As a result, it may also be the case that political intelligence traders may similarly face insider trading liability if they know that their tipper shared classified information covered by any Committee policy or national security law or agreement or practice of keeping such information confidential for national security purposes. This may similarly be the case for information obtained by Congressional Committees under seal or agreement of confidentiality.

---

[18]   See *O'Hagan*, 521 U.S. at 652.
[19]   See Bainbridge, supra note 2, at 295.

C.   Private Rights of Action

One interesting consequence of the STOCK Act is that private plaintiffs may obtain the right to sue members of Congress for violating the law. Section 20A(a) of the Securities Exchange Act provides a private right of action for investors who bought or sold securities contemporaneously with someone who engaged in a violation of the insider trading laws. Bainbridge notes that the immunities provided to a member of Congress for their official duties do not extend to lawsuits stemming from private litigation.[20] As such it would seem that the STOCK Act would allow private plaintiffs to bring private insider trading actions against members of Congress for trading that relates to their official duties, which may muddy the reach of congressional immunity for official acts.

For those members of Congress who engage in personal trading, this may result in politically motivated lawsuits designed to embarrass or harass (provided investors can meet the contemporaneous trading requirements). Elected officials or candidates hoping to harass incumbent members might bring frivolous litigation for various reasons.

If the required disclosures for a congressman's trades demonstrate a pattern of owning particular stocks, potential plaintiffs could easily purchase and sell stocks on a regular basis to meet the contemporaneous ownership rule. Litigation over what members of Congress knew when they traded, and why, might also provide a discovery window to learn a great deal of information under penalty of perjury about what would otherwise be confidential deliberations between members of Congress and other government officials.

V.   APPLICATION OF THE STOCK ACT TO THE POLITICAL INTELLIGENCE INDUSTRY

A.   Is Trading by Political Intelligence Professionals Prohibited by the STOCK Act?

In part an answer to this question depends on how the boundaries of the prohibition on government employees and elected officials are drawn. This chapter has noted the level of uncertainty present in an interpretation of the STOCK Act under the classical fiduciary-based theory of insider trading. It is also clear that the misappropriation theory of insider trading could apply to members of Congress, and indeed, other government employees, even before the STOCK Act was passed. It will therefore be impossible to sketch the full contours of how and to what extent the STOCK Act applies to the political intelligence industry. This subsection will, however, consider it to the extent possible.

The central case for this question is *Dirks*, since it established liability for tippees of corporate insiders in certain instances. The Court in *Dirks* notes that the "tippee's duty to disclose or abstain is derivative from that of the insider's duty" and that "[t]he tippee's obligation has been viewed as arising from his role as a participant after the fact in the insider's breach of a fiduciary duty."[21]

For example, the Court makes clear that "all disclosures of confidential corporate

---

[20]   See Bainbridge, supra note 2, at 302.
[21]   *Dirks*, 463 U.S. at 659.

information are not inconsistent with the duty insiders owe to shareholders." Thus in order for a potential tippee to understand whether he has committed insider trading, the uncertainty surrounding the circumstances that would constitute a breach of fiduciary duty on the part of the tipper in Congress or the government would be relevant.

Then we would need to consider the second prong of the *Dirks* test: whether the tipper enjoys some direct or indirect benefit that is either expected to translate into earnings in the future or that is intended to directly benefit a particular tippee. This leads to a number of difficult questions in the application of *Dirks* liability to political intelligence professionals. Does sharing information about legislative developments with someone who has donated to a congressman's political campaign amount to the type of quid pro quo covered by Dirks, since it is not necessarily a benefit that might translate into future earnings (but instead a donation to a political fund) and is further a recognized form of free speech?[22] And what about political donations to outside groups?

Some might wonder whether the SEC, as an agency under strict legislative oversight, might be unlikely to bring charges against members of Congress. It should be noted that the SEC doesn't necessarily have to target tipper members of Congress for it to bring a successful case against a tippee. *U.S. v. Evans* has held that tippee liability can be found even where no case was brought against the tipper of the confidential information.[23]

Dirks also provides that some outside parties may become temporary insiders for the purposes of *Dirks* tipper liability.[24] This opens up questions of whether analogous parties might become temporary insiders for purposes of political insider trading liability. In the congressional context, it is worth considering whether campaign staff become temporary insiders. For purposes of the executive branch, it is worth considering whether government contractors become temporary insiders.

There may be some room for the SEC to answer some of these questions by way of interpretive rulemaking, to the extent is has the existing authority under Section 10 of the Exchange Act to do so. And yet the SEC would not have extensive authority to promulgate outright bans of trading on particular sources of information, as it did with trading on information about tender offers under Rule 14, because it was not granted authority to do so by the STOCK Act.

In *O'Hagan* the Court found that Section 14 gave the SEC authority, in the case of tender offers, to prohibit certain acts that, though not fraudulent or deceptive, brought the risk that they would lead to deceptive conduct.[25] The Court held that Section 10 alone would not give the SEC sufficient authority for such a prophylactic rule. Since the STOCK Act merely adds an additional basis for a Section 10 violation by defining an additional type of activity as covered under the classical theory of insider trading, but does not provide additional authority as in Rule 14, any rulemaking under this section would be limited to actual fraudulent conduct rather than rules designed to prevent fraudulent practices through prophylactic measures. So, for instance, it would seem the SEC would not have the authority to affirmatively prohibit individuals donating to

---

[22]   See, e.g., Citizens United v. FEC, 130 S. Ct. 876 (2010).
[23]   See United States v. Evans, 486 F 3d 315 (7th Cir. 2007).
[24]   See *Dirks*, 463 U.S. at 655.
[25]   See *O'Hagan*, 521 U.S. at 673.

members of Congress from trading on information obtained from members of Congress across the board, since such a measure would cover innocent trading as well as deceptive conduct.

On the other hand, the SEC has interpreted through rulemaking instances in which a duty of trust and confidence is presumed to exist, as in Rule 10b5-2(b)(3) in which the Commission established the rebuttable presumption that the misappropriation theory of insider trading will apply "[w]henever a person receives or obtains material nonpublic information from his or her spouse, parent, child or sibling." It might therefore be able to establish rebuttable presumptions about certain types of relationship under the STOCK Act.

There are a number of profitable trading activities that will not be covered by the STOCK Act just as the insider trading laws do not cover them. As such, covered government employees and political intelligence firms will find their information and their services still have value even to the extent they make investment decisions on the basis of inside knowledge. For example, a decision not to purchase stocks, and a decision not to sell stocks in your portfolio, are both not covered by the insider trading laws precisely because no trade has occurred. So, for example, if a political intelligence firm learns, by way of what would otherwise be a violation of the STOCK Act, that the Chairman of the Federal Reserve is preparing to announce a dramatic decrease in interest rates, and the political intelligence firm advises its clients to hold on to stocks rather than sell them, and the clients take that advice, no actionable insider trading will have occurred.

B. Should Trading by the Political Intelligence Industry be Prohibited?

Many voices writing on the STOCK Act agree that information is contained within the halls of Congress and government that would be highly useful to the price discovery function of capital markets. A rule that paints with a broad brush to prohibit any transfers of information, regardless of whether equity or corruption concerns are implicated, should be compared against a more targeted approach that leaves open legitimate and efficient pathways for valuable information to be incorporated in the market price of traded stocks in real time.

Bainbridge briefly mentions expanding application of the STOCK Act to tippees by way of an explicit ban on all tippee trading, and suggests a ban that would prohibit all tippee trading with respect to information which a trader knew or should have known came from a member or staffer.[26] That observation exceeds the scope of his fairness argument, as it would extend a ban on outsider trading in this context that does not apply to all outside traders (a tippee trading on the basis of a tip from a tipper congressman without a quid pro quo benefit to the congressman would seem prohibited by Bainbridge's suggestion, but is not prohibited on the basis of a tip without an expected quid pro quo benefit to a corporate insider tipper). Manne's concerns about insider trading by government employees and elected officials are also not implicated in the context of outsider trading on the basis of government information in the absence of a quid pro quo benefit to the congressman or government employee.

---

[26]   See Bainbridge, supra note 2, at 306.

Prior discussions about various restrictions on information flows in the securities laws about the impact on the role of investment analysts and others trading on the basis of outside information also bear on this question. For example, one of the policy challenges the Supreme Court considered in *Dirks v. SEC* was a concern that "[i]mposing a duty to disclose or abstain solely because a person knowingly receives material nonpublic information from an insider and trades on it could have an inhibiting influence on the role of market analysts . . ."[27] The Court explores the fact that analysts can serve a useful function in questioning employees and investigating claims made by management about the value of a company using information available within the company. It is this justification that the Court uses to develop a foundation within fiduciary duty principles for tipper/tippee liability.

Kobayashi and Ribstein contrast instances of insider trading in which fiduciaries appropriate information obtained from inside companies in which they trade with outsider trading in which trading is informed by information obtained from outside a company in which trading occurs. Kobayashi and Ribstein emphasize that trading by outsiders, where fraud or misappropriation of information is not present, can help outsiders to capitalize on the production of socially beneficial information.[28] Political intelligence analysts can provide the type of socially valuable information that Kobayashi and Ribstein describe.

One also should not assume that political intelligence professionals merely transmit information to traders. They also apply unique analytical skills to the information to help determine the impact of a new law (or, for that matter, change in committee chairmanship or Senate or House procedural rule) and changes in probability of a particular outcome caused by developments affecting an uncertain event. In doing so they can produce new information if they have incentives to do so, and legal risk or even legal indeterminacy about their right to trade on that information can limit their incentives to actually produce the socially beneficial information.[29]

VI. CONCLUSION

Trading by political officials on the basis of official information is a highly controversial and ethically suspect practice, and suggests both equity and efficiency concerns that show the case against it is clear. It remains to be seen whether the STOCK Act will serve as an effective remedy to the problem. The STOCK Act takes a regime designed to deal with economic contractual relationships very much unlike the relationship between voters, the U.S. government, and employees and elected officials. The STOCK Act also takes a doctrinal scheme in the securities laws, which itself is grounded in an underlying state law fiduciary duty regime, and essentially graphs it into this sphere without tailoring it to this specific circumstance. It is therefore equally unclear whether the STOCK Act achieves its objective of preventing insider trading by members of Congress and whether the compro-

---

[27]   See *Dirks*, 463 U.S. at 658–659.
[28]   See Bruce H. Kobayashi and Larry Ribstein, Outsider Trading As An Incentive Device, 40 U. C. Davis L. Rev. 21 (2006).
[29]   See id. at 32.

mise leading to the legislation to exempt political intelligence firms is also fully realized. Further, the policy case for broad and outright prohibitions on trading by outside analysts in the political intelligence industry who assist investors in navigating the risks of government regulation and ownership has yet to be made.

10. What governmental insider trading teaches us about corporate insider trading
Sung Hui Kim

I. INTRODUCTION

There has been much academic debate about whether corporate insider trading should be banned. As Stephen Bainbridge recounts in the Introduction to this volume, that debate was sparked by Henry Manne's influential 1966 book, *Insider Trading and the Stock Market*.[1] Manne contended that corporate insider trading should be deregulated because the benefits to both society and the firm whose stock was traded outweighed the costs. He provided two basic rationales. First, Manne argued that corporate insider trading has the effect of moving securities prices toward the level that they would have reached had the inside information been made public. This increase in price accuracy helps allocate capital to its most productive uses.

Secondly, and more provocatively, Manne argued that corporate insider trading was "the most appropriate device for compensating entrepreneurs in large corporations."[2] Unlike ordinary managers whose service is easy to monitor and "can be purchased like any commodity in the marketplace," it is difficult to ascertain the value of an entrepreneur's services in the form of a predetermined salary. Instead, Manne argued, insider trading provides a means by which companies can compensate entrepreneurs for the value of their innovations. Securities prices tend to rise immediately following the public disclosure of the relevant innovation. Because such price increases roughly reflect the value of the innovation to the firm's business, insider trading enables entrepreneurs to recover a portion of the value of their innovative activity. And ultimately, according to Manne, society has a strong economic interest in incentivizing entrepreneurial innovations.

These claims have been thoroughly disputed,[3] and Manne himself has acknowledged difficulties with the second rationale, the compensation justification.[4] But my focus in this chapter is on an important but little-noticed distinction that Manne drew in his argument between *corporate* insider trading, which he defended, and *governmental* insider trading,[5] which he rejected. In his 1966 book, Manne explained that the compensation-

---

[1]   Henry G. Manne, Insider Trading and the Stock Market (1966).
[2]   Id. at 192.
[3]   See, e.g., Robert A. Prentice & Dain C. Donelson, Insider Trading as a Signaling Device, 47 Am. Bus. L. J. 1 (2010).
[4]   See Henry G. Manne, Insider Trading: Hayek, Virtual Markets, and the Dog that Did Not Bark, 31 J. Corp. L. 167, 173–74 (2005).
[5]   By "governmental insider trading," I refer to the practice of government officials, including members of Congress, trading on material nonpublic information in breach of their fiduciary duties. As I have argued elsewhere, members of Congress should be recognized as fiduciaries for purposes of federal insider trading law. See Sung Hui Kim, The Last Temptation of Congress:

for-innovation argument does not generally apply to government officials because "[v]ery often the government official's news will have been reported to him rather than developed by him or anyone in government."[6] Moreover, Manne argued that to the extent that a government official is responsible for innovations, those "innovations may injure a corporation economically as frequently as they benefit it."[7]And Manne could identify no "social, economic, or political interest in rewarding government officials simply for benefitting or injuring particular companies." In addition, allowing governmental insider trading might incentivize government officials to skew governmental processes to increase trading profits rather than serve the public interest. Finally, Manne warned against "the ease with which inside information can be utilized as a payoff device," which he identified as "the principal evil inherent in government insider trading." More than four decades later, Manne stood steadfast by his criticism of governmental insider trading. Manne stated *inter alia*:

> We do not want [government officials] to receive extra compensation or outside compensation for doing their jobs. And, of course, all too frequently their access to this information is merely another form of bribe, and that sure as hell is not legal.[8]

If even Manne, the most vocal defender of corporate insider trading, rejects governmental insider trading, it should not be surprising that there has been little academic or policy defense of the practice. Indeed, apart from Todd Henderson and Larry Ribstein, who urged, "Let members of Congress trade!,"[9] most academic commentators have expressed normative outrage at such actions.[10] To be sure, there has been a descriptive debate about whether certain forms of governmental insider trading, such as those made by members of Congress, violate existing federal securities law,[11] but there has been almost no normative debate about its impropriety.

Legislator Insider Trading and the Fiduciary Norm against Corruption, 98 Cornell L. Rev. (forthcoming 2013) [hereinafter Kim, Legislator Insider Trading].

[6] Id. at 193. Of course, the same could be said of corporate insider trading, since the vast majority of insider trading is done by employees who have not created the valuable information. See Prentice & Donelson, supra note 3, at 4.

[7] Of course, the same could be said of corporate insider trading, as insiders can benefit as much from bad news as good news. See id.

[8] See e-mail from Henry Manne to Pro.Con.org, procon.org (June 29, 2008), http://insidertrading.procon.org/view.source.php?sourceID=006015.

[9] M. Todd Henderson & Larry Ribstein, Let Members of Congress Trade!, politico.com (Dec. 1, 2011), http://www.politico.com/news/stories/1211/69601.html (last visited Nov. 19, 2012).

[10] See note 11 infra.

[11] Until Congress voted to formally ban congressional insider trading on March 22, 2012, many commentators believed that federal insider trading doctrine did not reach members of Congress. See, e.g., Stephen M. Bainbridge, Insider Trading Inside the Beltway, 36 J. Corp. L. 281, 285 (2011); Richard W. Painter, Getting the Government America Deserves: How Ethics Reform Can Make a Difference 163 (2009); Insider Trading and Congressional Accountability: Hearing Before the Comm. on S. Homeland Sec. & Gov't Affairs, 112th Cong. (Dec. 1, 2011) (statement of John C. Coffee Jr., Professor of Law). But see Donna Nagy, Insider Trading, Congressional Officials, and Duties of Entrustment, 91 B. U. L. Rev. 1105 (2011); Jonathan R. Macey & Maureen O'Hara, Regulation and Scholarship: Constant Companions or Occasional Bedfellows? 26 Yale J. Reg. 89, 107 (2009); Insider Trading and Congressional Accountability: Hearing Before the Comm. on

In this chapter, I unpack this normative consensus against governmental insider trading, with emphasis on congressional insider trading. Specifically, I argue that governmental insider trading should be seen as normatively problematic because it amounts to public corruption.[12] Indeed, Manne himself nodded to such an understanding by using words such as "payoff device" and "bribe" to describe the practice. It may seem pointless to tease out justifications for a conclusion that almost no one rejects, but there is a valuable payoff. When we examine more deeply the reasons why *public* corruption is problematic, we see that analogous reasons apply also to corruption in the *private* sector. And as I explain, just as governmental insider trading should be viewed as a form of public corruption, corporate insider trading should be viewed as a form of private corruption.

Although my argument applies generally to governmental insider trading, I focus on congressional insider trading because this type of governmental insider trading has received the widest public and scholarly attention. Section II briefly summarizes the evidence of governmental insider trading, with emphasis on recent empirical studies about trades made by members of Congress. Section III argues that governmental insider trading should be seen as a form of public corruption,[13] whose harms I articulate in section IV. Section V points out that as governmental insider trading should be seen as a form of public corruption, corporate insider trading should be seen as a form of private corruption with analogous harms. Thus, if one rejects governmental insider trading, one has good reason to reject corporate insider trading as well. Section VI concludes.

II.   THE EVIDENCE OF GOVERNMENTAL INSIDER TRADING

Governmental insider trading has been around since the founding of the Republic. In 1789, Alexander Hamilton, the first U.S. Secretary of Treasury, announced that the new American federal government would assume the Revolutionary war debts of states and the Continental Congress at face value. Prior to the announcement, the Assistant Secretary of Treasury, William Duer, leaked this information to speculators who invested on their own and on Duer's behalf in the debt certificates of southern states, which were then selling at a fraction of their face value.[14] As summed up by Charles Geisst, "Duer had

---

S. Homeland Sec. & Gov't Affairs, 112th Cong. (Dec. 1, 2011) (statement of Donald C. Langevoort, Professor of Law); Kim, Legislator Insider Trading, supra note 5.

[12]   Bainbridge, supra note 11, at 282 (arguing that permitting congressional insider trading "opens the door to corruption").

[13]   Section III is in large parts duplicative of Part III.B of Kim, Legislator Insider Trading, supra note 5.

[14]   Contemporaries faulted Duer at the time for driving the speculation. See Robert F. Jones, William Duer and the Business of Government in the Era of the American Revolution, 32 William & Mary Quarterly 393, 409 (1975); Cathy Matson, Public Vices, Private Benefit: William Duer and His Circle, 1776–1792, in New York and the Rise of American Capitalism: Economic Development and the Social and Political History of an American State, 1780–1870 (eds. William Pencak & Conrad Edick Wright), 72, 96 (1989); Edgar S. Maclay, ed., The Journal of William Maclay, United States Senator from Pennsylvania 1789–1791, vii, 175 (1965).

the distinction of being the first individual to use knowledge gained from his official position to become entangled in speculative trading; in effect, he was the first inside trader."[15]

William Duer may have been the first governmental insider trader but he wasn't the last. There have since been numerous suspicious cases,[16] but until 1995, evidence of governmental insider trading remained anecdotal. In 1995, Gregory Boller, a professor of marketing at the University of Memphis, investigated a random sample of 111 members of Congress from the Senate and the House of Representatives who purchased common stock from 1991 to 1993.[17] Boller found that 25 percent of the members sampled "showed stock transactions that directly coincided with legislative activity." For example, Senator Lloyd Bentsen (Democrat, Texas) had purchased stock in a dairy processor and sold it 10 months later—just days before the Justice Department began investigating the company for rigging bids to sell milk in public schools. Boller's more systematic research raised suspicions.

Indeed, it caught the eye of Alan Ziobrowski and his collaborators,[18] who analyzed all known senatorial stock market transactions between 1993 and 1998 and published their groundbreaking study in the *Journal of Financial and Quantitative Analysis*.[19] After poring through hundreds of pages of opaque and unaudited financial disclosure reports and using a calendar-time portfolio analysis, the researchers found that portfolios reconstructing approximately 6,000 reported common stock trades of U.S. senators outperformed the market by approximately 10 percent per year. By contrast, U.S. households performed on average worse than the market by −1.4 percent during the same period.

Perhaps Senators are just better educated and more financially savvy than the average household. But interestingly, Senators outperformed even corporate insiders, who beat the market by only 7 percent, and hedge funds, which beat the market by between 7 and 8 percent. Interestingly, political party affiliation did not predict returns in a statistically significant manner, but seniority did. Abnormally high returns were more common among the more junior Senators.

The study also produced evidence of uncanny timing. The "prices of common stocks bought by Senators tended to stagnate prior to purchase, soar after purchase, and then stagnate again after sale."[20] The authors concluded that "it seems clear that Senators have

---

[15]   Charles R. Geisst, Wall Street: A History: From Its Beginnings to the Fall of Enron 12 (2004). In response to the bond speculation, Congress enacted the Treasury Act of 1789, which prohibited and still prohibits certain officials from purchasing and disposing of state or federal government securities. Richard W. Painter, Bailouts: An Essay on Conflicts of Interest and Ethics when Government Pays the Tab, 41 McGeorge L. Rev. 131, 151 (2009).

[16]   See, e.g., Bud W. Jerke, Cashing In On Capitol Hill: Insider Trading and the Use of Political Intelligence for Profit, 158 U. Pa. L. Rev. 1451 (2010).

[17]   Gregory Boller, Taking Stock in Congress, by Joy Ward, Mother Jones (Sept./Oct. 1995 issue).

[18]   Megan McArdle, Capitol Gains: Are Members of Congress Guilty of Insider Trading—and Does It Matter?, theatlantic.com (Nov. 2011), http://www.theatlantic.com/magazine/archive/2011/11/capitol-gains/8692/ (last visited Nov. 19, 2012).

[19]   See Alan J. Ziobrowski et al., Abnormal Returns from the Common Stock Investments of the U.S. Senate, 39 J. Fin. & Quantitative Analysis 661 (2004) [hereinafter, Ziobrowski et al., Senate Study].

[20]   Matthew Barbabella et al., Insider Trading in Congress: The Need for Regulation, 9 J. Bus. & Sec. L. 199, 205 (2009) (interpreting the Ziobrowski study's findings).

demonstrated a definite informational advantage over other investors although the specific source(s) and nature of that information remain unknown."[21]

In 2011, the same research team turned its sights onto the House and examined 16,000 common stock trades made by approximately 300 members of the House of Representatives from 1985 to 2001.[22] The study found that a portfolio reconstructing these trades beat the market by over 6 percent annually—not as good as the Senators, but still abnormally high. The authors speculated that the smaller returns might arise from the fact that House members wield relatively less influence and thus may have less access to critical inside information.

In contrast to the Senate, political party affiliation mattered in the House: Democratic members enjoyed statistically significant better returns than Republicans. As a possible explanation, the authors pointed out that Democrats controlled the House for 10 of the 17 years covered in the study and were perhaps more entrenched in the House leadership and thus were more capable of exploiting the reins of power. And, as in the Senate, the most junior Representatives reliably outperformed their more senior colleagues. The authors speculated that this seniority effect could be caused by the fact that junior members tend to be in more financially precarious situations and accordingly are more motivated to trade on confidential information.

A third study, conducted by Andrew Eggers and Jens Hainmueller, complicates the picture. They reconstructed the portfolios of 453 members of Congress during a different and shorter time frame—between 2004 and 2008.[23] They found that many individual members generally did not beat the market. Indeed, their research suggested that Congress actually underperformed the market by 2 to 3 percent annually. It is not clear why their findings differ from the previous studies. Eggers and Hainmueller offer some explanations, including the possibility that members had changed their trading practices over time (e.g., moved more of their assets into qualified blind trusts) in response to increased scrutiny. (Even Ziobrowski's Senate study noted that for the years 1997 and 1998, Senators did not outperform the market—perhaps as a reaction to the bad publicity from Boller's research.[24]) Eggers and Hainmueller also speculate that perhaps the bull market of the 1990s provided more profit-making opportunities than the "relatively moribund and finally panic-stricken market" of the mid-2000s. It is also possible that members simply stopped reporting their incriminating transactions once they realized that academics and the media were watching them. After all, the disclosure reports are unaudited. Finally, it is always possible that one of the studies is wrong. Ziobrowski et al. have not released their full data set, and the Eggers–Hainmueller study has not been published in a peer-reviewed journal.[25]

---

[21]   Ziobrowski et al., Senate Study, supra note 19, at 676.

[22]   Alan J. Ziobrowski et al., Abnormal Returns From the Common Stock Investments of Members of the U.S. House of Representatives, 13 Business and Politics 1 (2011) [hereinafter, Ziobrowski et al., House Study].

[23]   Andrew Eggers & Jens Hainmueller, Political Investing: The Common Stock Investments of Members of Congress, 2004–2008, http://www.gsb.stanford.edu/facseminars/events/political_economy/documents/pe_10_10_hainmueller.pdf (last visited Nov. 19, 2012). The study analyzed 48,309 trades in 2,581 different stocks. Id.

[24]   Ziobrowski et al., Senate Study, supra note 19, at 676.

[25]   McArdle, supra note 18.

That said, even Eggers and Hainmueller's study—which found that members of Congress did not generally beat the market—discovered that members' investments in firms headquartered in their districts outperformed the market by about 4.5 percent per year. This finding is intriguing since, as the authors note, no research in recent decades has suggested that individual investors or money managers can outperform the market by investing in local companies. Also, members performed as well as the market with respect to investments in companies that contributed money to the member's election campaigns or lobbied the member's committee. In other words, members' investments in politically connected companies outperformed the rest of their investments. As a result, Eggers and Hainmueller conclude that "members of Congress seem to benefit as investors from knowledge of companies to which they are politically connected (and particularly those headquartered in their districts), but they seem not to invest enough in these connected companies to make up for the mediocre performance of the rest of their portfolios."[26]

In sum, what can we conclude about congressional insider trading based on these studies? According to the Efficient Capital Markets Hypothesis, a version of which has been supported by a wide body of empirical evidence, the "market incorporates all new information pertinent to stock values very quickly, with the result that future stock price changes and investment returns are unpredictable, rendering it impossible for investors to devise strategies based on available information that will consistently produce abnormal returns."[27] As a result, it should be extremely difficult to outperform the market unless one trades with an informational advantage over other investors. Corporate insiders, who normally have access to material information that is not generally available to the investing public, enjoy significant abnormal returns.[28] Apparently, so do members of Congress, especially regarding firms that are headquartered in their districts. All of this strongly suggests that members of Congress are trading with an informational advantage.

Given the foregoing evidence that some governmental insider trading may be taking place, one might ask what the big deal is? In other words, why is it wrong? I answer that question in the next two sections. In Section III, I argue that governmental insider trading can and should be seen as a form of public corruption. In Section IV, I describe why public corruption in the form of governmental insider trading is wrong by articulating its harms.

III. GOVERNMENTAL INSIDER TRADING AS PUBLIC CORRUPTION

As Justice Stewart said of obscenity, people seem to know public corruption when they see it, but it's hard to define.[29] One source of difficulty lies in the fact that what counts

---

[26] Eggers & Hainmueller, supra note 23, at 4.

[27] Ziobrowski et al., House Study, supra note 22, at 4.

[28] See, e.g., Jeffrey Jaffe, Special Information and Insider Trading, 47 J. of Business 410 (1974); Dan Givoly & Dan Palmon, Insider Trading and Exploitation of Inside Information: Some Empirical Evidence, 58 J. Bus. 69 (1985); H.N. Seyhun, Insiders' Profits, Costs of Trading, and Market Efficiency, 16 J. Fin. Econ. 189 (1986).

[29] See, e.g., Michael A. Genovese, Presidential Corruption: A Longitudinal Analysis, 136, in Corruption and American Politics (eds. Michael A. Genovese & Victoria Farrar-Myers) (2011)

as corruption is historically contingent. For example, it is today uncontroversial to say that a legislator accepting a bribe is corrupt. But in the nineteenth century, members of Congress openly accepted payments from companies lobbying to obstruct or advance particular legislation. For instance, Daniel Webster was on a retainer from the Bank of the United States to represent the bank's interests, and he unabashedly sent written reminders to replenish his bank account.[30] Bribing members of Congress was not formally banned until 1853. And even after the ban, members went undisciplined until public outrage erupted over the Credit Mobilier bribery scandal in the 1870s, which impelled Congress merely to censure the guilty members.[31] Not until more than a century later, in 1980, did the House finally expel a member for bribery.[32]

Also, what counts as corruption is culturally contingent.[33] Societies maintain different political systems with differing notions of accountability, cultivate different institutions of power with varying degrees of maturity and legitimacy, negotiate different boundaries between public and private domains, and draw on diverse relationships between power and wealth. Accordingly, societies necessarily experience corruption in diverse ways, making it difficult to define both precisely and universally. As summed up by John Kleinig and William C. Heffernan:

> Even if we confine ourselves to what we now familiarly speak of as public corruption, it soon becomes clear that what "we" consider to be corrupt is often contentiously so. One group's perquisite is another's corruption; one group's tradition of patronage is another's nepotism; one group's campaign contribution is another's bribery; one group's just rectification is another's misappropriation. Both historically and cross-culturally, instantiations of corruption have been contested, not only with respect to their identity but also, in certain instances, with respect to their undesirability.[34]

("[T]here is no commonly accepted definition of what constitutes corruption"); Michael Johnston, The Definitions Debate: Old Conflicts in New Guises, 12, in The Political Economy of Corruption (ed. Arvind K. Jain) (2001) ("No one has ever devised a universally satisfying 'one-line definition' of corruption"); Nathaniel Persily & Kelli Lammie, Perceptions of Corruption and Campaign Finance: When Public Opinion Determines Constitutional Law, 153 U. Pa. L. Rev. 119, 126–27 (2004) (noting that corruption means different things to the different Supreme Court Justices).

[30]   Daniel Webster, who served in the House and Senate and as Secretary of State, once reminded the President of the Bank of the United States, "If it be wished that my relation to the Bank be continued, it may be well to send me the usual retainers." Richard Allan Baker, The History of Congressional Ethics, in Representation and Responsibility: Exploring Legislative Ethics 8 (eds. Bruce Jennings & Daniel Callahan) (1985).

[31]   Dennis F. Thompson, Ethics in Congress: From Individual to Institutional Corruption 2 (1995).

[32]   The House voted unanimously to expel Michael J. "Ozzie" Myers, a Pennsylvania Democrat who accepted bribes in an undercover ABSCAM investigation. This was the House's first expulsion for corruption. Id. at 105, note 14. Four years earlier, the House had failed to expel Andrew J. Hinshaw, a California Republican, who had been convicted of accepting a bribe. Id. at 2.

[33]   See Jens C. Andvig & Odd-Helge Fjeldstad, Corruption: A Review of Contemporary Research 46 (2001) ("[W]hat is seen as corruption varies from one country to another"). That said, as Klitgaard notes, "Over a wide range of 'corrupt' activities, there is little argument that they are wrong and socially harmful," even across societies. Robert Klitgaard, Controlling Corruption 4 (1987).

[34]   John Kleinig & William C. Heffernan, The Corruptibility of Corruption, in Private and Public Corruption 3 (eds. William C. Heffernan & John Kleinig) (2004).

Moreover, even within a single society at a particular moment in time, there will be disagreement about what counts as "corrupt." For example, it has been well documented that elites and the public differ in what they regard as corrupt.[35] Also, an analysis of National Election Study surveys reveals that factors such as race, education, and income affect the likelihood that a respondent will perceive the government to be corrupt.[36]

Given such contingencies and controversies, my goal is not to proffer and defend some best definition of public corruption, which would attempt to specify a strict set of necessary and sufficient conditions that capture all instances of what people regard as corruption with no over- or under-inclusiveness. Indeed, the cognitive science of categories casts serious doubt on the success of any such project.[37] Instead, I offer something more modest, a definition that draws on rough consensus in the political science literature, jibes with general lay understandings, and performs useful analytic work in the narrow context of insider trading.

I start with the "classical" understanding of public corruption in political science. As Dennis Thompson explains:

> In the tradition of political theory, corruption is a disease of the body politic. Like a virus invading the physical body, hostile forces spread through the political body, enfeebling the spirit of the laws and undermining the principles of the regime. The form the virus takes depends on the form of government it attacks. In regimes of a more popular cast, such as republics and democracies, the virus shows itself as private interests. Its agents are greedy individuals, contentious factions, and mass movements that seek to control collective authority for their own purposes. *The essence of corruption in this conception is the pollution of the public by the private.*[38]

Thus, the classical understanding of public corruption is grounded in the notion that private interests somehow taint the public good.

More modern definitions of corruption build on this understanding but tend to drop the organic metaphors of disease, degeneration, or decay. They also tend to replace substance with procedure—the notion of substantive public good is replaced by the democratic process, which purifies private interests into legitimate public purposes.[39]

---

[35]   Matthew J. Streb & April K. Clark, The Public and Political Corruption 281, in Corruption and American Politics (eds. Michael A. Genovese & Victoria Farrar-Myers) (2011) (describing the perception gap in the views of the elites versus the public on corruption).

[36]   These factors, however, are less predictive than a respondent's political attitudes. See Persily & Lammie, supra note 29, at 153–67.

[37]   Since the 1970s, advances in the fields of cognitive psychology, cognitive linguistics, artificial intelligence, and anthropology have provided a persuasive account of how humans categorize people, things, and abstract concepts. Such an account discounts the role of deductive reasoning from abstracted principles. See, generally, George Lakoff, Women, Fire, and Dangerous Things: What Categories Reveal About the Mind (1987). For a specific exploration of these insights onto the legal profession, see Sung Hui Kim, Lawyer Exceptionalism in the Gatekeeping Wars, 63 SMU L. Rev. 73, 95–111 (2010). See also Daniel H. Lowenstein, Campaign Contributions and Corruption: Comments on Strauss and Cain, 1995 U. Chi. Legal F. 163, 164 (1995) (". . . concepts such as corruption cannot be applied satisfactorily to political life by deduction from general theoretical propositions").

[38]   Thompson, supra note 31, at 28 (emphasis added).

[39]   Id. at 28 (noting that the modern conception of corruption retains the notion of the "pollution of the public by the private" but replaces the "consensus on the public good" with the "democratic process").

Under most modern definitions, corruption involves an abuse of trust occasioned by an improper commingling of one's public role and private gain in derogation of predetermined democratic processes—essentially, an act that disrespects the sacred border between public and private. At minimum, there seems to be an academic consensus that public corruption entails an "abuse of public roles or resources for private benefit."[40] In short, public corruption is the use of public office for private gain.[41] Reflecting this simple core understanding, the very first page of the House Ethics Manual commands that members, officers, and employees of the House "should not in any way use their office for private gain."[42]

---

[40]   Michael Johnston, Democracy without Politics? Hidden Costs of Corruption and Reform in America, 16, in Corruption and American Politics (eds. Michael A. Genovese & Victoria Farrar-Myers) (2011).

[41]   See, e.g., Mark E. Warren, Political Corruption as Duplicitous Corruption, 37 Political Science and Politics 803 (2006) (noting the "received conception of political corruption" as "the abuse of public office for private gain"); Joseph S. Nye, Corruption and Political Development: A Cost–Benefit Analysis, 61 Amer. Pol. Sci. Rev. 417, 419 (1967) ("Corruption is behavior which deviates from the formal duties of a public role because of private-regarding (personal, close family, private clique) pecuniary or status gains; or violates rules against the exercise of certain types of private-regarding influence"); Susan Rose-Ackerman, Corruption and Government: Causes, Consequences, and Reform 91 (1999) (defining corruption as the "misuse of public power for private gain"); Thompson, supra note 31, at 7 (noting that all forms of corruption involve the "improper use of public office for private purposes"); Kleinig & Heffernan, supra note 34, at 3 ("If there is an orthodox account of corruption, it is that it consists in the improper use of public office for private gain"); Transparency International Corruption Perceptions Index 2011, transparency.org (June 26, 2012), http://cpi.transparency.org/cpi2011/in_detail/#myAnchor1 (last visited Nov. 19, 2012) (defining corruption as "the abuse of entrusted power for private gain"); World Bank Institute Control of Corruption Index, info.worldbank.org (June 26, 2011), http://info.worldbank.org/governance/wgi/pdf/cc.pdf (last visited Nov. 19, 2012) (noting that "Control of corruption captures perceptions to the extent to which public power is exercised for private gain . . .").

Two definitional issues are worth noting. First, many of the above cited definitions emphasize "misuse" (or "abuse") of public office for private gain. That, of course, raises the question of what counts as "misuse" versus acceptable "use." The same concern can be alternatively reframed as involving the distinction between "private gain" (which is improper) versus acceptable "gain," e.g., one's standard salary. For simplicity's sake, I would rather locate the disapprobation inherent in the term "misuse" in the term "*private* gain." As such, I define corruption simply as the *use* of public office for private gain.

Secondly, the definition of corruption that I have adopted is a narrow one—what political scientists categorize as *individual* corruption. But political scientists also refer to a broader *institutional* (or systemic form of) corruption. See, e.g., Thompson, supra note 31, at 25 (distinguishing individual and institutional corruption); Michael A. Genovese, The Politics of Corruption and the Corruption of Politics, 3, in Corruption and American Politics (eds. Michael A. Genovese & Victoria Farrar-Myers) (2011) (distinguishing individual and systemic corruption). With institutional/systemic corruption, public office is used not so much for private gain, such as lining one's pockets, but for political gain, such as furthering one's ideological causes, political party's fate, or even personal political ambitions. Trying to draw a bright line between institutional corruption and hardball politics is difficult. Thankfully, governmental insider trading falls squarely in the more easily defined category of individual corruption. For purposes of my analysis, I mean to emphasize private gain that is supererogatory and economic in nature. See discussion accompanying notes 43–47 infra.

[42]   H. Comm. on Standards of Official Conduct, 110th Cong., House Ethics Manual 1 (2008), ethics.house.gov, http://ethics.house.gov/Media/PDF/2008_House_Ethics_Manual.pdf (last visited Nov. 19, 2012).

A. Private Gain

Since at least Cicero, it has been "beyond debate that officials of the government are relied upon to act for the public interest not their own enrichment."[43] But not all forms of personal enrichment are dubious. After all, members are not required to make a vow of poverty before holding office. Indeed, the Founders endorsed the idea that members of Congress should be paid salaries on the view that being independently wealthy should not be a qualification for elected office.[44] Therefore, the notion of private gain must recognize that some forms of personal gain[45] are necessary or incidental to performing one's political role.

As proposed by Andrew Stark, "private gain" signifies that the public officials are enjoying the gain in question *outside* of their official roles. The "modifier *private* suggests a kind of gain—a trip on a corporate jet, attending an association meeting at a resort, an all-expense paid trip to a charity event—that does not, or ought not, or need not, redound to the official as part of his or her job."[46] Thus, private gain is a form of personal gain that is *supererogatory*—neither part of the explicit compensation allocated to the public official nor culturally viewed as an acceptable or unavoidable perquisite of the role.[47] Consequently, "[i]f the official's responsibilities required the official to board the corporate aircraft, or be present at the association meeting, or attend the charity event, then there would be no 'private' gain, just the exercise of office."[48]

B. From Public Office

It is not enough, however, that the gain be private. It must also somehow flow from the official's *public office*. In other words, there must be a proximate causal nexus between the public role and the private enrichment. At minimum it must be shown that she would never have received the invitation to ride the corporate jet, attend the association meeting at the resort, or participate in the all-expenses paid charity event *but for* her official public role. If the causal nexus is absent, the official's conduct is not improper because the opportunity did not flow from her public role. For example, if the official can demonstrate that prior to becoming a public official she had routinely received the same invitation to

---

[43] John T. Noonan, Jr., Bribes, 704 (1984).

[44] Thompson, supra note 31, at 50; The Records of the Federal Convention of 1787, vol. 1, 219 (ed. Max Farrand) (1966).

[45] By "personal gain," I mean to include gain that not only directly benefits the official in question but also inures to the official's family, relatives, or friends.

[46] Andrew Stark, Conflict of Interest in American Public Life 76 (2000) (defining the term "private gain from public office").

[47] Certain longstanding perquisites of congressional office would not ordinarily constitute "private gain" because they serve an important political function. For example, the purpose of the franking privilege is to aid communication with constituents. However, if the franking privilege is misused by members to assist in re-election efforts, it would amount to "private gain" under this definition. See Thompson, supra note 31, at 30, 73. Also, certain non-economic forms of personal gain, such as enhanced prestige or increased name recognition, are unavoidable consequences of holding office and thus unobjectionable.

[48] Stark, supra note 46 at 76.

attend the all-expenses paid charity event, the causal link would arguably be severed and the private gain would not be viewed as improper.[49] In addition, the official must have somehow intended to receive the gain in question in order for her conduct to be deemed improper. This is merely to acknowledge that inadvertent or accidental accruals of private gain can hardly be regarded as "corrupt."

Applying this basic definition, we can see why congressional insider trading can be described as corruption. First, such trading is private gain—a clear act of supererogatory financial gain. Profits earned from insider trading are not part of the explicit compensation allocated to members. Also, there is nothing in the job description of members of Congress or in the nature of their legislative tasks that requires them to use their own personal funds to trade in any stocks, let alone based on information gleaned through their work in Congress. Further, near unanimous public opinion against congressional insider trading strongly suggests that such trading is not culturally viewed as one of the acceptable or unavoidable perquisites of their jobs.[50] Moreover, no member has publicly defended this practice. In fact, when members are directly confronted by the press with allegations of insider trading, they react defensively and evasively.[51] Secondly, such trading opportunities flow from their public office, i.e., they would not have such lucrative trading opportunities *but for* the information gained by virtue of their office. Thus, congressional insider trading fits squarely within the definition of public corruption—the use of public office for private gain.

IV.   THE HARMS OF PUBLIC CORRUPTION

Even if, as a descriptive matter, governmental insider trading can be characterized as a form of public corruption, a skeptic might press the ultimate normative question: what's wrong with corruption? George Washington Plunkitt, the notorious New York state Senator and Tammany Hall politician, made just this challenge in a colorful speech back in 1905:

> Everybody is talkin' these days about Tammany men growin' rich on graft, but nobody thinks of drawin' the distinction between honest graft and dishonest graft. There's all the difference in the world between the two. Yes, many of our men have grown rich in politics. I have myself. I've made a big fortune out of the game, and I'm gettin' richer every day, but I've not gone in for dishonest graft—blackmailin' gamblers, saloonkeepers, disorderly people, etc.— and neither has any of the men who have made big fortunes in politics. There's an honest graft, and I'm an example of how it works. I might sum up the whole thing by sayin': "I seen my opportunities and took 'em.". . .

---

[49]   See id.

[50]   A recent public opinion poll reports that the "vast majority of Americans (86%) believe insider trading laws should be enforced against members of Congress." See New Judicial Watch—Harris Interactive Poll Sends Warning to Washington Politicians, judicialwatch.org (Jan. 20, 2012), http://www.judicialwatch.org/press-room/weekly-updates/new-poll-and-stealing-democracy/ (last visited Nov. 19, 2012).

[51]   See, e.g., Confronting Pelosi on Insider Trading, cbsnews.com (June 17, 2012, 3:55 pm), http://www.cbsnews.com/8301-504803_162-57323518-10391709/confronting-pelosi-on-insider-trading/?tag=segementExtraScroller;housing (last visited Nov. 19, 2012).

I'll tell you of one case. They were goin' to fix up a big park, no matter where. I got on to it, and went lookin' about for land in that neighborhood.

I could get nothin' at a bargain but a big piece of swamp, but I took it fast enough and held onto it. What turned out was just what I counted on. They couldn't make the park complete without Plunkitt's swamp, and they had to pay a good price for it. Anything dishonest in that?[52]

Plunkitt's defense of "honest graft" is refreshingly candid but ultimately unpersuasive. After all, but for Plunkitt's actions, the government could have bought that swamp for the "bargain" price that Plunkitt originally got it for. Instead, the government had no choice but to pay Plunkitt's higher, hold-out price, and thus suffered direct financial harm.

That said, in some cases, the financial harm to the government or to the general public is not so clear. For example, one common defense asserted by the bribe taker is that there is no victim.[53] Indeed, as already mentioned, Henry Manne has defended *corporate* insider trading on the grounds that it actually—on net—benefits investors.[54] The same defense has been made of congressional insider trading.[55] But such defenses (of corporate and congressional insider trading) understand harm too narrowly. Even if no primary harm to the government or other investors can be identified in the form of clear, direct, financial costs, tolerating public corruption in the form of governmental insider trading produces three distinct secondary harms captured by the terms temptation, distraction, and legitimacy.[56]

A.   Temptation Costs

Public corruption in the form of governmental insider trading tempts public officials into bad decision making. To make this claim, I have to offer some baseline of what counts, by contrast, as good governmental decision making. Keeping our focus on legislators, here is a thin account: legislative decision making should be driven by the merits of the underlying policy and be responsive to the interests of the Representative's constituents. This is a thin account in that I am specifying neither what counts as the "merits" nor how one goes about deciding them. Moreover, I am not specifying what it means to be "responsive"—whether a Representative acts on the basis of his own or his constituents' conception of their interests—which turns on whether one embraces a trustee or

---

[52]   William L. Riordan, Plunkitt of Tammany Hall: A Series of Very Plain Talks on Very Practical Politics (1993, 1905), reprinted in William Safire, Safire's New Political Dictionary: The Definitive Guide to the New Language of Politics (under entry "Honest Graft") 334 (1993).

[53]   Omar Azfar et al., The Causes and Consequences of Corruption, 573 Annals Am. Acad. Pol. & Soc. Sci. 42, 47 (2001).

[54]   Manne, supra note 1. See also Hsiu-Kwang Wu, An Economist Looks at Section 16 of the Securities Exchange Act of 1984, 68 Colum. L. Rev. 260 (1968). But see William K.S. Wang, Trading on Material Nonpublic Information on Impersonal Stock Markets: Who is Harmed, and Who Can Sue Whom under SEC Rule 10b-5?, 54 S. Cal. L. Rev. 1217, 1235 (1981).

[55]   See Henderson & Ribstein, supra note 9.

[56]   This is not to say that governmental insider trading is normatively problematic for consequentialist reasons only. There may also be deontological objections to the practice, which may not be well captured by terms such as "costs" or "harms."

delegate theory of representation.[57] Nor do I specify who counts as the Representative's "constituents," whether the relevant constituency is the Representative's electoral district or the public-at-large. That said, even under this minimalist account, deciding on the basis of one's private financial self-interest and ignoring or discounting the public's interest cannot be deemed a decision "on the merits" or one that is "responsive" to one's constituents.

Edmund Burke, who championed the trustee theory of representation, put this well in a speech in which he explained his role as a member of Parliament:

> Certainly, gentlemen, it ought to be the happiness and glory of a representative to live in the strictest union, the closest correspondence, and the most unreserved communication with his constituents. Their wishes ought to have great weight with him; their opinion, high respect; their business, unremitted attention. It is his duty to sacrifice his repose, his pleasures, his satisfactions, to theirs; and above all, ever, and in all cases, to prefer their interest to his own.[58]

According to Burke, it is neither indifference nor impartiality but sacrificing personal interests in favor of the constituents' interests that defines the essence of good legislative representation.

Now, what happens when we inject substantial financial temptation in the form of stock market trades based on information that few others have? Legislators are likely to succumb to this temptation and make decisions that they would not have made but for their financial self-interest. By definition, this deviation is bad because it departs from a decision based on the merits responsive to one's constituents.[59]

Moreover, when members base their legislative decisions on what maximizes their financial self-interest and not on what maximizes the public's welfare, they are invariably distorting government spending priorities and misallocating the financial resources of the federal government. For example, suppose that the Chair of the House Appropriations Committee believes that a particular military vehicle, manufactured by a small publicly traded corporation, is ultimately unsuitable for the Defense Department's purposes. But it is a close call because there is no obviously better alternative in the marketplace. Suppose further that this member's four children, who are each one year apart in age, will soon be attending college. If he advocates strongly in favor of the military vehicle, there is a good chance that the expenditure will be approved. And if he also purchases stock in advance, he stands to gain a hefty profit, which could help pay for tuition. Because of his personal financial situation, this member will be sorely tempted to advocate in favor of the military expenditure, notwithstanding his understanding of the merits. Such a decision risks a serious misallocation of government resources.[60] And it is not just that

---

[57]   The distinction between delegates and trustees in political theory is based on the "reasons for their decisions—whether they decide according to expressed preferences of the persons they represent [(delegate theory)], or according to representatives' judgments about the interests of the persons they represent [(trustee theory)]." Thompson, supra note 1, at 99–100.

[58]   Edmund Burke, Speeches at Mr. Burke's Arrival at Bristol, and at the Conclusion of the Poll, in The Works of the Right Honourable Edmund Burke 438, 446–47 (ed. Henry G. Bohn) (1954).

[59]   Members should not be beholden to influences that are decidedly irrelevant to the process of legislative deliberation. Thompson, supra note 31, at 20.

[60]   Indeed, studies indicate that corrupt procurements often lead to the diversion of government contracts toward suppliers of substandard quality, sometimes at higher prices and sometimes

legislators will be tempted to cast a bad *vote*. Temptation costs are likely to pervade all forms of legislative work, such as making phone calls, setting agendas, giving speeches, subpoenaing witnesses, asking questions in hearings, and so on. Indeed, entrepreneurial legislators might more proactively[61] try to hustle up trading opportunities by redirecting research resources, reorganizing their offices, and rewriting the rules of legislative ethics.[62]

True, financial temptation will not always change a legislator's behavior. Even in the case of outright bribery, one could imagine a situation in which the bribe does not actually lead to a bad decision. For example, suppose that, for a particular environmentally conscious member of Congress, a good decision—i.e., one based on the merits responsive to his constituents—would be to favor some carbon emissions cap on automobiles. Even if there were no bribe, he would vote in its favor. But he happens to be bribed to do so by an electronic car battery company, which would benefit from the legislation. Since the member would have voted in favor of the emissions cap regardless of the bribe, one could say that there was no consequential harm.[63] In a similar vein, apologists for corruption point out that bribes may occasionally lead to efficient outcomes.[64]

But this is ivory tower thinking. Yes, it is possible that isolated cases of bribery or other forms of corruption could fit into this scenario. But we will generally lack the evidence to be certain. In reality, perfect information is not available. There is often nothing in the nature of legislative acts (e.g., a vote in favor of or against proposed legislation) that provides obvious evidence of financially self-interested motivation. Take, for example, the investments of Representative Ron Paul (Republican, Texas). According to his financial disclosure for the year 2010, Paul owned $1.6 million to $3.5 million in gold-mining stocks, as well as a stake in three bear-market funds—funds designed to perform well when the S&P 500 and Nasdaq perform poorly. Previous disclosures from 1994 to 2002 reported that Paul held "semi-numismatic" coins worth

---

for inappropriate technologies. Tanja Rabl, Private Corruption and its Actors: Insights into the Subjective Decision Making Processes 64 (2008). Also, empirical work has found high levels of corruption to be associated with underinvestment in education (which provides fewer opportunities for bribery) and overinvestment in public infrastructure. Rose-Ackerman, supra note 41, at 2–3 (summarizing findings).

[61]   For example, with respect to bribery, economic research indicates that once bribery becomes pervasive in a society, government officials do not remain passive recipients of cash but rather become active extortionists of fees. Klitgaard, supra note 33, at 41–42. Citizens, too, increasingly "invest their energies in the pursuit of illicit favors . . ." Id. at 44.

[62]   Cf. Susan Rose-Ackerman, Corruption: Greed, Culture, and the State, 120 Yale L. J. Online 125, 135 (2010) (describing the potential effects of unchecked corruption).

[63]   Under federal law, acceptance of a bribe is illegal, regardless of whether the official's conduct was actually influenced. See, e.g., U.S. v. Valle, 538 F.3d 341, 346 (2008); U.S. v. Quinn, 359 F.3d 666, 675 (2004).

[64]   For reviews of arguments maintaining that corruption may occasionally be socially beneficial, see Rabl, supra note 60, at 64; Rose-Ackerman, supra note 41, at 21; Klitgaard, supra note 33, at 30–36. For critiques of such arguments, see Rose-Ackerman, supra note 41, at 26; Klitgaard, supra note 33, at 36 (concluding that corruption's "positive effects . . . were seldom encountered").

between $100,000 and $250,000, and over the past 16 years Paul has invested heavily in gold-mining stocks.[65]

Paul's policy positions as a legislator are remarkably consistent with his financial positions. Since December 2010, Paul has been the Chairman of the House Subcommittee on Domestic Monetary Policy.[66] In 2011, he voted against House Speaker John Boehner's plan to raise the nation's $14.3 trillion spending cap in an effort to avoid a default on U.S. debt.[67] And, since at least 1981, Paul has advocated returning the U.S. to the gold standard and for years has advocated abolishing the Federal Reserve Board.[68] A few years ago, Paul even told the *New York Times*, "We will go back to the gold standard, even if it takes the near-destruction of the dollar to get there."[69]

Were Paul's legislative judgments distorted by his financial investments?[70] Or did Paul simply put his money where his mouth is—which is why his investments track his policy convictions? How could we know? It is precisely the impossibility of ascertaining Paul's true motivations—whether he voted *because of*, *regardless of*, or *despite* private gain—that is the problem.

It is not just that third parties might not know what Paul's motivations are. Paul himself might not know since he, like everyone else, lacks introspective access into the more subtle yet pervasive causes of his own behavior.[71] Although we all want to believe that we are rational and deliberate authors of our own conduct, cognitive psychology teaches that our mental processes "operate to a great extent without our conscious awareness"[72] and much of our behavior is influenced by forces whose impact we tend to systematically dis-

---

[65]   Jim McTague, Candidate of Doom and Gloom, online.barrons.com (Aug. 20, 2011), http://online.barrons.com/article/SB50001424052702303822904576516114289723344.html (last visited Nov. 19, 2012).

[66]   Paul Appointed Chairman of Domestic Monetary Policy Subcommittee, paul.house.gov (Dec. 9, 2010), http://paul.house.gov/index.php?option=com_content&view=article&id=1806:paul-appointed-chairman-of-domestic-monetary-policy-subcommittee&catid=32:2010-press-releases (last visited Nov. 19, 2012).

[67]   McTague, supra note 65.

[68]   Ron Paul, End the Fed (2009).

[69]   Annie Lowrey, End the Fed? Actually, Maybe Not., slate.com (Feb. 9, 2011), http://www.slate.com/articles/business/moneybox/2011/02/end_the_fed_actually_maybe_not.2.html (last visited Nov. 19, 2012).

[70]   To clarify, I am not asserting that Paul's legislative judgments are, as a factual matter, distorted by his investments. As noted by Stark, "The problem, though, is that we cannot directly peer into an officeholder's mental state as she comes to judgment, cannot gauge the extent to which she remained admirably impervious to—or else was all-too-fallibly mindful of—her own interests. Since no law could effectively forbid officials from becoming judgmentally impaired by their own interests . . . conflict-of-interest regulation instead prohibits the holding of certain kinds of interest altogether." Stark, supra note 46, at 4.

[71]   See Richard E. Nisbett & Timothy DeCamp Wilson, Telling More than We Can Know: Verbal Reports on Mental Processes, 84 Psychol. Rev. 231 (1977); Timothy DeCamp Wilson & Richard E. Nisbett, The Accuracy of Verbal Reports About the Effects of Stimuli on Evaluations and Behavior, 41 Soc. Psychol. 118 (1978). See also Daniel Hays Lowenstein, On Campaign Finance Reform: The Root of All Evil is Deeply Rooted, 18 Hofstra L. Rev. 301, 325 (1989) (making a similar point with respect to the influence of campaign contributions).

[72]   Sung Hui Kim, The Banality of Fraud: Re-situating the Inside Counsel as Gatekeeper, 74 Fordham L. Rev. 983, 1026 (2005) [hereinafter Kim, Banality].

count.[73] And prominent among those pervasive, unconscious influences is the motivation of financial self-interest.[74]

Given this evidentiary uncertainty, *ex post* determination of whether some legislative decision making was altered by the potential for private gain will be costly, nearly impossible. Thus, it makes sense to adopt an *ex ante* prophylactic rule to prevent the temptation in the first place. In addition, a prophylactic ban on trading on material nonpublic information can be justified on accountability grounds. As Dennis Thompson has argued, citizens "have the right to insist, as the price of trust in a democracy, that officials not give reason to doubt their trustworthiness."[75] As a result, officials have a "responsibility not only to act for the right reasons but also to provide reasonable assurances that they are doing so" and "avoid acting under conditions that give rise to a reasonable belief of wrongdoing."[76]

B. Distraction Costs

Temptation to pursue one's financial self-interest, which potentially misallocates the government's financial resources, is not the only harm that can arise from public corruption. Another harm is the distraction occasioned by the excessive pursuit of private gain—in effect, the misallocation of a legislator's time. Consider, for instance, that Senator Kerry (Democrat, Massachusetts) and his wife completed 111 transactions (103 of which were buys) of pharmaceutical and health insurance companies in 2003 while the prescription drug benefit of the Medicare program was being debated in Congress.[77] Or consider that Congressman Jim Moran (Democrat, Virginia), a member of the Appropriations Committee, sold shares in 90 different companies on September 17, 2008—one day after members of Congress were briefed about the Administration's plan to bail out AIG.[78] The staggering volume of such trading activity raises a genuine question about whether these legislators are devoting sufficient attention and focus to perform their jobs competently. The distraction costs of corruption have been amply documented in numerous case studies, which observe that energies of corrupt bureaucrats are channeled toward the pursuit of "corrupt business interests, leaving behind what is their expected primary work."[79]

C. Legitimacy Costs

Finally, public corruption may generate another type of harm—one that is not localized but more systemic in nature and thus difficult to quantify. If citizens widely perceive

---

[73] See Don A. Moore & George Loewenstein, Self-Interest, Automaticity, and the Psychology of Conflict of Interest, 17 Soc. Just. Res. 189 (2004).

[74] See Kim, Banality, supra note 72, 1027–29. See also Lowenstein, supra note 71, at 324 (noting that "an individual whose own self-interest is at stake finds it difficult to view a situation dispassionately and objectively").

[75] Thompson, supra note 31, at 126.

[76] Id. at 23, 126.

[77] John Kerry, Financial Disclosure, 2003; Peter Schweizer, Throw Them All Out 17, 19 (2011).

[78] James Moran, Financial Disclosure, 2009; Schweizer, supra note 77, at 33.

[79] Klitgaard, supra note 33, at 38.

that legislators are not acting independently in the sense that they are making decisions to further their own financial self-interest, then the legitimacy of the legislature may be further undermined. This erosion of legitimacy may, in turn, translate into less citizen compliance with the law. By "legitimacy," I mean the property that a governmental authority, rule, or decision holds when the "relevant public regards it as justified, appropriate, or otherwise deserving of support for reasons beyond fear of sanctions or mere hope for personal reward."[80] A government that is perceived as sociologically legitimate is signified by an "active belief by [its] citizens, whether warranted or not, that particular claims to authority deserve respect or obedience for reasons not restricted to self-interest."[81]

Tom Tyler's groundbreaking 1990 panel study on legal compliance offers strong evidence to support the argument that when citizens believe that legal authorities violate norms of procedural fairness, the legitimacy of those legal authorities erodes, and citizens become less compliant with laws.[82] Using data collected from a random sample of 1,575 respondents and a subsequent random subset of 804 respondents, Tyler examined respondents' actual experiences with the police and courts, including changes in perceived legitimacy resulting from such experiences.[83] Because legitimacy is an abstract concept that is difficult to measure, Tyler identified two proxies that would serve as indirect measures or indicators of legitimacy: (1) citizens' self-reports of their perceived obligation to obey the law (irrespective of their personal views about whether the law was wrong or right); and (2) their general affective orientation toward legal authorities, i.e., the police and the courts. Tyler found that each indicator of legitimacy influenced citizens' actual compliance with the laws.[84]

But what then determined whether a person would have high or low indicators of legitimacy? Tyler found that a crucial determinant was the perceived fairness of the procedures that legal authorities followed, independent of the actual substantive outcome of those procedures.[85] Among the various factors relevant to common perceptions of procedural fairness were the honesty of the decision maker (whether the official was motivated to be just) and the decision maker's reliance on objective information to reach decisions.[86] To summarize, then, Tyler demonstrated that perceptions of procedural fairness predict indicators of legitimacy (measured as felt obligations to obey laws and as affective regard to legal authorities), which in turn predicts behavioral compliance.

Tyler made similar findings in subsequent research examining the legitimacy of members of Congress. Using both experimental and survey methodologies, Tyler found that citizens' judgments about the procedural fairness of congressional decision making independently influenced the legitimacy of members of Congress, as measured by respondents' proactive willingness to vote for political leaders, perceived obligations to

---

[80]   Richard H. Fallon, Jr., Legitimacy and the Constitution, 118 Harv. L. Rev. 1787, 1795 (2005).
[81]   Id.
[82]   See Tom R. Tyler, Why People Obey the Law 64 (1990).
[83]   Tyler, supra note 82, at 8–13.
[84]   Id. at 47, 62.
[85]   Id. at 102. Tyler generally refers to the fairness of the procedures followed as "procedural justice."
[86]   Id. at 164.

follow federal laws, and attitudinal support for authorities.[87] Citizens regarded legislators' honesty in their decision making, reliance on relevant information to reach decisions, and general trustworthiness as important components of procedural fairness.[88] In sum, Tyler's research shows that if citizens perceive that legal authorities, including the police, courts, and congressional Representatives, are making decisions based on unfair procedures, then citizens are less likely to: (1) accept those decisions; (2) regard those authorities as being legitimate; and (3) feel obligations to obey the laws. These findings are broadly consistent with empirical studies reporting cynicism, apathy, and regime instability in those developing countries that report widespread public perception of corruption.[89] What can we reasonably infer from this line of research? Insider trading by members of Congress and other government officials will be viewed by citizens as procedurally unfair—dishonest and corrupt. Casual empiricism, in the form of a review of public comments posted in response to on-line news reports of congressional insider trading, supports this hypothesis. Those comments condemn the practice of congressional insider trading as an "outrage" and "the very essence of corruption," denounce legislators-traders as "crooks [who] are taking advantage of their jobs to become richer" and "criminals," and urge that they be "prosecuted for betraying the public trust . . . and outright theft."[90] It should be no surprise, then, that the vast majority of Americans believe that insider trading laws should be enforced against legislators.[91] According to Tyler's research, to the extent that public perception of unfairness is widespread and endures, the legitimacy of Congress would erode, decreasing overall legal compliance. I do not want to overstate the point because, given today's cynical political climate, the government is probably viewed as procedurally unfair for myriad other reasons besides insider trading. That said, the fact that incremental harms to legitimacy are difficult to quantify should not lead one to dismiss the damage to governmental legitimacy as insignificant.

In sum, governmental insider trading constitutes public corruption, the use of public office for private gain. This is normatively problematic because it incurs temptation, distraction, and legitimacy costs.

V.   CORPORATE INSIDER TRADING AS PRIVATE CORRUPTION

Above I posited a plausible definition of public corruption—the use of public office for private gain—and articulated its various harms. But corruption is not constrained to the public sphere. As noted by John Kleinig and William C. Heffernan, "[c]orruption is not

---

[87]   Tom R. Tyler, Governing Amid Diversity: The Effect of Fair Decisionmaking Procedures on the Legitimacy of Government, 28 Law & Soc'y Rev. 809, 828 (1994).

[88]   Id. at 824.

[89]   Klitgaard, supra note 33, at 45.

[90]   See Insider: The Road to the Stock Act, cbsnews.com (June 17, 2012, 4:00 pm), http://www.cbsnews.com/video/watch/?id=7411992n&tag=component.0;topnews (last visited Nov. 19, 2012); Confronting Pelosi on Insider Trading, supra note 51 (comments on Sixty Minutes' report on governmental insider trading).

[91]   See supra note 50.

the exclusive failing of public officers; there may also be personal corruption, corrupt institutions, and corrupt cultures."[92] Even the *Oxford English Dictionary* refers to corruption within a "public corporation" in one of nine definitions listed for "corruption."[93] Indeed, there is no reason to think that the secondary harms associated with public corruption in terms of temptation, distraction, and legitimacy are unique to the public sector. For example, the misappropriation of funds is improper for the same reason regardless of whether the misappropriator is a public official or private citizen.[94] Assuming that corruption also afflicts the private sector, how would we define it? Unfortunately, defining "private corruption" is even more elusive than defining "public corruption." Unlike public corruption, private corruption has received almost no academic attention.[95] But here finally comes some of the payoff of examining corporate insider trading by way of governmental insider trading. We can craft a definition of private corruption by making minor modifications to our definition of public corruption (the use of public office for private gain).

Since we are addressing the private sphere, there is no "public office," but there is the position of being a fiduciary. Also, since we are exclusively in the private sphere, the term "private gain" fails to distinguish between the fiduciary's financial self-interest and that of the firm. Accordingly, a term such as "personal gain" can help distinguish between the two. By making these twin substitutions, we can define private corruption as the use of a fiduciary position for personal gain.[96]

Just as governmental insider trading could be seen as public corruption defined as the use of public office for private gain, corporate insider trading can be seen as private corruption defined as the use of one's fiduciary position for personal gain. First, such trading is a personal, self-serving, out-of-role activity undertaken by corporate insiders. There is nothing in the job description of officers or directors that requires them to use confidential information that they have gathered through their positions to employ personal funds to trade in securities. Nor are profits generated from insider trading generally regarded as an acceptable perquisite of executive status.[97] Secondly, such trading opportunities flow from their fiduciary position, i.e., they would not have such lucrative trading opportunities *but for* the information gained by virtue of their corporate positions.

---

[92]   Kleinig & Heffernan, supra note 41, at 3.

[93]   The sixth definition of "corruption" states: "Perversion or destruction of integrity in the discharge of public duties by bribery or favour; the use or existence of corrupt practices, *esp.* in a state, public corporation, etc." Oxford English Dictionary 974 (2nd ed. 1989).

[94]   Thompson, supra note 31, at 53.

[95]   See Rabl, supra note 60, at 18 (noting that "private corruption, that is, corruption in and between companies, is still a neglected topic").

[96]   For private corruption, "personal gain" is gain that not only directly benefits the fiduciary in question but also inures to the fiduciary's family, relatives, or friends.

[97]   A Business Week poll conducted in 1986 reported that 52 percent believed that insider trading should continue to be illegal. William A. Kelly, Jr. et al., Regulation of Insider Trading: Rethinking SEC Policy Rules, 7 Cato Journal 441 (1987). While this result does not seem like a serious indictment, more recent public reaction to the Martha Stewart scandal suggests that insider trading continues to be unpopular. See Alexandre Padilla, How Do We Think About Insider Trading? An Economist's Perspective on the Insider Trading Debate and its Impact, 4 J. L. Econ. & Pol'y 239, 253–54 (2008).

As already discussed, skeptics such as Henry Manne would retort, what's wrong with that? I maintain that private corruption in the form of corporate insider trading is harmful for the same types of reason that public corruption in the form of governmental insider trading is harmful. As noted, governmental insider trading is harmful because it tempts government officials, including members of Congress, into bad policymaking; distracts them from their tasks; and threatens to erode the legitimacy of government, including the legislative process. Analogously, corporate insider trading is harmful because it tempts corporate managers into bad decision making (i.e., making corporate decisions based on what maximizes the manager's own financial interests rather than the interests of the corporation); distracts them from their fiduciary tasks; and threatens to erode corporate legitimacy.

A.   Temptation Costs

First, the opportunity to profit from corporate insider trading tempts managers into making corporate decisions based not on the primary goal of enhancing corporate value[98] but rather on the goal of generating insider trading profits. These temptations can take myriad forms. Managers will be tempted to delay transmission of information to superiors until after the trade has been made; prematurely disclose information to the public once the trade has been made; select particular accounting practices in an effort to affect share prices and maximize insider returns; structure transactions in ways that maximize opportunities for keeping information secret; and select projects based not so much on their likely contribution to long-term corporate value but on their potential to produce dramatic price movements from which insiders can profit handsomely.[99]

Importantly, the temptation to introduce volatility into the share price is largely indifferent to the direction of the price movements.[100] After all, one can profit just as easily and as much from destroying corporate value and short selling as one can from increasing corporate value. To be sure, destroying corporate value may get an insider fired. However, in many cases the manager already expects to exit (regardless of the trading opportunity). To the extent that there are "last period agency costs,"[101] the manager may want to secure for himself a covert severance package on the way out, especially if destroying corporate value is easier than enhancing it (as it undoubtedly is).

---

[98]   In this chapter, I do not revisit the longstanding debate over the proper purpose of the corporation. See, e.g., Adolf A. Berle, Corporate Powers as Powers in Trust, 44 Harv. L. Rev. 1049 (1931); E. Merrick Dodd, For Whom Are Corporate Managers Trustees? 45 Harv. L. Rev. 1148 (1932). Suffice it to say that neither a shareholder- nor stakeholder-oriented view of corporate purposes would obviously endorse the practice of insider trading.

[99]   Stephen M. Bainbridge, Insider Trading, in III Encyclopedia of Law and Economics 772, 788–90 (eds Boudewin Bouckaert & Gerrit De Geest) (2000).

[100]   James D. Cox, Insider Trading and Contracting: A Response to the "Chicago School," 1986 Duke L. J. 628, 651–52 (1986); Saul Levmore, Securities and Secrets: Insider Trading and the Law of Contracts, 68 Va. L. Rev. 117, 149 (1982).

[101]   "Last period agency costs" occur when agents fear themselves to be in their last period of employment. Jennifer H. Arlen & William J. Carney, Vicarious Liability for Fraud on Securities Markets: Theory and Evidence, 1992 U. Ill. L. Rev. 691 (1992).

The opportunity to profit from corporate insider trading thus risks a serious misallocation of the corporation's financial resources. Instead of corporate value being the primary benchmark, the element of self-enrichment will distort corporate decision making. As Saul Levmore has written, "Overinvestment might develop in certain industries (or in exploration itself) and underinvestment in others, as insiders guide their firms into enterprises that generate 'events' that might be capitalized upon by traders in the stock market who have early access to the relevant information."[102] Moreover, if corporate insider trading goes unchecked by law, insiders will be tempted to reorganize their offices, rewrite corporate codes of conduct, and structure their activities in ways to generate larger insider trading profits.

At least one court has explicitly acknowledged that corporate insider trading generates just these temptation costs. In the 1969 case of *Diamond v. Oreamuno*,[103] a case of first impression for the New York Court of Appeals, shareholders filed a derivative action against the officers and directors of the company to account for gains generated from trades in the company's stock based on material nonpublic information "acquired by them solely by virtue of their positions" relating to an anticipated change in the company's earnings.[104] In rejecting the defendants' argument that damages must be specifically pleaded in order to state a claim based on a breach of fiduciary duty, the court noted that "unlike an ordinary tort or contract case," an action based on a breach of fiduciary duty "is not merely to *compensate* the plaintiff for wrongs committed by the defendant but, as this court declared many years ago . . ., 'to prevent them, by removing from agents and trustees all inducement to attempt dealing for their own benefit in matters which they have undertaken for others, or to which their agency or trust relates.'"[105]

Thus, the *Diamond* court allowed a breach of fiduciary duty claim for corporate insider trading to proceed based on the recognition that corporate fiduciaries should avoid "inducements" or temptations that compromise their ability to deal in matters relating to their trust. In highlighting the inchoate nature of the harms to be avoided, the court supported adopting an *ex ante* prophylactic ban on insider trading as a means of preventing temptations in the first place.

B.   Distraction Costs

Secondly, corporate insider trading may generate nontrivial distraction costs by "invit[ing] managers to devote some significant portion of the time and attention that they might otherwise devote to running the business to identifying trading profit opportunities."[106] Victor Brudney and Robert Clark warned about distraction costs but in a different context—relating to a fiduciary's misappropriation of corporate opportunities:

---

[102]   Levmore, supra note 100, at 149.

[103]   24 N.Y.2d 494, 248 N.E.2d 910 (N.Y. 1969).

[104]   24 N.Y.2d 496. The defendants knew that, as a result of increased expenses, their net earnings would decline significantly. Prior to the release of that information, they sold stock, avoiding a loss of $800,000. 24 N.Y.2d 497.

[105]   24 N.Y.2d 498–99 (citations omitted).

[106]   Donald C. Langevoort, Insider Trading: Regulation, Enforcement & Prevention, § 1:4 (2011).

The duties of the executives of a public corporation normally require full-time application of their managerial talents and energies and leave no room for active participation in the development or operation of other businesses. Correspondingly, their compensation arrangements are such that neither equity nor efficiency requires them to be allowed to take covert indirect compensation as they see fit.[107]

I do not want to overstate my case. The distraction costs posed by corporate insider trading are probably less than the distraction costs posed by misappropriating corporate opportunities. After all, the misappropriation and exploitation of a corporate opportunity should consume a significant amount of the insider's time. By contrast, an inside trade can be executed via a few text messages to one's broker. Similarly, the distraction costs posed by *corporate* insider trading may be less than the distraction costs posed by *governmental* insider trading. In many cases of governmental insider trading, the material nonpublic information will impact the stock prices of *multiple* issuers, e.g., various companies in a particular industry that may be impacted by proposed legislation. A member of Congress researching potential trades may thus be forced to research multiple companies in industries that are unfamiliar. By contrast, most (but not all) cases of corporate insider trading will involve information that impacts the stock prices of a single familiar issuer—the corporation for whom the corporate insider works. That said, the fact that distraction costs in some other context may be relatively large does not mean that the distraction costs in this context are absolutely small or trivial.

C.   Legitimacy Costs

Thirdly, corporate insider trading may undermine the legitimacy of corporate officials (and, derivatively, the corporation) in the eyes of public investors. As we learned above, perceptions of unfairness undermine the legitimacy of legal and political authorities. But what about the legitimacy of corporate authorities? Although "legitimacy" is normally used to refer to legal and political authorities, the concept can usefully be applied to the private sector. After all, corporate authorities can also command or lack the respect, support, and trust of the consuming or investing public. One need only be reminded of the rankings of "The Best & Worst Boards"[108] to understand that corporate authorities are judged not merely on shareholder returns but on perceptions of "good" or "bad" governance quality—criteria often associated with legal and political authorities. Unfortunately, there appears to be no empirical research that specifically examines the link between insider trading and corporate legitimacy.

However, one can draw inferences from studies building on Tyler's research and linking *employees'* fairness perceptions to their attitudinal support for corporate managers. For example, Roger Folger and Mary Konovsky conducted a survey of 217 first-line employees of a private manufacturing plant and found that employees' perceptions about the fairness of procedures used to determine pay raises positively correlated with their

---

[107]   Victor Brudney & Robert Charles Clark, A New Look at Corporate Opportunities, 94 Harv. L. Rev. 997, 1003 (1981).

[108]   See The Best & Worst Boards, businessweek.com (Oct. 7, 2002), http://www.businessweek. com/magazine/content/02_40/b3802001.htm (last visited Nov. 19, 2012).

organizational commitment and trust in their supervisors, independent of the substantive outcome of their pay raises.[109] Also, Brockner et al. conducted a study of 150 employees of a financial services organization and found that employees' perceptions about the fairness of the decision rule adopted to determine lay-offs positively correlated with employees' organizational commitment.[110] Both studies adopted similar definitions of "organizational commitment" as including: (1) a belief in or identification with the organization's goals or values; (2) a willingness to expend extra effort on the organization's behalf; and (3) an intention to remain with the organization.[111] In short, these studies suggest that attitudinal support for corporate authorities can erode as a function of the perceived fairness of corporate actions and decisions.

All of this begs the question: is corporate insider trading viewed as "unfair"? Justice Blackmun declared as much in his dissent in *Chiarella* and called insider trading "inherently unfair."[112] But commentators in the law and economics tradition have dismissed such claims as fuzzy, or in Manne's words "puerile."[113]

Of course, the fact that some elite academics dismiss unfairness arguments says little about how ordinary investors feel. The investing public is likely to view profits obtained through insider trading as a form of undeserved gain—an advantage accrued not through effort, ingenuity, or risk taking but through special access. And, in the case of insider trading by corporate insiders under the classical theory, this sense of unfairness is compounded by the fact that investors necessarily rely on corporate managers to produce information on which to assess corporate value. Just imagine the reaction if the viewing public found out that the host of the Jeopardy! quiz show was feeding clues to a friend contestant who just happened to trounce all his competitors. Or what if it was discovered that an Iron Chef competitor—tasked to create multiple delectable dishes all based on some "secret ingredient" that is dramatically revealed at the show's start—had known the secret all along, because of intimate access to the show's producer? Would there be a public relations disaster? Certainly. Would such outrage be dismissed as infantile jealousy of adept competitors? I doubt it. The point here is not to defend such reactions on grounds that would satisfy a moral philosopher but simply to predict the brute fact of public outcry.

Finally, beyond undermining the legitimacy of a single firm, if corporate insider trading is viewed as rampant and unchecked by law, the legitimacy of the entire U.S.

---

[109]   Roger Folger & Mary A. Konovsky, Effects of Procedural and Distributive Justice on Reactions to Pay Raise Decisions, 32 Acad. of Management J. 115, 125 (1989).

[110]   Joel Brockner, Tom R. Tyler, & Rochelle Cooper-Schneider, The Influence of Prior Commitment to an Institution on Reactions to Perceived Unfairness: The Higher They Are, the Harder They Fall, 37 Admin. Sci. Q. 241, 248–49 (1992).

[111]   Id. at 244; Folger & Konovsky, supra note 109, at 119 (referring to Organizational Commitment Questionnaire of Mowday et al.).

[112]   Chiarella v. US, 445 U.S. 222 at 248 (Blackmun J. dissenting).

[113]   Manne, supra note 4, at 182, note 60. As a result, unfairness claims have been mostly eclipsed by the popular property rights theory, which holds that the federal insider trading prohibition is most easily justified as a means of protecting property rights in information. See Jonathan R. Macey, From Fairness to Contract: The New Direction of the Rules Against Insider Trading, 13 Hofstra L. Rev. 9 (1984); Stephen M. Bainbridge, Insider Trading Under the Restatement of the Law Governing Lawyers, 19 J. Corp. L., 1 (1993).

securities markets may be put at risk. If the securities markets are viewed as rigged, then investors may lose confidence and refuse to participate in the markets, even if investing in publicly traded stocks would be the most profitable long-run investment strategy. Some evidence for this concern comes from the well-known "ultimatum games." These experiments demonstrate that people will often refuse to participate in what they perceive as an unfair transaction even if participating would further their financial self-interest.[114] In addition, some comparative empirical evidence suggests that nations with stricter insider trading laws enjoy lower costs of capital and more liquid securities markets,[115] indicating a possible inverse relationship between insider trading and investor confidence. Such loss of investor confidence would threaten the depth and liquidity of the markets. Indeed, this "investor confidence" rationale was specifically endorsed by the Supreme Court in *O'Hagan* to justify its extension of federal insider trading doctrine to include misappropriation theory.[116]

To be sure, this fear has been dismissed as just a bogeyman. For example, the much publicized insider trading scandals of the mid-1980s and subsequent robustness of the U.S. securities markets have been cited as evidence that insider trading does not seriously threaten investor confidence.[117] Of course, one could read the available evidence differently and emphasize the impact of the vigorous prosecution of insider traders and the swift passage of the Insider Trading and Securities Fraud Enforcement Act of 1988. On this interpretation, while investors were on notice that insider trading was common,[118] investors were also put on notice that—like other serious crimes—violations would be severely prosecuted.

VI. CONCLUSION

Commentators have correctly described federal insider trading doctrine as anomalous, odd, and incongruous.[119] But we should not be surprised by doctrinal incoherence when the very nature of the harms to be avoided is inchoate and systemic and therefore difficult to precisely define, locate, and quantify. The courts have responded to these complexities

---

[114]   See, e.g., Matthew Rabin, Incorporating Fairness into Game Theory and Economics, 83 Am. Econ. Rev. 1281 (1993); Colin Camerer & Richard H. Thaler, Anomalies: Ultimatums, Dictators and Manners, 9 J. Econ. Persp. 209 (1995).

[115]   Robert A. Prentice, The Inevitability of a Strong SEC, 91 Cornell L. Rev. 775, 831, note 347 (2006); Utpal Bhattacharya & Hazem Daouk, The World Price of Insider Trading, 57 J. Fin. 75, 97 (2002); Laura Nyantung Beny, Insider Trading Laws and Stock Markets Around the World: An Empirical Contribution to the Theoretical Law and Economics Debate, 32 J. Corp. L. 237 (2007).

[116]   U.S. v. O'Hagan, 521 U.S. 642, 658 (1997) (citations omitted) (noting that misappropriation theory is "well tuned to an animating purpose of the Exchange Act: to insure honest securities markets and thereby promote investor confidence").

[117]   Critics argue that these scandals had "put all investors on notice that insider trading is a common securities violation." Bainbridge, supra note 99, at 786.

[118]   See Padilla, supra note 97, at 253–54 (2008) (citing results of public opinion poll taken in the wake of the 1986 insider trading scandals, reporting that 69 percent of respondents believed that insider trading was common).

[119]   Bainbridge, Introduction to this *Handbook*.

by incrementally expanding federal insider trading doctrine to encompass temporary insiders, tippers, tippees, and even fiduciaries of firms not connected with the proscribed trades. This gradual expansion can be seen as judicial gropings to restrain a form of private corruption that, if left unchecked, could undermine investor confidence in the securities markets. The Supreme Court seemed to recognize that insider trading can generate these more systemic harms in *U.S. v. O'Hagan*:

> If the market is thought to be systematically populated with . . . transactors [trading on the basis of misappropriated information] some investors will refrain from dealing altogether, and others will incur costs to avoid dealing with such transactors or *corruptly* to overcome their unerodable informational advantages.[120]

In my view, understanding corporate insider trading as a form of private sector corruption helps explain why it is normatively problematic and should be proscribed. This insight about corruption came via a careful examination of governmental insider trading. Henry Manne was right. There is no good reason to tolerate governmental insider trading, given temptation, distraction, and legitimacy costs. But Manne was also wrong—since the same holds true for corporate insider trading.

---

[120] O'Hagan, supra note 116, at 658 (quoting Victor Brudney, Insiders, Outsiders, and Informational Advantages under the Federal Securities Laws, 93 Harv. L. Rev. 322, 356 (1979) (emphasis added).

11. A portrait of the insider trader as a woman
Joan MacLeod Heminway

The stock image of the perp walk for an insider trader is that of a besuited male—not too old, not too young—being led away by law enforcement officials (similarly clothed and also male). The suit and the age may be of marginal significance in this stereotypical profile. Yet the sex and gender[1] of the standard, run-of-the-mill insider trader is certainly male. This is, perhaps, unremarkable. Men have historically been the predominant trading participants in the securities markets. And so they must also be the predominant violators of trading rules, insider trading included.

Yet, since 2000, women have more frequently served as poster children for transgressions of US prohibitions on insider trading under § 10(b) of the Securities Exchange Act of 1934, as amended, and Rule 10b-5 as adopted under § 10(b) by the US Securities and Exchange Commission (SEC), either as defendants or as unwitting participants. Martha Stewart is undoubtedly the most visible example of a female image in an insider trading story. But other examples, not household names in other respects, also form part of a more visible presence of women in insider trading cases and controversies. These women include Carolyn Balkenhol, Danielle Chiesi, Randi Collotta, Nina Devlin, Kathryn Gannon (a/k/a Marilyn Star), Christie Heffner, Winnifred Jiau, Charlotte Ka On Wong Leung, Serenella Lina, Annabel McClellan, Donna Murdoch, Monie Rahman and Patricia Rocklage, to name a few.

Although it may be interesting and seemingly unusual to see more women as the veritable face of insider trading in the USA, one must wonder whether this change has any substantive significance. What, if anything, does sex or gender have to do with US insider trading regulation? This chapter first addresses that question and then explores (anecdotally and through extensions of existing sex and gender studies outside the insider trading realm) the potential roles and significance of sex and gender in insider trading in the USA. In particular, omnipresent public reports of insider trading cases in which material nonpublic information is shared between romantic partners (so-called "pillow talk" cases[2]) allow us to see women in a multiplicity of roles in insider trading schemes. The lack of empirical studies illuminating potential sexed or gendered information asymmetries,

---

[1] For a helpful and lucid discussion of sex and gender and its value in research and analysis (albeit in a different context), see Joan W. Scott, Gender: A Useful Category of Historical Analysis, 91 Am. Historical Rev. 1053 (1986). This chapter focuses on gender more than sex, while acknowledging that "the close association of gender and sex and the normative demands of conforming to the sex–gender stereotype for social recognition means that both the female sex and feminine gender are likely to be treated as equivalents." Alan Gregory et al., Does the Stock Market Gender Stereotype Corporate Boards? Evidence from the Market's Reaction to Directors' Trades, British J. of Mgmt. (forthcoming 2012) (early view at 2), available at http://onlinelibrary.wiley.com/doi/10.1111/j.1467-8551.2011.00795.x/abstract (last visited Nov. 20, 2012) (subscription required).

[2] See, e.g., Ellen Rosen, Rise in Insider-Trading Cases Shows the Perils of Pillow Talk, N.Y. Times, Aug. 24, 2007, at C6.

conceptions of duty and (more particularly) trust, risk preferences and senses of entitlement to insider trading proceeds also is a matter of concern. Although we can understand a few things about women as insider traders from existing theoretical, empirical, anecdotal and analytical information, many questions remain. Our understanding of the role that sex or gender may play in the construction and operation of insider trading prohibitions and enforcement efforts and the resulting overall picture of women as insider traders are both, as yet, incomplete.

I.   SEX OR GENDER AS A VALID LENS FOR INSIDER TRADING INQUIRY AND ANALYSIS

Insider trading law may interrelate with gender in a number of legally significant ways. For example, at a general level, the law of insider trading in the USA may be an expression of gendered principles. US insider trading law may be shaped by different conceptions of men and women and their roles in the economy and society. In addition (or instead), the operation of the rules governing insider trading in the USA may interact with gender in distinct ways: US insider trading regulation may engage men and women differently or it may have disparate impacts on market participants based on gender. Scholars have begun to explore these possibilities using theory and empirical data gathered in the lab and in the field. Insights from this work allow for a richer understanding and critique of the law governing insider trading regulation in the USA.

A.   Insider Trading as an Expression of Gendered Principles

Although its potential origins in gendered economic and societal conceptions may be non-obvious, the law of insider trading may be gender-constructed—at least in part. In 1998, Professor Judith Greenberg assessed the possible gendered nature of US insider trading regulation in a notable law review article.[3] In that work, she contended that insider trading law was shaped by the federal courts' perceptions of gendered roles in the economy and society—specifically, gendered roles that operate in markets and in families.

> [I]deas about gender, through their connection to the concepts of market and family, play a part in forming insider trading law. Insider trading law is understood to be law of and for the market, but not the family. Thus, concepts of "family" work to determine the limits of insider trading law.[4]

Specifically, Professor Greenberg concludes that "[i]nsider trading law today is premised on retaining the difference between markets and families, men and women."[5] She supports her argument by establishing the organizational utility of markets and family as a descrip-

---

[3]   Judith G. Greenberg, Insider Trading and Family Values, 4 Wm. & Mary J. of Women & L. 303 (1998).

[4]   Id. at 308.

[5]   Id. at 372.

tive dichotomy and illustrates the application of her thesis primarily through the analysis of an infamous insider trading case, *US v. Chestman*.[6]

The *Chestman* case is an early and interesting example of a pillow talk case—a special type of insider trading case, as earlier noted, typically based on the conveyance of material nonpublic information from one member of a romantically linked couple to the other.[7] In the *Chestman* case, a case involving material nonpublic information passed by a wife to her husband, the court found that kinship and marriage did not, alone, give rise to the requisite duty of trust and confidence on which insider status and insider trading liability are based.[8] Professor Greenberg notes that the result in *Chestman* reifies male/female distinctions rooted in the economic and social divide between the market and the family.[9] Specifically, Professor Greenberg notes that the *Chestman* court characterized the sharing of information and breach of trust between the wife and the husband in that case as ordinary marital relations and obligations that are not fiduciary in nature; they are matters of family and not of the market and therefore are not the basis of insider trading liability.[10] Professor Greenberg critiques this characterization and the resulting legal analysis in the case.[11]

At the same time, Professor Greenberg also notes that the court's view of the facts in *Chestman* paradoxically counters the traditional gendered roles of men and women in marriages.[12] In *Chestman*, the wife in the couple revealed material nonpublic information to her husband, who passed that information on to his broker. Would the result in *Chestman* have been different, we might ask, if the husband had revealed information to the wife and she had tipped or traded on it?

In 2000, nine years after the *Chestman* decision, the SEC adopted a rule to clarify the status of marital and other family relationships in misappropriation cases. Under Rule 10b5-2, the requisite duty of trust and confidence exists in a misappropriation case:

> Whenever a person receives or obtains material nonpublic information from his or her spouse, parent, child, or sibling; provided, however, that the person receiving or obtaining the information may demonstrate that no duty of trust or confidence existed with respect to the information, by establishing that he or she neither knew nor reasonably should have known that the person who was the source of the information expected that the person would keep the information confidential, because of the parties' history, pattern, or practice of sharing and maintaining confidences, and because there was no agreement or understanding to maintain the confidentiality of the information.[13]

---

[6]   947 F.2d 551 (2d Cir. 1991).

[7]   See supra note 2 and accompanying text; see also Chapter 1 in this volume; infra section III.

[8]   *Chestman*, 947 F.2d at 570–71.

[9]   Greenberg, supra note 3, at 331. ("An analysis of *Chestman* shows the importance of courts maintaining a clear line between market and family. Were this line to disappear, the distinction between family and market might be blurred, upsetting our notions of how to act in each realm and, thus, of male and female identity.")

[10]   Id. at 332–33.

[11]   Id. at 333–35.

[12]   Id. at 333. ("[T]he court viewed Keith and Susan Loeb's marriage as being a marriage of autonomous, self-sufficient individuals – a truly modern marriage.")

[13]   17 C.F.R. § 240.10b5-2(b)(2) (2012); see also Chapter 1 in this volume.

Rule 10b5-2 appears gender-neutral on its face. But the presumption of a duty based on the spousal relationship leaves open the possibility that a court may continue to explicitly or implicitly construct the law of insider trading based on gender through the ability of a recipient of material nonpublic information to rebut the presumed duty of trust and confidence by establishing the necessary facts, as expressly provided in the rule.

Professor Greenberg also invokes in her analysis another infamous insider trading case based on marital relations, *SEC v. Switzer*.[14] In the *Switzer* case, the husband in a married couple shared material nonpublic information with his wife for the purpose of coordinating their family activities and obligations. An acquaintance overheard the information, traded on it and tipped others. The court found no breach of duty in the husband's disclosure of the material nonpublic information to his wife under the circumstances.[15]

In describing and analyzing the *Switzer* case, Professor Greenberg notes the court's engagement with the gendered roles of the husband and wife in applying insider trading law to the facts of the case.

> [T]he court describes the conversation between husband and wife as one in which she is performing as a good wife, solicitous of his mental health . . . [S]he is described as the caring wife of separate spheres ideology. It is her job to provide solace and comfort to her husband as he deals with the troubles of the world.[16]

The stereotypical husband/wife relationship in the *Switzer* case provides a plausible explanation for the court's failure to find a breach of duty. The court may have been acting to preserve that traditional relationship and its role in the nuclear family.

Having established this gender-role premise, Professor Greenberg notes that several other, similar cases not involving heterosexual marital couples yield different results.[17] She finds the heterosexual marriage component to be compelling, if not dispositive, and ties the roles in this relationship back to her central theme: the market/family duality.

> According to the separate spheres ideology, the market is a male venue. Thus, the cases that involve the transfer of business information between men are more easily seen as involving market relations than those that involve the transfer of information among members of a heterosexual couple. Or, to phrase the point differently, relations between men and women are understood as predicated on an underlying sexual attraction and emotional attachment. These are characteristics associated with the family.[18]

In the aggregate, Professor Greenberg's analyses provide a reasonable basis for concluding that gender may have had a role in constructing US insider trading law.

The SEC's insider trading enforcement action against Martha Stewart also reveals potential gender-based roots for US insider trading regulation—or at least for the exercise of administrative enforcement discretion in insider trading cases. As a famous

---

[14]   590 F. Supp. 756 (W.D. Okla. 1984).
[15]   Id. at 766.
[16]   Greenberg, supra note 3, at 341–42.
[17]   Id. at 342–44.
[18]   Id. at 344.

television, radio and print publication personality, Martha Stewart represented a highly visible female example of insider trading to be held up for public pillory and contempt.[19] Although the SEC's case against Stewart (which involved a relatively small sum of money and was questionable on the merits for a number of reasons[20]) eventually was settled before trial, the public widely believes that Stewart was jailed for violating US insider trading prohibitions.[21] The SEC's enforcement activity more than served its purpose in personifying the modern insider trader as a woman.

The SEC's enforcement actions against Stewart can be seen as part of a larger strategy on the part of the agency to preserve and exercise its enforcement discretion with the aim of enhancing its own perceived value and serving related political aims.[22] In particular, during a time of deregulation and underfunding, it may be in the SEC's best interest to engage in high-profile enforcement activity.[23] By pursuing visible insider trading cases, the SEC may be able to improve its political leverage with the legislature, enabling it to garner additional funds and other support for its operations—while at the same time achieving specific and general deterrence aims.[24] Admittedly, visible enforcement activity was not necessarily a winning strategy for the SEC in the years immediately following the 2008 financial crisis (although the SEC's enforcement activity during that time may have prevented a more significant deterioration of its relationship with the US Congress). However, at the time the *Stewart* case was ripe for enforcement action, this strategy may have been employed with greater success.

Specifically, in early 2002 (when the SEC exercised its discretion to pursue Stewart for alleged insider trading violations), Stewart was highly visible as a public figure in a growing media/entertainment/publishing firm. Stewart's name was the business's headline, and she was a visible part of the entertainment piece of her business. Her image was recognizable to many in the United States and was associated with her name and her business. At a time when few women were recognizable as directors and officers of public companies, she was recognizable as a woman who started her own business and took it public. And, as one of few women having both the power and duties of an insider and the wealth to engage in relatively significant personal trading transactions in the market,

---

[19]   See generally Joan MacLeod Heminway, Was Martha Stewart Targeted?, in Martha Stewart's Legal Troubles 3–42 (Joan MacLeod Heminway ed., 2007) [hereinafter *Targeted*]; Joan MacLeod Heminway, Save Martha Stewart? Observations About Equal Justice in US Insider Trading Regulation, 12 Tex. J. Women & L. 247 (2003) [hereinafter *Equal Justice*].

[20]   Ray J. Grzebielski, Why Martha Stewart Did Not Violate Rule 10b-5: On Tipping, Piggybacking, Front-Running and the Fiduciary Duties of Securities Brokers, 40 Akron L. Rev. 55 (2007); Joan MacLeod Heminway, Martha Stewart: Insider Trader?, in Insider Trading: Global Developments and Analysis (Paul Ali & Greg N. Gregoriou eds., 2008).

[21]   Even reputable news outlets get this wrong. See, e.g., Congress Insiders: Above the Law?, 60 Minutes, CBSnews.com (November 11, 2011), available at http://www.cbsnews.com/8301-18560_162-57323221/congress-insiders-above-the-law/ (last visited Nov. 20, 2012).

[22]   See generally Harvey L. Pitt & Karen L. Shapiro, Securities Regulation By Enforcement: A Look Ahead At the Next Decade, 7 Yale J. on Reg. 149 (1990) (describing the interactions between SEC enforcement activity and the political realm, among other things).

[23]   See Stephen M. Bainbridge, Securities Law: Insider Trading 149 (2d ed. 2007); see also Pitt & Shapiro, supra note 22, at 184–89 (describing the importance of visibility to an effective, efficient enforcement program).

[24]   Bainbridge, supra note 23, at 149.

Stewart was a highly visible and desirable enforcement target for SEC enforcement action in part because she is a woman.

The Martha Stewart insider trading enforcement saga also exemplifies more generally a feminist construction of insider trading regulation (or, again, at least a feminist construction of enforcement discretion in the application of that body of regulation)—a construction that relies on unequal distributions of privilege and power as its core premises.[25] "Surely, there is a feminist tale to be told here—including that of male-dominated rule-makers and enforcement agents causing the fall of women who threaten their male power base and the resulting gender-infused *schadenfreude*—the joy experienced from another's misfortune."[26] In fact, it is possible that SEC enforcement discretion was exercised against Stewart at least in part because she is a woman.

> [T]he Martha Stewart investigation represents a highly publicized attempt to enforce US insider trading regulation against a woman. Accordingly, the SEC may be pursuing its insider trading enforcement action against Martha Stewart to hold her out as an example to other women (presumably as a deterrent) that alleged violations of US insider trading regulation committed by women will be vigorously pursued. . . . [S]trategic enforcement action is common and is an accepted part of overall enforcement discretion.[27]

The vagaries of insider trading regulation under § 10(b) and Rule 10b-5 create opportunities for enforcement of the law of insider trading in gender-specific ways that may reshape the contours of that law.[28]

Professor Theresa Gabaldon uses feminist analysis to examine US insider trading regulation in a 2002 article—together with Professor Greenberg's article, one of few full-length works in the area of feminism and securities regulation.[29] Like Professor Greenberg, Professor Gabaldon focuses on the nature of relationships in the context of insider trading's duty of trust and confidence in the USA. Specifically, she analyzes federal securities regulation rules (including those in US insider trading law) from the standpoint of trust-oriented relationships—noting both in-group and out-group manifestations and elements. She concludes, in relevant part, that:

> The predominant imagery of the federal securities laws is sketched by their recognized goals and enhanced by their detailed operative provisions. The central portrayals are of cold, hard, economically rational man. The usual offeror of securities is a predator, eager to sell nothing for something. His foil is a socially isolated widow or orphan who, if given enough (truthful) information will be made capable of rational, self-protective decision-making.[30]

---

[25]　Theresa A. Gabaldon, Feminism, Fairness, and Fiduciary Duty in Corporate and Securities Law, 5 Tex. J. Women & L. 1, 7 (1995) (referring to feminism's "insistent reliance on the springboard proposition that women occupy an unequal position in society").

[26]　Joan MacLeod Heminway, Martha Stewart and the Forbidden Fruit: A New Story of Eve, 2009 Mich. St. L. Rev. 1017, 1021 n.10.

[27]　Heminway, *Targeted*, supra note 19; Heminway, *Equal Justice*, supra note 19 (footnotes omitted).

[28]　Id.

[29]　Theresa A. Gabaldon, Assumptions about Relationships Reflected in the Federal Securities Laws, 17 Wis. Women's L. J. 215 (2002).

[30]　Id. at 247.

Insider trading law under § 10(b) and Rule 10b-5 can be viewed through this construct. The federal judiciary, as the key rule maker in US insider trading regulation, has largely been charged with identifying the predators whose activity needs to be channeled appropriately and the widows and orphans whose interests need to be protected. As such, Professor Gabaldon's portrayal of insider trading law in the USA also indicates that US insider trading regulation may be at least partially founded in gendered norms.

B.   The Interaction of Sex and Gender with the Operation of US Insider Trading Rules

Regardless of whether US insider trading regulation is constructed along gendered lines, its application and effects may differ based on categories of difference, including sex and gender. Increased knowledge of the biological and behavioral attributes of men and women gained from empirical studies has afforded researchers additional knowledge about innate and socialized differences in the sexes. This greater knowledge, when combined with theoretical frameworks and analysis, has enabled a richer study of the interrelation of insider trading with sex and gender.

Gender has become a more prevalent lens for inquiry and analysis as women have been moving in greater numbers into more diverse roles in the national economy and in society more generally. Women have increased their economic and financial market participation and visibility in varying sectors in the 20th and 21st centuries. Especially relevant to the subject of this chapter, women are more involved in buying and selling securities. Through empirical work on gender and securities trading, we have learned that women's behavior and outcomes in securities trading (as in other realms) are not always the same as those of men.[31] These differences in behavior and outcome may emanate from, or signal the need for changes in, the US securities regulation.

> [T]here is emerging evidence that women may behave and fare differently from men when they engage in securities trading transactions. These differences in behavior and outcome are increasingly important; around the world, growing numbers of women are investing in publicly traded securities and, as the publication of numerous female-targeted popular press books demonstrates, being encouraged to invest in the securities markets (and elsewhere) in greater amounts and with greater frequency. The increased participation of women in the securities markets may be or become market significant or legally significant.[32]

If these differences exist generally in securities trading transactions, they may also exist in trading contexts involving actual or potential contraventions of insider trading prohibitions. The identification of any salient differences in male and female insider trading may provide academics, policy makers and other interested parties with a new window on the efficacy of US insider trading regulation—a window that substantiates earlier analyses or illuminates new areas for consideration, study and potential action.

A number of important questions can be—and are beginning to be—asked about

---

[31]   Joan MacLeod Heminway, *Female Investors and Securities Fraud: Is The Reasonable Investor A Woman?*, 15 Wm. & Mary J. of Women & L. 291, 309–19 (2009).

[32]   Id. at 294–95.

gender differences in insider trading behavior and outcomes. Paramount among them: whether female insiders have access to the same kind and amount of undisclosed market-relevant (from a legal standpoint: material nonpublic) information as male insiders; whether female insiders trade while in possession of material nonpublic information as frequently as, and in volumes similar to, men; and whether women's trades while in possession of material nonpublic information are otherwise qualitatively different (made at different times, for different reasons and under other different circumstances). Empirical work has begun to answer these questions.

For example, a recent study finds that women may be less likely to benefit from insider trading because they are less likely to be in possession of material nonpublic information. In a study of insider trading behavior of senior corporate executives and directors in the USA between 1975 and 2008, researchers found that both male and female executives, board members and senior officers earned significant average positive excess returns from their securities purchases.[33] However, men earned greater excess returns on insider purchases on average than women in the same insider position, and men traded more frequently than women in the same insider position.

The coauthors tested four hypotheses as possible explanations for these results:

- an information access hypothesis, positing that men in the executive ranks have better access to beneficial information than women in the same positions;
- an overconfidence hypothesis, positing that men in the executive ranks are more overconfident than women in the same positions;
- a risk-aversion hypothesis, positing that men in the executive ranks are less (or no more) risk-averse than women in the same positions; and
- a use propensity hypothesis, positing that women in the executive ranks are less willing to use insider information than men in the same positions.[34]

The only hypothesis of the four that was supported by the tests performed in the study was the information access hypothesis. Although female executives do trade as much as (if not more than) male executives before significant events, male executives trade more overall and earn greater excess returns.[35] The researchers conclude that the sum total of the results of their study "suggest[s] that female executives may have limited access to inside information in comparison to their male counterparts."[36] Research conducted by graduate students in Sweden on trading in the securities of Stockholm Stock Exchange issuers also finds that male insiders earn higher abnormal returns than female insiders and attributes that difference to gender-related information asymmetries.[37]

---

[33]   See Sreedhar T. Bharath et al., Are Women Executives Disadvantaged? (June 24, 2009), http://ssrn.com/abstract=1276064 (last visited Nov. 20, 2012).

[34]   Id. at 3–4.

[35]   Id. at 4–5.

[36]   Id. at 5.

[37]   See Sverker Nordlander & Oscar Rheborg, An Insider Trading Cocktail—A Study on Gender Differences and the Implications of the Capital Insurance (Fall 2010), http://arc.hhs.se/download.aspx?MediumId=1086 (last visited Nov. 20, 2012).

A subsequent event study of director trades in the UK verifies the overall results of the US and Swedish studies: while all directors earned abnormal returns, men earned greater abnormal returns than women.[38] However, after measuring returns using a longer-term window, the UK study results changed dramatically. Over the longer term, women earned higher abnormal returns than men.[39] As a result, the study co-authors hypothesize that "the announcement period market reaction does not reflect the actual information-gathering capabilities of female directors, but reveals only the market's perception of such capabilities, which may have less to do with their actual capabilities and more to do with gender stereotyping."[40]

Finally, in an earlier UK study conducted by three of the same researchers, the co-authors found that abnormal returns for male and female directors of UK companies were similar after controlling for the category of director (executive versus non-executive).[41] The motivation for and findings of this study are founded in part in board demographics. Specifically, the researchers noted in describing the sample of firms being studied, that:

> [T]here are an average of 11.3 and 8.4 directors per company, respectively, but . . . females are underrepresented. Even more dramatically, females are more underrepresented with respect to executive directorships over non-executive directorships. The ratio of male non-execs to execs is 1.77, but the ratio of female non-execs to execs is 4.8. Hence any gender differences in directors' trading, since females are over-represented as non-executive directors relative to executive positions, may contaminate the information hierarchy effect measured only with respect to the category of the director.[42]

The results of the study expressly address the disentanglement of gender from director status in the United Kingdom and indicate that "the market reaction to a director's trade is not influenced by the gender of the director but is affected by the category of the director trading."[43]

Studies like these are beginning to reveal gender-based insider trading differences and to dispel certain commonly held beliefs about differences in male and female insider trading behaviors and outcomes. Data collected and analyzed in these studies should help theoreticians, researchers, policy makers and enforcement agents identify and better understand the legal significance of any identified differences in men's and women's behaviors and outcomes in insider trading contexts. For example, if US insider trading law protects or motivates men and women differently and that difference in protection or motivation is neither intended nor desirable, then changes in the law or in the enforcement of the law may be warranted.

---

[38]   Gregory et al., supra note 1.
[39]   Id. at 11.
[40]   Id. at 12–13.
[41]   Alan Gregory et al., Stock Market Patterns around Directors' Trades: Effects of Director Category and Gender on Market Timing (July 2009), https://business-school.exeter.ac.uk/docu ments/papers/finance/2009/0902.pdf (last visited Nov. 20, 2012).
[42]   Id. at 4.
[43]   Id. at 5.

II.   THE PERSISTENCE OF PILLOW TALK CASES AS AN EXPRESSION OF THE GENDER-CONSTRUCTION NORM

The theoretical and empirical background described in section I of this chapter offers a number of preliminary insights into the construction of US insider trading law and the difference in behavior and outcomes of female and male insider trading in the USA. These insights are important descriptors of insider trading realities as they relate to men and women. Some of these realities are more compelling than others.

Of particular note are the pillow talk cases,[44] which (as noted in section I) have received some theoretical, doctrinal and policy-oriented attention. A pillow talk case may involve either a heterosexual or homosexual relationship. In either case, much can be learned about the interaction of sex or gender and insider trading. Men and women may behave differently in mixed-sex (or mixed-gender) and same-sex (or same-gender) groups.[45]

A.   Legal and Empirical Observations about Pillow Talk Cases

The sharing of information between members of a couple in a pillow talk case is legally cognizable as a classic tipping case (if a corporate insider in the relationship inappropriately discloses material nonpublic information to the other individual in the relationship); a misappropriation case (if the individual in the relationship receiving the information breaches a duty of trust and confidence to the other individual in the relationship); or a misappropriation tipping case (if one individual in the relationship violates a duty of trust and confidence to someone outside the relationship by sharing material nonpublic information with the other individual in the relationship).[46] In each of these cases, the member of the couple receiving the information within the relationship may either trade on that information or tip it to someone outside the relationship. Thus, in the first form of pillow talk case, styled as a classic tipping case, an insider passes material nonpublic information to his or her romantic partner who either trades in securities of the issuer affiliated with the insider or re-tips the information to others who similarly trade. In the second form of pillow talk case, cognizable under Rule 10b5-2, a recipient romantic partner trades in securities or tips material nonpublic information in violation of his or her spousal (or other) duty of trust or confidence to the conveying romantic partner. In the third type of pillow talk case, a direct or indirect recipient of material nonpublic information violates a duty to the source of that information by tipping the information to his or her romantic partner who, in turn, either trades in securities of the issuer affiliated with the insider or re-tips to others who trade. Any of these forms of pillow talk case may involve one or more chains of tippees (i.e., more than just one or two tippees): the tippee or tippees of

---

[44]   See supra notes 2 & 7 and accompanying text.

[45]   See, e.g., Sander Hoogendoorn et al., The Impact of Gender Diversity on the Performance of Business Teams: Evidence from a Field Experiment 4 (Tinbergen Inst. Discussion Paper, Paper No 2011-074/3, 2011), available at http://papers.ssrn.com/sol3/papers.cfm?abstract_id=1826024 (last visited Nov. 20, 2012); Radosveta Ivanova-Stenzel & Dorothea Kübler, Gender Differences in Team Work and Team Competition 21–22 (July 9, 2009), available at http://www2.wiwi.hu-berlin.de/wtl/research/2007/IK090702.pdf (last visited Nov. 20, 2012).

[46]   See Chapter 1 in this volume.

an insider (or misappropriator) may re-tip some or all of the information to one or more secondary tippees, who may then further re-tip some or all of the information to one or more tertiary tippees, *ad infinitum*. Expert network insider trading cases, a significant target of the enforcement efforts of the SEC in the new millennium, fit this description and may involve pillow talk.[47]

Tipping and misappropriation cases have not been examined empirically in published studies. Because the existence and identity of a tippee or misappropriator typically is not known unless and until an inquiry and investigation by the SEC or another law enforcement authority is concluded and publicized, event studies, the *sine qua non* of empirical research in finance,[48] are not useful as a means of empirical study of tippee and misappropriator behavior. Said differently, one cannot measure the abnormal returns of a class of traders around a particular market-affecting event without knowing who comprises that class of traders, specifically or generally. Accordingly, event studies do not provide information about pillow talk cases.

One could gather and analyze, on the basis of gender, basic data on the pillow talk cases that have become public. While the data collection would be difficult and the sample size would be small, meaningful quantitative and qualitative empirical research using these data may help illuminate important aspects of this common form of insider trading. Qualitative research on pillow talk cases may be particularly instructive and may take many forms, including:

> [T]he analysis of information obtained through interviews, questionnaires or surveys, focus groups, reviews of historical documents (including correspondence and other communications), and direct participant observation captured in journal entries (or diaries). Study designs . . . [may] range from ethnographies (cultural examinations), to phenomenological research (experiential assessments), to approaches rooted in grounded theory (methods centered on theory formation and confirmation).[49]

Research of this kind may enable a better understanding of, for example, the types of relationship or the behavioral attributes of the individuals in a relationship that most commonly result in tipping, re-tipping or misappropriating information or in tippee or misappropriator trading. Studies of this kind may lead to new information about the relationship between gender and insider trading and the nature of women as insider traders.

B.   Anecdotal Observations about Pillow Talk Cases

In the absence of current empirical data and analysis on pillow talk cases, however, the anecdotal information that has surfaced in the news media provides snapshots of several variants of this form of insider trading case and the varied roles of women in these cases. Public reports indicate that pillow talk is a relatively common way of disseminating

---

[47]   See Ben Protess, Chiesi Sentenced to 30 Months in Galleon Case, DealBook, NYTimes.com (July 20, 2011), available at http://dealbook.nytimes.com/2011/07/20/chiesi-sentenced-in-galleon-insider-trading-case/ (last visited Nov. 20, 2012).

[48]   See Joan MacLeod Heminway, Theoretical and Methodological Perspectives, in The Sage Handbook of Corporate Governance 102–07 (Thomas Clarke & Douglas Branson eds., 2012).

[49]   Id. at 107.

material nonpublic information as part of alleged or actual insider trading violations. News stories published by *The New York Times* and reported on Fox News and other national media outlets in late 2007 noted that the SEC had brought seven pillow talk cases to that point in the year (after having brought only one case in all of 2006).[50] The *ABA Journal* noted a continued enforcement focus on pillow talk cases in 2008.[51] The pillow talk cases featured in these news stories comprise both simple tipping and misappropriation cases, in which the tipper and tippee are the only people engaged in the scheme, and more complex insider trading cases involving chains or networks of tippers and tippees. These cases often involve salacious facts and engage prurient interest.

In a case with facts close to those in *Chestman*, for example, Matthew Devlin, the husband of a public relations executive with advance knowledge of corporate transactions, acquired material nonpublic information from his wife (Nina Devlin, known as the "golden goose") and passed it on to others.[52] Similarly, William Marovitz, the husband of former Playboy Enterprises, Inc. chairman and chief executive officer Christie Hefner (daughter of Playboy founder Hugh Hefner), settled an SEC enforcement action alleging that he traded in Playboy stock while in possession of material nonpublic information about Playboy, despite significant compliance efforts over many years to prevent him from doing so.[53] In these cases, according to the publicized facts, men are using information extracted from seemingly unsuspecting women to trade or tip.

Turnabout is (as they say) fair play, however. Women also use material nonpublic information gleaned from their romantic relationships with men to trade or tip. Annabel McClellan, a San Francisco wife and mother, entered into a consent decree with the SEC to settle an insider trading case against her for tipping relatives about material nonpublic information on upcoming business transactions gained from her unwitting husband, a tax advisor who worked on mergers and acquisitions for Deloitte Tax L.L.P.[54] Adding

---

[50]   See Rosen, supra note 2; Lis Wiehl, Insider Trading: Pillow Talk Reveals Couples' Dirty Little Secrets, FoxNews.com (Oct. 30, 2007), available at http://www.foxnews.com/story/0,2933,305978,00. html (last visited Nov. 20, 2012).

[51]   See Martha Neil, NYSE Insider Trading Cases at Record High in 2008 as 'Pillow Talk' Increases, ABAJournal.com (Feb. 9, 2009), available at http://www.abajournal.com/news/article/08_insider_trading_hits_record_high_pillow_talk_a_growing_problem/ (last visited Nov. 20, 2012).

[52]   See Patricia Hurtado, Ex-Lehman Broker Devlin Sentenced to Three Years' Probation, Bloomberg.com (March 23, 2012), available at http://www.bloomberg.com/news/2012-03-23/ex-lehman-broker-devlin-sentenced-to-three-years-probation-1-.html (last visited Nov. 20, 2012); Holly M. Sanders, Flack Suspended in Pillow-Talking Case, N.Y. Post, Dec. 23, 2008, at 33.

[53]   See David S. Hilzenrath, SEC Charges William Marovitz, Spouse of Playboy's Christie Hefner, with Insider Trading, washingtonpost.com (Aug. 3, 2011), available at http://www.washingtonpost.com/business/economy/sec-charges-william-marovitz-spouse-of-playboys-christie-hefner-with-insider-trading/2011/08/03/gIQATSSqsI_story.html (last visited Nov. 20, 2012); Peter Lattman, Christie Hefner's Husband Is Accused of Insider Trading, DealBook, NYTimes.com (Aug. 3, 2011), available at http://dealbook.nytimes.com/2011/08/03/husband-of-playboy-executive-accused-of-insider-trading/ (last visited Nov. 20, 2012).

[54]   See Karen Gullo & Joshua Gallu, Ex-Deloitte Partner's Wife Settles SEC Case for $1 Million, Bloomberg.com (Oct. 17, 2011), available at http://www.bloomberg.com/news/2011-10-17/ex-deloitte-partner-s-wife-settles-sec-case-for-1-million-1-.html (last visited Nov. 20, 2012); Elizabeth Lesly Stevens, Lives With Polished Veneer Are Snared in S.E.C. Inquiry, NYTimes.com (Dec.

to the human interest of this story was the widely reported fact that McClellan also was co-developing "My Nookie," an adult-themed Web site and mobile app, during the time she was being investigated.[55]

In addition to the cases in which one romantic partner dupes another, there are cases in which husbands and wives or romantic partners collaborate to pass information to others in the market who trade or re-tip. A notable 2007 case of this kind involved an information technology specialist at MDS, Inc. who learned about a potential future tender offer by MDS for shares of Molecular Devices Corp. (and related merger negotiations), tipped his female romantic partner about the transaction and, together with the romantic partner, traded in Molecular Devices stock and call options.[56] In another, similar case involving a married couple (both lawyers), the wife both directly tipped a broker about material nonpublic information she acquired through her job at Morgan Stanley and tipped her husband on material nonpublic information, knowing he would share it with the broker.[57]

Perhaps most infamously, the highly publicized Galleon Group network insider trading cases include pillow talk components involving material nonpublic information gained in one romantic relationship as part of a collaborative network involving another romantic relationship. Danielle Chiesi, one of Raj Rajaratnam's informants, used a romantic relationship with an IBM executive to acquire material nonpublic information.[58] Chiesi also enjoyed a long-term romantic relationship with another participant in the insider trading network. In addition, her overall feminine wiles and flirtatious nature became gendered components of the case against her.[59] Wiretapped recordings of conversations between Chiesi and Rajaratnam reveal that Chiesi called Rajaratnam "honey" and "babe," and that, following Chiesi's successful solicitation of information from one male contact, Chiesi stated she had played the source of the information "like a finely tuned piano."[60] Chiesi's breach of trust and confidence was publicly revealed to be both personal and professional.

Romantic partners also may be involved in other ways in insider trading schemes. While not strictly pillow talk cases, they emanate from similar facts. In one recent case, for example, a former Goldman Sachs associate who obtained material nonpublic information from various sources (including confidential grand jury proceedings) made illegal trades through his girlfriend's account (as well as his aunt's account).[61] In a May 2012 complaint, the SEC alleged that a young woman used her boyfriend's account to make illegal trades based on material nonpublic information about the terms and timing

---

11, 2010), available at http://www.nytimes.com/2010/12/12/us/12bcmcclellan.html?pagewanted=all (last visited Nov. 20, 2012).

[55]   See Stevens, supra note 54.

[56]   See Rosen, supra note 2.

[57]   See id.; Larry Neumeister, Couple Pleads Guilty to Insider Trading, USATODAY.com (May 10, 2007), available at http://www.usatoday.com/money/economy/2007-05-10-1028951420_x.htm (last visited Nov. 20, 2012).

[58]   See Protess, supra note 47.

[59]   See id.

[60]   Id.

[61]   Michael J. de la Merced, Former Associate at Goldman Pleads Guilty, NYTimes.com (Aug. 29, 2007), available at http://www.nytimes.com/2007/08/29/business/29insider.html?ex=1346040000&en=daded0d369d41725&ei=5090&partner=rssuserland&emc=rss (last visited Nov. 20, 2012).

of a forthcoming acquisition of the company at which she worked as a legal assistant.[62] She also tipped her father.[63] Many insider trading cases, including pillow talk cases, also engage family members other than spouses.[64]

The pillow talk cases described here are a small sampling; nevertheless, they represent a diverse lot. The roles of women are varied. The analogy of some of these insider trading cases to prostitution is inescapable: man meets woman, gains her trust and confidence, and uses her in a scheme to make profits from an illegal enterprise. Yet, in other cases, the power dynamic of the roles, on its face, is reversed or more equal. It is hard to discern from these cases whether women engage with the law of insider trading on the same bases and under the same circumstances as men or whether they represent a distinct population from a regulatory standpoint. What we know from these public accounts is relatively superficial. With additional empirical research, however, these types of cases may offer new gender-based insights on US insider trading regulation.

III. THE OVERALL NEED FOR ADDITIONAL EMPIRICAL WORK TO FURTHER ENRICH UNDERSTANDING

Pillow talk cases are not the only type of insider trading case about which we lack empirical research on the basis of gender. As a whole, the gendered aspects of insider trading in the USA are understudied. As a result, our understanding of the role of sex and gender in insider trading is imperfect. There are many unsettled questions. We do not yet know whether women behave or fare differently from men in most aspects of insider trading. For example, women may or may not have the same capacity or desire to acquire material nonpublic information that men have. The studies cited in section I.B do not definitively answer that question.[65] Accordingly, while a woman may be in a role that puts her in the position of having a duty of trust and confidence (making her an insider for purposes of insider trading law under § 10(b) and Rule 10b-5), she may not have an inside line to the same quantity or quality of material nonpublic information to which a man in the same or a similar position has preferential access. A traditional feminist account of this type of information asymmetry and its relationship to the historical male orientation of enforcement and violations of US insider trading law might note that insider trading is a matter of privilege, and the male-dominance of illegal insider trading is yet another manifestation and extension of male privilege.

Researchers find that demographic majorities may use their in-group status to highlight and preserve the out-group status of demographic minorities in organizational management in a number of ways—although various factors may decrease the salience of the

---

[62]   See Sec's & Exch. Comm'n v. Milliard, CV12-73-M-DLC (D. Mont. filed May 7, 2012), available at http://www.sec.gov/litigation/complaints/2012/comp-pr2012-84.pdf (last visited Nov. 20, 2012).

[63]   Id.

[64]   See, e.g., Bruce Carton, New Form of Family Betrayal: Siblings, ComplianceWeek.com (Sept. 1, 2009), available at http://www.complianceweek.com/new-form-of-familial-betrayal-siblings/article/188095/ (last visited Nov. 20, 2012).

[65]   See supra notes 33–43 and accompanying text.

demographic differences.[66] From a structural perspective, board activity and decision-making may incorporate female directors in ways that handicap their ability to access material information. For example, evidence exists that female board members in the US historically served on less significant, less tactical board committees.[67] A marginalization of female corporate directors in board processes may reduce the quantity or quality of information available to those female directors. However, recent research reports indicate that, in particular in the years since the passage of the Sarbanes–Oxley Act in 2002,[68] women are beginning to assume more leadership roles on US corporate boards.[69] This trend may offset any perceived or actual informational imbalances between female and male directors. In addition, although the findings may be *sui generis* to Norway (which has a 40 percent gender quota rule for boards of public limited liability companies), female directors in Norway reported in a recent study that they are able to access important corporate information as board members.[70]

The mere fact that an information asymmetry may exist between men and women is not, in and of itself, legally significant. However, since US insider trading law is designed to address, among other things, certain kinds of information asymmetries, the existence of an information asymmetry challenges the notion that the same insider trading regulation for both men and women is needed to protect investors and markets. In US insider trading regulation, one size may not fit all.

The existence and nature of possible informational imbalances between male and female directors are not the only unresolved research questions relevant to gender and insider trading, however. Women may, for instance, have different conceptions of duty generally and different conceptions of a duty of trust and confidence, a core component of insider trading regulation in the USA. Different perceptions of duty may result in different types of breaches of duty. For example, there is evidence in the empirical literature that women and men trust differently, and those differences may have an impact on their behavior in relationships of trust.[71] Women may choose to breach duties in different circumstances than men breach those same duties because of their different understandings of the requisite duty. If women behave differently in relationships of trust and confidence based on a different notion of trust, then we may be over-regulating or under-regulating

[66] See James D. Westphal & Laurie P. Milton, How Experience and Network Ties Affect the Influence of Demographic Minorities on Corporate Boards, 45 Admin. Science Q. 366 (2000).

[67] See Diana Bilimoria & Sandy Kristin Piderit, Board Committee Membership: Effects of Sex-Based Bias, 37 Academy of Mgt. 1453 (1994).

[68] Pub. L. No 107-204, 116 Stat. 745 (codified in scattered sections of 11, 15, 18, 28 & 29 U.S.C.).

[69] See Dan R. Dalton & Catherine M. Dalton, Women and Corporate Boards of Directors: The Promise of Increased, and Substantive, Participation in the Post Sarbanes-Oxley Era, 53 Bus. Horizons 257, 261 (2010).

[70] See Beate Elstad & Gro Ladegard, Women on Corporate Boards: Key Influencers or Tokens?, J. Mgmt Gov. (Online First™), Nov. 23, 2010, available at http://ssrn.com/abstract=1582368 (last visited Nov. 20, 2012).

[71] See generally Rachel Croson & Uri Gneezy, Gender Difference in Preferences, 47 J. Econ. Lit. 448, 458–61 (2009); Joan MacLeod Heminway, Sex, Trust, and Corporate Boards, 18 Hastings Women's L. J. 173, 196 n. 117 (2007) (describing sex-based differences in trusting behavior and trustworthiness and relating them to the corporate governance context).

their conduct as compared with men. Which understanding of trust should govern and guide policy makers and regulators if two or more different types of trust are operative?

Women also may breach duties at different times and in different circumstances because of differences in their risk preferences. Some studies indicate that women may be more risk-averse than men in certain situations.[72] Moreover, a recent study of male traders in the City of London provides evidence that elevated steroid levels may change risk preferences, indicating a possible biological link between gender and risk-taking.[73] Women's distinct understandings of their duties in various insider trading contexts and the risks of proceeding in disregard of them may drive women to different patterns of compliance and non-compliance with US insider trading prohibitions.

Women also may have a different sense of entitlement to the profits that may be extracted from insider trading. Research indicates that women may be more other-regarding and less driven toward competitive behaviors than men, at least in certain contexts.[74] These attributes may lead women to make different decisions about taking insider trading proceeds for themselves (especially if they believe, however mistakenly, that others are harmed in the process) than men would make under similar circumstances. If insider trading is viewed as a tournament with winners and losers, women may just not want to play the game with the same frequency that men do. If that were to be proven true, it might impact the way in which, for example, scarce enforcement resources are allocated.

The hypotheses and observations made in the preceding paragraphs highlight a number of unanswered questions about sex or gender and insider trading founded in existing behavioral literature outside the insider trading context. These (and other) unanswered questions represent ready areas for empirical study that may help us to better understand and describe certain insider trading phenomena and give us information important to assessing the efficacy of existing insider trading rules and enforcement efforts. More— and more detailed—empirical analysis will help us complete our picture of female insider traders and better understand how they may differ from male insider traders. With this knowledge, we may be able to reform insider trading regulation and tailor insider trading enforcement to better protect investors and better assure honest, fair trading markets.

IV.   AN INCOMPLETE PORTRAIT OF THE INSIDER TRADER AS A WOMAN

Public reports indicate that women have growing and varied roles in insider trading violations in the USA. These new, diverse roles for women may be distinct or have distinctive characteristics—different from the roles historically and currently occupied by male insider traders. Scholarship in law and behavioral psychology and economics (among other areas of academic inquiry) has begun to identify and describe sex or gender differences in various contexts, but researchers have done little to study sexed or gendered

---

[72]   See, e.g., Croson & Gneezy, supra note 71, at 449–54.

[73]   John M. Coates & Joe Herbert, Endogenous Steroids and Financial Risk Taking on a London Trading Floor, 105 PNAS 6167 (Apr. 21, 2008).

[74]   See id. at 454–67.

aspects of insider trading doctrine or enforcement. Theoretical, doctrinal and empirical research and analysis can help fill this void and construct a more complete picture of the gendered construction and operation of US insider trading rules and the place of women in the overall insider trading puzzle.

Given that insider trading regulation in the USA is based on relationships (those founded on a duty of trust and confidence as well as, in tipping cases, the receipt of a personal benefit by a tipper),[75] the identification of sex and gender interactions with insider trading should help reveal more about the nature of relationships that commonly lead to insider trading liability. The *Dirks* case[76] and Rule 10b5-2[77] exemplify ways in which the federal courts and the SEC have struggled with the types of relationship that should be protected (e.g., under *Dirks*, the relationship between a truth-seeking broker-dealer/analyst and his information sources and clients) and those that may create liability (e.g., under Rule 10b5-2, the three identified relationships giving rise to a duty of trust and confidence in misappropriation cases) through the application of insider trading doctrine and the enforcement of its principles. Empirical research that illuminates the relationships that underlie violations of US insider trading law may help guide further rule-making initiatives or the exercise of insider trading enforcement discretion under § 10(b) and Rule 10b-5.

Although women have become more visible as participants in the securities markets and as alleged and actual transgressors of insider trading rules, the role of women in insider trading is still ill understood, except anecdotally. The portrait of the insider trader as a woman is a work in process. It is important that those of us who are engaged with the project keep the brush and palette in hand and continue painting until the full image is revealed in relevant detail. The resulting finished portrait of the insider trader as a woman may afford us important information not only about female insider traders, but also about insider traders and insider trading more generally.

---

[75]   See Chapter 1 in this volume.
[76]   Dirks v. SEC, 463 U.S. 646 (1983).
[77]   17 C.F.R. § 240.10b5-2 (2012).

PART 3

EMPIRICAL RESEARCH

12. Has illegal insider trading become more rampant in the United States? Empirical evidence from takeovers

Laura Nyantung Beny and H. Nejat Seyhun

I. INTRODUCTION

Insider trading[1] has long sparked popular outrage about the perceived excesses of Wall Street and corporate insiders' abuse of their privileged positions at the expense of ordinary investors (i.e., widows, orphans and the rest of us). This is especially true during economic recessions and capital market downturns, as in recent years. At such times, populist outrage over insider trading and other types of corporate fraud soars to peak levels. In turn, this places great pressure on regulators and prosecutors to pursue alleged inside traders with greater ferocity than in economically normal times.[2] Indeed, in the last few years, US federal authorities have increased the ante, enforcing insider trading laws with renewed vigor.

A prominent recent example is the Galleon case, the largest insider trading scandal in the USA in decades. This case ultimately resulted in 2011 in a criminal conviction and an 11-year prison sentence for Raj Rajaratnam, the man at the center of the scandal. The case involved widespread information networks and insider trading at several prominent hedge funds, including Galleon Management, LP, the former multi-billion dollar hedge fund founded and run by Mr. Rajaratnam. The US government alleged that various high-level executives at such illustrious companies as McKinsey & Co., Intel Corporation and IBM had provided material non-public information to the hedge funds. Through a complex network of business and personal relationships and information sharing, the Galleon scheme yielded more than $49 million in illegal profits or loss avoidance. The US Department of Justice (DOJ) and the Securities and Exchange Commission (SEC) aggressively pursued the alleged culprits in a variety of civil and criminal proceedings. Along the way, they have issued stern remarks in the press, presumably both to warn would-be offenders and to feed populist sentiment.

Furthermore, US authorities claim to have many more insider trading enforcement actions in the pipeline: "The current investigation—which traces its roots to an SEC inquiry in 2007 and FBI agents gaining court approval to use wiretaps to snare

---

[1] Insider trading is defined as trading by individuals or corporations based on illegally obtained material, non-public information. In most jurisdictions, including the USA, material information is information that reasonable investors would consider likely to affect the financial security's price, and non-public information is information that is not available to investors who are corporate outsiders.

[2] See Stuart Banner, Anglo-American Securities Regulation: Cultural and Political Roots, 1690–1860 (2002).

targets—has resulted in 66 people being charged with insider trading and related crimes, and 57 convictions, the largest crackdown on insider trading in modern law enforcement history."[3] According to federal law enforcement officials, cases have been "scheduled out" for the next five years and it is likely that "hundreds" of individuals will be charged in the coming years, including another hedge fund industry player of similar stature to Mr. Rajaratnam. SAC Capital and Citadel Investments are two of the large hedge funds that have been issued subpoenas in the current investigation.[4]

Another recent development is the increasing severity of punishment upon conviction for insider trading offenses. Both the probability of serving in prison as well as length of prison sentences have significantly increased. Between 1993 and 1999, fewer than 5 percent of defendants received prison sentences of two or more years upon conviction. This ratio increased to more than 25 percent between 2000 and 2009, and to about 50 percent between 2010 and 2012. These findings indicate an approximate ten-fold increase in the probability of receiving a prison sentence between the late 1990s and 2012. Similarly, the median length of prison sentences given by the courts also rose. Between 1993 and 1999, the median prison sentence was only 11.5 months. Between 2000 and 2010, the median prison sentence rose to 18 months. Finally, between 2010 and 2012 the median prison sentence for convicted defendants in New York federal courts rose to 2.5 years in prison, which indicates more than doubling of the length of prison sentences.[5] From all outward appearances, then, it appears that federal insider trading enforcement, convictions and sentences are on the rise. Indeed, in Section III we present evidence that civil enforcement has increased significantly over time.

How should we interpret this evidence of increased enforcement intensity? One explanation is that the USA (popular opinion, regulators, etc.) has become less tolerant of illegal insider trading. Another possibility is that insider trading has become more profitable in spite of enhanced enforcement efforts. As a consequence, there is more crime and thus more visible enforcement. While we are unable systematically to test the first explanation (increased intolerance), we can test the second explanation, which we refer to as the increased illegal trading hypothesis.

In this study, we test the increased illegal insider trading hypothesis by examining the pricing of common stock and options in the context of corporate takeovers. Corporate takeovers provide an excellent opportunity to engage in illegal insider trading in the common stock and call options of a target firm. Stock prices typically jump significantly on announcement of the takeover attempt. Call options on the target stock provide an even bigger windfall gain to option traders by enabling them to further leverage the announcement day returns on target shares.

We investigate our hypothesis using a sample of 1,177 tender offers between 1996 and 2011. We pursue two methodologies. First, we examine abnormal returns to target firms' stock around the takeover announcement. The increased illegal insider trading hypothesis

---

[3]   Charlie Gasparino & Sital Patel, *Here's a Tip: Insider Trading Cases Will Pile Up for Years*, FOX Business, February 21, 2012.

[4]   Id.

[5]   See Chad Bray & Rob Barry, *Long Jail Terms on the Rise*, The Wall Street Journal, October 13, 2011.

predicts that the pre-bid stock price run-up has increased over time, consistent with greater profitability and incidence of illegal insider trading.

Secondly, we examine the pricing of call options on target firms' stocks around the takeover announcement. If the increased illegal insider trading hypothesis is valid, the call options should exhibit increasing evidence of rich pricing prior to takeover announcements over time. That is, if increased insider trading is responsible for the pre-bid volume and price effects on bidder firms' stocks, we will observe an increase in the implied volatility of the target firms' stock because insiders will bid up the price of the target options by taking large options positions to benefit from the stock price run-up. Option prices are monotonically and positively related to option volatility. We implement the binomial option pricing model to compute implied volatilities.

Our results are consistent with the increased illegal trading hypothesis. We find that the average pre-announcement stock price run-up for target firms increased substantially between 1996 and 2011, which cannot be explained by changes in initial toehold investments but is consistent with an increase in the incidence of insider trading. We also find that implied option volatilities increase prior to the tender offer announcement date, consistent with the presence of illegal insider trading. Finally, we find a (weakly) positive relationship between implied volatility and the pre-bid price run-up, which is also consistent with our increased illegal insider trading hypothesis. Overall, our evidence suggests that the recent increase in US enforcement intensity is likely due to an increase in the incidence of illegal insider trading.

The chapter is organized as follows. Section II provides an overview of US federal insider trading law and presents SEC enforcement trends over time. Section III presents our hypotheses, empirical methodology, data and results. Finally, Section IV concludes.

II.   OVERVIEW OF US FEDERAL INSIDER TRADING LAW AND ENFORCEMENT

A.   Substantive Law

There are three main doctrines according to which trading on material non-public information is illegal under US federal laws. These are the disclose or abstain rule, misappropriation theory and Rule 14e-3 of the Securities Exchange Act.[6]

The disclose or abstain rule emerged from the US Supreme Court's interpretation of § 10(b) of the Securities Exchange Act of 1934 and Rule 10b-5 promulgated thereunder. In *Chiarella v. United States*[7] and *Dirks v. SEC*,[8] the Supreme Court held that the basis for insider trading liability is breach of a fiduciary duty that the defendant owes to contemporaneous traders. That is, if a corporate insider owes a fiduciary duty to shareholders trading contemporaneously, he or she has a duty to disclose the material non-public

---

[6]   See generally Stephen M. Bainbridge, Securities Law: Insider Trading (1999).
[7]   445 U.S. 222 (1980).
[8]   463 U.S. 646 (1983).

information or refrain from trading. The insiders upon whom such a fiduciary duty rests obviously include officers, directors and controlling shareholders.

However, US courts have also interpreted the disclose or abstain rule to include various corporate outsiders, deemed "constructive insiders," under certain circumstances. In particular, "[t]he outsider must obtain material nonpublic information from the issuer. The issuer must expect the outsider to keep the disclosed information confidential. Finally, the relationship must at least imply such a duty."[9] In addition, a "tippee" who has received material non-public information from an insider or constructive insider is also subject to the disclose or abstain rule if "the tipper has breached a fiduciary duty by disclosing information to the tippee, and the tippee knows or has reason to know of the breach of duty."[10]

The US Supreme Court endorsed the misappropriation theory in *U.S. v. O'Hagan*.[11] In this case, the Court held that an attorney (Mr. O'Hagan) violated § 10(b) of the 1934 Exchange Act and Rule 10b-5 when he bought shares and call options on the shares of a company that was the subject of a takeover and made a profit of over $4.3 million. Although the attorney was not an insider of either the takeover target or the acquiring firm, he worked for the law firm that was representing the latter firm (though he did not work on the acquisition). The Supreme Court held that he had engaged in illegal insider trading by virtue of the fact that he had misappropriated non-public information from the entity to whom he owed a fiduciary duty (the law firm), even though it was not the issuer of shares.

Finally, § 14(e) of the Exchange Act and Rule 14e-3 promulgated thereunder prohibit insider trading in the context of tender offers. Pursuant to Rule 14e-3, it is illegal for any person in knowing possession of material information about a tender offer to buy or sell a security while in possession of such information.[12] At first blush, the rule seems rather broad because it applies to anybody who possesses such information and trades without publicly disclosing it before trading. In addition, it does not matter whether she received the information directly or indirectly from the target, the offeror or a third person acting on their behalf; the prohibition still applies. Furthermore, liability under Rule 14e-3 does not require a pre-existing fiduciary relationship, but attaches to anybody who trades while in possession of the aforementioned information. Nevertheless, the scope of the rule is quite narrow. It only applies once the offeror has taken significant steps toward making its offer to the target company, and it only relates to information concerning a tender offer.

B.   US Enforcement Mechanisms and Recent Trends

While US insider trading laws have been relatively stable over the past decade, there have been significant changes in enforcement over time, as we demonstrate in this section. Federal insider trading laws may be enforced in several ways. First, the SEC may pursue civil actions and administrative proceedings. Secondly, private parties may bring civil

---

[9]   Stephen M. Bainbridge, Insider Trading: An Overview 2 (2000).
[10]   Id.
[11]   U.S. v. O'Hagan, 521 U.S. 642 (1997).
[12]   17 C.F.R. § 240.14e-3.

claims for damages under both state and federal laws. Finally, the DOJ may bring criminal charges.

The SEC may bring civil actions in federal district court against individuals suspected to have violated federal insider trading laws. The civil penalties it may pursue include "disgorgement of profits, correction of misleading statements, disclosure of material information, or other special remedies. Of these, disgorgement of profits to the government is the most commonly used enforcement tool."[13] The SEC may also initiate administrative proceedings against market professionals, resulting in disciplinary action such as censure, suspension, revocation of registration, etc.[14]

In the wake of several high-profile insider trading scandals in the 1980s, the US Congress increased the monetary penalty exposure of inside traders. In particular, the Insider Trading Sanctions Act of 1984 allowed for treble damages against persons who violate Rule 10b-5 or 14e-3. With the possibility of disgorgement, this means that those who violate insider trading laws face a potential monetary penalty of up to four times their illicit profits (or losses avoided) from engaging in insider trading. The Insider Trading and Securities Fraud Act of 1988 (ITSFA) further increased the array of enforcement measures available to the SEC.[15]

Private parties may also bring civil suits against inside traders. US courts have long interpreted Rule 10b-5 to contain an implied private right of action. In addition, pursuant to Exchange Act § 20A, private parties who traded contemporaneously with inside traders may sue for damages of up to the amount of profits (or loss avoided) by the inside traders. Private suits are, however, rare.

Finally, the SEC may request the DOJ to undertake a criminal prosecution against individuals suspected of having engaged in insider trading. Or, the DOJ may decide to prosecute on its own without a referral or request by the SEC. Violation of Rule 10b-5 or 14e-3 is a felony punishable by a fine of up to $5,000,000 and up to twenty years in prison. Criminal prosecutions have become increasingly frequent since the mid-1980s. The SEC and DOJ often work together on insider trading investigations, as the recent high-profile Galleon case illustrates, and appear to be publicly declaring their commitment to increased levels of cooperation.[16]

Over the past two decades, while private actions have seemingly remained relatively rare, public enforcement has increased significantly. Figure 12.1 presents enforcement actions initiated by the SEC during its fiscal years 1985, and 1990 through 2011.[17] The annual statistics presented in Figure 12.1 include both civil actions in federal district court

---

[13] Bainbridge, supra note 5, at 122.

[14] See id.

[15] See id.

[16] Referring to the Galleon hedge fund case, the SEC's Robert Khuzami recently stated that, "Our law enforcement agencies are together much more than the sum of our parts. That is why coordination, of which today's actions [parallel civil and criminal actions in the Galleon case] are a prime example, is critically important to the goal of rooting our fraud and misconduct in our markets." Robert Khuzami, SEC Director of Enforcement at *SEC v. Galleon Management, LP* Press Conference (Oct. 16, 2009), available at http://www.sec.gov/news/speech/2009/spch101609rk. htm (last visited Dec. 11, 2012).

[17] An SEC fiscal year begins on Oct. 1 of the prior calendar year. Thus, for example, fiscal year 2012 began on Oct. 1, 2011 and will end on September 30, 2012.

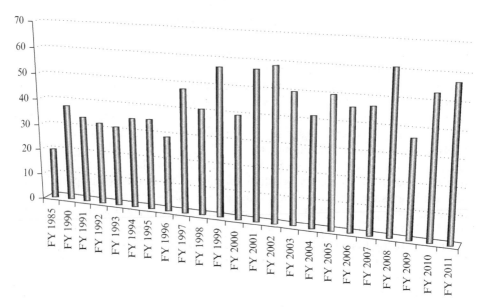

Source: http: www.sec.gov.

Figure 12.1   SEC enforcement actions, fiscal years 1985, 1990–2011

and administrative proceedings by the SEC. In most years, however, civil actions constitute the bulk of the SEC's enforcement measures.

As Figure 12.1 shows, the late 1990s marked a fundamental turning point in the SEC's
enforcement intensity. To put this evidence into perspective, in 1980 the SEC initiated a
mere 20 insider trading actions. This number had nearly doubled by 1990 to 38 enforcement actions. Between 1990 and 1995, the SEC brought an average of 34 enforcement
actions per fiscal year, while between 1995 and 2000 it brought an average of 42 enforcement actions per fiscal year. Then, between 2000 and 2005, the SEC brought an average
of 49 actions per fiscal year. The enforcement uptick that occurred in the late 1990s, and
continued through 2005, does not appear to have been a transitory, one-off reaction to
the dot.com boom and bust and the associated corporate and financial excesses. Indeed,
between 2005 and 2010 the SEC continued to launch an average of 49 insider trading
enforcement actions annually. Finally in fiscal year 2011, the SEC reports that it "brought
57 insider trading actions against 124 individuals and entities, a nearly 8 percent increase
in the number of filed actions from the prior fiscal year."[18]

While we do not have corresponding data on the number of criminal investigations or
cases initiated by the Justice Department over the past two decades, anecdotal evidence
suggests that criminal prosecutions have also increased during this period. For example, a
recent study conducted by the New York State Bar Association's Commercial and Federal
Litigation Section finds that the DOJ tends to bring criminal charges against individuals

---

[18]   Securities and Exchange Commission, SEC Enforcement Actions, Insider Trading Cases.
http://www.sec.gov/spotlight/insidertrading/cases.shtml (last visited Dec. 11, 2012).

sued by the SEC in New York federal courts.[19] It would seem to follow, then, that if civil suits have increased so too have criminal prosecutions, which tend to move in tandem (albeit not on a one-to-one basis) with SEC actions.[20] Moreover, the increased investigative collaboration between the SEC and the DOJ, as noted above, is likely to reinforce this trend. The use of technology, such as wiretaps and search warrants, has enhanced this collaboration as well as making it easier to secure insider trading convictions and/or guilty pleas.[21] The recent Galleon insider trading case, which entered the public spotlight in 2009, is an interesting example of the helpful role of technology in securing convictions.

Galleon was at one time a prestigious multi-billion dollar hedge fund, founded and controlled by Raj Rajaratnam. The SEC has charged Mr. Rajaratnam and nearly 30 other persons affiliated with Galleon with violating § 10(b) of the Securities Exchange Act of 1934 and Rule 10b-5 thereunder, and § 17(a) of the Securities Act of 1933. The charges allege "widespread and repeated insider trading at numerous hedge funds, including Galleon, and by other professional traders and corporate insiders in the securities of more than 15 companies. The insider trading generated illicit profits totaling more than $90 million."[22] In 2011, Rajaratnam was convicted on all counts and sentenced to 11 years in prison, the longest criminal sentence for insider trading thus far. Many defendants have pled guilty and several are aiding prosecutors in ongoing litigation. The case has involved close cooperation by the SEC's New York offices and the US Attorney's Office for the Southern District of New York and the Federal Bureau of Investigation.

Technology has played a critical role in the Galleon complex of cases, especially in enabling the conviction of Mr. Rajaratnam. Using taped conversations between Mr. Rajaratnam and his friends and business associates, the government was able to prove its allegations that he utilized his large network of contacts, including executives at major corporations such as Goldman Sachs, Intel, Proctor and Gamble, etc., to gather

---

[19]   http://www.nysba.org/Content/ContentFolders4/CommercialandFederalLitigationSection/ComFedReports/CRIMINALPROSECUTORIALDISCRETIONINTHEINSIDERTRADING CASES.pdf (last visited Dec. 11, 2012).

[20]   Note, however, that the DOJ does not pursue every individual that the SEC sues for insider trading. US Assistant Attorneys have prosecutorial discretion over whether or not to bring criminal charges. See id. Recent evidence suggests that, at least in New York, "licensed professionals stand a greater chance of being prosecuted than others (including officers of public companies); tippers tend to be treated more harshly than tippees; sole actors may be treated more leniently than those who advance a fraudulent scheme by tipping others; clients who made or stood to make less money, or avoid smaller losses, on their unlawful trading may be viewed more favorably than those who enjoy greater gains; those who consent up-front to settlements with the SEC do not tend to be prosecuted by the criminal authorities; and those who commit aggravating or additional stand alone crimes are more likely to find themselves defendants in parallel criminal cases." Id. at 14.

[21]   See, e.g., Morrison and Foerster, Insider Trading, Year-End Review (2011). Available at: http://www.mofo.com/files/Uploads/Images/2011-Insider-Trading-Review.pdf (last visited Dec. 11, 2012). See also Charlie Gasparino and Sital Patel, Here's a Tip: Insider Trading Cases Will Pile Up for Years, Fox Business, February 21, 2012, available at http://www.foxbusiness.com/industries/2012/02/21/heres-tip-insider-trading-cases-will-pile-up-for-years/#ixzz1tjeqKL3Y (last visited Dec. 11, 2012).

[22]   Securities and Exchange Commission, SEC Files Insider Trading Charges against Rajat Gupta, SEC Brings New Charges against Raj Rajaratnam, October 26, 2011, available at http://www.sec.gov/news/press/2011/2011-223.htm (last visited Dec. 11, 2012).

non-public information that he subsequently traded on. Without the wiretaps, the government's case would have been considerably more difficult to prove. The heart of the defense's legal theory was the mosaic theory. This is the notion that Mr. Rajaratnam gathered public information from various sources to create a trading strategy (and that he was very good at it, a financial wizard) but did not engage in illegal insider trading. Unfortunately for the defense, however, many of Mr. Rajaratnam's taped phone conversations were critical to his conviction.

The government faced similar challenges in making its case in the recent (June 2012) trial of Mr. Rajat Gupta. Mr. Gupta is former head of McKinsey and Company, and a former board member of Goldman Sachs and Proctor and Gamble. The SEC has charged Mr. Gupta with having supplied Mr. Rajaratnam with material non-public information concerning Goldman Sachs and Proctor and Gamble. According to the SEC, Galleon funds traded illegally on the basis of these tips, and made illegal profits (or avoided losses) greater than $23 million.[23] The SEC claimed that Mr. Gupta tipped Mr. Rajaratnam in violation of insider trading laws because of the two men's close personal relationship and extensive business dealings. Yet, Mr. Gupta never traded for his personal benefit. In spite of the fact that the evidence in Gupta's case was largely circumstantial, Mr. Gupta was convicted on three counts of securities fraud and one count of conspiracy for passing information about Goldman to Mr. Rajaratnam.[24] Mr. Gupta faces up to 20 years in prison for each of the fraud charges and up to five years for the conspiracy charge. The expected sentence under Federal guidelines is significantly lower.[25]

The Galleon case also illuminates US regulators' increasing scrutiny of so-called "expert network firms." These firms connect financial traders with industry consultants who provide them with industry- or company-specific information. They should only provide public information that can be found out through legal means. However, the SEC is concerned that expert network employees may sometimes be providing material, non-public information to traders in exchange for a fee. In 2010, for example, the SEC charged a French physician for tipping a hedge fund trader about adverse results of a clinical drug trial in which he had been involved. According to the SEC, the physician had been providing:

[C]onsulting services to the portfolio manager with whom he had developed a friendship over the years. The portfolio manager, based on the confidential information provided by Benhamou, ordered the sale of the entire position of HGSI stock held by six health care-related hedge funds that he co-managed (approximately 6 million shares). These sales occurred during the six-week period prior to HGSI's public announcement on Jan. 23, 2008, that it was reducing the dosage in one arm of the trial. Two million shares were sold in a block trade just before the markets closed on January 22. HGSI's share price dropped 44 percent by the end of the day on January 23. As a result of the sales, the hedge funds avoided losses of at least $30 million.[26]

---

[23] Id.

[24] Id.

[25] See Chad Bray et al., Insider Case Lands Big Catch, Wall Street Journal, Friday, June 15, 2012.

[26] Securities and Exchange Commission, SEC Charges Medical Researcher With Tipping Inside Information About Clinical Trial, November 2, 2010, available at http://www.sec.gov/news/press/2010/2010-209.htm (last visited Dec. 11, 2012).

The SEC has recently charged or investigated several more employees of expert network firms and hedge funds who use them in separate insider trading cases.[27] There are more cases in the pipeline and the impact on the hedge fund industry has been chilling.[28]

III.   HYPOTHESES AND METHODOLOGY

A.   Background

The presence of illegal insider trading can only be inferred. It cannot be directly measured because illegal inside traders typically do not declare their intent in advance nor do they admit to engaging in illegal insider trading after the fact. In this study, we examine price effects on stocks and options around the announcement of tender offers to indirectly detect the presence of illegal insiders.

Tender offers involve the efforts of accounting firms, investment banks, financial advisors, and executives of the bidder and target firms. Consequently, given that many people are involved in a takeover, there are potentially many opportunities to illegally share and use the privileged confidential information. As noted above, trading on the basis of non-public information about an upcoming tender offer is explicitly illegal under Rule 14e-3.[29] Nevertheless, if potential illegal traders think that they can escape detection or prosecution, they are likely to be tempted.

Recent developments in technology have created improved opportunities to hide one's transactions. The growth of online brokerage houses has allowed many investors to place trade orders anonymously. Secondly, many off-shore foreign tax havens are refusing to co-operate with US enforcement efforts. Given that more transactions can take place beyond the reach of US regulators, more people may be tempted to engage in illegal insider trading activities.

Takeovers are lucrative affairs. In a typical tender offer, stock prices rise significantly on

---

[27]   See Galleon Trial, Network Effects: A Massive Insider-Trading Trial Shakes Wall Street, The Economist, March 10, 2011.

[28]   Id.

[29]   The rule provides that:

As a means reasonably designed to prevent fraudulent, deceptive or manipulative acts or practices within the meaning of §14(e) of the Act, it shall be unlawful for any person described in paragraph (d)(2) of this section to communicate material, nonpublic information relating to a tender offer to any other person under circumstances in which it is reasonably foreseeable that such communication is likely to result in a violation of this section except that this paragraph shall not apply to a communication made in good faith,

i.   To the officers, directors, partners or employees of the offering person, to its advisors or to other persons, involved in the planning, financing, preparation or execution of such tender offer;

ii.   To the issuer whose securities are sought or to be sought by such tender offer, to its officers, directors, partners, employees or advisors or to other persons, involved in the planning, financing, preparation or execution of the activities of the issuer with respect to such tender offer; or

iii.   To any person pursuant to a requirement of any statute or rule or regulation promulgated thereunder.

the announcement of the tender offer. The increase in stock prices tends to be on the order of 20 to 30 percent. Evidence indicates that stock prices also tend to drift up prior to the announcement of the tender offer. Hence, corporate takeovers provide a perfect setting to exploit insider information. The large price increases on announcement provide excellent opportunities for illegal insider traders to buy the target shares before the announcement and thus profit illegally from the subsequent price increases.[30]

In an early study, Keown and Pinkerton examine stock price movements in 93 stocks that were eventually taken over during the period from 1975 to 1978.[31] They find a 13.25 percent run-up in stock prices during the 60 days before the takeover announcement. Most of this run-up occurs during the 20 days immediately preceding the takeover announcement. On announcement, stock prices further increase by another 13 percent. Hence, about half of the total stock price reaction occurs prior to the public disclosure of the takeover attempt. Keown and Pinkerton also find that the trading volume also abnormally increases during the same 20 days prior to takeover announcements. Keown and Pinkerton interpret their evidence as being consistent with illegal insider trading driving up both stock prices and trading volumes prior to the public announcements.

Subsequent studies also confirm the presence of pre-announcement run-ups in stock prices. For instance, studies by Asquith, Asquith and Mullins, and Dennis and McConnell all find similar stock price run-ups.[32] Furthermore, these studies also attribute the pre-announcement run-ups to illegal insider trading activity.

Various subsequent studies have investigated whether these run-ups in stock prices could be explained by alternative hypotheses. One such hypothesis is the presence of public information, such as rumors or 13-D filings, about the possibility of a tender offer, rather than insider trading.[33] In a test of the public rumor hypothesis, Jarrell and Poulsen study 172 tender offers from 1981 to 1985.[34] They find that the presence of rumors in the

---

[30]   A recent paper by Agrawal and Nasser finds that registered corporate executives and large shareholders refrain from profitable trading immediately before corporate takeovers. Hence, any illegal insider trading activity prior to the tender offers is most likely to come from affiliated persons rather than corporate executives. Anup Agrawal & Tareque Nasser, Insider Trading in Takeover Targets, J. Corp. Fin. (forthcoming 2012).

[31]   Arthur J. Keown & John M. Pinkerton, Merger Announcements and Insider Trading Activity: An Empirical Investigation, 36 J. Fin. 855 (1981).

[32]   Paul Asquith, Merger Bids, Uncertainty, and Stockholder Returns, 11 J. Fin. Econ. 51 (1983). Paul Asquith & David Mullins, The Gains to Bidding Firms from Mergers, 11 J. Fin. Econ. 121 (1983); Diane Denis & John McConnell, Corporate Mergers and Security Returns, 16 J. Fin. Econ 143 (1986).

[33]   Schedule 13-D is an SEC filing that must be submitted with ten days of acquiring a 5 percent or greater equity stake in any publicly held corporation. The filer must disclose his/her purpose in acquiring this block, including whether the filer intends to launch a takeover bid. Furthermore, 13-D filings must be updated to reflect any material changes, such as subsequent acquisition of disposition of more than 1 percent of the security for which an earlier filing was made. See, e.g., Michael C. Jensen & Richard S. Ruback, The Market for Corporate Control: The Scientific Evidence, 11 J. Fin. Econ. 5 (1983). However, John Pound and Richard Zeckhauser find that rumors accurately predict imminent takeover bids less than one-half of the time. John Pound & Richard Zeckhauser, Clearly Heard on the Street: The Effect of Takeover Rumors on Stock Prices, 63 J. Bus. 291 (1990).

[34]   G. Jarrell & A. Poulsen, Stock Trading before the Announcement of Tender Offers: Insider Trading or Market Anticipation? 8 J. L. Econ. & Org. 225 (1989).

news media is the most significant variable that explains the unanticipated premiums and pre-bid stock price run-ups that Keown and Pinkerton documented. Jarrell and Poulsen also find that subsequent illegal insider trading investigations do not explain the pre-bid run-ups. Accordingly, they interpret their evidence as being inconsistent with illegal insider trading and consistent with the public rumor hypothesis. However, Jarrell and Poulsen do not examine the source of the rumors. If the rumors about the tender offers were planted by those who acquired the information illegally, who took illegal stock positions and then spread the rumors, then pre-bid run-ups and illegal insider trading would be synonymous.

Holding all else constant, traders who obtain illegal insider trading information about a forthcoming takeover would have incentives to surreptitiously plant rumors in the financial press about the upcoming potential takeover. First, once they have taken their positions, any newspaper stories about the takeover result in increases in stock prices and give additional profits to illegal insider traders.[35] Secondly, the presence of rumors in the press gives the illegal insider traders a cover in case of a civil or criminal investigation. Illegal insiders can always point to the stories as to why they took up their stock positions in the target firms. Thus, it is not possible to clearly separate the rumor hypothesis from the illegal trading hypothesis.

In a cross-country study, Maug et al. examine pre-bid stock price run-ups in 48 countries in almost 19,000 takeover announcements.[36] They find that passing of the insider trading legislation affects the pre-bid stock price run-ups. In particular, they find that pre-bid stock price run-ups are significantly lower the more restrictive is a country's insider trading law, other things equal. This finding suggests that at least some of the pre-bid run-ups is due to illegal insider trading, which is reduced by the passing of tougher insider trading laws.

Illegal insider trading prior to takeovers has important public policy and economic consequences. Meulbroek and Hart find that the presence of illegal insider trading prior to takeovers is associated with about 10 percent higher takeover premiums.[37] Hence, illegal insider trading imposes costs on bidder firms' shareholders by increasing the cost of the takeovers. As the costs of successful takeovers increase, we would also expect a deleterious effect on the number of takeover attempts, potentially reducing the incidence of value-enhancing changes in corporate control.

B. Hypotheses and Methodology

In this study, we test whether illegal insider trading has become increasingly more common over time in the United States. We take two approaches to this question. First, we examine stock price run-ups prior to tender offer announcements over time. We

---

[35] See G. William Schwert, Markup Pricing in Mergers and Acquisitions, 41 J. Fin. Econ. 153 (1996).

[36] Ernst G. Maug et al., Insider Trading Legislation and Acquisition Announcements: Do Laws Matter? (2008), available at http://papers.ssrn.com/sol3/papers.cfm?abstract_id=868708 (last visited Dec. 11, 2012).

[37] Lisa Meulbroek & Carolyn Hart, The Effect of Illegal Insider Trading on Takeover Premia, 1 Eur. Fin. Rev. 51 (1997).

investigate whether the likelihood and magnitude of the pre-bid run-up in target firms' stock prices have increased over time. We also investigate whether bidder firms are more likely to make toehold investments in target firms over time and whether the price run-up can be explained by toehold investments.[38]

Secondly, to distinguish between the public rumor and illegal insider trading hypotheses, we examine the pricing of stock options on the target firms. Both hypotheses predict stock price run-ups, as discussed above. However, public information (including rumors) and insider information should have opposite effects on the volatility of the target stock returns. If the observed stock price run-ups are due to publicly known rumors about the possibility of a takeover, then we would expect the implied volatility of the options on the takeover target to decline both prior to the announcement as well as on the announcement date. This is because takeovers are volatility reducing events.

In some takeovers, the bidder firm announces a fixed price (a cash offer) for the target firm. The fact that the target price is fixed if the offer is successful reduces the volatility of the target firm's stock returns. Alternatively, instead of offering a fixed price, in some takeovers the bidder firms offer a fixed number of bidder shares for target shares (a stock exchange offer). We expect exchange offers to also reduce the volatility of target stock returns, since the volatility of the target shares is replaced by the volatility of the bidder shares. Bidder firms are typically much larger than target firms and therefore they are less volatile.

In short, if the pre-bid run-up in stock prices is due to public rumors about a prospective tender offer, we would expect the volatility of the target firms' stock returns to decline uniformly prior to the public announcement of the tender offers. As the run-up increases, volatility should decline more. This is because as the probability of the tender offer increases, there is a greater probability of a reduction in volatility of target returns. Hence, the public rumor hypothesis predicts a negative relation between the pre-bid run-up in stock prices and volatility of the returns to target firms.

In contrast, if illegal insider trading is driving the trading volume and price effects prior to corporate takeovers, then we would expect an increase in the implied volatility of the target firms' stock returns. This is because illegal insiders can exploit their information more efficiently by buying call options on the target firm instead of common stock. Call options typically provide additional leverage given by the elasticity of the option prices. By using call options illegal insiders can further leverage the announcement day returns. Thus, illegal insiders would be willing to bid up the price of the call options on a target firm in order to establish large options positions that would benefit from a run-up in the target stock price.

---

[38]　Toehold investments refer to the pre-announcement acquisition of shares by potential bidders. When any potential bidder acquires 5 percent of the outstanding shares, it needs to file a 13-D statement disclosing its position as well as its intent within ten days. Public disclosures of toehold investments are associated with positive stock price reactions. Toehold investments also help facilitate change of control. See generally W. Mikkelson & R. Ruback, An Empirical Analysis of the Interfirm Equity Investment Process, 14 J. Fin. Econ. 523 (1985); Clifford G. Holderness and Dennis P. Sheehan, Raiders or Saviors? The Evidence on Six Controversial Investors, 14 J. Fin. Econ. 555 (1985); D. Choi, Toehold Acquisitions, Shareholder Wealth, and the Market for Corporate Control, 26 J. Fin. & Quant. Anal. 391 (1991).

Holding current stock price, exercise price and maturity constant, option prices are monotonically and positively related to option volatility. Consequently, holding all else constant, if call option prices increase as a result of the illegal insider trading, then implied option volatilities should also increase.

In summary, the public rumor hypothesis predicts that the implied volatility of target stock returns will decrease prior to takeover announcements. In contrast, the illegal insider trading hypothesis makes the opposite prediction, in particular that the implied volatility of target stock returns will increase prior to takeover announcements. Implied volatility thus provides an excellent framework for investigating our illegal insider trading hypothesis.

To measure the implied volatility of the target returns, we follow Harvey and Whaley.[39] We implement the binomial option pricing model on American options with dividends numerically to compute the implied volatility estimates. We adopt the conventional assumption that any dividend paid on the underlying stock is known in advance. The advantage of the binomial option pricing model is that it can explicitly incorporate the fact that these options are American options subject to early exercise. Using the Newton–Raphson search procedure similar to that suggested by Manaster and Koehler,[40] we calculate the implied volatility for every call option transaction in our sample. More specifically, the following algorithm is employed: given an ith estimate implied volatility, the procedure suggests the $i + 1$th should be:

$$\sigma_{i+1} = \sigma_i - \frac{[C(\sigma_i) - C(\sigma^*)]}{vega} \qquad (12.1)$$

where $C(\sigma_i)$ is the price of the option with an implied volatility of σ_i computed from the binomial model, $C(\sigma^*)$ is the observed option price and $vega$ is the partial derivative of the option price with respect to volatility. We iterate on this procedure until the implied volatility has converged and the predicted price is equal to the market price.[41]

The literature on options valuation has uncovered systematic patterns on implied volatility as a function of the maturity and moneyness of the options.[42] To avoid confounding takeover related effects with well-known biases in binomial options pricing with respect

---

[39]   See Campbell R. Harvey & Robert E. Whaley, Market Volatility Prediction and the Efficiency of the S&P 100 Index Option Market, 30 J. Fin. Econ. 43 (1992); Campbell R. Harvey & Robert E. Whaley, Dividends and S&P 100 Index Option Valuation, 12 J. Futures Markets 123 (1992).

[40]   S. Manaster & G. Koehler, The Calculation of Implied Variances from the Black–Scholes Model: A Note, 37 J. Fin. 227 (1982).

[41]   We divide days to maturity into 180 intervals. The convergence criterion is set to 0.001 percent. That is, the algorithm is considered convergent if the estimated price is within 0.001 percent of the observed price. Ideally, the number of intervals should be dependent on the length of the days to maturity. However, there is a trade-off in terms of computation cost. We compare our estimates to the estimates we obtain from Black–Scholes when the underlying stock pays no dividends before expiration. Not surprisingly, they are very close to each other.

[42]   See e.g., Robert E. Whaley, Valuation of American Call Options on Dividend-Paying Stocks: Empirical Tests, 10 J. Fin. Econ. 29 (1982); Jeremy Stein, Overreactions in the Options Market, 44 J. Fin. 1011 (1989); Gurdip S. Bakshi et al., Empirical Performance of Alternative Option Pricing Models, 52 J. Fin. 2003 (1997).

Table 12.1   Characteristics of the tender offer sample

Subsample	Number of tender offers	Percent acquired	Total value acquired ($ million)	Initial toehold investment ($ million)	Probability of initial toehold (%)
1996–2000	647	95.9	642.7	279.1	33.6
2001–2005	259	95.7	800.4	13.9	97.6
2006–2011	271	94.2	1,392.6	21.7	93.0
Total	1,177	95.4	850.1	148.8	48.3

to maturity and moneyness, we restrict our attention to short-term options that extend beyond the takeover announcement date by no more than 30 days and are near the money. We define near the money options as with exercise prices within a 20 percent band of the current stock price. Changes in implied volatilities have been used in the literature to estimate price pressures on option prices.[43]

C.   Data and Results

Our corporate takeover data come from Securities Data Corporation (SDC) files from the Wharton Research database System (WRDS). Stock return data come from WRDS as well. Our options data come from Options Metrics Ivy DB Database. This database contains all exchange-traded options transactions after 1995.

To ensure availability of the options data, we focus on tender offers after 1995. To ensure that the potential stock price reaction on the announcement date is economically important, we also use only tender offers where the bidder firms were eventually successful in obtaining at least 50 percent of the target shares.

The sample characteristics of our tender offer database are shown in Table 12.1. Our database covers 1,177 tender offers from 1996 to 2011. Bidder firms acquired an average of 95.4 percent of the target firms through the tender offer. The average value of the target shares acquired equals $850 million.

As noted above, a pre-bid run-up in stock prices may be caused by toehold investments by the bidder firms that can also put upward pressure on target stock prices. Therefore, Table 12.1 also reports the average toehold investment by bidder firms, as well as the likelihood that a bidder firm made a toehold investment in a target firm. Just under half of the bidder firms bought a toehold in the target over the entire period (1996–2011). However, there is significant intertemporal variation in the probability of a toehold. During Period 1 (1996–2000), only 33.6 percent of the bidder firms bought a toehold investment in the target firms. During Period 2 (2001–2005), this ratio increased to 97.6 percent. In Period 3 (2006–2011), the toehold investment proportion declined slightly to 93.0 percent. As

---

[43]   See, e.g., Kaushik Amin et al., Index Option Prices and Stock Market Momentum, 77 J. Bus. 835 (2004); Xuewu Wang, Three Essays in Insider Trading (Sept. 3, 2011) (Ph.D. dissertation); H. Nejat Seyhun & Xuewu Wang, Return Predictability and Stock Option Prices, III(2) Int'l J. Appl. Fin. 171–205 (2012).

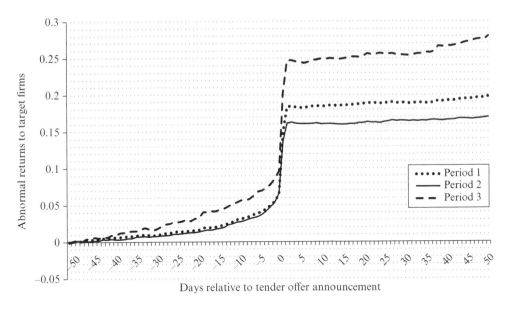

Figure 12.2   Cumulative average abnormal returns to target firms

explained below, however, the increased prevalence of toehold investments does not appear to explain the increase in pre-bid stock price run-ups over time.

Next, we compute abnormal returns to target firms. Abnormal returns are computed as the raw return minus the value-weighted market return from 50 days before the takeover announcement to 50 days after the takeover announcement. Implicitly, this approach assumes a Beta of 1 for all firms. Given the limited explanatory power of Beta, this simple market-adjusted return approach has been used frequently in the finance literature.[44]

Once we find the abnormal returns, we then average them for each event day relative to the takeover announcement date, which is defined as day zero. That is, we average the abnormal returns for each day from 50 days before to 50 days after the takeover announcement date. Finally, we calculate the cumulative average abnormal returns from 50 days before to 50 days after the tender offer announcement date.

Cumulative average abnormal returns to target firms are shown in Figure 12.2. We compute the cumulative average abnormal returns separately for the three sub-periods. As can be seen, stock prices rise abnormally prior to tender offers. During Period 1 (1996–2000), stock prices rise abnormally by about 20 percent. Furthermore, approximately one-third of the total run-up or about 7 percent rise occurs prior to the public announcement of the tender offer.

In Period 2 (2000–2005), stock prices rise about 17 percent from 50 days before to

[44]   See, e.g., Michael Gibbons & Patrick Hess, The Day of the Week Effects and Asset Returns, 54 J. Bus. 579 (1981); Werner De Bondt & Richard Thaler, Does the Stock Market Overreact, 40 J. Fin. 793 (1985); Stephen Brown & Jerold Warner, Using the Daily Stock Returns: The Case of Event Studies, 14 J. Fin. Econ. 3 (1985).

Table 12.2   Characteristics of the options sample

Subsample	Number of options	Maturity (days)	Moneyness of call options	Call implied volatility
1996–2000	17,692	55.74	0.992	0.59
2001–2005	6,323	57.76	0.989	0.48
2006–2011	21,916	58.16	0.990	0.41
Total	45,931	57.17	0.991	0.49

one day after the announcement date. Again, about one-third or about seven percentage points of the rise occur prior to the public announcement of the tender offer. Finally, during Period 3 (2006–2011), stock prices rise 28 percent from 50 days before to one day after the tender offer announcement date. In the most recent sub-period, about ten percentage points of the rise occur prior to the public announcement.

Figure 12.2 shows that the market reaction to tender offers has increased over time. Along with this increase, the incentives to trade on tender offer announcements have also increased since greater stock price movements indicate availability of greater abnormal, albeit illegal trading profits. Our evidence also indicates that instead of declining, the pre-bid run-up has increased over time. Compared with the pre-2006 periods, the pre-bid run-up during the last five years has increased by 50 percent (ten percentage points versus seven percentage points). The increase in pre-bid stock price run-up does not appear to be driven by changes in toehold investments over time. While the probability of a toehold investment increases from 33.3 percent to 97.6 percent between Periods 1 and 2, this change is not accompanied by a proportionate or even significant increase in the pre-bid run-up. Furthermore, although between Periods 2 and 3 the likelihood of a toehold investment declines slightly, the pre-bid price run-up increases significantly.

In short, the evidence in Figure 12.2 is consistent with the observation that higher levels of insider trading enforcement correspond to increased illegal insider trading activity, as reflected in a higher pre-bid stock price run-up.

We now turn to implied volatility tests. Sample characteristics of our options database are shown in Table 12.2. Our database contains about 45,000 options trades for firms involved in takeovers. The average remaining time to maturity is around 57 calendar days. The sample options tend to be at-the-money, with the average moneyness measure of the options about 1.0.[45] Average implied call volatility is about 50 percent.

We next examine the time series properties of the implied volatilities of call options on target firms around the takeover announcement. Figure 12.3 shows implied volatilities of call options around the tender offers. Overall, implied volatility of call options rises during the 50 days prior to the takeover announcement. On the takeover announcement date, the implied volatility falls by about half. Finally, during the 50 days after the takeover announcement date, the implied volatility rises slightly. Figure 12.3 shows no evidence of a fall in implied volatility prior to the announcement of the takeovers.

In Figure 12.4, we compute implied volatility for each of the three sub-periods sepa-

---

[45]   Moneyness of the options is defined as the stock price divided by the exercise price.

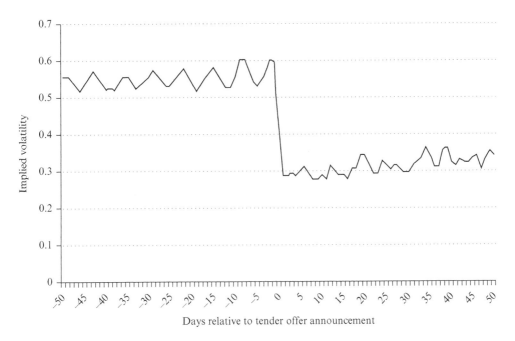

Figure 12.3   Implied option volatility relative to takeover announcement

rately. Evidence in Figure 12.4 indicates that in all three sub-periods, implied volatilities of call options of target firms decline on the public announcement of the tender offer. The magnitude of the decline is large and statistically significant. On average, volatility declines by as much as one-half of the pre-announcement day volatility. Hence, our evidence confirms that tender offers reduce volatility of target stocks' returns on announcement.

In contrast with the announcement day reaction, volatility of target stock returns does not decline prior to the announcement in any of the three sub-periods. In fact, volatility typically increases prior to the announcement of the takeovers in each sub-period. This figure is consistent with price pressure on call options, and inconsistent with the public rumor explanation. The public rumor hypothesis predicts a smoothly declining volatility prior to the announcement date as the tender offer is publicly anticipated. The lack of a smoothly declining implied volatility suggests that the tender offer announcement comes as a surprise to the market participants. Instead, consistent with the price pressure hypothesis, volatility increases prior to the tender offer announcement dates.

While not shown here, we undertook some additional tests. Specifically, the public rumor hypothesis predicts a negative relation between volatility and pre-bid run-up in stock prices. To test this hypothesis, we ran a regression of the changes in implied volatilities against the stock price run-ups. Our evidence suggests weakly positive relation between the two, instead of a negative relation as predicted by the public rumor hypothesis. This finding is inconsistent with the public rumor hypothesis.

Rising implied volatility prior to the public announcement of the takeover implies increasing price pressure on option prices as predicted by the illegal insider trading hypothesis. The fact that implied volatilities rise prior to tender offers can be seen

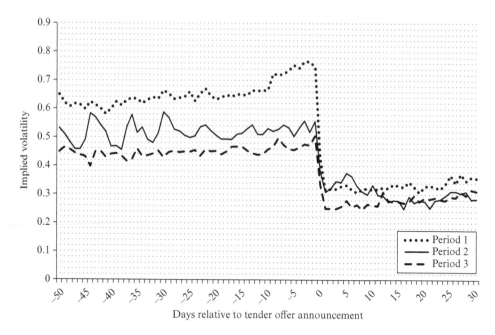

Figure 12.4   Implied option volatility relative to takeover announcement, by sub-period

from Figure 12.4. The increasing volatility is evident in all three sub-periods. Overall, Figure 12.4 is consistent with the presence of illegal insider trading prior to the announcement of the tender offers in all three sub-periods.

IV.   CONCLUSIONS

Recent evidence indicates increasing enforcement action against insider trading by the SEC and the DOJ. The SEC more than doubled its enforcement actions between 2005 and 2010 compared with the 1980s. At the same time, the severity of punishment for insider trading convictions has also increased. The probability of receiving a prison sentence upon conviction has increased almost ten-fold over the past 15 years. Similarly, the length of the median prison sentence upon conviction has more than doubled.

In this study, we investigate whether these increased enforcement actions correspond to increased illegal insider trading activity. We examine the pricing of common stocks and options around the announcement of tender offers to detect the presence of illegal insider trading. Our objective is to determine whether illegal insider trading occurs before tender offers and whether illegal insider trading has become more rampant over time. Our evidence indicates that the pre-announcement run-up in stock prices has become larger over time. During the 2006–2011 sub-period, the pre-bid run-up is 50 percent higher than in the pre-2006 period. We also find that toehold investments by bidders do not explain the time series variation in stock price behavior around takeovers.

The evidence from option pricing is also consistent with illegal insider trading at work. We find that the implied volatility of option prices increases before the announcement of tender offers and decreases on the announcement date. This evidence is consistent with a price pressure on call option prices prior to the announcement of the tender offers. Overall, our evidence suggests that the recent increased insider trading enforcement intensity in the USA most likely stems from an increased presence of illegal insider trading.

That insider trading has apparently increased over time raises significant legal and policy questions. One such question is whether enforcement efforts and expenses sufficiently deter insider trading. Relatedly, one may wonder whether the potential returns to illegal insider trading have become more lucrative the more stringent insider trading enforcement has become.

13. The changing demand for insider trading regulation
M. Todd Henderson

> Public policies are determined . . . by small minorities playing upon the fears and imbecilities of the mob—sometimes minorities of intelligent and honest men, but usually minorities of rogues.[1]

I. INTRODUCTION

Insider trading law sweeps broadly but uncertainly, leaving government officials wide discretion in the types of cases they can bring. This chapter presents some original research on which kinds of insider trading cases federal prosecutors decide to bring, and offers a theory to explain their choices. The data presented are consistent with a view that insider trading prosecutions are more a reflection of private interests than public ones. Trading on material, non-public information by certain individuals in certain circumstances is illegal. When it is illegal, the behavior is colloquially known as "insider trading," but this description is misleading. It is not illegal per se for company executives or other "insiders" to trade in their company's shares, and lots of people who are not company insiders can be liable for insider trading. Although the parameters of who can and cannot trade and based on what information are far from clear and still being worked out by the courts, there are severe legal consequences for those found to be on the wrong side of the line.

The direct consequences primarily flow from government action.[2] The Securities Exchange Commission (SEC) can bring civil charges against individuals, seeking disgorgement of profits earned, as well as other civil remedies, such as bans on serving in particular industries (e.g., brokerage) or in particular capacities (e.g., as a director or officer of a public company). Likewise, the Department of Justice (DOJ) can bring criminal charges against individuals, seeking to impose fines and deprive individuals of their liberty.

Notwithstanding the legal risk, there is abundant evidence of widespread and large-scale trading based on material, non-public information. Estimates put the amount of insider trading profits in the billions of dollars per year, and cases have been brought against corporate managers, stock brokers, college football coaches, celebrities, lawyers, and countless other types of individuals. Some of these people came by the material, non-public information by stealing it (what is known as "misappropriation" in the law of

---

[1]   H.L. Mencken, Notes on Democracy (1926).

[2]   Private plaintiffs may also sue seeking damages for ill-gotten gains, or use insider trading allegations as the basis for a securities class action suit for securities fraud by the firm in question. The former cases are quite rare, since trading is usually done on an anonymous exchange, while the latter cases implicate mostly liability for firms, not individuals.

insider trading), some by accident, and some by other means, such as legitimate research and aggregation of information from others.

With all these people trading in ways that implicate insider trading laws, government agents have significant discretion in the kinds of cases they bring. There is no shortage of potential defendants or theories on which to bring prosecutions. Prosecutors have charged big cases and small ones, cases against celebrities and no-names, and everything in between. For example, in recent years cases have been brought against celebrity CEOs, like Martha Stewart, and market professionals like hedge fund mogul Raj Rajaratnam. Stewart was sentenced to 18 months in prison for trading on non-public information to avoid less than $40,000 in losses, while Rajaratnam is serving an 11-year sentence for orchestrating an insider trading scheme that netted more than $60 million in profits.

Prosecutorial discretion is broad and relatively unchecked. There are no direct methods for policing prosecutorial choices, and the indirect methods, such as the ballot box, are unlikely to be highly responsive to the public interest. The SEC is regarded as a largely nonpartisan agency, as are the US attorneys who bring criminal cases. More importantly, insider trading prosecutions, while occasionally high profile, are a tiny fraction of the government workload—there are only about 30 to 40 cases brought per year in the entire country. Therefore, any claim that the decisions they make in this class of cases move elections strains credulity. It may be that nevertheless the public servants who make decisions pursue the public interest because this is their job and they feel the call of public service. The issue with insider trading, however, is that this public interest is quite contestable and hard to define.

One way to test whether prosecutions serve the public or some private interests is to examine the evidence about prosecutions to see if it fits better with an interest-group story or a public-interest one. The question is simple: is the enforcement of insider trading laws in the public interest? The evidence presented suggests that it is not.

II.   THEORIES OF REGULATION

There are two prevailing accounts of regulation. The first is the public-interest account. In this view, regulators are motivated primarily by pursuit of public welfare and regulations are promulgated largely to this end. In this account, prosecutors would ideally determine the social cost of particular conduct, and then, weighing the costs and benefits of bringing a case, prosecute cases in which there would be a net social gain.

The competing account is one in which regulators are influenced by the private interests of the regulated, and regulations are promulgated largely in proportion to the strength of these interests, whether or not they coincide with the public interest.[3] In this account, prosecutors would weigh the private costs, including their own, of particular actions, and bring cases in which there is a net private gain for the parties with the most to gain.

Since both accounts are plausible and are not mutually exclusive, determining which account best describes a particular regulatory scheme comes down to examining changes

---

[3]   See Sam Peltzman, Toward a More General Theory of Regulation, 19 J. Law & Econ. 211 (1976).

in regulatory approach and trying to explain them under the competing approaches. The debate about whether insider trading should be permitted, tolerated, or outlawed completely turns in large measure on which of these models more or less explains the current regulatory regime. Since it is difficult if not impossible to define the public interest in an area like insider trading, the most fruitful mode of analysis is to consider whether current regulations are consistent or inconsistent with the private-interest model.

A.   The Private-Interest Model of Insider Trading Regulation: Theory and Data

The leading theoretical account of the private-interest model of insider trading regulation is from David Haddock and Jonathan Macey. They view insider trading regulation as driven primarily by the private interests of those affected by the regulations operating on the SEC. They argue that "insider trading laws are not motivated primarily by concerns for efficiency, nor are they mistaken," but rather are deliberately designed to benefit a particular concentrated interest group or groups.[4] They identified two groups—managers of public companies (called "insiders") and licensed securities professionals (called "market professionals")—each of who are more concentrated and interested in insider trading rules than investors as a whole or the general public. Accordingly, they argue that insider trading regulations should reflect the relative influence of these two groups, since both have incentives to "support SEC actions that increase [their] group's net benefits."

Writing in 1987, Haddock & Macey described the rivalry for regulatory advantage between insiders and market professionals as generally favoring the latter. They start with the theory that when comparing the relative influence of groups, "the larger the proportion of its potential wealth that can be influenced by an agency's policy selection, the more an interest group can be expected to invest in influencing the agency" and therefore the more likely the agency is to favor that particular group.[5] Applying this theory to their two interest groups, they find market professionals have greater incentives to influence insider trading rules than firm insiders. Their intuition is straightforward: at that time, market professionals earned all of their income from trading profits, while corporate managers "merely augment[ed] their income by trading on inside information."[6] This is because "the bulk of [managers'] wealth, and hence the bulk of their time and effort, is associated more directly with managing the corporations that employ them."[7]

Insiders are not powerless in their model, but merely out-incentivized when it comes to routine trading on inside information. When it comes to other types of informed trades, specifically those surrounding takeovers, insiders have reason to care a lot more than market professionals about these profits and the consequences of pursuing them. Takeovers often result in insiders being ousted, and this means the battle over insider trading rules is about more than splitting the trading-profits pie. It is about

---

[4]   See David D. Haddock & Jonathan R. Macey, Regulation on Demand: A Private Interest Model, with an Application to Insider Trading Regulation, 30 J. Law & Econ. 311, 314 (1987).

[5]   Id. at 319.

[6]   Id. at 314–15.

[7]   Id.

protecting insiders' jobs and the wealth and fringe benefits that come with them. It may also be about protecting the utility of insiders that comes from achieving a particular corporate vision or strategy, or, perhaps more generally, the feeling of being in charge, completely.

Importantly for this account, insider trading rules influence the likely success of take-overs. In the 1980s, this was because, absent insider trading rules, bidders could leak information about future bids to friendly investors, known as arbitrageurs, who could then purchase large blocks of shares at relatively low prices. This would allow the bidder to more easily overcome managerial resistance by locking up votes in return for guaranteed profits. A liberal insider trading regime therefore would "seriously [threaten] the bulk of wealth of some managerial insiders" by threatening their jobs.[8] Importantly, Haddock & Macey claim this increased interest on the part of managers is not outdone by the interests of market professionals in these trades, since trades associated with takeovers "[account] for only a portion of the wealth of market professionals."[9] Therefore, their model predicts we should see insiders able to resist efforts of market professionals to expand trading opportunities involving takeovers.

Haddock & Macey use their model to explain the SEC's regulatory choices after an exogenous shock to existing rules from a 1980 Supreme Court decision. Before the shock, the SEC took the view that all traders should have access to the same information and that anyone with access to material, non-public information had an obligation to disclose the information before trading or abstain from trading.[10] Whatever its merits, this interpretation and practice put insiders and market professionals on relatively equal footing in terms of potential insider trading liability.

In *Chiarella v. U.S.*, however, the Supreme Court held the disclose-or-abstain rule applied only to traders who owed a fiduciary duty to those they were trading against.[11] (This modification of the SEC's rule was reaffirmed three years later in *Dirks v. SEC*.[12]) Since corporate managers clearly owe such a duty to their shareholders, and since using corporate information to earn trading profits would violate this duty under well-accepted corporate law doctrine, managers remained subject to insider trading rules. But securities market professionals owed no preexisting duty to strangers they traded against or to the shareholders of firms whose information they got by hook or by crook, and the rules did not apply to them. *Chiarella* and *Dirks* thus opened a wedge between the interest groups that the Haddock & Macey model predicted would be in some equilibrium before the decision.

Haddock & Macey's model predicts three things to flow from *Chiarella* and *Dirks*. First, SEC prosecutions would increasingly focus on insiders as opposed to market professionals. The intuition is obvious: the costs of prosecuting market professionals rises significantly post-*Chiarella* and *Dirks*, and market professionals would have incentives to encourage the SEC to divert resources in the direction of firm insiders. Haddock & Macey provide support for this prediction by showing that while about 50 percent of defendants

---

[8]   Id.
[9]   Id. at 316.
[10]   See, e.g., SEC v. Texas Gulf Sulphur, Co., 401 F.2d 833 (1968).
[11]   See Chiarella v. United States, 445 U.S. 222 (1980).
[12]   See Dirks v. SEC, 464 U.S. 646 (1983).

in insider trading cases before *Chiarella* and *Dirks* were insiders, this percentage rose to nearly 80 percent following the decision.[13]

Secondly, insiders, now threatened by the ability of market professionals to trade on inside information, especially on takeovers, would push back to protect against that area where they are especially threatened by trading, as opposed to merely not earning any extra trading profits. Haddock & Macey provide support for this prediction by describing how, following *Chiarella*, the SEC adopted a new rule—Rule 14e-3—that reinstated the ban on market professionals trading on material non-public information in the takeover context.[14]

Thirdly, market professionals, being given this great freedom to earn insider trading profits, would have increased incentives to police their own, since any deviations from the now-generous rules would involve dishonest brokers violating fiduciary duties, as this kind of behavior would implicate the trustworthiness of the entire industry. The authors support their prediction by pointing to the passage of increased penalties for insider trading in 1984[15] and the increased resources devoted to policing trading by the stock exchanges, which are controlled by market professionals.[16]

B.   Changes to the Private-Interest Account

In the over two decades since Haddock & Macey analyzed insider trading regulation through their private-interest model of regulation, several things have changed, both in terms of regulation and the underlying facts about the interest groups. This section analyzes these changes to see whether they are consistent with the Haddock & Macey account. If changes in regulation are consistent with predictions from changes in interest-group dynamics, then this would provide support for the private-interest model of regulation, and therefore a dramatic rethinking of our approach to insider trading. If, on the other hand, regulation cannot be explained by current incentives created by managers and market professionals, then we might view recent regulatory innovations as heading in the direction of the public interest.

Two changes over the past 20-plus years have fundamentally altered the interest-group dynamic, and these changes explain the current state of insider trading regulation.

The first big change of the past 20 years is the rise of stock and stock options as the predominant form of executive compensation. This has dramatically increased the stake firm insiders have in insider trading rules. Firm insiders now earn more than half of their annual income and an even larger component of their lifetime earnings from trades in firm stock. Since more of their wealth is in firm stock, insiders have reason to care a lot more about insider trading regulation than they did in 1987. This is true even for insiders who do not intend to trade on material, non-public information. So long as enforcement is imperfect and errors are possible in sorting between legal and illegal trades, insiders who are trading more will prefer regulations that are more permissive.[17]

---

[13]   See Haddock & Macey, Regulation on Demand, supra note 4 at 329, Table 1.
[14]   See SEC Securities Exchange Act Release No. 17120, 17 C.F.R. § 240.14e-3.
[15]   Insider Trading Sanctions Act, 15 U.S.C. § 78a, 21(d)(1); 32; 15(c)(4); 20 (1984).
[16]   See Haddock & Macey, Regulation on Demand, supra note 4.
[17]   See infra Section II.D.1.

The second big change is the rise of hedge funds as activist investors. Private investment pools have dramatically altered the scope and intensity of the takeover market by eschewing full-fledged takeovers, preferring instead to move quickly into large positions—a few percent—in a firm's stock, using that leverage to achieve changes in management or strategy, and then selling just as quickly to capture any increase in firm value. This means corporate changes can be done much faster and at much lower cost than 20 years ago. This in turn has generated instability and insecurity for corporate managers. For example, CEO turnover has fallen dramatically from about 15 years on average in the 1980s to less than five years on average today. In short, the takeover threat Haddock & Macey identified has been dramatically changed, from the fear of a takeover to proxy contests and other forms of activism, and the source of this expansion is activist investors, especially private funds or hedge funds.

Let's look at each of these changes in detail.

1.   CEO pay

The primary reason Haddock & Macey concluded that market professionals were a more powerful interest group than firm insiders was because securities professionals earned all of their income from trading, while insiders only earned a small part of their total compensation from trading. While this is still true for securities professionals, it has changed completely for insiders with the rise of firm equity as the dominant form of executive compensation.

As an initial matter, the absolute pay of firm insiders has increased dramatically over the past 20 years.[18] During the 1980s, the median pay of the CEO of the largest 50 American firms was $1.8 million. During the period 2000–2005, the median pay rose to $9.2 million.[19] Even more broadly, the median CEO pay of all the firms in the ExecuComp database (about 5600 firms) increased from about $500,000 in 1992 to over $1.3 million in 2009. This sharp rise in pay increases the incentives for firm insiders to care about insider trading rules, since they have more money at stake in the market.

Moreover the share of pay comprised of stock increased dramatically over the same period. Firm equity has become a much larger component of CEO pay over the past 20 years. During the late 1980s, less than 20 percent of total CEO compensation was in the form of firm equity, either restricted stock, stock grants, or options. By 2009, the share of total pay that was in the form of stock or options had risen to over 60 percent. Again, this was constant across all three sets of firms discussed above.[20] This means that the median CEO of the top 50 firms received about $450,000 in stock or stock options per year in the 1980s. Stock-based pay rose to over $5.5 million per year in the 2000s.[21] This is over a 12-fold increase in the annual incentives to care about insider trading rules. As expected given the annual increases in stock grants, the total stock portfolio of CEOs has also increased significantly over the past 20 years. During the late 1980s, the average portfolio value of stock and stock options for the top three executives for the 50 largest American

---

[18]   All figures in this section are in inflation-adjusted 2000 dollars.
[19]   See Carola Frydman & Dirk Jenter, Executive Compensation, Panel B (2010), available at http://ssrn.com/abstract=1582232 (last visited Nov. 29, 2012).
[20]   Id.
[21]   Id. at Panel A.

firms was about $2.5 million.[22] This amount rose to $12.1 million during the 2000s.[23] Again, this supports the claim that CEOs had much greater incentives to care about the stock price in 2007 than they did in 1987. The difference between a 5 percent return and a 15 percent return on sales of all shares would have been an additional million dollars in 2007 compared with 1987.

Not only were CEOs paid more in stock and did they hold more stock, but they were likely also to be trading significantly more stock in the 2000s than they were in the 1980s and 1990s. According to a recent empirical study of over 8400 firm insiders at over 3000 publicly traded firms, the average top executive sold over $7 million in firm shares per year over the period 2001–2007.[24] There are no good data available about CEO trading in firm stock from the 1980s, but since the average CEO was earning less than $500,000 in stock-based compensation per year, it seems reasonable to conclude that the volume of trading was significantly lower.

Not only are today's CEOs trading much more in volume, many are earning large, abnormal trading profits on these trades. According to the study cited above, some of the insiders (at about 1200 firms) sold about $8 million in firm shares per year, earning abnormal returns of about 12 percent on these sales.[25] This means these sales were generating abnormal profits of about $1 million per year, which is greater than the value of all the shares granted to the average CEO during the 1980s. Moreover, this sales figure includes only sales as reported under certain trading plans, so it does not necessarily include open-market purchases and sales. This means that whatever proclivity CEOs have for open-market purchases would have to have changed dramatically for there to be any doubt about the conclusion that insiders care about trading rules far more today than just two decades ago.

2.   Role of hedge funds

The other pillar of Haddock & Macey's interest-group analysis was the conclusion that firm insiders would care more than market professionals about insider trading surrounding takeovers. This section describes how the rise of activist investors, largely through unregulated pools of private money, known broadly as hedge funds, has dramatically increased the threat firm insiders face from market professionals. In addition, it shows how this change in the market can be expected to alter the Haddock & Macey analysis and thus the state of insider trading law.

In the most comprehensive analysis of the rise of hedge funds and their implications for firms, Professors Alon Brav, Wei Jiang, Randall Thomas, and Frank Partnoy conclude that "hedge funds increasingly engage in a new form of shareholder activism and monitoring that differs fundamentally from previous activist efforts by other institutional investors."[26] They show how activist hedge funds have targeted hundreds of companies

---

[22]   Id. at 42, Table 2.

[23]   Id.

[24]   See M. Todd Henderson et al., Strategic Disclosure of Rule 10b5-1 Plans, Univ. of Chicago Working Paper, (2010), available at http://papers.ssrn.com/sol3/papers.cfm?abstract_id=1137928 (last visited Nov. 29, 2012).

[25]   See id.

[26]   Alon Brav et al., Hedge Fund Activism, Corporate Governance and Firm Performance, 63 J. Fin. 1729 (2008).

and "[d]uring the year after the announcement of activism, average CEO pay declines by about one million dollars, and the CEO turnover rate increases by almost 10 percentage points."[27] The authors also show how the number of companies targeted with such activism is in the hundreds. There was nothing like this kind of activism in the 1980s or the 1990s, and executives today face a much greater chance of being subjected to ouster or a large pay cut as a result of trading by hedge funds.

While there was a robust takeover market in the late 1980s, it was driven by junk bond investors who financed the activities of corporate raiders like Carl Ichan and T. Boone Pickens who engaged in large and expensive takeovers of a few firms. In contrast, hedge funds today deploy vastly more capital and across a much wider range of firms. In short, they have brought discipline to countless more firms than the takeover wave of the 1980s. This insecurity is reflected in commentary about hedge fund activism. Recent news stories describe the "Attack of the Hungry Hedge Funds,"[28] note that "Hedge Funds Are the New Sheriffs of the Boardroom,"[29] call them "The New Raiders,"[30] and characterize their actions as "To Battle, Armed with Shares."[31] These articles describe how "corporate boards are adjusting to a new reality: the activist investor, armed with a handful of shares and a megaphone, is changing corporate America and the deal-making landscape."[32] Hedge fund managers describe their actions in this way as well: "We're putting together a war machine . . . and no company will be safe."[33]

Although the first hedge fund started in 1949, 20 years later the SEC counted only 140 investment partnerships that could be considered hedge funds.[34] There were a few prominent hedge funds operating during the 1970s, 1980s, and 1990s, but neither hedge funds nor any other shareholder pools were significant players in disciplining corporate managers when Haddock & Macey were writing. As summarized by Linda Chatman Thomsen, the former head of enforcement at the SEC, and her coauthors, "until the 1990s, hedge funds operated in relative obscurity and drew little public attention."[35]

Today, hedge funds are not obscure but are rather a central player in a much revitalized and much more widespread market for corporate control. The growth of the private capital industry has been remarkable. Three years after Haddock & Macey's analysis, the hedge fund industry deployed about $40 billion of unleveraged, managed assets.[36] The industry had grown to over $500 billion by 2000, and according to a 2003 SEC

---

[27] Id.

[28] See Mara Der Hovanesian, Attack of the Hungry Hedge Funds, Bus. Wk., Feb. 20, 2006, at 72.

[29] Allan Murray, Hedge Funds Are the New Sheriffs of the Boardroom, Wall St. J., Dec. 14, 2005, at A2.

[30] Emily Thornton, The New Raiders, Bus. WK., Feb. 28, 2005, at 32.

[31] Andrew Ross Sorkin, To Battle, Armed with Shares, N.Y. Times, Jan. 4, 2006, at Cl.

[32] Id.

[33] Justin Hibbard, Take Your Best Shot, Punk, Bus. Wk., Nov. 7, 2005, at 118.

[34] Barry Eichengreen of the University of California at Berkeley and Donald Mathieson of the International Monetary Fund in a report on hedge funds.

[35] Linda C. Thomsen et al., Hedge Funds: An Enforcement Perspective, 39 Rutgers L. J. 541 (2007–2008).

[36] SEC, Implications of the Growth of Hedge Funds: Staff Report to the United States Securities And Exchange Commission (2003).

report, there were 6000 to 7000 hedge funds operating in the United States, managing approximately $600 to $650 billion in assets.[37] The best estimates suggest there are about 9000 funds operating today, managing more than $1.1 trillion in assets.[38] This represents growth of about 3000 percent over the past 15 years. Importantly for an analysis of insider trading law, these assets are not sitting on the sidelines or investing passively.

Hedge funds are following relatively aggressive strategies of trading and activism that are changing the way insiders think about their relationship with market profession-als. This is driven by several factors, some having to do with the nature of hedge funds, some having to do with the general light touch regulatory environment for hedge funds, and some having to do with regulatory changes that make activism by hedge funds (and others) easier.

The nature of hedge fund investing is different from other institutional investing in several key ways, each of which facilitates hedge fund activism in trying to influence corporate policies.

First, hedge funds are free to take large stakes in individual firms and hold them for long periods, since laws or regulations that require other institutional investors to maintain diversified portfolios do not generally apply to hedge funds. In addition, hedge funds are not bound by rules requiring certain investors, like mutual funds, to have their shares be redeemable on demand. Investors in mutual funds can force a fund to sell securities immediately to satisfy redemption requests, whereas hedge funds can contract with investors to make investments not redeemable for many years. These features allow hedge funds to hold large stakes in individual companies over long time horizons, and thereby increase their leverage over firm policies, as well as their ability to control the board.

Secondly, hedge funds operate more freely than other institutional investors due to a relatively light-touch regulatory approach. Hedge funds are not covered by the limitations on derivatives trading and margin trading found in the Investment Company Act.[39] In addition, hedge funds do not operate under strict fiduciary duty requirements that other institutional investors, such as pension funds, are subjected to under federal law govern-ing retirement plans.[40] Hedge funds also do not have significant conflicts of interest or political commitments due to their typical independence. This allows them increased flex-ibility in the nature and scope of attacks they can mount on corporations. As the former head of SEC enforcement recently concluded, "hedge funds often pursue more aggressive investment strategies because they do not operate under the regulatory restrictions and fiduciary safeguards applicable to mutual funds and other regulated entities that favor relative returns to average investors."[41]

Thirdly, hedge funds are somewhat freer in their ability to implicitly coordinate activi-ties in a way that avoids federal disclosure requirements, and thereby makes any takeover attempts quicker and stealthier, giving targets less time to mount a defense. Current law requires that investors taking greater than a 5 percent stake in a company must file a

---

[37]   Id.
[38]   Linda C. Thomsen et al., supra note 35, at 551.
[39]   Section 12(a), Investment Company Act of 1940.
[40]   The Employment Retirement Income Security Act of 1974 (ERISA), 29 US § 1002 *et seq.*
[41]   Linda C. Thomsen et al., supra note 35, at 550.

Schedule 13D "beneficial ownership report" with the SEC stating, among other things, their precise holdings and intentions. Such filings, which must happen within 10 days of crossing the 5 percent threshold, give target companies opportunities to put in place a legal, structural, public relations, or deal-based defense to any attack on corporate policy. This allows firms to raise the costs of takeovers, and therefore make them less likely.

Fourthly, hedge funds have greater ability to use material, non-public information. Actively managed money is a more costly strategy than passive investing (e.g., investing in an index fund), so funds must be able to earn higher returns in order to attract capital. For activist funds, this typically comes from two sources: first, being able to effectuate changes in management, strategy, operations, or the like as a result of being the largest single shareholder in a firm or being the lead wolf in a pack; and, secondly, using information obtained by its privileged position to time the entry and exit from the firm in a profitable manner.

If funds cannot time their trades based on privileged information, they may not be able to justify the 20-percent-of-profits fee they typically charge. The point is simple: the better able funds are to trade ahead of the market based on inside information, the greater their returns will be relative to the market returns. In addition, if activism is known to the market, the greater the need for opportunistic timing of trades. This is because other investors not sharing profits with the hedge fund may be able to mimic their investments. If an investor knows about a fund's activist investment, the investor can simply make the same trades, while saving the 20 percent fee. To earn these returns (and thus attract capital) and avoid these problems, funds looking to exit with advantageous timing may often be skirting the line of trading based on material, non-public information.

Hedge funds get access to this important inside information from a variety of sources. For one, activism frequently involves close interaction with target firms. Hedge funds often take significant stakes in target firms, seek board representation, provide alternative funding sources (e.g., PIPE investments), and otherwise communicate with (and pressure) the board and managers about their current strategy. In the largest study to date on hedge fund activism, the authors found that in nearly 50 percent of cases of activism during the early 2000s, the hedge fund planned to "communicate with the board/management on a regular basis."[42] This means funds will very frequently come into possession of material, non-public information about target companies. As the former head of enforcement at the SEC recently wrote, "[i]n the course of acquiring a substantial interest in or providing financing to companies, hedge funds may become privy to non-public information not available to the companies' stockholders."[43]

Even hedge funds without an activist role in a particular company may have something close to informational parity with insiders given the nature of the hedge fund industry. For one, funds are often affiliated with larger financial entities, like investment or commercial banks, and information leakage between departments (driven by the need to earn outsized profits) is well documented. In addition, hedge funds are privileged clients of investment banks, since fund trading, which is the largest component of non-computerized trades,

---

[42]   Brav et al., *supra* note 26, at 1743, Table I, Panel B.
[43]   Thomsen et al., *supra* note 35, at 579.

represents a significant part of bank profits.[44] Hedge funds are "inextricably interwoven with the core of the U.S. financial system—for example, commercial banks, investment banks, large financial institutions, pension funds, insurance companies, endowments, foundations, municipalities, and other public funds" and therefore operate at the center of the information web for public companies.[45] For example, because investment banks in the prime brokerage business for hedge funds have other clients, including public companies, the potential for information sharing, either explicitly or implicitly, is significant.[46] Inside information could also come from CEOs, who may be investors in funds, or brokers who are affiliated with activist hedge funds. Another source of inside information is seen in cases showing how funds have frequently tapped networks of former employees of firms and other "experts" on their business to come into possession of material, non-public information.

These traits of, strategies of, and regulatory environment for hedge funds generate significant pressure on and uncertainty for firm insiders. The threat to employment and income that used to come from an unlikely takeover of the entire firm has morphed into a much more likely threat of pressure from activist investors. The takeover market in the 1980s was like a lightning strike; today it is more like a sustained rain.

This is not just a theoretical claim. According to a comprehensive dataset and analysis by Brav et al., firm insiders face large personal costs as a result of hedge fund activism. The Brav study first documents widespread and effective activism on the part of hedge funds over the past decade. The authors identify over 1000 instances of hedge fund activism against public companies during a six-year period from 2001 to 2006. This means that the average public company faced a nearly 20 percent chance of being the target of an activist hedge fund over this period. Since funds target smaller and underperforming/ under-valued firms, this percentage significantly underestimates the threat for these firms.

The threat is real because funds are highly effective as activists. In nearly 550 cases of specific activism on subjects such as capital structure, business strategy, sale of the company, and governance, the authors find that hedge funds are successful or partially successful in 67 percent of cases. The success of this activism on CEOs is manifest in two primary ways.

First, CEO turnover increases as a result of hedge fund activism. The study shows that "[o]ne year after [hedge fund] targeting, however, the turnover rate at the targeted companies is 12.4 percentage points higher than that of their matched peers."[47] Off of a base rate turnover of about 13 percent over the period 2001 to 2006, activism implies a doubling of the risk of losing one's job for the average targeted CEO over this period. More specifically, the authors find that hedge funds are successful in their goal of removing a CEO of an underperforming company in nearly 40 percent of cases, and that even when they fail to remove the CEO, in another 30 percent of cases the fund or funds "achieve partial success, involving the CEO staying on but agreeing to adopt policies along the lines proposed by the fund."[48]

---

[44]   Roel C. Campos, Comm'r, U.S. Sec. and Exch. Comm'n, Remarks Before the SIA Hedge Funds & Alternative Investments Conference (June 14, 2006).

[45]   Thomsen et al., supra note 35, at 550.

[46]   Id.

[47]   Brav et al, supra note 26 at 1770.

[48]   Id.

Another recent study corroborates the claim that the pressure on CEOs has increased significantly over the past 20 years. Lucian Taylor examined changes in firm leadership over the period 1970 to 2006 to develop a model of CEO turnover.[49] His raw data show that the number of "forced" CEO successions (over roughly the same number of firms) increased from 44 during the 1980s to 58 during the period 2000 to 2006, and the percentage of CEO successions that were "forced" increased from about 14 percent during the 1980s to 26 percent during the period 2000 to 2006.[50] The time trend is fairly linear over the period 1970 to 2006, with the percentage of forced successions rising from about 8 percent in the period 1970 to 1974 to about 25 percent by 2005 to 2006. (As an important control, the number and percentage of "unforced" successions did not increase in the same way: both were higher in the earlier time period.) In addition, the percentage of forced successions per year increased from an average of about 1.75 percent during the 1980s to 3.75 percent during the period 2000 to 2006.

Overall turnover of CEOs has also increased. The best estimates of CEO turnover in the period before Haddock & Macey were writing are about 7 percent per year.[51] According to data from Kaplan and Minton, the standard turnover rate for CEOs of the largest 500 U.S. firms increased from an average of 10 percent per year for the period 1992 to 1997 to an average of over 13 percent per year for the period 1998 to 2007.[52] More recent data suggest this trend is only increasing: the rate has been over 14 percent since 2005, and was nearly 17 percent in 2008. This means turnover has almost doubled since the early 1990s, and this change is even greater when compared with the 1980s.

Secondly, hedge fund activism has lowered the pay of those executives who survive an attack. Brav et al. examined CEO pay at firms targeted by hedge funds relative to pay at a matched set of firms (i.e., the same industry, the same size, and the same value).[53] They found that CEOs of targeted firms were paid significantly more (by about $1 million) than CEOs of peer companies. But in the year following hedge fund involvement with the firm, the CEOs of the peer companies were compensated at similar levels.[54] This means that activism results in a reduction in pay of nearly $1 million for the CEO of a targeted firm.

This result obtains even when correcting for the interaction between turnover and pay. After all, the change in pay may reflect the possibility that new CEOs are paid less. The authors show that conditional on having the same CEO before and after an activist hedge fund takes a position in the firm, the CEO's pay goes from being nearly $500,000 greater than matched firms to more than $700,000 less following activism.[55] This change of about

---

[49]   Lucian A. Taylor, Why Are CEOs Rarely Fired? Evidence from Structural Estimation, 65 J. Fin. 2051 (2010) (Table 2).

[50]   Id

[51]   According to data from Michael Weisbach, the CEO turnover rate during the period 1974 to 1983 was about 7 percent per year. Weisbach documents 286 CEO changes during a 10-year period for 367 firms. This yields a turnover percentage of about 7 percent (286/(10*367). Michael S. Weisbach, Outside Directors and CEO Turnover, 20 J. Fin. Econ. 20 (1988).

[52]   Steven N. Kaplan & Bernadette A. Minton, "How Has CEO Turnover Changed?" Working Paper (2010), available at http://faculty.chicagobooth.edu/steven.kaplan/research/km.pdf (last visited Nov. 29, 2012).

[53]   Brav et al., supra note 26.

[54]   Id. at 1732.

[55]   Id. at 1770.

$1.2 million is a significant amount of CEO pay. During this period, the average CEO of a firm likely targeted by hedge funds (i.e., small to mid-cap firms) was paid about $2–3 million,[56] meaning a nearly 50 percent pay change as a result of hedge fund activism. Even for CEOs of larger firms, who averaged about $5–6 million during the period of the Brav et al. study, a change of more than $1 million in pay is undoubtedly a significant event. In sum, Brav et al. conclude that "[d]uring the year after the announcement of activism, average CEO pay declines by about one million dollars, and the CEO turnover rate increases by almost 10 percentage points."[57] The authors document managerial hostility to hedge fund activism, noting that it "may stem from its negative impact on CEO pay and turnover even if it ultimately creates value for shareholders."[58]

C.   Insider Trading Prosecutions Today

This section presents evidence on how the SEC's insider trading policies have changed since the time of Haddock & Macey's account, and argues that these changes follow as expected from the changing interest-group dynamic described above. Specifically, the enforcement profile identified by Haddock & Macey—over 70 percent of cases brought against firm insiders—has changed to focus more on market professionals. In addition, while back then insiders were more likely than market professionals to face criminal sanctions for insider trading offenses, today the opposite is true. Finally, the SEC rules at that time treated insiders more strictly than market professionals, while today new SEC rules greatly expand the ability of insiders to trade based on inside information.

1.   Targets

The targets of SEC enforcement of insider trading law have changed significantly over the past 20 years, and they have done so in ways consistent with the changing interest-group incentives described above. Haddock & Macey report that during the 17 years of their study (1970–1987) about 70 percent of the SEC's insider trading cases were brought against insiders, while about 16 percent were brought against market professionals. This was consistent with their explanation of the incentives for each of these groups at the time—insiders as a group had much less interest in insider trading regulation given the small part it played in insider utility.

To see how the enforcement has changed since 1987, a dataset of all SEC prosecutions for insider trading for the years 1982 to 2009 was assembled by the author. Defendants were coded as "insiders" or "market professionals" as per the methodology used by Haddock & Macey.[59] The result is a database of over 830 insider trading defendants over a 27-year period. The SEC brings charges against an average of about 30 defendants per

---

[56]   Frydman & Jenter, Executive Compensation, supra note 19, at Table 1.

[57]   Brav et al., supra note 26, at 1732.

[58]   Id.

[59]   This chapter applies the following classifications, as used by Haddock & Macey: insiders who trade for their own accounts are classified as "insiders"; brokers who trade for their own account or those of their clients are classified as "market professionals"; a lawyer who trades based on information gleaned from his work with a firm, or a lawyer tipped by an insider is classified as an "insider"; a broker tipped by an insider is classified as "both".

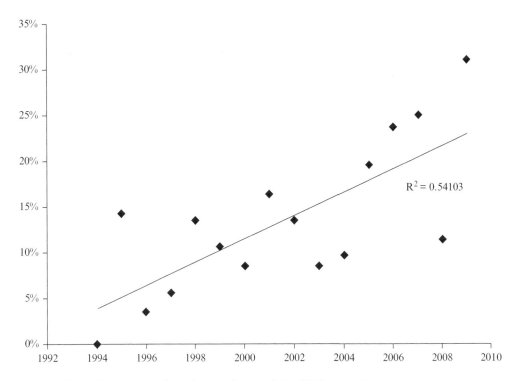

Figure 13.1   Percentage of market professionals in SEC case mix

year, ranging from about 20 to 50. The database allows one to compare the change in the mix of enforcement cases between insiders and market professionals.

The shift in favor of insiders and against market professionals over the past two decades is significant. The percentage of all SEC cases brought against market professionals in the dataset increased from about 10 percent prior to 1990 to more than 22 percent during the period 2004 to 2009. In other words, the risk for market professionals has more than doubled since the time of Haddock & Macey's analysis. Furthermore, the percentage of market professionals prosecuted by the SEC was over 30 percent in 2009; this was the highest percentage of market professionals prosecuted in the history of the SEC. The preliminary data from 2010 and 2011 suggest an even greater and more sustained shift toward allocating SEC and DOJ resources toward market professionals and therefore away from firm insiders. Another way of seeing this is to consider that of the top seven years in terms of percentage of market professionals as defendants, five were since 2000. Similarly, of the bottom seven years in terms of the percentage of market professionals as defendants, only one was in the past 10 years.

The trend in risk of civil prosecution for market professionals relative to insiders is shown in Figure 13.1. Although there is year-to-year variation in the percentage of SEC cases targeting insiders compared with market professionals, the increasing focus on market professionals in the SEC's case mix is obvious from the data. Given the relatively small number of cases each year, a single large scandal or two can distort the numbers for a particular year. But the upward trend in enforcement against market professionals is clear.

This change in enforcement priority from an insider-dominated mix of cases to a more balanced portfolio of insider and market professional cases is consistent with the story above about how market changes give insiders greater incentives to care about insider trading rules.[60]

2. Criminal cases

Market professionals today not only face a greater risk of civil liability from an SEC action, but also a significantly greater risk of criminal liability from a parallel DOJ action. Haddock & Macey did not address this issue, perhaps because in the period before 1987 there were too few criminal prosecutions to yield any meaningful comparisons across the type of defendant: out of 117 total insider trading defendants from 1982 to 1987, only five were prosecuted criminally (about 4 percent of all defendants).

But the use of criminal sanctions has increased dramatically. The recent spate against hedge fund managers and their associates is illustrative of a broader trend.[61] There were over 80 criminal cases brought against individuals involved in insider trading over the period 2001 to 2009. In fact, there were more criminal insider trading prosecutions in each of the past 10 years than in 54 years of the insider trading prosecutions up to the point when Haddock & Macey were writing.

The rise in criminal risk has not been equal for insiders and market professionals. During the period 1989 to 1997, about 13 percent of insiders charged in a civil case by the SEC were prosecuted criminally by the DOJ for insider trading or related matters; only 4 percent of market professionals sued by the SEC were charged criminally. In the past five years, the risk of criminal prosecution for insiders has remained the same—about 14 percent were charged—but the criminal risk rose to nearly 40 percent for market professionals. In other words, while insiders faced similar criminal prosecution risk in the past five years compared with earlier periods, the risk for market professionals increased by about 10 times.

D. Rule Changes

Not only did the government change its litigation policies by altering the civil and criminal enforcement mix, but it also promulgated two new rules that tilt the playing field in ways favorable to insiders. One of them is especially worth considering.[62]

---

[60] A study of insider trading prosecutions in New York yields similar results. See Criminal Prosecutorial Discretion in Insider Trading Cases: Let's Look at the Numbers, available at http://www. nysba.org/Content/ContentFolders4/CommercialandFederalLitigationSection/ComFedReports/ CRIMINALPROSECUTORIALDISCRETIONINTHEINSIDERTRADINGCASES.pdf (last visited Nov. 29, 2012) (finding dramatic shift in case mix toward market professionals).

[61] At this writing, there are at least as many individuals under criminal indictment for insider trading in one scandal as in the entire five-year period preceding Haddock & Macey. See M. Todd Henderson, The Changing Demand for Insider Trading Law, Working Paper 2012 (on file with author).

[62] The second rule change, passed at the same time as Rule 10b5-1 noted above, leveled the playing field between insiders and market professionals somewhat, by clarifying the scope of the misappropriation theory in ways that are more likely to implicate market professionals.

1.   Rule 10b5-1

The first new rule has enabled insiders to dramatically expand their ability to earn abnormal returns on trades in their firms' shares. In October 2000, the SEC promulgated Rule 10b5-1, which provides an affirmative defense that reduces trade-related litigation risk for insiders who enter into trading plans when they do not possess material, non-public information, even if they possess such information at the time they execute the trades. This affirmative defense allows more trading flexibility because it absolves insiders from having to cancel pre-planned trades or disclose subsequently obtained material, non-public information before pre-planned trades are executed.

According to the SEC, the purpose of Rule 10b5-1 was to provide a vehicle through which insiders could more readily diversify their firm-specific holdings. In other words, to give greater opportunities for uninformed trading, and thereby reduce the frequency of informed trading. Linda Chatman Thomsen, the former head of the SEC Division of Enforcement, stated that "the idea [of Rule 10b5-1] was to give executives opportunities to diversify or become more liquid through the use of plans with prearranged trades without facing the prospect of an insider trading investigation."[63]

There were two stated motivations for the Rule. The first was a desire to increase trading and compensation efficiency by lowering the cost for insiders who were not trading on inside information to signal this to the market. The Rule was a way of mitigating the market-for-lemons problem, and therefore would encourage "good" trades from insiders while discouraging "bad" ones. If market observers cannot readily sort between these types, they will apply a discount to all shares. Rule 10b5-1 allows the good type to distinguish themselves, and thereby save this amount.

The second was a desire to increase the power of the SEC to go after "bad" trades. Before the Rule was promulgated, some courts permitted a defense to insider trading when insiders offered evidence that although they possessed material, non-public information, they did not actually use the information to motivate their trades.[64] The SEC claimed it needed only to show possession. The Rule tried to resolve this issue by adopting the broader possession standard, which seems to give the SEC more power to police insider trading against firm insiders.

But recent research shows there is more to Rule 10b5-1 than this account suggests. Two recent empirical analyses show that insiders using the Rule actually outperform insiders not using the Rule, meaning the Rule does not in practice reduce the potential to trade on the basis of inside information, but actually the opposite. These studies show insiders use the Rule to earn extraordinary abnormal returns of 12 to 24 percent per year based on exploiting their informational advantage.

---

[63]   See Speech by SEC Staff: Opening Remarks Before the 15th Annual NASPP Conference, October 10, 2007.

[64]   In SEC v. Adler, the Eleventh Circuit held that the government had to prove not only that an insider "possessed" inside information at the time of trading, but also that the insider "used" the information to make the trading decision. The Court, however, also created a rebuttable presumption of use where the government showed the defendant was aware of the information. SEC v. Adler, 137 F.3d 1325 (11th Cir. 1998). The Ninth Circuit adopted the same "use" standard in U.S. v. Smith, 155 F.3d 1051 (9th Cir. 1998), while also holding that a presumption of use was impermissible in criminal cases.

One of these studies by Todd Henderson, Alan Jagolinzer, and Karl Muller shows the primary mechanism insiders use to exploit the Rule is an SEC interpretation that gives insiders a virtually costless option on future sales.[65] Here is how it works. The SEC determined that an insider who entered into a plan to trade in the future could later cancel that plan, even if the insider based that cancellation on material, non-public information.[66] This means an insider with uncertainty about the future stock price can enter into a plan to sell her shares sometime in the future knowing that if the future turns out to be brighter than she thought, she can cancel the planned sales. In this way, the Rule effectively legalizes trading on material, non-public information, since it allows insiders to opportunistically plan sales and use cancellations in combinations that exactly replicate trades based on inside information. And, as shown in Henderson et al., the SEC's decision not to require disclosure of either plans or cancellations makes the option embedded in the Rule costless (or nearly so) since market participants will not necessarily observe plans or cancellations and therefore be unable to impose costs for what may be bad conduct by insiders.

The empirical and theoretical research shows insiders used the Rule, as designed and interpreted by the SEC, to sell tens of billions of dollars in shares per year and to earn larger profits from these sales than they could have had they not used the Rule.[67] For the firms in the Henderson et al. study, there was a total of about $10 billion in stock sales in the first year of 10b5-1 use for insiders shown to be exploiting the Rule.[68] As noted above, the average return for these insiders was about 12 percent better than the expected market return. These data suggest insiders earned about $1.2 billion in abnormal returns based on material, non-public information.[69] This amounts to about $1 million in excess returns available to each insider by using the Rule.

If one views the Rule through the lens of the SEC pursuing the public interest, then the current state of the Rule looks like a big mistake—the results run directly counter to the SEC's assessment of what the public interest requires, i.e., informational parity between traders. But, if one believes that what appear to be regulatory mistakes are only reflections of relevant private interests, the Rule simply may be a result of increased influence of corporate managers on SEC policies. Insiders cannot as easily impact courts, which continue to take a rather dim view of insiders trading against individuals to whom they owe fiduciary duties, as they can the SEC, so it makes sense that the latter is where they would seek a change in the law.

The Rule might even be justified as a quid pro quo of sorts in which the SEC was "compensating" insiders for liberalized rules about proxy communications and a regulatory light touch when it came to hedge funds and other activist investors. Such a bargain could arise from specific bundling of rules in which direct trade-offs and payments are made, or from an updating process in which rules issued at a specific time (t_2) are designed

---

[65] Henderson et al., Strategic Disclosure of Rule 10b5-1 Plans, supra note 24.

[66] See SEC Division of Corporation Finance, Manual of Publicly Available Telephone Interpretations, Fourth Supplement, Rule 10b5-1, Question 15 (issued May 2001).

[67] Henderson et al., Strategic Disclosure of Rule 10b5-1 Plans, supra note 24.

[68] See id.

[69] About 1100 insiders sold an average of $8.2 million in stock in the first year after 10b5-1 was used for the first time. See id. at Table 2.

to ameliorate negative impacts arising from other rules issued at an earlier time (t_1). It appears from the timing in this case that this is an example of the latter, at least insofar as Rule 10b5-1 (promulgated in 2000) is associated with the proxy-rule changes (promulgated in the 1990s).

The story might look something like this. There was a fairly robust market for corporate control in the 1980s. According to Mergerstat, there were over 750 mergers or acquisitions from 1985 to 1990, about 25 percent of which were hostile. Owing in part to the recession of 1991, M&A activity fell in the early 1990s, but as a measure of the market for corporate control, the number of hostile deals fell by over 12 percentage points. Poison pills were becoming more common as a defense during this time, as were defenses involving the relatively onerous proxy rules described above. To reinvigorate the market for corporate control, or, looking at it a slightly different way, to empower shareholders who might be disadvantaged by more entrenched managers, the SEC decided to modernize the proxy rules. Perhaps the SEC intended to simply restart the market for corporate control that had existed in the recent past. There is some evidence that this occurred: in the late 1990s, the number of mergers and acquisitions rose to yearly totals not seen since the mid-1980s, and the percentage of hostile deals increased to nearly 15 percent. This reversion might not have necessitated a change in insider trading policy; instead we might have expected the SEC to have simply replicated the 1980s policy. But the rise of hedge funds, which the SEC failed to regulate for a variety of reasons, was a confounding factor that dramatically increased the threat to CEOs. From the perspective of the SEC, this confluence of rule changes and the rise of private money might have been beneficial for society and shareholders generally, given the relatively low-cost discipline that hedge funds bring. But given this threat, CEOs could be expected to push back against hedge funds, calling for registration, tighter regulations, and so forth. One way for the SEC to placate this demand to some extent would be to focus more insider trading resources on hedge funds. A few criminal prosecutions would send a powerful deterrent signal against the worst type of conduct of hedge funds, something even other hedge funds might approve of, and would raise the costs for all hedge fund activism given the imperfections of the legal system and internal controls at funds.

Importantly, the timing of Rule 10b5-1 corresponds well with the changes in the civil and criminal prosecution mix noted above. The emphasis of the SEC in bringing civil cases changed dramatically in the period after 2000, with the SEC bringing many more cases against securities market professionals than it ever had in the past. In addition, this was exactly the same time that the SEC began to refer (and the DOJ began to accept) many more securities market professionals for criminal prosecution than it had in the past. The three big changes in SEC policy—two that made insider trading much more risky for market professionals and one that made insider trading much less risky for insiders—happened at around the same time, and at a time in which the changes in the underlying interest-group dynamic had reached a point of critical mass.

Two other factors support the interest-group account for Rule 10b5-1. First, the Rule has not been amended or repealed despite the empirical evidence of its effects on insider trading. The evidence in the two studies mentioned above is well known to SEC officials, including the head of the Division of Enforcement quoted above. In addition, documents from J.P. Morgan, revealed by Wikileaks, show that investment advisors were aware of the "loophole" in the Rule and how insiders could exploit it to earn insider trading profits.[70] And yet, the Rule and the various interpretations that generate these profit-making opportunities remain unchanged nearly five years after first being exposed.

Secondly, the SEC could have achieved the goal of increasing diversification-trading opportunities for insiders in a much more simple and obvious way. Most obviously, there was no reason why the interpretations that led to the loopholes in the Rule needed to be decided the way they were. Cancelling a planned trade under the Rule based on material, non-public information could be "in connection with the purchase or sale of a security," as required by statute for the SEC to act, even if it might not be for planned trades not under the Rule. In addition, there was no legal or obvious policy reason why the SEC would not require disclosure of plans or, at the very least, the disclosure of cancelled trades. More interestingly perhaps, the SEC could have required insiders wanting litigation prophylaxis to issue trading instructions, such as dollar or share amounts to be sold, to an unaffiliated and anonymous third person (intermediated by the SEC), who would then execute the trades without any contact with the insider. This would guarantee the insider the opportunity to diversify the portfolio and eliminate the risk of gaming the system. Presumably this system or others the mind could imagine were not adopted because of the influence of firm insiders on the regulatory process.

2.   Targeting hedge funds

The model of regulation developed in this chapter supports the targeting of hedge funds. The targeting of market professionals generally and hedge funds specifically is openly admitted by the SEC. The new Director of Enforcement at the SEC, Robert Khuzami, made this clear in an interview with Bloomberg Business week, which summarized his enforcement priorities as follows: "Setting Sights On: Insider trading at hedge funds."[71] This is consistent with the data presented above and with the private-interest model. The private-interest model not only predicts SEC enforcement would tilt in the direction of market professionals and away from firm insiders, but it also predicts the subset of market professionals that would be specifically targeted. The model predicts firm insiders would use their limited lobbying or influencing resources to go after the weakest subgroup of securities market professionals in terms of influence. This group is arguably hedge funds, at least during the period of interest.

As described above, hedge funds are a relatively new subset of market professionals. They are also a highly diffuse group—anyone can start their own hedge fund and as a result there are upwards of 10,000 individual funds of varying sizes. This contrasts with just a handful of traditional investment professionals, such as large investment banks and broker-dealers. Accordingly, traditional investment professionals are better able to overcome collective action problems that might reduce the efficacy of influence peddling, are more aligned in interest, know the ways in which influence can best be achieved, and have better relationships with regulators, as a result of familiarity, shared employees, and so forth.

---

    [70]   See Kevin Wilson et al., Whistleblower Exposes Insider Trading Program at J.P. Morgan, Wikileaks, available at mirror.wikileaks.info/wiki/wikileaks/index.html (last visited Nov. 29, 2012).
    [71]   Mike Dorning, The Power Brokers: Fifteen Regulators, Lawmakers, and Lobbyists Shaping the Torrent of Regulations, Bloomberg Businessweek, Jan. 24–30, 2011.

Although hedge funds are represented by a trade association, which can help mitigate these problems, until recently hedge funds were not collectively very active in policy-making circles in Washington. In 2008, hedge funds spent about $6 million on lobbying expenditures.[72] In contrast, according to the web site opensecrets.org, the securities industry spent nearly $95 million. Several individual investment companies, like Merrill Lynch, Goldman Sachs, and Morgan Stanley, each spent between two and five million dollars on lobbying.

The private-interest model also predicts a response from hedge funds. There is some evidence of this. During the period 2006 to 2008, the financial-services industry as a whole increased lobbying expenditures by 38 percent; large hedge funds and their trade group, the Managed Funds Association, increased lobbying expenditures by over 700 percent. In light of this, a weak prediction is that we should see over the medium term a change in SEC policy to reflect this increased organization and effort on the part of hedge funds and other activist investors.

A final point is worth making about hedge funds, and it supports the conclusion that the targeting of hedge funds is not motivated by the public interest. The argument is that insider trading by hedge funds is more socially valuable than similar trading by other market professionals. Here is why. As described above, one situation in which hedge funds commonly trade on the basis of material, non-public information involves the market for corporate control, broadly conceived. And this trading is thought to be necessary for hedge funds to profitably engage in activism, which has led to increased pressure on corporate managers. Insofar as this revitalized market for corporate control is socially beneficial, and insofar as its profitability depends on trading on insider information, then we can think of insider trading profits as the price of better corporate decision making and governance. Just as society gives monopoly rights as an incentive for the production and revelation of valuable inventions, so too can we think of the profits hedge funds earn from insider trading as the necessary price for their role in policing corporate managers.

In contrast, while others trading on material, non-public information may be providing some value from their trades, it is likely much less than that provided by hedge fund trades. For instance, a broker with access to a firm's earnings a few hours or days ahead of the public release may trade on this information and move the price closer to its true value a few hours or days before it otherwise would, but this is likely to be much less valuable from a social welfare or shareholder welfare perspective than the ousting of an entrenched CEO, the reduction in pay of an overpaid CEO, or the change in strategy for an underperforming firm.

If this is correct, then holding everything else constant, trades by hedge funds engaged in activism are more socially valuable than similar trades by insiders, market professionals, or their tippees. This would mean a regulator pursuing the public interest, as opposed to its own interest or that of powerful groups of regulated parties, would target trades that were less socially valuable. That the SEC has nevertheless tilted the playing field consciously in favor of insiders and has decided to specifically focus on insider trading at

---

[72]   See, Susan Pulliam and Tom McGinty, US: Hedge Funds Boost Profile in Lobbying, Wall St. J., June 22, 2009.

hedge funds suggests either a different view of the public interest or enforcement decisions based on the relative power of private interests.

III.   CONCLUSION

This chapter argues that the current state of insider trading law and enforcement is best explained by an examination of the current interest-group dynamics between firm insiders and securities market professionals, as opposed to some abstract notion of the public interest. The data reveal a dramatic change in the target of government insider trading prosecutions, both in civil and criminal cases, over the past two decades. This is best explained by the relative changes in the interest-group dynamics, as insiders have much greater incentive to care about insider trading enforcement given their increased trading in company shares and the greater role trading plays in corporate takeover battles. It seems that, just as in 1987, insider trading law and enforcement are not based on efficiency or a mistake, but rather a reflection of the private interests. This should make us think again about the wisdom of the entire enterprise.

14. Insider trading: what is seen and what is not seen
Alexandre Padilla

> He generally, indeed, neither intends to promote the public interest, nor knows how much he is promoting it. . . . [H]e intends only his own security; and by directing that industry in such a manner as its produce may be of the greatest value, he intends only his own gain, and he is in this, as in many other cases, led by an invisible hand to promote an end which was no part of his intention. Nor is it always the worse for the society that it was no part of it. By pursuing his own interest he frequently promotes that of the society more effectually than when he really intends to promote it.[1]

I. INTRODUCTION

After handing an eleven year jail sentence to Raj Rajaratnam, Federal District Court Judge Richard J. Holwell commented that "insider trading is an assault on the free markets," adding that "his crimes reflect a virus in our business culture that needs to be eradicated."[2] More recently, the *Wall Street Journal* reported that the FBI was building cases on 120 people for illegal insider trading. In addition, the FBI released a new public-service announcement against insider trading featuring Michael Douglas. Douglas, of course, famously portrayed Gordon Gekko in Oliver Stone's movie, *Wall Street*, which character was largely inspired by Ivan Boesky, one of the (in)famous convicted insider traders of the late 1980s.[3] In this public-service announcement, Douglas introduces himself as the actor who played Gordon Gekko. Douglas adds that, while the movie and his character were fictional, the problem is real and he encourages contacting the local FBI office to report insider trading.[4]

Such visceral negative reactions to insider trading are not new.[5] We can trace such

---

[1]   Adam Smith, An Inquiry into the Nature and Causes of the Wealth of Nations. Book IV, Chapter 2: Of Restraints upon the Importation from Foreign Countries of such Goods as can be Produced at Home (Edwin Cannan, ed. 1904).

[2]   See Peter Lattman, Galleon Chief Sentenced to 11-Year Term in Insider Case, Dealbook New York Times, Oct. 13, 2011, available at http://dealbook.nytimes.com/2011/10/13/rajaratnam-is-sentenced-to-11-years/ (last visited Nov. 28, 2012). Beyond the fact that financial markets are definitely not free markets as they are among the most regulated markets in the U.S., and also in most countries that have financial markets, this paper's motivation is largely inspired by Judge Holwell's statement.

[3]   See Wall Street, directed by Oliver Stone, 20th Century Fox, 1987.

[4]   See Jenny Strasburg & Reed Albergotti, Insider Targets Expanding, Wall St. J., February 28, 2012, at A1.

[5]   We use a very general definition of insider trading adopted in the literature, which is the use of material nonpublic information about a corporation in a securities transaction. Insiders are traditionally defined as any individual who has access or has been given access to inside information. The U.S. legislation uses the same definition of insider trading. However, it introduces a distinction within the class of insiders by differentiating registered (inside) insiders from (unregistered) outside

reactions as far back as Henry Manne's law classes. Manne describes in *Insider Trading and the Stock Market* a student's reaction to his arguments on insider trading during class. She stomped her foot and insisted, "I don't care; it's just not right!"[6] Such vehement opposition to the idea that some people in the corporate world—the insiders—can make profits or avoid losses "simply" by trading on information not available to most investors and the general public is still the predominant idea. Insiders remain in the eyes of the general public, the media, the Congress, lawmakers, and Hollywood the villains of free markets and capitalism.[7]

But is it really the case? It might be so that insiders are greedy individuals. It might be so that insiders are self-interested and only care about making profits or avoiding losses. However, borrowing Adam Smith's words, is it possible that insiders, while pursuing their own gains, are "led by an invisible hand to promote an end which was no part of their intention?" Is it possible that "by pursuing their own interest they frequently promote that of the society more effectually than when they really intend to promote it"?

There is a difference between what people perceive insider trading is and what insider trading actually is. The fact that a majority of people believes that insider trading harms markets does not mean that insider trading actually harms markets.[8] As Bastiat once wrote, there is what is seen and there is what is not seen.[9] Often, people only focus on what is seen and overlook what is not seen. Some actions, behaviors, institutions, laws, or policies may have immediate observable positive effects, but these can also produce negative

---

insiders (tippees). Registered insiders (or corporate insiders) are defined by § 16 of the Securities Exchange Act of 1934 as every director and officer of the corporation plus any owners of more than 10 percent of the corporation's equity. They are required by § 16(a) to report periodically all their trade in equity securities to the Securities Exchange Commission (SEC). Unregistered insiders (or outside-insiders) are also in possession of material nonpublic information but are not required to report their transactions to the SEC. Unregistered insiders' acquisition of inside information can be direct in the course of their work (investment bankers, lawyers, risk arbitragers, accountants, financial printers) or indirect by the intermediary of registered insiders (tippees).

[6] See Henry G. Manne, Insider Trading and the Stock Market, 233 n. 42 (1966). Roy A. Schotland discusses similar reactions from the legal community, as well as at least one SEC official after Manne's book was published. See Roy A. Schotland, Unsafe at any Price: A Reply to Manne, Insider Trading and the Stock Market, 53 Va. L. Rev. 1425 (1967).

[7] James B. Stewart's Den of Thieves (2nd ed. 2010) illustrates perfectly that perception of insiders being the villains of the capital markets who, indulging themselves in their greedy pursuit of money, "put the financial system and world economy in jeopardy" (p. 8). See also Alexandre Padilla, How do we Think About Insider Trading? An Economist's Perspective on the Insider Trading Debate and its Impact, 4 J. Law, Econ & Policy, 239 (2008), in which he assesses the impact that Henry Manne had on how insider trading is perceived. In this article Padilla argues that, while the academic literature on insider trading has moved away from dogmatic and emotional arguments, in the political realm and in the public, emotions and dogmatism are still dominating the discourse on insider trading.

[8] Neither is the argument that most countries have and enforce laws prohibiting insider trading so insider trading must be harmful to markets valid. The political voting process or polls are poor tools to assess whether a practice or behavior is harmful or beneficial.

[9] See Frédéric Bastiat, Oeuvres complètes de Frédéric Bastiat, mises en ordre, revues et annotées d'après les manuscrits de l'auteur. Vol. 5 Sophismes économiques. Petits pamphlets II: Ce qu'on voit et ce qu'on ne voit pas, 1854–1855, pp. 336–392, available at http://oll.libertyfund.org/title/2346 (last visited Nov. 28, 2012).

effects—only visible in the long run—that outweigh these positive effects. Alternatively, some actions, behaviors, institutions, laws, or policies may have immediately observable negative effects but in the long run we might see positive effects emerge that outweigh these negative effects.

Therefore, in the light of Bastiat's observations, is it possible that the costs insider trading creates that people perceive immediately are outweighed by benefits that will only be perceived in the long run? Alternatively, is it conceivable that perceived benefits of insider trading laws will be outweighed by costs in the long run?

Manne definitely thought so. He was the first scholar to suggest that insider trading might actually not be harmful to markets. Manne's main argument was that insider trading could actually improve the operation of markets as the nonpublic information upon which insiders trade is being inputted into the stock price, moving the stock price toward its more accurate value.[10] Another argument advanced by Manne was that insider trading could serve as a compensation mechanism to reward the entrepreneurial activities of insiders.[11] Therefore, according to Manne, allowing insiders to trade on the information their work generated would spur entrepreneurial activities, which the society would benefit from. Manne did not deny that insider trading had some costs but he argued that the long-term benefits would far exceed those short-term costs.[12] While Manne's arguments generated some emotional replies, they also generated a very prolific literature attempting to assess his arguments and the costs and benefits of insider trading. The purpose of this chapter is not to offer a new survey of the literature on insider trading.[13] Instead the contribution of this chapter is more modest. First, in the light of Judge Holwell's assertion, it revisits the conclusions of the empirical literature keeping in mind Adam Smith's and Frederic Bastiat's observations. Secondly, this chapter relies on Hayek's work on the role of knowledge in the operation of markets and the price system as a mechanism to allocate resources to their most valued uses and applies it to the case of insider trading.[14] We argue that, properly understood, insider trading could enhance the operation of markets and produce unintended long-term benefits that outweigh the costs that insider trading might create. Also, this chapter argues that insider trading laws have unintended consequences that might outweigh the benefits that the empirical literature argues that insider trading laws generate.

Because District Court Judge Richard J. Holwell's comment on the nature of insider trading is a positive statement about an empirical question, section II focuses attention

---

[10]   See Henry G. Manne, In Defense of Insider Trading, 44 Harvard Bus. Rev. 113 (1966), for a summary of his arguments presented in his 1966 book.

[11]   Id. at 117–119.

[12]   Manne indeed argued that insider trading mostly harmed short-term investors and speculators but not long-term investors. See Henry Manne, Insider Trading and the Stock Market 102 (1966).

[13]   For an overview of the literature on insider trading, see Stephen M. Bainbridge, Insider Trading, in Encyclopedia of Law & Economics 772 (Boudewijn Bouckaert & Gerrit De Geest eds., 1999).

[14]   Alexandre Padilla, Insider Trading: Is There an Economist in the Room?, 24 J. Private Enterprise 113, 115–116 (2009), makes a similar point in explaining that Manne's argument can be interpreted from a Hayekian perspective. See also Henry G. Manne, Insider Trading: Hayek, Virtual Markets, and the Dog that Did Not Bark, 41 J. Corp. L. 167 (2005).

on the empirical literature assessing the effects of insider trading laws on capital markets. The section then discusses some of the potential limits of this literature and argues that the empirical literature overlooks the unintended consequences that insider trading laws generate. In other words, following Bastiat, this section argues that the literature ignores what is not immediately seen when it comes to insider trading laws. Section III offers a perspective, built upon Hayek's work on the role of knowledge and the nature and role of prices in allocating resources to their most valued uses, as to why some of the costs of insider trading might be outweighed by other unintended benefits. Section IV offers concluding remarks about some directions on further empirical research.

II.   INSIDER TRADING LAWS AND THE STOCK MARKET: THE EMPIRICAL LITERATURE

While there is a very prolific literature about the merits of Henry Manne's thesis, most of the debate has largely been grounded on theoretical arguments. Because insider trading is by and large illegal, it has been very difficult to empirically assess the validity of either side of the debate. As a result, most empirical studies, instead of measuring the impact of insider trading on capital markets, have focused on the alternative hypothesis, which is to measure the impact of insider trading laws or the absence of insider trading laws on capital markets.

A.   Insider Trading Laws and the Stock Market

Most empirical studies attempting to measure the effects of insider trading laws on capital markets focus on a few key variables: ownership concentration, market liquidity, and cost of equity.[15] Market liquidity and the cost of equity are particularly important for corporations when it comes to attracting investors and raising financing through equity. Market liquidity refers to the transaction costs associated with buying and selling stocks.[16] A market is considered liquid when prices at which stocks are bought or sold are extremely close to the market prices, and variations between market prices and the prices at which stocks are bought (premium) or sold (discount) are due to the size of the block of stocks bought or sold.[17] In short, market liquidity refers to the easiness of buying and selling stocks. Market liquidity is very important to investors, particularly when it comes to selling their stocks and, especially, when they try to sell large blocks of stocks. Therefore, when markets are less liquid, investors will bid lower prices, ask a higher return on equity, and buy smaller blocks of stocks to compensate for the risks incurred when they buy stocks. As a result, it becomes more costly and difficult for corporations to raise financing through equity.

---

[15]   Dispersed ownership, liquidity, and cost of equity are obviously interconnected. More dispersed ownership means more liquid markets, while more liquid markets means lower cost of equity.

[16]   See Albert Kyle, Continuous Actions and Insider Trading 53 Econometrica 1315, 1316 (1985).

[17]   Id. at 1317.

Bhattacharya and Daouk analyze fifty-one countries over twenty years and study whether insider trading laws have any effects on the cost of equity.[18] More particularly, they look at whether the existence of insider trading laws has any impact on cost of equity. They find that adopting insider trading laws has no impact on cost of equity. However, after the first prosecution under insider trading laws, the cost of equity decreases significantly from 0.3 percent when they use the credit rating approach to 7 percent when using an international capital asset pricing model approach.[19] Bhattacharya and Daouk conclude that their results are statistically and economically significant. However, they are reluctant to attribute causality. They note there is an endogeneity problem they have not addressed, which is associated with the fact that, when government enforces insider trading laws, it is probably because cost of equity is too high. Secondly, they note the fact that first enforcement of insider trading laws is also associated with an increase in country credit ratings, which makes the stock market attractive to outside investors.[20]

Building on Bhattacharya and Daouk, Beny also does a cross-country analysis of insider trading laws and measures their effects on stock market performance by looking at the stringency of insider trading laws as opposed to whether countries have insider trading laws and enforce them or not.[21] She observes that, in countries where insider trading laws are more stringent, ownership is more dispersed and stock markets are more liquid.[22] More particularly, it seems that the determining factor is when insider trading is subject to criminal sanctions.[23] Like Bhattacharya and Daouk, Beny is careful in emphasizing that her results only show a significant statistical correlation and not proof. However, she does believe that her results are consistent with the pro-regulation argument that insider trading laws have positive externalities on stock markets and, therefore, they do not support deregulating insider trading and leaving it to private contracting.[24]

B.   Insider Trading Laws: What is Not Seen

As we have discussed, the empirical literature shows that adopting and enforcing laws that prohibit insider trading promote capital market development by increasing market liquidity and decreasing the cost of capital. These studies conclude that even though we only observe a correlation, and it does not necessarily mean causation, the results support regulating insider trading.

There is little doubt that the question as to whether insider trading is harmful for the development of capital markets is an empirical one. However, one cannot ignore the

---

[18]   Uptal Bhattacharya & Hazem Daouk, The World Price of Insider Trading, 57 J. Fin. 75 (2002).

[19]   Id. at 78.

[20]   Id. at 104.

[21]   Laura Nyantung Beny, Insider Trading Laws and Stock Markets Around the World: An Empirical Contribution to the Theoretical Law and Economics Debate, 32 J. Corp. Law 237 (2007). See also Laura Nyantung Beny, Do Insider Trading Laws Matter? Some Preliminary Comparative Evidence, 7 Am. L. & Econ. Rev. 144 (2005).

[22]   Id. at 280.

[23]   See Beny, supra note 21, at 174.

[24]   Id. at 281.

several difficulties that arise when trying to answer this question. This does not mean that we should not attempt to answer the question empirically but rather it means that we should be aware of these issues and be very cautious about the conclusions we derive from these studies.

First, these studies do not necessarily prove that insider trading is actually harmful to capital markets. What they show is that when countries enforce laws regulating insider trading, capital markets tend to perform better than markets where such laws are either nonexistent or unenforced. However, empirical studies have shown that insider trading laws are largely ineffective in preventing the type of insider trading that these laws prohibit.[25] Therefore, it cannot be argued that insider trading or the absence thereof is the reason some capital markets are more or less developed than others because insiders are still trading on the basis of inside information on these markets regardless of whether insider trading is being regulated. If insider trading regulation *per se* does not explain capital market development, one needs to look for another possible explanation as to why this correlation exists.

An alternative interpretation, implied in these studies, is not that insider trading harms capital markets because it is "bad" but rather that the public will not invest in capital markets if they believe that insiders are buying and selling on the market using nonpublic information and, therefore, it is "bad" for capital markets' development to allow insider trading. However, this interpretation does not meet the eye test.

Several surveys have been conducted in the wake of insider trading scandals and they all show that a majority of adults surveyed believed that insider trading was common among investment professionals.[26] For example, after the crackdown on insider trading in 1986 that saw Dennis Levine, Michael Milken, Ivan Boesky, and Martin Siegel all indicted on charges of insider trading, a poll conducted for *Business Week* by Louis Harris & Associates showed that, out of 1,248 surveyed adults, "only 52 percent of respondents said insider trading should be illegal, while 41 percent said insider trading was just a case of people making money because they knew information that other people do not."[27] More importantly, the poll also showed that 53 percent of the respondents would buy stocks in a company if they received an information tip about an impending takeover

---

[25]   For studies finding that insider trading laws are largely ineffective in preventing insider trading, see James H. Lorie & Victor Niederhoffer, Predictive and Statistical Properties of Insider Trading, 11 J. Law & Econ. 35 (1968); Jeffrey F. Jaffe, Special Information and Insider Trading, 47 J. Bus. 410 (1974); Joseph E. Finnerty, Insiders and Market Efficiency, 31 J. Fin. 1141 (1976); H. Nejat Seyhun, Insiders' Profits, Cost of Trading, and Market Efficiency, 16 J. Fin. Econ. 189 (1986); H. Nejat Seyhun, The Effectiveness of the Insider Trading Sanctions, 35 J. L. & Econ. 149 (1992); Lisa Meulbroek, An Empirical Analysis of Illegal Insider Trading, 47 J. Fin. 1661 (1992); J. Carr Bettis et al., The Effectiveness of Insider Trading Regulations, 14 J. Applied Bus. Res. 53 (1998). For more theoretical perspectives on the effectiveness of insider trading regulation, see Matthew Spiegel & Avanidhar Subrahmanyam, The Efficacy of Insider Trading Regulation, Working Paper 257, Berkeley, University of California, Institute of Business and Economic Research (1995); Alexandre Padilla, Can Regulation of Insider Trading Be Effective? in Insider Trading: Regulatory Perspectives 75–109 (C. Vidya ed. 2007); Alexandre Padilla, Should the Government Regulate Insider Trading? 22 J. Libertarian Stud. 379 (2011).

[26]   See Padilla, supra note 7, at 253–256 (discussing these surveys).

[27]   See Associated Press, Poll: Few People Fault "Insider" Traders, Anchorage Daily News, Aug. 15, 1986, at B4.

from a friend who was an insider in the company.[28] In other words, combined with the fact that empirical evidence shows that insider trading laws are largely ineffective in discouraging inside trading, these surveys show that not only is the general public fully aware that insider trading laws are ineffective in discouraging insider trading but they are still investing despite knowing that they are at risk of trading with insiders.[29]

A second aspect these studies seem to underestimate is that there might be some trade-offs associated with greater dispersion of stock ownership, greater liquidity, and less insider trading.[30] Bhide argues that insider trading laws and the resulting greater dispersion of stock ownership and market liquidity have unintended consequences that might translate into corporate mismanagement.[31]

When a stockholder actively engages in monitoring the management, such activity generates positive externalities for the other shareholders. In other words, while the costs are borne exclusively by the shareholder actively monitoring the management, all the shareholders share the benefits. When stock ownership is greatly dispersed, only owners of large blocks of stocks have any incentives to monitor management as they have more at stake than small shareholders for which monitoring management is a net cost. Being able to actively monitor management is essential for large shareholders to protect their interests and minimize the risks of mismanagement. Large shareholders are often able to sit on the board of directors, which allows them to actively monitor, influence, and prevent management from expropriating shareholders.[32] In addition, when sitting on the board of directors, large shareholders often have access to inside information, which allows them to evaluate more accurately management's performance and disentangle endogenous from exogenous factors affecting corporation performance.[33] Therefore, being able to sit on the board of directors and accessing inside information are essential for large shareholders to protect their interests. However, liquidity is as essential for large shareholders, particularly when the factors affecting firm performance are exogenous and therefore selling their stocks is the only solution for large shareholders to minimize their losses.[34]

---

[28] Id. To be sure survey results ought to be taken cautiously as people might not answer questions truthfully. They might answer questions by attempting to guess what the average opinion will be or based on what they think the average opinion is of what is right or wrong. However, it is doubtful that people would actually acknowledge that they would violate insider trading laws if they had such opportunity offered to them if they did not mean it. Actually, one might suspect that, with regard to this specific question, people who said they would not trade after a tip from a friend might not be totally truthful if they thought that answering positively would shed a negative light on their moral integrity.

[29] See Robert E. Wagner, Gordon Gekko to the Rescue? Insider Trading as a Tool to Combat Accounting Fraud, 79 U. Cin. L. Rev. 973, 1001–1004 (2011).

[30] Laura Nyantung Beny, Do Investors in Controlled Firms Value Insider Trading Laws? International Evidence, 4 J. L. Econ. & Pol'y 267 (2008), does attempt to answer that question empirically.

[31] Amar Bhide, The Hidden Costs of Stock Market Liquidity, 34 J. Fin. Econ. 31 (1994). See also Alexandre Padilla, The Regulation of Insider Trading as an Agency Problem, 5 Fla. St. U. Bus. L. Rev. 64 (2005–2006).

[32] Andrei Shleifer & Robert W. Vishny, Large Shareholders and Corporate Control, 94 J. Pol. Econ. 461 (1986).

[33] See Padilla, supra note 31, at 67 & note 12.

[34] Id. at 69.

As we have seen above, market liquidity is essential for raising equity finance and empirical evidence suggests that insider trading laws contribute to increased market liquidity.[35] However, these laws might actually raise market liquidity above the optimal level by discouraging large ownership and active monitoring of management. More particularly, as determined by § 16 of the Securities Exchange Act of 1934, owners of more than 10 percent of equity, along with every officer and director of the corporation, are considered insiders.[36] By making large shareholders insiders, § 16 raises the risks and costs for shareholders to own large blocks of stocks by reducing the liquidity of the stocks owned by large shareholders. As a result, incentives to own large blocks of stocks, serve on the board of directors, and actively monitor the management disappear or are significantly reduced. To protect the liquidity of their stock portfolios, many investors prefer to keep their ownership below 10 percent to avoid triggering the insider status.[37] This decrease in large stock ownership and resulting increase in stock dispersion have an impact on the structure of boards of directors toward more nonexecutive outside directors with little financial interest in the company. They also reduce incentives for board members to actually monitor and control management and increase incentives for board members to collude with management and expropriate shareholders.[38]

Beny uses firm-level data from a cross-section of large firms from twenty-seven developed countries to empirically assess whether insider trading laws reduce intra-firm efficiency and result in more shareholders' expropriation from managers or controlling shareholders.[39] Her findings are that countries with more stringent insider trading laws and enforcement tend to exhibit higher corporate value in common law countries. On the other hand, in civil countries, the stringency of insider trading laws and enforcement has no impact on corporate value.[40] Beny suggests that the difference in effects between common law and civil law countries could be interpreted as insider trading laws impacting monitoring positively in common law countries but not in civil law countries.[41] She suggests that this difference might be due to the fact that in civil law countries the enforcement of such laws is more lax than in common law countries.[42]

However, there are two points that need to be emphasized in this discussion. First, while Beny's empirical research seems to contradict the argument that insider trading laws aggravate agency problems, her study cannot really explain the difference in the performance of corporations between common law and civil law countries. One explanation that Beny does not mention, for example, is Mark Roe's hypothesis that degree of capital market development, share ownership dispersion, liquidity, corporate value, and specifically the degree of shareholder expropriation is independent of the legal system in

---

[35]   See supra note 21 and accompanying text.
[36]   Securities Exchange Act of 1934 § 16, 15 U.S.C. 328 (2012), available at http://www.sec.gov/about/laws/sea34.pdf (last visited Nov. 28, 2012).
[37]   Padilla, supra note 31, at 69–70.
[38]   Id. at 70–71 (citing Oliver Hart, Corporate Governance: Some Theory and Implications, 105 Econ. J. 678, 681–682 (1995)).
[39]   Beny, supra note 30.
[40]   Id. at 291.
[41]   Id. at 292.
[42]   Id. at 293.

which these firms operate but rather depends on the political and ideological system in which those firms operate.[43] In other words, it is not so much that common law systems are more apt to protect investors, shareholders, and property rights in general than civil law systems, but rather that the type of ideologies underpinning the political system dictate whether investors and property rights in general will be protected or not. Countries where the political ideology is more left leaning are more anti-capital and more pro-labor and countries where the political ideology is more right leaning are more pro-capital and less pro-labor. As a result, capital markets are more developed and more liquid, and exhibit higher corporate valuation, in countries where the ideology underpinning the politics is more pro-capital.[44] Therefore, we arrive at this apparent contradiction in which civil law countries (typically more left leaning) often tend to enforce insider trading laws more strongly than common law countries (typically more right leaning), but then have less developed and liquid capital markets, less dispersed ownership, and lower corporate valuation than in common law countries that have laws that protect better investors and property rights.[45] The contradiction can be resolved by Roe's hypothesis. Left-leaning governments might be more inclined to enforce insider trading laws because they are more anti-capital and insider trading commonly involves large shareholders and corporate managers who also are shareholders, than right-leaning governments whose enforcement of insider trading laws aims at protecting investors and, more particularly, minority (non-controlling) shareholders from being expropriated by controlling shareholders (managers or large shareholders).

Secondly, the studies suggesting that insider trading laws have significant positive externalities on stock market development and corporate valuation do not address the other evidence that the countries observing a greater number of fraudulent accounting scandals seem to be those that have seen an increase in the stringency of their insider trading laws.[46] In other words, insider trading laws may encourage investment while not discouraging insider trading but, at the same time, they unintentionally give the opportunity to management to misappropriate shareholders as they manipulate earnings to hide low productivity, boost stock prices, and make profitable trades.[47] In addition, these studies do not address the fact that, contrary to insider trading, fraudulent accounting causes an

---

[43]   Mark J. Roe, Strong Managers, Weak Owners: The Political Roots of American Corporate Finance (1994). See also Mark J. Roe, Political Determinants of Corporate Governance (2003); Mark J. Roe, Legal Origins, Politics, and Modern Stock Markets, 120 Harv. L. Rev. 462 (2006).

[44]   See Mark J. Roe, Political Preconditions to Separating Ownership from Corporate Control, 53 Stan. L. Rev. 539 (2000); and Laura N. Beny, What Explains Insider Trading Restrictions? International Evidence on the Political Economy of Insider Trading Regulation, John M. Olin Center for Law & Economics, Working Paper No.08-001, Social Sciences Research Network Electronic Paper Collection 47 (2008). Available at: http://ssrn.com/abstract=304383 (last visited Nov. 28, 2012). See also Marco Pagano & Paolo Volpin, The Political Economy of Corporate Governance, 95 Am. Econ. Rev. 1005, 1027 (2005).

[45]   Beny, supra note 44.

[46]   Simi Kedia & Thomas Philippon, The Economics of Fraudulent Accounting, 22 Rev. Fin. Stud. 2169, 2195 (2009).

[47]   Id. at 2171. See also Arturo Bris, Do Insider Trading Laws Work? 11 Eur. Fin. Mgmt 267, 309 (2005) (showing that insider trading laws increase the incidence and profitability of insider trading but also that the toughness of insider trading laws reduces the incidence of insider trading).

amplification of business cycles and is accompanied by misallocation of resources in the form of excessive hiring and investment to mimic good management.[48]

A review of empirical studies assessing the benefits of insider trading laws shows that they appear to discount significantly the direct and indirect costs of insider trading laws that can translate in higher costs than those of insider trading.[49]

III.   COULD INSIDER TRADING BE NOT HARMFUL TO MARKETS?

As we have seen, the empirical studies analyzing the effects of insider trading laws on capital markets development, while very important, highlight a significant problem when it comes to studying the effects of insider trading on capital markets: they do not prove that insider trading is actually harmful to capital markets. At best, they show that people are more willing to invest when laws against insider trading exist and are enforced because they might think they are less likely to buy or sell stocks from insiders. In reality, the empirical evidence shows that, while the general public might oppose insider trading because they do not want to buy or sell stocks from individuals who are better informed than they are, they still invest in capital markets despite knowing that insider trading is common. Moreover, we have seen that there are hidden costs associated with increased market liquidity and dispersed ownership that translate into management entrenchment, shareholder expropriation, and fraudulent accounting, which lead to excessive investment and resource misallocation in the economy.

A.   "The Use of Knowledge in Society"[50]

The early twentieth century was marked by the socialist calculation debate during which economists considered whether a centrally planned economic system where the factors of production are owned by the state could be as efficient as, if not more efficient than, a market economy where most factors of production are owned by individuals or groups of individuals, in allocating resources to their most valued uses.[51] The debate opposed two groups of economists. Ludwig von Mises and Friedrich Hayek argued that central planning could not be as efficient as a market economy while Oskar Lange, H.D. Dickson, Fred M. Taylor, Abba P. Lerner, and E.F.M. Durbin argued that socialism under the proper conditions could be as efficient as a decentralized economic system where the primary

---

[48]   Id. at 2195.

[49]   While Kedia and Philippon assume that managers engage in fraudulent accounting with the purpose to engage in insider trading, one can assume that managers engage in fraudulent accounting with the myopic purpose of keeping their positions within the firm and not be the victim of myopic minority shareholders who are more concerned about short-term performance than long-term performance. Id. at 2171.

[50]   The title of this section is inspired by Friedrich A. Hayek, The Use of Knowledge in Society, 35 Am. Econ. Rev. 519 (1945).

[51]   For a recent discussion of the socialist calculation debate, see Bruce Caldwell, Hayek and Socialism, 35 J. Econ. Lit. 1856 (1997). See also Don Lavoie, A Critique of the Standard Account of the Socialist Calculation Debate, 5 J. Libertarian Stud. 41 (1981).

allocations of the resources would be made via the market.[52] The details and outcome of the debate are not as important for our discussion as the implications of the debate as they relate to the understanding of the nature and role of prices when it comes to the allocations of resources in the economy. According to Mises and Hayek, monetary prices can only emerge in a system where factors of production are owned privately as opposed to being owned by the state so they can be the objects of exchange for the purpose of allocating them to various alternative lines of production. In this regard, it is out of the competition for these resources with alternative uses that are valued differently by all individuals that prices emerge. Without prices, there is no mechanism to calculate profits and losses and without such a mechanism we cannot decide how to allocate scarce resources. Without a price mechanism, we are left "groping in the dark."[53] Lange replied to Mises's criticism of the absence of a price mechanism as a mechanism to allocate resources in the economy by arguing that the central planning board could mimic the market mechanism by applying a trial and error procedure. Lange argued that through this method the central planning board would sooner or later succeed in finding the correct set of prices. In addition, Lange argued that the central planning board, having a much wider knowledge than any single individual and entrepreneur in the competitive market process, would be able to find the right equilibrium prices faster.[54] However, Mises and Hayek replied separately that Lange was ignoring the fundamental role that profit-seeking entrepreneurs play in an ever-changing price structure. Entrepreneurs rely on current prices in their future-oriented production decisions, which affect the allocation of resources in the economy, to make judgments about future prices that are brought about by their decisions but also the consumption and production decisions of millions of individuals whose tastes and preferences constantly change. However, according to Mises, for the system to work, it needs well-defined and enforced property rights to get the proper information and incentives necessary to perform that entrepreneurial function.[55]

Hayek went a step further and explained that the decisions of these entrepreneurs do more than just affect future prices to improve the allocation of resources in the economy. These decisions, Hayek told us, are not only based on technical or scientific knowledge, they are also based on the "knowledge of the particular circumstances of time and place" that these entrepreneurs rely on when they make their decisions.[56] This knowledge, which is localized and tacit knowledge, is the product of experience and as such cannot be communicated to a central planning board in the same fashion that scientific or technical knowledge can be communicated to individuals.[57] Prices convey more than just information about the decisions of a myriad of individuals; prices also convey the local and tacit knowledge dispersed among a myriad of individuals that they rely on to make these decisions. In a sense, that knowledge dispersed among thousands of individuals is being crystalized in its most essential and understandable form in prices. Therefore, according to Hayek, the most significant aspect of the price system is "the economy of knowledge

---

[52] Don Lavoie, supra note 51, at 41; see also text accompanying note 3 supra.
[53] Caldwell, supra note 51, at 1859.
[54] Id. at 1862.
[55] Id. at 1863–1864.
[56] Hayek, supra note 50, at 521.
[57] Caldwell, supra note 51, at 1866.

with which it operates, or how little the individual participants need to know in order to be able to take the right action."[58] Without prices, individuals would be required to collect an astronomical amount of knowledge and, more particularly, experience to acquire that local knowledge to be able to decide where to allocate their resources, to make production decisions.

In the light of the socialist calculation debate, one can understand the crucial role that the price system plays in allocating resources in the economy but also the importance of allowing entrepreneurs to use their local and tacit knowledge in their business decisions. The corollary of this is that any regulation or legislation that prevents entrepreneurs from using their knowledge of the particular circumstances of time and place inherently hinders the effectiveness of the price system by distorting the signals they send to the other market participants.

B.   The Use of Inside Knowledge in Capital Markets

Hayek's fundamental contribution to understanding the nature and role of prices is essential to understand how insider trading can enhance the operation of markets as opposed to hindering it. More particularly, his emphasis on the importance of local knowledge, which Hayek calls "knowledge of the particular circumstances of time and place," can help us appreciate the role that insiders play in enhancing the operation of capital markets. Most insiders, whether they are directors, officers, large shareholders, or others acquire the nonpublic material corporate information either in the course of their work or while sitting on the board of directors as large shareholders traditionally do.[59] In other words, that knowledge that insiders produce and acquire via the course of their work is the product of experience; it is that knowledge of the particular circumstances of time and place described by Hayek. Their decisions to buy or sell stocks, which affect stock prices, are often based on inside information.[60] The changes in prices resulting from insiders' decisions therefore incorporate that inside information that market participants do not necessarily know but will help them make decisions. On the other hand, preventing insiders from trading on this information distorts the price signal that market participants receive.[61]

When one understands the role that insiders play in the markets, one can also recognize another function insiders are playing: that of whistleblowing. Wagner suggests that, under very specific conditions, insiders should be allowed to sell their stocks based on negative (inside) knowledge. In doing so, insiders selling their stocks in face of bad news

---

[58]   Hayek, supra note 50, at 527.

[59]   That information is not tacit, and certainly can be communicated, but it does not necessarily mean that investors once in possession of this knowledge would necessarily understand or know what to do with it. On the other hand, price changes can serve as a starting point for decision making.

[60]   Sometimes people make decisions without fully being aware of all the knowledge they are using to make their decision.

[61]   Beny, supra note 21, at 280 also argues that insider trading laws improve price informativeness. Obviously, this goes against Hayek's theory. However, Beny does not address the empirical literature that shows that insider trading laws fail in general to deter insider trading.

serve as whistleblowers to inhibit corporate frauds and, more particularly, accounting frauds such as earnings manipulations.[62] Allowing insiders to sell their stocks in the presence of fraudulent accounting would actually dissuade management from engaging in fraudulent accounting because the resulting drop in prices would communicate different information to minority shareholders to sell and outside investors not to invest in the company. In doing so, managers, tempted to hide the low productivity of their business by manipulating earnings and hiring and investing excessively, would be discouraged from doing so because most investors and minority shareholders rely on price changes in their decision making. As Hayek mentions, market participants do not need to know exactly why the prices are dropping other than they should no longer allocate resources toward this specific line of production or business.[63] In this regard, allowing insiders to sell their stocks in the case of negative news or in the presence of fraudulent accounting will save resources and avoid misallocation of resources for a longer period of time, reducing the magnitude of business cycle.[64]

C. Empirical Evidence

There is empirical evidence that insiders, when trading, use knowledge of particular circumstances of time and place as it applies to the environment in which they work and that this knowledge is being communicated to markets months, sometimes years, ahead. We find such evidence at both the firm level and the market level that insiders rely on their knowledge of the particular circumstances of time and place to sell their stocks. This evidence is particularly important with regard to investment and allocation of resources in the economy.

At the firm level, Seyhun and Bradley investigate insider trading preceding corporate bankruptcy announcements. They find that insiders do "bail out" on their stockholders prior to filing a bankruptcy petition as far back as five years before the filing date and their selling volume increases up to the announcement month.[65]

When looking at registered insider trading prior to bankruptcy petition filing, Seyhun and Bradley find that "insiders are significant net sellers of their firm's shares in the

---

[62] See Wagner, supra note 29 at 981–984.

[63] Hayek, supra note 50, at 526.

[64] It is true that individuals buying from insiders selling will lose. However, one can argue that these individuals would have bought this company's stock regardless. Another argument is that allowing insiders to sell on bad news would aggravate the moral hazard problem encouraging insiders to make decisions against the shareholders' interests to drive down prices. It is difficult to see why insiders would manufacture bad news if there is no profit to be made. The main argument against insider trading is that allowing insider trading would give incentives to insiders to manufacture good news to drive up prices to profit from the price swing. Manufacturing bad news will not allow insiders to make any gains. Allowing insiders in presence of bad news enable them to minimize their losses, which would discourage them to manufacture good news to avoid those losses or, as in the case of the whistleblower argument, to encourage insiders to signal to the market participants that some of the information provided to the market by the company is inaccurate and they should not invest in the company or should withdraw investment from the company.

[65] H. Nejat Seyhun & Michael Bradley, Corporate Bankruptcy and Insider Trading, 70 J. Bus. 189, 214 (1997).

months and years preceding a bankruptcy filing."[66] They observe that, in the fifth year before filing a bankruptcy petition, insider selling represents a total disinvestment of $716,000 per firm. When compared with the fact that the returns to the stockholders of these firms are significantly negative in the fourth year before filing, the data suggest that "insiders possess privileged information regarding the future price of their firms' securities."[67] Moreover, Seyhun and Bradley observe that the trading pattern by top executives and officers shows that they have more information regarding their firms' future situation than other insiders.[68]

At the market level, Marin and Olivier investigate insider sales and stock market crashes.[69] They focus on individual stocks traded on the NYSE, Amex, and NASDAQ between 1986 and 2002.[70] Marin and Olivier's findings are consistent with Seyhun and Bradley's results that insiders' sales associated with corporate bankruptcies are not necessarily driven by their need for liquidity and diversification. Their study shows that insider sales in the distant past are a strong indicator of market crashes resulting from informed investors getting out of the market.[71] On the other hand, when insiders sell in the recent past, the likelihood of a crash is low because insiders are bound by § 16(b) of the Securities Exchange Act of 1934.[72] Their results show that the timing of insiders' sales is not strategic as to avoid SEC prosecution because the likelihood of being prosecuted by selling on bad news is much lower compared with buying on good news, as documented by Meulbroek.[73]

These studies are important as they indicate that when insiders sell they communicate their knowledge of the particular circumstances of time and place to the market; this knowledge is being crystallized into the stock prices and sends a signal to the market where to allocate or not allocate the resources in the economy. On the other hand, these studies show that when insiders are highly constrained by insider trading laws, as they cannot sell their stocks, they may have incentives to engage in fraudulent accounting to hide poor performance and postpone drops in the company's stock prices.[74]

IV. CONCLUDING REMARKS

Is insider trading an assault on free markets? The answer to this empirical question is not as clear-cut as Judge Richard J. Holwell seemed to imply in his comments during Raj Rajaratnam's sentencing hearing. The empirical literature is still struggling to find any causality between insider trading laws and capital market development. As we have seen, the correlations that these studies have found are problematic in their interpretation and,

---

[66]   Id. at 205.

[67]   Id. at 201.

[68]   Id. at 214.

[69]   Jose M. Marin & Jacques P. Olivier, The Dog That Did Not Bark: Insider Trading and Crashes, 63 J. Fin. 2429 (2008).

[70]   Id. at 2430.

[71]   Id. at 2453.

[72]   Id. at 2455.

[73]   Id. at 2458–2459. See also Meulbroek, supra note 25, at 1669.

[74]   Wagner, supra note 29, at 976–980. See also Kedia & Philippon, supra note 46, at 2169–2170.

often, the conclusions do not meet the eye test or other empirical results. The fact that stock markets with higher corporate valuation seem to exhibit more fraudulent accounting scandals, crashes, and resulting amplified business cycles in countries that have the most stringent insider trading laws also raises questions about what constitutes healthy capital markets and how we measure corporate performance.[75] There seems to be a trade-off between trying to reduce the amount of informational asymmetry between market participants and, at the same time, unintentionally allowing people who benefit from an informational asymmetry to distort the signal that the general public receive, leading to misallocation of resources in the economy and amplified business cycles. The contribution of this chapter is to revisit Henry Manne's argument that insider trading improves capital market and intra-firm efficiency. This chapter argues that inside information is the knowledge of the particular circumstances of time and place described by Hayek and, therefore, that preventing insiders from using that knowledge distorts the signals that stock prices send to market participants, leading to greater market instability and also to more shareholder expropriation. This chapter offers the alternative hypothesis that under some circumstances insider trading would benefit stock markets and lead to less shareholder expropriation.

To be sure, the chapter does not truly answer the questions asked in the introduction. Instead, in response to Judge Holwell's statement, it argues that another line of empirical research ought to be explored that would consist in trying to measure empirically what would be the optimal level of insider trading or alternatively the optimal level of insider trading regulation.[76] Given that most countries have insider trading laws with various degrees of stringency and enforcement, a first step would be to measure empirically the direct and indirect costs of insider trading laws and their enforcements and compare them with the expected benefits.

---

[75] For a critique of using Tobin's Q as a measure of corporate performance, see Philip H. Dybvig & Mitch Warachka, Tobin's Q Does Not Measure Performance: Theory, Empirics, and Alternative Measures (2011), available at http://ssrn.com/abstract=1562444 (last visited Nov. 28, 2012).

[76] Except in Beny, supra note 44, at 50 & note 135, there does not seem to be any mention in the literature that the optimal amount of insider trading is not zero, and Judge Holwell's statement implies that the optimal amount of insider trading is zero. Obviously, from a pure economic viewpoint, as the optimal rate of pollution or crime is not zero, even if insider trading has negative externalities, the optimal amount of insider trading is not zero.

15. The political economy of insider trading laws and enforcement: law vs. politics? International evidence

Laura Nyantung Beny

I. INTRODUCTION

Despite theoretical arguments that stock markets are more efficient when insiders are allowed to trade freely,[1] many increasingly regard insider trading as a threat to stock market integrity and efficiency.[2] By 2000, eighty-seven countries had enacted insider trading legislation and thirty-eight had prosecuted insider trading at least once.[3] However, these laws vary in stringency and many of them were enacted only recently, often long after the stock market came into existence.[4] Enforcement intensity also varies across countries, with some countries regularly enforcing insider trading laws and others allowing insiders to trade with impunity notwithstanding the laws on the books.[5] This study aims to provide at least a partial explanation of the differential timing of insider trading legislation and enforcement across countries.

The results may inform the academic debate about insider trading regulation, which centers on the question of whether such regulation is efficient or inefficient. There are vocal advocates on both sides of the debate. Those who oppose insider trading regulation argue that, at best, it simply redistributes rents among private parties at the cost of regulation[6] and, at worst, may reduce efficiency by distorting managerial incentives[7] or reducing the accuracy of stock prices.[8] In contrast, proponents of insider trading regulation argue

---

[1] See, e.g., Henry Manne, Insider Trading and the Stock Market (1966); Dennis Carlton & Daniel Fischel, The Regulation of Insider Trading, 35 Stan. L. Rev. 857 (1983).

[2] Franklin A. Gevurtz, The Globalization of Insider Trading Regulation, 15 Transnat'l Law. 63, 67–68 (2002).

[3] See Utpal Bhattacharya & Hazem Daouk, The World Price of Insider Trading, 57 J. Fin. 75, 80–84 (2002); Gevurtz, supra note 2, at 65.

[4] See infra Table 15.3.

[5] See infra Table 15.3.

[6] See, e.g., David Haddock & Jonathan Macey, Controlling Insider Trading in Europe and America: The Economics of the Politics, in Law and Economics and the Economics of Legal Regulation 149 (J. Matthias Graf von den Schulenburg & Goran Skogh eds., 1986) [hereinafter Haddock & Macey, Controlling Insider Trading]; David Haddock & Jonathan Macey, Regulation on Demand: A Private Interest Model, with an Application to Insider Trading Regulation, 30 J. L. & Econ. 311 (1987) [hereinafter Haddock & Macey, Regulation on Demand]; Carla Tighe and Ron Michener, The Political Economy of Insider-Trading Laws, 84 Am. Econ. Rev. 164–168 (1994).

[7] See, e.g., Carlton & Fischel, supra note 1, at 869–872.

[8] See, e.g., id. at 868.

that such regulation increases market efficiency by encouraging broader investor participation, increasing liquidity (share trading), and improving share price accuracy.[9]

Legal academics not only disagree about the effect of insider trading regulation on
stock markets, they also disagree about its genesis. Those who oppose such regulation
often rely on the private interest theory of regulation to explain how these laws, despite
their presumed inefficiency, are enacted to satisfy influential private interests.[10] In contrast, those who support insider trading restrictions rely on the public interest theory of
regulation to explain how insider trading regulation is enacted to address market failures.[11] The two theories are rarely merged into a single framework.

However, because insider trading and its regulation concern the distribution of property rights to use private corporate information, the issue has both private (distributional)
and public (efficiency) dimensions. Both dimensions are taken into account in the political
economy model outlined in this study. Like the private interest theory of insider trading
regulation, the analysis can accommodate the enactment of socially inefficient regulation.
At the same time, it can also accommodate the enactment of socially efficient regulation,
even though some private constituencies may benefit from such regulation.

It would be ideal to test the model directly using international data. However, that
requires data on underlying private preferences and social costs across countries. Such
data are usually unobservable in a single country, let alone internationally. I therefore
focus on several observable factors that existing theories suggest may explain the diversity
of insider trading policies across countries. These factors are financial development, legal
origin, political openness, and ideology. More specifically, the investor model, the legal
origins theory of finance, and the political theory of finance suggest that countries with
more developed stock markets, common law legal systems, and more democratic and
right-leaning political systems, respectively, ought to be more inclined to regulate insider
trading than other countries. Examining whether these factors help explain the relative
timing of enactment and enforcement of insider trading legislation across countries may
in turn shed light on the underlying preferences and social costs and thus inform the
debate.

The main finding, based on data from a cross-section of countries between 1980 and
1999, is that a country's political system—not its legal or financial system—best explains
its proclivity to regulate insider trading. Specifically, more democratic nations enacted
and enforced insider trading laws earlier than less democratic nations, controlling for
wealth, financial development, legal origin, and other factors. Furthermore, controlling
for the same factors, left-leaning governments were latecomers to insider trading legislation and enforcement relative to right-leaning and centrist governments.

---

[9] See, e.g., Reinier Kraakman, The Legal Theory of Insider Trading Regulation in the United
States, in European Insider Dealing 39 (Klaus Hopt & Eddy Wymeersch eds., 1991); Mark Klock,
Mainstream Economics and the Case for Prohibiting Insider Trading, 10 Ga. St. U. L. Rev. 297,
325–333 (1994).

[10] See Haddock & Macey, Regulation on Demand, supra note 6; David Haddock & Jonathan
Macey, A Coasian Model of Insider Trading, 80 Nw. U. L. Rev. 1449 (1987) [hereinafter Haddock
& Macey, Coasian Model].

[11] See, e.g., James D. Cox, Insider Trading and Contracting: A Critical Response to the Chicago
School, 1986 Duke L. J. 628, 653 (1986).

The findings are generally consistent with the political theory of capital market development and inconsistent with the legal origins theory of capital market development. They also challenge theoretical claims that insider trading restrictions are market inhibiting because the kinds of governments that appear more inclined to regulate insider trading are precisely the governments that are generally thought to pursue market-promoting policies.

The chapter is organized as follows. Section II sketches a political economy model of insider trading regulation that integrates both private (distributional) and public (efficiency) considerations. Section III then presents four empirically testable hypotheses about the comparative timing of insider trading legislation and enforcement across countries. Section IV explains the empirical methodology. Section V describes the data and presents the results. Section VI concludes.

II.   THE POLITICAL ECONOMY OF INSIDER TRADING

Insider trading legislation concerns the allocation of property rights to use and benefit from private corporate information.[12] Insider trading laws therefore have an important influence on the distribution of private rents among corporate insiders and outsiders.[13] When insider trading is unregulated, by default, the government assigns the property rights to private corporate information to corporate insiders, enabling them to maximize their private rents from the use of such information. In contrast, when insider trading is prohibited, the state removes insiders' monopoly on the use of private corporate information and thus redistributes private rents to outsiders. The preferences and relative political influence of insiders and outsiders are thus important determinants of the government's insider trading policy. However, insider trading regulation does not just affect the distribution of private rents. It also affects capital market efficiency and thus overall economic efficiency. In this section, I present a political economy analysis of insider trading regulation that integrates both distributional and economic efficiency concerns.

A.   The Private Constituencies: Insider Trading Creates Winners and Losers[14]

1.   The potential winners: corporate insiders and their friends
Corporate insiders include managers, board members, and controlling or large shareholders. Their status gives them privileged access to corporate information and thus a probable

---

[12]   Stephen M. Bainbridge, Securities Law: Insider Trading (2007); Jonathan Macey, Insider Trading: Economics, Politics, and Policy (1991); Zohar Goshen & Gideon Parchomovsky, On Insider Trading, Markets, and "Negative" Property Rights in Information, 87 Va. L. Rev. 1229 (2001); Kimberly Kraweic, Fairness, Efficiency, and Insider Trading: Deconstructing the Coin of the Realm in the Information Age, 95 Nw. U. L. Rev. 443 (2001).

[13]   See supra note 12.

[14]   While unconvincing, some argue that insider trading produces no net gainers or losers. See, e.g., William J. Carney, Signalling and Causation in Insider Trading, 36 Cath. U. L. Rev. 863 (1987). If that were true, insider trading arguably would not be such a controversial political economic issue.

trading advantage relative to outsiders. Evidence suggests that insiders make superior profits relative to public investors and other participants in the stock market even when they trade on the basis of publicly available and thus immaterial information.[15] Insider trading on the basis of material, non-public information is probably even more profitable, especially in stock markets where there are relatively few constraints on self-dealing by insiders. Professor Arturo Bris, for example, presents international evidence that suggests insider trading on the basis of private information about corporate takeovers is very profitable and insider trading profits vary inversely with the stringency of insider trading laws.[16]

Relatives, friends, and business associates who trade on the basis of private information received from insiders are also likely to profit.[17] So, too, may politicians and government bureaucrats who receive private information in exchange for economic or political favors.[18]

2. The potential losers: information, liquidity traders, and small investors

Outsiders who stand to lose from insider trading include information traders, liquidity traders, and possibly minority shareholders. Information traders receive most of their income from stock trading and are insiders' main competitors for trading profits. They include market professionals, such as analysts, broker-dealers, market makers, and other sophisticated investors. While their knowledge or ability to process corporate information is superior to those of other outside investors, they experience direct losses from insider trading. Informed traders consistently lose relative to insiders when the latter trade on the basis of material, non-public information because, although they are well informed relative to outsiders, informed traders are at a distinct informational disadvantage vis-à-vis insiders.[19]

Liquidity traders are investors who trade frequently and thus benefit from low trading costs. They include institutional investors, such as pension funds, mutual funds, insurance companies, and index traders. Their trading is largely driven by exogenous factors such

---

[15] See, e.g., Leslie Jeng et al., Estimating the Returns to Insider Trading: A Performance-Evaluation Perspective, in R. Econ. & Stat. 453 (2003); Nejat Seyhun, The Effectiveness of Insider-Trading Sanctions, 35 J. L. & Econ. 149 (1992). A few commentators contend that insiders' profits are offset by reductions in their salaries. See, e.g., Carlton & Fischel, supra note 1. However, this claim rests on the unrealistic assumption that insiders' trades are transparent. See Kraakman, supra note 9, at 50.

[16] Arturo Bris, Do Insider Trading Laws Work? 11 Eur. Fin. Mgmt 267, 269 (2005).

[17] Outsiders who receive private information from insiders are often called "tippees." See, e.g., Chiarella v. United States, 445 U.S. 222 (1980).

[18] In India, for example, "the broker-promoter-politician-fund manager nexus . . . these days accounts for the biggest chunk of insider trading." Sucheta Dalal, Nabbing Insider Traders: Easier Said Than Done, Rediff, Aug. 16, 2000, available at http://www.rediff.com/money/2000/aug/16dalal.htm (last visited Dec. 11, 2012).

[19] See Nicholas Georgakopoulos, Insider Trading as a Transactional Cost: A Market Microstructure Justification and Optimization of Insider Trading Regulation, 26 Conn. L. Rev. 1 (1993); Goshen & Parchomovsky, supra note 12; Haddock & Macey, Regulation on Demand, supra note 6; Jhinyoung Shin, The Optimal Regulation of Insider Trading, 5 J. Fin. Intermediation 49 (1996). In other work, I find a positive relationship between the stringency of insider trading laws and stock price informativeness, indirectly suggesting that information traders are discouraged by insider trading. Laura N. Beny, Do Insider Trading Laws Matter? 7 Am. L. & Econ. Rev. 144 (2005) [hereinafter Beny, Do Laws Matter?].

as portfolio realignment or short-term consumption rather than by new information. Theoretical[20] and empirical[21] studies suggest that insider trading increases transaction costs. Thus, liquidity traders stand to lose from insider trading because they trade frequently enough to be harmed by greater transaction costs.

It is less clear how insider trading affects uninformed, small outside shareholders who trade infrequently and own minority equity stakes in firms. They may be indirectly harmed if institutional investors who experience increased trading costs as a result of insider trading pass on greater mutual and pension fund fees to them. In addition, if insider trading raises agency costs (i.e., causes managers to behave in ways that reduce corporate value) and the market systematically underestimates the amount of such trading, small outside investors will be harmed because they will be buying shares at a higher price than their actual value. In contrast, if insider trading reduces agency costs and the market underestimates the amount of such trading, minority shareholders will benefit because they will be buying shares at a lower price than their actual value. Recent evidence suggests that some outside shareholders value insider trading restrictions.[22]

B. Social Costs

Apart from its private distributional effects, theory and evidence suggest several ways in which insider trading may harm stock markets and the economy as a whole.

1. Price informativeness and capital allocation

Information traders play a positive role in price formation, both in the extent and kind of information that is impounded in stock prices.[23] They are rewarded for this by the profits they earn in trading against less informed investors. They maximize their profits by gathering firm-specific information until the marginal cost exceeds the marginal benefit of gathering such information. The collective trading of many such traders leads to more efficient capitalization of firm-specific information into stock prices,[24] making stock prices more informative.[25]

Professor Jeffrey Wurgler shows that capital is more efficiently allocated in the economy

---

[20]   See, e.g., Lawrence Glosten & Lawrence Harris, Estimating the Components of the Bid/Ask Spread, 21 J. Fin. Econ. 123 (1988); Shin, supra note 19.

[21]   See, e.g., Thomas Copeland & Dan Galai, Information Effects and the Bid–Ask Spread, 38 J. Fin. 1457 (1983); Glosten & Harris, supra note 20; Hans Stoll, Inferring the Components of the Bid–Ask Spread: Theory and Empirical Evidence, 44 J. Fin. 115 (1989).

[22]   See Laura N. Beny, Do Investors in Controlled Firms Value Insider Trading Laws? International Evidence, 4 J. L. Econ. & Pol'y 267 (2008); Art Durnev & Amrita Nain, Does Insider Trading Regulation Deter Private Information Trading? International Evidence, 15 Pacific-Basin Fin. J. 409 (2007).

[23]   Goshen & Parchomovsky, supra note 12; Randall Morck et al., The Information Content of Stock Markets: Why Do Emerging Markets Have Synchronous Price Movements? 58 J. Fin. Econ. 215 (2000).

[24]   Sanford Grossman, On the Efficiency of Competitive Stock Markets Where Traders Have Diverse Information, 31 J. Fin. 573 (1976); Andrei Shleifer & Robert Vishny, The Limits of Arbitrage, 52 J. Fin. 35 (1997).

[25]   Kenneth French & Richard Roll, Stock Return Variances: The Arrival of Information and the Reaction of Traders, 17 J. Fin. Econ. 5 (1986); Richard Roll, R^2, 43 J. Fin. 541 (1988).

when a greater amount of firm-specific information is capitalized into stock prices.[26] It thus follows that if insider trading discourages information traders, it imposes a negative externality on the economy by reducing the informativeness of stock prices,[27] even if not all traders are discouraged. Consistent with this, in other work I document a positive relationship between stock price informativeness and the stringency of insider trading laws.[28] Thus, capital allocation may be less efficient in countries with lax insider trading legislation and enforcement.

2. Capital constraints and the cost of capital

Capital constraints limit the range of feasible investments in the economy, in turn constraining economic growth.[29] A lower cost of capital makes investments more profitable and encourages the entry of new entrepreneurs into the capital market. Using international time series data, Professors Utpal Bhattacharya and Hazem Daouk demonstrate that the initial enforcement of insider trading legislation is followed by a 5 percent decrease in the cost of capital.[30] Their finding suggests that capital is more expensive in countries where the public perceives insider trading to be unregulated. This implies that enforcing insider trading legislation could ultimately lead to greater economic growth by reducing the cost of capital. Conversely, countries with lax insider trading legal regimes may not be maximizing growth.

3. Transaction costs and liquidity

Liquid markets are valuable because greater liquidity makes purchasing and disposing of shares on short notice at the appropriate price easier for investors. The more liquid the market, the more willing investors should be to participate in it. Professors Yakov Amihud and Haim Mendelson confirm that investors value liquidity by showing that companies whose shares are more liquid must pay investors a lower expected rate of return than companies with less liquid shares.[31] In other words, their evidence shows that companies with more liquid shares have a lower cost of equity capital. Liquid markets may also mitigate agency costs, by lowering the opportunity cost of monitoring and facilitating the market for corporate control.[32] As noted above, however, evidence suggests that insider trading increases transaction costs and thus reduces stock market liquidity.

---

[26] Jeffrey Wurgler, Financial Markets and the Allocation of Capital, 58 J. Fin. Econ. 187 (2000).

[27] Morck et al., supra note 23, present cross-country evidence that stock price informativeness and investor protections are positively correlated, implying that beneficial arbitrage activity is greater in countries where the threat of expropriation is lower.

[28] Beny, Do Laws Matter?, supra note 19; see also Nuno Fernandes & Miguel A. Ferreira, Insider Trading Laws and Stock Price Informativeness 22 Rev. Fin. Stud. 1845 (2009).

[29] See generally Bekaert et al., Does Financial Liberalization Spur Growth, 77 J. Fin. Econ. 3 (2005).

[30] Bhattacharya & Daouk, supra note 3.

[31] Yakov Amihud & Haim Mendelson, Asset Pricing and the Bid–Ask Spread, 17 J. Fin. Econ. 223 (1986).

[32] See, e.g., Markus Berndt, Global Differences in Corporate Governance Systems, in Konomische Analyse des Rechts [Economic Analysis of Law] 3 (Peter Behrens et al. eds., 2002); Ernst Maug, Insider Trading Legislation and Corporate Governance, 46 Eur. Econ. Rev. 1569,

In short, there are several potential channels through which insider trading may reduce both stock market efficiency and overall economic efficiency.

C.   A Political Economy Model of Insider Trading Regulation

According to the public interest theory of regulation, governments intervene in markets to correct their failures and thus promote efficiency.[33] From this perspective, insider trading regulation can be seen as an attempt by the government to address a market failure that market participants are unwilling or unable to solve through private contracting.[34] A fundamental weakness of the public interest theory of regulation, however, is that it is vague about the mechanisms through which a social desire to correct a market failure gets translated into public policy.[35] As Professors Shleifer and Vishny argue, however, "institutions supporting property rights are created not by the fiat of a public-spirited government but, rather, in response to political pressure on the government exerted by owners of private property."[36]

Thus, for example, the mere fact that insider trading may be thought to be inefficient does not lead to the automatic enactment of insider trading legislation. Market inefficiencies can persist for long periods without governmental intervention, due not just to the costs of regulation but also to effective opposition to reform from private parties who stand to lose from insider trading regulation. The private interest theory of regulation is also deficient in that it tends to consider competition between special interest groups as the sole determinant of who wins the regulatory game.[37] Theorists of this stripe generally view regulatory intervention as inefficient, downplaying the reality that regulation sometimes does enhance economic efficiency.[38]

1575, 1580 (2002). But see Amar Bhide, The Hidden Costs of Stock Market Liquidity, 34 J. Fin. Econ. 31 (1993) (arguing that greater liquidity hinders corporate monitoring).

[33]   See Richard Posner, Theories of Economic Regulation, 5 Bell J. Econ & Mgmt. Sci. 335 (1974).

[34]   See, e.g., Cox, supra note 11.

[35]   Posner, supra note 33.

[36]   Andrei Shleifer & Robert Vishny, The Grabbing Hand: Government Pathologies and their Cures 10 (1998).

[37]   E.g., Sam Peltzman, Toward a More General Theory of Regulation, 19 J. L. & Econ. 211 (1976); George Stigler, The Theory of Economic Regulation, 2 Bell J. Econ. & Mgmt. Sci. 3 (1971). David Haddock and Jonathan Macey apply this type of model to insider trading regulation, and argue that insider trading legislation is the result of demand from powerful special interests. Haddock & Macey, Regulation on Demand, supra note 6.

[38]   Edward Glaeser, Simon Johnson & Andrei Shleifer, Coase versus the Coasians, 116 Q. J. Econ. 853 (2001) aptly note how the Coasians are more Coasian than Coase was himself. They also show how securities laws can increase economic efficiency. See also Simeon Djankov, Edward Glaeser, Rafael La Porta, Florencio Lopez-de-Silances & Andrei Shleifer, The New Comparative Economics, 31 J. Comp. Econ. 595–619, 607, 612–613 (2003) ("not all institutional failure should be blamed on politics. In fact, politics often moves societies toward institutional efficiency rather than away from it . . . even when some interest groups obstruct change, Coasian bargaining often leads to efficient institutional choice" and citing U.S. progressive reforms as an example of efficiency-increasing regulation); Steven P. Croley, Public Interested Regulation, Fla. St. U. L. Rev. 1 (2000) (arguing that regulation may sometimes be in the public interest, i.e., increase economic efficiency); Susan M. Phillips and J. Richard Zecher, The SEC and the Public Interest, 25 (1981) (leaning

As Professor Gary Becker recognizes, the impetus for policy change lies somewhere between public and private interest theories of regulation.[39] Accordingly, his model of interest-group competition integrates the two approaches.[40] In Becker's model, consistent with the private interest theory of regulation, interest groups support policies that maximize their private rents. Those with the most at stake do not automatically prevail, however. Who prevails among private constituencies depends on several factors that influence the relative efficiency of their political expenditures, such as group wealth, social and political networks, and size.[41] It also depends on the social welfare implications of the competing preferences. This is the novel aspect of Becker's model: efficiency plays an explicit role in the outcome of competition among private parties. Specifically, efficiency enters the model in that an interest group has an inherent advantage in the competition if its preferred policy raises social welfare and an inherent disadvantage in the competition if its preferred policy lowers social welfare.[42]

Becker's framework can be applied to the contest over insider trading regulation. The status quo is unregulated insider trading. Market participants who wish to overturn the status quo must prevail upon the state to enact and enforce insider trading legislation. Corporate insiders may resist insider trading regulation by various means, including monetary payments to politicians and, importantly, information tip-offs to politicians and market professionals. If insiders are able to co-opt market professionals, who include information and liquidity traders, they may easily succeed in maintaining the status quo because in many stock markets small outside investors are a relatively unorganized group whose relatively small individual stakes provide little financial incentive to lobby.[43] Thus, on the face of it, it seems as though corporate insiders could often easily defeat insider trading regulation.

However, applying Becker's integrated public–private framework, insider prevalence cannot be taken for granted. If insider trading is inefficient, as it may be in some markets, insiders will be inherently disadvantaged in the competition over regulatory policy relative to outsiders. While they may be able to overcome this disadvantage in some contexts, they may not be able to do so in others.

---

toward public choice (private interest) theory of regulation but acknowledging that public choice and efficiency might in some cases merge).

[39]   Gary Becker, A Theory of Competition Among Pressure Groups for Political Influence, 98 Q. J. Econ. 371 (1983).

[40]   Id

[41]   Smaller, more cohesive groups are often thought to be more influential than larger groups because they are better able to control free-riding among their members. See generally Mancur Olson, The Logic of Collective Action (1965). However, smaller size need not always give a group a political advantage. Being larger may increase the influence of special interest groups, if the scale effect outweighs the free-riding effect of an increase in group size. Becker, supra note 39.

[42]   A group that favors an inefficient policy may overcome its inherent disadvantage, however, if it is able to exert greater political influence than the competing group. Becker, supra note 39.

[43]   However, normative factors, like a sense of what is fair, may cause small investors to have strong feelings about the matter. Furthermore, as the investor class in a country expands, outside investors may become more organized and begin to lobby based on their collective financial interests. See infra Section III.A.

III.   TESTABLE HYPOTHESES

While it would be ideal to test the political economy model in Section II directly, data on the underlying private preferences and social costs are unavailable across countries. Thus, in this section I focus on three relatively more observable factors—financial development, law, and politics—that existing theories suggest may explain the diversity of insider trading policies across countries. I discuss these theories and present four testable hypotheses.

A.   Finance: The "Investor Model"[44]

As the stock market develops, outside investors may become more effective at exerting political pressure on the state to adopt greater investor protections via numerous channels.[45] First, as the size of the domestic investor class increases, their wealth and influence become more important relative to those of corporate insiders. Outside investors' influence may increase even more relative to insiders' if they include foreign investors from countries where restrictions on insider trading are the norm.[46] Secondly, as stock markets develop, institutions may emerge to mitigate the free-riding problems that stymie collective action by small outside investors.[47] Investor associations are an example. In the United States, for example, the Investor's Clearinghouse is an online forum run by the Alliance for Investor Education,[48] which disseminates information on a wide variety of investment topics, including financial fraud.

Market professionals may also become more cohesive and develop interests increasingly distinct from those of corporate insiders. Institutional investors, for example, may begin to share information on issues of collective concern, like corporate governance and securities fraud. One U.S. example is Institutional Investor Online.[49] The site provides

---

[44]   See Peter A. Gourevitch & James Shinn, Political Power and Corporate Control 96–123 (2005). ("In the investor model, the owners of firms and external providers of capital work out a 'good governance' bargain through a combination of private ordering and public regulations, thus providing protections for minority shareholders.")

[45]   See, e.g., Marco Pagano & Paolo Volpin, Shareholder Protection, Stock Market Development, and Politics, 4 J. Eur. Econ. Assoc. 315–341 (2006) (presenting a model with mutual feedback between stock market development and investor protection, where greater investor protection leads to a broader stock market, which in turn broadens the shareholder base and increases political support for shareholder protections).

[46]   Bekaert et al. argue that "[i]t is possible that the enactment of . . . [insider trading laws] [is] particularly valued and perhaps demanded by foreigners before they risk investing in emerging markets." Bekaert et al., supra note 29, at 35. The internationalization of stock markets has led to a proliferation of regulatory harmonization efforts among countries under the auspices of institutions like the International Organization of Securities Commissions (IOSCO) and bilateral agreements between the U.S. Securities and Exchange Commission (SEC) and foreign market regulators. Arguably, this has generated a "race-to-the-top" in the sense that many countries have agreed to amend their laws in order to satisfy minimum standards of securities regulation.

[47]   Mechanisms that reduce free-riding problems increase the "productivity" of political expenditures. See Becker, supra note 39.

[48]   http://www.investoreducation.org/index.cfm (last visited Dec. 11, 2012).

[49]   http://www.iimagazine.com/.

articles about a range of issues of concern to institutional investors, like the dangers of investing in overseas markets, like China, that are rife with insider trading and market manipulation.[50] The international edition[51] monitors corporate performance in many countries, including emerging markets, like Brazil and India, and often ranks companies based on their corporate governance practices.[52]

Stock exchanges, seeking to maximize trading volume and thus commissions, may begin to engage in self-regulation long before formal legislative action is taken. This occurred in the U.S. and the United Kingdom as their stock markets were developing.[53] Private stock exchanges in the two countries regulated their members, which include stock-issuing firms and market professionals like broker-dealers, imposing listing requirements and disclosure and anti-manipulation rules. In turn, self-regulation by market professionals may stimulate legislative action that leads to formal stock market regulation.[54]

Thus, as the stock market increases in significance, constituencies that favor liquidity and an orderly market may increase private demand for regulatory oversight that is likely to include insider trading legislation and enforcement. Furthermore, as these constituencies become more organized and resource-endowed they pose a greater political threat to the insider-dominated status quo.

As the stock market develops, the social cost of insider trading may increase and thus strengthen the efficiency case for insider trading legislation, as well. Research suggests that insider trading becomes more profitable (and thus more tempting) and socially costly as the stock market becomes more liquid.[55] Applying the model outlined in Section II, this would imply an increase in outside investors' relative advantage (or a decrease in their relative disadvantage) in the political competition over insider trading policy.

In summary, as the stock market develops, both private and public forces are likely to bring insider trading policy to the forefront of public and legislative debate and increase outsiders' ability to challenge the insider-dominated status quo.[56] These observations lead to the first prediction:

---

[50] See, e.g., Kevin Hamilton, Laissez Regulators, Institutional Investor, Oct. 25, 2002, http://www. iimagazine.com/article.aspx?articleID=1036391.

[51] http://www.iimagazine.com/default.aspx?theme=International.

[52] See, e.g., "Institutional Investor Releases Inaugural Ranking of Asia's Top Executives and Shareholder-Friendly Companies," Institutional Investor, http://www.iimagazine.com/RankingsAsiaTopExec.aspx.

[53] John Coffee, The Rise of Dispersed Ownership: The Roles of Law and the State in the Separation of Ownership and Control, 111 Yale L. J. 1 (2001). According to Professor Coffee, "[b]y a variety of means, including a substantial self-regulatory component, both the United States and the United Kingdom developed legal and institutional mechanisms that enabled dispersed ownership to persist." Id. at 44; see also Brian Cheffins, Does Law Matter? The Separation of Ownership and Control in the United Kingdom, 30 J. Legal Stud. 459 (2001).

[54] See Coffee, supra note 53, at 67–68 (arguing that private parties may eventually perceive self-regulation to be insufficient because of enforcement deficiencies).

[55] See Maug, supra note 32, at 1579–1585.

[56] See Coffee, supra note 53, at 65. ("Legislative action seems likely to follow, rather than precede, the appearance of securities markets, in substantial part because a self-conscious constituency of public investors must first arise before there will be political pressure for legislative reform that intrudes upon the market.")

Hypothesis 1   A country with a more developed stock market is more likely to enact and enforce insider trading legislation than a country with a less developed stock market.

However, a country's legal and political systems will also affect outsiders' ability to overcome the status quo, as discussed next.

B.   Legal Origins Theory of Finance

According to the legal origins theory of finance, a primary determinant of a country's financial development is its legal origin.[57] Fundamental differences among legal systems generate differences in investor protection laws, which support different levels of financial development. In particular, the legal origins theory of finance holds that the common law is more conducive to minority investor protection than civil law.[58] Thus, small investors are more willing to invest in firms in common law countries than in civil law countries, where they fear being robbed by insiders and large shareholders. The result is that common law countries develop deep stock markets with diffuse ownership, while stock markets in civil law countries remain shallow and firms must rely on traditional forms of finance, like banks, related firms, and founding families.[59] Accordingly, stock ownership and control are relatively concentrated in civil law countries.[60]

The legal origins theory of finance suggests that corporate insiders and dominant shareholders are likely to pose a greater obstacle to the enactment and enforcement of insider trading legislation in civil law countries than in common law countries.[61] That is the private interest side of the political equation. On the public side, the theory suggests that there will be a greater efficiency imperative for insider trading regulation and enforcement in common law countries than in civil law countries. As explained above, as the stock market develops and equity finance becomes more important to the economy, the public interest case for insider trading regulation is likely to increase. Common law systems may be more responsive to this imperative because, presumably, they are more accommodating of "the changing needs of society."[62]

---

[57]   See, e.g., Rafael La Porta et al., Law and Finance, 106 J. Pol. Econ. 1113 (1998) [hereinafter La Porta et al., Law and Finance]; Rafael La Porta et al., Legal Determinants of External Finance, 52 J. Fin. 1131 (1997) [hereinafter La Porta et al., Legal Determinants].

[58]   The factors that presumably drive the legal and financial differences between common law and civil law countries are the existence of fiduciary duties in common law systems and their absence in civil law systems, the supposedly greater flexibility of common law judges compared with civil law judges, and the "over-regulation" of markets in civil law countries. See Mark J. Roe, Legal Origins, Politics, and Modern Stock Markets, 120 Harv. L. Rev. 462, 464 (2006) [hereinafter Roe, Legal Origins].

[59]   La Porta et al., Law and Finance, supra note 57; La Porta et al., Legal Determinants, supra note 57.

[60]   La Porta et al., Law and Finance, supra note 57; La Porta et al., Legal Determinants, supra note 57.

[61]   See Maug, supra note 32, demonstrating that controlling shareholders may benefit from lax insider trading laws. In a similar vein, Harold Demsetz, Corporate Control, Insider Trading and Rates of Return, 76 Am. Econ. Rev. 313 (1986) and Bhide, supra note 32, argue that insider trading legislation reduces controlling shareholders' profits.

[62]   This is the dynamic "law and finance theory." See Thorsten Beck, Asli Demirguc-Kunt, &

In summary, legal origins theory suggests that common law countries are more likely to enact and enforce insider trading legislation in response to private and public demand than civil law countries. This is the second prediction:

Hypothesis 2   A common law country is more likely to enact and enforce insider trading legislation than a civil law country with the same level of stock market development.

C.   The Political Theory of Finance

The political theory of finance emphasizes the centrality of politics, rather than legal origin, to financial market development.[63] According to the theory, public policies governing financial markets are jointly determined by competing preferences, the distribution of power, the openness of the political process, and ideology.[64] This section focuses on the last two factors, which are more measurable than the others.

First, as Professors Gourevitch and Shinn note, "[t]o obtain the most advantageous rules each player needs a way of getting the political system to reflect its preferences."[65] Other things equal, it should be harder for outsiders to challenge the status quo (unregulated insider trading, or an as yet non-enforced insider trading ban) in countries with relatively closed and undemocratic political systems. In the latter systems, insiders, the incumbents, are likely to have greater influence on the political process.

> Weak democracies have formalized elections and means of leadership succession, but are quite vulnerable to manipulation by elites and special interest groups. Money, guns, poverty, weak civil service systems, and ignorance can all contribute to a system unable to enforce its rules and regulations. . . . In a corrupt democracy, investors feel insecure, and [outside stock ownership] will not take place.[66]

In contrast, when the political process is open and contestable, outsiders have a greater chance of influencing national policy.[67] In short, outsiders are more likely to get the political system to reflect their preferences in democracies than in authoritarian states. In addition, ideology is critical. In particular, as Professor Roe notes, "[t]he first order

---

Ross Levine, Law, Politics, and Finance, World Bank Policy Research Paper 2585 (2001). See also Paul G. Mahoney, The Common Law and Economic Growth: Hayek Might be Right, 30 J. Legal Stud. 503 (2001).

[63]   E.g., Marco Pagano & Paolo Volpin, The Political Economy of Corporate Governance, 95 Am. Econ. Rev. 1005, 1027 (2005); Raghuram Rajan & Luigi Zingales, The Great Reversals: The Politics of Financial Development in the Twentieth Century, 69 J. Fin. Econ. 5 (2003); Roe, Legal Origins, supra note 58; Mark Roe, Political Preconditions to Separating Ownership from Corporate Control, 53 Stan. L. Rev. 539 (2000) [hereinafter Roe, Political Preconditions]; Mark Roe, Rents and their Corporate Law Consequences, 53 Stan. L. Rev. 1463 (2001); Lucian A. Bebchuk & Zvika Neeman, Investor Protection and Interest Group Politics, 23 Rev. of Fin. Stud. 1089 (2009); Beck, Demirguc-Kunt, & Levine, supra note 62.

[64]   See, e.g., Gourevitch & Shinn, supra note 44, at 58. ("Policy . . . is the output of preferences and power resources mediated by political institutions.")

[65]   Id. at 57.

[66]   Gourevitch & Shinn, supra note 44, at 81; see also Daron Acemoglu, Why Not a Political Coase Theorem? Social Conflict, Commitment, and Politics, 31 J. Comp. Econ. 620–652 (2003).

[67]   See Bebchuk & Neeman, supra note 63.

condition is a polity that supports capital markets."[68] In his labor model of politics and finance, Professor Roe suggests that left-leaning governments tend to eschew investors and capital market regulation and focus on workers and labor market regulation. This relative neglect of capital markets does not necessarily stem from hostility toward capital owners, although it may.[69] The salient assumption is that left-oriented states and legislatures tend to devote their political energy and resources to labor-protective redistributive policies.[70] Thus, other things equal, left-leaning governments may be less likely to redistribute property rights in inside information from the corporate elite (managers and dominant shareholders) and their associates to outside investors than right-leaning or centrist governments. In fact, keeping corporate information inside the firm may be an explicit outcome of the state's political bargain with corporate insiders in a left-leaning, pro-labor regime.[71]

The foregoing considerations yield this study's final predictions:

Hypothesis 3a   A country with a more democratic political system is more likely to enact and enforce insider trading legislation than a country with a less democratic political system with the same level of stock market development.

Hypothesis 3b   A country with a left-leaning government is more likely to enact and enforce insider trading legislation than a country with a right-leaning government and the same level of stock market development.

---

[68]   Roe, Legal Origins, supra note 58, at 464.

[69]   Roe notes that "[i]n social democracies – nations . . . whose governments play a large role in the economy, emphasize distributional considerations, and favor employees over capital-owners when the two conflict – public policy emphasizes managers' natural agenda and demeans shareholders' natural agenda." Roe, Political Preconditions, supra note 63, at 3–4. Professor Roe maintains that social democracies "do not want unbridled shareholder wealth maximization, and, hence [emasculate] shareholder wealth maximization institutions." Id. at 4. Professor Coffee disagrees, arguing that a more "feasible political explanation is . . . that power seeking nationalists could use banks as their agents and that banks, once entrenched, had natural reason to resist the rise of rivals for their business." Coffee, supra note 53, at 53. Professors Rafael La Porta et al., The Quality of Government, 15 J. L., Econ. & Org. 222 (1999) [hereinafter La Porta, Quality of Government], also emphasize the role of state intervention in markets, arguing that for historical and cultural reasons Europeans support greater state intervention than Americans.

[70]   Roe supports this claim with empirical evidence that shows an inverse correlation between labor power and investor protections and ownership diffusion, a common measure of stock market development. Roe, Legal Origins, supra note 58, at 497. But see Paul Mahoney, The Origins of the Blue-Sky Laws: A Test of Competing Hypotheses, 46 J. L. & Econ. 229 (2003) (finding that the progressive lobby strongly influenced the adoption of securities regulation by forty-seven of the forty-eight U.S. states between 1911 and 1931).

[71]   In the corporatist model of sectoral conflict, corporate insiders and workers may align to ensure that both are entrenched. See, e.g., Gourevitch & Shinn, supra note 44, at 64–65. ("[S]olidarities are often based on sectors, on 'bosses and workers' within a particular business sector who share interests, along with the inside blockholders who join them.") See also Marco Pagano & Paolo Volpin, The Political Economy of Corporate Governance, 95 Am. Econ. Rev. 1005 (2005) ("show[ing] that entrepreneurs and workers can strike a political agreement by which low investor protection is exchanged for high employment protection").

Table 15.1   Summary of hypotheses

Hypothesis	Summary
Hypothesis 1	A country with a more developed stock market is more likely to enact and enforce insider trading legislation than a country with a less developed stock market.
Hypothesis 2	A common law country is more apt to enact and enforce insider trading legislation than a civil law country with the same level of stock market development.
Hypothesis 3a	A country with a more democratic political system is more likely to enact and enforce insider trading legislation than a country with a less democratic political system with the same level of stock market development.
Hypothesis 3b	A country with a left-leaning government is more likely to enact and enforce insider trading legislation than a country with a right-leaning government and the same level of stock market development.

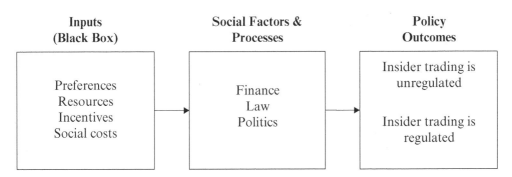

Figure 15.1   Illustration of possible causal mechanisms

Table 15.1 summarizes the hypotheses, while Figure 15.1 presents a stylized illustration of possible causal mechanisms.

IV.   METHODOLOGY: DURATION ANALYSIS

The regression analysis covers countries that had not enacted or enforced insider trading legislation as of 1980. I first examine the enactment of insider trading legislation. The null hypothesis is that in any given year between 1980 and 1999, all countries that had not yet enacted insider trading laws were equally likely to enact them and only chance determined whether a country would move from the group of countries with no insider trading laws to the group that had enacted such laws. The alternative hypothesis is that this process was not random, but that because of country-specific conditions some countries had a greater probability of enacting insider trading legislation than others in any particular year between 1980 and 1999. More specifically, I have postulated that finance, law, and politics affect the likelihood that a country will move from "have not" to "have" status with respect to insider trading legislation. Thus, I test both the proposition that the time to adopting insider trading legislation, given that a country had no such legislation in 1980, was non-random and that the time to adoption can be explained by the factors identified in my hypotheses.

There are compelling reasons to think that enforcement rather than enactment is the real turning point for a country's stock market. Enforcement, because it requires an expenditure of scarce resources, demonstrates political and legal will to give the insider trading prohibition teeth.[72] In contrast, the enactment of insider trading legislation may be relatively costless. Thus, I also examine the timing of enforcement. I take two approaches. First, I examine the probability that a country enforced insider trading legislation between 1980 and 1999. Under this approach, the question is: what determined how soon after 1980 a country initially enforced insider trading legislation? Framed this way, the question implicitly assumes that the meaningful switch from "have not" to "have" status occurs not when a country enacts insider trading legislation but when it enforces such legislation for the first time. Secondly, I examine the probability that a country enforced insider trading legislation between the year of enactment and 1999. The question here is: what determined how long it took a country to put its insider trading legislation to work? In both cases, as for enactment, I simultaneously test whether the time to enforcing insider trading legislation was non-random and whether it can be explained by the factors identified in my hypotheses.

The methodology is duration, or survival analysis.[73] This technique seeks to identify for each point in time the probability that a nation will move to the group of "have" countries rather than "survive" as a member of the "have not" group of countries. In duration or survival analysis the hazard rate, $h(t)$, is the probability or "risk" that an event occurs at a particular time, t, given that it has not already occurred. As explained above, I am interested in three hazard rates: (1) the probability or "risk" that a country had passed insider trading legislation in year t, given that it had not yet passed such legislation as of 1980; (2) the probability or "risk" that a country had enforced its insider trading legislation for the first time in year t, given that it had not yet enforced such legislation as of 1980; and (3) the probability or "risk" that a country had enforced its insider trading legislation for the first time in year t, given that it had not yet enforced such legislation since enacting it.

I test whether the three hazard rates are influenced by the hypothesized factors, i.e., whether the probability or "risk" of the event in question (enactment or enforcement) varies with country-level financial, legal, and political factors. I use a Weibull proportional hazards regression, which has the following form:

$$h[t,x(t),b] = h_o(t)\exp[x(t)'b] \tag{15.1}$$

where $h(t)$ is the hazard rate at time t, b is a vector of maximum-likelihood regression coefficients to be estimated by the model, x is a vector of independent or explanatory

---

[72]   See, e.g., Howell E. Jackson & Mark J. Roe, Public and Private Enforcement of Securities Laws: Resource-Based Evidence, 93 J. Fin. Econ. 207 (2009).

[73]   For a more thorough explanation of analytical methods for survival time data see William Greene, Econometric Analysis (1997); J. Kalbfleisch & R. Prentice, The Statistical Analysis of Failure Time Data (1980); Nicholas Kiefer, Economic Duration Data and Hazard Functions, 26 J. Econ. Lit. 646 (1988).

variables, and $h_0(t)$ is the baseline hazard rate. The baseline hazard rate, $h_0(t)$, equals pt^{p-1}, where p is a parameter estimated from the data.[74] The model assumes that the hazard rates are independent across countries, but not within countries over time. The model is also dynamic in that it follows each country over time and therefore permits the social context (e.g., financial development and politics) to vary over time.

The Weibull regression is convenient because it lends itself to intuitive interpretation. In particular, a transformation of equation (15.1) yields the following relationship:

$$\ln(T) = x'b + e \qquad (15.2)$$

Equation (15.2) means that the log of the expected time (denoted as T) to the event of interest is a linear function of the explanatory variables and an error term. In the regressions, therefore, T is the expected time in years from the base year until a country's enactment or initial enforcement of insider trading legislation. The regression coefficients, b, signify the percentage change in the expected time to enact or initially enforce insider trading legislation for a one-unit change in the corresponding explanatory variable. Thus, a positive b implies that an increase in the explanatory variable increases the expected time to or "risk of" the enactment or initial enforcement of insider trading legislation. Conversely, a negative b means that an increase in the explanatory variable decreases the expected time to or "risk of" the enactment or initial enforcement of insider trading legislation.[75]

V. DATA AND RESULTS

A. Data Description

This section describes three sets of variables: the dependent variables, the explanatory variables, and the control variables.

1. Dependent variables
In the late 1990s, Professors Bhattacharya and Daouk sent a survey to the national regulator and main stock exchange in each country with a stock market.[76] Their survey posed two simple questions: (1) when did the country enact insider trading legislation; and (2) when did the country enforce such legislation for the first time? I use the information they gathered from their survey to determine the timing of a country's enactment and enforcement of insider trading legislation.

---

[74] See Kiefer, supra note 73.

[75] For example, if the regression yields a negative coefficient on civil law origin when I estimate equation (15.2) for the time to enacting insider trading legislation, the appropriate interpretation would be that on average civil law countries are at a greater "risk" of enacting such laws, or enact earlier, than common law countries. Conversely, if the regression yields a positive coefficient on civil law origin, the appropriate interpretation would be that on average civil law countries are at a lesser "risk" of enforcing insider trading laws, or enforce later.

[76] Bhattacharya & Daouk, supra note 3.

2. Explanatory variables

I use three measures of stock market development. First, stock market capitalization relative to GDP (in constant 2000 US$) gauges the economic significance of the stock market. Secondly, stock market turnover is the ratio of the value traded relative to the value of the stock market. Finally, the value of shares traded relative to GDP (in constant 2000 US$) gauges the significance of stock trading to the overall economy. The last two variables are liquidity measures. Annual values of these data are available at the World Bank's World Development Indicators (WDI) database online.[77]

To classify a country's legal system as a common law or civil law system, I rely on two sources. The first source is the work of Professors La Porta et al.[78] They grouped countries into four legal categories: English common law, French civil law, German civil law, and Scandinavian civil law. I code French, German, and Scandinavian civil law countries as belonging to the civil law family. The variable *Civil* equals 1 for the latter countries and 0 for English common law countries. For the countries that La Porta et al. did not report on, I fill in the gaps with the U.S. Central Intelligence Agency's (CIA's) classifications of national legal systems that are available in its publication, the World Factbook.[79]

For openness/competitiveness of the political process, I use three variables. The first variable is the "fractionalization" of the legislature and comes from the Database of Political Institutions assembled by Beck et al.[80] This variable measures the probability that two officers randomly chosen from the legislature are from different political parties and ranges from 0 to 100 percent. A higher value suggests a more competitive legislature, i.e., that more political actors are "willing to act independently in the consideration of any given policy change."[81] Conversely, a lower value suggests a less competitive legislature.[82] The second variable, also from the Database of Political Institutions, is a measure of political checks and balances. It is the average of four alternative measures of political checks and balances and ranges between 1 and 10.[83] A higher value corresponds to more political checks and balances and a lower value corresponds to fewer political checks and balances. The third variable, from the Polity IV Database,[84] measures the general openness of political institutions. It ranges between 0 and 10, with 10 indicating the greatest degree of openness and 0 the least.

---

[77]   World Bank World Development Indicators, http://data.worldbank.org/data-catalog/world-development-indicators (last visited Dec. 11, 2012).

[78]   La Porta et al., Law and Finance, supra note 57; La Porta et al., Legal Determinants, supra note 57.

[79]   CIA World Factbook, https://www.cia.gov/library/publications/the-world-factbook/index.html (last visited Dec. 11, 2012).

[80]   Thorsten Beck et al., New Tools and New Tests in Comparative Political Economy: The Database of Political Institutions, World Bank Policy Research Working Paper 2283 (2000).

[81]   Id. at 19.

[82]   Id.

[83]   These measures, created by Beck et al., take into consideration both the number of pivotal decision makers (i.e., those "whose agreement is necessary before policies can be changed") and "the effectiveness of electoral checks on government decision makers." Id. at 22, 26. The measures "count the number of veto players in a political system, adjusting for whether these veto players are independent of each other, as determined by the level of electoral competitiveness in a system, their respective party affiliations, and the electoral rules." Id. at 27.

[84]   Center for International Development and Conflict Management, Polity IV Database, http://www.cidcm.umd.edu/polity (last visited Jan. 21, 2008).

Finally, using principal components analysis,[85] I combine the three political process variables into a single variable, called *Democracy*. I use this combined variable to investigate the political Hypothesis 3a.

For political ideology, I again rely on the Database of Political Institutions. The database includes information on the political orientation of the largest party in the government. The dummy variable *Left* equals 1 if the largest party is communist, socialist, social democratic, or left-wing, and 0 otherwise. The dummy variable *Center* equals 1 if the largest party is centrist or its "position can best be described as centrist (e.g., because the party advocates the strengthening of private enterprise but also supports a redistributive role for government, for example in the form of a tightly knit safety net)," and 0 otherwise.[86] Finally, the dummy variable *Right* equals 1 if the largest party is conservative, Christian democratic, or right-wing, and 0 otherwise.

3. Control variables
In addition to the explanatory variables that I use to investigate the hypotheses, I include several variables in the regressions to control for other factors that may influence policy outcomes.

First, I control for GDP per capita because wealthier countries tend to have stronger government institutions, rule of law traditions, and regulatory resources than poorer countries.[87]

Secondly, I control for government quality. Professors La Porta et al. demonstrate that "good" governments protect property rights and promote the rule of law and thus facilitate orderly societies, markets, and economic prosperity.[88] As a proxy for "good" government, I use an index of corruption assembled by Professor Mauro.[89] The index ranges from 0 (most corrupt) to 10 (least corrupt).

Thirdly, I control for religious affiliation. For reasons that are not entirely understood, empirical evidence suggests that Protestant countries have "better" governments than Catholic and Muslim countries.[90] I create dummy variables for *Protestant*, *Catholic*, *Muslim*, and *Other* to describe the dominant religion in each country.[91]

Finally, anything that directs the public's attention to the stock market and increases concern that it is run fairly and efficiently may increase demand for insider trading

---

[85] See I. T. Jolliffe, Principal Component Analysis (2002).

[86] Beck et al., supra note 80, at 15.

[87] See, e.g., Douglass North, Structure and Change in Economic History (1981); La Porta et al., Quality of Government, supra note 69.

[88] La Porta et al., Quality of Government, supra note 69.

[89] Paolo Mauro, Corruption and Growth, 110 Q. J. Econ. 681 (1995). This control is justified by cross-country empirical studies showing that there is a significant negative correlation between corruption and the rule of law and financial openness. See Zvika Neeman, M. Daniele Paserman, & Avi Simhon, Corruption and Openness, B. E. J. Econ. Anal. Pol., 8(1), December 2008.

[90] La Porta et al., Quality of Government, supra note 69, show that religion is a satisfactory instrument for the quality of institutions and government.

[91] The dummy variable *Protestant* equals 1 if the dominant religion is Protestant, and 0 otherwise. The dummy variable *Catholic* equals 1 if the dominant religion is Catholic, and 0 otherwise. The dummy variable *Muslim* equals 1 if the dominant religion is Muslim, and 0 otherwise. The dummy variable *Other* equals 1 if the dominant religion consists of religions besides Protestant, Catholic, and Muslims, and 0 otherwise.

legislation. One such factor may be rapid growth in the economic significance of the stock market and the resulting growth of the investing class. Rapid decline in the stock market may have a similar effect. As they experience a decline in their financial wealth, investors may demand greater legal protection, especially if they attribute the decline to corporate fraud.[92] In short, other things constant, investor demand for insider trading legislation and enforcement may increase on the heels of dramatic growth or decline of the stock market. I control for this possibility using the five-year rate of growth in stock market capitalization relative to GDP. I use the five-year growth rate because any policy response is likely to follow with a time lag.

The data and their sources are described in Table 15.2.

B.   Descriptive Statistics

Table 15.3 presents the comparative experiences of stock markets until 1999. For each of the one hundred and three countries reported, Table 15.3 presents the year in which the country's main stock exchange was established, the year (if any) in which the country's insider trading legislation was enacted, and the year (if any) in which such legislation was initially enforced.

Table 15.3 illustrates the wide range of experiences across countries. For example, the oldest stock exchange was established in Germany in 1585. The youngest stock exchange was established in Kazakhstan in 1997. The earliest insider trading legislation was passed in 1934 in the United States. Some countries, like Bulgaria, Swaziland, and Kuwait, had not yet regulated insider trading as of 1999. The United States was also the first country to enforce its insider trading laws while it took some countries three decades longer to enforce (and sometimes to enact) insider trading legislation. For example, Spain and Oman did not enforce their insider trading laws until 1998 and 1999, respectively. The non-enforcing group as of 1999 included both developed markets such as Austria, Ireland, Luxembourg, and New Zealand and emerging markets such as Mexico and Russia. Note that the average years of enactment and initial enforcement of insider trading legislation are roughly similar between developed and emerging stock markets. This means that emerging stock markets tend to enact and enforce insider trading laws when their stock markets are relatively younger, and suggests that it is not a history of experience with stock trading per se that leads to insider trading legislation.

While Table 15.3 presents data for all countries with a stock market as of 1999, the descriptive statistics are calculated using fewer countries. To start with, they exclude the nine countries that enacted insider trading legislation before 1980[93] and Yugoslavia,

---

[92]   See generally, Mark Roe, Backlash, 98 Colum. L. Rev. 217 (1998); Stuart Banner, Anglo-American Securities Regulation: Cultural and Political Roots, 1690–1860 (2002).

[93]   Brazil, Canada, France, Mexico, Nigeria, Singapore, South Korea, Sweden, and the United States enacted insider trading legislation before 1980. The United Kingdom is excluded from the duration analysis below because it enacted insider trading legislation in 1980, the first year of the empirical analysis, though it is included in calculation of the descriptive statistics presented in this section. Countries are also dropped from the enactment duration regression for all the years after the year in which they enacted insider trading legislation and from the enforcement regression for all the years after they enforced insider trading legislation.

Table 15.2   Description of variables and sources

Variable	Description and source
Year main stock exchange was established	The year in which the country's main stock exchange was established. Bhattacharya & Daouk, supra note 3, at 80–84.
Year insider trading law was enacted	The year in which the country passed insider trading legislation. Bhattacharya & Daouk, supra note 3, at 80–84.
Year insider trading law was initially enforced	The year in which the country initially enforced its insider trading legislation. Bhattacharya & Daouk, supra note 3, at 80–84.
Gross Domestic Product (GDP) per capita	Annual per capita GDP in constant US$ (2000) for the years 1980–1997. World Bank World Development Indicators, supra note 77; United Nations Statistics, http://unstats.un.org /unsd/default. htm.
Stock market capitalization relative to GDP	Annual stock market capitalization (number of outstanding shares multiplied by their market value) divided by GDP in constant US$ (2000) for the years 1980–1999. World Bank World Development Indicators, supra note 77.
Total value of stocks traded relative to GDP	Annual total value traded divided by stock market capitalization in constant US$ (2000) for the years 1980–1997. World Bank World Development Indicators, supra note 77.
Stock market turnover	Annual total value of shares traded on the stock exchange divided by GDP for the years 1980–1997. World Bank World Development Indicators, supra note 77.
Legal family	A dummy variable that signifies the country's legal origin. The variable equals 1 if the country has a civil law system and 0 if the country has a common law system. CIA World Factbook, supra note 79; La Porta et al., Law and Finance, supra note 57, at 1130–1131.
Political openness score	This variable measures the general openness of political institutions, measured annually over 1980–1999. The variable ranges between 0 and 10, with 10 signifying the highest degree of political openness and 0 signifying the lowest degree of political openness. The eleven-point scale is constructed additively. Center for International Development and Conflict Management, Polity IV Database, supra note 84.
Fractionalization of the legislature	This variable measures the annual probability that two officers chosen at random from the legislature are members of different parties. The index ranges between 0% and 100% and is assigned a missing value if the country has no parliament. The variable was reported for the years 1980–1995. Beck et al., supra note 80; http://siteresources.worldbank.org/ INTRES/Resources/469232-1107449512766/DPI2010_ stata9.zip.

Table 15.2   (continued)

Variable	Description and source
Average political checks and balances	This variable equals the average value of four measures of political checks and balances, measured annually over 1980–1995. The measures incorporate both the number of decision makers "whose agreement is necessary before policies can be changed" and "the effectiveness of electoral checks on government decision makers." The variable ranges between 1 and 10, with 10 signifying the most checks and balances and 0 signifying the fewest checks and balances. Beck et al., supra note 80; http://siteresources.worldbank.org/INTRES/Resources/469232-1107449512766/DPI2010_stata9.zip.
Democracy index	Composite of preceding three political process variables, calculated using principal components analysis.
Ideology of the largest government party	Dummy variables for the ideology of the largest party in the government. The dummy variable Left equals 1 if the largest party is communist, socialist, social democratic, or left-wing, and 0 otherwise. The dummy variable Center equals 1 if the largest party is centrist or its "position can best be described as centrist (e.g., party advocates strengthening private enterprise in a social-liberal context)," and 0 otherwise. A party is "[n]ot described as centrist if competing parties 'average out' to a centrist position (e.g., party of 'right-wing Muslims and Beijing-oriented Marxists')." The dummy variable Right equals 1 if the largest party is conservative, Christian democratic, or right-wing. Ideology was reported for the years 1980–1995. Beck et al., supra note 80; http://siteresources.worldbank.org/INTRES/Resources/469232-1107449512766/DPI2010_stata9.zip.
Corruption score	"The degree to which business transactions involve corruption or questionable payments." The index ranges between 0 and 10. 0 signifies the highest degree of corruption or side payments in business dealings, while 10 indicates the lowest degree of corruption or side payments in business transactions. The corruption index for a given country is the average value over the years 1980–1983. Mauro, supra note 89, at 708–710.
Religious affiliation	Dummy variables for the dominant religious affiliation of the country's population. The dummy variable Protestant equals 1 if the dominant religion is Protestant, and 0 otherwise. The dummy variable Catholic equals 1 if the dominant religion is Catholic, and 0 otherwise. The dummy variable Muslim equals 1 if the dominant religion is Muslim, and 0 otherwise. The dummy variable Other equals 1 if the dominant religion consists of religions besides Protestant, Catholic, and Muslims, and 0 otherwise. CIA World Factbook, supra note 79; La Porta et al., Quality of Government, supra note 69, at 268–276.

Table 15.3   Comparative experiences

Country	Year of establishment of main stock exchange	Year insider trading law enacted	Year of first enforcement of insider trading law
Developed Stock Markets			
Australia	1859	1991	1996
Austria	1771	1993	None
Belgium	1801	1990	1994
Canada	1878	1966	1976
Denmark	1919	1991	1996
Finland	1912	1989	1993
France	1826	1967	1975
Germany	1585	1994	1995
Hong Kong	1891	1991	1994
Ireland	1793	1990	None
Italy	1806	1991	1996
Japan	1878	1988	1990
Luxembourg	1929	1991	None
Netherlands	1600s	1989	1994
New Zealand	1870	1988	No
Norway	1819	1985	1990
Singapore	1930	1973	1978
Spain	1831	1994	1998
Sweden	1863	1971	1990
Switzerland	1938	1988	1995
United Kingdom	1773	1980	1981
United States	1792	1934	1961
Developed Average	**1828**	**1990**	**1994**
Emerging Stock Markets			
Argentina	1854	1991	1995
Armenia	1993	1993	None
Bahrain	1987	1990	None
Bangladesh	1954	1995	1998
Barbados	1987	1987	None
Bermuda	1971	None	None
Bolivia	1979	None	None
Botswana	1989	None	None
Brazil	1890	1976	1978
Bulgaria	1991	None	None
Chile	1893	1981	1996
China	1990	1993	None
Colombia	1928	1990	None
Costa Rica	1976	1990	None
Croatia	1918	1995	None
Cyprus	1996	1999	None
Czech Republic	1871	1992	1993
Ecuador	1969	1993	None
Egypt	1890	1992	None
El Salvador	1992	None	None

Table 15.3   (continued)

Country	Year of establishment of main stock exchange	Year insider trading law enacted	Year of first enforcement of insider trading law
Emerging Stock Markets			
Estonia	1996	1996	None
Ghana	1989	1993	None
Greece	1876	1988	1996
Guatemala	1986	1996	None
Honduras	1992	1988	None
Hungary	1864	1994	1995
Iceland	1985	1989	None
India	1875	1992	1998
Indonesia	1912	1991	1996
Iran	1966	None	None
Israel	1953	1981	1989
Jamaica	1961	1993	None
Jordan	1978	None	None
Kazakhstan	1997	1996	None
Kenya	1954	1989	None
Kuwait	1984	None	None
Latvia	1993	None	None
Lebanon	1920	1995	None
Lithuania	1926	1996	None
Macedonia	1996	1997	None
Malawi	1996	None	None
Malaysia	1973	1973	1996
Malta	1992	1990	None
Mauritius	1988	1988	None
Mexico	1894	1975	None
Moldova	1994	1995	None
Mongolia	1991	1994	None
Morocco	1929	1993	None
Namibia	1992	None	None
Nigeria	1960	1979	None
Oman	1988	1989	1999
Pakistan	1947	1995	None
Palestine	1995	None	None
Panama	1990	1996	None
Paraguay	1977	1999	None
Peru	1951	1991	1994
Philippines	1927	1982	None
Poland	1817	1991	1993
Portugal	1825	1986	None
Romania	1882	1995	None
Russia	1994	1996	None
Saudi Arabia	1984	1990	None
Slovakia	1991	1992	None
Slovenia	1924	1994	1998

Table 15.3 (continued)

Country	Year of establishment of main stock exchange	Year insider trading law enacted	Year of first enforcement of insider trading law
Emerging Stock Markets			
South Africa	1887	1989	None
South Korea	1956	1976	1988
Sri Lanka	1896	1987	1996
Swaziland	1990	None	None
Taiwan	1961	1988	1989
Tanzania	1998	1994	None
Thailand	1974	1984	1993
Trinidad	1981	1981	None
Tunisia	1969	1994	None
Turkey	1866	1981	1996
Ukraine	1992	None	None
Uruguay	1867	1996	None
Uzbekistan	1994	None	None
Venezuela	1840	1998	None
Yugoslavia	1894	1997	None
Zambia	1994	1993	None
Zimbabwe	1896	None	None
Emerging Average	**1933**	**1991**	**1995**

Note: The data in this table come from Bhattacharya and Daouk, supra note 3, at 80–84.

leaving a total of ninety-three countries. Ideally, this would translate into 1860 country-year observations per variable, i.e., one observation for each of the ninety-three countries in each of the twenty years from 1980 to 1999. However, consistently measured data for all of the countries and years are unavailable, so the results are based on fewer than 1860 country-observations. Countries are also automatically dropped (or censored) from the duration analysis for all the years after the year in which they enacted (or enforced) insider trading legislation. Accordingly, I note the number of observations underlying the duration regressions presented below.

Table 15.4 presents summary statistics of the main variables. Table 15.5 reports average correlations between the year in which insider trading legislation was enacted or first enforced and the explanatory variables, and is thus more interesting from the perspective of the hypotheses. A negative coefficient suggests that an explanatory variable is associated with earlier enactment or enforcement insider trading legislation, and vice versa. The most striking feature of Table 15.5 is the high proportion of statistically significant correlations spanning all variable categories (most are significant at the 1 percent level). The timing of insider trading legislation and enforcement seems to be systematically and statistically significantly related to the explanatory variables rather than a mere coincidence.

The following relationships are statistically significant in Table 15.5. Wealthier countries and countries with more developed stock markets tend to have enacted and enforced insider trading legislation earlier, respectively, than poorer countries and countries with less developed stock markets. Common law countries tend to have passed insider trading

Table 15.4   Summary statistics

Variable	Number of observations	Mean	Std dev.	Min.	Max.
Age of main stock exchange	93 countries	1929	77 years	1586	1998
Year law enacted	93 countries	1991	4.5 years	1980	1999
Year law first enforced	27 countries	1994	2.7 years	1989	1999
Gross Domestic Product (GDP) per capita	1737	$7,563	$9,506	$130	$53,420
Stock market capitalization relative to GDP	1128	0.4	0.5	<.01	5.7
Stock market turnover	1037	0.4	0.5	<.01	5.3
Total value of stocks traded relative to GDP	1120	0.2	0.4	0	6.5
Fractionalization of the legislature	1023	0.5	0.3	0	0.9
Average political checks and balances	1112	2.8	1.4	1	9.5
Political openness score	1167	6.3	4.0	0	10
Corruption score	900	6.9	2.4	1.5	10
Civil law	93 countries	71%			
Left	798	40%			
Center	798	10%			
Right	798	50%			
Protestant	1840	10%			
Catholic	1840	30%			
Muslim	1840	20%			
Other religions	1840	40%			

Note: The maximum number of observations for time-varying variables is 1860 country-year observations. The variables are described in Table 15.2.

legislation earlier than civil law countries, but to have enforced such laws later than civil law countries. Countries with more open political systems and countries with non-left-leaning governments generally passed and/or enforced insider trading laws earlier, respectively, than countries with less open political systems and countries with left-leaning governments, consistent with Roe's political theory of finance.[94] Less corrupt countries tend to have enacted and enforced such laws sooner than more corrupt countries. Finally, predominantly Protestant countries tend to have enforced (not enacted) insider trading laws sooner than predominantly Catholic and Muslim countries.[95] Aside from the finding that civil law countries on average enforced insider trading legislation earlier than common law countries, the results in Table 15.5 are largely consistent with the hypotheses presented in Section III.

---

[94]   Roe, Legal Origins, supra note 58.
[95]   Table 15.5 also suggests that countries that enact insider trading legislation earlier tend to enforce them earlier as well. This is not surprising because laws cannot be enforced until they have been enacted, so a positive correlation would be expected even if the time from enactment to the first enforcement were a random process.

Table 15.5   Correlations

Variable	Year law enacted	Year enforced
Year law enacted	1.00	
Year law first enforced	0.536[a]	1.00
	(0.000)	
Gross Domestic Product (GDP) per capita	−0.275[a]	−0.386[a]
	(0.000)	(0.000)
Stock market capitalization relative to GDP	−0.133[a]	−0.175[a]
	(0.000)	(0.000)
Total value of stocks traded relative to GDP	−0.092[a]	−0.284[a]
	(0.003)	(0.000)
Stock market turnover	−0.072[b]	−0.317[a]
	(0.026)	(0.000)
Civil law	0.188[a]	−0.161[a]
	(0.000)	(0.000)
Composite democracy index	−0.189[a]	−0.046
	(0.000)	(0.377)
Left	0.142[a]	0.145[a]
	(0.000)	(0.005)
Center	−0.051	0.108[b]
	(0.163)	(0.038)
Right	−0.113[a]	−0.194[a]
	(0.002)	(0.000)
Corruption score	−0.174[a]	−0.268[a]
	(0.000)	(0.000)
Protestant	−0.024	−0.164[a]
	(0.341)	(0.000)
Catholic	0.033	0.221[a]
	(0.120)	(0.000)
Muslim	0.039	0.415[a]
	(0.127)	(0.000)
Other religions	−0.045[c]	−0.330[a]
	(0.078)	(0.000)

Note: The variables are described in Table 15.2. The numbers in parentheses are the probability levels (p-values) at which the null hypothesis of zero correlation can be rejected in two-tailed tests. The superscripts a, b, c denote statistical significance at the 1%, 5%, and 10% levels, respectively.

C.   Results of Duration Analysis

1.   Enactment of insider trading legislation

The measured duration (i.e., the time at "risk" of enacting legislation) for each country is the period between 1980 and the year in which the country enacted insider trading legislation. If a country had not enacted insider trading legislation between 1980 and 1999, it is considered to have been at "risk" for enactment during the entire period.

The results are presented in Table 15.6. The first four columns (1–4) show the individual factors – finance, law, and politics – that correspond, respectively, to Hypotheses 1, 2

Table 15.6   *Weibull regressions of expected time to enactment of insider trading legislation*

Explanatory variable	H1 Finance (1)	H2 Law (2)	H3a Democ. (3)	H3b Ideology (4)	All (5)
GDP per capita					6.20×10^{-6}
					(0.00)
Market capitalization/GDP	0.02				−0.21
	(0.14)				(0.24)
Civil law		0.14			0.10
		(0.11)			(0.31)
Democracy (combined variable)			−0.13^c		−0.36^b
			(0.64)		(0.18)
Center-dominated government				0.15	0.16
				(0.24)	(0.30)
Right-dominated government				−0.05	−0.09
				(0.13)	(0.17)
Corruption index					0.09
					(0.08)
Catholic					−0.09
					(.022)
Muslim					0.38
					(0.35)
Other religion					−0.51^b
					(0.24)
Five-year growth of market capitalization/GDP					0.01
					(0.03)
Number of countries	72	92	63	56	23
Number of observations	538	1160	556	458	172
Likelihood ratio	0.02	1.65	3.95	0.77	11.49
P-value of chi^2	0.89	0.20	0.05	0.68	0.40

Note: The regression is a Weibull hazard model, $\ln(T) = x'b + e$ where the dependent variable ln(T) is the log of the expected time to enactment of insider trading legislation between 1980 and 1999. Each explanatory variable, described in Table 15.2, is measured in each year during the period that a country is at "risk," except the years for which the variable is missing. For Hypothesis 2, the omitted dummy variable is common law. Thus, the coefficient on the civil law dummy variable measures the effect of having a civil law system on the probability of enacting insider trading legislation relative to the effect of having a common law system. For Hypothesis 3, the omitted dummy variable is left government. Thus, the coefficients on the right and center dummy variables measure the effect of having a right or center government on the probability of enacting insider trading legislation relative to the effect of having a left government. The regression constant is not reported. The superscripts b and c, respectively, denote the 5% and 10% significance levels.

and 3. Column 5 shows the full model with the control variables. Contrary to Hypothesis 1, in column 1 the coefficient on stock market capitalization relative to GDP is positive, suggesting that more developed stock markets took longer to enact insider trading legislation. However, the coefficient is insignificant. Column 2 reports that the coefficient on civil law legal origin is positive. This suggests that, as Hypothesis 2 predicts, civil law countries were less apt than common law countries to enact insider trading legislation between 1980 and 1999. Again, however, the coefficient is insignificant. In column 3, the coefficient on the democracy index is negative and significant at the 10 percent level. Consistent with Hypothesis 3a, this means that stronger democracies were more likely to enact insider trading during the period than weaker democracies. In column 4, the ideology variables are insignificant, although the coefficient on the right government dummy variable is negative, consistent with Hypothesis 3b. In the full model, reported in column 5, the coefficient on the democracy index remains negative and is significant at the 5 percent level, although several observations are lost.

In summary, the results in Table 15.6 suggest that political openness was the dominant factor in countries' adoption of insider trading legislation between 1980 and 1999. This finding is consistent with the notion that outsiders have a comparative advantage over corporate insiders in strong democracies with open political institutions. Numerically, the regression in column 5 suggests that if a country had experienced a one-unit increase in its composite democracy index it would have experienced a 36 percent decrease in its expected time to enact insider trading legislation between 1980 and 1999, other things constant.

2. Enforcement of insider trading legislation

As explained above, I measure the duration until initial enforcement of insider trading legislation in two ways. Under the first approach, the duration (i.e., the time at "risk") for each country is the time between 1980 and the year in which the country first enforced its insider trading legislation. If a country had not enforced insider trading legislation between 1980 and 1999, it is considered to have been at "risk" for enforcement during the entire period.

Table 15.7 presents the results for the first approach in Panel A. In column 1, the coefficient on stock market capitalization is negative and significant at the 5 percent level. This result is consistent with Hypothesis 1 and suggests that countries with more significant stock markets were more likely to enforce insider trading legislation between 1980 and 1999 than countries with less significant stock markets. As for legal family, in column 2, the coefficient on civil law origin is negative, which is inconsistent with the legal family theory because it implies that civil law countries were more prone to enforce insider trading legislation than common law countries between 1980 and 1999. However, the coefficient on civil law is insignificant in column 2. Consistent with Hypothesis 3a, column 3 suggests that stronger democracies were more likely to enforce insider trading laws during the period than weaker democracies. The coefficient on the democracy index is negative and significant at the 1 percent level. Column 4 shows that right-leaning governments were more prone to enforce insider trading laws between 1980 and 1999 than left-leaning governments, consistent with Hypothesis 3b, but this result is only marginally significant (p-value = 11 percent).

The full model is shown in column 5. There, the coefficient on the democracy index remains negative and is significant at the 5 percent level. More specifically, the regression in column 5 suggests that a country that had increased its democracy score by one point would have experienced a 17 percent reduction of its expected time to enforce insider trading legislation during the period, other things constant. In addition, the coefficient on the right government dummy variable remains negative and becomes significant at the 1 percent level. This result implies that, other things constant, a country whose government

Table 15.7　*Weibull regressions of expected time to enforcement of insider trading legislation*

(Panel A)

Explanatory variable	H1 Finance (1)	H2 Law (2)	H3a Democ. (3)	H3b Ideology (4)	All (5)
GDP per capita					6.20×10^{-6} c
					(5.38×10^{-6})
Market capitalization/GDP	-0.16b				-0.11
	(0.08)				(0.09)
Civil law		-0.06			-0.25b
		(0.11)			(0.12)
Democracy (combined variable)			-0.21a		-0.17b
			(0.08)		(0.08)
Center-dominated government				0.00	-0.20
				(0.26)	(0.14)
Right-dominated government				-0.23†	-0.22a
				(0.14)	(0.08)
Corruption index					0.00
					(0.02)
Catholic					0.02
					(0.09)
Muslim					1.83
					(577.74)
Other religion					-0.28b
					(0.12)
Five-year growth of market capitalization/GDP					-0.01
					(0.00)
Number of countries	91	93	70	61	29
Number of observations	981	1647	817	703	307
Likelihood ratio	3.21	0.29	10.97	3.88	28.74
P-value of chi²	0.07	0.59	0.00	0.14	0.00

Notes:
† p-value = 11%
The regression is a Weibull hazard model, $\ln(T) = x'b + e$ where the dependent variable $\ln(T)$ is the log of the expected time to initial enforcement of insider trading legislation between 1980 and 1999. Each explanatory variable, described in Table 15.2, is measured in each year during the period that a country is at "risk," except the years for which the variable is missing. For Hypothesis 2, the omitted dummy variable is common law. Thus, the coefficient on the civil law dummy variable measures the effect of having a civil law system on the probability of initially enforcing insider trading legislation relative to the effect of having a common law system. For Hypothesis 3, the omitted dummy variable is left government. Thus, the coefficients on the right and center dummy variables measure the effect of having a right or center government on the probability of initially enforcing insider trading legislation relative to the effect of having a left government. The regression constant is not reported. The superscripts a, b, and c, respectively, denote the 1%, 5%, and 10% significance levels.

(Panel B)

Explanatory variable	H1 Finance (1)	H2 Law (2)	H3a Democ. (3)	H3b Ideology (4)	All (5)
GDP per capita					−0.00[a]
					(0.00)
Market capitalization/GDP	−0.43				−0.07
	(0.29)				(0.31)
Civil law		−0.53			−0.54
		(0.34)			(0.41)
Democracy (combined variable)			−0.53[b]		−0.19
			(0.23)		(0.21)
Center-dominated government				0.01	−0.33
				(0.86)	(0.47)
Right-dominated government				−0.65	−0.54[b]
				(0.46)	(0.28)
Corruption index					0.05
					(0.07)
Catholic					−0.03
					(0.38)
Muslim					6.30
					(1317)
Other religion					−0.37
					(0.43)
Five-year growth of market capitalization/GDP					−0.02 (0.04)
Number of countries	74	75	56	51	28
Number of observations	443	487	261	245	135
Likelihood ratio	2.22	2.62	7.23	2.88	24.92
P-value of chi^2	0.14	0.11	0.01	0.24	0.01

had moved from left to right would have experienced a 22 percent decrease in its expected time to enforce insider trading legislation between 1980 and 1999. These results support the political theory of finance.[96] Counterintuitively to the legal origins perspective, the regression in column 5 suggests that civil law countries had a 25 percent lower expected time to enforce insider trading legislation than common law countries during the period, other things constant. Also, while financial development is independently significant in column 1, it is not significant in the full model. Finally, column 5 shows that wealthy countries, as measured by per capita GDP, were slightly more likely than poor countries to enforce insider trading legislation between 1980 and 1999. This result is not surprising,

---

[96] See, e.g., Roe, Legal Origins, supra note 58.

because enforcement involves a significant expenditure of resources.[97] However, the coefficient is relatively small.

Under the second approach, the duration (i.e., the time at "risk") for each country is the time between the year in which the country enacted insider trading legislation and the year in which the country first enforced such legislation. If a country had enacted but not enforced insider trading legislation between 1980 and 1999 it is considered to have been at "risk" for enforcement over the entire period between the year when the country enacted the law and 1999.

The results are reported in Panel B of Table 15.7. In column 1, the coefficient on stock market capitalization is negative, as expected, but it is only marginally significant. Column 2 shows that legal origin is insignificant. In column 3, the coefficient on the democracy index is negative and significant at the 5 percent level. Consistent with Hypothesis 3a, this result suggests that strong democracies tended to enforce their insider trading laws sooner after enacting such laws than weak democracies. In column 4, although the coefficient on the right government variable is negative as predicted, the coefficients on both ideology variables are insignificant.

Finally, column 5 reports the full model for the second measure of enforcement. The coefficient on the democracy index remains negative but becomes insignificant, while the coefficient on right ideology remains negative and becomes significant at the 5 percent level. Thus, the results in column 5 confirm the finding in Panel A that right-leaning governments tended to be more inclined to enforce insider trading legislation than left-leaning governments between 1980 and 1999. The coefficient on civil law origin is negative and insignificant.

In summary, the enforcement regressions reinforce the preeminence of political explanations over financial and legal explanations of a country's insider trading regime.

D.   Robustness Checks

I check the robustness of the results in several ways. First, I run the enactment regressions without the European Community (EC) members. These countries were required, pursuant to the EC Insider Trading Directive of 1989, to enact minimum insider trading legislation by June 1, 1992.[98] Thus, a potential criticism of the enactment regressions is that they include European countries with strong democracies that did not necessarily choose to but were required to enact insider trading legislation. However, when I exclude the EC countries, the political explanations of enactment (i.e., democracy and ideology) become even more influential.[99] Secondly, I run the same regressions using the liquidity measures of stock development (stock market turnover and value traded relative to GDP) in place of stock market capitalization relative to GDP. This also does not change the

---

[97]   See generally Jackson & Roe, supra note 72.

[98]   89/592/EEC of November 13, 1989. See generally, European Insider Dealing, supra note 9; Amy E. Stutz, A New Look at the European Economic Community Directive on Insider Trading, 23 Vand. J. Trasnat'l L. 135 (1990).

[99]   When I exclude the EC members, the coefficient on the democracy index is −1.13 and significant at 1 percent and the coefficient on right government is −0.79 and significant at 1 percent. Compare these results with the corresponding results in column 5 of Table 15.6.

core results. Thirdly, in case a different dynamic affected relatively young stock markets during the period in question, I run the same regressions excluding countries whose stock markets were established after 1975. I repeat this for countries whose stock markets were established after 1980 and 1990, as well. These modifications do not change the main results either. Finally, I run country random effects logit regressions for each of the duration measures on all of the explanatory and control variables. The results are similar to those of the Weibull regressions.

VI. CONCLUSION

This study first sketched a political economy model of insider trading regulation that encompasses both private and public interest theories of regulation. Because the underlying dynamics of this model are unobservable across countries, I then shifted the analysis to a higher degree of generality to facilitate empirically testable hypotheses about the comparative timing of enactment and enforcement of insider trading regulation across countries.

The results are consistent with Roe's labor-versus-capital political theory of finance and suggest that politics is the first-order determinant of comparative insider trading policies. In particular, political openness and ideology most aptly explain the comparative timing of insider trading regulation and enforcement across countries. The results show that more democratic political systems enacted and enforced insider trading laws earlier than less democratic or authoritarian political systems, controlling for wealth, financial development, legal origin, etc. The results also show that left-leaning governments were relative latecomers to insider trading legislation and enforcement relative to right-leaning and centrist governments, controlling for the same factors as above. In contrast to the political theory of finance, the legal family theory of finance does not explain the differential timing of insider trading regulation and enforcement across countries.[100] In fact, the results suggest that civil law countries may sometimes be more inclined than common law countries to enforce insider trading regulations, contrary to the legal family theory of finance.

This study's findings have important implications for the longstanding debate about insider trading regulation. While the private interest theory of insider trading regulation posits that insider trading regulation is inefficient, this view is increasingly challenged by the accumulating international evidence on the beneficial effects of insider trading regulation. The latter evidence suggests that stock markets become more informationally efficient and liquid and the cost of capital falls after insider trading laws have been enacted and/or enforced. The evidence presented in this chapter strengthens that challenge because it suggests that the kinds of governments that are more prone to regulate insider trading

---

[100] For existing critiques of the legal origins approach, see, e.g., Gourevitch & Shinn, supra note 44, at 85–87; Katharina Pistor et al., Law and Finance in Transition Economies, 8 Econ. Transition 325 (2000); Roe, Legal Origins, supra note 58, at 470–482; Sonja Fagernäs, Prabirjit Sarkar & Ajit Singh, Legal Origin, Shareholder Protection and the Stock Market: New Challenges from Time Series Analysis, Centre for Business Research, University of Cambridge Working Paper No. 343 (2007).

are precisely the governments that are generally believed to pursue market-promoting, not market-inhibiting, policies.[101] Market-oriented democracies are more likely to have a polity willing and able to overcome entrenched insider opposition to capital market development than authoritarian states.

The foregoing result, however, does not prove that right- and center-leaning democracies adopt more efficient insider trading laws than left-leaning autocracies. This study does not address cross-country variation in the substantive content of these laws, but merely examines the determinants of the relative timing of a country's switch from "have not" to "have" status regarding the existence and enforcement of insider trading laws. A more complete picture would emerge if it were possible to estimate the relationship between financial development, legal origin, and politics, respectively, and the stringency of the substantive rules over time. Such an analysis could reveal a more complex (i.e., non-linear) relationship between the explanatory variables and insider trading policy. It may reveal, for example, that the stringency of a country's insider trading law increases in its level of democracy. If overly restrictive insider trading laws are inefficient, such a finding would suggest that stronger democracies tend to adopt inefficient insider trading policies. Alternatively, it may reveal that stronger democracies adopt moderately stringent laws rather than excessively restrictive laws or no laws at all.[102]

In short, there is a genuine question of whether securities regulation takes the form of a Laffer curve, where both too little and too much regulation are undesirable. Future research on this question would be of great interest and import.

---

[101]   See generally Donald Whittman, Why Democracies Produce Efficient Results, 97 J. Pol. Econ. 1395 (1989); Kevin Grier & Michael Munger, On Democracy, Regime Duration, and Economic Growth (unpublished manuscript, on file with author) (2006); Djankov et al., supra note 38; Acemoglu, supra note 66.

[102]   Richard Epstein suggests that "the light touch version [i.e., moderate insider trading laws] is in line with voluntary arrangements and thus imposes relatively little costs on firms and gives them this advantage. The firm decision [to privately prohibit insider trading] is bonded and backed by the government. It is like the food companies that love federal inspection within limits because it strengthens their claim for selling good food. But once the laws become too strong, then they no longer replicate what the firms want and become a drag." Conversation between the author and Professor Epstein. For one example of "light touch" regulation, see Adam C. Pritchard, Self-Regulation and Securities Markets, Reg. 32 (2003).

PART 4

GLOBAL PERSPECTIVES

Section A

Asia

16. The regulation of insider trading in China: law and enforcement

Hui Huang

I. INTRODUCTION

What explains the differing pace of financial development and economic growth across nations? Beginning in the late 1990s, four financial economists – Professor Rafael La Porta, Florencio Lopez-de-Silanes, Andrei Shleifer and Robert Vishny (known collectively as 'LLSV') – offered the so-called 'legal origins' theory, arguing in a series of studies that the legal regime for effective investor protection is a prime factor in shaping financial development.[1] This line of research has generated much controversy. One of the main criticisms levelled at it is that it focuses too much on the law on paper with little regard to its enforcement.[2]

The lack of consensus in the debate is mainly attributable to the lack of accurate information and in particular, empirical data. Most of the research surrounding the debate has indeed been drawn from advanced economies, such as the USA and the UK,[3] and, to a lesser extent, from some developing countries such as India where English is a widely used language and there is thus relatively easy access to relevant information.[4] In contrast, much less research has been done on China, despite the fact that it is now the world's second largest economy with the fastest growth rate. This is mainly because of considerable difficulties involved in data collection in relation to the subject matter.

This chapter represents an attempt to contribute to the debate by examining both the rules and enforcement of insider trading regulation in China. This chapter will demonstrate that the Chinese insider trading regulation is essentially transplanted from overseas jurisdictions, particularly the USA, and as a result there are few substantive doctrinal differences that appear to be more than trivial. However, the formal legal rules can be very different from the reality of actual practice, particularly in developing countries such as China. Indeed, research into the efficacy of insider trading regulation shows the key issue not to be whether a country has the formal regime of insider trading regulation, but whether it actually enforces the regulation.[5] In this connection, the chapter will go beyond

---

[1]   See, e.g., Rafael La Porta et al., Legal Determinations of External Finance, 52 J. Fin. 1131 (1997); Rafael La Porta et al., Law and Finance, 106 J. Pol. Econ. 1113 (1998).

[2]   See, e.g., John C. Coffee, Jr., Law and the Market: The Impact of Enforcement, 156 U. Pa. L. Rev. 229 (2007).

[3]   See, e.g., John Armour et al., Private Enforcement of Corporate Law: An Empirical Comparison of the United Kingdom and the United States, 6 J. Empirical Legal Stud. 687 (2009).

[4]   See, e.g., Bernard S. Black & Vikramaditya S. Khanna, Can Corporate Governance Reforms Increase Firm Market Values? Event Study Evidence from India, 4 J. Empirical Legal Stud. 749 (2007).

[5]   See, e.g., Utpal Bhattacharya & Hazem Daouk, The World Price of Insider Trading, 57 J. Fin. 75 (2002).

the formal rules to look at various enforcement mechanisms of insider trading regulation, including public and private enforcement. Methodologically, apart from the traditional tool of case study, it will conduct a comprehensive empirical study of insider trading cases in China from 1991 to 2011, in an effort to show how Chinese insider trading regulation has been enforced in practice.

The chapter proceeds as follows. To set the stage, Section II first provides an overview of insider trading regulation in China, discussing the legal framework and the extent of insider trading. Section III then conducts a detailed analysis of the key elements of insider trading law, including the types of insiders, the scope of inside information and subjective elements, in light of recent cases from a comparative perspective. This is followed by a critique of the theoretical basis of China's insider trading law, which sheds light on the problems with the application of specific rules. Section IV focuses on the issue of enforcement, empirically examining all reported insider trading cases in China over the research period. The final section then briefly concludes.

II.   BACKGROUND

A.   The Regulatory Framework

The current regulatory regime for China's financial markets is sectors-based, with three specialist commissions, namely the China Securities Regulatory Commission (CSRC), the China Banking Regulatory Commission (CBRC) and the China Insurance Regulatory Commission (CIRC), responsible for regulating the securities, banking and insurance sectors, respectively.[6] The CSRC is the national regulatory body with authority over both securities and futures markets, and is therefore charged with the task of fighting insider trading in China.

The history of the regulation of insider trading in China can be traced back as early as 1990 when the stock market was at its very early stage.[7] Drawing upon overseas experiences, particularly the USA, which is the pioneer in the field,[8] China has established a relatively complete regulatory regime regarding insider trading, even though, as shall be discussed later, it is not without problems.[9] The key provisions in Chinese insider trading regulation, that give technical effect to the regulatory goals, are now enshrined in the *Securities Law of the People's Republic of China* ('Securities Law').[10] The Securities Law paid a fair amount of attention to insider trading, devoting as many as five articles on

---

[6]   For more discussion of the institutional structure of financial regulation in China, see Hui Huang, Institutional Structure of Financial Regulation in China: Lessons from the Global Financial Crisis, 10 J. Corp. L. Stud. 219 (2010).

[7]   For a discussion of the historical development of China's insider trading regulatory regime, see Hui Huang, International Securities Markets: Insider Trading Law in China 19–22 (2006).

[8]   Id. at 25.

[9]   See infra Section III.

[10]   Zhonghua Renmin Gongheguo Zhengquanfa (中华人民共和国证券法) [Securities Law of the PRC] (promulgated by the Nat'l People's Cong., 29 December 1998, effective 1 July 1999) [hereinafter Securities Law].

issues such as the definition of insider, the scope of insider information and the types of prohibited activities.[11] On 29 March 2012, the Supreme People's Court and the Supreme People's Procuratorate jointly issued a judicial interpretation to provide guidance on the handling of criminal insider trading cases ('Judicial Interpretation on Insider Trading Law in Criminal Cases').[12] Apart from the key insider trading provisions noted above, there are also other sources of law regulating insider trading indirectly as preventative measures. For instance, Article 142 of the *Company Law of the People's Republic of China* stipulates that traditional insiders such as directors, supervisors and senior management cannot sell the shares they hold in their company within one year from the time of listing and within six months of their resignation from the company.[13] Further, Article 13 of the *Rules on Administrating the Shares Held by Directors, Supervisors and Senior Management in Their Company and Changes to Their Shareholdings* provides for black-out periods during which directors, supervisors and senior management are not allowed to trade shares in their company.[14] Another preventative measure is contained in Article 3 of the *Notice on Regulating the Information Disclosure Issue of Listed Companies and the Behaviour of Relevant Parties Concerned*, requiring that, at the stage of planning major events which may affect the share price of a listed company, parties who may be privy to the planning exercise, such as the directors, supervisors, senior management of the company, parties directly involved in the event and market intermediaries retained for the exercise, have a duty of confidentiality before public disclosure of the event.[15]

Finally, Article 47 of the Securities Law, modelled after Section 16(b) of the US *Securities and Exchange Act of 1934*,[16] prohibits so-called 'short-swing trading'. Specifically, it requires directors, supervisors, senior managers and substantial shareholders of a listed company (a shareholder holding 5 per cent or more of the outstanding shares) to disgorge to the company any short-swing profits, namely profits made from any purchase and sale (or sale and purchase) of the company's equity securities in any six month period.[17]

---

[11]   These Articles will be examined in detail in Section III.

[12]   Zuigao Renmin Fayuan, Zuigao Renmin Jianchayuan Guanyu Banli Neimu Jiaoyi and Xielu Neimu Xinxi Xingshi Anjian Juti Yingyong Falv Ruogan Wenti de Jieshi (最高人民法院、最高人民检察院关于办理内幕交易、泄露内幕信息刑事案件具体应用法律若干问题的解释) [Judicial Interpretation on Several Issues concerning the Application of Insider Trading Law in Criminal Cases] (promulgated on 29 March 2012, effective from 1 June 2012).

[13]   Zhonghua Renmin Gongheguo Gongsifa (中华人民共和国公司法) [Company Law of the PRC] (promulgated by the Nat'l People's Cong., 29 December 1993, effective 1 July 1994) rt. 142 [hereinafter Company Law].

[14]   Shangshi Gongsi Dongshi, Jianshi he Gaoji Guanli Renyuan Suochi Bengongsi Gufen jiqi Biandong Guanli Guize (上市公司董事监事和高级管理人员所持本公司股份及其变动管理规则) [Rules on Administrating the Shares Held by Directors, Supervisors and Senior Management in Their Company and Changes to Their Shareholdings] (promulgated by the China Securities Regulatory Commission, 5 April 2007), Art. 13.

[15]   Guanyu Guifan Shangshi Gongsi Xinxi Pilu ji Xiangguan Gefang Xingwei de Tongzhi (关于规范上市公司信息披露及相关各方行为的通知) [Notice on Regulating the Information Disclosure Issue of Listed Companies and the Behaviour of Relevant Parties Concerned] (promulgated by the China Securities Regulatory Commission, 29 January 2008), Art. 3.

[16]   15 U.S.C. § 78p(b) (1994).

[17]   Securities Law, supra note 10, at Art. 47.

B.   The Extent of Insider Trading

In comparison to most Western countries, China's securities market is very young, with the two national stock exchanges – namely the Shanghai Stock Exchange and the Shenzhen Stock Exchange – being established only in the early 1990s. Even though China's securities market has a short history, it has made remarkable progress so far and played an increasingly important role in China's economic development. By the end of 2010, just two decades after their establishment, the two stock exchanges were home to an aggregate of 2062 listed companies, with a combined market capitalization of CNY 26.54 trillion (roughly USD 4.11 trillion),[18] ranked the world's second largest securities market.[19]

Insider trading appears to be a very serious problem in China. In 2003, this author carried out the first field work of its kind on insider trading in China, using semi-structured and in-depth interviews to obtain empirical data on issues such as the incidence of insider trading in China.[20] Despite some concerns, this methodology has proved to be of particular value in collecting useful first-hand information in the area of insider trading, due to the fact that insider trading is by nature a hidden form of misconduct and thus there are no readily observable data. One can, of course, compile a list of reported cases, but it by no means paints a complete picture of the extent of insider trading, simply because many insider trading activities have gone undetected and the reported cases may just be the tip of the iceberg.

My 2003 study found that insider trading was widespread in China.[21] Nine years on, the insider trading problem is likely to remain the same, and in fact may be more severe than before as a result of the new developments of the markets. For instance, a growth enterprise market (GEM) was established in the second half of 2009; the systems of short sale and margin lending have been implemented on a trial basis from 31 March 2010; and index futures were introduced on 16 April 2010. These market developments pose new challenges for China in its battle against insider trading, because they could increase both the opportunity for and the scope of insider trading. In the face of this, the CSRC, on 16 November 2010, together with several other government agencies such as the Ministry of Public Security, the Ministry of Supervision and the National Bureau of Corruption Prevention, issued a joint circular on the need to strengthen efforts to crack down on insider trading in China.[22] It states that:

---

[18]   See the official website of the China Securities Regulatory Commission at http://www.csrc. gov.cn/pub/zjhpublic/G00306204/zqscyb/201106/t20110602_196073.htm (Statistics of April 2011) (last accessed 8 January 2012).

[19]   Ma Yuan, Market Capitalization of China's Exchanges Rank World's No.2 (4 January 2011), http://english.caing.com/2011-01-04/100213646.html (last accessed 28 November 2012).

[20]   Huang, supra note 7, at 37–46.

[21]   Id. at 40.

[22]   Guanyu Yifa Daji he Fangkong Ziben Shichang Neimu Jiaoyi de Yijian (关于依法打击和防控资本市场内幕交易的意见) [Opinion on Preventing and Combating Insider Trading in the Capital Markets in accordance with the Law] (promulgated by the China Securities Regulatory Commission, the Ministry of Public Security, the Ministry of Supervision, the State-owned Assets Supervision and Administration Commission, and the National Bureau of Corruption Prevention, 16 November 2010) [hereinafter Opinion on Preventing and Combating Insider Trading].

At present, the situation we face in preventing and fighting insider trading in the capital markets is very dire. The identities of insiders are very complicated, the trading methods very elusive, the operating forms very secretive, and the detection work very difficult. With the introduction of index futures, insider trading has become more complicated and more secretive.[23]

III.   WHAT CONSTITUTES INSIDER TRADING IN CHINA?

A.   Who is an Insider?

As discussed above, Chinese insider trading law is heavily influenced by the US experience. In general, China's insider trading law centres upon primary insider trading situations, and extends liability to those who trade on the basis of misappropriated information. Aside from trading, tipping and procuring are also prohibited.[24]

Article 73 of the Securities Law generally prohibits persons with knowledge of inside information on securities trading from using such inside information to trade securities.[25] Other Articles, however, restrict this wide net. Article 74 lists some specific types of persons that are considered to be 'persons with knowledge of inside information'.[26] According to this list, statutory insiders can be categorized into several groups. The first group is corporate directors and officers, including directors, supervisors, managers, deputy managers and other senior management persons of the corporation[27] and its holding corporation.[28] Secondly, apart from the members of senior management, lower-level employees are also deemed insiders if they have obtained inside information in connection with their employment.[29] This category may represent the largest number

---

[23]   Id. at ¶1.
[24]   Securities Law, supra note 10, at Art. 76.
[25]   Securities Law, supra note 10, at Art. 73.
[26]   Under this provision, 'insiders' include:

1.   directors, supervisors, managers, deputy managers and other senior management persons concerned of companies that issue shares or corporate bonds;
2.   shareholders who hold not less than 5 per cent of the shares in a company;
3.   the senior management persons of the holding company of a company that issues shares;
4.   persons who are able to obtain material company information concerning the trading of its securities by virtue of the positions they hold in the company;
5.   staff members of the securities regulatory authority, and other persons who administer securities trading pursuant to their statutory duties;
6.   the relevant staff members of public intermediary organizations who participate in securities trading pursuant to their statutory duties and the relevant staff members of securities registration and clearing institutions and securities trading service organizations; and
7.   other persons specified by the securities regulatory authority under the State Council.

Securities Law, supra note 10, at Art. 74.
[27]   Securities Law, supra note 10, at Art. 74(1).
[28]   Securities Law, supra note 10, at Art. 74(3).
[29]   Securities Law, supra note 10, at Art. 74(4).

of insiders. Thirdly, substantial shareholders are also insiders for the purpose of insider trading law.[30]

The above three groups are all traditional corporate insiders, but the insider trading prohibition is not limited to them. There are two more groups of persons who are nominal outsiders but nevertheless subject to the prohibition. One group corresponds to what is called temporary or constructive insiders in the USA, namely a variety of nominal outsiders who participate in securities trading pursuant to their statutory duties or private contracts, such as underwriters, accountants, lawyers, consultants, and the staff members of securities registration and clearing institutions.[31] The other group are regulatory officials, namely persons who have regulatory authority over securities trading.[32]

While defining insiders by means of enumeration has the benefit of providing specific guidance, it could potentially be narrowing, thereby inviting loopholes in an unintended manner. Elsewhere this author has discussed in detail some groups of people who may possess material, non-public information and yet could circumvent the prohibition to trade affected securities with impunity, such as retired corporate officers and tippees.[33] Potentially, the last subsection of Article 74 may plug these loopholes, as it is a catch-all provision referring to 'other persons' specified by the CSRC. To date, the CSRC has not issued any formal regulation to provide further details on the scope of the provision.[34]

A recent high-profile case sheds some light on the persons who may potentially fall within this category. In the *Li Qihong* case,[35] Mrs. Li was then the mayor of the city of

---

[30]   Securities Law, supra note 10, at Art. 74(2). In China, a shareholder with 5 per cent or more of the shares issued by a listed company is considered to be a substantial shareholder.

[31]   Securities Law, supra note 10, at Art. 74(6).

[32]   Securities Law, supra note 10, at Art. 74(5).

[33]   Hui Huang, The Regulation of Insider Trading in China: A Critical Review and Proposals for Reform, 17 Austl. J. Corp. L. 281, 294–96 (2005).

[34]   The CSRC has issued an internal guidance document, listing several other types of people as insiders under the last subsection of Article 74. *See* Zhongguo Zhengquan Jiandu Guanli Weiyuanhui Guanyu 'Zhenquan Shichang Caozong Xingwei Rending Zhiyin (Shixing)' ji 'Zhengquan Shichang Neimu Jiaoyi Xingwei Rending Zhiyin (Shixing)' de Tongzhi (中国证券监督管理委员会关于 ' 证券市场操纵行为认定指引（试行） ' 及 ' 证券市场内幕交易行为认定指引（试行）的通知') [Notice of the CSRC Regarding the Printing and Distribution of the '(Provisional) Guide for the Recognition and Confirmation of Manipulative Behaviour in the Securities Markets' and the '(Provisional) Guide for the Recognition and Confirmation of Insider Trading Behaviour in the Securities Markets'] (promulgated by the China Securities Regulatory Commission on 27 March 2007) [hereinafter the 2007 CSRC Guide on Insider Trading]. Article 6(2) of the above document elaborates on the category of 'other people' within the meaning of Article 74 of the 2005 Securities Law.

It should be noted however that the 2007 CSRC Guide on Insider Trading is strictly for the CSRC's internal use only. The 2007 CSRC Guide on Insider Trading serves the purpose of helping CSRC staff to better understand the insider trading law and ensuring consistency of enforcement standard. To date, it has never been publicly referred to as a legal basis in any administrative penalty decisions on insider trading. For a more detailed discussion of the 2007 CSRC Guide on Insider Trading, see Nicholas Calcina Howson, Enforcement Without Foundation? Insider Trading and China's Administrative Law Crisis, Am. J. Comp. L. 955 (2012) (arguing that the 2007 CSRC Guide on Insider Trading is void and unenforceable).

[35]   Li Qihong's Insider Trading Abyss, Sina 新闻中心 (14 May 2011), http://news.sina.com.cn/c/2011-05-14/170822464899.shtml (last accessed 28 November 2012).

Zhongshan of Guangdong Province. She was in charge of the asset restructuring exercise of a listed company which was majority-owned by the Zhongshan government. Mrs. Li divulged the confidential information on the restructuring matter to her husband and sister-in-law, who subsequently traded shares of the said company at a huge profit. The CSRC later conducted an investigation into the matter, and Mrs. Li was accused of insider trading before the Intermediate People's Court of Guangzhou City on 6 April 2011. This case shows that government officials other than those in the regulatory body, namely the CSRC, are included in the category of 'other persons'.

Apart from the above primary insider trading instances, China has also introduced the misappropriation theory from the USA to expand the scope of its insider trading regulation.[36] Under Article 76, a person who has illegally obtained material non-public information has an insider's duty and thus is prohibited from trading on the basis of the information.[37] As noted previously, the Judicial Interpretation on Insider Trading Law in Criminal Cases has recently been issued to provide further guidance on the application of insider trading law in China. Under Article 2 of the above instrument, a person may be found to have illegally obtained inside information if the inside information is obtained in the following three circumstances: (1) through such means as theft, cheating, tapping, spying, extraction, bribery and private trading; (2) from the close relatives of primary insiders, or people with other types of close relationships with primary insiders; (3) from people who have contact with primary insiders during the sensitive period of the inside information.[38] This provision casts a very wide net and provides a clear legal basis for pursuing tippee liability.

B. What is Inside Information?

Article 75(1) of the Securities Law generally defines what constitutes 'inside information' in China, providing that:

> Inside information is information that is not made public because, in the course of securities trading, it concerns the company's business or financial affairs or may have a major effect on the market price of the company's securities.[39]

However, this broad standard may be too vague and indeterminate, making it potentially very difficult to resolve litigation, and for insiders to decide whether they must disclose information before trading. In order to give some guidance and facilitate its application, Article 75(2) itemizes some specific types of facts that are regarded as inside information,[40]

---

[36] For discussion of the misappropriation theory, see infra Section III.D.
[37] Securities Law, supra note 10, at Art. 76.
[38] Judicial Interpretation on Insider Trading Law in Criminal Cases, Art. 2.
[39] Securities Law, supra note 10, at Art. 75(1).
[40] According to this provision, 'inside information' includes:

1. the major events listed in the second paragraph of Article 62 of this law;
2. company plans concerning distribution of dividends or increase of registered capital;
3. major changes in the company's equity structure;
4. major changes in security for the company's debts;

including the so-called 'major events' as listed in Article 67 under the regime of continuous information disclosure.[41]

As with the scope of insiders, there is also an open-ended category of inside information, referring to 'other information' as determined by the CSRC. Recent cases have provided some insights into what information might be included under this category. In the *Pan Haishen* case, the alleged insider trading was based on non-public earning forecasts. Looking into the words of the provisions, neither Article 67 nor Article 75 explicitly covers this type of inside information, and thus the CSRC held that it fell into the catch-all category.[42]

C.   Subjective Elements

1.   Is negligence enough?

The insider trading provisions in the Securities Law do not directly address the issue of subjective elements. For criminal liability, the Criminal Law generally requires actual

---

5.   any single mortgage, sale or write-off of a major asset used in the business of the company that exceeds 30 per cent of the asset concerned;
6.   potential liability for major damages to be assumed in accordance with law as a result of an act committed by a company's director(s), supervisor(s), manager(s), deputy manager(s) or other senior management person(s);
7.   plans concerning the takeover of listed companies;
8.   other important information determined by the securities regulatory authority under the State Council to have a significant effect on the trading prices of securities.

Securities Law, supra note 10, at Art. 75(2).

[41]   A listed company is obligated to disclose, by submitting an ad hoc report on the 'major events' to the CSRC and to the stock exchange where it is listed. Under Article 67, the types of 'major events' include:

1.   a major change in the company's business guidelines or scope of business;
2.   a decision made by the company concerning a major investment or major asset purchase;
3.   conclusion by the company of an important contract which may have an important effect on the company's assets, liabilities, rights, interests or business results;
4.   incurrence by the company of a major debt or default on an overdue major debt;
5.   incurrence by the company of a major deficit or incurrence of a major loss exceeding 10 per cent of the company's net assets;
6.   a major change in the external production or business conditions of the company;
7.   a change in the chairman of the board of directors, or not less than one-third of the directors or the manager of the company;
8.   a considerable change in the holdings of shareholders who each hold not less than 5 per cent of the company's shares;
9.   a decision made by the company to reduce its registered capital, to merge, to divide, to dissolve or to file for bankruptcy;
10.   major litigation involving the company, or lawful cancellation by a court of a resolution adopted by the shareholders' general meeting or the board of directors;
11.   other events specified in laws or administrative regulations.

Securities Law, supra note 10, at Art. 75.

[42]   Zhongguo Zhengjianhui Xingzheng Chufa Juedingshu 2008 No. 12 (中国证监会行政处罚决定书 2008 年 12 号) [Administrative Penalty Decision of the CSRC, 2008, No. 12] (promulgated by the China Securities Regulatory Commission, 16 March 2008).

intent or recklessness as to the existence of the facts and intentionality to engage in illegal behaviour, stipulating 'the crime is constituted as a result of clear knowledge that one's own act will cause socially harmful consequences, and of hope for or indifference to the occurrence of those consequences'.[43] Insider trading liability is no exception, and thus for criminal liability to attach to insider trading, there should be the presence of either intention or recklessness.[44]

In non-criminal settings, however, the CSRC has recently held that negligence may be sufficient to sustain administrative penalties for insider trading. In the *Kuang Yong* case, Mr. Kuang Yong was involved in the negotiation of a backdoor listing deal. He often had telephone calls at home, discussing the progress of the deal. His wife overheard some of the calls and, after working out what it was about, traded relevant shares at a profit. In August 2010, the CSRC found that Mr. Kuang negligently divulged inside information, and imposed a fine of RMB 30,000 on Mr. Kuang for his negligent behaviour.

Although the above case shows the intensified effort of the CSRC to combat insider trading, it has arguably gone too far in allowing mere negligence to be the basis of insider trading liability. First, at the conceptual level, the term 'tipping' connotes a conscious transfer of inside information and thus its blameworthiness. In the USA, tipping liability even further requires a 'personal benefit' test, namely 'whether the insider receives a direct or indirect personal benefit from the disclosure, such as a pecuniary gain or a reputational benefit that will translate into future earnings'.[45] Secondly, for practical purposes, it would be simply too easy to attract insider trading liability on the basis of negligence, as overhearing or even eavesdropping is very hard to avoid in the real world. In contrast, for insider trading liability to arise under Rule10b-5 in the USA, there is a requirement of scienter. Although the term 'scienter' has never been clearly defined, it generally refers to intent and in some cases, recklessness, but certainly not mere negligence.[46]

2. The 'use or possession' debate

It is hardly surprising that for the purpose of insider trading liability, the precondition for those to be considered as insiders is that they actually possess inside information. In China, the statutory phrase 'persons with knowledge of inside information' ('*Zhixi Neimu Xinxi de Zhiqing Renyuan*') suggests that possession of inside information is required for insider trading liability to attach.[47] Further, for insider trading liability to occur, a necessary element is the defendant's knowledge of the nature of the information, or, more accurately, the knowledge that the possessed information is material and non-public. In China, there are two tests for proving the defendant's knowledge that the information is inside information; namely, the subjective knowledge test to prove the insider 'knew' and the objective knowledge test to prove that the insider 'ought to have reasonably known'.[48]

---

[43] Criminal Law, supra note 65, at Art. 14. The Criminal Law distinguishes between intentional crimes and negligent crimes. Criminal liability is to be imposed for negligent crimes only when the law explicitly stipulates. Id. at Art. 15.

[44] Id. at Art. 180.

[45] Dirks v. SEC, 463 U.S. 646, 663 (1983).

[46] William K.S. Wang & Marc I. Steinberg, Insider Trading 171 (1996).

[47] Securities Law, supra note 10.

[48] Id.

While it is conceptually straightforward about the possession requirement as discussed above, the crux of the issue lies in proving it. Indeed, the evidentiary problem has now been regarded as the biggest difficulty facing Chinese regulators in fighting against insider trading. The CSRC has long tried to solve the issue by exploring the possibility of reversing the burden of proof.

The CSRC has gained strong support from the Supreme Court in this aspect. On 13 July 2011, the Supreme Court held a symposium on issues associated with conducting judicial review of administrative penalties the CSRC makes for insider trading, and clearly supported the idea of reversing the burden of proof in such cases.[49] Further, on 1 June 2012, the newly issued Judicial Interpretation on Insider Trading Law in Criminal Cases makes formal provision for the reverse of burden of proof in the criminal prosecution of insider trading cases. Under Article 1 of this instrument, the types of insiders as enumerated in Article 74 of the Securities Law, such as directors and senior managers, will be presumed to possess relevant inside information; under Article 2, the same presumption of possession of inside information applies to the close relatives of primary insiders, or people with other types of close relationships with primary insiders, or people who have contact with primary insiders during the sensitive period of the inside information, if their relevant transactions are 'obviously abnormal'.

Article 3 provides guidance on when transactions may be considered 'obviously abnormal': in making such determination, one needs to take into account the totality of the circumstances, including the degree of time matching, the degree of trading deviation and the degree of interest connectedness:

1. the time when an account is opened, an account is closed, a fund account is activated or trading (custody) is designated or designated trading (custody transfer) is revoked is basically consistent with the time when the insider information is formed, changed, or disclosed;
2. the time of funds change is basically consistent with the time when the insider information is formed, changed, or disclosed;
3. the time when the securities or futures contract related to insider information is purchased or sold is basically consistent with the time when the insider information is formed, changed, or disclosed;
4. the time when the securities or futures contract related to insider information is purchased or sold is basically consistent with the time when the insider information is obtained;
5. the purchase or sale of a securities or futures contract is clearly different from the normal trading habit;
6. the purchase or sale of a securities or futures contract, or the intensive holding of a securities or futures contract clearly deviates from the fundamentals reflected by the disclosed securities or futures information;

---

[49]   最高人民法院关于审理证券行政处罚案件证据若干问题的座谈会纪要   [Minutes of the symposium held by the Supreme Court on various issues associated with conducting judicial review of the evidence in securities administrative penalty cases] (issued by the Supreme Court on 13 July 2011).

7. the withdrawal from and deposit in the account are relevant to or have interest relations with the person who has access to or illegally obtains such insider information; and

8. any other obviously abnormal transactions.

The above presumption of possession of inside information can be rebutted if the defendant can show that they have justifiable reasons or justified information sources for the seemingly abnormal transactions.

The next logical question is whether *mere possession* of inside information at the time of trading is sufficient for one to attract liability, or more specifically, whether the imposition of liability presupposes a further showing that the insider actually *used* the information. In other words, is it required to prove a causal connection between the possessed inside information and the defendant's trading? This issue is known as the 'possession versus use' debate in the USA, and at the international level there are four different approaches to the issue: the strict possession, strict use, modified use and modified possession tests.[50]

It was not until a recent case in 2008 that the CSRC had a chance to decide on the above issue. In the case of *Deng Jun & Qu Li*,[51] Mr. Deng and Mrs. Qu were senior management of a company which was the target of a takeover. At the initial stage of the takeover negotiation, the bidder company sent two officers to the target company to do preliminary due diligence, and for confidentiality reasons, the two officers did not disclose their identities. But Mr. Deng and Mrs. Qu managed to work out who the two visitors were, and traded relevant shares at a profit. During the CSRC investigation, Mr. Deng and Mrs. Qu argued that they did not have knowledge of the takeover and, more importantly, they traded shares not because of the alleged inside information but because of their independent research on the price movement of the relevant stock.[52] In response, the CSRC essentially adopted the modified use test, under which the actual use of inside information is a requisite element of liability but, in order to alleviate the evidentiary problem, a rebuttable inference of use applies to people in possession of inside information. As Mr. Deng and Mrs. Qu did not successfully adduce evidence to rebut the inference, they were held to have used the information to trade.

The CSRC's position has been supported by the judiciary in the recently issued Judicial Interpretation on Insider Trading Law in Criminal Cases. Article 4 of this instrument provides that a transaction conducted by a person in possession of inside information would not be treated as inside trading if the transaction is conducted according to pre-existing written contract, plan or instruction, or based on other legal source of information or other legal grounds.[53]

---

[50] See Hui Huang, The Insider Trading 'Possession versus Use' Debate: An International Analysis, 33 Sec. Reg. L. J. 130 (2006).

[51] Zhongguo Zhengjianhui Xingzheng Chufa Juedingshu (2008) No. 46 (中国证监会行政处罚决定书 2008 年 46 号) [The Administrative Penalty Decision of the CSRC, 2008, No. 46] (promulgated by the China Securities Regulatory Commission, 10 November 2008).

[52] The Administrative Penalty Commission of the CSRC, Explanations on Securities Administrative Penalty Cases 4 (2009).

[53] Judicial Interpretation on Insider Trading Law in Criminal Cases, Art. 4.

D.   Revisiting the Unclear Theories of China's Insider Trading Law

The preceding discussion has provided an updated examination of the core elements of China's insider trading law in light of recent cases, and from a comparative perspective, has pointed out some problems therein with respect to the scope of insiders, inside information and subjective elements. At a fundamental level, those problems actually have their root in the confusion around the theory of insider trading liability in China.

As discussed above, China's insider trading law has benefited greatly from overseas experiences, notably those of the USA. Unfortunately, however, China's legislators appear to have simply put all of them together, without paying adequate attention to how they relate to each other and how they will function as a whole. Indeed, over time, under the general anti-fraud provision of Rule 10b-5, US courts have developed several different and even conflicting theories of insider trading liability:[54] first, the equality of access theory was adopted in *SEC v. Texas Gulf Sulphur Co.* by the Second Circuit in 1968;[55] then the Supreme Court replaced it with the classical theory in *Chiarella v. United States*[56] and further expanded the scope of the classical theory to the tipping situation in *Dirks v. SEC*;[57] finally endorsing the misappropriation theory to complement the classical theory in *United States v. O'Hagan*.[58]

As discussed previously, Article 73 generally provides that 'persons with knowledge of inside information on securities trading are prohibited from taking advantage of such inside information to engage in securities trading'.[59] A literal reading of this article suggests that China adopts the equality of access theory. This implies that anyone with unequal access to inside information would generally be subject to the prohibition.

However, the above situation does not sit comfortably with Article 74 or Article 76. As discussed above, Article 74 curbs the broad nature of Article 73 by enumerating specific types of persons who are regarded as insiders.[60] The list seems to be wholly based on the *Chiarella–Dirks* classical insider trading theory. First, it covers traditional insiders, such as directors, officers and substantial shareholders. Secondly, constructive or temporary insiders – staff members of intermediaries including underwriters, accountants, consultants and lawyers – are also listed. Moreover, Article 76 essentially introduces the misap-

---

[54]   For a detailed discussion of the evolution of US insider trading jurisprudence from a comparative perspective, see Huang, supra note 50, at 297–303.

[55]   401 F.2d 833 (2d Cir. 1968), cert. denied, 394 U.S. 976 (1969). Under this theory, anyone with unequal access to inside information, whether they are corporate insiders or outsiders, has a duty of disclosure before trading and, if they fail to disclose, they will breach the duty and thus Rule 10b-5.

[56]   445 U.S. 222 (1980). Under this theory, insider trading liability under Rule 10b-5 occurs only when one party owes a fiduciary duty to the other party with whom they are trading.

[57]   463 U.S. 646 (1983) (holding that tippees can be held liable on the grounds that they violate their fiduciary duty inherited from tippers/insiders who breach their fiduciary duty to disclose confidential information in the first place).

[58]   521 U.S. 642 (1997). Under this theory, insider trading liability arises when the insiders breach their fiduciary duty owed to the source of the inside information, as distinct from the party with whom they trade.

[59]   Securities Law, supra note 10.

[60]   See supra Section III.A.

propriation theory by reference to 'other persons who have illegally obtained such insider information'.[61] Thus, it appears that Articles 74 and 76 have jointly imported the classical theory and the misappropriation theory, which are collectively called 'fiduciary duty-based theories' by this author elsewhere.[62] It is thus not unfair to say that when enacting the Securities Law, China's legislators appear to have failed to fully understand the nature and functioning of the US insider trading regime.

This is well illustrated in the recent controversy over the issue of front-running, a practice dubbed 'rat-trading' in China, where fund managers trade for their own accounts, prior to placing an order for the fund, to take advantage of any change in the market price of financial instruments resulting from the order for the fund. The first such case reported in China is the *Tang Jian* case.[63] In March 2006, Mr. Tang Jian, the then assistant fund manager of an influential fund management company in China, allegedly traded a stock ahead of the execution of his fund's order to purchase the same stock. As the fund's order involved a large quantity of the stock, the price of the stock rose significantly after the completion of the fund's order. Mr. Tang then sold his stock, reaping a big profit in April 2006. He repeated this pattern of trading in May 2006.

This case generated considerable debate in China as to the nature of front-running. There is little doubt that Mr. Tang, as a fund manager, stood in a fiduciary relationship with the unit holders of the fund, and therefore his behaviour of front-running the fund's order constituted a breach of fiduciary duty. Indeed, Mr. Tang profited at the expense of the unit holders, because his personal trading may have increased the price at which the fund's order was executed. This problem also has a broad negative impact on investor confidence as it undermines the integrity of the market. It is thus clear that front-running has harmful effects and should be regulated.[64] But the more difficult question is how to regulate it and, in particular, whether front-running is actually a form of insider trading and hence should be subject to insider trading law.

In April 2008, the CSRC held that front-running was not insider trading (without providing any reasons in its ruling), and punished Mr. Tang merely on the basis of his breach of fiduciary duty. At that time, breach of fiduciary duty only attracted administrative and civil liabilities, so Mr. Tang did not receive criminal sanctions. This result was widely criticized as unsatisfactory, prompting the legislature, namely the National People's Congress (NPC), to hastily add a provision to the *Criminal Law of the People's Republic of China* to make front-running a criminal offence on 28 February 2009.[65]

The chaos surrounding the regulation of front-running could have been avoided if the CSRC had a better understanding of the underlying theories of, and thus the functioning

---

[61] Id.

[62] Huang, supra note 50, at 281.

[63] Zhongguo Zhengjianhui Xingzheng Chufa Juedingshu 2008 No. 22 (中国证监会行政处罚决定书 2008 年 22 号) [The Administrative Penalty Decision of the CSRC, 2008, No. 22] (promulgated by the China Securities Regulatory Commission, 8 April 2008).

[64] For a detailed discussion of the theoretical bases for regulating liability, see, e.g., Jason Carley, The Future of Front-running, 13 Co. & Sec. L. J. 434 (1995).

[65] Zhonghua Renmin Gongheguo Xingfa Xiuzhengan (7) (中华人民共和国刑法修正案) [The Seventh Amendment to the Criminal Law of the PRC] (promulgated by the Standing Committee of the NPC, 28 February 2009) [hereinafter Criminal Law].

of, the overseas insider trading laws on which China's law is modelled. By the early 1990s, US commentators were already arguing that front-running could constitute insider trading under Rule 10b-5 based on the misappropriation theory, as the fund manager owes a fiduciary duty to the fund which is the source of the information about imminent orders.[66] This view was essentially adopted in a case decided in 2004, where a broker, knowing of a large imminent order from a client, put through a transaction on another client's behalf, thus benefiting from the pre-warning.[67] Similarly, in Australia, which adopts the insider trading theory of equality of access, front-running has long been seen as a form of insider trading, the rationale being that the front-runner enjoys unequal and privileged access to the information about large or market-sensitive orders.[68]

As discussed above, China's insider trading law appears to have transplanted both the equality of access theory and the fiduciary duty-based theories consisting of the classical theory and the misappropriation theory. However, the CSRC failed to use either of them to deal with the issue of front-running, which has resulted in a problem with the scope of China's insider trading regulation. In order for Chinese insider trading regulation to be more effective, it is imperative that its theoretical basis be clarified and streamlined. This author has suggested that the equality of access theory is preferable to the fiduciary duty-based theories, especially in the context of China.[69]

IV.   HOW IS THE LAW ENFORCED?

A.   Overview of Enforcement Mechanisms

In China, there are generally three types of legal liability, namely administrative liability, civil liability and criminal liability. However, as to insider trading, only administrative and criminal liability are available at the moment. According to Article 202 of the Securities Law, in the case of insider trading, administrative liability could be imposed:

> [The inside trader] shall be ordered to dispose of the illegally obtained securities according to law, his illegal gains shall be confiscated and, in addition, he shall be imposed a fine of not less than the amount of but not more than five times the illegal gains, or a fine of not more than the value of the securities illegally purchased or sold.[70]

Article 202 also provides that if an insider trading case is serious enough to constitute a crime, criminal liability shall be pursued.[71] Criminal liability is set out in detail in Article 180 of the Criminal Law which states:

---

[66]   Mark S. Howard, Front-running in the Marketplace: A Regulatory Dilemma, 19 Sec. Reg. L. J. 263, 278 (1991).

[67]   United States v. Martha Stewart and Peter Bacanovic, 305 F. Supp. 2d 368 (S.D.N.Y. 2004). For a critique of this case, see Ray J. Grzebielski, Why Martha Stewart Did Not Violate Rule 10b-5: On Tipping, Piggybacking, Front-running and the Fiduciary Duties of Securities Brokers, 40 Akron L. Rev. 55 (2007).

[68]   See CARLEY, supra note 64, at 434–35.

[69]   Huang, supra note 50, at 281.

[70]   Securities Law, supra note 10, at Art. 202.

[71]   Id.

[Inside traders] shall be sentenced to not more than five years in prison or criminal detention, provided the circumstances are serious. They shall be fined, additionally or exclusively, a sum not less than 100 per cent and not more than 500 per cent as high as their illegal proceeds. If the circumstances are especially serious, they shall be sentenced to not less than five years and not more than 10 years in prison. In addition, they shall be fined a sum not less than 100 per cent and not more than 500 per cent as high as their illegal proceeds.[72]

The newly issued Judicial Interpretation on Insider Trading Law in Criminal Cases provides further guidance as to what constitutes 'serious circumstances' and 'very serious circumstances' within the meaning of the above-mentioned Article 180 of the Criminal Law. The circumstance that would be considered 'serious' includes: (1) the accumulative trading amount of securities is more than 500,000 yuan; (2) the accumulative amount of used margin for futures trading is more than 300,000 yuan; (3) the accumulative amount of profits gained or losses avoided is more than 150,000 yuan; (4) insider trading is conducted or insider information is leaked more than three times; or (5) any other serious circumstance.[73] Moreover, 'very serious circumstances' include: (1) the accumulative trading amount of securities is more than 2,500,000 yuan; (2) the accumulative amount of used margin for futures trading is more than 1,500,000 yuan; (3) the accumulative amount of profits gained or losses avoided is more than 750,000 yuan; or (4) any other very serious circumstance.[74]

Under the Securities Law, nothing has been said about private civil liability for insider trading except a simple provision that generally prioritizes private civil liabilities for all securities violations. Article 232 of the Securities Law reads:

> If the property of a person, who violates the provisions of this Law and who therefore bears civil liability for damages and is required to pay a fine, is insufficient to pay both the damages and the fine, such person shall first bear the civil liability for damages.[75]

However, the Securities Law does not devote any specific provisions to civil damages payable to the aggrieved party by a person who has engaged in insider trading. No provisions in the Securities Law expressly address the issues concerning civil remedies, such as the standing of the plaintiff and measure of damages, rendering private civil liabilities virtually unavailable in practice and thus making Article 232 illusory.[76] To be sure, a private right of action could be theoretically based on the existing general contract law or on the tort regime. However, due to the special nature of insider trading such as the impersonality and anonymity of exchange transactions, it is extremely difficult, if not impossible, in terms of causation and reliance, to assert insiders' liability on those conventional grounds.

---

[72]   Criminal Law, supra note 65, at Art. 180.
[73]   Judicial Interpretation on Insider Trading Law in Criminal Cases, Art. 6.
[74]   Ibid., Art. 7.
[75]   Securities Law, supra note 10, at Art. 232.
[76]   For an in-depth analysis of the issues concerning private civil liability for insider trading, see Hui Huang, Compensation for Insider Trading: Who should be Eligible Claimants?, 20 Austl. J. Corp. L. 84 (2006).

B.   Empirical Data: Cases from 1991–2011

1.   Methodology

This section endeavours to provide insights into the way in which China's insider trading law has been enforced in practice. To this end, I examine all insider trading cases reported nationwide until the end of May 2011, covering a period of about 20 years since the birth of Chinese securities markets as marked by the establishment of the two national stock exchanges in Shanghai and Shenzhen. I conducted an exhaustive search of relevant cases, using the following means.

To begin with, I accessed all reported decisions on administrative enforcement on the official website of the CSRC. According to Article 184 of the Securities Law, 'all the decisions reached by the [CSRC], on the basis of the results of its investigations, to impose penalties on illegal acts in relation to securities, shall be made public'.[77] The CSRC publicizes all of the cases it handles on its official website, which is freely accessible to all. The website provides a comprehensive source of information regarding enforcement action by the CSRC.

As the official website of the CSRC only contains administrative penalty decisions made by the CSRC, I then searched all reported insider trading cases adjudicated by the court in a widely used electronic database of Chinese law,[78] with search terms based on the relevant legislative provisions. This produced a very small number of criminal cases on insider trading. I discovered that this database is incomplete, for it omitted even some of the well-known cases. I therefore also searched media reports on the internet, and this returned good results, which provided useful information about both closed and pending cases.

2.   Empirical findings

The above searching efforts produced a total of 39 cases, which is believed to be adequate to conduct statistical analysis. Each case in the data set was read and analysed according to the relevant research questions: (1) the year in which the case was heard; (2) the identity of the insider; (3) the nature of the inside information; and (4) the use of criminal enforcement.

Table 16.1 divides the study period into several five-year windows in an effort to show temporal changes to the intensity of insider trading enforcement in China.[79] As the table shows, there are two peaks in the record of cases, one during the 1996–2000 period and the other in the 2006–2010 period.[80] This is evidence that insider trading is highly likely to happen in a bull market. The Chinese securities market experienced rapid development

---

[77]   Securities Law, supra note 10, at Art. 184.
[78]   See http://Chinalawinfo.com (last accessed 8 January 2012).
[79]   Note that each of the cases listed here involves either enforcement action by the CSRC or criminal prosecution in the court. There is a pattern that the CSRC does not bring enforcement action against insider trading once criminal enforcement is pursued. Thus, there is no duplication of cases in the data set, for no cases attracted both administrative penalty and criminal penalty. Further, there are a very small number of cases where private civil suits followed the public enforcement. These private civil suits are not included in order to avoid double counting. For more discussion on private enforcement, see infra Section IV.C.
[80]   Within the period from 2006 to 2010, the total number of 25 insider trading cases shows a steady increase across the five years: one in 2007; four in 2008; six in 2009 and fourteen in 2010.

Table 16.1   When was the case heard?

Time range	Number of cases	Percentage
1991–1995	2	5
1996–2000	7	18
2001–2005	3	8
2006–2010	25	64
2011–	2	5
Total	39	100

Table 16.2   Who was the insider?

Types of insiders	Number of cases	Percentage
Traditional insiders	36	70
Constructive insiders	5	10
Government officials	3	6
Listed companies themselves	3	6
Others	4	8
Total	51	100

during the above-mentioned periods. For instance, in 1996 the market became bullish and was so overheated that the government had to cool it down by a series of measures.[81] Again, China had another round of feverish bull market from 2006, thanks to the state share reform, with the Shanghai Stock Exchange Composite Index surging from the low level of 998 points on 6 June 2005 all the way up to the record high of 6124 points on 16 October 2007.[82]

Two reasons can be advanced to explain the phenomenon that insider trading is more likely to occur during periods of heightened market activities in a bull market. On the one hand, a bull market provides more opportunities for insider trading. In a bull market, share prices are highly volatile and there are a lot of investment activities. The volatility of the market offers more chances for profitable speculations such as insider trading. On the other hand, a bull market may make it safer to commit insider trading because the chance of detection becomes lower. Thus, the volatility in share prices encourages insider trading to a significant degree.

Table 16.2 examines the identity of the person(s) committing insider trading either by directly trading or by tipping others to trade. There are 51 cases listed, which is more than the number of cases overall, as in some cases there were more than one insider defendant.[83] The table shows that traditional insiders, such as company directors, senior management

---

[81]   Huang, supra note 7, at 51.
[82]   See Shanghai Stock Exchange, http://www.sse.com.cn/sseportal/ps/zhs/home.html (last accessed 8 January 2012).
[83]   Note that the number does not include secondary insiders, namely tippees. This is because tippees are normally the spouse, relatives and friends of the primary insider/tipper, and they usually

Table 16.3   What was the inside information about?

Content of inside information	Number of cases	Percentage
Mergers and acquisitions	22	57
Major contracts or investments	6	15
Earnings	5	13
Dividend distribution plan	2	5
Capital increase	2	5
Others	2	5
Total	39	100

and officers, account for most of the insiders involved in the cases. However, there are also other types of insiders. In particular, up to five insiders in the cases were investment bankers (so-called 'constructive insiders') who were retained to provide a professional service and thus got access to inside information.

It is also worth noting that in three cases the listed companies themselves committed insider trading in relation to their own shares, but these cases are all before 2000. There is a discernible trend that more and more insider trading cases involve individual insiders. It is easier to detect insider trading committed by entities than natural persons because more people are involved in the former situation. This development suggests that insider trading becomes increasingly concealed and thus makes it more difficult to detect.

Table 16.3 reveals that a majority of insider trading cases are based on inside information concerning mergers and acquisitions (M&A). This may be explained by at least three factors. The first is that takeovers always result in major price movements and thus create a favourable environment for committing insider trading. In the context of takeovers, insider trading is typically committed through buying shares ahead of information disclosure on takeovers and thereafter selling them at a profit. Secondly, the fact that many people are involved in preparing takeovers and thus the relevant information may be easily leaked out increases the chance of insider trading. Finally, China's legal regime for M&A is far from effective, particularly in relation to information disclosure, providing a fertile breeding ground for inside trading.[84]

Table 16.4 presents a significant finding about China's insider trading enforcement, namely the aggressive use of criminal sanctions in recent years, particularly after 2008. Out of 39 insider trading cases examined in this study, criminal prosecutions have been brought in up to 10 cases, or about 26 per cent of all cases.

It is fair to say that criminal prosecutions of insider trading have had a slow start in China – although criminal liability for insider trading has been available since 1997, it was not employed until 2003 in the *Shenshen Fang* case. In the ensuing five years, there was only one more criminal inside trading case, namely the *Changjiang Konggu* case. This

---

have no relationship with the company whose shares were traded. Including tippees in the table would thus distort the picture of the persons likely to commit insider trading.

[84]   For more discussion on China's takeover law, see Huang, The New Takeover Regulation in China: Evolution and Enhancement, 42 Int'l Law. 153 (2008).

Table 16.4   How has criminal enforcement been used?

Name	Year	Profit (Chinese yuan)	Penalty (Chinese yuan)	Decided or pending
Li Qihong case	2011	19,830,000		Pending
Tianshan Fangzhi case	2011	1,737,423.84	• Disgorgement of illegal profit • Fine of 3 million yuan • Three-year imprisonment	Decided
Huang Guangyu case	2010	306,000,000	• Fine of 0.6 billion yuan • Nine-year imprisonment	Decided
Guang Yawei case	2010	Not specified		Pending
Gao Yangcai case	2010	Not specified		Pending
Liu Baochun case	2010	About 7,000,000		Pending
Dong Zhengqing case	2009	22,846,712.42	• Disgorgement of illegal profit • Fine of 3 million yuan • Four-year imprisonment	Decided
Hangxiao Ganggou case	2008	40,370,000	• Disgorgement of illegal profit • Fine of 40,370,000 yuan • Two and a half-year imprisonment	Decided
Changjiang Konggu case	2003	9,600,000	• Disgorgement of illegal profit • Fine of 100,000 yuan • Three-year imprisonment	Decided
Shenshen Fang case	2003	780,000	• Disgorgement of illegal profit • Fine of 800,000 yuan • Three-year imprisonment	Decided

situation was criticized by many commentators – including this author – who called for greater use of criminal prosecutions to increase deterrent effects.[85] Fortunately, since 2008 criminal prosecutions of insider trading have regained momentum. A spate of criminal cases has been reported, and the penalties imposed therein have been very severe in some cases, even by international standards.

For instance, in the high-profile *Huang Guangyu* case, during the period from April to September 2007, Mr. Huang bought RMB 1 billion-worth of shares in a company called Beijing Zhongguancun, making use of the inside information on the corporate restructuring of the said company. When the information was publicly disclosed and the share price rose accordingly, Mr. Huang made a profit of RMB 0.3 billion on the book. However, he continued to hold the shares rather than sell them to realize the profit, and

---

[85]   See, e.g., Huang, supra note 7, at 48–50; Han Shen, A Comparative Study of Insider Trading Regulation Enforcement in the USA and China, 9 J. Bus. & Sec. L. 41, 71–2 (2009).

eventually suffered a huge loss of up to 65 per cent of the purchase value due to the share price plunge during the global financial crisis of 2008. In 2010, Mr. Huang was sentenced to nine years in prison and fined RMB 0.6 billion (roughly US $93 million).[86] Two points are worth noting about this case. First, both the imprisonment term and the amount of monetary penalty are the highest so far in China's insider trading enforcement history. Secondly, this case suggests that insider trading liability may arise, regardless of the actual result of the trading. This position has also been confirmed by the CSRC in its enforcement actions.[87]

C. Analysis and Policy Implications

The above empirical data show that in recent years, there has been a significant increase in the number of insider trading cases, with a growing tendency to use criminal sanctions. This comes as China has vowed to strengthen its enforcement efforts, and launched a nationwide high-profile crackdown against insider trading. This is a very encouraging development of insider trading enforcement in China, but more still needs to be done.

Indeed, although China's recent record of insider trading enforcement seems to compare favourably with that of the UK,[88] it clearly falls far behind the USA, where between 2001 and the autumn of 2006, over 300 insider trading enforcement actions were brought by the Securities and Exchange Commission (SEC) against more than 600 individuals and entities.[89] Thus, the following text will discuss in more detail the issues on public and private enforcement, and set out policy recommendations to enhance the efficacy of China's insider trading law.

1.   Public enforcement
In overseas jurisdictions, when examining the intensity of public enforcement, commentators often look at two aspects: enforcement outputs (namely enforcement actions brought and penalties imposed) and enforcement inputs (namely the budget and staff size of the regulator).[90] These data are, of course, relevant in measuring enforcement intensity, but there is one more important dimension to the question, which is the institutional structure and governance framework of the regulator. Indeed, research focused exclusively on the

---

[86]   Note that Mr. Huang was convicted of other crimes in addition to insider trading, and thus the overall imprisonment term is 14 years.

[87]   See, e.g., Zhongguo Zhengjianhui Xingzheng Chufa Juedingshu (Qu Xiang) 2008 No. 49 [The Administrative Penalty Decision of the CSRC (Qu Xiang), 2008, No. 49] (promulgated by the China Securities Regulatory Commission, 20 November 2008) (administrative penalty was imposed, even though the insider trading resulted in a loss rather than a profit).

[88]   During the period from 2001 to 2007, the Financial Services Authority (FSA) in the UK reportedly brought only eight insider trading cases. See Grant Ringshaw, Hot on the Trail of the Insider Dealers, Sunday Times (London), 13 May 2007, Bus. 8 (Eng.). Further, there had been few recorded criminal prosecutions of insider trading in the UK by 2007.

[89]   Illegal Insider Trading: How Widespread Is the Problem and Is There Adequate Criminal Enforcement? Hearing Before the S. Comm. on the Judiciary, 109th Cong. 12 (2006) (statement of Linda Thompson, Director, Division of Enforcement, SEC).

[90]   Howell Jackson & Mark J. Roe, Public and Private Enforcement of Securities Laws: Resource-Based Evidence, 93 J. Fin. Econ. 207 (2009).

inputs and outputs of enforcement implicitly treats the processor in the middle – i.e., the regulator – as a black box. This methodology may work only when the regulator can be sufficiently trusted in terms of its independence and accountability.

Where regulatory independence and accountability are in question, enforcement inputs and outputs data may not tell the full story. In this case, even if the enforcement agency is seemingly strong both in terms of inputs (well funded and well staffed) and outputs (a good number of enforcement actions), one should not jump to any final conclusion, because the enforcement activity may be conducted in a dubious way. This unfortunately appears to be the case in China, as illustrated in the following two examples.

The first example is the *Huang Guangyu* case, discussed earlier. Mr. Huang was once the richest self-made man in China and even today is widely regarded as one of the most talented Chinese businessmen. In April 2009, when he was detained for market misconduct, he had just turned 40 and attempted suicide in the detention centre. This was quite surprising, as Mr. Huang reportedly had a very strong mind and had experienced many ups and downs in his life. Many believed that his suicide attempt was not due to the problem of market misconduct, but to political pressure. Indeed, soon after Mr. Huang's detention, a number of high-ranking officials were detained and penalized, showing that Mr. Huang was entangled in far more serious political corruption problems than mere commercial crimes. It was widely suspected that this background had something to do with the severe penalty Mr. Huang finally received for the commercial crimes.

The other case concerns Ms. Li, who at the time was a regulatory official of the CSRC. It was reported that Ms. Li got divorced from her husband, and they had a bitter property dispute. In 2008, Ms. Li's ex-husband and ex-mother-in-law reported to the CSRC that Ms. Li had sent mobile messages containing inside information to her mother, and provided evidence such as the call record and trading account. Less than two days later, the CSRC responded that it had conducted an internal investigation and found no evidence of Ms. Li committing insider trading. Despite strong calls from the public, the CSRC refused to comment on the evidence supplied by the informants and no further investigation was carried out.

The above two cases provide some useful information which cannot be obtained from the data on enforcement inputs and outputs. To be sure, it is important to give more resources – such as funding and staff – to the regulator in order to enhance its enforcement efforts. But that is not enough. Indeed, there should be a mechanism in place to ensure that regulatory resources are actually used in a fair, transparent and efficient way. This requires that the CSRC enjoys more independence, while at the same time subjecting it to more scrutiny.

2.   Private enforcement

The picture of securities law enforcement would not be complete without having a look at the issue of private enforcement. There has been an international debate on the utility of private enforcement vis-à-vis public enforcement of securities law. Some have argued that private enforcement played a more important role than public enforcement in the development of securities markets,[91] while others have found a dominance of public enforcement

---

[91]   See Rafael La Porta et al., What Works in Securities Laws?, 61 J. Fin. 1, 20 (2006).

over private enforcement.[92] Regardless of the relative performance of public and private enforcement, it is generally accepted that private enforcement is a necessary and appropriate supplement to governmental enforcement to deter insider trading. If this is the case even in the USA, where the SEC is relatively well resourced and efficient, it should be more so in China where, as discussed above, public enforcers may fail to act due to lack of independence and accountability in addition to the general issue of resource constraints.

As noted earlier, although the Securities Law in principle provides for private action against insider trading, the functioning of that system is hampered by the absence of detailed implementing rules. Indeed, in the open-market setting, private civil liability for insider trading has long raised some extremely difficult questions. In the USA, this problem has been aptly captured by Professor Clark, who pointed out:

> Once a private right of action under Rule 10b-5 was implied and recognized, there was bound to be a period of painful growth, as the courts struggled to give shape and meaning to the standard list of elements of a tort action as applied to the new context. Who was to have standing to bring private actions? Who could be sued? What exactly would constitute the duty imposed? What would be needed to show a violation of the duty and causation of injury? What would the measure of damages be?[93]

If the Western judges, who are usually chosen from among leading lawyers in relevant areas, find it difficult to handle the complex issues over private enforcement of insider trading law, then the Chinese judges, who are ill-equipped in terms of education and experience, may only find it even harder. This situation has been well illustrated in the three circulars the Supreme People's Court of China (SPC) issued in relation to the hearing of civil cases arising from securities fraud. First, on 21 September 2001, the SPC issued a circular to refuse to accept civil remedy cases over securities frauds such as misrepresentation, market manipulation and insider trading, citing that the judiciary did not have the necessary expertise and resources to hear those difficult cases. Due to mounting public pressure, however, the SPC soon issued an additional circular on 15 January 2002 to agree in principle to accept and hear civil cases arising from securities misrepresentation, and then on 9 January 2003 issued a third circular to provide detailed rules on the hearing of such cases.

Importantly, under the two SPC circulars issued in 2002 and 2003, it is clearly stipulated that securities civil cases can be brought against misrepresentation only, to the exclusion of other types of securities fraud such as insider trading. On 30 May 2007, however, Mr. Xi Xiaoming, the vice-president of the SPC, stated at a national conference on the adjudication of civil and commercial cases that courts should also accept securities civil cases arising from insider trading and market manipulation. Mr. Xi's statement was later distributed as the SPC's official document to the courts at all levels across the nation.[94] Since then, there have been some attempts to bring civil cases in the context of insider trading. On 4 September 2008, *Chen Ningfeng v. Chen Jianliang*, the first civil compensation case

---

[92]   Jackson & Roe, supra note 90.
[93]   Robert C. Clark, Corporate Law 316 (1986).
[94]   Civil Compensation Cases against Insider Trading and Market Manipulation Are Imminent (18 November 2007), http://npc.people.com.cn/GB/6543957.html (last accessed 28 November 2012).

over insider trading, was heard before the Intermediate People's Court of Nanjing. This civil case piggybacked on an administrative penalty decision by the CSRC imposed earlier on Mr. Chen Jianliang for insider trading.[95] Significantly, the hearing of the civil case was conducted and ended in an unusual way. First, only Mr. Song Yixin, the attorney for the plaintiff, appeared at the hearing, with the plaintiff, the defendant and the attorney for the defendant all being absent. Secondly, an assistant to the attorney for the defendant delivered to the court a statement of the plaintiff requesting the withdrawal of the suit. Thirdly, the statement of the plaintiff was made without the knowledge of the plaintiff's own attorney. Finally, the court allowed the case to be withdrawn.

In comparison, the 2009 case of *Chen Zuling v. Pan Haishen* produced the first judgment on civil claim for insider trading in China.[96] Like the case discussed above, this case followed an administrative penalty decision by the CSRC against Mr. Pan Haishen for insider trading. Since the CSRC had earlier found Mr. Pan guilty of insider trading, the court went directly to examine the issues specific to civil claims, and in particular whether there was causation between the plaintiff's trading and the defendant's insider trading. In this case, the defendant's insider trading took place on 16 April 2007, more than two months before the plaintiff's trading, which was on 18 June 2007. Further, the plaintiff did not suffer a loss but rather made a profit from his trading. In the end, the court rejected the case, on the grounds that no causal link existed between the plaintiff's trading and the defendant's insider trading.

Although these two cases did not succeed, their significance should not be understated. They have opened the door to civil action against insider trading, attracting considerable social attention to the new concept of private enforcement of insider trading regulation in China. Indeed, there have been more cases filed recently for civil remedies against insider trading, including those based on the high-profile insider trading case of *Huang Guangyu* discussed earlier. These cases are representative of the tendency for public and private enforcement to be used on a cumulative and overlapping basis. This is a welcome development in terms of increasing the deterrent threat for insider trading as well as generating some compensation for aggrieved investors. For instance, in the case of *Chen Ningfeng v. Chen Jianliang*, it is likely that the defendant had offered compensation to the plaintiff privately outside the court in return for the plaintiff agreeing to withdraw the case. On the other hand, there is much to be desired in relation to private enforcement of insider trading regulation in China. The bringing of civil cases against insider trading has a shaky legal basis: such cases are allowed only under a conference speech of an SPC vice-president, while the two formal circulars issued in 2002 and 2003 remain unchanged that only cases arising from misrepresentation can be accepted. Further, the above-noted conference speech only calls for the courts to accept securities civil cases arising from insider trading, without providing detailed guidance on how such cases should be adjudicated. Indeed, civil suits against insider trading involve some different and more complicated

---

[95]   Zhongguo Zhengjianhui Xingzheng Chufa Juedingshu 2007 No.15 (中国证监会行政处罚决定书 2007 年 15 号) [Administrative Penalty Decision by the CSRC, 2007, No. 15] (promulgated by the China Securities Regulatory Commission, 28 April 2007).

[96]   Chen Zuling v. Pan Haishen (2009) Yi Zhong Min Chu Zi No. 8217 (Civil Judgment, The First Intermediate Court of Beijing, 2009) (陈祖灵诉潘海深证券内幕交易赔偿纠纷案（2009）一中民初字第8217号，北京市第一中级人民法院民事判决书).

issues than those in the context of misrepresentation. It is thus imperative that, like the circular issued in 2003 on civil cases arising from misrepresentation, a new circular be formally issued to clarify the rights of action and provide detailed rules with respect to civil cases arising from insider trading.

V.   CONCLUSION

Twenty years on, it is fair to say that China has made a great achievement in gradually setting up a regulatory regime for insider trading in line with international experiences. There remain, however, problems and uncertainties in relation to some of the key elements of insider trading regulation, such as the types of insiders, the scope of inside information and the requisite state of mind. These problems arise essentially because of the confusion surrounding the theoretical basis of China's insider trading law, which borrows from various overseas experiences without adequate attention paid to their mutual relationships and compatibility with local conditions in China.

In recent years, China's securities markets have experienced significant developments, such as the introduction of index futures, which provide new opportunities for committing insider trading and thus new challenges for the regulator. This has prompted Chinese authorities to strengthen their efforts to crack down on insider trading, making more use of criminal sanctions and increasing the level of penalties. As a result, there has been a surge in the number of insider trading cases since 2006. This body of cases provides insights into how the law has been interpreted and enforced in practice. It is found, for instance, that the ways of committing insider trading have become increasingly concealed and sophisticated, making it more difficult for regulators to detect, and that a majority of insider trading cases have occurred in the context of M&A.

Despite the recent progress on the enforcement front, more needs to be done. Apart from the obvious suggestion to give more resources to the regulator, the issues of regulatory independence and accountability must be properly addressed in order to ensure the integrity and efficacy of public enforcement. This is particularly important in a transitional and emerging market like China where the rule of law is yet to be fully established. On the other hand, private enforcement is an integral part of the enforcement picture, no matter how important it is relative to public enforcement. It is particularly important in China as it may help to mitigate the issues of regulatory independence and accountability. At present, however, private civil suits against insider trading are operating in a legal limbo due to the lack of implementing rules. Finally, apart from ex post enforcement, it is also important to have in place an effective system of ex ante prevention, such as improving the legal regime for information disclosure and strengthening internal control systems of relevant entities to prevent inside information being abused.

17. Punishing possession—China's all-embracing insider trading enforcement regime
Nicholas Calcina Howson

I. INTRODUCTION

The domestic capital markets of the People's Republic of China ("PRC" or "China") have come a very long way in just over two decades. With an initial market capitalization of just US$ 2 billion in 1991,[1] by the first quarter of 2011 the aggregate market capitalization of the more than 2000 issuers listed on the Shanghai and Shenzhen stock exchanges exceeded US$ 4.2 trillion, a sum that excludes the market capitalization of PRC-domiciled or offshore-domiciled but PRC-controlled issuers listing on foreign exchanges.[2]

It is therefore no wonder that the world's attention has fixed on the Chinese securities markets, paralleling an awed fascination with the PRC's unprecedented economic growth over three decades. Notwithstanding this impressive expansion of domestic exchanges and Chinese issuer participation in the global capital markets, the building and staffing of a securities regulatory system from scratch, and the rise of a relatively autonomous Chinese financial press, the Chinese markets continue to be plagued by volatility and dysfunction. One of the most widely acknowledged problems is securities fraud, specifically insider trading, which has been pervasive in the Chinese markets since the establishment of the Shanghai and Shenzhen exchanges in 1990–91.[3]

Insider trading takes many forms in the PRC. Certainly the classic situation—where insiders use non-public material information from and regarding their own company to trade in the stock of that company prior to an announcement affecting the market price of that company's securities—occurs very frequently. The case against insiders at Zhejiang Hangxiao Steel Structure Co., Ltd. is an example. In the period after a March 2007 announcement of a large infrastructure contract won by the firm in Angola, the company's stock rose 150 percent. Insiders who purchased before the announcement and sold afterwards were to said to have profited by over US$ 5 million. The big Angola contract

---

[1]   Or 10.8 billion renminbi yuan ("RMB") at the official 1991 RMB:US$ exchange rate of 5.32:1. See Feng Wei, The Shanghai and Shenzhen Exchanges: Business Operation, Governance Structure and Regulatory Function (Asian Development Bank, 2000), at 332 (Table 20-1), available at: http://www.adb.org/documents/books/demutualization_stock_exchanges/chapter_20.pdf (last visited Dec. 1, 2012).

[2]   See KPMG and FTSE Group, China's Capital Markets: The Changing Landscape, June 2011, available at: http://www.kpmg.com/cn/en/IssuesAndInsights/ArticlesPublications/Documents/China-Capital-Markets-FTSE-201106.pdf (last visited Dec. 1, 2012).

[3]   See: Ling Huawei, Qiao Xiaohui, Fu Tao & Hu Runfeng, Neimu Jiaoyi "Wenyi" [The Insider Trading "Plague"], 186 CAIJING, May 28, 2007, at 66–69 (hereinafter, "Insider Trading Plague"); and Shen Han, A Comparative Study of Insider Trading Regulation Enforcement in the U.S. and China, 9 J. Bus. & Sec. L. 41, 56–60 (2007).

proved to be fictitious, causing a huge price slump, but only after the insiders had dumped their pre-announcement purchases at the high end.[4] At the same time, a good deal of the activity commonly understood or reported as "insider trading" in China is more closely akin to securities trading manipulation by what the Chinese idiom broadly labels "[casino] dealers" (zhuangjia). For instance, "front running" by "rat-cellars" (laoshucang)—where mutual fund managers purchase the stock of an issuer before the fund they direct makes purchases of the same stock (triggering a price rise in the stock)—is also said to infect the high volume domestic securities fund industry. A variant of this is a common breaching of the state–private gap in China, where non-insider private fund managers are tipped by non-insider state-owned mutual funds that they are about to purchase a given issuer's stock, with an inevitable price rise upon the large state mutual funds' purchase becoming known (and the state tipper and private tippee splitting the extraordinary profits).[5] Accordingly, administrative enforcement actions and even criminal prosecutions for this kind of activity are effected pursuant to statutory prohibitions on "manipulative securities trading", and not "insider trading."

At the same time, enforcement against insider trading has been anemic. One author reviewing the period between 2002 and the end of 2006, or the period prior to the issuance of what this chapter calls the 2007 Insider Trading Guidance Provisions, notes the application of administrative sanctions by the China Securities Regulatory Commission ("CSRC") in 196 cases of securities fraud, only one of which (in 2004) relates to insider trading.[6] A review of the year in securities regulation for 2009 by Shanghai Stock Exchange officials[7] listed only six completed enforcement actions, but also noted wide press coverage of four other insider trading scandals involving government officials straddling political and economic power. Likewise, a close review of publicly announced enforcement decisions[8] by the CSRC shows few that are related to insider trading, and invariably only with respect to minor actors.

The reasons for this weak enforcement record are well known, and include: regulatory resource constraints; low levels of investigatory sophistication and deficient technical means; difficulties in contemporaneous detection and obtaining evidence;[9] the regulator's inability to act as a civil action plaintiff (and thus extract information and/or settlements

---

[4] See Insider Trading Plague, supra note 3, at 67. For similar breaches see also the Lin Shiquan and Liu Yang enforcement decisions infra.

[5] See Gady Epstein, "Market Maker," Forbes, Jan. 28, 2008, available at: http://www.forbes.com/global/2008/0128/050.html (last visited Dec. 1, 2012).

[6] See Han, supra note 3, at 57. See also Benjamin L. Liebman and Curtis J. Milhaupt, Reputational Sanctions in China's Securities Market, 108 Colum. L. Rev. 929, 942 (2010) (for 2001–06: "the number of [CSRC] sanctions seems rather modest given the ubiquity and severity of the problems with . . . insider trading . . . in China's stock markets").

[7] See Wu Weiying & Pu Lifen, 2009 Nian Zhongguo Zhengquan Fazhi Pingshu [2009 China Securities Rule of Law Commentary], 2 Zhengquan Fayuan [Securities Landscape] 361, 373–74 (2010).

[8] Posted continually at: http://www.csrc.gov.cn/pub/zjhpublic/index.htm?channel=3300/3313 (last visited Dec. 1, 2012).

[9] "With respect to the investigation of insider trading, [we] face two issues: difficulties in obtaining evidence and recognition . . .," May 2007 statement by a CSRC No.1 Enforcement Department official, Insider Trading Plague, supra note 3, at 66.

from market participants); constraints on the private civil action applicable across China's corporate law and securities law regimes; the uneven competence, autonomy and independence of China's judiciary; and—of overwhelming importance in the Chinese context—the political and economic power of some of the most flagrant violators, whether individuals or institutions. Some analysts even point to a conflict in the role of China's securities regulator, the CSRC: tasked on one side with the protection of investors and market transparency, and on the other side with "provid[ing] the [state-owned enterprises] with preferential access to the financial resources of the capital market for the best interests of the government."[10]

Whatever the reasons for it, lackluster enforcement against insider trading in China can fuel a vicious circle: obstacles to robust enforcement can ensure that the costs of insider trading are minimal or non-existent, especially when compared with the benefits on offer, which in turn only encourages further insider trading in the Chinese markets.

II.   LEGAL AND REGULATORY NORMS FOR INSIDER TRADING IN THE PRC

The legal and regulatory norms governing insider trading have developed quickly in the PRC, and concurrent with (or sometimes even before) the formal, legal, establishment of the PRC's domestic capital markets and stock exchanges. With the establishment of China's first post-1949 exchanges, the governments of Shanghai (on November 27, 1990) and Shenzhen (on May 15, 1991) promulgated municipal-level "measures" that explicitly prohibited "insider trading" (neimu jiaoyi).[11] In April 1993, the State Council Securities Commission (SCSC)—the State Council department originally above the newly established CSRC—promulgated the first national regulation concerning securities issuance and trading, the Provisional Regulations on the Administration of Stock Issuance and Trading ("SCSC Issuance and Trading Regulations") which also explicitly prohibited "insider trading." That prohibition was echoed in the September 1993 Provisional Measures on Prohibiting Securities Fraud Behavior issued by the SCSC ("SCSC Securities Fraud Measures"). In October 1997, the national legislature of the PRC amended the Criminal Law to include the crime of "insider trading," but without any elaboration on the elements of this new crime (other than heightened mens rea-type requirements which work across the Criminal Law).

Only in 1999, with passage of the PRC's first Securities Law, was insider trading

---

[10]   Han, supra note 3, at 58 (pointing to the "quota" system discontinued more than a decade ago, and the continued presence of poorly performing state-owned enterprises listed on China's domestic capital markets). This author does not concur with Han Shen's notion of a conflicted CSRC, a view informed by almost 20 years of interaction with the CSRC and its officers.

[11]   See Article 39 of the November 27, 1990 Shanghaishi Zhengquan Jiaoyi Guanli Banfa [Shanghai Municipal Measures on the Administration of Securities Trading], and Article 43 of the May 15, 1991 Shenzhenshi Gupiao Faxing Yü Jiaoyi Guanli Zanxing Banfa [Shenzhen Municipal Interim Measures on the Administration of Stock Issuance and Trading]. The Chinese "neimu jiaoyi" for "insider trading" is a neologism that first entered China's regulatory lexicon in the October 1990 Provisional Measures on the Administration of Securities Companies [Zhengquan Gongsi Guanli Zanxing Banfa].

extensively described and prohibited in a non-criminal "law," a formulation largely carried over into the revised Securities Law effective on January 1, 2006 ("2006 PRC Securities Law"). The 2006 PRC Securities Law also contains related prohibitions on "short swing trading" and "manipulative securities trading."[12] The short swing profits rule is modeled on U.S. 1934 Securities Exchange Act, Section 16(b), and forces directors, supervisory board members, senior management and substantial shareholders (5 percent or above) to disgorge to the corporation profits arising from trading within a six month window. There are no scienter requirements or affirmative defenses under Chinese law for breach of the short swing trading prohibition. Company directors also have direct personal liability for entity short swing trading. Interestingly, if the company board does not seek such disgorgement, even after shareholder demand, the shareholders have a legal right to implement a kind of ad hoc derivative action, and sue for disgorgement "acting in the company's interest." (This is not to be confused with the PRC's corporate derivative action, also established in the 2006 PRC Company Law.)

On March 3, 2007, the CSRC conceived its internal "guidance document" (zhidaoxing wenjian) on the 2006 PRC Securities Law statutory prohibition on "insider trading," the (Provisional) Guide for the Recognition and Confirmation of Insider Trading Behavior in the Securities Markets ("Insider Trading Guidance Provisions").[13] The Insider Trading Guidance Provisions by their own terms are not "public," understood as a term of art under Chinese legislative and rule-making practice,[14] they are not posted on the CSRC website and are not included in any form of legislative or regulatory gazette, and therefore are not norms of which market participants have any formal notice. Moreover, they are not a species of any of the legally enforceable legal-regulatory norms permitted in the Chinese system. Instead, they are only non-legal and non-regulatory guidance directed to CSRC staff, subordinate securities regulatory bodies, and the Shanghai and Shenzhen exchanges regarding the application of law and the implementation of administrative enforcement.

Finally, on May 22, 2012 the Supreme People's Court and the Supreme People's Procuratorate of the PRC jointly released an "Explanation" governing the enforcement of China's statutory insider trading prohibition, but only with respect to criminal prosecutions ("Criminal Enforcement Explanation").[15]

---

[12]   2006 PRC Securities Law, Arts. 47 (short swing trading) and 77 (manipulative securities trading).

[13]   Zhongguo Zhengquan Jiandu Guanli Weiyuanhui Guanyu Yinfa "Zhengquan Shichang Caozong Xingwei Rending Zhiyin (Shixing)" Ji "Zhengquan Shichang Neimu Jiaoyi Xingwei Rending Zhiyin (Shixing)" De Tongzhi [Notice of the CSRC Regarding the Printing and Distribution of the "(Provisional) Guide for the Recognition and Confirmation of Manipulative Behavior in the Securities Markets" and the "(Provisional) Guide for the Recognition and Confirmation of Insider Trading Behavior in the Securities Markets"] (not promulgated but distributed internally by the CSRC, Mar. 27, 2007), available at: http://vip.chinalawinfo.com/ NewLaw2002/SLC/slc.asp?db=chl&gid=144622 (last visited Dec. 1, 2012) (a CSRC notice which distributes guidance provisions for both insider trading and manipulative securities trading (the latter actionable under Article 77 of the 2006 PRC Securities Law)).

[14]   They are, however, widely available, for instance on the subscriber on-line collection of Chinese laws and regulations ChinaLawInfo, available at: http://www.chinalawinfo.com.

[15]   Zuigao Renmin Fayuan, Zuigao Renmin Jianchayuan Guanyu Banli Neimu Jiaoyi, Xielu Neimu Xinxi Xingshi Anjian Juti Yingyong Falü Ruogan Wenti De Jieshi [Supreme People's Court, Supreme People's Procuratorate Explanation Regarding Certain Specific Law Application Issues in

III. INSIDER TRADING REGIME(S)

China's insider trading regulatory regime is plagued by contradictions which arise in two contexts: (1) within the formal provisions of the Securities Law itself; and (2) as between the system articulated in the statute, on the one hand, and as articulated and enforced via agency action of dubious legality, on the other. The latter conflict, between the 2006 PRC Securities Law regime and administrative enforcement under the 2007 Insider Trading Guidance Provisions which cuts the insider trading breach out of a whole new cloth, is the more pronounced—a problem implicitly recognized with the release of the Criminal Enforcement Explanation in May 2012, which attempts to draw at least criminal enforcement practice back within the bounds of the statutory scheme. As I will describe below, this second, non-law-based, structure authorizes enforcement of insider trading liability against mere possessors of non-public material information who happen to trade securities during an ex post-determined price-sensitive period. The 2006 PRC Securities Law, conversely, describes something closer to a "classical" or fiduciary duty-based theory of insider trading liability alongside a separate "misappropriation"-type basis. I have argued that the 2007 Insider Trading Guidance Provisions are void and unenforceable, and subject to legal challenge on their face or as applied.[16] Notwithstanding, because the CSRC enforces insider trading law in China pursuant to both sets of norms, in this chapter I examine the entirety of the PRC insider trading prohibition derived from both the 2006 Securities Law and the 2007 Insider Trading Guidance Provisions.

A. The Statutory Scheme

The 2006 PRC Securities Law addresses insider trading at eight places.[17] In U.S. jurisprudential terms, the regime introduced in the 2006 statute rejects the equal access theory while adhering to the *Cady, Roberts/Chiarella* line (but with defendants identified in the Securities Law or an authorized regulatory enactment), and adding an *O'Hagan*-like misappropriation basis.

Article 73 of the Securities Law prohibits (1) "persons with knowledge of inside information" and (2) those "who have illegally procured inside information," from "using" inside information to engage in securities trading activities. On a first view, the 2006 PRC Securities Law rejects the confines of a classical theory by broadening the scope of

---

the Handling of Criminal Cases of Insider Trading and the Communication of Inside Information] (passed by the Sup. People's Ct. Adjudication Comm. Oct. 31, 2011 and the Supreme People's Procuratorate Feb. 27, 2012, issued May 22, 2012), available at http://www.court.gov.cn/qwfh/sjfs/201205/t20120522_177170 (last visited Dec. 1, 2012).

[16] See Nicholas Calcina Howson, Enforcement Without Foundation? Insider Trading and China's Administrative Law Crisis, 60 Am. J. Comp. L. 955 (2012) (hereinafter "Enforcement Without Foundation").

[17] See 2006 PRC Securities Law, Arts. 5 (basic prohibition against insider trading), 47 (short swing trading by insiders), 73–76 (elaborated provisions on insider trading, analyzed here), 180 (power of CSRC to stop trading in suspect securities) and 202 (administrative penalties and measures). Criminal prosecution for the established crime of insider trading (at Article 180 of the PRC Criminal Law) is explicitly authorized at Article 231, while civil damages (and, perhaps, a private claim in damages) are given a legal basis in the final clause of Article 76.

defendants from status insiders to those who simply have knowledge of inside information. For scholars familiar with U.S. jurisprudence, this regime initially looks like the *SEC v. Texas Gulf Sulphur*[18] equal access theory expansion of *Cady, Roberts & Co.*,[19] which extended insider trading liability from corporate insiders to anyone in possession of non-public material information. (*Texas Gulf Sulphur* was subsequently cut back to the "classical" or fiduciary duty-based theory in *Chiarella v. United States*,[20] so that liability was narrowed to those in breach of a fiduciary or special relationship of trust and confidence with the trading counterparty.[21]) If this initial reading was accurate, the 2006 PRC Securities Law would have represented a significant departure from the earliest iterations of insider trading law in China, which addressed only the actions of formal status insiders in the style of *Cady, Roberts*.[22]

On closer inspection, however, the 2006 statute does no such thing, for Article 74 of the 2006 PRC Securities Law narrows the scope of possible defendants to "include" (baokuo) a roster of traditional company, market and regulatory insiders, and other persons stipulated in regulation by the CSRC. Those statutory persons with knowledge of insider information are: directors, supervisory board members and senior managers of the issuer; 5 percent or more shareholders of the company and its/their directors, supervisory board members and senior managers, and the actual controlling shareholders of the company and its/their directors, supervisory board members and senior managers; directors, supervisory board members and senior managers of companies controlled by the issuer (appropriately adjusted in the 2007 Insider Trading Guidance Provisions, Article 6(2)(ii), to mean: "the controlling shareholders of the issuer or listed company, other companies controlled by the actual control party, and their directors, supervisory board members and senior management"); people whose executive or staff position in the company provides access to inside information; CSRC staff and others who administer or regulate securities issuance and trading; and securities sponsors, underwriters, securities exchange personnel, securities registration personnel and securities service institution personnel (which presumably includes lawyers and accountants).

A critical question is whether the Chinese characters "baokuo" for "include" or "including" in Article 74 mean "including only" or "including without limitation." Increasingly, Chinese statutes follow contemporary Chinese language contractual drafting conventions, so that if the drafter seeks to codify the "including without limitation" idea, the character phrase "baokuo danbuxianyu" is used. That phrase is not employed in the 2006 statute. Accordingly, the effect of Article 74 is to limit the scope of insider trading defendants qua "persons with knowledge of inside information" to those persons or institutions listed in the article itself. In U.S. jurisprudential terms, the 2006 regime

---

[18]   SEC v. Texas Gulf Sulphur, 401 F.2d 833 (2d Cir. 1968), cert. denied 394 U.S. 976 (1969).

[19]   Cady, Roberts & Co., 40 S.E.C. 907 (1961).

[20]   Chiarella v. United States, 445 U.S. 222 (1980).

[21]   Outside of the tender offer context, where the equal access theory lives on in the U.S. Securities and Exchange Commission's 1934 Securities and Exchange Act Rule 14e-3, 17 C.F.R. § 240.14e-3.

[22]   See Article 81 of the SCSC Issuance and Trading Regulations, and Article 5 of the SCSC Securities Fraud Measures.

rejects the equal access theory while adhering to the *Cady, Roberts/Chiarella* line, with parties potentially liable identified in or via the Securities Law.

In direct tension with the 2006 PRC Securities Law declaration of fealty to classical insider trading doctrine at Article 74 are: (1) the second prong of Article 73 (read in conjunction with a phrase in Article 76); and (2) the significant delegation of regulatory authority to the CSRC in Article 74(vii).

The second prong of Article 73 along with one clause of Article 76 provides a separate misappropriation basis for insider trading. Those liable for insider trading sourced in misappropriation—described as "those who have illegally procured inside information" (feifa huoqu neimu xinxi de ren)—are identified separately from, and do not have to be in the class of, "persons with knowledge of inside information" enumerated in Article 74. In U.S. jurisprudential terms, this tracks the 1997 *United States v. O'Hagan*[23] innovation, creating an expanded basis of insider trading liability for traders who breach a fiduciary duty or other special relationship with the source of the inside information (recall that per *Chiarella* the special duty or relationship must be with the trading counterparty). In such cases, the government only needs to demonstrate: (1) "illegal procurement" of information; (2) that such information is "inside information"; (3) use of that inside information to trade; and (4) trading of securities (of an issuer related in some way to the information). There is no requirement that the people who engage in misappropriation and trading be members of the Article 74 enumerated class of "persons with knowledge of inside information."

The last clause of 2006 PRC Securities Law Article 74 authorizes the CSRC to identify by regulation "others" aside from the traditional insiders enumerated in Article 74(i)–(vi) as "persons with knowledge of inside information." (There was no need to instruct the CSRC to augment the scope of defendants guilty of misappropriation because there is no defined class of "persons who have illegally procured inside information.") Given the strong focus on statutorily enumerated insiders described above, the grant of regulatory authority to the CSRC in Article 74(vii) to widen the scope of "persons with knowledge of inside information" originally represented a very significant nod in the direction of loosening the under-inclusive list of insider trading defendants. It was also consistent with larger patterns in PRC legislative practice designed to allow a certain level of generality in law, while conferring significant discretion on administrative institutions.

In defining what the prohibited "use" of inside information is, the 2006 PRC Securities Law at Article 76 elaborates on the legal duties of (1) those "with knowledge of inside information", and (2) those who have misappropriated inside information, duties which again seem to track, in part, the U.S.-style, disclose or abstain from trading rule: people in possession of inside information (relevant to specific) securities trading are prohibited from (1) purchasing or selling that company's securities (2) disclosing such information, or (3) suggesting that others purchase or sell such securities, in each case at any time before such inside information is publicly disclosed. Article 76 of the 2006 PRC Securities Law—and specifically the clause prohibiting "suggesting that others purchase or sell such securities"—therefore forms an additional basis in Chinese law for insider trading liability, or what other jurisdictions call "tipper" liability. This liability exists even where the

---

[23]   United States v. O'Hagan, 521 U.S. 642 (1997).

defendant has not actually engaged in securities trading, though assuredly "used" inside information. Conversely, "tippees" are not subject to insider trading liability, at least insofar as they are not "persons with knowledge of inside information" per Article 74, or have not engaged in misappropriation of inside information under Articles 73 and 76.

The 2006 PRC Securities Law sets out a statutory definition of "inside information," while granting the CSRC authority to "recognize and confirm" other information that is inside information. In U.S. terms, the focus of these determinations is on the materiality (or "importance") of the information, and the degree to which it is public. The earliest definition of inside information under Chinese law came in 1993 at Article 5 of the SCSC Securities Fraud Measures, which stipulated that "inside information" consists of important (zhongda) non-public information known by traditional (status) insiders which might influence the price of securities traded in the market, but then also listed 25 other kinds of "important" information. Article 75 of the 2006 PRC Securities Law (largely tracking Article 69 of the 1999 PRC Securities Law) defines "inside information" broadly as: "non-public information relevant to a company's business or financial affairs or which may have a major (zhongda) effect on the market price of that company's securities." The Chinese character set "zhongda," translated here as "important" or "major," can be understood as the equivalent of "material." There is a much theoretical writing in the PRC on how to evaluate "importance" (zhongdaxing) or materiality, including a focus on standards objective (did the information in fact have a significant effect on price?) and subjective (would or did the information impact the decisions of a normal or reasonable investor?).[24] There is no indication that these considerations are employed in actual enforcement.

Article 75 then lists items that are deemed to be inside information, including a cross-reference to the Securities Law Article 67(2) list of major events subject to U.S. Securities and Exchange Commission (SEC) Form 8-K-like continuing disclosure. These items include: (1) the major (zhongda) events listed in Article 67(2) of the 2006 PRC Securities Law; (2) company plans for distribution of dividends or increase of registered capital; (3) major changes in the company's capital structure; (4) major changes in the company's debt security/guaranties; (5) any single mortgage, sale or write-off of a major business asset of the company which exceeds 30 percent of the (value of) the asset; (6) potential liability for major damages to be assumed under law as a result of behavior by a company's directors, supervisory board members or senior management personnel; (7) plans related to the acquisition of a listed company; and (8) other important (zhongyao) information recognized and confirmed by the CSRC to have a significant effect (xuanzhu yingxiang) on the trading price of securities. The cross-reference to Article 67(2) of the 2006 PRC Securities Law imports the following items into the statutory definition of "inside information": (1) a major change in a company's business program or scope of business; (2) a decision by the company regarding a major investment or asset disposition; (3) conclusion by the company of an important (zhongyao) contract which may produce a significant (zhongyao) effect on the company's assets, liabilities, rights and

---

[24]   See for example: Ye Lin, Neimu Jiaoyi De Falü Guanzhi [The Insider Trading Legal Regime], in ZHENGQUANFA JIAOCHENG [SECURITIES LAW] 314–15 (Ye Lin, Duan Wei, Wang Shihua & Wang Huajie, eds., 2010).

interests or business results; (4) the company's incurrence of a major debt or default on a significant (zhongda) debt that is past due; (5) a major deficit or losses incurred by the company; (6) a major change in the external conditions affecting production or business of the company; (7) a change in the chairman of the board, or not less than one third of the directors or the manager of the company; (8) a relatively significant (jiaoda) change in the holdings or control of shareholders who hold 5 percent or more of the company's shares or the company's controlling shareholders; (9) a decision by the company to reduce its registered capital, to merge, split or dissolve, or to file bankruptcy; (10) (information relating to) major litigation involving the company, or voiding or declaration of non-effectiveness under law of a shareholders' meeting or board resolution; (11) the establishment of a criminal investigation regarding the company or where judicial institutions have taken criminal enforcement measures against company directors, supervisory board members or senior management personnel; and (12) other events stipulated in regulation by the CSRC. Only item (11), criminal investigation or criminal enforcement against company officials, is new when compared with the same definitional clause in the 1999 PRC Securities Law.

The significant aspect of this statutory definition of inside information is the two bites of the apple given to the CSRC. First, the catch-all delegation of authority to the CSRC at Article 75(viii) allows the securities regulator to "recognize and confirm" other important information that has "a significant effect" on the trading price of securities. Secondly, the cross-reference in Article 75(i) to Article 67(2)(xii) of the 2006 PRC Securities Law gives the CSRC authority to stipulate in regulation other important (zhongda) events that can be imported into the definition of inside information. These two invitations, different in nature (one allows mere "recognition and confirmation," the other requires "stipulation in regulation"), are taken up with gusto in the 2007 Insider Trading Guidance Provisions described below.

At this stage of exposition, it is important to note two things about Article 75 and the definition of inside information: First, the statutory provisions give meaning to a specific defined term—"inside information" (neimu xinxi)—which is one of the elements neces-sary to make out insider trading liability under Articles 73, 74 and 76 of the 2006 PRC Securities Law. Secondly, neither Article 75 nor any other statutory provision alludes to a "price-sensitive period." Each of these aspects will become important in the analysis of the 2007 Insider Trading Guidance Provisions, below, where the term "inside informa-tion" is a defined term used in a completely different architecture of the insider trading prohibition, and certain information becomes actionable "inside information" only when those in possession of it trade during a "price-sensitive period."

In sum, the statutory forms of Articles 73–76 of the 2006 PRC Securities Law—if undisturbed by the subsequent 2007 Insider Trading Guidance Provisions—create a system whereby only specifically enumerated traders may have liability, a structure which can be both overbroad and under-inclusive.

It is potentially overbroad given the clear liability for innocent traders who are part of the Article 74 enumerated class and who trade while merely in possession of statutorily defined inside information. One aspect of the over-broadness problem, at least with respect to liability for "persons with knowledge of inside information," is the failure of Chinese law to require any scienter or breach of duty on the part of those in possession of inside information who trade in the relevant securities before public disclosure of the information. (This problem does not apply to those who have misappropriated inside information under Articles 73 and 76, as their illegal procurement of inside information serves as an adequate proxy for fault or breach. Nor does this critique apply to the crime of insider trading under Article 231 of the Securities Law, Article 180 of the PRC Criminal Law and the 2012 Criminal Enforcement Explanation, which requires some showing of intentionality, interpreted as actual intent or recklessness.[25]) This raises the very strong possibility of strict liability for certain individuals who trade innocently in the relevant securities while they happen to be in possession of inside information. Professor Huang Hui, also the author of a chapter on the PRC in this volume, has attempted to imply something less draconian than strict liability when writing about the analogous provisions of the 1999 PRC Securities Law. He understands the defendant's "knowledge that the possessed information is material and non-public" as a necessary element[26] in establishing the case, and further divines a necessary causal link between the defendant insider's position and the acquisition of information, such that "persons with knowledge of inside information" are prohibited from trading only if they have access to the information because of their connection with the company whose securities are affected, by virtue of their office or profession.[27] Professor Huang seems to conjure critical elements out of thin air: what he understands as a kind of breach of duty/scienter "lite" element and what he later calls a "causal link" between trader status and "acquisition" (or even possession) of information. This effort to read some kind of intentionality requirement into the statute ultimately fails,[28] and it is instead clear that—at least insofar as the statute is concerned—there is strict liability for the 2006 PRC Securities Law Article 74 enumerated persons who happen to possess inside information at the time they trade in securities of the company.

The structure is under-inclusive for traders not part of the Article 74 enumerated class but who trade on statutorily defined "inside information," even apparently "tippers" alluded to in Article 76 (unless such "tippers" are also guilty of misappropriation). Two other kinds of transactions, punished by almost any coherent insider trading enforcement regime, fall outside of the Article 73–76 system: (1) "tippee" trading; and (2) where an individual who acts as the financial advisor to an acquiring company trades in the stock of a listed target (defined here in short form as "tippees" and "M&A advisors" respectively). In neither case (and other than tippees or M&A advisors who have also engaged in misappropriation) is there any basis for the assertion of insider trading liability against such persons trading on non-public material information under the 2006 PRC Securities Law. "Tippees" are exculpated because Article 76 only prohibits "tipping" (although "tippees" would have liability if coincidentally members of the Article 74 enumerated class of persons with knowledge of inside information, or their gaining the tip involved

---

[25]   PRC Criminal Law, Art. 14. Merely negligent behavior is only subject to criminal prosecution when the Criminal Law explicitly says so. Id., Art. 15.

[26]   See Hui Huang, The Regulation of Insider Trading in China: A Critical Review and Proposals for Reform, 17 Austl. J. Corp. L. 281, 291–92 (2005).

[27]   Id. at 294–95.

[28]   As Professor Huang also recognizes: "This issue ["possession versus use"] is largely ignored in China ... the issue deserves careful attention, particularly given the stiff liability of insider trading." Id. at 292.

some kind of misappropriation of inside information). "M&A advisors" (again, unless guilty of misappropriation) are also not liable because they are outside of the enumerated class of traders listed in Article 74, as they are not employed at the company which issues the traded stock.

B. The Agency's Parallel and Conflicting Enforcement Regime

The CSRC evidently created the 2007 Insider Trading Guidance Provisions in response to the invitation at Article 74(vii) of the 2006 PRC Securities Law (and the more suitable invitation at Article 75(viii) of the same statute, calling for CSRC "recognition and confirmation" of important information that has a significant effect on securities' trading prices). However, the job was botched badly, with the CSRC issuing non-administrative regulatory norms of doubtful legality[29] that far exceed the statutory invitation.[30] While the Insider Trading Guidance Provisions do widen very significantly the defined scope of "people with knowledge of inside information" under Article 74, they then go many steps further to recast entirely insider trading in China and create new and additional bases for liability, far beyond that ever contemplated in China's 2006 Securities Law. The result, in U.S. jurisprudential terms, is non-public guidance—not law or administrative regulation—that provides for a *Texas Gulf Sulphur* theory of liability targeting anyone simply in possession of inside information who trades. Recall that the 2006 PRC Securities Law provides for a much narrower version of liability, applicable only to specific insiders identified in, or pursuant to, the statute, plus what aspires to be liability connected to misappropriation.

How do the 2007 Guidance Provisions accomplish this wholesale restructuring of PRC insider trading law? Article 12 of the Insider Trading Guidance Provisions (under a Section IV entitled "The Recognition and Confirmation of Insider Trading Behavior") ignores entirely the statutory scheme and sets forth a brand new architecture establishing the elements of insider trading, as follows:

Article 12: Securities trading activity that conforms to the following conditions shall constitute insider trading:
(1) the person undertaking the behavior is an insider;
(2) the information involved is inside information;
(3) the subject person buys or sells related securities during the price-sensitive period of the inside information, or suggests that other persons buy or sell related securities, or reveals the information.

---

[29]   See Enforcement Without Foundation, supra note 16. This problem is apparent in other key areas of PRC regulation and enforcement. See Wei Cui, What is the "Law" in Chinese Tax Administration? 19:1 Asia Pac. L. Rev. 75 (2011) (regarding the issuance and application of ultra vires tax "circulars" by the PRC Ministry of Finance and the State Taxation Administration, and the latter's 2010 regulation designed to legalize tax rule-making).

[30]   By their explicit terms, the Guidance Provisions apply to trading of publicly issued and stock exchange-listed securities (Article 4(2)), and are to be "referred to" with respect to insider trading identified at other State Council-approved trading venues. This limitation does not amount to much, as all insider trading enforcement actions are with respect to securities traded on the Shanghai and Shenzhen exchanges (and might only be useful as a defense for state-owned enterprise insiders and political cadres illegally and personally trading in non-listed, non-tradable shares in listed PRC issuers, whose actions bring other bases for liability).

This formulation is at substantial variance with, and goes far beyond, the insider trading regime as it is defined in Articles 73–76 of the 2006 PRC Securities Law described above.

The Insider Trading Guidance Provisions at Articles 5 and 6 create a new defined term, "insider" (neimuren), which term does not appear in the 2006 PRC Securities Law. The Securities Law never mentions, or addresses the liability of, "insiders," but only "persons with knowledge of inside information," people guilty of misappropriation, and either of the foregoing who tip others. The Insider Trading Guidance Provisions, authorized to elaborate the class of persons included in the category of "persons with knowledge of inside information," do exactly the opposite at Article 6(1) and reverse-merge the 2006 PRC Securities Law Article 74(i)–(vi) statutory list of "persons with knowledge of inside information" into the Guidance Provisions-created category of "insiders." The statutorily ungrounded definition of "insider" is then further expanded in Articles 6(2)–(5) of the Provisions to include:

- the issuer (as a "person with knowledge of inside information");
- the controlling shareholder of the issuer, entities controlled by the actual control party of the issuer, and their respective directors, supervisory board members and senior management (as "persons with knowledge of inside information");
- any party involved in a listed company's merger, acquisition or reorganization and their relevant personnel (as "persons with knowledge of inside information");
- persons who gain inside information in the performance of their work (as "persons with knowledge of inside information");
- the partners and spouses of those natural persons included in Article 74(i)–(vi) of the Securities Law (i.e., the statutorily defined "persons with knowledge of inside information");
- the parents or children or other relatives of any natural persons included in the above categories who come into possession of inside information;
- those who employ illegal methods such as trickery, coaxing, eavesdropping, monitoring, secret trading etc. to gain inside information;
- those who gain inside information through other channels.

Finally, Article 5 of the Insider Trading Guidance Provisions stipulates that such insiders may be legal persons as well as natural persons. Perhaps most egregiously expansive in the new formulation is the substance of Article 6(5) of the Guidance Provisions, the last bullet above, which deems anyone "who gains inside information through other channels" to be an "insider" for enforcement purposes. This is tantamount to declaring that trading while in mere possession of inside information (and during a price-sensitive period) is a basis for insider trading liability in the PRC.

As noted above, Article 75 of the 2006 PRC Securities Law defines "inside information" and lists items that are deemed to be inside information. The statute also delegates to the CSRC the power to "recognize and confirm" other important information that has "a significant effect on the trading price of securities." The CSRC's 2007 Insider Trading Guidance Provisions respond to this delegation, but in a way that looks past the statute. Most importantly, the Guidance Provisions define "inside information" not for the 2006 PRC Securities Law (and Articles 73, 74 and 76 which invoke use of such information as an element to make out the breach), but instead under the Guidance Provisions, and specifically the new and independent invocation of "inside information" in the Article 12 prohibition set forth above. Thus, instead of using the Guidance Provisions to fill out the meaning of the statute, the Guidance Provisions use the statute to fill out, in part, the meaning of a newly employed term in the Provisions. Article 7 of the Provisions changes ever so slightly the general definition of "inside information" in the preamble to Article 75 of the Securities Law, stating that "inside information" under the Provisions means "non-public[31] information relevant to a company's business or financial affairs or which may have a major effect on the market price of *a* company's securities. . . ." Compare this formulation with the Securities Law Article 75 language, which focuses on information that may have a "major effect on the market price of *that* [gai] company's securities." This very small difference may be designed to facilitate CSRC enforcement against defendants who trade in the securities other than firms where they are classical insiders, such as the insider trading M&A advisors described above.

At Article 8, the Provisions then reverse-merge 2006 PRC Securities Law Article 67(2) (piggy-backing onto Article 67(2)(xii)'s delegation to the CSRC of all Form 8-K-type events which have a "relatively significant" effect on the securities price), Article 75(ii)– (vii) and Article 75(viii)'s delegation of the power to determine "inside information" into the Provisions' own definition of "inside information." Further, the Provisions at Article 8(5) declare simply that inside information under the same Guidance Provisions is "other important information that has a significant effect (xuanzhu yingxiang) on the trading price of securities"—which language tracks exactly the precise delegation made to the CSRC under Article 75(viii) of the 2006 PRC Securities Law. In conversational terms, the statute authorizes the regulator to "define X to include whatever the regulator thinks has the properties of Y," and the regulator responds with "We hereby define X to include whatever we think has the properties of Y," without elaboration. In short, the Guidance Provisions here do not sharpen or define the CSRC's enforcement power in any signifi- cant way, and instead offer somewhat tautological expressions of authority and coverage. Happily, the Guidance Provisions at Article 9 do state what information that has "a sig- nificant effect on trading prices of securities" means: in normal circumstances, informa- tion that immediately upon disclosure and for a specified period causes the company's trading price to depart significantly from the market index or the index for like issuers, or that causes significant volatility in the broad market index.

Finally, Article 10 of the 2007 Insider Trading Guidance Provisions injects a totally new concept into the determination of what "inside information" is, such that specific information becomes actionable only when those in possession of it trade securities during a "price-sensitive period." That period is defined in the Insider Trading Guidance Provisions to extend from the time when the inside information begins to be constituted to the moment when the information no longer has an effect on securities prices (the definition is further refined in the 2012 Criminal Enforcement Explanation with the elaboration of yet another new legal term with no statutory basis, "inside information sensitive period"). This new concept is the result of a drafting difference between the 2006 PRC Securities Law and the 2007 Insider Trading Guidance Provisions. As noted above, Article 76 of the Law states that people with knowledge of inside information relevant to specific securities are prohibited from doing certain things before such inside information

---

[31]   The meaning of "public" is defined at Article 11 of the Insider Trading Guidance Provisions.

is "publicly disclosed." Article 12(3) of the Guidance Provisions changes that prohibition to apply to a "price-sensitive period" (jiage mingan qi), which is not bounded by the moment such information becomes "publicly disclosed." Instead, the CSRC Guidance Provisions extinguish traders' legal obligations at the moment when "the information no longer has an effect on securities prices"—a time very difficult for any trader in possession of inside information to determine with certainty.

In sum, the 2007 Insider Trading Guidance Provisions explode the bounds of the 2006 PRC Securities Law. Whereas under the 2006 Law only a narrowly defined class of "persons with knowledge of inside information" or those who engaged in misappropriation (acting directly or as tippers) could be liable for specifically defined insider trading, under the CSRC's 2007 Guidance Provisions any person simply in possession of information (and thus an "insider" under the Provisions) that is determined to be "inside information" who "purchases or sells relevant securities, or suggests that another purchase or sell such securities, or communicates such inside information" during a "price-sensitive period" is liable for insider trading.[32]

The result is a kind of strict liability under the Insider Trading Guidance Provisions for anyone trading in securities when deemed to be in possession of inside information and during a price-sensitive period. To be fair, the liability is not absolutely strict, as the same Guidance Provisions introduce a scienter-like requirement—"whether or not [the defendant] knew or was informed of [zhicai] inside information"—but only for: (1) "the parents or children or other relatives of any natural persons" included in the expanded scope of "persons with knowledge of inside information" in the 2007 Guidance Provisions;[33] and (2) "those who employ illegal methods such as trickery, coaxing, eavesdropping, monitoring, secret trading, etc. to gain inside information" and "those who gain inside information through other channels."[34] This will be cold comfort for the huge class of other potential defendants, for at the same time the 2007 Guidance Provisions make insider trading liability only stricter for: (1) the "persons with knowledge of inside information" originally listed in the 2006 PRC Securities Law at Article 74(i)–(vi); and (2) the expanded scope of such persons, reversing the burden of proof so that such defendants will be liable for insider trading during the price-sensitive period unless "they have sufficient evidence to demonstrate that they did not know or were not informed of inside information."[35]

How do these major differences between the statute and CSRC enforcement "guidance" work out in potential application to culpable trading? Here I give two examples. First, "tippees" (as defined above) who are not guilty of misappropriation and who trade during the price-sensitive period would be liable under the CSRC Insider Trading

---

[32]   It should be noted that the Provisions, at Article 19, provide diverse bases for exculpation, ranging from blanket exculpation (e.g., stock buy-backs or transactions pursuant to triggered mandatory offers) to knowledge defenses and even the broad discretion of the CSRC.

[33]   Limited to: the securities issuer; the controlling shareholder of the issuer, companies controlled by the actual control party of the issuer, and their respective directors, supervisory board members and senior management; any party involved in a listed company's merger, acquisition or reorganization and their relevant personnel; and persons who gain inside information in the performance of their work.

[34]   Insider Trading Guidance Provisions, Art. 14(2).

[35]   Id.

Guidance Provisions, although not under the 2006 PRC Securities Law. Likewise, M&A advisors (as defined above) consulting for an acquirer and trading in the shares of a target company during a price-sensitive period would be liable for insider trading under the CSRC Guidance Provisions, but not under the Securities Law. To be very clear, the issue is not that the CSRC has broadened the scope of "persons with knowledge of inside information" under Article 74 of the 2006 PRC Securities Law, something that agency was perfectly entitled to do. Instead, the problem is that the CSRC has created a whole new class of defendants—outside of "persons with knowledge of inside information" and those guilty of misappropriation (acting directly or as "tippers")—called "insiders" who can now be exposed to serious liability if they trade during a price-sensitive period with respect to any securities (i.e., not the securities of the company relevant to their status), and with a new burden of proof which almost assures their guilt (unless they can prove a negative, that they did not know or were not informed of the inside information).

IV.   SANCTIONS AND PENALTIES

Insider trading prohibitions in the PRC are enforced through administrative and criminal penalties. There is a question as to the grounds for a private right of action in damages for other market participants.

Article 202 of the 2006 PRC Securities Law provides the basis for administrative enforcement and penalties, which include: disposition of the illegally traded securities, confiscation of illegal proceeds, and the levy of administrative fines ranging from one to five times illegal proceeds. The Insider Trading Guidance Provisions, at Articles 21–23, describe how the CSRC calculates "proceeds." Articles 24 and 25 of the Provisions present guidelines for CSRC determination of the relative severity of administrative sanctions. (Provision is also made for penalizing traders who do not realize gains from illegal insider trading, or only de minimus gains.) Fines and warnings may also be levied on or directed at natural persons involved with insider trading by legal entities. Personnel from securities regulatory institutions who engage in insider trading are subject to the heaviest administrative penalties. Article 180 of the PRC Criminal Law (buttressed by the 2006 PRC Securities Law's Article 231) provides for criminal penalties against insider trading, including imprisonment for up to ten years and criminal fines (one to five times illegal proceeds). As noted above, in May 2012 criminal enforcement of the insider trading prohibition was sharply narrowed with issuance of the Supreme People's Court and the Supreme People's Procuratorate joint Criminal Enforcement Explanation, which reasserts the 2006 PRC Securities Law limitation on "persons with knowledge of inside information" as only those listed in Article 74 of the statute and elaborates slightly on what constitutes misappropriation and tipping of inside information.

The grounds for a private civil action, difficult in any case given causation and reliance elements and the competence of China's developing judiciary, are a bit murkier under PRC law. Article 207 of the superseded 1999 PRC Securities Law referred to "civil damages" arising in connection with insider trading, but made no mention as to how any victim of a defendant's adjudicated insider trading might sue for such damages. There is a similar, if stronger, hint of a private claim at Article 76 of the 2006 PRC Securities Law, which holds: "Where investors have experienced losses from insider trading behavior, the [inside] traders should bear compensation liability in accordance with law." (The same clause appears at Article 77 with respect to manipulative securities trading.) However, there is no further elaboration of, or legal basis for, a private civil claim in the 2006 PRC Securities Law, which means that Chinese victims of someone else's insider trading would have to rely on a private suit in tort (or "rights infringement" (qinquan) under the PRC system) or possibly contract. Any effort by PRC plaintiffs to make out such a claim would very likely be met with a denial by the Chinese judiciary because of the absence of a clear "legal basis" (falü yiju) in statute for the claim. As one authoritative PRC securities law specialist concludes, "thus there is still no way to fully protect the compensation [rights] for investors who are harmed by insider trading behavior."[36]

V.   ENFORCEMENT AGAINST INSIDER TRADING PURSUANT TO STATUTE AND "GUIDANCE"

In specific insider trading enforcement actions, the CSRC is generally conforming to its reputation for seriousness of purpose, technical competence and independence. For instance, the agency is rapidly developing a kind of insider trading-specific "common law" addressing complex issues of legal presumption, burdens of proof and scienter.[37] Yet, from a higher level, the CSRC is engaging in enforcement behavior which is arguably extra-legal: for, regardless of the clear conflict between the two regulatory structures described in statute, on the one hand (modified "classical" plus *O'Hagen* misappropriation), and internal agency "guidance," on the other (*Texas Gulf Sulphur* or mere possession of material, non-public information while trading), the CSRC is actively enforcing insider trading liability under the extremely broad theory promised by the defective 2007 Insider Trading Guidance Provisions, and in situations where the explicit terms of the 2006 PRC Securities Law do not provide for liability. PRC academics note this,[38] and a glance at the most recent enforcement decisions posted on the CSRC website confirms the problem.

A 2011 enforcement decision[39] shows how liberally the CSRC mis-applies Article 74 of the PRC 2006 Securities Law, in that the defendant is pronounced "a person with knowledge of inside information" simply because he "participated in . . . [the reverse-merger]

---

[36]   Ye, supra note 24, at 312.

[37]   See Wu & Pu, supra note 7, at 374 (describing CSRC jurisprudence in 2009 regarding: burden of proof on a trader's defense that alleged inside information was developed from independent analysis; definition of "knowing" (or should have known) inside information; liability for traders who engage in insider trading only to incur losses and thus have no proceeds from breach; and the evidentiary approach to use of proxy accounts for insider trading).

[38]   Ye, supra note 24, at 319. ("The [Insider Trading Guidance Provisions] clearly stipulate that where insider trading with respect to any exchange-issued or -listed securities is identified, the Guidance Provisions are to be applied. If insider trading is identified on any other State Council-approved securities exchange, enforcement is to be implemented with reference to the Guidance Provisions.")

[39]   See Zhongguo Zhengjianhui Xingzheng Chufa Juedingshu (Liu Yang) [China Securities Regulatory Commission Administrative Punishment Decision (Liu Yang)] (2011) No. 24, issued June 14, 2011.

related affairs." This is not the same thing provided for under Article 74(iv) ("persons who are able to obtain relevant inside information concerning the company by virtue of the position they hold in the company"), which is unavailable precisely because the defendant comes into possession of important information about a company—the target—different from the one he is employed at. Nor does the CSRC make any effort to base his liability in the misappropriation prong of the statute. The CSRC is clearly relying upon the wider basis for insider trading liability provided in the 2007 Insider Trading Guidance Provisions.

In another 2011 enforcement action,[40] the CSRC does not indicate how the defendant qualifies as one of the persons enumerated in Article 74 of the 2006 PRC Securities Law, concluding simply that he became a "person with knowledge of inside information." He is not identified as an officer or shareholder of the selling controlling shareholder of the issuer, although he is identified as the top executive of another entity which may be a shareholder of the issuer holding more than 5 percent of the issuer per Article 74(ii) of the Securities Law. Nowhere in the decision does the CSRC feel the need to articulate how this defendant qualifies as a "person with knowledge of inside information," or if he is guilty of misappropriation of the information, no doubt because they are relying upon the broader basis for insider trading liability provided for in the 2007 Insider Trading Guidance Provisions.

In a standard 2010 husband–wife/tipper–tippee case,[41] the CSRC simply declares the husband/tipper to be a "person with knowledge of inside information" without tying his status to the enumerated persons under Article 74. Nor does the CSRC independently identify him as a person guilty of misappropriation under Articles 73 and 76. He may be a tipper of non-public material information, but because he is neither a "person with knowledge of inside information" nor guilty of misappropriation, technically he is not subject to the tipping prohibition under Article 76. Thus, as a person who has merely come into possession of inside information, it is unclear how he is an insider trading defendant under the 2006 PRC Securities Law, unless the CSRC is using the broad basis for enforcement provided for under the 2007 Insider Trading Guidance Provisions. Secondly, the wife is a tippee-trader of inside information, and again there is no connection between her possession of the information and any kind of misappropriation. She is therefore not an appropriate defendant under the 2006 PRC Securities Law, and the only way in which the CSRC can accomplish enforcement against her is via the 2007 Insider Trading Guidance Provisions.

There remains a question as to whether the PRC People's Procuratorate was or is using the extra-legal coverage of the Insider Trading Guidance Provisions to establish the elements of the crime of insider trading via Article 180 of the PRC Criminal Law, thereby resulting in the imprisonment of certain persons. The real picture of criminal enforcement of the insider trading prohibition and Article 180 of the Criminal Law is obscured because

---

[40] See Zhongguo Zhengjianhui Xingzheng Chufa Juedingshu (Lin Shiquan) [China Securities Regulatory Commission Administrative Punishment Decision (Lin Shiquan)] (2011) No. 26, issued June 29, 2011.

[41] See Zhongguo Zhengjianhui Xingzheng Chufa Juedingshu (Jia Huazhang and Liu Rong) [China Securities Regulatory Commission Administrative Punishment Decision (Jia Huazhang and Liu Rong)] (2010) No. 53, issued Dec. 21, 2010.

criminal judgments are not publicized or reasoned in the way civil and administrative law cases increasingly are. Instead, criminal defendants are simply reported to be guilty of "insider trading" and then subject to criminal punishment. Given the CSRC's very cavalier attitude toward extra-legal insider trading enforcement, it is not unreasonable to think that the People's Procuratorate—as advised by the expert agency charged with enforcement, the CSRC—has also used the defective Guidance Provisions in the criminal sphere. This is certainly the implication of the rather sudden release of the 2012 Criminal Enforcement Explanation, which strongly reasserts the primacy of the statutory architecture over the unbounded 2007 Insider Trading Guidance Provisions in respect of criminal prosecutions.

VI.   CONCLUSION

The foregoing analysis tells us that the CSRC is presently enforcing the 2006 PRC Securities Law prohibitions on insider trading not in accordance with the narrow theory set out in the Securities Law itself, but pursuant to the very expansive theory that lives through the ultra vires 2007 Insider Trading Guidance Provisions. Stuck with a statutory scheme that looks like a loose assemblage of the *Cady, Roberts*/*Chiarella* line and *O'Hagen* misappropriation, the Chinese securities regulator nonetheless wields a stick that tracks the broad enforcement regime implied in *Texas Gulf Sulphur*. It is also highly likely that the PRC public prosecutor has used the defective Insider Trading Guidance Provisions as the sole basis for enforcement of the crime of insider trading in cases where the alleged behavior of defendants does not come within the scope of the 2006 PRC Securities Law and the PRC Criminal Law. If nothing else, examples of extra-legal enforcement in the administrative sphere demonstrate clear violations of the 1996 Law of the PRC on Administrative Punishments, which forbids the imposition of administrative punishments without a statutory basis, makes invalid administrative punishments imposed not in accordance with law, and forbids the imposition of administrative punishment under law other than in accordance with publicly promulgated norms. Extra-legal enforcement in the criminal sphere is only more problematic, and contrary to a number of key Chinese laws and policy statements, from the PRC Law on Legislation to the PRC Constitution.

Interestingly, the serious problem of illegality and mismatch regarding insider trading enforcement described in this chapter does not pertain with respect to the separate prohibition against "manipulative securities trading" under Article 77 of the 2006 PRC Securities Law. For such manipulation, the CSRC is perfectly in compliance with the law in providing mere "guidance" for enforcement,[42] because Article 77 is drafted at a high level of generality, Article 77(iv) provides a broad catch-all against "other methods" of manipulation with no specific required elements to make out "manipulation" (such as scienter, purchase or sale of securities, etc.), and the statute makes no affirmative delegation of regulatory power to the CSRC or any other agency. Accordingly, the CSRC is free under the statute to enforce against such manipulative trading in any way it determines,

---

[42]   Which it did at the same time it issued the defective Insider Trading Guidance Provisions in 2007.

and without reference to any notified or universally applicable administrative law norm—something I argue it cannot do with respect to insider trading.

Some, noting the anemic enforcement against rampant insider trading in the Chinese capital markets and less attuned to legal niceties in a transitional legal system, may see extra-legal and over-broad enforcement by the PRC securities regulator or the public prosecutor as a positive phenomenon. How else, other than by the most aggressive and far-reaching enforcement design and practice, can the Chinese regulator punish brazen violators whose virtually costless behavior only fuels the vicious circle that leads to ever-increasing insider trading and market manipulation? After all, they point out, many of the people made insider trading defendants are in fact guilty of trading on non-public material information, even if their behavior does not breach the narrowly drawn statutory prohibition.

Others, even if they do not overly object to the legal infirmities of the CSRC Guidance Provisions-based enforcement regime, will recognize that the illegality of insider trading enforcement norms casts a significant shadow over the PRC securities regulator's ability to govern China's capital markets, and thereby ensure the perceived transparency and information symmetry critical to sustaining investor confidence and participation. Any successful legal challenge to administrative or criminal enforcement of the insider trading prohibitions by defendants would constitute a body blow to the regulator's hard-earned reputation for competence, regulatory power and technical sophistication, and confirm what many small investors already understand as the unlevel playing field characterizing China's "casino" markets. Moreover, it would contribute to the vicious circle whereby the apparent costs of engaging in insider trading are virtually nil, encouraging in turn expanded illegal activity going forward.

The only thing we can say for certain at this point is that the PRC does in fact enforce against insider trading in the Chinese domestic markets under the widest theory known to securities regulation, and a theory that is radically different from the one provided for in national law—assessing liability and levying punishment for trading in securities when merely in possession of broadly defined inside information. Whether the very wide net aggressively cast over insider trading, specifically, is a good thing for the development of China's capital markets, generally, is a question that will only be understood well into the future, and as those same capital markets and their investor participants become ever more integrated with global securities markets and transnational regulatory regimes.

APPENDIX: SELECTED STATUTORY PROVISIONS

2006 PRC Securities Law

Article 73. It is prohibited for those with knowledge of securities trading [related] inside information or those who have illegally procured inside information to use inside information in undertaking securities trading activities.

Article 74. Persons with knowledge of securities trading [related] inside information include:

(i)   directors, supervisory board members, and senior managers of the issuer;

(ii)   5 percent or more shareholders of the company and its/their directors, supervisory board members and senior managers, and the actual controlling shareholders of the company and its/their directors, supervisory board members and senior managers;

(iii)   directors, supervisory board members and senior managers of companies controlled by the issuer;

(iv)   people whose executive or staff position in the company provides access to inside information;

(v)   Securities Regulatory Organ [CSRC] staff and others who pursuant to their legally stipulated duties administer or regulate securities issuance and trading;

(vi)   relevant securities sponsors, underwriters, securities exchange personnel, securities registration and settlement personnel, and securities service institution personnel; and

(vii)   other persons stipulated in regulation by the State Council Securities Regulatory Organ [the CSRC].

Article 75. Inside information means non-public information relevant to a company's business or financial affairs or which may have a major effect on the market price of that company's securities in the course of securities trading activities. The following information all constitutes inside information: . . . (viii) other important information recognized and confirmed by the State Council Securities Regulatory Organ [the CSRC] to have a significant effect on the trading price of securities.

Article 76. Those with knowledge of inside information related to securities trading and those who have illegally procured inside information may not, prior to public disclosure of the inside information, purchase or sell that company's securities, or disclose such information, or suggest that others purchase or sell such securities. . . .

2007 Insider Trading Guidance Provisions

Article 12. Securities trading activity that conforms to the following conditions shall constitute insider trading: (1) the person undertaking the behavior is an insider; (2) the information involved is inside information; and (3) the subject person buys or sells related securities during the price sensitive period of the inside information, or suggests that other persons buy or sell related securities, or [publicly] reveals the [inside] information.

18. Insider trading regulation in Japan
J. Mark Ramseyer

Investors will always bring different amounts of information to the market. They will bring different analytical talents and different levels of sophistication. Precisely because men and women shrewder and wiser than us buy and sell in the market, we who are more naive can trade at prices that incorporate available information. When Congress passed the federal regulatory framework in the early 1930s, it provided that firms could recover insider profits from a narrow band of investors in a narrow set of trades. But further than that it did not go. Insider trading was not a crime.

That state of affairs was one the Securities and Exchange Commission (SEC) and the courts would change. Through aggressive prosecution and compliant adjudication, insider trading in the USA has become a crime. Citing the general anti-fraud rule, the SEC and the courts now routinely send inside traders to prison.

Occupied by the USA for seven years at mid-century, Japan inherited a securities law modeled on the two US statutes. As in the USA, firms could recover the profits earned by designated insiders in designated trades. Further the law did not go. Insider trading was not a crime.

Many scholars and bureaucrats thought this unfortunate. Without criminal penalties against insider trading, they argued, investors would lack faith in the market. They would avoid stocks and bonds. Because investors would avoid them, so would the firms. Absent criminal penalties against insider trading, Japan could not develop a healthy and robust securities market.

The critics won, and in 1988 the Diet declared insider trading criminal. Investors could now safely "trust the market." And within two years, that market collapsed. Once insider trading became a crime, the volume of shares traded plummeted, and the market capitalization of Japanese firms disappeared. Two decades later, the market has yet to recover.

To tell this story, I first outline the legal context to the Japanese insider-trading ban (Section I). I explain the law (Section II.A–B) and survey its enforcement (Section II.C). I conclude with a short look at the securities market (Section III).

I. INTRODUCTION

At least since the late 1940s, Japanese corporate law has held directors and officers to a duty of loyalty. Japanese securities law has required them to disgorge their short-swing profits (a § 16(b) equivalent).[1] It has contained an anti-fraud rule (a Rule 10b-5 equivalent).[2] But for 40 years, Japanese courts saw virtually no litigation over insider

---

[1] Securities Exchange Act of 1934, as amended, § 16(b).
[2] 13 F.R. 8183, Dec. 22, 1948, as amended at 16 F.R. 7928, Aug. 11, 1951.

trading. They saw no litigation, either civil or criminal, under any of these provisions. Academic commentators thought this a Bad Thing. At the government advisory committee on securities regulation in 1988, they argued that if insider trading were "allowed to continue, the health and fairness of the securities market would suffer. The trust of investors in the markets would disappear. To retain that health and trust, the regulation of insider trading was essential."[3] Along the same line, a standard securities handbook declared that "insider trading blocks the fair development of prices, and erodes the trust of investors in securities markets. Necessarily, it prevents the healthy development of those markets."[4]

And so in 1988 the Japanese Diet passed a statute. To facilitate § 16(b)-equivalent claims, it told designated insiders to report their trades to the regulators. It ordered those regulators to scour the reported trades and notify firms of any claims they should raise. To facilitate criminal prosecutions of insider trading, the Diet passed an additional, entirely new framework. It specified the people subject to its new insider trading ban. It detailed the firms and trades covered. It listed the information that could be material and authorized detailed rules about what counted as disclosure.

Draft it and they will sue. Firms still never sue for insider trading under the corporate fiduciary duty provisions. Prosecutors still never file charges under the old Rule 10b-5 equivalent. But since 1988, firms have regularly claimed and recovered under the Sec.-16(b) analogue. Prosecutors have regularly charged investors for criminal insider trading under the new statutory sections.

Investor faith and trust in the market? Once the new rules took effect, investors massively pulled their funds. From 1988 to 1990, the number of shares traded on Japanese exchanges fell from 283 billion to 123 billion. By 1992, they had fallen to 66 billion. In the four years after the Diet banned insider trading, in other words, the number of shares traded fell by an astonishing 77 percent (Figure 18.1). Perhaps banning insider trading reassures investors about the integrity of the securities markets. But only perhaps. If the Japanese experience suggests anything at all, it suggests exactly the opposite.

II. INSIDER TRADING LAW

A. Corporate Law

1. In the USA

Suppose a CEO knows his firm's stock is underpriced. He approaches a shareholder and offers to buy his stock. Under some traditional (i.e., pre-1934) American case law, he owed a fiduciary duty to that shareholder. If he bought the stock without disclosing what he knew of the underpricing, he violated that duty and owed the shareholder his profit.[5]

---

[3]   Quoted in Wataru Ota, Insaidaa torihiki kisei [The Regulation of Insider Trading] in Yoshiro Miwa, Hideki Kanda & Noriyuki Yanagawa, eds., Kaisha ho no keizaigaku [The Economics of Corporate Law] 345, 345 (Tokyo: University of Tokyo Press, 1998).

[4]   Sin Nihon shoken chosa sentaa, ed., Shoken handobukko (dai 3 ban) [Securities Handbook (3d. ed.)] 513 (Tokyo: Toyo keizai shimpo sha, 1989).

[5]   Hotchkiss v. Fischer, 16 P.2d 531 (Kan. 1932).

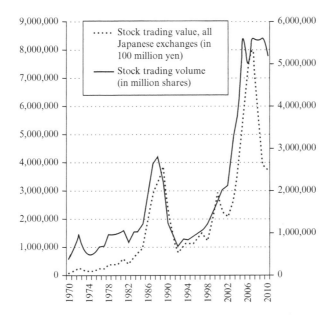

Note: Left axis gives trading value; right axis gives trading volume.

Source: Tokyo Stock Exchange, at http://www.tse.or.jp/market/data/value/index.html (last accessed July 1, 2011).

Figure 18.1   Stock trading value and volume (all Japanese exchanges)

Other cases found no such duty to shareholders.[6] And even those that did describe officers as agents for the shareholders did not necessarily stop them from selling their stock on inside information. After all, the buyer became a shareholder only after he bought the stock. At the time of the purchase, he was not yet a shareholder—and the CEO owed him no duty.[7] Absent a fiduciary duty, non-disclosure is not fraudulent: *caveat emptor*.

Nonetheless, that a CEO was not the shareholders' fiduciary did not mean he could keep his profits. The question for the courts was not whether he was a fiduciary. He was. It was whether he was a fiduciary to the shareholders, or "only" to the corporation. By standard agency principles, agents may not make "secret profits" on opportunities they acquire through their agency. Instead, they owe their profits to their principal.[8] If a CEO serves as agent for his firm, then he owes his insider trading profits to it. As the Second Restatement of Agency put it:[9]

> [If a director] has "inside" information . . . [, then] profits made by him in stock transactions undertaken because of his knowledge are held in constructive trust for the principal. He is also liable for profits made by selling constructive information to third persons, even though the principal is not adversely affected.

---

6   Hooker v. Midland Steel Co., 74 N.E. 445 (Ill. 1905).
7   Joseph v. Farnsworth Radio & Television Corp., 99 F. Supp. 701 (S.D.N.Y. 1951).
8   Reading v. Regem [1948] 2 K.B. 268 (1948); Tarnowsky v. Resop, 51 N.W.2d 801 (Minn. 1952).
9   Restatement (2d) of Agency, § 389 Comment c.

And so the US courts sometimes (but not always) held. Officers who traded on information they acquired through their position could find that they owed their profits to the firm.[10]

2. In Japan

The Japanese Corporate Code similarly requires fiduciary duties of directors.[11] It declares a director an agent of the firm (Corporate Code, § 330) and imposes on him a duty of loyalty to it (§ 355).[12] According to the Supreme Court, the duty follows from the general fiduciary duty that the Civil Code imposes on all agents.[13] Although the Corporate Code does not explicitly require a fiduciary duty of non-director officers, officers are agents too. By the Supreme Court's logic, they owe fiduciary duties to the firm as well.

Formally, directors and officers would seem to owe the firm any profits they made on inside information. Given that they owe their duties to the firm, however, they apparently do not owe them to the shareholders. If they trade on inside information, they thus would not (absent more) owe those shareholders their profits. Instead, by the logic of the Second Restatement, they would owe those profits to the firm.

Some commentators do imply that directors should pay their insider profits to their firm. "Where a fiduciary transacts with a third party for himself," writes Michio Hamada, professor of law at Nagoya University, he should be "deemed to have engaged in the transaction for the benefit of his principal."[14] When he sells, he "acquires the proceeds for the sake of his beneficiary. As a result, that beneficiary can demand that he transfer those proceeds to it."

It has been a route the courts did not take. I found no corporate law cases that held insiders liable to the firm on their trades. Neither did I find any commentary that claimed that courts actually did so. Instead, Hideki Kanda, professor of law at the University of Tokyo, explains that such an approach would not fit well with the language of the Code.[15] Elsewhere (§ 423; § 266 of the pre-2004 Commercial Code), the Corporate Code specifies the scope of a director's liability to the firm in elaborate detail. Should he cause it to pay too large a dividend, he is liable for the excess. Should he waste corporate assets, he is liable for the loss. In a variety of situations, the statute details what he owes. By the usual implication, if it does not detail something, he does not owe it. As the statute does not tell him to pay the firm his insider profits, he does not owe them.

B. Securities Law

1. In the USA

At the time that the lawyers in the American-dominated occupation rewrote Japanese corporate and securities law in the late 1940s, US regulators expected courts to police

---

[10]   Diamond v. Oreamuno, 248 N.E.2d 910 (1969).

[11]   Kaisha ho [Corporate Code], Law No. 86 of July 26, 2005.

[12]   Prior to 2005, § 254 of Shoho [Commercial Code], Law No. 48 of Mar. 9, 1899, declared the director an agent of the firm. Section 254-3 expressly imposed a duty of loyalty.

[13]   Arita v. Kojima, 596 Hanrei jiho (S. Ct. June 24, 1970); see Minpo [Civil Code], Law No. 89 of April 27, 1896, Secs. 644–646.

[14]   Michio Hamada, Shoho [Commercial Code] 139 (Tokyo: Iwanami shoten, 2001).

[15]   Hideki Kanda, Kaisha ho [Corporate Law] 204-05 (Tokyo: Kobundo, 11th ed. 2009).

insider trading through § 16(b) of the 1934 Securities Exchange Act.[16] If an officer, director, or dominant (over 10 percent) shareholder made money buying and selling his firm's stock within a six-month period, the corporation could sue him for his gains (the section imposes no criminal sanctions). If he refused to pay and blocked the suit, a shareholder could sue derivatively to enforce its right. To let investors learn about the insiders' profits, § 16(a) required officers, directors, and dominant shareholders regularly to disclose their trades.

Although US firms still recover profits under § 16(b), the provision no longer lies at the core of insider trading jurisprudence. Instead, § 10(b) of the 1934 Act has taken its place.[17] For the last four decades, American regulators and courts have policed insider trading through the anti-fraud provisions of § 10(b)'s Rule 10b-5:[18]

It shall be unlawful for any person . . .
(a) To employ any device, scheme, or artifice to defraud,
(b) To make any untrue statement of a material fact or to omit to state a material fact necessary in order to make the statements made . . . not misleading, or
(c) To engage in any act, practice, or course of business which operates . . . as a fraud or deceit . . .,
in connection with the purchase or sale of any security.

For the violators, criminal penalties apply. Sometimes courts impose civil sanctions as well.

Rule 10b-5 says nothing about insider trading, of course. As eventually articulated by the Supreme Court, the rule (sort of) applies anyway because: (1) the rule bans fraud in connection with the purchase or sale of securities; (2) non-disclosure is fraudulent when a trader owes a fiduciary duty to his counter-party; and (3) officers and directors owe that fiduciary duty to their shareholders. Table those court opinions that declare that directors and officers owe this fiduciary duty only to the firm itself. Table too the fact that an insider who sells his stock may trade with someone who is not yet (at the moment of purchase) a shareholder at all. Invoke propositions (1) through (3) anyway, and the courts can (sort of) plausibly declare insider trading (by officers and directors) a violation of Rule 10b-5.

The SEC adopted Rule 10b-5 in 1942, but it did not adopt it to ban insider trading. It began applying it to insider trading only in the early 1960s. William Cary (of "race for the bottom" fame) taught corporate law at Columbia, but from 1961 to 1964 chaired the SEC. In the Commission's internal, uncontested consent opinion to *In re Cady Roberts*,[19] he announced that an investor who traded on nonpublic information violated Rule 10b-5:[20]

An affirmative duty to disclose material information has been traditionally imposed on corporate "insiders," particularly officers, directors, or controlling stockholders. We, and the courts

---

[16] Securities Exchange Act of 1934, as amended, 15 U.S.C. § 78a et seq.
[17] Securities Exchange Act of 1934, as amended, § 10(b).
[18] 13 F.R. 8183, Dec. 22, 1948, as amended at 16 F.R. 7928, Aug. 11, 1951.
[19] In re Cady, Roberts & Co., 40 S.E.C. 907 (1961). See generally Kenneth G. Patrick, Perpetual Jeopardy (Macmillan, 1972); J. Mark Ramseyer, Business Organizations 211–12 (Aspen, 2012) and sources cited therein.
[20] Id. at 911.

have consistently held that insiders must disclose material facts which are known to them by virtue of their position but which are not known to persons with whom they deal and which, if known, would affect their investment judgment.

As Cary well knew, the statement was preposterous legal history. The SEC had taken no such position. Neither had the courts. Cary was trying to move the SEC into an entirely new field, and praying the courts would follow. They did. The Second Circuit adopted this logic in 1969 in *Texas Gulf Sulphur*,[21] and the modern 10b-5-based insider trading jurisprudence began.

Some observers never reconciled themselves to the change, of course. Justice Powell was one. "The SEC," he insisted, "should have gone to Congress long ago" instead of inventing "expansive rules" that pushed the "vague language" of § 10(b) "to the edge of rationality."[22] He fought a losing cause. The lower courts went with Cary rather than Powell, and by the 1980s the use of 10b-5 as an insider trading ban had become the norm.

2.   Section 16(b) in Japan

The US-imposed Securities and Exchange Act (SEA)[23] of 1948 blended the 1933 and 1934 US securities statutes. In § 189, the SEA included a § 16(b) equivalent. It had started with a § 16(a) equivalent too, but the Diet repealed it in 1953.[24] Given that the repealed section had mandated the disclosure of the trades covered by the 16(b) equivalent, its repeal left shareholders with no way to learn about insider trades. Predictably, they abandoned § 189. As of 1983, University of Tokyo securities law professor Makoto Yazawa could report only one § 189 claim in over 30 years.[25]

All this changed with the massive insider trading initiative of 1988.[26] That year, the Diet reintroduced a § 16(a) analogue in § 188.[27] In its eventual form, officers and principal shareholders (over 10 percent) reported their trades to the Financial Services Agency. If the Agency decided that an insider owed profits to the firm, it ordered him to pay. If he refused, it notified the company. If within 30 days the company failed to demand the money from him, it reported the trades to the public.[28]

---

[21]   Securities & Exchange Commission v. Texas Gulf Sulphur Co., 401 F.2d 833 (2d Cir.), cert den'd sub nom. Coates v. S.E.C., 394 U.S. 976 (1969).

[22]   Quoted at Kurt A. Hohenstein, Fair to All People: The SEC and the Regulation of Insider Trading, at Virtual Museum & Archive of the History of Financial Regulation, www.sechistorical. org/museum/galleries/it (last accessed July 1, 2011).

[23]   Shoken torihiki ho [Securities Exchange Act], Law No. 25 of 1948.

[24]   Louis Loss, Makoto Yazawa & Barbara Ann Banoff, Japanese Securities Regulation 194 (Tokyo: University of Tokyo Press, 1983); Hideki Kanda, supervising ed., Chukai Shoken torihiki ho [Annotated Securities Exchange Act] 1173 (Tokyo: Yuhikaku, 1997).

[25]   L. Loss, et al., supra note 24, at 194.

[26]   Law No. 75 of 1988.

[27]   See H. Kanda, Chukai, supra note 24, at 1173. The provision would eventually become § 163 of the Financial Products Transaction Act (FPTA).

[28]   In its current form, FPTA, §§ 163, 164(4), 164(7); Hiroyuki Ishizuka, Kin'yu shohin torihiki ho Q&A 100 [Financial Products Trading Act, Q&A 100] 200–203 (Tokyo: Nihon keizai shimbun sha, 2006); H. Kanda, Chukai, supra note 24, at 1173; Yu Kimeda, supervising ed., Insaidaa torihiki kisei no jitsumu [The Regulatory Practice of Insider Trading] 449 (Tokyo: Shoji homu, 2010).

The current § 16(b) equivalent appears in § 164 of the Financial Products Trading Act (FPTA; the renamed SEA):

> For the purpose of preventing the unfair use of secrets obtained by an officer or principal shareholder of a listed company by reason of his office or status, any profit realized by him from any purchase of a specified security of the listed company and sale within a period of six months, or from any sale of a specified security and purchase within a period of six months, shall be recoverable by the listed company.

With a § 16(a) analogue available, firms and shareholders have filed claims. Some appear in the press—e.g., a 2008 claim against the US-based activist fund Steel Partners.[29] Others appear among reported judicial opinions. Courts uphold the provision against constitutional challenges (violation of property rights). Consistently, they take a prophylactic approach similar to that in the USA. Firms need not show any damages, for example, and need not show that the defendant had access to any inside information.[30]

3. Rule 10b-5 in Japan

The Americans also imposed on Japan a Rule 10b-5 equivalent. The provision currently appears in § 157 of the FPTA (formerly SEA, § 58):

> No person shall engage in any of the following acts:
> (a) Employ any unfair device, scheme, or artifice in connection with the purchase or sale (or other transaction or derivative transaction) of a security.
> (b) Use any document (or make any statement) containing a fraudulent statement of a material fact or omitting to state a material fact necessary in order to make the statement made not misleading, in connection with the purchase or sale (or other transaction or derivative transaction) of a security, in order to acquire money or other property.
> (c) Employ a fraudulent market with the intent of inducing a purchase or sale (or other transaction or derivative transaction) of a security.

Violations give rise to criminal penalties.

Prosecutors and judges have not used the provision to police insider trading. Recall, however, that the SEC did not write Rule 10b-5 in 1942 to police insider trading anyway. It wrote it to ban fraud, and only under Cary's chairmanship in the early 1960s did it sweep

---

[29] Japan Law Express, July 12, 2008, japanlaw.blog.ocn.ne.jp/japan_law_express/2008/07/post_3726.html (last accessed July 1, 2011); Reuters July 11, 2008, http://jp.reuters.com/article/businessNews/idJPJAPAN-32708220080711 (last accessed July 1, 2011). See also claim by Fisuko on Korean investor Cho Bijun: JC-NET, 4/24/10, at n-seikei.jp/2010/04/post-718.html (last accessed July 1, 2011); JASDAQ's instructions to Paint House to assert claim against Lotus: ja.wikipedia.org/wiki/TMC (last accessed July 1, 2011).

[30] [No names given], 1777 Hanrei jiho 36 (Sup. Ct. Feb. 13, 2002) (statute is constitutional), aff'g, 56 Sanhan minshu 346 (Tokyo High Ct. Sept. 28, 2000), aff'g, 56 Saihan minshu 340 (Tokyo D. Ct. May 24, 2000); K.K. Bando hoteru v. Yomeishu seizo, K.K., 1428 Hanrei jiho (Tokyo High Ct. May 27, 1992) (no need to show damages or inside information), aff'g, 1428 Hanrei jiho 143 (Yokohama D. Ct. Sept. 24, 1991); [No name given], 1444 Hanrei jiho 139 (Tokyo D. Ct. Oct. 1, 1992); Y.G. Sanwa Entaapuraizu v. Min. of Finance, 764 Hanrei taimuzu 150 (Tokyo D. Ct. Nov. 2, 1990) (Min. Finance determination of liability is not administrative disposition); Nikko, K.K. v. Y.G. Sanwa Entaapuraizu, 857 Kin'yu shoji hanrei 24 (Kobe D. Ct. July 27, 1990).

insider trading within the ambit of fraud. In effect, Japanese prosecutors and judges stayed with the American SEC's original plan for the rule.

Section 157 began as a general anti-fraud provision, and so it has stayed. As of 2010, courts have published only three opinions interpreting it, and none involves insider trading. In 1963, the Tokyo High Court convicted a trader of securities fraud—but not insider trading.[31] In two cases from 2000, the Supreme Court affirmed lower court opinions acquitting Nomura Securities directors of § 157 violations in reimbursing a major client for securities losses.[32] The case law on § 157 has gone no farther.[33]

4.   The 1988 amendments

(a)   Overview   In 1988, Japan passed a series of changes to let regulators police insider trading.[34] The economy had boomed spectacularly in the 1960s. After an oil-cartel-induced recession in the 1970s, it boomed again. To fund their growth, firms listed their shares on the stock market. In 1970, 1580 firms listed their stock on the Japanese stock exchanges, for a total market capitalization of 16.8 trillion yen. By 1980, 1729 firms listed their shares at a market capitalization of 80.0 trillion, and by 1987, 1912 listed shares worth 345.6 trillion (Figure 18.2).

Despite this phenomenal market performance, some scholars and bureaucrats still thought the situation unacceptable. Without criminal and civil penalties against insiders, they argued, investors would not trust the stock market. Worried that insiders rigged the game, investors would avoid it. And if investors avoided it then firms would avoid it too. Without heavier sanctions for insider trading, argued scholars and bureaucrats, the Japanese economy could never grow.

To solve this perceived problem, the Diet passed a statute. Under the new regime, if an officer or director bought or sold his firm's stock while holding material nonpublic information, he faced criminal penalties. If he bought or sold shares in a tender offer target, he faced criminal penalties. And if a tippee with that nonpublic information bought or sold stock, he faced the penalties too.

The rules detail a formalistic regime. It is much more formal than the Rule 10b-5 criminal (and civil) jurisprudence in the USA, but less formal than that of § 16(b). It covers a narrower set of trades than Rule 10b-5 and a broader set than § 16(b).

(b)   Who is covered?   The 1988 rules apply to a discrete group of specified insiders. The list is exclusive: if a trader is not on it, he is not subject to the rules.

---

[31]   Japan v. Uchimura, 5 Kakyu saiban keishu 651 (Tokyo High Ct. July 10, 1963).
[32]   Ikenaka v. Tabuchi, 1549 Hanrei Jiho 11 (Tokyo High Ct. Sept. 26, 1995), aff'd, 1729 Hanrei jiho 28 (S. Ct. July 7, 2000); Kawai v. Tabuchi, 1064 Kin'yu shoji hanrei 21 (Tokyo High Ct. Jan. 27, 1999), aff'd, 1096 Kin'yu shoji hanrei 9 (S. Ct. July 7, 2000).
[33]   Shinsuke Matsumoto, Saishin Insaidaa torihiki kisei [New: Insider Trading Regulation] 12 (Tokyo: Shoji homu, 2006) (no cases applying § 58 to insider trading); Y. Kimeda, supra note 28, at 3, 7 note 6 (same).
[34]   FPTA, §§ 166, 167; SEA §§ 190-2, 190-3.

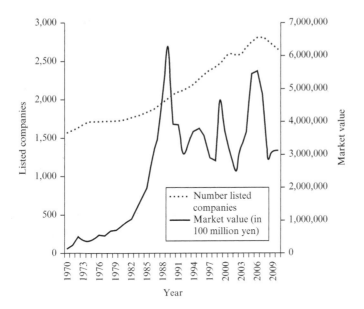

Source: See Figure 18.1.

Figure 18.2   Number and market value of listed companies (all Japanese exchanges)

(I)   EMPLOYEES   The statute applies to officers, directors, and others who work at the firm.[35] Note that it bans them from trading only on information they acquire on the job. Suppose a friend tips a fellow employee information over drinks after work. The employee is not liable as an employee. Instead, he is liable only as a tippee. Although he is liable in either case, the distinction matters—because if he tips someone else, that other person would be liable only if he (the tipper) learned the information as an employee rather than a tippee. As explained below, secondary tippees may safely trade under the 1988 rules.[36]

(II)   MAJOR SHAREHOLDERS   The Japanese Corporate Code gives shareholders with at least a 3 percent stake access to the corporate books.[37] If a shareholder acquires information through that access, he may not trade on it (FPTA, § 166(a)(2)). If other investors (e.g., creditors) obtain similar access, they may not trade on the information either.

(III)   LEGAL AUTHORITIES   People (e.g., regulators) with legal authority over a company may not trade on any information they acquire through their authority (§166(a)(3)).

(IV)   CONTRACT PARTNERS   A firm (or person) that obtains information about another firm through its contractual ties or through negotiations over contractual ties may not

---

[35]   FPTA, § 166(a)(1); S. Matsumoto, supra note 34, at 44–46.
[36]   See Y. Kimeda, supra note 28, at 50.
[37]   Kaisha ho, § 433; see S. Matsumoto, supra note 34, at 46–48.

trade.[38] The rule may cover attorneys, accountants, and bankers, as all three work for (or with) a firm under contract—though if they are also agents of the firm, they may fall within the category of "employees" (above) as well.[39]

(v)   FORMER INSIDERS   Anyone subject to the ban will continue to be covered by it for a year after his affiliation with the firm ends (§ 166(a)). Rather than ask when an insider's fiduciary duty to the firm stops, the Japanese statute imposes a bright-line one-year rule.

(VI)   TENDER OFFERORS   A person who acquires information from his affiliation (whether by employment, stock holdings, legal authority, or contractual ties) to the acquirer in a tender offer may not trade.[40]

(VII)   TIPPEES   If an insider (by any of the definitions above) conveys information to someone else, that tippee may not trade.[41] The coverage does not turn on whether anyone breached a fiduciary duty by tipping—all tips are off limits.[42] It does turn on whether the disclosure was intentional—if someone merely overhears a thought-to-be-confidential comment, he may freely trade.[43]

Because the ban covers only those who hear from a defined insider, secondary and tertiary tippees may freely trade. Note, however, that someone who works with a primary tippee (e.g., a newspaper editor who employs an investigative reporter who learns inside information) is not a secondary tippee. Instead, he is a co-primary tippee.[44]

(c)   What information is material?   The 1988 statute also lists information that is material, but this list is not exclusive. Instead, all information that an investor would consider important in deciding whether to buy or sell is material.[45] Note that an investor violates

---

[38]   FPTA, § 166(a)(4); see, e.g., [No names given], 1845 Hanrei jiho 147 (S. Ct. Dec. 3, 2003). In some respects, this takes a different approach from footnote 22 of Dirks v. Securities & Exchange Commission, 463 U.S. 646, 662 note 22 (1983), though it is consistent with later lower court cases like Securities & Exchange Commission v. Lund, 570 F. Supp. 1397 (C.D. Cal. 1983).

[39]   FTPA, § 166(a)(1). Compare S. Matsumoto, supra note 34, at 50–54, with Y. Kimeda, supra note 28, at 41, 62–63. In fact, this distinction should not make a difference. In other words, rather than sweep lawyers and accountants into the ban by calling them "temporary insiders," Dirks, 463 U.S. at 655 note14, Japanese law covers them in the statute as either contractual partners or agents.

[40]   FPTA, § 167. Japan takes an approach analogous, in other words, to Rule 14(e)-3 of the 1934 Act. Rather than worry about "fiduciary duties" or "misappropriation," Chiarella v. United States, 455 U.S. 222 (1980); United States v. O'Hagan, 521 U.S. 642 (1997), it employed a bright-line rule in the statute.

[41]   FPTA, § 166(c); e.g., [No names given], 244 Shiryo shoji homu 206 (Nagoya D. Ct. May 27, 2004).

[42]   Dirks, 463 U.S. at 660 (tippee may trade if tip was not fiduciary duty breach).

[43]   Y. Kimeda, supra note 28, at 70–71. Compare this with SEC v. Switzer, 590 F. Supp. 756 (W.D. Okla. 1984) (tippee may trade on overheard information because careless conversation may be a duty of care violation, but does not generate a gain to the tipper, and the Dirks rule hinges on a fiduciary duty breach from which the tipper gains).

[44]   S. Matsumoto, supra note 34, at 56; Y. Kimeda, supra note 28, at 69–70.

[45]   FPTA, § 166(b)(4); S. Matsumoto, supra note 34, at 139–144; e.g., [No names given], 1438 Hanrei jiho 151 (Tokyo D. Ct. Sept. 25, 1992).

the statute if he trades while holding material nonpublic information; he need not have used it in deciding whether to buy or sell. Note too that the statute authorizes the government to specify events that it exempts as de minimis—and that the Ministry of Finance maintains such an exempt-event list.[46]

Acting through its board of directors (or other mechanism), a firm might decide to do something that would affect an investor's decision to hold its stock.[47] Alternatively, it might decide not to pursue an option it had earlier announced it would follow. Both can give rise to illegal insider trading. As illustrations, the statute lists such actions as stock issues, capital reductions, stock buy-backs, stock splits, dividend issues, mergers, business sales, business purchases, liquidations, and new products or technologies (§ 166(b)(1)).

The firm might also encounter new constraints or possibilities.[48] Again, the events can give rise to illegal insider trading. As illustrations, the statute lists natural disasters, stock sales by major investors, stock purchases by outside investors, and the delisting of the firm's stock (§ 166(b)(2)).

A firm may find that its earlier announcements or financial projections were wrong. They may have been overly optimistic. They may have been unduly pessimistic. In either case, the errors will matter to investors, and an insider who trades on them will violate the insider trading ban (§ 166(b)(3)).

(d)   What firms are covered?   Section 16(b) in the USA applies only to exchange-listed or very large firms; Rule 10b-5 applies to all corporations. The insider trading ban in Japan sweeps closer to § 16(b) than Rule 10b-5: it applies only to exchange-listed companies.[49] If a firm lists at least one type of security on an exchange, then the insider trading ban applies to all of its securities—including those it does not list.[50]

(e)   What information is nonpublic?   Although the 1988 statute states that insiders may not trade on information before other investors have had the chance to incorporate it into their decisions, it authorizes the Financial Services Agency (FSA) to issue bright-line rules about the required disclosure (§ 166(d)). The Agency has. For example, it specifies that if insiders want to rely on disclosure to the press, they must disclose the information to at least two firms (e.g., newspapers, the public television network NHK) and wait at least 12 hours.[51]

---

[46]   FPTA, § 166(b); Kaisha kankeisha to no tokutei yuka shoken to no torihiki kisei ni kansuru naikaku furei [Cabinet Order Regarding Regulation of Trades in Specified Securities, Etc., by Corporate Related Parties, Etc.], Min. Finance Order 10 of Feb. 3, 1989.

[47]   E.g., [No names given], 1679 Hanrei jiho 11 (S. Ct. June 10, 1999); K.K. MAC asetto manejimento, 1299 Hanrei taimuzu 99 (Tokyo High Ct. Feb. 3, 2009).

[48]   E.g., [No names given], 1671 Hanrei jiho 45 (S. Ct. Feb. 16, 1999).

[49]   See §§ 163(a), 166, as interpreted by Shikko rei § 27-2. Although the statute applies to the over-the-counter market as well as the organized exchanges, because JASDAQ has become an exchange the OTC market has effectively disappeared. See S. Matsumoto, supra note 34, at 39.

[50]   Y. Kimeda, supra note 28, at 19.

[51]   Kinyu shohin torihikiho shikko rei Seirei 321 of Sept. 30, 1965, § 30(a). Alternatively, insiders may disclose to the Tokyo Stock Exchange through its Timely Disclosure Network. Id.; see S. Matsumoto, supra note 34, at 20, 183–191.

(f)   What securities are covered?   The 1988 rules cover stocks and bonds, along with derivatives and other options. Bonds are covered only if the inside information affects default risk.[52] Options are covered at the time of acquisition—not exercise. Note that options are covered only if bought from a third party—not if acquired from the firm itself.[53]

(g)   What are the penalties?   An investor who violates the rules is subject to a trivial fine (up to 5 million yen). He must, however, disgorge to the state all revenues (all proceeds—not just all profits) from the insider trading.[54] He also faces a possible prison term of up to five years (FPTA, § 197-2(m)). Corporations are subject to fines of up to 500 million yen (§ 207).

5.   The 2004 reforms

In 2004, the Diet added to the 1988 criminal provisions an administrative surcharge regime. Quite what problem it saw with the criminal framework is unclear. To convict a defendant, the government had to prove "intent."[55] But the intent that it needed to show was nothing more than the facts of the trade in question—those it would have to show in an administrative proceeding anyway. It did not need to show that the defendant knew the law, or that he knew that what he did was illegal. Certainly, it did not need to prove that he intended to defraud.[56]

Commentators argued that criminal prosecutions created too much work for the government. Administrative proceedings would be simpler, they argued.[57] To be sure, criminal proceedings brought heavier penalties. If convicted, a defendant owed all the proceeds from his trades to the state—not just a surcharge calculated from his profits. He risked time in prison. He incurred substantial social stigma. Given those higher costs, a rational defendant would invest more resources contesting the charges. Yet if the higher penalties made defendants fight harder, the government could demand lower penalties. It did not need a separate administrative proceeding.

Maybe criminal prosecutions brought other problems. Perhaps the higher burden of proof raised the government's costs. Perhaps some of the (intentionally) rigid procedural rules raised those costs. Perhaps the government could more easily add staff to the Securities Exchange Surveillance Commission (SESC) than to the prosecutors' offices. Or perhaps it found it too hard to convince overworked prosecutors to spend time on victimless financial crimes.[58]

---

[52]   Section 166(f)(6); Shikkorei, supra note 51, § 32-2; Min. Finance Order, supra note 46, at § 5; see Y. Kimeda, supra note 28, at 14, 245 note 487; S. Matsumoto, supra note 34, at 209–210.

[53]   FPTA, § 166(f)(2-2); S. Matsumoto, supra note 34, at 174–182, 195, 204; Y. Kimeda, supra note 28, at 21.

[54]   FPTA, § 198-2; S. Matsumoto, supra note 34, at 265–266; [No names given], 1139 Hanrei taimuzu 311 (Tokyo D. Ct. May 2, 2003).

[55]   S. Matsumoto, supra note 34, at 267.

[56]   See S. Matsumoto, supra note 34, at 273; Y. Kimeda, supra note 28, at 5 (no need to show profit from information, no need to show intent to make money, no need to show use of information); [No names given], 5 Saihan keishu 2354 (S. Ct. Nov. 15, 1951).

[57]   S. Matsumoto, supra note 34, at 274.

[58]   Y. Kimeda, supra note 28, at i (prosecutors focused on cases showing mala in se).

Whatever the logic, the government argued that an administrative option would let it pursue more cases and in 2004 obtained a civil surcharge regime. Suppose someone violates the 1988 insider trading statute (the same FPTA, §§ 166–167, that carry criminal sanctions). Under the new regime, the government may sue him in an administrative forum for his net profits.[59]

The concept of the surcharge is simple. Take an investor who sells high on inside information. He owes the government the amount he receives, less the lowest stock price over the two weeks after the information's disclosure (FPTA, § 175(a)). If he buys low on undisclosed information, he owes the difference between the price he paid and the highest price over the two weeks after the disclosure.

C. Enforcement

The SESC at the FSA coordinates enforcement activities. As of mid-2011, it employed a staff of about 400, and assigned a quarter to insider trading and securities disclosure.[60] To identify the problematic trades, the staff works with the stock exchanges. In 2005, the Tokyo Stock Exchange investigated about 8000 transactions, issued warnings when it thought it appropriate, and reported problematic trades to the SESC.[61] The Commission also takes tips from the general public—during the year ending mid-June 2009, about 4800 tips. Most of these involved market manipulation, but it did receive about 500 tips on insider trading.[62]

The Commission investigates transactions it considers problematic. The most serious of these it routes to the prosecutors' office. The less egregious it handles through the administrative proceedings. In 2005, it surveyed 7500 trades for possible insider trading connections, and more closely investigated 500.[63]

The result is a modest but regular level of enforcement (Table 18.1).[64] In 2006, the government levied an administrative surcharge on eight insiders for their trading; in 2009,

---

[59] If prosecutors demand disgorgement in a criminal charge, the surcharge remedy disappears as superfluous. FPTA, § 185-7, 185-8; see Y. Kimeda, supra note 28, at 414; S. Matsumoto, supra note 34, at 273–277.

[60] Tokyo Stock Exchange (TSE) and SESC websites.

[61] S. Matsumoto, supra note 34, at 27–28; TSE and SESC websites.

[62] SESC website.

[63] S. Matsumoto, supra note 34, at 29–30.

[64] The numbers are surprisingly hard to confirm. Part of the confusion apparently comes from the fact that the number of "warnings" does not equal the number of defendants—some warnings apply to multiple defendants, while some defendants violate multiple provisions. Part of the confusion comes from the fact that the surcharge is imposed not just on insider trading but on selected other securities violations as well—from April 2005 to May 2008, the SESC imposed a surcharge on 52 people, but 13 of the 52 involved fraudulent disclosure offenses. And part of the confusion comes from the fact that the prosecutors' office generally discloses only the total number of defendants prosecuted for securities offenses as a whole—in 2007 the government prosecuted 7 people specifically for insider trading but 67 people for securities-related crimes. See Shoken torihiki to kanshi iinkai, Kin'yu shohin torihiki ho ni okeru kachokin jireishu [Cases Regarding the Surcharge Under the Financial Products Transactions Act] ii (June 2008) (hereinafter Jireishu, 2008); Homu sho, Hanzai hakusho tab. 1-3-2-7 (Tokyo: Homu sho, 2010).

Table 18.1   Insider trading enforcement levels

A. Administrative warnings and surcharge

	Defendants				Per warning surcharge (/1000)
	Insiders		Tippees		
	Non-TO*	TO**	Non-TO	TO	
2006	8	0	0	0	4468
2007	9	0	4	3	2475
2008	14	1	2	2	3480
2009	13	4	12	9	1295

B. Criminal prosecutions

2004	4
2005	5
2006	8
2007	4

Notes:
"Warnings" are "kankoku" for insider-trading violations. The columns give the number of defendants. Some defendants were warned on multiple counts, while some warnings applied to multiple defendants.
*   Not related to a tender offer.
**   Related to a tender offer.
Years are from April to March.
Per warning surcharge is the total surcharge collected in the year, divided by the number of administrative warnings imposed.

Sources: Shoken torihiki to kanshi iinkai, Kin'yu shohin torihiki ho ni okeru kachokin jireishu [Cases Regarding the Surcharge Under the Financial Products Transactions Act] (June 2010); Shoken torihiki to kanshi iinkai, Kachokin jireishu no kohyo to insaidaa torihiki jian no keiko nitsute [Regarding the Publication of Surcharge Cases and the Trends in Insider-Trading Cases] (July 2010); Sadakazu Osaki, Tekihatsu ga aitsugu insaidaa torihiki [Disclosure of Insider Trading Continues] (Tokyo: Nomura Research Institute, 2008).

it imposed the surcharge on 38 insiders. In 2004 and 2007, it prosecuted four people for criminal insider trading; in 2006, it prosecuted eight.

For the most part, the SESC collects only small amounts through the surcharge. In 2009, it took an average of 1.3 million yen (about $14,000) per case. Of all surcharge actions brought by May of 2009, in 60 percent it collected less than 100,000 yen (about $1050).[65]

III.   THE ECONOMY

The Japanese stock market boomed during the 1980s. The market capitalization of Japanese firms grew from 71 trillion yen at the start of 1980 to 611 trillion by the close of 1989. Then, it collapsed. It has yet to recover. Real estate prices plummeted at the same time.

---

[65]   Jireishu, 2008, supra note 64.

What caused the massive collapse remains a puzzle. Writers often attribute it to a "bubble," but the comment does not much help. If writers mean that in retrospect prices were too high, they merely restate the question. Given what happened, stock prices in 1989 were indeed "too high." The point is "correct." It is also trivial.

Other writers sometimes describe the collapse as a true bubble: informed investors knew that prices were too high, but bought anyway because they hoped to sell before prices fell. Models of "rational bubbles" notwithstanding, this is obviously hard to fit with rational behavior. It leaves unanswered why rational investors would buy high knowing that the price was about to fall, and phrases like "contagion" just restate the question.

Worse, the notion of a true bubble is inconsistent with much of the rest of the story. Japanese developers bought land in the 1980s, and on it built condominiums, golf courses, and office buildings. These were decidedly long-term projects: developers do not build office buildings on short-term projections. And they were projects that made financial sense only if prices stayed high long term. Real investors, using real money, built real skyscrapers—on the premise that prices would not fall.

Yet asset prices did fall. I do not know why they fell, but I know that the insider-trading ban took effect in 1989. The market collapsed the next year and—20 years later—has yet to recover. If insider trading bans help assure investors of the integrity of the market, Japan offers no evidence of the phenomenon. If insider trading bans help insure the growth of the market, Japan provides no evidence of this either.

IV. CONCLUSIONS

The US-controlled Allied occupation imposed on Japan an American-style corporate and securities law. US law did not ban insider trading at the time, and neither did the new Japanese law. Only in the 1960s did US prosecutors and judges start to criminalize insider trading. Their Japanese counterparts did not follow their lead, and as of the mid-1980s had left insider trading largely unregulated.

In 1988, the Japanese Diet banned and criminalized insider trading. Rather than use a maddeningly imprecise rule like 10b-5, it carefully specified which investors, which trades, and which contexts would trigger the ban. Perhaps it was the kind of statute Justice Powell had in mind when he urged Congress to draft new legislation rather than follow Cary's lead and attack insider trading through the vague anti-fraud provisions of Rule 10b-5.

Commentators in Japan urged the Diet to adopt the legislation because they hoped—they said—to restore investor confidence in the stock market. Only with a ban on insider trading would Japan acquire a healthy market. If the ban restored investor confidence, it did not show. Shortly after the ban took effect, the Japanese stock market collapsed.

Section B

Australasia

19. Insider trading in Australia
Keith Kendall and Gordon Walker

I. INTRODUCTION

As a former British colony, Australia is a common law country. At Federation in 1901, the then six separate colonies became States,[1] with the formation of a central government at the federal level. This federal system, in which legislative competency is split between two levels of government, has shaped the form and history of securities regulation (as a subset of corporate law) in Australia. This introduction provides the context in which the Australian insider trading regime has been developed.

In 2012, Australia constitutes a medium-sized economy with GDP of USD 1.5 trillion and a population base of approximately 22 million.[2] The main securities market is the Australian Securities Exchange (ASX), which is a national operation. The national market was formed in 1987 through the amalgamation of the previously independent State stock exchanges.[3] As of March 2012, there were 2,223 companies listed on the ASX and market capitalization was AUD 1.3 trillion[4] (the eighth largest in the world and second largest in the Asia-Pacific).[5]

Prior to the introduction of the present system, securities regulation (and corporate law in general) was regulated in Australia at the State level. Insider trading was not recognized as a problem in Australia until the 1970s with the release of the Rae Report, which investigated securities activity in the Australian market during the mining boom of the 1960s and early 1970s and found instances of extensive insider trading activity had taken place.[6] State legislation was progressively introduced to regulate insider trading in the wake of the Rae Report's findings. For example, § 75A of the Securities Industry Act 1970 (NSW) imposed criminal and civil liability for trading for the purpose of obtaining a financial advantage by a person associated with a corporation if that person possessed specific price-sensitive information relating to the corporation which was not generally known.

---

[1] New South Wales, Victoria, Queensland, South Australia, Western Australia and Tasmania. During the process leading up to the formation of the Commonwealth of Australia at Federation, New Zealand (as a British colony at that time with the same status as the Australian colonies) considered joining the Commonwealth as a State, but removed itself from the process, eventually becoming a sovereign nation in its own right.

[2] Australia, Central Intelligence Agency—The World Factbook, available at http:// www.cia. gov/library/publications/the-world-factbook/geos/as.html (last accessed December 4, 2012).

[3] History, The ASX Group, available at http://www.asxgroup.com.au/history.htm (last accessed December 4, 2012).

[4] Approximately USD 1.4 trillion.

[5] The Australian Market, The ASX Group, available at http://www.asxgroup.com.au/the-australian-market.htm (last accessed December 4, 2012).

[6] Senate Select Committee on Securities and Exchange, Parliament of Australia, Australian Securities Markets and their Regulation (1974) (hereinafter "Rae Report").

In 1980, the Commonwealth Government introduced the Securities Industry Act 1980 (Cth), which was designed to serve as a model for uniform State-based legislation. At this time, the first national corporate regulator, the National Companies and Securities Commission (NCSC) was established. This form of legislative co-operative scheme, in which States enacted their own legislation based on a model put forth at the Commonwealth level, was to serve as the model for corporate and securities regulation in Australia until 2001.[7]

The current regulator is the Australian Securities and Investments Commission (ASIC), which draws its regulatory authority from the Australian Securities and Investments Commission Act 2001 (Cth). Among other things, ASIC registers companies, investigates breaches of the law and enforces the law. ASIC enforces the law by bringing civil proceedings or referring suspected criminal conduct to the Commonwealth Director of Public Prosecutions (the Commonwealth DPP). In 2010, ASIC's functions were expanded to include the supervision of trading on Australia's licensed equity, derivative and futures markets.[8]

As noted, the first impetus to regulate insider trading in any meaningful way had its genesis in the Rae Report of 1974. The outcome of that inquiry was the State-based legislative scheme modeled on the Securities Industries Act 1980 (Cth). Notwithstanding the reform represented by the statutory scheme, it was argued that the prohibition was ineffectual and/or did not go far enough.[9] Others argued that the prohibition was unjustified.[10] In light of these criticisms, the NCSC commissioned the Anisman Report to investigate options for further reform.[11] The Anisman Report recommended retention of the insider trading prohibition, regarding insider trading as "essentially a problem of non-disclosure"[12] and suggested broadening the provisions to remove any undue restrictions (such as the requirement for an insider to be connected with the issuer).[13]

While the initial response to the Anisman Report was largely negative,[14] the Commonwealth Government commissioned a further inquiry into reforming the insider trading provisions in 1989, headed by Alan Griffiths.[15] This inquiry was driven by anecdotal and empirical evidence subsequent to the Anisman Report which showed that

---

    [7]   Gregory Lyon & Jean du Plessis, The Law of Insider Trading in Australia 5 (2005); R. P. Austin & I. M. Ramsay, Ford's Principles of Corporations Law 43–47 (14th ed., 2010); Baxt, Black & Hanrahan, Securities and Financial Services Law, 29–47 (7th ed., 2008).

    [8]   Greg Yanco, "Market Supervision Moves to ASIC—What does it Mean for Brokers?" (June 9, 2010), available at http://www.asic.gov.au/asic/pdflib.nsf/LookupByFileName/speech-market-supervision-moves-to-asic-Greg-Yanco.pdf/$file/speech-market-supervision-moves-to-asic-Greg-Yanco.pdf (last accessed December 4, 2012).

    [9]   Philip Anisman, Insider Trading Legislation for Australia: An Outline of the Issues and Alternatives vi (1986) (hereinafter "Anisman Report").

    [10]   Id.

    [11]   Id.

    [12]   Id. at 2.

    [13]   See discussion in id. at 15–48.

    [14]   Lyon & du Plessis, supra note 7, at 7.

    [15]   House of Representatives Standing Committee on Legal and Constitutional Affairs, Fair Shares for All—Insider Trading in Australia (1989) (hereinafter "Griffiths Report").

insider trading was widespread in Australia, difficult to detect and unnecessarily difficult to prosecute successfully under the existing regime.[16]

The Griffiths Report made a total of 21 recommendations, including the removal of any requirement for a connection with the issuing company (Recommendation 2), clarification of the definition of "inside information" and important constituent elements (Recommendation 3) and a substantial increase in maximum penalties (Recommendation 11). Subsequent to these recommendations, the insider trading prohibition in Australia was broadened significantly, particularly in regard to the definition of "insider." Consistent with Recommendation 2, the reforms (implemented in 1991) removed any requirement that an insider have a connection with the issuing company, requiring instead mere possession of inside information.[17] This standard has been maintained through to the present day and has served as a model for other jurisdictions.[18] These reforms were introduced through a new co-operative statutory scheme, in which the States implemented uniform legislation based on the Commonwealth Government's Corporations Law.[19] In 2001, the States referred their legislative powers over corporations to the Commonwealth Government, which allowed the passage of the Corporations Act 2001 (Cth)[20] at the Commonwealth level.[21] While the 2001 developments incorporated some significant and substantial reforms to the regulation of corporations and securities markets in Australia, the insider trading provisions have remained predominantly the same in most material respects since the 1991 reforms.

In considering the proposed reforms over the last three decades, a good deal of attention has been given to the policy basis on which the insider trading prohibition is to be justified. During this time, the following justifications have been identified:[22]

- fiduciary duty;
- misappropriation;
- market fairness;
- market efficiency.

Of these four bases, it is the market fairness theory (sometimes referred to as the equal access theory[23] or access to information theory[24]) that underpins the shape of the Australian provisions most strongly. Equal access to information was put forward in the Anisman Report as sufficiently broad to deal with most of the concerns regarding coverage of undesirable behavior and consistent with market integrity objectives, although

---

[16]   Id at 2.
[17]   Elements of the reasoning behind this recommendation are set out below in the discussion of the definition of insider under the current provisions; for the full reasoning as set out in the Griffiths Report. Id. at 22–23.
[18]   See chapter in this volume on New Zealand's legislation.
[19]   Austin & Ramsay, supra note 7, at 45.
[20]   All subsequent legislative references, unless noted otherwise, will be to this statute.
[21]   Austin & Ramsay, supra note 7, at 46.
[22]   See, e.g., Companies and Securities Advisory Committee (CASAC), Insider Trading—Discussion Paper 13 (June 2001).
[23]   Lyon & du Plessis, supra note 7, at 8–9.
[24]   Baxt, Black & Hanrahan, supra note 7, at 692.

falling short of providing total coverage.[25] Despite such qualifications, the Griffiths Report considered this policy basis as the most consistent with promoting investor confidence (through promotion of market integrity) and adopted this theory as its guide in reforming the prohibition.[26]

In essence, the market fairness theory maintains that "each and every participant in the securities market should be afforded equal access to inside information."[27] Rather than requiring the information to be in the possession of each and every investor (including potential investors), emphasis is placed on investors having an equal *opportunity* to access the relevant information.[28] This policy basis is evident in the current provisions through, for example, the focus on the use of inside information[29] in the definition of "insider" (which looks only to possession of inside information) and the means by which information may be made generally available. The policy basis for the provisions can influence judicial interpretation of the terms used in the statute. For example, equality of access and the concomitant requirement for market fairness were particularly influential in the *Firns*[30] decision, in which the New South Wales Criminal Court of Appeal was required to consider whether an individual had breached the prohibition by trading on information observed overseas and, in particular, whether an "unfair advantage" had been obtained.[31]

II.   THE PRESENT LEGISLATION

The current prohibition against insider trading in Australia is contained in Part 7.10 which is a substantive re-enactment of Division 2A of the former Corporations Law.[32] The operative provision is § 1043A(1), which states:

Subject to this Subdivision, if:
(a) A person (the insider) possesses inside information; and
(b) The insider knows, or ought reasonably to know, that the matters specified in paragraphs (a) and (b) of the definition of inside information in section 1042A are satisfied in relation to the information;
the insider must not (whether as principal or agent):
(c) apply for, acquire, or dispose of, relevant Division 3 financial products, or enter into an agreement to apply for, acquire, or dispose of, relevant Division 3 financial products; or
(d) procure another person to apply for, acquire, or dispose of, relevant Division 3 financial

---

[25]   Anisman Report, supra note 9, at 11–13.

[26]   Griffiths Report, supra note 15, at 17.

[27]   Justin Mannolini, Insider Trading—The Need for Conceptual Clarity, 14 C&S L. J. 151, 154 (1996).

[28]   See, e.g., Baxt, Black & Hanrahan, supra note 7, at 692.

[29]   This was emphasized in the Griffiths Report, which foreshadowed the 1991 reforms; Griffiths Report, supra note 15, at 22.

[30]   R. v. Firns (2001) 51 NSWLR 548. This decision is discussed later in this chapter.

[31]   Id. at 558. The court also went on to consider the influence of the market efficiency justification; id. at 561.

[32]   The only difference from the previous provision was the extension of the prohibition from trading in a company's securities to Division 3 financial products. In essence, this change extended the range of financial instruments that insiders are prohibited from trading. See also Ashley Black, Insider Trading and Market Misconduct, 29 C&S L. J. 313, 315 (2011).

products, or enter into an agreement to apply for, acquire, or dispose of, relevant Division 3 financial products.

Failure to comply with this section is a criminal offense and may also give rise to civil liability. Section 1043A(2) contains a similarly structured prohibition on tipping.[33]

The elements of the offense of insider trading appear on the face of the legislation. The physical element is the possession of inside information. The requisite mental state is knowledge or constructive knowledge that the information is inside information. When prosecuted as a criminal offense, these elements must be proved by the prosecution beyond a reasonable doubt.[34]

Section 1043A is laden with defined terms. "Division 3 financial products" are essentially any tradeable financial instrument, including derivatives and government-issued securities.[35] The prohibition covers a wide variety of securities, with very few restrictions. There is no requirement that the relevant securities be tradeable on a public exchange.[36]

A.   Definition of Insider

The only definition contained within § 1043A(1) itself is that of "insider," which is the core of the claim made in this chapter that Australia's prohibition is one of, if not the widest in the world. Unlike other comparable jurisdictions, such as the United States, which require some sort of connection between the party and the company whose securities are being traded, § 1043A(1) identifies an insider merely as someone in possession of inside information. This possession standard means that any party, regardless of relationship or position in respect of the relevant company, may come within the prohibition. This was a deliberate design intent behind § 1043A's predecessor, § 1002G of the Corporations Law.

The Griffiths Report, which was the result of the formal inquiry into strengthening Australia's insider trading laws and led to the introduction of the relevant provisions in the Corporations Law (re-enacted in the present legislation), noted that the previous requirement for a connection with the company was "too restrictive"[37] and "unnecessarily complicates the issue."[38] The Griffiths Report went on to state that "It is the use of the information, rather than the connection between a person and a corporation, which should be the basis for determining whether insider trading has occurred."[39]

The possession standard casts a very wide net. Any legal person, including a corporation, who possesses inside information comes within the definition of insider. Defining an insider in these terms is a clear embodiment of the equal access theory justifying prohibiting insider trading, since an unrestricted definition of insider is a necessary prerequisite for a prohibition that focuses on the use of information only.

---

[33]   Discussed later in this chapter.
[34]   Lyon & du Plessis, supra note 7, at 58.
[35]   Corporations Act 2001, § 1042A.
[36]   The tipping offense applies only to listed securities; id. § 1043(2)(c).
[37]   Griffiths Report, supra note 15, at [4.3.1].
[38]   Id. at [4.3.5].
[39]   Id.

B.   Definition of Information

Because an insider is defined as someone merely in possession of inside information, the notion of what constitutes such inside information takes on particular importance. Inside information is a subset of the broader concept of "information," requiring this latter notion to be defined before the prohibition has any content.

"Information" is defined in § 1042A as including suppositions and other matters that are insufficiently definite to merit disclosure to the general public and matters relating to a person's intentions. This inclusive definition goes no further than making explicit that these aspects are covered. In the result, an examination of judicial consideration of the term is required to identify its parameters.

An early prohibition on insider trading in Australia required that information be "specific,"[40] leading the Supreme Court of New South Wales to hold that information needed to be of a concrete kind, rather than general or loose deductions.[41] The legislative requirement that information be specific was removed from the subsequent New South Wales legislation.[42] Considering this later provision, Justice Young in *Hooker Investments v. Baring Bros*[43] expanded upon the *Ryan v. Triguboff* approach, holding that information as used in the legislation included "factual knowledge of a concrete kind *or* that obtained by means of a hint or veiled suggestion from which one can impute knowledge."[44]

In interpreting the Victorian legislation in place at that time,[45] which had no explicit requirement that information be specific, Justice McInerney in *Commissioner for Corporate Affairs v. Green*[46] rejected a submission that information could not include "rumour, possibility or speculative suggestion nor information of a kind that is preliminary or uncertain."[47] Referring favorably to Justice McInerney's approach in *Green*, Justice Young in *Hooker Investments* drew a vague distinction between information and knowledge:

> I wonder . . . whether it is safe to equate information and knowledge. Information is often defined as knowledge acquired, derived or inculcated by observation, reading or study or by what one is told; but in some cases information implies lack of knowledge such as, for instance, where one says he is informed of a thing but he does not know whether or not his information is true.
>
> In my mind information [in the legislation] goes further than knowledge and includes the situation where someone has been informed of something which he does not know to be true nor does he care whether it is true or not. In other words, information may include a rumour that something has happened with respect to a company which a person neither believes nor disbelieves.[48]

---

[40]   Securities Industry Act 1970 (NSW), § 75A.
[41]   *Ryan v. Triguboff* [1976] 1 NSWLR 588, 599.
[42]   Securities Industry Code (NSW), § 128.
[43]   *Hooker Investments Pty Ltd v. Baring Bros Halkertson & Partners Securities Limited* (1986) 10 ACLR 462.
[44]   Id. at 463 (emphasis added).
[45]   Companies Act 1961 (Vic.), § 124(2).
[46]   [1978] VR 505.
[47]   Id., at 511.
[48]   Hooker Investments v. Baring Bros (1986) 10 ACLR 462, 467–468.

Justice Young's comments seem to extend the concept of information beyond whatever limits one may impose on the notion of knowledge. Indeed, if knowledge is regarded as an understanding of objective true fact (as Justice Young seems to suggest), § 1042A appears to incorporate this view, by explicitly including matters for which truth is not a prerequisite (such as supposition). The distinction is a fine one and it is debatable whether much hinges on defining where knowledge ends and information begins. For example, a submission in *R. v. Rivkin*[49] seeking to rely on Justice Young's comments, was rejected by the New South Wales Court of Criminal Appeal as being "of the most technical kind that are entirely lacking in merit."[50]

Indeed, the law has been developed such that the concept of information is now regarded as being of wide import. The inclusive definition contained in § 1042A was first introduced in the 1991 reforms as § 1002A(1) of the Corporations Act 1989. The legislative history makes it clear that the expanded definition was designed to overcome concerns that the term "information" would not encompass "supposition, intentions, and other matter not sufficiently certain to require its release to the public."[51] Subsequent interpretation has confirmed the wideness of the definition to be applied, with the New South Wales Court of Criminal Appeal holding in *Hannes v. DPP (No 2)*[52] that information may be imprecise[53] and the Federal Court in *ASIC v. Citigroup Global Markets*[54] rejecting a submission that information does not include a person's internal thought processes.[55]

C. Definition of Inside Information

Having established that the concept of information, as used in the insider trading provisions, is a wide concept with few restrictions, the focus moves to a subset of this notion— inside information. Given that the definition of information is very wide, its precise parameters are not especially important.[56]

"Inside information," however, is the sole criterion by which a person is identified as being prohibited from trading in particular securities under § 1043A. Consequently, identifying information that falls into this category takes on a singular importance. Section 1042A defines inside information as information that is:

(a) not generally available;
(b) if it was generally available, a reasonable person would expect it to have a material effect on the price or value of particular Division 3 financial products.

---

[49] (2004) 59 NSWLR 284; [2004] NSWCCA 7.
[50] Id. at [131] (note that this paragraph is not reproduced in the official report).
[51] Explanatory Memorandum to Corporations Legislation Amendment Bill 1991 (Cth), [319].
[52] Hannes v. Director of Public Prosecutions (No 2) (2006) 60 ACSR 1.
[53] Id. at 111.
[54] Australian Securities and Investments Commission v. Citigroup Global Markets Australia Pty Ltd (No 4) (2007) 160 FCR 35.
[55] Id. at 106.
[56] The boundaries defining information are important only to the extent that anything beyond those limits cannot constitute inside information. As the prohibition's true focus is on the narrower notion of inside information, identifying the precise limits of information is of minimal consequence in light of the foregoing analysis.

This definition introduces two new concepts into the matrix: general availability and material effect. These are now considered.

1.   Information that is not generally available

The requirement that information must not be generally available has been a feature of the Australian prohibition on insider trading since its early days.[57] Such a requirement would seem to be intuitive. Because the reasoning for banning insider trading essentially comes down to preventing parties from obtaining an unjustifiable profit from using an informational advantage, a threshold requirement must be that the information used to gain that profit must not be widely available. If the information is widely available, then it is difficult to see where the informational advantage lies, undermining the basis for which the party with that information is prevented from trading.

Unlike the predecessors to the Corporations Law, the current legislation provides some guidance as to when information is regarded as generally available. Section 1042C states:

> (1) For the purposes of this Division, information is generally available if:
>   (a) it consists of readily observable matter;
>   (b) both of the following subparagraphs apply:
>   (i) it has been made known in a manner that would, or would be likely to, bring it to the attention of persons who commonly invest in Division 3 financial products of a kind whose price might be affected by the information; and
>   (ii) since it was made known, a reasonable period for it to be disseminated among such persons has elapsed; or
>   (c) it consists of deductions, conclusions or inferences made or drawn from either or both of the following:
>   (i) information referred to in paragraph (a);
>   (ii) information made known as mentioned in subparagraph (b)(i).

There are two basic pathways by which information can qualify as generally available under § 1042C (noting that the third listed is a derivation from the first two). These are the readily observable and publishable information tests.

(a) Readily observable test   The readily observable test contained in § 1042C(1)(a) raises a number of questions that have not been entirely resolved. Writing shortly after the readily observable test was incorporated into the insider trading prohibition, Bostock dissected this test, noting that neither the statute nor the legislative history provides guidance, for example as to how the information needs to be observable to be regarded as readily observable.[58] Nor is light shed on to whom the information needs to be readily observable. An example is provided of a confidential company memorandum found lying in the street;[59] it is certainly readily observable to the party who picked it up, but it seems at odds with the general notion of what constitutes generally available information. This simple case study would seem to suggest that there is a requirement for opportunity for a broader group to observe the information that does not appear on

---

[57]   See, e.g., Securities Industry Act 1980 (Cth), § 128.
[58]   T.E. Bostock, Australia's New Insider Trading Laws, 10 C&S L. J. 165, 171 (1992).
[59]   Id.

the legislation's face.[60] Lyon and du Plessis condense Bostock's critique to three open questions:

- By what means must the information be readily observable?
- Readily observable to whom?
- Observable where?[61]

A handful of cases have provided the courts with the opportunity to consider the requirement of readily observable. To be readily observable, it is enough that the information *may* be observed; there is no requirement that it actually *be* observed.[62] Further, the test as to whether information is readily observable is objective and hypothetical.[63] In an increasingly internationalized and integrated securities market, the question of where the information needs to be readily observable also raises concerns about the intended scope and purpose of the prohibition, as demonstrated by the following cases.[64]

The decisions in *R. v. Firns*[65] and *R. v. Kruse*[66] provide an excellent illustration of the problems that may arise under § 1042C as it currently stands. Both decisions emanate from the same fundamental facts. A mining company (Carpenter), which was listed on the ASX, received a favorable court ruling in the Supreme Court of Papua New Guinea regarding a mining license in July 1995. Kruse, an officer of Carpenter, was present in the court at the time judgment was handed down. Very soon after the judgment, Kruse purchased shares in Carpenter through a broker in Australia, which were sold four days later for a profit of AUD 50,000.

Firns was the son of another director in Carpenter, the latter also being present in the court at the time the judgment was handed down. Soon after the judgment, the director phoned Firns (who was in Australia) and instructed him to purchase shares in Carpenter. Some 400,000 shares were purchased (in Firns' wife's maiden name), which were subsequently sold for a profit.

The central issue in both cases was whether the relevant information (the court judgment) was readily observable as required under § 1002B of the Corporations Law (the forerunner to § 1042C). At first instance, Kruse was found not guilty of insider trading (i.e., the information was readily observable), but the opposite outcome occurred in the *Firns* litigation.

In both cases, the court had to consider whether the information had to be readily

---

[60] Bostock goes through the example provided in the legislative history of excess stocks held in a company's yards as an illustration of information that is to be regarded as readily observable but may not be regarded as disseminated; id.

[61] Lyon & du Plessis, supra note 7, at 37.

[62] R. v. Firns (2001) 51 NSWLR 548, 564; ASIC v. Citigroup Global Markets Australia Pty Ltd (No 4) (2007) 160 FCR 35, 107.

[63] ASIC v. Citigroup Global Markets Australia Pty Ltd (No 4) (2007) 160 FCR 35, 106, citing R. v. Firns (2001) 51 NSWLR 548, 565.

[64] See also discussion in Black, supra note 32, at 318.

[65] (2001) 51 NSWLR 548.

[66] Unreported, New South Wales District Court, December 2, 1999, No98/11/0908. The description and analysis provided here rely on the material provided in Lyon & du Plessis, supra note 7, at 37–40.

observable in Australia. The only material difference in the facts between *Kruse* and *Firns* was the location of the defendant at the relevant time. Kruse was in Papua New Guinea and observed the information first hand, whereas Firns was in Australia and received the information via a telephone call. In *Kruse*, O'Reilly DCJ emphasized the public nature of the court ruling, with the matter listed the previous day and the presence of journalists and photographers as well as lawyers in the court at the time judgment was handed down.[67] Such circumstances were very public and would render the information imparted on that occasion as readily observable within the ordinary meaning of those words.[68] Importantly, while "the facts must be directly observable in the public arena . . . that public arena need not be confined to [Australia]."[69]

Judge Sides in *Firns* at first instance noted the same circumstances surrounding the occasion of the judgment, particularly the presence of members of the press.[70] His Honor, though, regarded the term "readily observable," as used in the legislation, as requiring that the information be readily observable in Australia.[71]

The decision at first instance was overturned on appeal in the Supreme Court of New South Wales.[72] In the majority's judgment, Mason P held that judicially adding the words "within Australia" to the readily observable requirement altered the statutory charge to the defendant's detriment.[73] Having established that § 1002B did not restrict the relevant class of persons to whom the information needs to be readily observable to those located within Australia, Mason P applied the principles of open justice to regard a decision handed down in open court to be readily observable.[74]

(b) Publishable information test   Section 1042C(1)(b) contains what is sometimes referred to as the publishable information test, which is an alternative means by which information may qualify as generally available. There are two components to this test: the information has been made known in a manner at least likely to come to the attention of regular investors and a reasonable period of time for dissemination has elapsed. The first requirement consists of two aspects, namely the manner of publication and the class of person likely to invest in relevant financial instruments. The legislation does not provide any further guidance as to the content or intended application of these criteria.

In respect of the manner of publication, § 1042C(1)(b) is more limited than the suggestion originally in the draft legislation put forward as part of the Anisman Report.[75] There, information was to be regarded as "public information" (and, therefore, not brought within the prohibition) if it was made known through a filing, press release or some other manner likely to bring the information to the attention of a reasonable investor.[76] The

---

[67]   R. v. Kruse, 4–6, as reproduced in Lyon & du Plessis, supra note 7, at 39.

[68]   Id.

[69]   Id.

[70]   R. v. Firns, unreported New South Wales District Court, 2–4, as reproduced in Lyon & du Plessis, supra note 7, at 38.

[71]   Id.

[72]   R. v. Firns (2001) 51 NSWLR 548.

[73]   Id. at 565.

[74]   Id. at 566.

[75]   Anisman Report, supra note 9, at 134.

[76]   Id. (§ 1(1)(g) of the draft legislation).

specific examples were not replicated in the later Griffiths Report, the draft legislation for consultation or the final statutory provisions. No explanation for this exclusion was provided at any stage. The current provision, which refers only to the manner of dissemination in general terms, allows the courts the ability to assess whether the manner is appropriate in the circumstances on a case by case basis. For example, if the issue of a press release in a particular setting may not be regarded as sufficient in itself to bring the information to the attention of reasonable investors, the wording of § 1042C allows the courts to conclude that that is not a means meeting the provision's requirements. This would not be the case under the Anisman draft legislation (noting that the reasonable period of time for dissemination requirement was applicable only to the general manner means of dissemination and not the specific examples).[77]

With the benefit of hindsight,[78] not identifying particular means by which the information is to be deemed to be generally available assists with § 1042C's continued applicability, due to the extreme pace of change in communications technology. Although in the context of information that is readily observable, Mason P noted the effect advances in communications technology can have on how the requirements of the prohibition on insider trading are interpreted.[79]

The second aspect is identifying the class of persons who are likely to invest in the financial instruments whose price might be affected by the information. Some limited guidance is provided in the legislative history as to this requirement's content. Selective disclosure will be insufficient: "It would not be sufficient for information to be released to a small sector of the investors who commonly invest in the securities. The information must be made known to a cross section of the investors who commonly invest in the securities."[80] Further, the legislative language is explicit in that the class of investors is those who "commonly invest" in the relevant securities. This is broader than current holders of those securities and encompasses potential investors.[81] As such, disclosure to the present shareholder base is unlikely to be adequate to render the information generally available under § 1042C(1)(b).

The second component of the publishable information test is that a sufficient period of time has elapsed for the information to be disseminated among the relevant class of investors. As with this test's first component, little legislative guidance is provided. A good deal of attention was devoted to this matter in the Griffiths Report, which acknowledged arguments both in favor of and against prescribing minimum time periods.[82] For example, there was a concern that small investors could be disadvantaged if an insider was able to walk straight from a press conference disclosing price-sensitive information to the telephone and place an order to trade shares in the relevant

---

[77]   Id. (§ 1(1)(g)(iii) of the draft legislation).

[78]   A necessary supposition, since the legislative history gives no indication as to why the specific examples were not included in the final legislation.

[79]   R. v. Firns (2001) 51 NSWLR 548, 564–565.

[80]   Explanatory Memorandum to the Corporations Legislation Amendment Bill 1991 (Cth), [328].

[81]   Keith Kendall & Gordon Walker, Insider Trading in Australia and New Zealand: Information that is "Generally Available," 24 C&S L. J. 343, 348 (2006).

[82]   Griffiths Report, supra note 15, at [4.5.1]–[4.5.5].

company.[83] Ultimately, it was concluded that while the absence of specific time constraints may disadvantage small investors compared with market professionals, any such time limit would be arbitrary and unrealistically long in some cases.[84] As such, the overriding concern was that such rigid periods would penalize the diligent.[85] Such concerns have proven to be prescient, as developments in communications technology since the Griffiths Report was published (in 1989) have reduced the time it takes to disseminate information; for example, a press release in the late 1980s that may not have been readily available to most investors until published in the following day's press may now be available almost immediately upon being published on an appropriate internet site.[86]

At this point, it is worth noting that the disadvantage of small investors, presumably with no special access to inside information, is negated to an extent by virtue of § 1043M(2). This subsection provides a defence to a person who trades on information where that person came into possession of that information purely by the information having been published in the manner described in § 1042C(1)(b)(i) (i.e., in a manner likely to bring it to the attention of regular investors).[87] This provides an effective distinction between parties with special access to price-sensitive information and those investors who happen upon the relevant, for example, press release before it is widely known.[88] Consequently, such uninformed investors may be at an advantage compared with (traditional)[89] insiders in that they are not constrained in their trading by being required to wait for an appropriate time to have elapsed for the information to be disseminated before trading.[90]

(c) Information analysis   A third means is provided for in § 1042C by which information may be regarded as generally available. This is where the person has unique information, but that information was derived from information that falls within § 1042C(1)(a) and/ or § 1042C(1)(b)(i). In other words, a market participant will not be brought within the insider trading provisions merely because they drew a conclusion that no one else drew (and traded based on that conclusion), so long as that conclusion was based on information that was readily observable or had been appropriately published.[91] Further, there is no requirement that the information have been disseminated for any particular period of time.[92] This arises from the fact that § 1042C(1)(c) draws upon § 1042(1)(b)(i) (the manner of publication requirement) but makes no mention of § 1042C(1)(b)(ii) (the dissemination requirement).[93] This last observation increases the importance of accurately identifying

---

[83]   Id. at [4.5.2].
[84]   Id. at [4.5.5].
[85]   Id.
[86]   Kendall & Walker, supra note 81, at 348.
[87]   Corporations Act 2001 (Cth), § 1043M(2).
[88]   Lyon & du Plessis, supra note 7, at 35.
[89]   In the sense of those with special access to inside information, rather than those in mere possession of that information as provided for in the Australian system.
[90]   Of course, as has been noted in other contexts in this chapter, developments in communications technology are likely to erode any informational advantage arising in this manner.
[91]   See ASIC v. Citigroup Global Markets Australia Pty Ltd (No 4) (2007) 160 FCR 35, 107.
[92]   Id.
[93]   See also Rhys Bollen, Research Analysts and the Australian Insider Trading and Misleading or Deceptive Conduct Regimes, 21 C&S L. J. 430, 439–440 (2003).

the source of the information that the defendant relied upon. If the relevant information is merely the relevant (for example) press release, the defendant must wait for an appropriate amount of time for that information to be disseminated throughout the market. However, if the press release contains some morsel of information that leads the defendant to a particular conclusion, then it appears that the defendant may trade immediately. The same would seem to apply if the press release contained a nugget of information that provided the last link in a chain of reasoning leading the defendant to that conclusion (assuming that the other links are either readily observable or have been similarly published). For example, if a company announced via a press release that a particular deal with a Chinese company had fallen through and the defendant wanted to sell their shares as a direct result of that information, then the defendant would need to wait an appropriate period of time for the information to be disseminated. If, however, the defendant was aware of the importance of this particular deal because of the increase in competition from India and the United States and based on the company's profit forecasts as disclosed in the previous year's financial report, and concluded that the company's profitability would now be substantially reduced as a result of the deal not proceeding, then it appears that the defendant could trade immediately. This illustrates the importance and difficulty inherent in identifying, first, the relevant information and, secondly, the source of that information, both of which are necessary to determine whether the information (however identified) qualifies as inside information. This is in addition to the difficulties already canvassed in respect of what would constitute an appropriate period of time if the defendant needs to wait for the information to be disseminated. Unfortunately, the courts have not had an opportunity to consider these matters.[94]

2.   Material effect

Even if the information is not generally available, § 1042A also requires that, to qualify as inside information, the information must be reasonably expected to have a material effect on the company's securities. Section 1042D provides guidance as to when information can be expected to have a material effect on the price of the relevant securities. It states:

> For the purposes of this Division, a reasonable person would be taken to expect information to have a material effect on the price or value of particular Division 3 financial products if (and only if) the information would, or would be likely to, influence persons who commonly acquire Division 3 financial products in deciding whether or not to acquire or dispose of the first mentioned financial products.[95]

First, the test is objective because of explicit reliance on what "a reasonable person would be taken to expect." Secondly, the test is whether the information would be likely to influence a trading decision of a regular investor. As to this second aspect, there is no specific requirement that the information would have a particular effect on the security's price (e.g., the price would be expected to move by a minimum percentage). Consequently, it may be argued in appropriate circumstances that an expected effect that may be regarded

---

[94]   See examples provided in Michael Gething, Insider Trading Enforcement: Where Are We Now and Where Do We Go From Here?, 16 C&S L. J. 607, 613 (1998); Lyon & du Plessis, supra note 7, at 51–53; Anisman, supra note 9, at 44.

[95]   Corporations Act 2001 (Cth), § 1042D.

as nominal and unlikely to be influential in one situation would be significant and influential in another scenario (e.g., if there is a very thin market for the securities or some slight negative news has a disproportionate effect as the rest of the market is strongly positive).

The notion of material effect was considered in *Citigroup* on two occasions. The first was in considering the price sensitivity of the identity of the bidder in an expected takeover. Considering the expert evidence led by both sides, the court held that as the price of the relevant shares had moved to such an extent after a takeover became expected but before the identity of the likely bidder was known there would likely have been little further effect on the share price.[96] As a consequence, at the point in time when the impugned trading took place, the court held that the information would not have had the required material effect.[97]

The second occasion was in relation to information as to the timing of the takeover bid. It was held that this information would be price sensitive within the test provided for in the legislation.[98] A concerning aspect of this part of the judgment is its seeming reliance on hindsight. While on a careful reading, it is apparent that the court did reach this conclusion without depending on observed price movements, the reasoning moves straight into a short discussion of the price movements around the time of the relevant announcement to illustrate the information's price sensitivity.[99] The concern is that this passage could be misinterpreted as a precedent for judging materiality with the benefit of hindsight, which would further add to the uncertainty already present as to the location of the boundary between legitimate and proscribed market conduct.

3. Deeming

Section 1042G attributes the actions and characteristics of its officers to the body corporate for the purposes of the insider trading prohibition. "Officer" is defined broadly in § 9 and includes a person who makes decisions affecting a substantial part of the corporation's business, a person who has the capacity to affect significantly the corporation's financial standing and a person with whose instructions the corporation's directors are accustomed to act.[100] This extended meaning of "officer" was considered in the *Citigroup* case, where the Federal Court held that a trader with a daily limit of AUD 10 million was not in a position to affect significantly the corporation's business so as to come within this definition.[101] In coming to this conclusion, Justice Jacobson held that,[102]

> It is true that [the trader's] daily limit was large when expressed in dollar terms and could potentially amount to considerable financial exposure over a number of days. But I do not consider that this of itself is sufficient to make him a person who had the capacity to affect Citigroup's financial standing within para (b)(ii). A loans officer at a large branch may, for example, in

---

[96]   ASIC v. Citigroup Global Markets Australia Pty Ltd (No 4) (2007) 160 FCR 35, 109.
[97]   Id.
[98]   The reported judgment refers to § 1043D, but this would seem to be a reporting error, as § 1043D does not deal with any aspect of price sensitivity or materiality. Consequently, it may be surmised that the court was actually referring to § 1042D; see id. at 110.
[99]   Id.
[100] Definition of "officer," § 9(b).
[101] ASIC v. Citigroup Global Markets Australia Pty Ltd (No 4) (2007) 160 FCR 35, 99–101.
[102] Id. at 101.

general terms, have the capacity to affect the bank's standing if he or she lends recklessly, but the loans officer is an employee, not an officer of the corporation.

Section 1042H provides a similar deeming for actions and knowledge of partners in a partnership to the other members in that partnership. These attribution provisions need to be read subject to the relevant exception and defense provisions (discussed below), in particular the Chinese wall defenses.[103]

D. Prohibited Conduct

There are three forms of prohibited conduct under § 1043A: trading, procuring and tipping. To be affected by the prohibition, a person need only be in possession of inside information and know (or ought reasonably to know) that that information is inside information. While the preceding analysis demonstrates that there are a number of matters that make identifying information as inside information less than clear cut in many situations, once the inside information has been identified as such, mere possession is enough to bring the holder within the prohibition. No other criteria, such as a connection with the company, are required.

1. Trading
Section 1043A(1)(c) prohibits an insider from (whether as principal or agent) applying for, acquiring or disposing of relevant financial instruments. Insiders are also restrained from agreeing to engage in these forms of conduct. This is a narrower range of prohibited conduct than was the case under previous legislation, which also included offers and attempts to buy or sell securities.[104]

2. Procurement
Section 1043A(1)(d) extends the prohibition to insiders from procuring another person to engage in the conduct identified in § 1043A(1)(c). Without limiting the meaning "procuring" would otherwise be taken to have, § 1042F(1) includes inciting, inducing or encouraging an act or omission on the part of another person.

3. Tipping
The prohibition against acts often referred to as "tipping"[105] is included in § 1043A(2). This is where an insider is banned from communicating the information (or causing the information to be communicated) to another person where the insider knows (or reasonably ought to know) that that other person is likely to engage in conduct referred to in § 1043A(1) (i.e., trade themselves or procure another person to trade). Unlike § 1043A(1), the tipping prohibition also requires the relevant financial securities to be tradeable on an Australian financial market.[106] Securities are still treated as being tradeable for the purposes of the tipping prohibition even if the issuing company has had trading in its securities suspended.[107]

---

103 Section 1043F (for bodies corporate) and § 1043G (for partnerships).
104 Lyon & du Plessis, supra note 7, at 59.
105 Id. at 62.
106 Section 1043(2)(c).
107 Section 1042E.

III.   EXCEPTIONS AND DEFENSES

The legislation provides for several exceptions and defenses from liability and/or prosecution for breaching the insider trading prohibition in § 1043A.[108] Under § 1043M(1), the prosecution is not required to prove the non-existence of any facts that would make out any such exception or defense. Consequently, the burden to prove these facts falls upon the defense, which, under the Commonwealth Criminal Code, must be proved on the balance of probabilities.[109]

The first exception is contained in § 1043B, which applies when a member of a registered scheme withdraws their investment. For the exception to apply, the amount paid to the member must be calculated with reference to the value of the underlying assets held through the scheme. Baxt, Black and Hanrahan explain that this exception is necessary to permit buyback covenants contained in unregistered schemes.[110] This is because the responsible entity will at times be in possession of inside information when required to redeem a member's interests.[111]

Underwriters could potentially be caught by the prohibition in § 1043A(1) against applying for financial instruments while in possession of inside information, since their involvement in underwriting an issue of securities could provide them access to such price-sensitive information that is not generally available. As a consequence, an exception is provided for underwriters who acquire financial securities under an underwriting arrangement,[112] entering into an underwriting agreement[113] or disposing of the securities that were acquired under the underwriting agreement.[114] The exception applies only to those securities acquired under the underwriting agreement; it does not apply to the same kind of securities in the issuer if those specific securities are not acquired under that agreement.[115] An exception to the prohibition against tipping is provided for in § 1043C(2) for parties seeking to secure the services of a potential underwriter.

An exception is provided for parties who are required to acquire financial securities under a legal requirement.[116] A similar exception is allowed for parties who are required to communicate inside information under the Corporations Act.[117]

Sections 1043F and 1043G provide for the Chinese wall defense for bodies corporate and partnerships respectively. Under § 1043F, a body corporate will not breach the insider trading prohibition by entering into a transaction or agreement at a time when an officer of the body corporate is in possession of inside information if,

---

[108]   The legislative distinction between exceptions and defenses is not especially clear. At first blush, it appears that exceptions refer to civil liability, whereas defenses seem to relate to criminal prosecutions. However, the terms are used apparently interchangeably at times; see Lyon & du Plessis, supra note 7, at 71.
[109]   Criminal Code (Cth), § 13.5.
[110]   Baxt, Black & Hanrahan, supra note 7, at 720.
[111]   Id.
[112]   Section 1043C(1)(a).
[113]   Section 1043C(1)(b).
[114]   Section 1043C(1)(c).
[115]   Baxt, Black & Hanrahan, supra note 7, at 720.
[116]   Section 1043D.
[117]   Section 1043E.

1. the decision to enter into the transaction or agreement was made on behalf of the body corporate by a person (or persons) other than the officer in possession of the inside information;
2. the body corporate at that time had in place arrangements that could reasonably be expected to prevent the communication of that inside information to the person (or persons) who made the decision to enter into the transaction or agreement; and
3. the inside information was not actually communicated.

The adequacy of Chinese walls within an investment bank was considered in the *Citigroup* decision.[118] The Federal Court confirmed that, to be an adequate Chinese wall, the relevant policies do not have to meet "the practical impossibility of ensuring that every conceivable risk is covered by written procedures and followed by employees."[119]

The defense available for partnerships under § 1043G is structured in a similar way to that for bodies corporate under § 1043F.

Section 1043H provides an exception where the relevant inside information is the insider's knowledge of their own intentions. A similar exception is available for bodies corporate under § 1043I(1). Further, if one of the body corporate's officers or employees knows of the body corporate's intentions and came into that information through their employment with the body corporate, then the body corporate will not breach § 1043A by that fact alone.[120]

An exception is provided for in § 1043J for officers of a body corporate who enter into transactions or agreements on behalf of their employer where the inside information is knowledge that the body corporate proposes to enter into transactions in relation to the financial securities of another entity. To illustrate this exception, Baxt, Black and Hanrahan provide the example of a body corporate purchasing shares in another body corporate in anticipation of making a takeover bid for that second body corporate.[121]

Section 1043K provides an exception for financial services licensees (and their representatives) where they trade on behalf of unrelated clients, so long as appropriate policies are in place to ensure that the inside information is not communicated to the principal and that no such communication took place.

Finally, § 1043M provides for positive defenses from allegations of a breach of the insider trading prohibition. The trading or procuring offenses may be defended if the defendant can prove[122] that the information came into their possession solely by virtue of being published in a manner described in § 1042C(1)(b)(i) (a manner likely to bring it to the attention of regular investors).[123] A similar defense is available against a charge of tipping.[124] Alternatively, it is a defense if the counterparty to the transaction knew, or ought reasonably to have known the information prior to entering into the transaction

---

[118] ASIC v. Citigroup Global Markets Australia Pty Ltd (2007) 160 FCR 35, 110–112.
[119] Id. at 112.
[120] Sections 1043I(2) and (3).
[121] Baxt, Black & Hanrahan, supra note 7, at 725.
[122] As noted earlier, the burden of proof for the elements of these defenses rests with the defense; supra note 109.
[123] Section 1043M(2)(a).
[124] Section 1043M(3)(a).

or agreement (in the case of trading or procuring)[125] or the recipient of the information knew or ought reasonably to have known of the information before the communication (in the case of tipping).[126]

IV.   PENALTIES

Insider trading under the Corporations Act may be sanctioned as either a criminal or civil offense. Criminal penalties for both individuals and bodies corporate are imposed under § 1311 and are set under item 310 of Schedule 3. For individuals, the penalty is up to 10 years' imprisonment and/or the greater of 4,500 penalty units[127] and three times the amount of benefits derived (not necessarily by the defendant) that are reasonably attributable to the commission of the offense. For bodies corporate, the penalty for a criminal conviction is the greater of 45,000 penalty units[128] and three times the value of the total benefits derived from the insider trading offense. If those total benefits cannot be valued, then the alternative penalty is 10 percent of the body corporate's turnover in the 12 months ending in the month when the body corporate committed (or began committing) the offense.

Civil penalties are provided for in § 1317E. The insider trading offenses are listed in §§ 1317(1)(jf) and (jg), qualifying them as "financial services civil penalty provisions" as defined under § 1317DA. Under § 1317G, if convicted of an insider trading offense as a civil matter, a court may order an individual to pay a fine of up to AUD 200,000 or a body corporate pay a fine of up to AUD 1 million if the contravention of insider trading prohibition:

(a) Materially prejudices the interests of traders in the relevant financial products;
(b) Materially prejudices the issuer of the relevant financial products or, if the issuer is a corporation or a scheme, the members of the issuer; or
(c) Is serious.

Only ASIC can seek an order under § 1317E and, therefore, seek the penalties set out under § 1317G.[129] ASIC must bring the civil action within six years of the contravention.[130]

Section 1317HA also provides for compensation orders for damages suffered by another person (which may include a corporation) or a registered scheme.[131] In assessing damages, the court may consider the amount of profits derived from the offense[132] or

---

[125]   Section 1043M(2)(b).
[126]   Section 1043M(3)(b).
[127]   As at May 2012, a "penalty unit" is defined in § 4AA of the Crimes Act 1914 (Cth) (for the purposes of Commonwealth offenses) as AUD 110. This means that the fine for a criminal conviction for an individual under § 1311 is AUD 495,000.
[128]   AUD 4,950,000 (as at May 2012).
[129]   Section 1317J.
[130]   Section 1317K.
[131]   The operative provision from which such compensation orders may be sought is § 1043L.
[132]   Section 1317HA(2).

the diminution of the value of any property held by a scheme.[133] The court is empowered under § 1043N to relieve a person from any compensation order applicable under § 1317HA if the defenses available under § 1043M are made out. Section 1317S provides additional avenues for the court to relieve a person wholly or partly from liability under § 1317HA where the person has acted honestly and the court believes they should fairly be excused for the contravention.

V.   ENFORCEMENT

A.   Institutional Arrangements

The ASX and ASIC use the SMARTS surveillance system supplied by NASDAQ OMX. The SMARTS Integrity Platform is an extensive market surveillance solution consisting of 12 modules. It takes a real-time data feed directly from the trading engine of the exchange and processes it in real time, automatically detecting anomalies and producing alerts. The SMARTS Integrity Platform has been adopted by over 40 exchanges and regulators.[134] Prior to 2010, market surveillance was carried out solely by the ASX using SMARTS. In 2010, responsibility for market supervision was transferred to ASIC, which also uses SMARTS technology.

The present division of responsibility can be summarized as follows: as stated, ASIC has responsibility for supervision of real-time trading on Australian domestic markets and is responsible for enforcing laws against misconduct on Australian financial markets. ASX Compliance Pty Ltd is responsible for monitoring and enforcing compliance with ASX operating rules. Matters arising before the transfer of responsibility for market supervision to ASIC on August 1, 2010 are referred to the Disciplinary Tribunal. Matters arising after August 1, 2010 are referred to the ASX Chief Compliance Officer. The ASX is obliged under the Corporations Act 2001 and pursuant to a Memorandum of Understanding with ASIC dated October 28, 2011 (available at the ASX website) to notify ASIC of various matters including any suspected contraventions of the Corporations Act or the operating rules. Information about the number and type of referrals made by ASX to ASIC is published in the ASX Compliance Monthly Activity Report.

B.   Market Supervision by ASIC

The Market and Participant Supervision Unit at ASIC comprises four teams: real-time market surveillance, relationship management, participant compliance and market analysis. The market surveillance team uses SMARTS technology and contains several former ASX personnel. Preliminary analysis of a suspected insider trading matter is done by the real-time surveillance team, the misconduct and breach reporting unit and the participant compliance team. The matter then proceeds to the market analysis team for

---

[133]   Section 1317HA(3).
[134]   See http://www.smartsgroup.com/index.php/solutions/smarts-integrity-platform.html (last accessed December 4, 2012).

further assessment and a recommended course of action, which may include a referral to a deterrence unit for investigation. ASIC deterrence teams contain former ASX investigators. For example, the deterrence team dedicated to market integrity matters was built around staff from ASX investigations and enforcement units. A "Triage Committee" then prioritizes matters and, where appropriate, the markets deterrence teams at ASIC take matters to court.[135]

C.   Enforcement by ASIC

ASIC's approach to enforcement appears in Information Sheet 151.[136] ASIC states that its strategic priorities include confident investors and fair and efficient financial markets. Hence, ASIC will use deterrence to achieve its strategic priorities in cases of serious misconduct which impacts on market integrity or the confidence of investors and has serious consequences for investors. ASIC has the option of pursuing civil penalties or referring criminal offenses to the Commonwealth DPP. Criminal prosecution is reserved for the most serious misconduct such as insider trading where the maximum penalty is up to 10 years.

In striking contrast to the position in New Zealand (which has substantially similar laws), ASIC has a strong record in pursuing insider conduct matters.[137] For example, there were seven insider trading verdicts and judgments in the period July 1, 2009 to June 30, 2011 and 10 insider trading verdicts and judgments in the period January 1, 2011 to December 31, 2011.[138] A later report noted seven insider trading matters pending.[139] Indeed, there is some evidence that Australia's global ranking as a force against insider trading is climbing.[140] Interestingly, it is not traditional insiders such as company directors who feature heavily in recent prosecutions. One report noted that seven out of eleven

---

[135]   This summary derives from Yanco, supra note 8.

[136]   ASIC, ASIC's Approach to Enforcement, Information Sheet 151, available at http://www.asic.gov.au/asic/pdflib.nsf/LookupByFileName/INFO-151-ASIC's-approach-to-enforcement.pdf/$file/INFO-151-ASIC's-approach-to-enforcement.pdf (last accessed December 4, 2012).

[137]   See Hannah Low, ASIC Doubles the Danger for Insiders, The Aus. Fin. Rev., November 9, 2011, at 8. The number of people convicted for market manipulation and insider trading has doubled since ASIC took over from the ASX due to its broad investigative powers. Sixteen criminal actions relating to market and insider trading charges have been brought since January 2009. Id.

[138]   See ASIC Report 277, ASIC Supervision of Markets and Participants: July to December 2011 (February 2012), available at http://www.asic.gov.au/asic/pdflib.nsf/LookupByFileName/rep277-published--7-February-2012.pdf/$file/rep277-published--7-February-2012.pdf (last accessed December 4, 2012).

[139]   See ASIC Report 281, ASIC Enforcement Outcomes: July to December 2011 (March 2012), available at http://www.asic.gov.au/asic/pdflib.nsf/LookupByFileName/rep281-published-29-March-2012.pdf/$file/rep281-published-29-March-2012.pdf (last accessed December 4, 2012).

[140]   Andrew Main, We're Getting SMARTS, All Right, The Aus. Fin. Rev., February 8, 2012, at 42.

people prosecuted for insider trading recently came from the ranks of corporate advisors, lawyers and accountants.[141]

VI.   CONCLUDING REMARKS

The preceding analysis demonstrates that Australia has had, for the last 20 years, a particularly broad prohibition against insider trading, as measured by world standards. The essential component of this claim is the definition of "insider" in § 1043A, which looks only to the possession of inside information. Compared with most other jurisdictions, which usually require some form of connection to the issuing company, Australia may be regarded as having one of the broadest, if not the widest prohibition in the world.

Despite the longevity and the prescriptiveness of the current regime, a degree of uncertainty surrounds particular elements of these provisions. In particular, matters such as when information is to be considered generally available and what constitutes sufficient dissemination have caused problems in the past. Given the severe penalties associated with breaching the insider trading provisions, which include up to 10 years' imprisonment for individuals, it is reasonable to expect that the boundary between acceptable and unacceptable behavior should be drawn more clearly. Alternatively, this vagueness may cause the courts to err on the side of caution and construe the provision in a defendant-friendly manner (consistent with the overriding innocent until proven guilty standard in criminal prosecutions). Such an outcome will inevitably lead to claims from the regulator that the prohibition is unenforceable in its current form and needs to be strengthened further. Either way, it is safe to conclude that Australia's insider trading provisions are likely to see further reform.

---

[141]   Patrick Durkin, 7 of 11 Insiders were Advisers, The Aus. Fin. Rev., February 8, 2012, at 9. (ASIC said the majority of insider trading cases arose from misuse of confidential information by advisors on big corporate deals.) See also James Frost, ASIC Warns Advisory Firms Over Insider Trading Leaks, The Australian, February 8, 2012, at 42.

20. Insider trading law in New Zealand
Gordon Walker and Andrew F. Simpson

I. INTRODUCTION

The first set of statutory controls on insider trading in New Zealand were enacted in 1988 and applied (with amendments) until 2008. The 1988–2008 insider trading regime is generally regarded as having failed. The various reasons for that failure include: the lack of or limitations on regulatory enforcement powers; insufficient funding for the regulator; over-reliance on private enforcement; poor regulatory design; and weak disclosure obligations on directors and officers before 2004. Consequently, New Zealand implemented its second and current insider trading regime in February 2008. This regime followed and sought to improve upon the insider trading legislation applying in Australia. Thus, for all practical purposes, the New Zealand insider trading regime has closely resembled Australia's since 2008. Australia and New Zealand have the most expansive insider trading regimes in the world, potentially applying to any person in possession of inside information. There is one key difference between them, however: Australia's insider trading laws are much more aggressively enforced than are New Zealand's, where the majority of pre-2008 regime cases have been unsuccessful or settled and no prosecutions have been launched under the post-2008 legislation. This introduction briefly describes the governmental and legal systems, the main securities markets and the principal legislation.

New Zealand is a sovereign independent unitary state, which has a constitutional monarchy, a "Westminster style" unicameral legislature and a sophisticated common law legal system derived from United Kingdom origins.[1] The population base is small (approximately 4.4 million in 2012). New Zealand securities markets are characterized by relatively low trading volumes and market capitalization. The principal securities markets are the three markets operated by the New Zealand Exchange Limited (NZX).[2] In March 2012, market capitalization of the NZX was approximately NZD57 billion.

The principal sources of New Zealand securities law are the Securities Act 1978 and the Securities Markets Act 1988 (SMA). It is expected that these two statutes will be repealed when the Financial Markets Conduct Bill 2011 is passed. The most important regulations are the Securities Regulations 2009 (as amended).

The Securities Act 1978 introduced New Zealand's first separate securities legislation directed at the primary market. Before that time, the subject was embedded in company

---

[1]   The court hierarchy comprises the District Court, the High Court, the Court of Appeal and (since 2003) the Supreme Court of New Zealand. Securities litigation usually commences in the High Court. New Zealand courts are bound by precedent decisions of higher courts in the appellate hierarchy. Decisions of courts in other common law jurisdictions are of persuasive authority.

[2]   The NZX operates three markets: the New Zealand Stock Market (NZSX), the New Zealand Debt Market (NZDX) and the New Zealand Alternative Market (NZAX). Before demutualization, the NZX was known as the New Zealand Stock Exchange (NZSE).

legislation such as the Companies Act 1955 and the common law. The collapse of a merchant bank—Securitibank—provided the impetus for the present Securities Act.[3] Securitibank had attracted funds in a manner that avoided the prospectus provisions of the former Companies Act 1955. The legislative response embodied in the Securities Act 1978 was designed to regulate the activity of fund raising generally and defeat technical avoidance of the prior law.[4]

The SMA was the first major attempt to regulate the secondary market, including insider conduct. In contrast to the position in the USA, where insider trading is regulated by Securities and Exchange Commission (SEC) rulemaking (see the Introduction to this volume), the SMA established a statutory regime directed at insider conduct, which—with some amendments—applied for twenty years. Following the failure of the 1988–2008 experiment with private enforcement of insider trading prohibitions, the post-2008 regime was modeled on the Australian legislation. The Financial Markets Conduct Bill 2011 is proposed to repeal the Securities Act 1978 and the SMA, and replace both statutes with one omnibus Act covering the primary and secondary markets. As of December 2012, the relevant clauses of the Financial Markets Conduct Bill 2011 as reported back from the Commerce Committee do not change the current regime in any substantial manner. In May 2011, the Financial Markets Authority (FMA) replaced the Securities Commission as the principal regulator. One consequence of the legislation establishing the FMA is that "securities regulation" is no longer a distinct body of law in New Zealand: it is now subsumed under the rubric of financial markets law.[5]

Section II of this chapter provides an historical overview of insider trading regulation at common law, under the Companies Act 1993 and under the SMA in the period 1988–2008. For the 1988–2002 period, the *Wilson Neill* litigation is emblematic of design flaws and other problems. The period 2002–2008 is briefly discussed. In Section III an analysis of the present statutory insider trading regime in New Zealand as influenced by the regional free trade agreement between Australia and New Zealand is provided. Section IV concludes by noting a puzzling "enforcement deficit" in comparison to Australia.

II. HISTORICAL OVERVIEW

Regulation of insider trading in New Zealand has been markedly changeable. Insider trading prohibitions were enacted in 1988, amended in 2002 and amended again in 2006. The latter amendments became effective in 2008.[6] It is not expected that the Financial

---

[3] See Frank Partnoy, Why Markets Crash and What Law Can Do About It, 61 U. Pitt. L. Rev. 741 (2000).

[4] For a full review of the history of securities regulation in New Zealand until 1998, see Gordon Walker, Reinterpreting New Zealand Securities Regulation, in Securities Regulation in Australia and New Zealand 88–126 (Gordon Walker ed., 1998).

[5] See Philipp Maume & Gordon Walker, A New Financial Markets Law for New Zealand, 29 C&S L. J. 455 (2011).

[6] For a comprehensive review of the law on insider trading before and after the 2006 amendments to the SMA, see Shelley Griffiths, The Secondary Market, in Company and Securities Law in New Zealand 1061, 1083 (John Farrar ed., 2008).

Markets Conduct Bill 2011 will change the present insider trading regime in any significant way. Since 1988, the rationales underlying prohibition of insider trading have shifted from fiduciary or similar relationships to an "equal access" rationale. The latter rationale derives from the position in Australia where a 1989 report entitled *Fair Shares for All* formed the policy basis for reform in 1991.[7]

A. Insider Trading at Common Law

Until 1988, any person incurring loss as a consequence of insider trading by another could seek recourse only at common law or under company legislation. In the leading case of *Coleman v. Myers*,[8] the New Zealand Supreme Court (as it then was) and, on appeal, the New Zealand Court of Appeal considered a claim for restitution or damages brought by minority shareholders in a family-owned private company. Two directors of the family company had acquired all of the shares in the company, financing those acquisitions by the subsequent sale of surplus assets owned by the company. Among other causes of action, the minority shareholders claimed they had been induced to sell their shares at an under-value by certain misrepresentations and non-disclosures on the part of the two directors. The Court of Appeal held the directors owed a fiduciary duty to the company's shareholders and breached that duty by misleading the other shareholders and failing to disclose certain material information:

> [I]n the setting seen here there must be an obligation not to make to shareholders statements on matters material to the proposed dealing which are either deliberately or carelessly misleading. And in my opinion there must at least be an obligation to disclose material matters as to which the director knows or has reason to believe that the shareholder whom he is trying to persuade to sell is or may be inadequately informed.[9]

The Court of Appeal (and Justice Mahon in the Supreme Court) expressly denied any fiduciary duty owed by directors to shareholders generally,[10] but were prepared to recognize a fiduciary duty arising in the circumstances of the particular case. Justice Cooke stated:

> In the circumstances of this case it seems to me obvious that each of the respondent directors did owe a fiduciary duty to the individual shareholders. To that extent I fully agree with Mahon, J. Broadly, the facts giving rise to the duty are the family character of the company; the positions

---

[7] Robert Austin & Ian Ramsay, Ford's Principles of Corporations Law 563 (14th Ed. 2010). "The central recommendation of the Committee was that the 'person connected' criterion should be removed, principally in the interests of simplicity. On this approach, anyone in possession of inside information who knows its significance would be precluded from trading." Id.

[8] [1977] 2 NZLR 225 (SC, CA).

[9] Id. at 333 (Cooke, J).

[10] Justice Mahon considered the decision to the contrary in Percival v. Wright [1902] 2 Ch 421 (in which Justice Swinfen Eady had declined to find a fiduciary duty was owed by directors to shareholders with whom they were dealing) to be wrongly decided, while Justices Cooke and Casey in the Court of Appeal considered it not to lay down a general proposition and not to have relevance in the instant case.

of father and son in the company and the family; their high degree of inside knowledge; and the way in which they went about the takeover and persuasion of shareholders.[11]

Since it is clear that in the general run of cases directors' fiduciary duties are owed to the companies they direct and not to shareholders in those companies, plaintiff shareholders seeking compensation at common law for harm occasioned by insider trading will have to demonstrate that in the particular circumstances they reposed trust and confidence in the directors sufficient to give rise to a fiduciary relationship between the parties.[12] It seems that such a relationship will normally arise only in smaller private companies, though exceptionally it might arise in an unlisted public company.[13]

B.   Insider Trading under the Companies Acts

Historically, company legislation in New Zealand followed United Kingdom models until the Companies Act 1993 was enacted, which Act was modeled on U.S. and Canadian company law.[14] The current Companies Act 1993 imposes particular restrictions on directors. Relevantly, § 145(1) states that, subject to specified exceptions:

> A director of a company who has information in his or her capacity as a director or employee of the company, being information that would not otherwise be available to him or her, must not disclose that information to any person, or make use of or act on the information.

Section 148 requires a director to disclose to the board his or her dealings in the company's shares. Section 149 goes further and restricts a director who possesses company information by virtue of his or her position as a director "which is information material to an assessment of the value of shares" from acquiring such shares unless the consideration given or received "is not less than the fair value of the shares or securities."[15] In the same circumstances, a director may not dispose of such shares unless the consideration is "not more than the fair value" of those shares or securities. "Fair value" must be determined on the basis of all information known to the director or publicly available at the relevant

---

[11]   [1977] 2 NZLR 225 (CA) at 330.

[12]   Justice Woodhouse stated that "while it may not be possible to lay down any general test," relevant factors included a "dependence upon information and advice, the existence of a relationship of confidence, the significance of some particular transaction for the parties, and of course the extent of any positive action taken by or on behalf of the directors to promote it." Id. at 325.

[13]   In Cottom v. GUS Properties Ltd. (1995) 7 NZCLC 260, 821, the Court of Appeal confirmed the applicability of the *Coleman v. Myers* decision and discussed that decision in the context of a non-listed company with 200 shareholders. The Court was prepared to find that directors "intending to participate as purchasers in the share exchange, owed a duty to shareholders to ensure they were fully informed of relevant matters known to the directors before making a decision to sell." Id. at 260, 827 (McKay, J.).

[14]   See Gordon Walker et al., Commercial Applications of Company Law in New Zealand 28–30 (4th ed. 2012).

[15]   Companies Act 1993 (NZ) § 149(1). Section 149(2) provides that "the fair value of shares or securities is to be determined on the basis of all information known to the director or publicly available at the time." The law on § 149 is discussed in Peter Watts et al., Company Law in New Zealand 528–530 (2011).

time.[16] Under § 149(4), the director is liable to the person from whom the shares were purchased or to whom they were sold for the difference between the sale price and the fair value of the relevant shares or securities.[17] Subsection 149(6) states, however, that nothing in § 149 applies in relation to a company to which Part I of the SMA applies. Thus, where the insider trading regime under Part I of the SMA applies, § 149 of the Companies Act 1993 does not apply. This means that § 149 cannot apply to a "public issuer" as defined in the SMA but can apply to companies that are not publicly listed on a registered exchange in New Zealand.

Some qualifications to the § 149(6) carve-out must be recognized. The FMA is now empowered by Part 2 of Schedule 1 of the FMA Act to enforce the Companies Act 1993 where that Act relates or applies to "financial market participants." Under § 4 of the FMA Act, a company that has offered shares to the public (an issuer) is a financial market participant and accordingly all breaches of the Companies Act by unlisted issuers and their directors and senior managers fall under the FMA's powers.[18] A further qualification flows from § 13 of the SMA, which prohibits conduct in relation to any dealings in securities that is misleading or deceptive or likely to mislead or deceive. Section 13(2) states that this section applies more broadly than the rest of Part I of the SMA, "and so applies to securities whether listed or non-listed and to all dealings in securities (not only trading)." Accordingly, § 13(2) may be applicable to facts falling within § 149.

C.   The Securities Markets Act 1988

New Zealand's securities markets are regulated under the Securities Act 1978 and Securities Markets Act 1988, both of which, in amended form, remain in force as of December 2012. The Securities Act 1978 originally aimed to promote investor protection by a combination of disclosure requirements and private rights of action. The Securities Amendment Act 1988 (which was amended and renamed in 2002 as the Securities Markets Act 1988) brought New Zealand's first statutory proscription of insider trading into effect in December 1988. The SMA was motivated in large part by the government's desire to restore investor confidence in New Zealand's capital markets, following the worldwide crash of share markets in October 1987.[19] As it transpired, however, New Zealand's securities markets were among the slowest in the world to recover from "Black Monday."[20] Arguably, obstacles to private enforcement of the

---

[16]   Companies Act 1993 (NZ) § 149(2).

[17]   The leading case is Thexton v. Thexton [2002] 1 NZLR 780 (CA). In that case, the policy behind § 149 was said to be "abstain or pay fair value."

[18]   See the definition of "financial markets participant" in Financial Markets Authority Act 2011 (NZ) § 4.

[19]   "Market capitalisation had grown from $17,600m [NZD] at the end of 1985 to $42,436m at the end of 1986. By 31 December 1987 market capitalisation had actually fallen to $24,200m. The collapse of the sharemarket was followed some 12 months later by the collapse of the commercial property market and the demise of several major financial institutions whose investment and property base had been cut away . . . ." Peter McKenzie, Reflections on a Decade with the Securities Commission 1985–1995, 7 Canterbury L. Rev. 215 (1996).

[20]   Brian Gaynor, Securities Regulation in New Zealand: Crisis and Reform, in Securities Regulation in Australia and New Zealand 11 (Gordon Walker & Brent Fisse, eds., 1994).

insider trading prohibition may have been one of the factors in the slow post-crash recovery of the markets.

The insider trading prohibitions in Part I of the SMA (as originally enacted) applied to the conduct of "insiders" in relation to the securities of any "public issuer," by parties in possession of "inside information"[21] (these terms being defined in SMA § 2). Four principal prohibitions were set out, each of which was subject to particular exceptions. First, § 7 imposed liability on an "insider" in possession of inside information about a public issuer for buying or selling securities of that public issuer. Secondly, § 9 imposed liability on an insider in possession of inside information about a public issuer for "tipping" any other person. Thirdly, § 11 imposed liability on an insider of one public issuer in possession of inside information about a second public issuer for buying or selling securities of the latter public issuer. Fourthly, § 13 imposed liability on an insider of one public issuer in possession of inside information about a second public issuer for "tipping" any other person regarding the securities of the latter public issuer. For the purposes of §§ 9 and 13, "tipping" occurred if the insider advised or encouraged any person to buy or sell; advised or encouraged any person to advise or encourage another to buy or sell; or communicated information to another person knowing or believing that other would either buy or sell or advise or encourage another to buy or sell.[22] In each case, insiders were potentially liable to the person from whom the insider bought the relevant securities or to whom the insider sold the relevant securities, and to the public issuer.[23] The quantum of liability was the loss incurred by the counterparty or, in cases in which the public issuer was the plaintiff, the amount of any gain made or loss avoided as a result of the trading plus any amount which the Court considers to be an appropriate pecuniary penalty. Pecuniary penalties were capped at the greater of the total consideration paid or received, or three times the gain made or loss avoided.[24] Amounts recovered by public issuers were to be held on trust for distribution in accordance with Court directions, e.g., to present or past members of the issuer.[25] No criminal sanctions attached to insider trading at this time. Originally, the Securities Commission had no power to pursue an insider trading prosecution. It was up to the aggrieved shareholder to pursue private enforcement. This policy was quite unrealistic. Consider the position of the average investor trading on the NZSE (as it then was) and make the unlikely assumption that such investor has clear evidence of insider trading by a counterparty. Civil legal aid would be unavailable to such an investor, whose decision to litigate would turn on considerations of quantum of loss and the cost of litigation. If the loss was modest, the investor would have no incentive to litigate, as litigation costs would be prohibitive. Next, assume a high net-worth individual or company with a suspicion of insider trading by the counterparty and substantial losses but no clear evidence of breach. Again, the decision to litigate would turn on cost/benefit considerations. Assuming the affected

---

[21] Interpretive issues in the meaning of "inside information" under the SMA are explored in Keith Kendall & Gordon Walker, Insider Trading in Australia and New Zealand: Information that is "Generally Available," 24 Co. & Sec. L. J. 343 (2006).
[22] Securities Markets Act 1988 (NZ) §§ 9(1) and 13(1).
[23] Securities Markets Act 1988 (NZ) §§ 7(2), 9(2), 11(2), 13(2).
[24] Securities Markets Act 1988 (NZ) §§ 7(3), 9(3), 11(3), 13(3).
[25] Securities Markets Act 1988 (NZ) § 19.

trader is in the business of trading shares, the rational decision might be to take a tax loss and not litigate.

To assist potential plaintiffs, former § 17 of the SMA allowed present or past members of a public issuer to seek the Securities Commission's approval for the issuer to obtain, at the issuer's expense, a barrister's or solicitor's opinion on whether or not the issuer had a cause of action against the insider. Former § 18 provided that a public issuer's right of action against an insider might be exercised by a member of the issuer, with the Court's leave. This innovation immediately introduced the possibility of a "free rider" problem, however, whereby the well-resourced shareholder might seek to shift litigation costs to the company, at the expense of all shareholders.

Private enforcement of the insider trading prohibitions was first tested in New Zealand in the emblematic *Wilson Neill* litigation.[26] This litigation highlighted design flaws in the original legislation. In July 1991, Wilson Neill Ltd (WNL) had placed 13 million shares with various institutional investors at NZD0.40 per share, after Magnum, another WNL investor, had decided not to acquire those shares pursuant to an option. By the end of 1991, the shares were worth only NZD0.10 each. The complaining shareholders (institutional investors and one private investor) alleged that WNL had a right of action against Magnum, WNL's then Chief Executive and certain other executives and associated companies on the basis that those insiders had allegedly sold WNL shares while in possession of material non-public information concerning the company's unfavorable prospects. With the Securities Commission's approval, the complaining shareholders required WNL to obtain an opinion from a leading Queen's Counsel, who considered WNL had a reasonably good cause of action against two of the alleged insiders but that the position in respect of Magnum and two others was much more equivocal. The complaining shareholders sought to rely on SMA § 18 to require WNL to exercise the alleged right of action. Although the complaining shareholders were at liberty to sue in respect of their own cause of action for losses they sustained, requiring the issuer to bring suit would have two advantages for them: first, it was only in relation to the issuer's cause of action that the Court was entitled to award a pecuniary penalty; secondly, the issuer would be liable to pay the shareholders' costs in taking the issuer's case.[27]

In the High Court, Justice Heron was satisfied that "good reason for not bringing the action" had been shown,[28] so refused to grant leave under SMA § 18 to the complaining shareholders. Justice Heron's decision was upheld in the Court of Appeal, which took a broad view of the "good reason" ground for denying leave:

---

[26] Colonial Mutual Life Assurance Society Limited v. Wilson Neill Limited [1993] 2 NZLR 617 (HC); Colonial Mutual Life Assurance Society Limited v. Wilson Neill Limited (No. 2) [1993] 2 NZLR 657 (HC); Colonial Mutual Life Assurance Society Ltd. & Ors. v. Wilson Neill Ltd. & Ors (1994) 7 NZCLC 260, 401; Colonial Mutual Life Assurance Society Ltd. v. Wilson Neill Ltd. [1994] 2 NZLR 152 (CA). For a full discussion, see Craig Mulholland, Insider Trading in New Zealand: Aspects of the Wilson Neill Case, in Securities Regulation in Australia and New Zealand 641 (Gordon Walker & Brent Fisse, eds., 1994).

[27] Colonial Mutual Life Assurance Society Limited v. Wilson Neill Limited (No. 2) [1993] 2 NZLR 657 (HC) at 664.

[28] Id. at 681.

What may constitute good reason, however, is not restricted. Considerations including the strength or weakness of the case, the financial position of the public issuer on which the costs of the action will fall (subject only to any order ultimately made against the defendant) and the interests of other shareholders must be among the total circumstances of the case open to be taken into account.[29]

Both Courts evidently entertained concerns regarding the effect that granting leave would have on WNL as a whole and on its shareholders generally.[30] Both Courts observed that the complaining shareholders were in a position to litigate their claims in their own names and at their own expense.[31] Quite possibly Parliament had in mind shareholders of smaller resources when it enacted SMA §§ 17–19. The *Wilson Neill* decisions, however, signaled to prospective litigants that the Courts would not lightly "allow a free hand to a third party to undertake complex litigation at the expense of a public company containing many shareholders . . ."[32]

The approach the New Zealand Courts adopted toward SMA § 18 proceedings significantly diminished the utility to complainant shareholders of the procedure for issuer funding of actions against alleged insiders. Several different problems contributed to the inutility of § 18. First, the legislation itself was silent on important questions of procedure. While a number of these questions were resolved in the course of the various *Wilson Neill* hearings, those hearings may well have deterred potential applicants from availing themselves of what was probably perceived as an uncertain and costly avenue of redress. Secondly, the procedure *Wilson Neill* demanded under § 18 involved "three different trials at three different levels of proof,"[33] with concomitant expense. Thirdly, directors of the issuer who were innocent of wrongdoing can be expected to oppose the proceedings: they may sympathize with the accused insiders if they were also directors ("boardroom bias") or might simply be resistant to the company suffering the expense and adverse publicity that proceedings would entail. Fourthly, the Courts' concern to avoid burdening shareholders with the expense of litigation that is potentially beneficial only to a small sub-set of shareholders reveals a fundamental flaw in the regime: the benefits are concentrated while the costs are diffuse. The risk of plaintiff "free-riding" therefore arises. The costs of any issuer-funded insider trading litigation under § 18 are borne, ultimately, by all of

---

[29] Colonial Mutual Life Assurance Society Ltd v. Wilson Neill Ltd [1994] 2 NZLR 152 (CA) at 160.

[30] [1993] 2 NZLR 657 (HC) at 682; [1994] 2 NZLR 152 (CA) at 161.

[31] "[T]he availability of proceedings to the complaining shareholders in their own right is critical. They are substantial investors in the marketplace and can foot it with the others" [1993] 2 NZLR 657 (HC) at 679 (Heron, J.). "If the institutional appellants wish to litigate their claims against Magnum they remain free to do so in their own names in exercise of their own alleged causes of action. The litigation should not be pursued at the cost of the other shareholders in Wilson Neill." [1994] 2 NZLR 152 (CA) at 162 (Cooke, P.).

[32] [1993] 2 NZLR 657 (HC) at 682 (Heron, J.).

[33] "First, there is the shareholders request to the [New Zealand Securities Commission] that a barrister be appointed at the company's expense to investigate. The barrister then has to report as to whether or not there are grounds for mounting an insider-trading case (trial one). Second, application has to be made to a judge to obtain leave to issue proceedings (trial two). Third, if shareholders want to bring action in the name of the public issuer, then leave of the court is also required (trial three)." Mulholland, supra note 26 at 655.

the members, most of whom are likely to have suffered little or no loss as a result of the impugned conduct. The shareholders who are motivated to use the § 18 procedure are likely to be relatively well-resourced investors, with a relatively large stake in the issuer, who have suffered a sufficiently large loss to make the application worthwhile. If the Courts are skeptical of the desirability of issuers funding litigation to the benefit of well-resourced applicants, and are careful to prevent litigation costs being transferred to investors unaffected by insider conduct, then such a procedure can have only a very limited scope of application in practice.

D.   The Securities Markets Amendment Act 2002

Following a period of weak enforcement—and after the Russell Committee[34] and Roche Committee[35] had each reported on proposals for regulatory reform—the SMA was amended with the objective of enhancing enforcement. The Securities Markets Amendment Act 2002 took effect in December 2002,[36] amending the Securities Markets Act 1988 by adding new §§ 18A–18E, which continued in force until the Securities Markets Amendment Act 2006 commenced in February 2008.

Under the new § 18A, the former Securities Commission gained the power to exercise a public issuer's right of action against an insider, if the Commission considered it in the public interest to do so. The Commission could commence proceedings without the leave of the Court, if the public issuer did not object, or with the Court's leave if the public issuer objected.[37] The Commission could also take over proceedings commenced by the public issuer or another, with the Court's leave.[38] The Court was required to grant leave if satisfied it was in the public interest for the proceedings to be brought or continued, and for the Commission to conduct the proceedings.[39]

The Commission used its new powers in two instances. First, it commenced action in 2004 in relation to alleged insider trading in Tranz Rail shares in 2002. It was alleged that individuals had sold Tranz Rail shares while in possession of inside information. The sales had occurred in 2002, some two and a half years before proceedings were commenced; however, the Limitation Act 1950 provided that where a penalty is in issue proceedings must be commenced within two years of the date the cause of action arose. This proved fatal to the Commission's case.[40] The second case concerned an allegation of insider trading in relation to Provenco shares in 2003. This claim was settled in 2005.

---

[34]   See Andrew Simpson, The First and Second Spenser Russell Reports on Securities Law Reform in New Zealand, 11 C&S L. J. 188 (1993).

[35]   See Andrew Simpson, The Roche Report on Securities Law Reform in New Zealand, 11 C&S L. J. 331 (1993).

[36]   Provisions in the same amending Act to enhance insider disclosure obligations commenced on a later date. Securities Markets Amendment Act 2002 (NZ) § 2(2).

[37]   Securities Markets Act 1988 (NZ) § 18B(1), (2)(a).

[38]   Securities Markets Act 1988 (NZ) § 18B(2)(b).

[39]   Securities Markets Act 1988 (NZ) § 18B(3).

[40]   Securities Commission v. Mildavia Rail Investments BVBA [2007] 2 NZLR 454 (CA).

III.   CURRENT INSIDER TRADING REGULATION

Insider trading in New Zealand is currently regulated under the SMA as amended by the Securities Markets Amendment Act 2006, which went into effect in February 2008.[41] This legislation may best be understood in the context of the prior experiment with private enforcement, described above, and the forces impelling further reform of financial markets regulation in New Zealand.

Three key drivers have impelled recent financial market reforms in New Zealand: globalization, the regional free trade agreement with Australia and domestic politics. First, the globalization of securities markets means that New Zealand's markets are profoundly affected by international conditions and events.[42] So, for example, it was the worldwide stock market crash of 1987 that provided the impetus for the first statutory regime directed at insider conduct under the SMA. The global financial crisis of 2008 also prompted major reform[43] including the establishment of the FMA as the new market regulator,[44] pursuant to the Financial Markets Authority Act 2011, and the introduction to Parliament of the Financial Markets Conduct Bill 2011.

Secondly, the Closer Economic Relations (CER) Agreement—the regional free trade agreement between Australia and New Zealand—has functioned as an umbrella agreement for a set of downstream agreements with soft and hard law consequences.[45] One downstream outcome of the CER Agreement is the inter-governmental project to coordinate business laws in the two countries.[46] This project finds expression in the Memorandum of Understanding between the Government of New Zealand and the Government of Australia on Coordination of Business Law (Business Law MOU).[47] The Business Law MOU is soft law that has led to hard law consequences.[48] Pursuant to the Business Law MOU, New Zealand has adapted the Australian statutory regime on continuous disclosure and insider conduct. Similarly, the Financial Markets Conduct Bill 2011 borrows heavily from the Australian Corporations Act 2001.

Thirdly, domestic political imperatives have prompted reforms including the introduction of the SMA in 1988. The Financial Markets Conduct Bill 2011 is also driven in large part by the political objectives of the center-right National Party that now governs New Zealand with support from the ACT Party and Maori Party. One objective is to partially

---

[41]   Securities Commission, New Securities Law for Investment Advisers and Market Participants 2008: A Guide to New Requirements under the Securities Markets Act 1988 (2008).

[42]   See Gordon Walker & Mark Fox, Globalization: An Analytical Framework, 3 Ind. J. Global Legal Stud. 375 (1996); Franklin Gevurtz, The Globalisation of Insider Trading Prohibitions, 15 Transnat'l Law 63 (2002).

[43]   See Philipp Maume & Gordon Walker, Capital Markets Matter: A New Era in New Zealand Securities Regulation, 29 C&S L. J. 184 (2011).

[44]   See Phillip Maume & Gordon Walker, Goodbye to All That: A New Financial Markets Authority for New Zealand, 29 C&S L. J. 239 (2011).

[45]   See Gordon Walker, The CER Agreement and Trans-Tasman Securities Regulation: Part 1, 19 J. Int'l Banking L. & Reg. 390 (2004).

[46]   See id.

[47]   See id. The third and current version of the Business Law MOU was signed in June 2010.

[48]   See id. Compare Chris Brummer, Soft Law and the Global Financial System: Rule Making in the 21st Century (2012).

remedy the damage caused by the collapse of finance companies in the global financial crisis.[49] The government's desire to strengthen domestic investor confidence in the regulatory regime prior to privatizing certain state-owned enterprises is another objective.[50]

A.   Insider Trading Prohibitions since 2008

A major overhaul of insider trading regulation under the SMA came into force in February 2008, on commencement of the Securities Markets Amendment Act 2006. As stated, the reforms were based on the Australian model,[51] largely following Part 7.10 of Division 3 of the Corporations Act 2001 (Cth). The Australian regime is the most expansive in the world, being directed at "a person" who "possesses inside information,"[52] although the wide ambit of the Australian provisions is qualified by a set of statutory carve-outs. It is expected that the cognate New Zealand statutory prohibition will remain largely unaffected by the Financial Markets Conduct Bill, introduced to New Zealand's Parliament in late 2011. Indeed, that Bill will move the New Zealand law even closer toward the Australian model.

Part 1 of the SMA creates three criminal offenses in relation to insider trading in relation to securities: the trading offense (§ 8C), the disclosing offense ("tipping") (§ 8D) and the advising or encouraging offense (§ 8E). In addition, § 11E provides that the same three offenses apply to insider trading in relation to futures contracts. We discuss elements common to all of the insider trading provisions, then the characteristics of each offense.

1.   Territorial scope

While the SMA is silent as to territorial scope, it is clear that the insider trading regime is confined to conduct relating to trading or holding (or advising or encouraging another to trade or hold) securities of a public issuer which are listed on a registered exchange's securities market in New Zealand.[53] *Securities Commission v. Mildavia Rail Investments BVBA*[54] concerned the sale of shares in the listed company Tranz Rail Limited. Justice Williams held that the Court had jurisdiction in respect of insider trading claims brought by the Securities Commission against a non-resident foreign national (Mr. Ferenbach) and a non-resident foreign entity (Berkshire Fund III) under the Courts' general jurisdiction and the former § 42 of the SMA (now repealed).

---

[49]   See Mark Fox, Gordon Walker and Alma Pekmezovic, Corporate Governance Research on New Zealand Listed Companies, 29 Ariz. J. Int'l & Comp L. 1 (2012).

[50]   See Mixed Ownership Model Bill 2012 for the New Zealand government's proposal to sell stakes in certain state-owned enterprises.

[51]   See Keith Kendall & Gordon Walker, Insider Trading in Australia and New Zealand: Information that is Generally Available, 24 C&S L. J. 343 (2006). For an overview of the Australian law on insider trading, see Robert Austin & Ian Ramsay, Ford's Principles of Corporation Law § 9.600 et seq. (14th ed. 2010). See also Ashley Black, Insider Trading and Market Misconduct, 29 C&S L. J. 313 (2011).

[52]   Corporations Act 2001 (Cth) § 1043A(1)(a).

[53]   In a similar fashion, the powers of the FMA insofar as they relate to "financial markets" apply to financial markets in New Zealand: Financial Markets Authority Act 2011 (NZ) § 4.

[54]   [2006] 2 NZLR 207 (HC).

2. "Securities"

The relevant insider trading must involve trading in securities, continuing to hold securities, or advising or encouraging another to trade or hold securities.[55] Section 2 of the SMA defines the term "security" in some detail. In particular, paragraphs (b) and (d) of the definition apply to the insider trading prohibitions under Part 1 of the SMA. Paragraph (b) provides that the security must have been allotted and listed on a registered exchange's market. Paragraph (d) extends the meaning of a security to include what might be described as relevant interests in securities.

3. "Public issuer" of securities

New Zealand's insider trading provisions apply to any person who is "an information insider of a public issuer."[56] A "public issuer" is defined as meaning "a person who is a party to a listing agreement with a registered exchange," or was so at the time of conduct to which the Act applied.[57] The term "registered exchange" means a person who holds a market registration under § 36F of the SMA.[58] The NZX is a "registered exchange" for the purposes of the SMA and the three markets operated by the NZX are accordingly registered securities markets operated by a registered exchange (the NZX). Together, these provisions mean that the insider trading regime is confined to conduct relating to trading or holding (or advising or encouraging another to trade or hold) securities of a public issuer which are listed on a registered exchange's securities markets in New Zealand.[59]

4. "Information insider"

An "information insider" is defined as a person who: (a) has material information relating to the public issuer that is not generally available to the market; and (b) knows or ought reasonably to know that the information is material information; and (c) knows or ought reasonably to know that the information is not generally available to the market.[60] A public issuer may be an information insider of itself.[61] "Inside information" is information in respect of which a person is an information insider of the public issuer in question.[62]

The first limb of the definition of "information insider" requires that the insider must have "material information." "Information" is not specifically defined but SMA § 3 defines "material information" in relation to a public issuer as information that: (a) a reasonable person would expect, if it were generally available to the market, to have a material effect on the price of listed securities of the public issuer; and (b) relates to particular securities, a particular public issuer or particular public issuers, rather than to securities generally or public issuers generally. Whether a reasonable person would expect that the

---

[55] Securities Markets Act 1988 (NZ) §§ 8C, 8D, 8E.
[56] Securities Markets Act 1988 (NZ) §§ 8, 8C, 8D, 8E.
[57] Securities Markets Act 1988 (NZ) § 2.
[58] Securities Markets Act 1988 (NZ) § 2.
[59] In a similar fashion, the powers of the FMA insofar as they relate to "financial markets" apply to financial markets in New Zealand: Financial Markets Authority Act 2011 (NZ) § 4.
[60] Securities Markets Act 1988 (NZ) § 8A.
[61] Securities Markets Act 1988 (NZ) § 8A(2).
[62] Securities Markets Act 1988 (NZ) § 8B.

material information, if it were generally available to the market, would have a material effect on the price of the public issuer's listed securities is an objective test.

The second limb of the definition requires that the putative "information insider" have actual or constructive knowledge that the information is such "material information."

The third limb of the definition of "information insider" requires that the relevant material information must be actually or constructively known by the insider to be "not generally available to the market." Section 4 of the SMA provides that information is generally available to the market: (a) if it is information that has been made known in a manner that would, or would be likely to, bring it to the attention of persons who commonly invest in relevant securities and, since it was made known, a reasonable period for it to be disseminated among those persons has expired; or (b) if it is likely that persons who commonly invest in relevant securities can readily obtain the information by observation, use of expertise, purchase from other persons or any other means; or (c) if it is information that consists of deductions, conclusions or inferences made or drawn from either or both of the previous two kinds of information.[63]

Pursuant to § 8A, it must also be proved that the information insider knows or ought reasonably to know that the information is material information and knows or ought reasonably to know that the information is not generally available to the market.

5.   The offenses

The trading offense is committed where, the elements described above being present, an information insider of a public issuer trades in securities of the public issuer.[64] Secondly, the disclosing offense is committed where, the elements described above being present, an information insider (A) of a public issuer directly or indirectly discloses inside information to another person (B), provided A knows or ought reasonably to know or believe that B will trade or is likely to trade securities of the public issuer or, if B is already a holder of those securities, continue to hold them or advise or encourage another person (C) to trade or hold them.[65] Thirdly, the advising or encouraging offense is committed where, the elements described above being present, an information insider (A) of a public issuer either: (1) advises or encourages another person (B) to trade or hold securities of the public issuer; or (2) advises or encourages (B) to advise or encourage another person (C) to trade or hold those securities.[66]

B.   Exceptions and Defenses

There are eight exceptions or "safe harbors" to the prohibitions on insider conduct[67] and five affirmative defenses.[68] The accused party bears the onus of proving each of the statutory affirmative defenses but only to the civil standard of "balance of probabilities."

The first statutory defense is "absence of knowledge of trading." A person who can

---

[63]   See Kendall and Walker, supra note 21.
[64]   Securities Markets Act 1988 (NZ) § 8C.
[65]   Securities Markets Act 1988 (NZ) § 8D.
[66]   Securities Markets Act 1988 (NZ) § 8E.
[67]   Securities Markets Act 1988 (NZ) §§ 9–9G.
[68]   Securities Markets Act 1988 (NZ) §§ 10–10D.

prove (on the balance of probabilities) that he or she did not know, and could not reasonably be expected to know, that he or she traded the securities has a defense in any "trading offense" proceeding under § 8C.[69]

Secondly, it is a defense in a proceeding for trading or disclosing (under §§ 8C or 8D) to prove that "the inside information was obtained by research and analysis" rather than directly or indirectly from the public issuer concerned.[70] The same defense applies in a proceeding under § 8E where the advice or encouragement was based on inside information obtained by research and analysis.[71] "Research" means "planned investigation undertaken to gain new knowledge and understanding."[72]

Thirdly, it is a defense to the trading offense and the disclosing offense if the accused can prove that the other party to the transaction, or the recipient of the disclosure, "knew or ought reasonably to have known the same inside information" before the transaction or the disclosure took place.[73] Where disclosing or advising or encouraging is alleged, a related defense arises if the accused can prove that he or she has the insider information (or is an information insider) only through acting as the other party's adviser in relation to trading or holding the securities in question.[74] The adviser must be "acting in a professional capacity," including as a lawyer, accountant or investment adviser.[75]

Fourthly, in a trading offense proceeding, it is a defense if the accused can prove that the relevant securities were traded under a fixed trading plan or under options having a fixed exercise price and that the trading plan was entered into or the options were acquired prior to the accused obtaining the inside information and without any intent to evade the prohibition.[76] A "fixed trading plan" must be fixed for a period of time and the investor must have no right to withdraw before the expiry of the period and no influence over trading decisions during that period.[77]

Finally, a "Chinese wall defense" protects a person accused of any of the three insider trading offenses where "arrangements existed that could reasonably be expected to ensure that no individual who took part in the active decision received, or had access to, the inside information" or was influenced by a person with inside information; and every person with inside information and every participant in the decision acted in accordance with the arrangements; and no decision participant received or had access to inside information.[78]

The insider trading prohibitions do not apply to forms of behavior specified under SMA §§ 9–9G. These excepted forms of conduct include: trading activity and disclosures that are required by an enactment;[79] acquisitions, disclosures and advice or encouragement that occur under an underwriting or sub-underwriting agreement or for the purpose

---

[69]   Securities Markets Act 1988 (NZ) § 10.
[70]   Securities Markets Act 1988 (NZ) § 10A(1).
[71]   Securities Markets Act 1988 (NZ) § 10A(2).
[72]   Securities Markets Act 1988 (NZ) § 10A(3).
[73]   Securities Markets Act 1988 (NZ) § 10B(1) and (2).
[74]   Securities Markets Act 1988 (NZ) § 10B(3).
[75]   Securities Markets Act 1988 (NZ) § 10B(4).
[76]   Securities Markets Act 1988 (NZ) § 10C(1).
[77]   Securities Markets Act 1988 (NZ) § 10C(2).
[78]   Securities Markets Act 1988 (NZ) § 10D.
[79]   Securities Markets Act 1988 (NZ) §§ 9, 9A.

of negotiating such;[80] trading as an agent who acts on specific instructions to trade securities, without having received inside information, advice or encouragement;[81] specified trading, disclosing and advising in connection with a takeover offer under the Takeovers Code;[82] redemption of units in a unit trust at a price based on the underlying value of the assets;[83] and trading by the Reserve Bank of New Zealand in securities issued by itself or by the Crown.[84]

C.   Penalties and Civil Remedies

Contravention of §§ 8C to 8E is a criminal offense.[85] Section 43 provides for a criminal penalty for the criminal liability established in § 8F. For an individual, the maximum penalty is imprisonment for a term not exceeding five years or a fine not exceeding NZD300,000 or both; for a company, the maximum penalty is a fine not exceeding NZD1,000,000. Civil liability also attaches such that an "aggrieved person" may seek to recover compensation for loss or damage. Civil remedies are available for breach of the insider trading prohibition.[86] First, the FMA may seek a pecuniary penalty and declaration of contravention.[87] The maximum amount of a pecuniary penalty for a contravention of an insider trading prohibition is the greater of: (a) the consideration for the transaction that constituted the contravention (if any); or (b) three times the amount of the gain made, or the loss avoided, by the person in carrying out the conduct; or (c) NZD1,000,000.[88] Secondly, an "aggrieved person" who has suffered loss, or who is likely to suffer loss, may apply for a compensatory order.[89]

D.   Further Reform: The New Financial Markets Law

The three drivers of financial market reform in New Zealand referred to earlier in this chapter (i.e., globalization, the regional free trade agreement with Australia and domestic politics) continue to operate. In 2011, a new Financial Markets Authority was established under the Financial Markets Authority Act 2011 (FMA Act).

The new financial markets law rests on three core definitions which appear in § 4 of the FMA Act. The first core definition is "financial markets," which means the financial markets in New Zealand. The second core definition is "financial markets legislation." The meaning of this term is set out in Schedule 1 of the FMA Act, which is divided into two parts. Part 1 of Schedule 1 includes the Securities Act 1978 and the SMA. Part 2 encompasses other legislation including the Companies Act 1993. The relevance of the

---

80   Securities Markets Act 1988 (NZ) § 9C.
81   Securities Markets Act 1988 (NZ) § 9D.
82   Securities Markets Act 1988 (NZ) § 9E.
83   Securities Markets Act 1988 (NZ) § 9F.
84   Securities Markets Act 1988 (NZ) § 9G.
85   Securities Markets Act 1988 (NZ) § 8F.
86   Securities Markets Act 1988 (NZ) § 42R.
87   Securities Markets Act 1988 (NZ) §§ 42T–42Z.
88   Securities Markets Act 1988 (NZ) § 42W.
89   Securities Markets Act 1988 (NZ) §§ 42ZA, 42ZB.

division is that the FMA's power to monitor compliance with and investigate conduct that may contravene various Acts applies without restraint to the statutes listed in Part 1 of Schedule 1. Hence, the FMA's powers extend directly to the regulation of insider conduct. As stated, Part 2 of Schedule 1 includes the Companies Act 1993 but here the FMA's powers only apply to the extent that the relevant Acts apply or relate to "financial markets participants." This third core term is defined in § 4 of the FMA Act as, inter alia, a person "who is, or is required to be, registered, licensed, appointed, or authorized under . . . any of the Acts listed in Part 1 of Schedule 1" and includes an unlisted issuer, its directors and senior managers. Because the powers of the FMA apply to the Acts listed in Part 2 of Schedule 1 insofar as they "relate . . . to financial markets participants," a director or senior manager of an unlisted issuer may be subject to the FMA's powers in relation to insider conduct.[90] In addition, the FMA has the power (subject to considerations such as the public interest) to exercise a person's right of action in respect of insider trading under § 34 and subsequent sections of the FMA Act. In the result, the FMA has ample powers—including enhanced information gathering and enforcement powers under Part 3 of the FMA Act—to pursue insider conduct. In striking contrast to Australia, however, no prosecutions for insider trading have been initiated since 2008. As a generalization, the predecessor of the FMA (the former Securities Commission) did not have a good track record on enforcement. One key reason was the lack of adequate funding.[91] Although the precise details of the funding of the new FMA have not been announced, some form of industry levy is likely to be the prime means of funding the new body along with governmental subvention. The enforcement policy of the FMA will be critical to its success or failure. The FMA has announced its enforcement policy.[92] It has stated, for example, that it will actively enforce compliance with the new licensing regime for trustees and statutory supervisors from October 2011.[93] The FMA's prosecution of the cases connected with failed finance companies provides some grounds for confidence in this policy. A mix of criminal and civil proceedings had been instituted against the directors of ten finance companies by October 2012.[94] In total twenty-five investigations were continuing while twenty-six cases had been referred to another regulator, concluded with another enforcement option or closed.[95] On the other hand, there appear to have been no proceedings taken in respect of insider trading in the four years since the new regime came

---

[90] See Gordon Walker et al., Commercial Applications of Company Law in New Zealand 320 (4th ed. 2012).

[91] "It is clear from the review team's surveys and research that under-resourcing is at the heart of many of the Commission's current problems." Michel Prada and Neil Walter, Report on the Effectiveness of New Zealand's Securities Commission 28 (2009) (hereinafter "Prada Report").

[92] See Financial Markets Authority, FMA Enforcement Policy, available at http://www.fma.govt.nz/laws-we-enforce/enforcement/fma-enforcement-policy/ (last accessed November 29, 2012). See also, FMA, Inquiries, Investigations and Enforcement Report (August 2012), available at www.fma.govt.nz (last accessed December 3, 2012).

[93] Ibid.

[94] See FMA, Finance Company Cases before the Court, available at http://fma.govt.nz/laws-we-enforce/enforcement/prosecutions-and-proceedings (last accessed November 29, 2012).

[95] See FMA, Status of Investigations into Failed Finance Companies (Non-Bank Deposit Takers), available at http://www.fma.govt.nz/laws-we-enforce/enforcement/prosecutions-and-proceedings (last accessed November 29, 2012).

into effect in February 2008. We explore possible reasons for this puzzling phenomenon in the conclusion to this chapter.

IV.   CONCLUSION: THE ENFORCEMENT DEFICIT

New Zealand's insider trading regime has never been characterized by active and rigorous enforcement. It is striking that the former Securities Commission did not originally have an enforcement function at all. A former Chairman of the Securities Commission, Peter McKenzie, has observed:

> The enforcement of the Securities Act and the Companies Act remained with the Registrar of Companies and the Corporate Fraud Squad of the Police, and when it was later established, the Serious Fraud Office. The Commission's statute did not make it a corporate policeman. *Both the government and the business community wished to establish a much less interventionist body* than the SEC in the United States or the ASC in Australia. The Commission was to be a regulatory watchdog with power to bark, but the biting was to be left to others.[96]

Although fundamental reforms aligned the New Zealand insider trading regime with that of Australia from February 2008, there has been much less enforcement activity in New Zealand than in Australia. All of the insider trading cases reported since 2008 were commenced under the pre-2008 insider trading regime. The Annual Reports of the Securities Commission for the years 2008 to 2011 reveal that no prosecutions for insider trading occurred in these years. The 2008/09 financial review of the Securities Commission by Parliament's Commerce Committee mentions no prosecutions for insider conduct.[97] The 2009 Prada Report makes no mention of any insider trading prosecutions. In September 2011 the FMA announced its enforcement policy[98] but in the first twelve months following its inception (in May 2011) the FMA launched no prosecutions for insider conduct. By contrast, the Australian Investments and Securities Commission recorded a total of thirty-three referrals of insider trading matters to the Deterrence section in the period August 1, 2010 to December 31, 2011.[99]

Nevertheless, it seems likely that insider trading continues to occur in New Zealand. The Special Division report in the Annual Reports of the New Zealand Markets Disciplinary Tribunal disclose that the Division received a total of thirty-nine SMARTS alerts in the period from January 2009 to December 2011.[100] If the SMARTS alerts indicate prima facie that some insider trading is occurring, it would seem puzzling that no insider trading enforcement actions have been commenced since 2008.

---

[96]   Peter McKenzie, Reflections on a Decade with the Securities Commission, 6 Canterbury L. Rev. 217 (1996) (emphasis added).

[97]   Report of the Commerce Committee, 2008–09 Financial Review of the Securities Commission (2009).

[98]   See supra note 92.

[99]   ASIC, Report 277, ASIC Supervision of Markets and Participants: July to December 2011 (February 2012).

[100]   The SMARTS system provides electronic surveillance of market activity and generates alerts in relation to suspicious activity that may warrant further investigation.

In the early years of insider trading regulation in New Zealand, it appears that the lack of enforcement powers in the regulator, combined with sub-optimal regulation (private enforcement was inhibited by the inbuilt "free-rider" problem) and chronic underfunding resulted in a lack of enforcement by the former Securities Commission.[101] In more recent years, as amendments have increased the regulator's powers, other causes must be sought.

One factor possibly contributing to the lack of insider trading enforcement action is that such enforcement may have been "crowded out" by a focus on prosecutions relating to the collapse of finance companies since 2007. The FMA cannot prosecute every breach that comes to its attention, since it must make efficient and effective use of its finite resources. Accordingly, even well-founded suspicions of insider trading might not be investigated or prosecuted if other enforcement matters (e.g., those associated with finance company collapses) are considered as taking priority.

A second possible factor in the enforcement deficit may be that the insider trading regime overall is working quite well, by reason of the continuous disclosure obligations[102] rather than the conduct prohibitions. Research by finance scholars supports this hypothesis. In a paper published in 2004, Ahmad Etebari, Alireza Tourani-Rad and Aaron Gilbert examined transactions disclosed by corporate insiders for a sample of ninety-three listed companies during the 1995–2001 period, during which disclosure obligations were "two-tiered."[103] The authors drew attention to the differential between the "immediate disclosure" obligations of substantial shareholders and the "delayed disclosure" required of directors and executives.[104] A key finding of the study was that large abnormal gains to insiders came "largely from transactions involving delayed disclosure" whereas "transactions involving immediate disclosure earn insignificant returns."[105] A 2007 paper by Aaron Gilbert, Alireza Tourani-Rad and Piotr Wisniewski examined the effect on the market of SMA amendments requiring all corporate insiders to disclose details of their trading within five trading days and increasing the enforcement powers of the Securities Commission.[106] Their results

---

[101]   Compare Tomasz P. Wisniewski & Martin T. Bohl, The Information Content of Registered Insider Trading under Lax Law Enforcement, 25 Int'l Rev. L. & Econ. 169 (2005).

[102]   An effective continuous disclosure regime reduces the incidence of insider trading by narrowing the information asymmetry between insiders and the market generally.

[103]   Ahmad Etebari et al., Disclosure Regulation and the Profitability of Insider Trading, 12 Pacific-Basin Fin. J. 479 (2004).

[104]   Etebari, Tourani-Rad, & Gilbert state that:

Until recently, disclosure laws in New Zealand regarding insider trading were vastly different from those of other developed countries. Under the [SMA] only substantial shareholders (SSH), those shareholders with over 5% of the company's shares, were required to disclose their trading in a timely fashion and even then only when their holding changed by a cumulative 1% since the previous disclosure. As for directors and executives, only company directors were required to disclose their trading in their annual report, while executives who were non-board members were not required to disclose their trading at all. This meant that only large shareholders disclosed trading in a timely fashion, within five days of the trade, while ordinary directors disclosed, on average, 9–10 months after the transaction.

Id. at 481.

[105]   Id. at 479.

[106]   Aaron Gilbert et al., Insiders and the Law: The Impact of Regulatory Change on Insider Trading, 47 Mgmt Int'l Rev. 748, 763 (2007). A new Part 2 was inserted in the SMA by Securities

"provided strong evidence that the regulatory changes have resulted in a significant reduction of the microstructure effects of insider trading."[107] The authors concluded that "the change in regulations has had a positive impact on the market."[108]

Because the Securities Commission's enforcement powers were increased around the same time that disclosure requirements were tightened,[109] it is difficult to be certain as to which of those changes caused the effects observed by Gilbert, Tourani-Rad and Wisniewski. In the absence, however, of any high-profile prosecutions, it seems unlikely that the changes to enforcement powers have substantially deterred insider conduct. If Etebari, Tourani-Rad and Gilbert are correct that rules requiring prompt disclosure by insiders are associated with much lower returns on insider transactions, then stricter disclosure may have caused insider trading in New Zealand to diminish in both frequency and economic impact, making prosecutions a less urgent priority. It is possible, therefore, that the imposition of enhanced disclosure obligations on insiders is a factor in the low incidence of insider trading prosecutions in New Zealand in recent years. This is not to say, however, that continuous disclosure rules supplant either insider trading rules or their enforcement. The rigorous enforcement of the insider trading prohibitions by an expert and well-resourced regulator will continue to be critical to the credibility of New Zealand's securities markets.

Markets Amendment Act 2002 (NZ) § 16, providing for continuous disclosure by public issuers; disclosure by directors and officers; and disclosure of interests of substantial security holders in public issuers. Id.

[107]   Gilbert, supra note 106, at 763.

[108]   Id.

[109]   The Securities Markets Amendment Act 2002 (NZ) commenced on December 1, 2002, except for the disclosure amendments, which commenced on May 3, 2004.

Section C

Europe

21. UK insider dealing and market abuse law: strengthening regulatory law to combat market misconduct

Kern Alexander

Insider dealing and market manipulation legislation and regulation have been considered necessary to promote the efficient pricing of securities and to enhance the integrity of the capital markets.[1] Insider dealing is not a victimless crime; it is both a manifestation of inefficient markets and a considerable corporate governance problem.[2] Market manipulation involves deliberate acts or statements intended to create false or misleading impressions about a particular issuer(s) of securities or to engage in behaviour that would distort the functioning of the market that could lead to unusual and sharp price swings in securities and related volatility which can undermine investor confidence and financial stability. Both insider dealing and market manipulation have been recognized as criminal offences in all European Economic Area (EEA) countries and in most other jurisdictions with developed financial markets. Moreover, the European Union Directive[3] on Insider Dealing and Market Manipulation requires EU member states to create a civil offence for insider dealing and market manipulation known as the 'Market Abuse' offence.

The chapter analyses the UK criminal law of insider dealing and the civil or regulatory law of market abuse to show how it has evolved and been utilized by UK authorities since the financial crisis of 2007–08 to control market misconduct. Although the substantive law has generally remained the same since before the crisis, UK authorities are increasing the number of investigations and enforcement actions to counter the reputation of the City of London as a 'light touch' jurisdiction that has tolerated market misconduct. Insider dealing is a criminal offence defined under Part V of the Criminal Justice Act 1993. In contrast, market abuse is a civil offence as set forth in §§ 118–123 of the Financial Services and Markets Act 2000. The chapter will review the UK insider dealing law and analyse some related issues concerning the difficulty and complexity of its application. It will then discuss the UK market abuse offence and its development under the EU Directive on Insider Dealing and Market Manipulation.[4] The final section discusses efforts by the UK

---

[1]   See Kern Alexander, Insider Dealing and Market Abuse: The Financial Services and Markets Act (FSMA) 2000, ESRC Centre for Business Research, University of Cambridge, Working Paper 222, 19–20 (2000); see also, Emilios Avgouleas, The Mechanics and Regulation of Market Abuse, 11–14 (2005).

[2]   Insider dealing laws are generally considered to be necessary because they address a particular manifestation of the principal – agent problem in corporate governance in which firm agents extract rents from the firm by using privileged or confidential information belonging to the firm.

[3]   Directive 2003/6/EC of the European Parliament and Council of 28 January 2003, *OJ* L96/16.

[4]   Directive 2003/6/EC of the European Parliament and Council of 28 January 2003.

Financial Services Authority (FSA) to develop a more proactive posture in dealing with market misconduct by using more regulatory enforcement actions to target market abuse.

The regulation of insider dealing under United Kingdom law traditionally had the objective of protecting shareholders against the misuse of privileged or confidential information belonging to the company by corporate insiders who were in a position to utilize the information for their gain at the expense of the company and its shareholders. In contrast, regulatory controls on market manipulation were designed to prevent misleading statements and practices concerning issuers and their securities and behaviour that would distort the markets.[5] The criminal law was the main legal vehicle through which authorities sought to control insider dealing and market manipulation. In recent years, policymakers have recognized that insider dealing and market manipulation also pose risks to the efficient functioning of capital markets and, when complex financial instruments or trading strategies are involved, can lead to serious market distortions and liquidity risks.[6] The EU and its member jurisdictions have adopted the civil or regulatory offence of market abuse requiring a lower standard of proof to impose liability. The market abuse offence is designed not only to protect shareholders against the misuse of proprietary information belonging to the company and others to whom a fiduciary duty is owed, but also to promote a more efficient functioning of financial markets by fostering minimum standards of fair dealing and transparent practices that reduce market distortions and control systemic risks.[7]

In today's globalized financial markets, there is a general acceptance of the impropriety and economic inefficiency of insider dealing and market manipulation. Indeed, the International Organization of Securities Commissions (IOSCO) expressly recognizes market abuse and insider dealing to be a threat to the integrity and good governance of financial markets that can, in certain circumstances, undermine systemic stability in those markets. Accordingly, IOSCO has adopted international standards for the efficient regulation of securities markets that contain recommended prohibitions on market abuse and insider dealing that are designed in part to control systemic risks and enhance financial stability.[8]

---

[5]   See FSMA, 2000, c. 8, § 397 (1) (a)–(c) (containing the criminal offences of misleading statements and misleading practices). The FSA obtained a criminal conviction under § 397 (1)(c) in 2005 against a company and its directors for making a profit forecast to the market which was dependent on three contracts which did not exist. See R. v. Rigby and Rowley (2005) (unreported). Moreover, section 397 (3) defines the criminal offence of market manipulation as engaging in any course of conduct which creates a false or misleading impression as to the market or price or value of relevant investments if that is done for the purpose of creating that impression and of inducing another person to buy, sell, subscribe for, or underwrite those investments.

[6]   European Central Bank, Financial Stability Report 2 (January 2011).

[7]   Systemic risk has become an important focus of the regulatory reform agenda but its definition has been much disputed by academics and policymakers. See Eilis Ferran & Kern Alexander, The European Systemic Risk Board, 35 Eur. L. Rev. 751–776 (2010).

[8]   See International Organization of Securities Commissions, Objectives and Principles of Securities Regulation (2001).

I.   THE EVOLUTION OF THE UK INSIDER DEALING OFFENCE

In the United Kingdom insider dealing can be defined as trading in organized securities markets by persons in possession of material non-public information and has been recognized as a widespread problem that is extremely difficult to eradicate. Some of the insider dealing is based on corporate information, i.e. information about a company's finances or operations. In recent years, however, most of the important dealing cases have concerned mergers and acquisitions due largely to the explosive growth in takeover activity during the past decade. Indeed, the bankers, lawyers, public relations advisors and others who receive advance knowledge of proposed takeovers, which invariably occur at a substantial premium over the existing market price of the acquired company's shares, face a strong temptation to make a quick profit from inside information. Moreover, advances in technology have made it possible for traders using electronic trading networks and algorithmic traders to take advantage of privileged inside information and to manipulate markets.[9] Notwithstanding the fact that for over twenty years the abuse of this information has been a serious criminal offence, studies conducted by the FSA indicate that there is considerable evidence that such information is abused in a significant percentage of cases.[10] This indicates that the control of insider dealing is a complex issue in regard to which the criminal justice system can only achieve so much.

The general criminal law has always sought to protect the integrity of public markets. There were very early common law offences that criminalized attempts to interfere with the proper operation of the markets. The possibility of civil liability for breach of fiduciary duty existed for directors and officers who benefited from inside information or who illicitly disclosed privileged information. The scope of action for shareholders, however, was limited because of the rule in *Percival v. Wright*[11] that company directors owed no duties to shareholders. The possibility of civil liability also existed for primary insiders for breach of confidence and for tippees as constructive trustees.[12] Moreover, since the eighteenth century, Parliament and the City of London have adopted a number of measures aimed at promoting the integrity of investment banks, securities brokers and other financial intermediaries.

Although the effectiveness of these measures has been questioned by some economists and market participants,[13] there has always been the recognition that manipulative and fraudulent conduct has especially serious implications for the efficient operation of capital markets because of the threat posed to individual investors. Indeed, maintaining the integrity and fairness of financial markets has generally been viewed as a prerequisite for their efficiency. Yet, the use of information obtained in privileged circumstances has

---

[9]   See Kern Alexander, Market Structures and Market Abuse, in J. Barth and M. Taylor, Safeguarding Financial Stability, the Encyclopaedia of Financial Globalization 120–133 (2012).
[10]   See Paul Barnes, Stock Market Efficiency, Insider Dealing and Market Abuse 152–161 (2009).
[11]   Percival v. Wright (1902) 2 Ch. 421.
[12]   See Brenda Hannigan, Insider Dealing, 8–9 (2nd ed. 1994).
[13]   See Henry Manne, Insider Trading and the Stock Market (1966); Jan Engelen & Luc Van Liedkerke, The Ethics of Insider Trading Revisited, 74 J. Bus. Ethics 497 (2007).

not always been considered objectionable, let alone unfair. For example, some economists have suggested that certain restrictions on insider dealing might actually undermine efficiency in financial markets and increase agency problems.[14]

Until 1980, the restrictions on insider dealing in the United Kingdom were extremely limited. There was no specific legislation other than the requirements in the Companies Acts for directors, members of their families and substantial shareholders to report dealings in the shares of their companies. While these disclosure obligations were justified on a number of grounds, a significant one was that this would discourage the abuse of inside information. Whether reporting such transactions does have such an effect is open to debate. In any case, these provisions were poorly policed.[15] We have also seen that the common law provided no real possibility for those who dealt with those who abused inside information to seek recovery in the civil courts.[16] The use of inside information absent some affirmative obligation to disclose it, did not, and probably in most cases still does not, give rise to a cause of action in the civil law. The most significant element of regulation was that provided by a range of self-regulatory and professional bodies in the City of London. For example, the City Panel on Takeovers and Mergers[17] and the London Stock Exchange[18] had adopted rules and guidelines that restricted insider dealing and the 'tipping' of inside information in the early 1970s. There was considerable scepticism, however, as to how effective they were in practice. The self-regulatory bodies in the City of London increasingly recognized that for effective enforcement, particularly where there was an international element in the transaction, statutory powers were required. Consequently, by 1980, many in the City recognized the need for insider dealing to be made a specific criminal offence.

The Companies Act 1980 included the specific criminal offence of insider dealing in limited circumstances.[19] This new criminal offence supported the growing recognition in UK company law that fiduciary duties designed to protect the company and shareholders against insider dealing on the grounds that trading on the basis of inside information was a form of theft from the company and indirectly extracted rents from shareholders was inadequate and that stricter criminal sanctions were needed.[20] The scope of criminal liability for the insider dealing offence was widened under Part V of the Criminal Justice Act 1993 (CJA 1993) by expanding the definition of the terms 'insider' and 'securities'.[21] The CJA 1993 expansion of the offence of insider dealing was enacted as a result of the

---

[14]   See Steven Shavell, Risk Sharing and Incentives in the Principal and Agent Relationship, 10 Bell J. Econ. 55–73 (1979).

[15]   See Kern Alexander, et al., Insider Dealing and Market Abuse 31–33 (2002). By contrast, the US enacted anti-market manipulation legislation in 1934 in §§ 9 and 10(b) of the Securities Exchange Act of 1934. 15 U.S.C. 78(i), 78(j).

[16]   Percival v. Wright (1902), 2 Ch. 421.

[17]   City Code on Takeovers and Mergers, Rule 4.1.

[18]   The London Stock Exchange, Model Code for Securities Transactions by Directors of Listed Companies (Yellow Book) §§ 5.43–5.48 (1987).

[19]   Part V of the Companies Act 1980 first introduced the offence of insider dealing in certain specified circumstances. See Companies Act 1980, §§ 68–73.

[20]   Companies Act 1980, Part V.

[21]   Criminal Justice Act 1993, c. 36 (Eng.).

UK Government's implementation of the 1990 European Community Insider Dealing Directive.[22]

The CJA 1993 prohibited three classes of conduct in certain circumstances: (1) dealings in price-affected securities based on inside information; (2) encouraging another to deal in price-affected securities based on inside information; and (3) knowingly disclosing inside information to another. Regarding market manipulation, the Financial Services Act 1986 created two criminal offences consisting of (1) misleading statements, and (2) misleading practices.[23] The traditional UK approach to controlling insider dealing and market manipulation was therefore to use the criminal law,[24] which often proved ineffective in curtailing the rampant abuse of insider information and manipulative practices in UK securities markets.

A.   The Criminal Justice Act 1993 (Part V)[25]

The CJA 1993 Part V provides for the offence of insider dealing that seeks to prevent individuals from engaging in three classes of conduct in particular circumstances. First, the Act prohibits dealing in price-affected securities on the basis of inside information.[26] Secondly, it prohibits the encouragement of another person to deal in price-affected securities on the basis of insider information; and, thirdly, it prohibits knowing disclosure of insider information to another.[27] To prove an offence under § 52, it was necessary to demonstrate two elements: (1) the status of the person charged as an insider; and (2) the type of information in the person's possession to be inside information. Section 52 provides in the relevant part:

(1) An individual who has information as an insider is guilty of insider dealing if, in the circumstances mentioned in subsection (3), he deals in securities that are price-affected securities in relation to the information.

(2) An individual who has information as an insider is also guilty of insider dealing if –

---

[22] Council Directive 89/552 of 13 November 1989 co-ordinating regulations on insider dealing, *OJ* EC 18 Nov. 1989, L 334/30.

[23] FSA, 1986, §§ 47(1) (misleading statements) & 47(2) (misleading practices). The Financial Services and Markets Act 2000 replaced the Financial Services Act 1986. In particular, it replaced § 47 with new provisions prohibiting misleading statements and practices in § 397 (1)–(3) FSMA. See supra note 4 and accompanying text.

[24] As discussed above in note 13, Parliament amended the Companies Act in 1980 to criminalize insider dealing. In 1985 Parliament expanded the insider dealing offence to include tippees by enacting the Companies Securities (Insider Dealing) Act 1985 ('the 1985 Act'). See Companies Securities (Insider Dealing) Act 1985, § 24 (prohibiting individuals who had access to material non-public information by virtue of their position with the company from trading in the company's securities and created a tipping offence and a tippee offence). The UK statutory approach was built on earlier common law offences that criminalized attempts to interfere with the proper operation of the markets, but which created offences that were narrow in scope and thereby difficult for prosecutors to prove in a court of law. Consequently, the 1985 Act resulted in few prosecutions and even fewer convictions.

[25] Criminal Justice Act 1993, c. 36 (Eng.). The CJA 1993 Pt V came into force on 1 March 1994 together with two ancillary statutory instruments (both reproduced in the 'Rules and Regulations'); namely, the Insider Dealing (Securities and Regulated Markets) Order 1994 and the Traded Securities (Disclosure) Regulation 1994. The relevant provisions are in the 'Ancillary Acts.'

[26] CJA 1993 Pt V, § 52(1).

[27] CJA 1993 Pt V, § 52(1) and (2).

(a) he encourages another person to deal in securities that are (whether or not that other knows it) price-affected securities in relation to the information, knowing or having reasonable cause to believe that the dealing would take place in the circumstances mentioned in subsection (3); or

(b) he discloses information, otherwise than in proper performance of the functions of his employment, office or profession, to another person.

(3) The circumstances referred to above are that the acquisition or disposal in question occurs on a regulated market, or that the person dealing relies on a professional intermediary or is himself acting as a professional intermediary.

Criminal liability for each offence may only attach to an individual because the term 'individual' is defined to exclude corporations and other entities (e.g. public authorities). The definition of individual did cover, however, unincorporated partnerships or firms comprising a collection of individuals. Moreover, it should be noted that a company could be liable for insider dealing by committing the secondary offence of encouraging another person to deal.

To commit the offence of insider dealing, an individual must have information as an insider, which is defined in the CJA 1993 § 57 as follows:

(1) . . . a person has information as an insider if and only if –

(a) it is, and he knows that it is, inside information, and

(b) he has it, and knows that he has it, from an inside source.

(2) For the purposes of subsection (1), a person has information from an inside source if and only if –

(a) he has it through

(i) being a director, employee or shareholder of an issuer of securities; or

(ii) having access to the information by virtue of his employment, office or profession; or

(b) the direct or indirect source of his information is a person within paragraph (a).

The CJA 1993 § 57 created a distinction between a primary insider (a person who has direct knowledge of inside information) and a secondary insider (a person who learns inside information from an inside source). The primary insider usually obtains inside information through being a director, employee or shareholder of an issuer of securities or any person who has information because of his employment or office. A secondary insider obtains inside information either directly or indirectly from a primary insider. Section 57 would impose liability on brokers or analysts as secondary insiders if they act on 'market intelligence' that they know comes from a primary insider.

The insider dealing offence can only be committed if the acquisition or disposal of securities occurs on a regulated market or if the person dealing relied on a professional intermediary or is himself a professional intermediary.[28] The CJA 1993 defines 'professional intermediary' as a person who carries on a business of acquiring or disposing of securities (whether as principal or agent) or a business of acting as an intermediary between persons taking part in any dealing in securities.[29] Individuals employed by such a person to carry out these activities are also defined as 'professional intermediaries'. The

---

[28]   CJA 1993 § 52(3).
[29]   CJA 1993 § 59(1)(a).

definition of professional intermediary does not include a person whose activities are merely incidental to other activities or if those activities are only conducted occasionally.[30] The CJA 1993, § 59 defines 'professional intermediary' as follows:

(1) a professional intermediary is a person –
   (a) who carries on a business consisting of an activity mentioned in subsection (2) and who holds himself out to the public or any section of the public (including a section of the public constituted by persons such as himself) as willing to engage in any such business; or
   (b) who is employed by a person falling within paragraph (a) to carry out any such activity.
(2) The activities referred to in subsection (1) are –
   (a) acquiring or disposing of securities (whether as principal or agent); or
   (b) acting as an intermediary between persons taking part in any dealing in securities.

Under this definition, a person will rely on a professional intermediary only if the professional intermediary either acquires or disposes of securities (whether as principal or agent) in relation to the dealing or acts as intermediary between persons taking part in the dealing.[31] If deals in securities do occur on a regulated market (i.e. investment exchange), the insider dealing offence will be relevant unless the transaction is truly a private deal off the market without the intervention of a market professional.

The offence of insider dealing cannot apply to anything done by an individual acting on behalf of a public sector body in pursuit of the government's economic policies (e.g. managing monetary policy through the adjustment of exchange rates, interest rates or the public debt or foreign exchange reserves).[32] The purpose of these exclusions is to permit government policymakers to have sufficient discretion to manage the economy in the public interest. These exclusions, however, would not apply to the government's sale of shares in a privatization.[33]

B. The Elements of the Dealing Offence

The two essential requirements for the dealing offence are that: (1) an individual must have information as an insider; and (2) the insider must deal in securities that are price-affected securities in relation to the information.[34] With respect to inside information, the prices of price-affected securities will likely be significantly affected if information related to such securities is made public.[35] Accordingly, if an insider has inside information, he must not deal in the securities to which that information relates. The CJA 1993 adopts a broad definition of 'dealing in securities' to cover any acquisition or disposal of a security, including an agreement to acquire or dispose of a security and the entering into a contract

---

[30] CJA 1993 § 59(3)(a)–(b).
[31] CJA 1993 § 59(4).
[32] CJA 1993 § 63(1).
[33] These exclusions would not apply or exempt the setting of the London Inter-bank Offered Rate ('LIBOR'), which is calculated daily based on estimates by large banks of their cost of borrowing funds in fifteen different currencies in the inter-bank loan market.
[34] CJA 1993 § 52(1).
[35] CJA 1993 § 56(2).

which creates the security or the bringing to an end of such contract.[36] Moreover, such acquisitions or disposals are within the definition irrespective of whether they are made by an individual as principal or as agent.

The securities to which the Act applies are price-affected securities which are defined in the CJA 1993, Schedule 2. They include shares and debentures in companies, as well as their derivatives. They also include gilts and local authority stock (even of foreign public bodies) and their derivatives. Contractual rights for difference (e.g. derivatives) are also included. The list conforms to the EC Directive on Insider Dealing,[37] so that not only corporate securities and instruments based on such securities are included, but also that other contractual rights in other futures and derivatives markets are covered.

The relevant time at which to consider whether or not an offence has been committed would appear to be at the time of agreement to acquire or dispose of the security. At that time, if the individual had inside information about these securities he will have committed an offence. However, if he received inside information only after making the agreement, he will probably not have violated the provision if he completes the deal and actually acquires or disposes of the securities. On the other hand, if the individual had the inside information at the time when he agreed to acquire or dispose of the security, it would seem that he will still have committed an offence, even if he does not complete the bargain.

The acquisition or disposal may be made by an individual acting either as principal or agent. Accordingly, if an agent has inside information, he will be within the scope of the offence if he deals in the relevant securities even though, in a direct sense, he will not gain from the transaction. This has special relevance to a trader who is engaged in a transaction as agent to benefit his principal. The fact that the individual deals as agent and not principal is irrelevant. However, where the agent deals on an execution basis only, such an approach hardly seems justified and is unfair to the principal who gave the instruction if the agent then feels inhibited from processing the order. Fortunately, it appears that a defence in this situation would allow the agent to act on instructions notwithstanding that, incidentally, he has inside information.[38]

A person is also regarded as dealing in securities if he procures, directly or indirectly, an acquisition or disposal of the securities by another person.[39] Such procurement may occur in a number of ways, including where the person who actually acquires or disposes of the security is acting as an agent, nominee or at the direction of another in relation to the acquisition or disposal of a security.[40] This aspect of the definition of 'dealing in securities' is designed to cover transactions through an agent or nominee where the principal has relied on inside information without purchasing or selling the securities himself. Transactions are also covered that are undertaken at the direction of a sole shareholder who uses its influence over a company to deal in its shares.[41]

The buying or selling need not necessarily relate to securities of the company with

---

[36]   CJA 1993 §55(3)(b).
[37]   Art. 1(2) Council Directive 89/552/EEC.
[38]   CJA 1993 § 53(1)(c).
[39]   CJA 1993 § 55(1)(b).
[40]   CJA 1993 § 55(4).
[41]   *See* Parliamentary Debates, House of Commons, Standing Committee B, 10 June 1993, column 171 (per the Economic Secretary).

which the person concerned is in an access relationship. It is also the case that dealing in the securities of related companies on the basis of relevant unpublished information would also be considered insider dealing. Dealings in securities other than equity securities that are price-affected by the information would be considered to be insider dealing in the UK and most other jurisdictions. Thus, acquiring options to acquire or dispose of underlying securities would be objectionable, as would dealing in other types of derivative securities. The question is simply whether the decision to deal in the relevant securities is influenced by the information that the person concerned has acquired and is using improperly.

The term 'insider dealing' is wide enough to encompass deals on or off an organized securities market. While a number of legal systems have effectively confined the operation of their legal rules to transactions that occur on an organized securities exchange or on or through an organized over-the-counter market, the elements of the abuse are the same whether the transaction is on a market or in a private direct transaction. One of the reasons why jurisdictions have confined the operation of their laws to public markets is the idea that the wrong indicated by insider dealing is one against the market as a whole. It saps confidence in the integrity and fairness of the market. Consequently, some countries have made available only their criminal laws to sanction this essentially public wrong or, rather, crime. Off-market transactions are left to the ordinary law that governs the commercial dealings of private persons. The fallacy is to attribute the description of insider dealing to one type of transaction and not to the other. While there may be justifications for distinguishing market and off-market insider transactions in regard to the remedies that are made available and in relation to enforcement, the nature of the abuse and its elements are the same. Therefore, it is appropriate to regard insider dealing as taking place on organized markets as well as in private and even face-to-face transactions.

Regarding the case of primary insiders, the classic example that is often given of insider dealing is where a director of a company learns in a board meeting that his company's profit forecasts are about to be revised to a significant extent and then goes onto the stock market and trades on the basis of this information before it is made publicly available. In such circumstances, he has clearly taken advantage of his position and the information that came to him by virtue of his seat on the board. He has manifestly misused the confidential information that was entrusted to him in the proper performance of his duties as a director or, in the words of US federal law, misappropriated it. It would also be generally regarded as falling within the notion of insider dealing if he persuaded another person to deal in the securities of his company or disclosed the information to a third person knowing that he would be likely so to deal or otherwise misuse the information.

In the case of other primary insiders, it is not, of course, only company directors that will in the ordinary course of their duties acquire price-sensitive information. Indeed, it is probably more likely that in most companies there are many other insiders who will come into possession of such information rather more regularly than the directors. Having regard to the obvious relationship that a director has to his company, it remains to be seen whether such persons would be rash enough to risk exposure to public criticism by engaging in insider dealing. Furthermore, it cannot be taken for granted that most company directors would be willing to risk their position and the financial and other benefits that arise as a result of their office by engaging in abusive deals.

The notion of insider dealing is broad enough to encompass all those who, by virtue of their position in the company or who, by their business or professional relationship with the company, are likely to have access to privileged information. For the sake of convenience, it is perhaps useful to describe such persons as primary insiders. They are all subject to the common denominator of enjoying a special relationship with the company that gives them access to the price-sensitive information in question. Indeed, in US jurisprudence, they have often been referred to as 'access insiders'. Debate has taken place as to whether those who obtain such information in breach of their duties attaching to the relationship in question should be regarded as primary insiders. For example, is it appropriate to regard an office cleaner, who, while having access to a company's premises by virtue of her employment directly or indirectly with the company, obtains price-sensitive information by rummaging in the rubbish bins, as a primary insider? Although it is arguable that all those who abuse price-sensitive information should be sanctioned, for the sake of convenience in drafting rules and laws, most jurisdictions distinguish between those who obtain such information in the proper and lawful exercise of the duties attaching to the relationship that they have with the relevant company and those who do so essentially outside the scope of those responsibilities.

Regarding secondary insiders, it is also considered to be insider dealing when a person, while not in an access relationship to the issuer, acquires the relevant information in circumstances where he knows that it is unpublished price-sensitive information and comes from an insider source and then deals or encourages another to deal. Thus, although the office cleaner in the example referred to above might not be considered to be a primary insider, her abuse of the information obtained from what she appreciates is an 'inside source' would generally be considered to amount to insider dealing. In some cases, it will even be considered objectionable for this tippee or secondary insider to pass the information on to yet another person in circumstances where they know or should appreciate that the information is likely to be misused.

Regarding inside sources, the law and, indeed, morality in most societies necessitates proof of a relationship between the source of the information and the person who is to be accused of insider dealing. The price-sensitive information must be obtained by virtue of this relationship. It is the relationship that taints it and renders improper its use for personal benefit. Of course, the notion of relationship is stretched far beyond what the law would normally consider to be relationships of a fiduciary quality or, for that matter, necessarily giving rise to a duty of confidentiality. The extent to which it is necessary to establish that the relevant information is obtained by virtue of the privileged access that the relationship gives to the person concerned is a matter for debate. Logically, if the information can be shown to have been obtained from some other and outside source, then its use by a person who is clearly in a special relationship with the company should not be considered to be insider dealing. However, in most systems of law, there will be a 'presumption' that if a primary insider is in possession of price-sensitive information in regard to the securities of the issuer with which he has an access relationship, then the 'inside information' was obtained pursuant to this relationship.

In considering the definition of inside information, one should accept the premise that information itself is a very vague and ill-defined concept in most legal systems. However, in the context of insider dealing, it is generally not necessary to refine a definition that does more than indicate that it possesses a quality sufficient to influence the decision of the person who has access to it to deal in particular securities. In other words, the information that the person accused of insider dealing has in his possession must be such as would influence his decision to buy or sell. In the UK, as in most legal systems, it is enough if the information would influence the mind of a person who would be likely to deal in the relevant securities. Thus, materiality is objective and is determined by reference to the particular class or group of investors that would ordinarily be likely to deal in the securities in question. This gives the test of materiality sufficient flexibility to accommodate narrow and highly specialized markets. The more specific and precise the information is, the more likely it is that it will influence the mind of a reasonable person.

The information must be inside information. In other words, it must have a quality that ties it to the issuer in whose securities the dealing takes place. We have already discussed this issue in terms of the relationship that the person accused of insider dealing must have, directly or indirectly, with the source of the information. Obviously, relevance will be bound up with materiality in most conceivable cases. The information need not be generated within, by or for the benefit of the issuer in whose securities the dealing takes place. For example, it would be objectionable for a director of a company that intends to make an attractive takeover offer for the securities of another company to deal in the securities of that other company on the basis of this knowledge. The information in such a case may be regarded as being inside information obtained through his insider nexus with his company, but its relevance is to the market in that other issuer's securities.

While the information involved in most cases of insider abuse will be confidential or at least obtained in a relationship that might be expected to give rise to obligations of confidentiality, it is not always that the information will be such that could be protected as 'confidential' information. Indeed, there will be cases where the information is too tentative to be protected as proprietary information, but which would still meet the test of materiality. It is also the case that there will be situations when the information is not confidential to a particular person or entity. In the result, it is clear that inside information is not always confidential information. Of course, in the United States, the courts have fashioned the so-called 'misappropriation theory' to justify liability for insider dealing. This approach sanctions the 'misappropriation' of information that belongs to another person. Dealing on the basis of such information will constitute a misappropriation, as will improperly disclosing it to another in circumstances where that other utilizes it. The notion that information belongs to another person who will often obtain the same by the inside source is a difficult one for many legal systems. For example, while many legal systems are prepared to protect confidential information as if it were a form of property, not all by any means consider information capable of being a species of property.[42]

Regarding unauthorized disclosures, it has already been pointed out that most systems of insider dealing regulation would regard disclosing inside information to another person, without the appropriate authority, in circumstances where that other person is likely to abuse the information, as a form of insider dealing. Of course, merely disclosing information, even if there is an expectation that the recipient will himself deal, is not 'dealing' in any real sense of the word. While it is possible and commonplace to attribute the transactions of an agent to the principal and therefore the deals of the agent to the

---

[42]   See, e.g., Oxford v. Moss (1978) 68 Cr. App. R. 183 (holding that information was not property for the purpose of the law of theft).

deals of the 'insider', it is less easy to describe procuring or encouraging the dealing of another as insider dealing. Nonetheless, the term 'insider dealing' is often employed in such an expansive manner, as it is in the UK.

Where a person, without authority, discloses unpublished and material information in the knowledge that the recipient might well utilize the information for dealing, then it is at least arguable that the person should be held responsible for what is indirectly the exploitation of the information in question. In the UK, as in most systems of law that regard such unauthorized disclosures as tantamount to insider dealing, it matters not whether the recipient actually engages in transactions which would themselves be considered insider dealing. For example, while the informant might be culpable, the recipient who deals on the basis of the information may not be aware that the information emanates from an inside source. Of course, a failure to appreciate the status of the information might well in any case bring into issue its materiality.

Such conduct will, however, only be considered objectionable when the primary insider discloses the relevant information without proper authority. It is not always easy to decide if a particular disclosure is legitimate or not. As a general rule, if the disclosure is made with the actual or implied authority of the person concerned to make or authorize disclosure, then it will not be objectionable. There may be cases where, while the relevant officer of the company has authority to disclose information, he does so not for a proper purpose, but perhaps to facilitate improper transactions on the part of another. In most systems of law, agents have authority only to engage in actions that are properly motivated. Therefore, a disclosure that is motivated by improper considerations, such as a desire to promote a false market, would not be legitimate and justifiable even when a primary insider has no authority to disclose information. It may well be on the facts appropriate and legitimate for him to do so, for example 'blowing the whistle' on misconduct. Provided that such is done for a purpose that would be considered proper and is not dishonest, it is hard to see that such conduct could be described as fostering insider abuse. The line between what is acceptable and what is not is not always clear. Difficulties have arisen in the case of selective disclosures to analysts and private briefings, as we shall see in the discussion of the market abuse offence.

Section 402 of the Financial Services and Markets Act 2000 authorizes the FSA to enforce the criminal offence of insider dealing.[43] Over the years, responsibility for prosecuting crimes involving insider dealing has proved to be something of a 'hot potato' and has been shared by several UK agencies and prosecuting authorities. The police have never been particularly enthusiastic about such cases and the Serious Fraud Office has taken the view that the vast majority would not come within its statutory remit. Indeed, several years ago the SFO dismissed such offences as being of a 'technical and regulatory' nature. With the realization that 'real' criminals may engage in the deliberate gathering and exploitation of price-sensitive information attitudes have possibly changed, and even the Serious Organized Crime Agency has exhibited some interest. However, given the FSA's exclusive responsibility for policing the market abuse regime it is sensible that the FSA is now the lead prosecutor for cases under the Criminal Justice

---

[43]   See Financial Services and Markets Act 2000, c. 8 (Eng.), § 402 (authorizing FSA to bring insider dealing prosecutions and imposing seven year custodial sentence for insider dealing).

Act.[44] It should be remembered, however, that serious cases of insider abuse will often involve other criminal conduct and more general offences, such as money laundering and terrorist financing.

II.   THE MARKET ABUSE OFFENCE

In 2000, the UK Parliament enacted the Financial Services and Markets Act 2000, which created a civil offence for market abuse, enhanced criminal penalties for insider dealing, and created three criminal offences for misleading statements and practices.[45] Section 118 FSMA created three distinct categories for the market abuse offence: (1) misuse of information; (2) creating false or misleading impressions; and (3) market distortion. Unlike the above criminal offences, the market abuse offence could be enforced in regulatory administrative proceedings in which unlimited civil penalties could be imposed based on a lower evidentiary standard defined as the regular user test. Significantly, the market abuse offence was concerned not only with protecting legally privileged information belonging to issuers of securities against abusive behaviour by insiders and other third parties, but also was directed against behaviour that could undermine market confidence, including systemic stability. The market abuse offence was designed therefore to enhance market confidence and investor protection by prohibiting *any* person – not just insiders who owed a duty to corporate issuers not to benefit from the use of inside information – from misusing information (i.e. legally privileged information), or creating false or misleading impressions in the market, or distorting the market concerning qualified investments traded on recognized exchanges. By defining the offence in broad terms, the regulatory authority could police the market for behaviour that was not only abusive to particular issuers, but to the market as a whole. As discussed below, the EU Market Abuse Directive 2003 has required the UK to elaborate the definition of market abuse in key areas.

A.   What Constitutes Market Abuse

In contrast to the criminal offence of insider dealing, the statutory framework creating the market abuse offence is very broad, covering 'behaviour' that is both on market and off market, including trading activity and disseminating false or misleading information. The Market Abuse Directive extended the three categories of market abuse under the original § 118(2)(a)–(c) – misuse of information, creating false or misleading impressions, and market distortion – to seven categories as set forth in § 118(2)–(8):

---

[44]   The FSA has so far secured eleven further convictions in relation to insider dealing: Christopher McQuoid and James William Melbourne in March 2009; Matthew and Neel Uberoi in November 2009; Malcolm Calvert on 11 March 2010; Anjam Ahmad on 22 June 2010;Neil Rollins on 21 January 2011; Christian and Angie Littlewood on 8 October 2010; Helmy Omar Sa'aid on 10 January 2011; and Rupinder Sidhu on 15 December 2012. As of July 2012, the FSA is prosecuting eleven other individuals for insider dealing.

[45]   FSMA, 2000, §§ 118–123 (Market abuse regime), and § 402 (authorizing FSA to bring insider dealing prosecutions and imposing seven year custodial sentence for insider dealing); and § 397 (1)–(3) creating three criminal offences for making misleading statements and acts.

(1) insider dealing; or

(2) improper disclosure of inside information; or

(3) misuse of relevant information where the behaviour falls below the standard of behaviour reasonably expected by a regular user of the market or a person in the position of the alleged abuser; or

(4) manipulating transactions in the relevant market unless for legitimate reasons and in conformity to accepted market practices on the relevant market; or

(5) manipulating devices; or

(6) information dissemination that gives or is likely to give a false or misleading impression; or

(7) misleading behaviour or distortion of the market where the behaviour falls below the standard of behaviour reasonably expected by a regular user of the market or an alleged abuser;

unless such behaviour conforms with a rule which expressly provides that behaviour which conforms with the rule will not amount to market abuse; or conforms with Commission Regulation 2273/2003/EC which implements the Market Abuse Directive in relation to exemptions for buy-back plans and stabilization of financial instruments; or does not amount to market abuse under the Code of Market Conduct, or some other FSA position.

In addition, the UK regime maintains its separate civil offence of requiring or encouraging another to commit market abuse if the act in question would have amounted to market abuse if committed by the requirer or encourager.[46] It states in relevant part that the requirement or encouragement offence can be committed if 'by taking or refraining from taking any action, a person has required or encouraged another person or persons to engage in behaviour which if the person themselves engaged in such behaviour would amount to market abuse'.[47] In considering whether to bring an action for this offence or the market abuse more generally, the FSA will take account of factors such as acceptable market practices and level of knowledge and skill of the person concerned.

B.   Prescribed Markets, Qualifying Investments and the Jabre Case

The FSA enforcement action against the hedge fund manager Phillipe Jabre and his employer GLG Partners raised an important issue regarding the scope of the term 'qualifying investments'. In the *Jabre* case,[48] the defendant Jabre had entered into agreements to short sell the stock of the Japanese bank Sumitomo Mitsui Financial Group (SMFG) a few days after receiving price-sensitive information about the bank from a Goldman Sachs salesman. Jabre argued that his conduct in short selling SMFG stock was not, as a matter of law, market abuse contrary to § 118 because his trades in SMFG shares occurred on the Tokyo Stock Exchange and therefore were not qualifying investments on a prescribed market. He argued that it would violate the 'territoriality' principle for a market

[46]   FSMA 2000, § 123 (1)(b) (authorizing the FSA to impose a penalty on a person if it is satisfied that that person, by taking or refraining from taking any action, has required or encouraged another person or persons to engage in behaviour which, if engaged in by the encourager, would amount to market abuse.

[47]   Id.

[48]   Jabre v. Financial Services Authority (Jurisdiction) [2006], Court of Appeal – United Kingdom Financial Services and Markets Tribunals, 10 July 2006 (Eng.) (hearing on appeal by Mr. Jabre of the Financial Service Authority's Decision Notice to Philippe Jabre and to GLG Partners (28 February 2006)).

abuse penalty to be imposed in the exercise of the FSA's power under § 123. The FSA found, however, that Mr. Jabre's behaviour did occur in relation to qualifying investments (SMFG shares) that were traded on a prescribed market. SMFG's shares were qualifying investments of a corporate body (SMFG) and, crucially, those shares were quoted at the relevant time on the London Stock Exchange's SEAQ International Trading System, which was a market to which § 118 applied.[49] Jabre contended that the actual shares he shorted were not traded by him on the London market, but rather on the Tokyo market, and that the term 'qualifying investments' applied only to the shares actually traded, and not to all the shares of the same kind. Moreover, he argued that the purpose of § 118 (prior to the Market Abuse Directive) was to regulate conduct in relation to UK markets, and not in respect of markets outside the UK which were not prescribed by the UK Treasury; and that his conduct on the Tokyo market had no effect on the shares listed on the London market and therefore could not constitute market abuse simply because the shares in question were listed on both markets.

The Tribunal rejected this argument by reasoning that the statutory phrase 'traded on a market to which this section applies' in subsection (1)(a) does not mean that the actual shares traded had to be the same shares that were subject to the abusive behaviour. The Tribunal held that behaviour constituting market abuse 'does not require the identification of any particular shares as being the qualifying investments to which the behaviour relates'. Indeed, the Tribunal reasoned that, if Jabre's argument were accepted, it would be nearly impossible for a regulator in market abuse cases involving, for example, disclosing inside information or disseminating false rumours, to identify any particular share or group of shares which were the subject of wrongful behaviour. Moreover, Jabre's assertion that his conduct on the Tokyo market did not have an effect on the London market was inapposite because the real issue was whether Jabre's behaviour on the Tokyo market could be reasonably expected to undermine confidence in the shares traded on the London market. The Tribunal held that Jabre's insider dealing by shorting the shares of the Japanese bank, wherever it occurred, had the effect of destroying confidence in the global market for the bank's securities and therefore constituted market abuse with respect to qualifying investments on UK prescribed markets.

C. The Duty to the Market

The *Jabre* case also highlights the duty of market participants to the market to maintain transparency and overall market confidence. An important aspect of the market abuse offence was that, unlike the criminal offence of insider dealing, it established a duty to the market for anyone whose conduct – whether on or off market – was defined as being market abuse. This meant that it was not necessary for prosecutors to prove that the defendant breached a duty to an investor or to the company or firm whose financial

---

[49] The Tribunal observed that SEAQ International (the Stock Exchange Automatic Quotation System for international equity market securities) is a quote-driven trading service in which securities traded on SEAQ International required at least two market makers registered with the London Stock Exchange and that two-way prices must be displayed on the LSE system for the security in question. SEAQ International was a prescribed market because of its link with the LSE, and SMFG's shares, which were listed on the LSE system through SEAQ, were qualifying investments.

instruments were being traded. It was sufficient for the regulator to show on a balance of probabilities that the behaviour in question in respect of qualifying investments had impacted the market itself by undermining investor confidence and the integrity of the market as perceived by regular users of the market. In imposing liability, however, the FSA may still under certain circumstances need to show that the state of mind of the alleged abuser was relevant for committing the offence.

Market abuse is therefore defined as behaviour which occurs in relation to qualifying investments admitted to trading on a prescribed market, or in respect of which a request for admission to trading has been made. It also applies to qualifying investments and to investments that are related to qualifying investments. These related investments can be traded on exchanges that are not prescribed UK exchanges. For instance, related investments could be traded on prescribed exchanges or off exchange in other EEA jurisdictions, or on or off exchange outside the EEA, if they relate to qualifying investments on a UK prescribed market. Although relevant in some circumstances, the state of mind of the market abuser is not necessarily relevant for a successful prosecution of the civil offence.

III.   EU INSIDER DEALING AND MARKET MANIPULATION DIRECTIVE

The EU Insider Dealing and Market Manipulation Directive[50] has defined insider dealing as a form of market abuse that can constitute both a civil and a criminal offence. The Directive expands the scope of personal liability for primary insiders by excluding any requirement that they have 'full knowledge of the facts' in order for criminal or civil liability to be imposed. The repeal of this requirement recognizes the market reality that primary insiders may have access to insider information on a daily basis and are aware of the confidential nature of the information they receive. In addition, the Directive adopts an information connection requirement to the definition of secondary insider.[51] According to this definition, a secondary insider would be any person, other than a primary insider, 'who with full knowledge of the facts possesses inside information.' They would be subject to the same prohibitions on trading, disclosing and procuring as primary insiders.

The UK regulations implementing the Directive replace the original § 118(2)(a)–(c) with new definitions of who are the 'insiders' and of what constitutes 'inside information'. Rather than having three definitions of abusive behaviour in § 118, there are now seven categories which provide more specific definitions of prohibited or restricted behaviour.

---

[50]   Directive 2003/6/EC of the European Parliament and of the Council of 28 January 2003 on insider dealing and market manipulation (market abuse) [2003] *OJ* L96/16.

[51]   Directive 2003/6/EC, Article 2 (prohibiting 'any person . . . who possesses inside information from using that information by acquiring or disposing of, or by trying to acquire or dispose of, . . . either directly or indirectly, financial instruments to which that information relates'), and Article 4 (prohibiting 'any person', . . . 'who possesses inside information while that person knows, or ought to have known, that it is inside information' from disclosing inside information to any other person). See EC Market Abuse Directive [2003], *OJ* L96/21, Arts 2, 3 and 4.

This includes 'behaviour' 'where an insider deals, or attempts to deal, in a qualifying investment or related investment on the basis of inside information relating to the investment in question'. By § 118A, behaviour is taken into account only if it occurs 'in the United Kingdom' or is taken outside the UK with respect to a qualifying investment (or related investment) on a prescribed UK market or a qualifying investment (or related investment) on a market prescribed by another EEA state. This provides extraterritorial jurisdiction for the FSA or other EEA authorities to enforce their market abuse legislation against parties who engage in behaviour outside their territory that amounts to market abuse if it relates to qualifying investments on prescribed markets in an EEA member state.

Section 118B defines 'insiders' as any person who has inside information, among other things, 'as a result of having access to the information through the exercise of his employment, profession or duties'. The term 'insiders' also applies to any person who has inside information as a result of his membership of the administrative, management or supervisory bodies of an issuer of qualifying investments, or as a result of his holding in the capital of an issuer of qualifying investments, or as a result of his criminal activities, or obtained by other means and which he knows, or could reasonably expect to know, is inside information.

Section 118C defines 'inside information' for the purposes of Part VII of the Act as the following:

> (2) In relation to qualifying investments, or related investments . . . inside information is information of a precise nature which –
> (a) is not generally available;
> (b) relates, directly or indirectly, to one or more issuers of the qualifying investments or to one or more of the qualifying investments; and
> (c) would if generally available, be likely to have a significant effect on the price of the qualifying investments or on the price of the related investments . . .

This broad definition of 'inside information' derives from the Directive's definition of inside information as 'precise, not been made public, relates directly or indirectly to issuers, and if made public, would have a significant effect on price of qualifying investments (i.e., financial instruments actually issued by the issuer)'. Information is regarded as generally available to users of the market if it can be 'obtained by research or analysis conducted' by or on their behalf.

The EU Market Abuse Directive's broader definition of inside information has reinforced the powers of the FSA to bring market abuse cases based on misuse of information and privileged or confidential information that is leaked by insiders. This was demonstrated in the FSA's enforcement action in 2008 against Richard Ralph and Philip Boyens. This case showed how insiders who acquire inside information in relation to their professional and employment duties can be subject to civil liability for market abuse.[52] In this case, Mr. Ralph, a former UK Ambassador to Belgium, was, at the relevant time, the executive chairman of AIM-listed, Monterrico Metals plc (Monterrico) when he asked

---

[52] FSA Notice to Richard Ralph (12 November 2008/Ralph); and FSA Notice to Philip Boyen (12 November 2008/Boyen).

Mr. Boyen to buy £30,000 ($46,500) worth of shares on his behalf. At the time, it was public information that the company was in takeover talks, but Mr. Ralph also knew that a takeover had been agreed in principle at a premium price that substantially exceeded the then share price. Mr. Ralph was involved in the takeover discussion and knew he was not allowed to deal in the company's shares while the material information on the takeover had not been disclosed. He nevertheless directed his broker to execute trades on his behalf before the material inside information was disclosed.[53]

IV.   POST-CRISIS FSA ENFORCEMENT

The UK Financial Services Authority was criticized in several government reports and by the House of Commons Treasury Committee for following a 'light touch' prudential regulatory approach and for failing to investigate and enforce effectively investor protection, market abuse and insider dealing rules before the global credit crisis began in 2007. Between 2003 and 2007, the FSA brought only nine enforcement actions for market abuse and insider dealing. After the crisis began, however, since 2007 the FSA has toughened its approach considerably by embarking on a number of high profile investigations, including pre-dawn raids on banks and investment firms, and increasing the number of enforcement actions against those accused of market abuse or insider dealing. For example, the FSA has averaged since 2008 fifteen enforcement actions a year involving alleged market abuse and has imposed over £214 million ($331.4 million) in civil fines.[54] Regarding the criminal offence of insider dealing, it has obtained eleven convictions and prosecuted an additional sixteen cases in 2012. Indeed, the FSA's enforcement approach has become more aggressive in order to send a message to the market that market misconduct will not be tolerated and it has enhanced its co-ordination in cross-border prosecutions with foreign regulators.[55] This was demonstrated in the case against James and Miranda Sanders, which resulted in the FSA obtaining convictions in May 2012, when these British defendants were convicted for illicitly using inside information about US issuers to trade index futures on a London exchange.[56]

The FSA's stricter approach was demonstrated in several highly publicized cases in 2011 and 2012 involving senior bankers and fund managers who allegedly leaked insider information on UK-listed companies in violation of the UK market abuse regime. Specifically, the FSA imposed a civil penalty of £450,000 ($725,000) on Ian Hannam,

---

[53]   See FSA Notice to Richard Ralph (12 November 2008/Ralph); and FSA Notice to Philip Boyen (12 November 2008/Boyen). Ralph agreed to a fine of £117,691.41, while Mr. Boyen agreed to a fine of £81,982.95.

[54]   See supra note 44 and accompanying text.

[55]   In the recent FSA insider dealing enforcement action against James and Miranda Sanders, FSA acting director of enforcement and financial crime, Tracy McDermott, said that the FSA is sending 'a clear message about our willingness, and ability, to tackle serious, organised insider dealing'. In cases involving cross-border investigations and enforcement, the FSA acting enforcement director has observed that the FSA 'and our overseas counterparts, are committed to working together to tackle abuse wherever it occurs'. See http://www.fsa.gov.uk/library/communication/pr/2012/060.shtml (last accessed 8 October 2012).

[56]   Id.

JP Morgan Chase's global head of equity capital markets, in April 2012 for illicitly disclosing inside information to a third party investor about the likelihood of a takeover of a company by one of Mr. Hannam's clients. Mr. Hannam has appealed the penalty to the UK Financial Markets Tribunal on the grounds that the information he disclosed was not privileged inside information and that he did not make a profit or avoid a loss personally on the leaked information. Nevertheless, the UK Listing Authority has strict prohibitions on insiders leaking inside information to third parties outside of approved reporting channels. This type of unauthorized disclosure of inside information constitutes misuse of privileged information, a form of market abuse which, although it may not be criminal insider dealing, is a civil offence for which unlimited fines can be imposed.

The other high profile case involves prominent investment manager David Einhorn[57] and his hedge fund Greenlight Capital,[58] which together were fined £7.2 million for trading on the basis of confidential information in the shares of a British pub chain. In this case, Mr. Einhorn and Greenlight Capital traded on the basis of inside information about a UK listed company. Mr. Einhorn denied wrongdoing by arguing that he committed the trades in question in New York and that he did not fully understand the breadth of the market abuse offence. He decided not to appeal the FSA's decision and to pay a settlement.[59]

The FSA enforcement approach aims to expose and deter market abuse which has been rife in UK financial markets for many years. Prior to 2007, many traders in the UK markets were aware that the benefits of engaging in market abuse and insider dealing, such as passing on inside information, far outweighed the potential costs of being caught, in part because the penalties were low and enforcement unlikely. However, after a number of parliamentary hearings that exposed the FSA's passive posture as a supervisor, the FSA has taken on a more proactive stance in enforcing prudential regulation and conduct of business rules. As discussed, this has resulted in increased enforcement of market abuse and insider dealing laws. The FSA, however, will be disbanded in 2013 as new UK legislation that restructures financial regulation will take effect. The FSA will be replaced by a Twin Peaks regulatory model consisting of a Prudential Regulatory Authority (PRA), whose responsibility will be to supervise financial institutions, and a Financial Conduct Authority (FCA), whose responsibility will be to protect investors and consumers and enforce conduct of business rules. Under the Financial Services Act 2013, the FCA will be the primary enforcer of the UK market abuse regime and insider dealing laws. Most of the FSA's enforcement and market conduct divisions will be transferred to the FCA, where it is expected that the tougher enforcement will be continued.

The FSA's efforts to strengthen regulatory controls and enforcement against market misconduct have come in for criticism by industry practitioners and their lawyers and

---

[57] See FSA Decision Notice to David Einhorn (12 January 2012). The FSA imposed a fine of £3,638,000 for engaging in market abuse in violation of § 118(2) FSMA.

[58] See FSA Decision Notice to Greenlight Capital, Inc. (12 January 2012). The FSA decision imposed on Greenlight Capital, Inc. a fine of £3,650,795, pursuant to § 123(1) of FSMA for engaging in market abuse in violation of § 118(2) FSMA.

[59] FSA Decision Notice, supra note 57.

by some politicians.[60] The case involving Ian Hannam has attracted much controversy because it involves a banker accused by the FSA of misuse of information (the market abuse civil offence) even though he was not alleged to have made a profit or avoided a loss by trading on such information. Moreover, the case involves the definition of insider or privileged information and the burden of proof that the FSA is required to meet in a civil action to establish that the information is inside information. Also, the FSA has used new powers provided under the Financial Services Act 2010 to ban financial professionals found liable for market abuse or other market misconduct.[61]

These cases demonstrate that the UK and EU securities laws have a broader definition of market misconduct that would violate the market abuse rules whereas similar conduct under US securities laws may not attract liability. For example, the definition of what constitutes insider information under US criminal law must be proved beyond a reasonable doubt and the defendant is entitled to a jury trial. By contrast, under the UK market abuse regime, what constitutes inside or privileged information need only be proved on the balance of probabilities (more likely than not) and the case would be heard before an administrative tribunal. Under UK law, one type of market abuse could be the sharing of information that later turns out to be significant or market moving, but at the time of the leak did not appear to the insider who leaked the information to be market moving. The FSA would only have to prove on the balance of probabilities that the accused knew or should have known that the information was inside or privileged information and therefore could only be disclosed lawfully to a third party through approved regulatory channels. Lawyers advising market professionals have complained that this has created ambiguity and uncertainty regarding what they can or cannot disclose to clients or other third parties. Indeed, some have observed that the FSA Handbook rules are not clear and that the FSA is not providing adequate guidance to market practitioners about what they can and cannot disclose. This ambiguity, however, in defining new and untested areas of conduct as market abuse, is part of the FSA's new approach to stricter regulation that is judgment led and forward looking.[62] The FSA's judgment-led supervisory and regulatory approach aims to strike a balance between a legalistic rules-based approach of defining what is and what is not market misconduct with a more forward-looking approach that grants discretion to the supervisor to use its judgment to respond to changes and innovations in the marketplace that might constitute a new form of market abuse but have not yet been defined as such by the regulator in its rulebook. This proactive, forward-looking and judgment-led approach to regulation has become official policy of the UK Treasury and is an overriding theme in the Financial Services Act 2013, which replaced the FSA with the PRA and FCA in early 2013.

---

[60]   See Allister Heath, Murdoch and Hannam's Departures Symbolise Power Shift, City AM, 4 April 2012, at 2 (British MP David Davis criticized the FSA market abuse enforcement action against Ian Hannam as 'un-British' and that the regulator's disciplinary process was against traditional principles of English law and that the offence of misuse of information charged by the FSA was an 'incredible extension of what constitutes insider trading by the FSA').

[61]   Several recent FSA decision orders imposing substantial penalties and banning orders are under appeal (including the appeals of two traders from Cantor Fitzgerald who appealed their fines and banning orders in early 2012) and will be ruled on in late 2012 by the Upper Tribunal.

[62]   See Hector Sants, Financial Services Authority Chief Executive Officer, Oral Evidence before the UK Parliament's Joint Committee on the Draft Financial Services Bill (11 November 2011) at 17–18.

It is generally accepted among market practitioners that before the FSA adopted this more proactive regulatory approach, market participants had rarely been charged with market abuse, let alone the criminal offence of insider dealing, which required prosecutors to prove beyond a reasonable doubt that the defendant knew or should have known that he was an insider and that he knew or should have known that he possessed inside information. Nevertheless, the FSA's tougher enforcement approach since 2007 and the new judgment-led regulation approach have had the effect of deterring market misconduct and led to a greater number of enforcement actions for market abuse and criminal prosecutions for insider dealing. The FSA asserts that its more aggressive enforcement posture has deterred significant amounts of market misconduct, especially with respect to insider dealing during takeovers. The FSA provides data to suggest that in 2009 unusual share price movements occurred before 30 per cent of UK-based mergers and acquisitions, which suggests the likelihood of leaked inside information before the official takeover announcement. By 2011, however, the figure had dropped to 20 per cent. This lower figure has been attributed to an increase in the number of publicized investigations, enforcement actions, convictions and penalties. Although it remains debatable whether the FSA's more proactive enforcement posture has actually deterred insider dealing and market abuse, it certainly marks an important move away from its previous 'light touch' enforcement approach that had resulted in pervasive market misconduct to a less cavalier, more compliance-based approach to market conduct.

In addition, the FSA's more proactive enforcement approach has benefited from greater resources that are derived from fees charged by the FSA to authorized firms and approved persons. In 2007, the FSA's budget for its enforcement division was £32 million; by 2012, this had increased to over £70 million. This has allowed the FSA to double the size of its enforcement division to approximately 400 staff, which includes lawyers, accountants, forensic experts, former police officers and intelligence officers. The enforcement division has been transferred to the new Financial Conduct Authority when the FCA takes up its powers in early 2013. Indeed, the FSA's acting head of enforcement has stated that despite its impending demise the FSA will be as active as ever in enforcing market abuse and insider dealing laws.[63] Moreover, the transfer of market abuse oversight and enforcement to the FCA in 2013 is part of a longer-term plan to maintain credible deterrence so that when the FCA takes up its new role it will continue with the judgement-led supervisory and enforcement approach that the FSA has already begun and which is mandated in the newly adopted Financial Services Bill 2012.

V. SUMMING UP

The regulation of insider dealing and market abuse has and will no doubt continue to raise a host of issues that would not ordinarily be encountered in the control of other anti-social conduct. The sophistication of financial markets, within which the law and

---

[63] See Martin Wheatley, Acting Director of the Financial Conduct Authority, Oral Evidence before the UK Parliament's Joint Committee on the Draft Financial Services Bill (24 October 2011) at 12.

regulatory mechanisms operate, compounds the practical and legal difficulties confronting those seeking to administer and apply the law. While the control of insider dealing and market abuse has much in common with the prevention and interdiction of money laundering and even corruption, the crafting of legislation and developing a supporting regulatory framework will involve issues of peculiar complexity and sensitivity. Despite these problems, the efficacy of anti-insider dealing and market abuse regulation has, in many countries, become almost a litmus test for the efficiency and competence of the wider regulatory structure overseeing the markets and the conduct of business in the financial sector.

In practical and political terms, the control of insider dealing and market abuse is a significant issue. While the various philosophical justifications for regulation may be argued about, it is the case that in many countries it is now recognized that the presence of such laws and regulation is required if investor confidence in the integrity of the markets is to be preserved and promoted. A somewhat cynical perspective might suggest that it matters little if the empirical evidence is equivocal as to the extent of the problem of insider dealing and market abuse and the harm it creates. If enough people think it occurs, for whatever reason, and consider it to be unfair, confidence in the reputation and therefore the efficiency of the market will be eroded. Consequently, those who are responsible for the protection of the markets have a responsibility to act. Whether this involves the use of the criminal law, or the civil law of market abuse, or some other regulatory mechanism, it is in the 'public good' that it be seen that insider dealing and market abuse are not condoned.

22. Insider trading in European law
Katja Langenbucher

The history of European insider trading law starts as late as 1966 with an expert report for the European Commission, advocating a new legal framework for "The development of a European Capital Market." Named after one of its authors, the "Segré Report" viewed insider trading as a "technical" problem, relating to directors or executives dealing in shares of their company.[1] Only in 1989 did the European Council pass a directive in order to coordinate the widely differing insider trading regimes in the Member States.[2] Fourteen years later, the European Parliament and the Council enacted a new directive addressing both insider trading and market manipulation as the two most prominent threats to smoothly working capital markets.[3] In 2011, the European Commission published proposals for both a directive and a regulation to update and expand its legal regime on insider trading and market manipulation.

US law has heavily influenced European insider trading law. This is particularly true with regard to legal concepts such as inside information, materiality and models of the reasonable investor's behavior. Surprisingly, however, European law deviates quite markedly from US law as far as policy issues are concerned. It references concepts that have long been dismissed in US law, such as the integrity of capital markets, and the necessity to place investors on an equal footing and to protect them from what is perceived as an injury resulting from the improper use of inside information. In contrast, the misappropriation theory endorsed by US courts, the Securities and Exchange Commission (SEC) and legal scholars alike[4] has not gained a strong foothold in European law.

---

[1]   Report of a Group of Experts Appointed by the EEC Commission, The Development of a European Capital Market, at ch. 1 ¶ 8(iii) (November 1966).

[2]   Council Directive 89/592/EEC of November 13, 1989 coordinating regulations on insider dealing, 1989 O.J. (L 334) 30 [hereinafter cited as 1989 Directive]. As an example highlighting the differing regimes consider Germany on the one hand (insider trading not addressed by any legal rule) and the UK on the other (first consolidated statutory regulation of insider trading by the Company Securities (Insider Dealing) Act 1985, which entered into force on July 1, 1985).

[3]   Directive 2003/6/EC of the European Parliament and of the Council of January 28, 2003 on insider trading and market manipulation (market abuse), 2003 O.J. (L 96) 16 [hereinafter cited as MAD].

[4]   See Chapter 1 of this book [Stephen M. Bainbridge, An Introduction to the *Research Handbook on Insider Trading*], at 8.

I.   THE ANATOMY OF INSIDER TRADING LAW IN EUROPE

A.   The Impact of European Law on National Laws of the Member States

European insider trading law thus far consists of one core directive (the MAD) and two implementing directives,[5] with the proposal for a regulation and a directive currently pending.

Regulations and directives are distinct instruments of European law. The former are binding in their entirety and directly applicable in all Member States, Art. 288 para. 2 TFEU.[6] The latter are binding solely with regard to the ends to be achieved and to the Member States addressed. Directives grant discretion as to the choice of form and methods employed by the national authorities in transposing them into national law, Art. 288 para. 3 TFEU.[7] There are varying degrees of discretion offered: some directives contain precise rules of considerable detail; others are broad and principle-based. Some set a minimum standard only;[8] others proscribe Member States to "gold-plate" the directive by adopting or maintaining more stringent national rules.[9] The European Court of Justice[10] has added to the effectiveness of directives by recognizing a principle of "harmonious interpretation" which requires the national courts to interpret any relevant national law in the light of directives.[11]

The number of directives by far exceeds the number of regulations to be found in European securities and capital markets law.[12] This is due to the flexibility directives accord to both the European lawmaker—with regard to the necessary degree of specificity of legal rules—and to the Member States—by respecting variations in their legal systems, and their political and administrative arrangements.[13] Corroborating this fact, the European law on insider trading has so far come exclusively in the form

---

[5]   Commission Directive 2003/124/EC of December 22, 2003 implementing Directive 2003/6/EC of the European Parliament and of the Council as regards the definition and public disclosure of inside information and the definition of market manipulation, 2003 O.J. (L 339) 70 [hereinafter cited as Directive 2003/124]; Commission Directive 2004/72/EC of April 29, 2004 implementing Directive 2003/6/EC of the European Parliament and of the Council as regards accepted market practices, the definition of inside information in relation to derivatives on commodities, the drawing up of lists of insiders, the notification of managers' transactions and the notification of suspicious transactions, 2004 O.J. (L 162) 70 [hereinafter cited as Directive 2004/72].

[6]   Consolidated Version of the Treaty on the Functioning of the European Union, May 9, 2008, 2008 O.J. (C 115) 47, 171–172 [hereinafter TFEU].

[7]   See generally Paul Craig & Gráinne de Búrca, EU Law 105–106, 190–216 (5th ed. 2011).

[8]   See, e.g., Commission Proposal for a Directive of the European Parliament and of the Council on criminal sanctions for insider dealing and market manipulation, recital (15), COM (2011) 654 final (Oct. 20, 2011) [hereinafter cited as Proposal/Directive].

[9]   See, e.g., Directive 2004/39/EC of the European Parliament and of the Council of April 21, 2004 on markets in financial instruments amending Council Directives 85/611/EEC and 93/6/EEC and Directive 2000/12/EC of the European Parliament and of the Council and repealing Council Directive 93/22/EEC, Art. 31 para. 1, 2004 O.J. (L 145) 1, 25.

[10]   Hereinafter cited as ECJ.

[11]   Case C-14/83, Von Colson and Kamann v. Land Nordrhein-Westfalen, 1984 E.C.R. 1891; see further Craig & de Búrca, supra note 7, at 200–207.

[12]   There are approximately 20 regulations and 70 directives.

[13]   Craig & de Búrca, supra note 7, at 106.

of directives.[14] The proposal for a regulation on insider dealing currently under way[15] marks an exception to this rule. The EU Commission has attracted considerable criticism precisely for choosing a regulation rather than a directive,[16] yet has remained unimpressed, stressing the benefits of reduced regulatory complexity and greater legal certainty.[17]

For the ensuing discussion it is helpful to keep in mind that the "European law on insider trading" consists of a set of core rules that is applicable in every Member State either directly or after having been transposed into national law. This set of harmonized core rules is supplemented by bodies of national law that differ among the Member States.[18]

B.   The Market Abuse Directive

European law views insider trading and market manipulation as two forms of "market abuse," which hinder "prompt and fair disclosure of information to the public"[19] and threaten "the smooth functioning of securities markets."[20] This link between disclosure and acceptable market behavior is displayed in the list of policy statements underlying the directive[21] as well as in its dogmatic structure: the existence of inside information triggers both a prohibition on insider trading and a disclosure requirement.[22]

The MAD contains definitions of inside information, of persons qualifying as insiders and details of the prohibition on the use of inside information. Furthermore, it stipulates duties to disclose inside information to the market and identifies the market places and the transactions covered.

1.   The scope of the MAD

The MAD applies to issuers of financial instruments such as securities, units in collective investment undertakings, futures, certain swaps and options, derivatives and other instruments if they are either admitted to trading on a regulated market in at least one Member State or their value depends on a financial instrument of this kind.[23] According to Art. 7 MAD some transactions of Member States, the European System of Central Banks, national central banks and some officially designated bodies are exempt from its scope. Furthermore, exemptions apply to trading in own shares pursuant to "buy-back" programs under Art. 8 MAD.

---

[14]   See 1989 Directive, supra note 2; MAD, supra note 3.

[15]   Commission Proposal for a regulation of the European Parliament and of the Council on insider dealing and market manipulation (market abuse), COM (2011) 651 final (Oct. 20, 2011) [hereinafter cited as Proposal/regulation].

[16]   EU Economic and Social Committee, March 14, 2012, at 1, 3.

[17]   Proposal/regulation, supra note 15, at 5.

[18]   On UK law, see Chapter 21 of this book [Alexander Kern, UK Insider Dealing and Market Abuse Law].

[19]   MAD, supra note 3, recital (24).

[20]   MAD, supra note 3, recitals (2), (12), (15).

[21]   I.e., the so-called "recitals."

[22]   On this combination technique see infra Section I.B.5.

[23]   The details are to be found in MAD Art. 1 para. 3.

2. The definition of inside information

According to Art. 1 MAD:

> For the purposes of the MAD, inside information shall mean information of a precise nature which has not been made public, relating, directly or indirectly, to one or more issuers of financial instruments or to one or more financial instruments and which, if it were made public, would be likely to have a significant effect on the prices of those financial instruments or on the price of related derivative financial instruments.[24]

As far as commodity derivatives are concerned, information is considered inside information if users of the relevant markets would, according to common practices, "expect to receive" such information.[25]

3. The definition of insiders

The MAD contains broad definitions of persons who possess inside information and therefore are addressees of the directive's prohibitions. Art. 2 para. 1 sub-para. 2(a), (b), (d) cover classic insiders: officers, directors and certain employees, shareholders and persons who gain inside information through criminal behavior.[26] The provision seems to be somewhat broader than its US equivalent as far as shareholders are concerned. Whereas the Securities Exchange Act § 16(b)[27] applies only to shareholders owning more than 10 percent of the company's stock, the directive addresses any person who possesses inside information "by virtue of his holding in the capital of the issuer."[28]

Persons qualifying as "constructive insiders" or as insiders on the basis of a "non-traditional relationship" under US law[29] may be captured by Art. 2 para. 1 sub-para. 2(c) if they have access to information in a professional context.[30] Persons who decide on transactions on behalf of a legal person who is considered to be an insider without being the issuer of the financial instrument in question are covered by Art. 2 para. 2. In addition to those more specific rules, Art. 4 extends insider trading prohibitions far beyond the scope of US law to so-called "secondary insiders," i.e., any person "who possesses inside information while that person knows, or ought to have known, that it is inside information."[31]

---

[24]   MAD Art. 1 para. 1 sub-para. 1. This includes information conveyed by clients to persons charged with the execution of orders concerning financial instruments, MAD Art. 1 para. 1 sub-para. 3.

[25]   MAD Art. 1 para. 1 sub-para. 2; see infra note 83 on the proposed reformulation.

[26]   MAD Art. 2 para. 1 sub-para. 2 reads: "[A]ny person who possesses that information: (a) by virtue of his membership of the administrative, management or supervisory bodies of the issuer; or (b) by virtue of his holding in the capital of the issuer; or . . . (d) by virtue of his criminal activities."

[27]   15 U.S.C. § 78p(b); on § 16(b)'s prophylactic approach to insider trading, see generally James D. Cox et al., Securities Regulation 918–931 (6th ed. 2009).

[28]   MAD Art. 2 para. 1 sub-para. 2(b).

[29]   Bainbridge, supra note 4, at 11.

[30]   MAD Art. 2 para. 1 sub-para. 2(c) reads: "[A]ny person who possesses that information . . . (c) by virtue of his having access to the information through the exercise of his employment, profession or duties." For an exception to this rule, see infra text accompanying notes 36 and 41 et seq.

[31]   MAD Art. 4; see infra Section II.A.2.

4. The prohibition on using inside information

Quite similar to US law, the MAD's prohibitions can roughly be divided into two categories: trading and tipping. While the prohibition on trading closely resembles US law, the rule on tipping is rather broad and unfettered by an equivalent of the US misappropriation theory.[32]

Instances of trading are addressed by Art. 2 para. 1, which bars an insider in possession of inside information from using:

> [T]hat information by acquiring or disposing of, or by trying to acquire or dispose of, for his own account or for the account of a third party, either directly or indirectly, financial instruments to which that information relates.[33]

It may be regarded as an example of the incorporation of US standards into European insider trading law that the "use versus possession" debate between the SEC and the US Supreme Court[34] is implicitly contained in the wording of Art. 2 para. 1. We will see below that the ECJ has displayed a strong preference towards the view defended by the SEC.[35]

US lawyers will find another parallel between the MAD and the SEC's practice regarding Rule 10b5-1(c)(1)(i)(A):[36] according to Art. 2 para. 3, an insider purchasing or selling a security on the basis of a contract which was concluded before the person possessed inside information does not violate the insider trading prohibition. Tipping situations are captured by Art. 3. Limbs (a) and (b) of that rule encompass any disclosure of inside information to another person unless such disclosure occurs in a normal professional context[37] as well as "recommending or inducing another person, on the basis of inside information, to acquire or dispose of financial instruments to which that information relates."

5. The duty to disclose

We have seen above that the existence of inside information has two legal consequences: a prohibition of insider transactions and a duty to disclose inside information to the market.[38] This distinguishes the European approach from US law, which does not recognize a general duty to disclose inside information under Rule 10b-5.[39]

---

[32] See infra Section II.
[33] MAD Art. 2 para. 1; see infra Section II.A.2.
[34] See Stephen M. Bainbridge, An Overview of US Insider Trading Law: Lessons for the EU? 7–8 (UCLA School of Law, Law & Economics Research Paper Series, Research Paper No. 05-5, January 2005), available at http://papers.ssrn.com/sol3/papers.cfm?abstract_id=654703 (last accessed December 5, 2012); Hei Huang, The Insider Trading "Possession Versus Use" Debate: An International Analysis, 33 Sec. Reg. L. J. 130 (2005); Karen Schoen, Insider Trading: The "Possession versus Use" Debate, 148 U. Pa. L. Rev. 239 (1999).
[35] See infra Section I.C.3.
[36] 17 C.F.R. § 240.10b5-1(c)(1)(i)(A).
[37] For case law on this point, see infra Section I.C.1.
[38] See supra text accompanying note 22.
[39] Cox et al., supra note 27, at 694; see most recently Matrixx Initiatives, Inc. v. Siracusano, 131 S.Ct. 1309, 563 U.S. (2011).

Instead, the European duty to disclose bears some similarities to current reporting requirements under Form 8-K and the listing standards of the various stock exchanges.[40]

MAD Art. 6 para. 1 puts the issuer under an obligation to inform the market of inside information if three conditions are met: (1) he is an issuer of financial instruments; (2) the inside information directly concerns the issuer; and (3) there is no permission to delay disclosure. Under Art. 6 para. 2 an issuer is allowed to delay public disclosure if such disclosure would prejudice the issuer's legitimate interests, provided there is no danger of misleading the public and the issuer is able to ensure confidentiality.

C.   The Case Law of the ECJ

The ECJ does not settle legal disputes between private individuals but may be invoked by referral of a national court pursuant to Art. 267 TFEU if a question on the interpretation of EU law arises in a legal dispute before the national courts of a Member State. It is important to bear in mind that the court's competence is referral-based, hence it is not comparable to an appeal system. The national court decides whether it ought to refer a question on the interpretation of EU law to the ECJ. When it has clarified the question referred, the ECJ sends the case back to the national court in order for it to apply EU law, as interpreted by the ECJ, to the case at hand and decide the dispute.[41]

Thus far, the court has heard three cases on insider law. Two of these cases were decided under the 1989 Directive, the third under the MAD. A fourth case is currently pending.

1.   The case *Grøngaard & Bang*: disclosing inside information in a professional context
Grøngaard & Bang concerned a Danish case relating to a supervisory board member, Mr. Grøngaard, who, according to co-determination laws, held his board position by virtue of being a member of a labor union.[42] In his capacity as a board member, Grøngaard received information on an imminent merger which he passed on to his superior, the head of the labor union, Mr. Bang. Bang informed a member of his staff, who ended up trading on the information. The Danish authorities brought charges against all three of them. In this context, the Danish court asked the ECJ to clarify the scope of the 1989 Directive as far as employee-elected board members are concerned.

The legal rule in question has remained unchanged since 1989. MAD Art. 3(a) prohibits the disclosure of inside information to a third party unless "such disclosure is made in the normal course of the exercise of his employment, profession or duties."

While the rule's wording does not lend itself to cover Grøngaard, who passed on information to his supervisor in a professional context, the court relied on an especially narrow reading. It held that the normal exercise of professional duties to which the rule refers requires a "close link" between the disclosure and the exercise of the board member's pro-

---

[40]   Cox et al., supra note 27, at 694; see also Peter Versteegen, § 15 WpHG, in Kölner Kommentar zum WpHG [Cologne Commentary on the Wertpapierhandelsgesetz [WpHG] [Securities Trading Act]] ¶ 42–43 (Heribert Hirte & Thomas M.J. Möllers eds., 2007) (F.R.G.) [hereinafter cited as Kölner Kommentar].

[41]   See Craig & de Búrca, supra note 7, at 442.

[42]   Case C-384/02, Grøngaard & Bang, 2005 E.C.R. I-9939.

fessional duties and disclosure is "absolutely necessary" for the exercise of those duties.[43] The court's reasoning stressed the importance of investors' confidence in a functioning securities market, which it viewed as depending on "being placed on an equal footing and protected against the improper use of inside information."[44]

2. The case *Georgakis*: "taking advantage" of inside information

The case *Georgakis* concerned members of a Greek family who were both board members and blockholders of a listed company.[45] They engaged in a number of transactions commonly referred to as "painting the tape" in order to artificially augment the volume of trading. Today, such behavior would qualify as market manipulation and fall within the scope of MAD Art. 5. However, there was no prohibition of market manipulation under the terms of the 1989 Directive, which accounts for the fact that the Greek court referring the case to the ECJ tried to subsume the transactions in question under an insider trading prohibition.

The relevant legal rule in 1989 required the insider to "take advantage" of inside information.[46] Under this rule, the ECJ correctly denied the applicability of the trading prohibition since the entire Georgakis family took part in those transactions. Consequently, none of them took advantage of inside information with regard to their respective counterparty. What remains of interest today is the fact that the ECJ once again stressed the importance of protecting investor confidence and placing investors on an equal footing.[47]

3. The case *Spector*: "using" inside information

Spector was the first case decided under the MAD.[48] The Belgian company Spector Photo Group NV bought shares in order to implement a stock option scheme offered to its employees. Those transactions were spread over five installments, with the last one undergoing a number of changes as to price limits, the number of shares concerned and timing. A week later, the company announced positive news to the market causing the share price to rise significantly. The Belgian financial services authority fined both the company and its director. The latter challenged this in court, claiming that the Belgian authority had failed to prove a causal link between their knowledge/possession of the positive news and the transaction concerning the purchase of shares. Hence, neither the company nor its director had "used" the inside information that they possessed.

The issues to be discussed in the *Spector* case bear a close resemblance to the

---

[43]   Id. at ¶ 56; Heinz-Dieter Assmann, § 14 WpHG, in WpHG-Kommentar [Commentary on the WpHG] ¶ 74b (Heinz-Dieter Assmann & Uwe H. Schneider eds., 6th ed. 2012) (F.R.G.) [hereinafter cited as Assmann/Schneider]; Eberhard Schwark & Dominik Kruse, § 14 WpHG, in Kapitalmarktrechtskommentar [Commentary on Capital Markets Law] ¶ 46–47 (Eberhard Schwark & Daniel Zimmer eds., 4th ed. 2010) (F.R.G.) [hereinafter cited as Schwark/Kruse].

[44]   Id. at ¶ 33.

[45]   Case C-391/04, Georgakis, 2007 E.C.R. I-3741.

[46]   Today, MAD Art. 2 prohibits the insider from "using" inside information, see supra Section I.B.4 and infra Section I.C.3.

[47]   Georgakis, supra note 45, at ¶ 37; see also Schwark/Kruse, supra note 43, § 13 WpHG at ¶ 16–17.

[48]   Case C-45/08, Spector Photo Group, 2009 E.C.R. I-12073.

well-known US "use-or-possession" debate.[49] The wording of MAD Art. 3 requires the insider to "possess" information and "use" it by purchasing or selling relevant shares. While this could be construed as the MAD following the "use" approach, the ECJ, somewhat comparable to its argument in *Grøngaard & Bang*, went for a narrow interpretation. It held that there is a rebuttable presumption of "use" if the insider is in possession of relevant information. Recognizing the need for exceptions, the court acknowledges a right to rebut the presumption, yet without offering a bright line between situations that violate the prohibition and those that do not. In order to distinguish these cases, it refers us back to the policies underlying the MAD. In the same vein as *Grøngaard & Bang* and *Georgakis*, the ECJ points to the need to ensure "equality between the contracting parties in stock-market transactions" and to avoid unjustified economic advantages at the expense of outsiders.[50] Insider trading's "essential characteristic consists in an unfair advantage."[51]

4.　The pending case *Geltl v. Daimler*: preliminary information

The German Federal Court of Justice has referred the *Geltl* case to the ECJ.[52] The CEO of DaimlerChrysler, Jürgen Schrempp, stepped down from his position in July 2005, a fact which resulted in a significant rise of the stock price. Investors sued the company when it became clear that a series of intermediate steps, such as discussions with supervisory and regular board members, members of the marketing department and employee representatives, had preceded the official decision taken by the supervisory board. DaimlerChrysler had not revealed any of those steps to the market, arguing that the resignation as such, not the discussions leading up to it, was inside information. The investors claimed that they had sold their shares during the period preceding the official resignation and would not have done so had they known of the impending resignation. Under German law, DaimlerChrysler would be liable to those investors if it failed, deliberately or through gross negligence, to disclose inside information that directly concerned the company.[53] The rule is somewhat comparable to a private cause of action under Rule 10b-5, the main difference being that it extends far beyond the scope of an affirmative duty to disclose inside information imposed under Rule 10b-5.

Seen from the perspective of US law, the case is not necessarily about insider trading but rather about disclosure, given that the company is alleged to have failed to inform the public about a material fact. European law links both concepts quite narrowly:[54] the existence of inside information triggers a prohibition on trading under MAD Art. 2 as

---

[49]　See Katja Langenbucher, The "Use or Possession" Debate Revisited—Spector Photo Group and Insider Trading in Europe, 5 C.M.L.J. 452, 460, 466 (2010).

[50]　Spector Photo Group, supra note 48, at ¶ 48–49.

[51]　Id. at ¶ 52.

[52]　Bundesgerichtshof [BGH], Nov. 22, 2010, Neue Zeitschrift für Gesellschaftsrecht [NZG] [New Journal of Company Law] 109 (2011) (F.R.G.). The ECJ rendered his decision on *Geltl* after this chapter had been submitted: Case C-19/11, Geltl v. Daimler AG, Judgment of the Court announced on June 28, 2012, available at http://curia.europa.eu/juris/document/document.jsf?text=&docid=124466&pageIndex=0&doclang=EN&mode=lst&dir=&occ=first&part=1&cid=526619.

[53]　Wertpapierhandelsgesetz [WpHG] [Securities Trading Act], July 26, 1994, BGBl. I at 1749, last amended by Gesetz, Dec. 22, 2011, BGBl. I at 3044, § 37b para. 1.

[54]　See supra text accompanying notes 22 and 37; infra Section II.

well as a disclosure obligation under Art. 6, the latter presupposing that the information directly concerns the issuer. Hence, the question referred to the ECJ under European law is relevant to both the disclosure obligation and the trading prohibition.

a. Is there such a thing as preliminary inside information? We have seen above[55] that information of a precise nature, having the potential to significantly impact market prices, qualifies as inside information under MAD Art. 1. This definition is further qualified by Art. 1 para. 1 of Directive 2003/124:

> [I]nformation shall be deemed to be of a precise nature if it indicates a set of circumstances which exists or may reasonably be expected to come into existence or an event which has occurred or may reasonably be expected to do so and if it is specific enough to enable a conclusion to be drawn as to the possible effect of that set of circumstances or event on the prices of financial instruments or related derivative financial instruments.

With regard to the potential to have a significant price effect, Art. 1 para. 2 of Directive 2003/124 states that such information "shall mean information a reasonable investor would be likely to use as part of the basis of his investment decisions." Those rules suggest a number of things. Clearly, the official resolution of the supervisory board on the CEO's resignation qualifies as inside information as of the day on which it was taken. Furthermore, during the months preceding the board resolution, Schrempp's resignation was an "event" which "may reasonably be expected" to occur. Hence, the company was supposed to scrutinize on a daily basis whether the probability of his resignation had increased. Once it reached the conclusion that the resignation was indeed "reasonably to be expected" to occur, DaimlerChrysler was under the obligation to disclose this assessment.

During this same period, certain events such as a conversation between Schrempp and the board members or the passing on of information to the marketing department potentially qualify as inside information in their own right. Obviously, preliminary information of this kind does not fall under the relevant rule as clearly as the result finally reached,[56] because it will be more complicated to decide whether preliminary information is "specific" enough and whether it is likely to have a significant price effect as required by Art. 1 para. 1, 2 of Directive 2003/124. The latter is closely connected to an assessment of the probability of the final result coming into existence. In other words: if DaimlerChrysler discloses the fact that its CEO has come to an agreement with the supervisory board members concerning his resignation and the vote thereupon is impending, this information will be very specific and is very likely to affect the share price. If DaimlerChrysler discloses the fact that the CEO discussed plans to resign over lunch with his wife, who also happens to be employed by the company as a personal assistant, this information is clearly less specific. Its potential to impact the share price depends on how the market will assess the probability of the plan actually materializing. Of course, it might also depend

---

[55] See supra Section I.B.2.

[56] Holger Fleischer, Ad-hoc Publizität beim einvernehmlichen vorzeitigen Ausscheiden des Vorstandsvorsitzenden—Der DaimlerChrysler Musterentscheid des OLG Stuttgart [Ad-hoc Disclosure in the Case of a Mutually Agreed Early Resignation of the CEO—The Higher Regional Court of Stuttgart's Model Decision in DaimlerChrysler], NZG 401, 404 (2007).

on whether market participants anticipate short-term price reactions to the lunchtime talk alone, irrespective of the probability of the CEO actually resigning. It follows that a piece of preliminary information could be both specific and able to impact market prices while, at the same time, the—potential—end result cannot yet reasonably be expected to occur.

b.   "Reasonable expectations" and the probability/magnitude approach   The referral by the German Federal Court of Justice concerns two questions. The first relates to the somewhat protracted process of decision-making leading up to the CEO's resignation. The appeals court had argued that any such preliminary step must be exempt from disclosure as long as it cannot be said that it is reasonably to be expected that those future events will come into existence, in order not to flood the market with information about future events.[57]

The second referral question inquires when an event "may reasonably be expected to occur" under Art. 1 para. 1 of Directive 2003/124. More specifically, the court wants to know whether the ECJ is leaning towards the concept of adopting a certain probability threshold or towards a "probability/magnitude" approach.

The General Advocate issued his opinion in March 2012.[58] With regard to the first question, he points out that there is nothing in the text of the MAD or Directive 2003/124 to suggest that preliminary steps of a staggered process of decision-making are exempt from the disclosure requirement imposed by MAD Art. 6 para. 1. Rather, they would qualify as inside information if the rule's other conditions were met, i.e., that they are specific and capable of significantly affecting market prices.[59]

On the second question, the General Advocate seems to embrace the US "probability/magnitude" approach. He explicitly rejects the notion of a probability threshold requirement,[60] in essence having recourse to many of the reasons cited by the US Supreme Court in its dismissal of the "agreement-in-principle" test.[61] Remember, however, that the scope of the relevant European ad hoc disclosure obligation extends far beyond that of Rule 10b-5.[62]

Instead of a probability threshold, the General Advocate suggests introducing a "multi-factor test" for inside information. His basic argument for extending the directive's current scope runs as follows: although Art. 1 para. 1 of Directive 2003/124 requires

---

[57]   Oberlandesgericht [OLG] [Higher Regional Court] Stuttgart, Feb. 15, 2007, NZG 352, 357–58 (2007); OLG Stuttgart, Apr. 22, 2009, NZG 624, 626–627 (2009).

[58]   Case C-19/11, Geltl v. Daimler AG, Opinion of Advocate General Mengozzi delivered on Mar. 21, 2012, available at http://curia.europa.eu/juris/document/document.jsf?docid=120661&pageIndex=0&doclang=EN&mode=lst&dir=&occ=first&cid=388454 (last accessed December 5, 2012) [hereinafter cited as Opinion of GA Mengozzi].

[59]   Id. at ¶ 35–56; Christian Pawlik, § 13 WpHG, in Kölner Kommentar, supra note 40, at ¶ 15; cf. Assmann/Schneider, supra note 43, § 13 WpHG at ¶ 28a.

[60]   Id. at ¶ 81; see Fleischer, supra note 56, at 404 et seq.; Lars Klöhn, Der gestreckte Geschehensablauf vor dem EuGH—Zum DaimlerChrysler-Vorlagebeschluss des BGH [The Elongated Course of Events Before the European Court of Justice—Note on the Referral of the German Federal Court of Justice in the DaimlerChrysler case], NZG 166, 168 et seq. (2011); cf. Assmann & Schneider, supra note 43, § 13 WpHG at ¶ 25b.

[61]   See Basic v. Levinson, 485 U.S. 224, 233–236 (1988).

[62]   See supra Section I.B.5.

(a) "precision," which refers to reasonably expecting the occurrence of an event, and (b) a certain degree of specificity, those two conditions are to be blended into one comprehensive test.[63] A high degree of (a) will be able to compensate for a low degree of (b), and vice versa.[64]

c. The "reasonable investor" and the "total-mix" test   Given the already broad scope of the European rule, the General Advocate's reading of Directive 2003/124 just outlined calls for a qualifying factor. It seems that, to this end, the General Advocate relies on the concept of the "reasonable investor" in Art. 1 para. 2, claiming that:

> [T]he definition of reasonableness . . . must be constructed by reference to the "reasonable investor" . . ., an investor who tests information concerning the occurrence of future sets of circumstances or events against an objective criterion of reasonableness, rather than in relation to merely speculative purposes.[65]

Using the model of a "reasonable investor" to guard against what the US Supreme Court termed an "avalanche of trivial information,"[66] however, needs to be carefully fitted into the inner workings of the directive. Art. 1 para. 2 of Directive 2003/124 takes the point of view of the "reasonable investor" in order to determine whether the information is likely to impact market prices. By contrast, "reasonableness" under Art. 1 para. 1 seems to be assessed from the company's point of view, seeking to assess whether the chances of a future event materializing are high enough to justify alerting the markets. Blending both paragraphs suggests that even if an issuer considers those chances to be quite uncertain, it still needs to disclose the information to the market if there is a possibility of a "reasonable investor" being interested in such preliminary news.

Why would we assume that a "reasonable investor" cares about preliminary news which the issuer regards as not yet justifying disclosure? That assumption is unconvincing if the "reasonable investor" reacts only to information that is vested with a certain probability to materialize or to have an impact on the issuer's fundamental value. In this case, he probably does not care what Schrempp and his wife discussed over lunch. As a consequence, preliminary information of this kind would not be price-significant, and the "reasonable investor" and the issuer would concur. We could, however, picture the "reasonable investor" as anticipating short-term price swings and taking advantage of them, irrespective of whether the information relates to a highly probable event or one with implications for the issuer's fundamental value.[67] If we adhere to this view, even information at a very early stage of a decision-making process is "likely to have a significant effect on the prices of financial instruments" under Art. 1 para. 2 of Directive 2003/124.

The General Advocate seems to dislike the second option when viewing the "reasonable investor" as being dismissive of "merely speculative purposes."[68] Instead of betting

---

[63] Opinion of GA Mengozzi, *supra* note 58, at ¶ 69–95.

[64] *Id.* at ¶ 70.

[65] *Id.* at ¶ 71.

[66] *TSC Industries, Inc. v Northway, Inc.*, 426 U.S. 438, 448–449 (1976); *Basic v. Levinson*, 485 U.S. 224, 231–232 (1988).

[67] See Klöhn, *supra* note 60, at 170.

[68] Opinion of GA Mengozzi, *supra* note 58, at ¶ 71.

on short-term profits, the "reasonable investor" evaluates whether a particular event "could come about,"[69] thus re-introducing the concept of probability through the back door. Defining his model investor in more detail, the General Advocate draws a parallel to the US "total mix test."[70] The "reasonable investor" is interested in any information that would significantly alter the total mix of information available to him.[71]

The ECJ will have the chance to carefully mold this standard to fit the European directive's framework. We have seen earlier that its definition of inside information is significantly broader than the duty of disclosure under Rule 10b-5. Given that the US Supreme Court, applying an already narrow rule, is still "careful not to set too low a standard of materiality,"[72] this task is even more pressing for the ECJ, which is already working with a much wider rule.

D. The Current Reforms

The European Commission[73] is currently working on two proposals for reform. One is a directive concerning sanctions for market abuse. The other aims at consolidating and extending the prohibitions on market abuse in the form of a regulation.[74]

1. The proposal for a directive on criminal sanctions for insider dealing and market manipulation[75]

The MAD instructs Member States to prohibit insider dealing. However, it does not call for criminal sanctions. The proposal on introducing mandatory criminal penalties reacts to the fact that the sanctioning regimes of the different Member States have been viewed as heterogeneous and in some cases weak.[76] In order to strengthen the effective sanctioning of market abuse, the proposal lays down minimum rules on criminal sanctions. Art. 3 of the proposal/directive asks the Member States to ensure:

> [T]hat the following conduct constitutes a criminal offence, when committed intentionally:
> (a) when in possession of inside information, using that information to acquire or dispose of financial instruments to which that information relates for one's own account or for the account

---

[69]   Id. at ¶ 72 and note 16; Fleischer, supra note 56, at 405.

[70]   Opinion of GA Mengozzi, supra note 58, at note 15.

[71]   See TSC Industries, Inc. v. Northway, Inc., 426 U.S. 438, 449 (1976) (holding that "there must be a substantial likelihood that the disclosure of the omitted fact would have been viewed by the reasonable investor as having significantly altered the 'total mix' of information made available"); Basic v. Levinson, 485 U.S. 224, 231–232 (1988); Matrixx Initiatives, Inc. v. Siracusano, 131 S.Ct. 1309, 1318, 563 U.S. (2011).

[72]   TSC Industries, Inc. v Northway, Inc., 426 U.S. 438, 448–449 (1976); Basic v. Levinson, 485 U.S. 224, 231–232 (1988).

[73]   Hereinafter cited as the Commission.

[74]   On directives and regulations in EU law generally, see supra Section I.A.

[75]   See supra note 8.

[76]   European Securities and Markets Authority, Report on the actual use of sanctioning powers under MAD, at ¶ 17–81, ESMA/2012/270 (Apr. 26, 2012), available at http://www.esma.europa.eu/system/files/2012-270.pdf (last accessed December 5, 2012); Report by the High-Level Group on Financial Supervision in the EU, at ¶ 84 (Feb. 25, 2009), available at http://ec.europa.eu/internal_market/finances/docs/de_larosiere_report_en.pdf (last accessed December 5, 2012).

of a third party. This also includes using inside information to cancel or amend an order concerning a financial instrument to which that information relates where that order was placed before entering into possession of that inside information; or
(b) disclosing inside information to any other person, unless such disclosure is made in the lawful course of the exercise of duties resulting from employment or profession.

Art. 5 aims at criminalizing inciting, aiding and abetting, and attempt. Art. 7 extends criminal liability to legal entities.

2.   The proposal for a regulation on insider dealing and market manipulation[77]

Opting for a regulation instead of a directive, the pending proposal for a regulation on insider dealing and market manipulation does not grant legislative discretion to Member States.[78] Should it enter into force as planned, there will be one uniform regime covering market manipulation and insider trading throughout the European Union.

Its most distinctive feature is an extension of the current regime's scope in a number of ways. As far as insider trading is concerned, the proposal reaches beyond regulated markets so as to encompass new markets, trading facilities and financial instruments traded over-the-counter (see a. below). The definition of inside information and the prohibited types of transactions are widened (see b. below). Minimum rules on sanctioning are introduced (see c. below). Furthermore, the proposal expands the rules on market manipulation and directors' dealings as well as the competences of authorities to search private premises and seize documents. Whistleblowers are protected and incentivized.

a.   Reaching beyond regulated markets   The MAD only covers transactions on "regulated markets." According to Art. 1 para. 13 of Directive 93/22/EEC,[79] a market is a "regulated market" if it functions regularly and appears on a list of regulated markets drawn up by each Member State, and provided its conditions of operation are governed by regulations of the competent authorities, and it meets certain reporting and transparency requirements. This concept falls short of capturing trades on multilateral trading facilities,[80] organized trading facilities[81] and financial instruments traded over-the-counter[82] only. Hence, Art. 2 para. 1(b) of the proposal/regulation includes transactions on an MTF or an OTF; Art. 2 para. 1(c) extends the scope of regulation to transactions relating to financial instruments which are traded on a regulated market, an MTF or an OTF. The proposal further includes the auctioning of emission allowances concerning the European Union's climate policies.

Spot markets are outside the scope of the MAD, which covers financial and derivative markets only. The proposal does not intend to change this regime as a whole, but suggests spreading its reach to transactions of this kind which are related to financial and

---

[77]   Supra note 15.
[78]   On the difference between directives and regulations see supra Section I.A.
[79]   Council Directive 93/22/EEC of May 10, 1993 on investment services in the securities field, 1993 O.J. (L 141) 27.
[80]   Hereinafter cited as MTF.
[81]   Hereinafter cited as OTF.
[82]   Hereinafter cited as OTC.

derivative markets. As to insider trading, it advocates a more comprehensive definition of inside information.

b. Expanding the term "inside information" and the transactions covered One of the proposal's more drastic suggestions is an extension of the meaning of "inside information."[83] Not only does it move beyond MAD Art. 1 in encompassing emission allowances and auctioned products based thereon and align the somewhat vague definition relating to commodity derivatives to the general definition of inside information.[84] It also adds a sweeping new definition, according to which inside information is any information:

> [R]elating to one or more issuers of financial instruments or to one or more financial instruments, which is not generally available to the public, but which, if it were available to a reasonable investor, who regularly deals on the market and in the financial instrument or a related spot commodity contract concerned, would be regarded by that person as relevant when deciding the terms on which transactions in the financial instrument or a related spot commodity contract should be effected.[85]

Note, however, that the drafters of the proposal realized the vagueness of their new definition. Departing from the MAD's concept of linking insider trading prohibitions and reporting requirements, the proposal separates both aspects. If information falls under the proposed definition of inside information but is not precise enough to warrant disclosure to the market, the insider trading prohibition applies, yet no reporting requirement ensues.[86]

Whereas the MAD thus far captures only the acquisition or disposal of financial instruments by insiders, the proposal adds the attempt to cancel or amend an order. If a legal person qualifies as an insider, the proposal covers not only natural persons who took part in the decision-making but also those who merely "influence" the decision to carry out a transaction.

c. Introducing minimum rules on sanctioning MAD Art. 14 requires Member States to provide for an effective and dissuasive sanctioning regime, leaving them with considerable discretion as to the form and substance of such regimes. Art. 26 of the proposal/regulation reaches out further, by stipulating a minimum catalogue of administrative

---

[83] See supra Section I.B.2. After this chapter had been submitted, several changes to Art. 6 para. 1(e) of the proposal/regulation were made. For the latest news see amendments of European Parliament on the proposal/regulation on May 11, 2012, available at http://www.europarl.europa.eu/sides/getDoc.do?pubRef=-//EP//NONSGML+COMPARL+PE-489.421+01+DOC+PDF+V0//EN&language=EN; ECON – Report on proposal/regulation on Oct. 22, 2012, available at http://www.europarl.europa.eu/sides/getDoc.do?pubRef=-//EP//NONSGML+REPORT+A7-2012-0347+0+DOC+PDF+V0//EN.

[84] Instead of referring to information which users of derivative markets would "expect to receive" (MAD Art. 1 para. 1 sub-para. 2), Art. 6 para. 1(b) of the proposal/regulation singles out information which has a significant effect on the prices of derivatives or related spot commodity contracts.

[85] Art. 6 para. 1(e) of the proposal/regulation.

[86] Proposal/regulation, supra note 15, at ¶ 3.4.2.1.

measures and sanctions. This includes, among other things, cease-and-desist orders, "naming and shaming" instruments, and corrections of false or misleading statements, as well as banning insiders from exercising functions in investment firms. The proposal for a directive on criminal sanctions adds the threat of jail time.[87]

II.   WHAT IS DIFFERENT ABOUT INSIDER TRADING LAW IN EUROPE?

The preceding overview on insider trading law has illustrated the pronounced influence of US law on European regulation. This is particularly true with regard to the integration of the US debate on "possession versus use," tests such as "probability/magnitude" and the "total mix of information," and the "reasonable investor" serving as a guideline for assessing the materiality of inside information.

Of course, there are marked differences as well. Arguably the most notable divergence is the difference in the underlying policy reasons. European law does not subscribe to any version of a misappropriation theory. Instead, it proscribes insider trading on grounds of market integrity and fairness. This accounts for the comparatively broader scope of European insider trading law, which applies as soon as we find a person profiting from an information asymmetry. Thus, it encompasses not only classic insiders but reaches far beyond US law's "constructive" and "non-traditional" insiders, without imposing the somewhat artificial need to show some form of misappropriation (see A. below). However, the clear focus on market integrity has its downsides, too. Under European law, possession of inside information triggers not only a prohibition on trading but also a disclosure requirement. While this seems to flow naturally from the overall goal of promoting market integrity, it also carries the risk of flooding the market with irrelevant information, thereby increasing volatility (see B. below).

A.   The Policy Question: Integrity of Markets or Misappropriation?

1.   The victimless crime and the fairness argument

The way in which a legal system defines the term "insider" is central to understanding the policies underlying its insider trading law. From a US point of view, classical insiders have a special relationship to the issuer, typically requiring a fiduciary duty. Duties of this nature make the misappropriation theory applicable to officers, directors and large shareholders as well as certain mid-level corporate employees.[88] With ties to the issuer becoming more far-fetched, the application of the misappropriation theory becomes more complicated. This is true not only for tipping situations but also for so-called "constructive insiders" as well as "non-traditional" relationships.[89]

By contrast, European law does not encounter similar problems. Since insider trading is not viewed as a breach of fiduciary duty or as the insider misappropriating information

---

[87]   See supra Section I.D.1.

[88]   Bainbridge, supra note 4, at 9 et seq.

[89]   See id. at 22–28.

from the issuer or someone else, European law's comprehensive definition of an "insider" allows for catching any of the situations which appear difficult from a US perspective. The underlying goal, which possibly reminds a US reader of cases such as Texas Gulf Sulphur,[90] is twofold:[91] the MAD aspires to preserve the "integrity of financial markets" by aiming at "full and proper market transparency," thereby "strengthening public confidence in securities and derivatives."[92] To this rather market-driven approach, the ECJ adds a focus on fairness to the individual investor:

> [T]he purpose of the prohibition . . . is to ensure equality between the parties in stock-market transactions by preventing one of them who possesses inside information and who is, therefore, in an advantageous position vis-à-vis other investors, from profiting from that information, to the detriment of those who are unaware of it . . . The essential characteristic of insider dealing thus consists in an unfair advantage.[93]

What can we learn from this approach? European law embraces fairness arguments in insider trading much more readily than US law.[94] It is not fundamentally sceptical about imposing a general duty on capital markets participants not to use inside information to the disadvantage of another party. Nor does it view the party transacting with the insider as making an independent decision to buy or sell. Rather, the insider's counterparty is regarded as being treated unfairly by the insider who profits from an incomplete disclosure of relevant facts.[95]

Consequently, Henry Manne's analysis of insider trading as a "victimless crime"[96] does not have a strong foothold in European law. This is related to European law's openness towards recognizing a duty not to act unfairly vis-à-vis investors on capital markets. It can also be traced back to an argument of inadmissible hypothetical causality:[97] if the insider knowingly causes a loss to his counterparty there is no reason for him to escape liability because another market participant would have caused the same loss unintentionally.

2. Primary and secondary insiders

Despite its comprehensive scope, it is not necessarily the mere possession of inside information that triggers a prohibition on trading under European law. Some limitations are made with regard to the person being aware of his possession of inside information. Under MAD Art. 2 para. 2 such awareness is presumed for classical insiders (sometimes termed "primary insiders"). According to MAD Art. 4, anyone who does not belong to

---

[90] SEC v. Texas Gulf Sulphur Co., 401 F.2d 833 (2d Cir. 1968) (en banc), cert. denied 394 U.S. 976 (1969).

[91] For more detail, see Langenbucher, supra note 49, at 462–465.

[92] MAD, supra note 3, recitals (12), (15); proposal/regulation, supra note 15, recital (2).

[93] Spector Photo Group, supra note 48, at ¶ 48.

[94] For a critical discussion of the policy debate in the US, see Bainbridge, supra note 4, at 19 et seq.

[95] Cf. id. at 37 ("It is . . . the nondisclosure that causes the harm, rather than the mere fact of trading.")

[96] Henry Manne, Insider Trading and Property Rights in New Information, 4 Cato J. 933, 937 (1985).

[97] Langenbucher, supra note 49, at 464.

this group but is in possession of inside information (a so-called "secondary insider") qualifies as an insider solely if he knows or ought to know that the information in question is inside information.[98]

The group of secondary insiders is considerably larger than the group of tippees, "constructive" and "non-traditional" insiders in US law. Thus, it comprises not only employees and business connections of the issuer but also the notorious taxi driver overhearing the CEO's conversation on the backseat, or the seatmate on an airplane catching an unintentional glimpse of the papers on the seat next to him.

Just like regular primary insiders, a person qualifying as a secondary insider is the addressee of every permutation of the insider trading prohibition. The logic underlying the comprehensive scope is based on considerations of fairness and market integrity. Both the taxi driver and the seatmate, if they are aware of being in possession of privileged information, have an advantage over the person with whom they intend to transact. European law denies them a good reason to profit from this windfall.

It should be noted that the Commission's proposal discussed above,[99] while slightly reformulating the relevant rules, does not change the substance of the definitions or re-orientate the policies underlying them. "Market integrity" and achieving a "level playing field" continue to figure prominently in the text of the proposal. "Investor protection" has, moreover, been added as yet another goal of the market abuse regime.[100]

B.   Defining Inside Information: The Risks of Over- and Under-inclusiveness

One of the most challenging tasks any insider trading law faces is to draw a line between irrelevant facts and material information. A rulemaker will typically weigh the potential damage of being over-inclusive against the risks of drafting an under-inclusive rule. Being over-inclusive is not only objectionable with regard to sanctions. If a duty to disclose applies, over-inclusiveness also carries the risk of flooding the markets with irrelevant information. As we have seen above, European law, but not US law, links prohibitions on insider trading and reporting requirements.[101] As a result, one would expect US law to embrace a more comprehensive approach to disclosure, and European law to draft its rules more narrowly in order to avoid a disclosure-overload. In fact, the contrary is the case.

In distinguishing relevant from irrelevant information, US law relies on "materiality" from the point of view of a "reasonable investor." Information is "material" if there is a "substantial likelihood that the disclosure of the omitted fact would have been viewed by the reasonable investor as having significantly altered the 'total mix' of information made available."[102]

At first glance, European law employs a very similar test.[103] According to MAD Art. 1 para. 1 any information qualifies as inside information if it "would be likely to have a

---

[98]   See supra text accompanying note 31.
[99]   See supra Section I.D.2.
[100]   Proposal/regulation, supra note 15, at 2–3 and recitals (8), (26).
[101]   See supra Section I.B.5.
[102]   TSC Industries, Inc. v. Northway, Inc., 426 U.S. 438, 449 (1976).
[103]   See supra Sections I.B.2. and I.C.4.c.

significant effect on the prices of financial instruments." The existence of a significant price effect depends on whether "a reasonable investor would be likely to use [this information] as part of the basis of his investment decisions."[104]

In addition to the "reasonable investor" test, information has to be of a "precise nature" in order to qualify as inside information under European law. Discussing the case *Geltl v. Daimler* above, we have seen that the required "precision" is contingent, first, on the event at hand having occurred or warranting the reasonable expectation that it will occur. Secondly, it is subject to the information being specific, thereby allowing for an assessment of its possible effect on the prices of relevant financial instruments.[105]

However, the requirement of information being "precise" enough to warrant both a trading prohibition and a disclosure requirement seems to matter less to today's rulemakers. This is noticeable not only from General Advocate Mengozzi's opinion discussed above,[106] but also from the Commission's proposal. If the novel definition of "inside information" that is currently proposed by the Commission is adopted,[107] there would no longer seem to be a need to decide upon information being "precise" or to determine the significance of its effect on market prices. Instead, it would appear that the "reasonable investor" is to become the only guideline in distinguishing material from irrelevant information.

Although seemingly a move towards US law, this definition is considerably broader than its US counterpart. It catches information as soon as it is "relevant," without restraining its scope to "important" facts. In addition, it entirely dispenses with the need for a "substantial likelihood" of the model investor taking the relevant information into account when entering into a transaction.

The broadened scope of the proposal accounts for the criticism that has been leveled at the Commission. Some commentators claim that it intends to subsume information of an imprecise nature as well as information lacking a significant effect on market prices under its new definition of inside information.[108] Arguably, however, the Commission's proposal is open to another reading. The accompanying explanatory memorandum suggests that widening the definition of inside information is aimed at catching situations which are not yet ripe for disclosure to the market but nevertheless already warrant a prohibition on insider trading. Pertinent examples include preliminary contract negotiations, plans

---

[104]   See Art. 1 para. 2 of Directive 2003/124.

[105]   See supra Section I.C.4.

[106]   See supra text accompanying notes 58 et seq.

[107]   See supra Section I.D.2.b. See supra note 83.

[108]   See Deutsches Aktieninstitut [DAI] [German Share Institute], Comment on the proposals for a regulation on insider dealing and market manipulation (market abuse) and for a Directive on criminal sanctions for insider dealing and market manipulation 3–5 (Jan. 16, 2012), available at http://www.dai.de/internet/dai/dai-2-0.nsf/0/189B7C078F402D02C12579B200 4113B3/$FILE/AB494BC767678F78C12579610034CFCE.pdf?openelement&cb_content_name_ utf=2012-01-16%20DAI-Comment%20MAD%20final.pdf (last accessed December 5, 2012); Bundesverband deutscher Banken [Federal Association of German Banks], Stellungnahme zu den Legislativvorschlägen der Europäischen Kommission vom 20.10.2011 [Comment on the EU Commission's Proposal/Directive and Proposal/Regulation of Oct. 20, 2011] 5 (November 30, 2011), available at http://www.bankenverband.de/downloads/122011/dk-stn-2011-11-30- stellungnahme-mad-mar-final.pdf (last accessed December 5, 2012).

for public offerings or conditions of marketing financial instruments.[109] Interestingly, the Commission seems to assume that these situations are either not yet precise or do not yet have the necessary market impact to qualify as inside information under the MAD.[110] Should the ECJ follow the suggestions of the General Advocate in *Geltl v. Daimler*, which is still pending, this assumption does not necessarily hold true. Remember that the General Advocate proposes a comprehensive test for deciding upon the requisite degree of "precision." A low degree of precision may be compensated by a high degree of market impact, and vice versa, with the "reasonable investor" being the arbiter of what is to qualify as inside information.[111] Hence, the General Advocate suggests reading the current requirements of the MAD *de lege lata* along the same lines that the Commission envisages for the future.

What implications does this have for the Commission's proposal? There are good reasons to assume that the seemingly all-embracing new definition of "inside information" needs to be understood in the context of the Commission's literal approach towards interpreting the MAD strictly on the basis of its wording, instead of covering imprecise pieces of information through the adoption of a multi-factor balancing test. Two things follow from this. First, the Commission's definition of "inside information," covering facts which a reasonable investor would deem relevant despite their lack of precision, lends itself to an interpretation along the lines of the materiality test deployed by US law as well as to the General Advocate's multi-factor balancing test. Special care should be attributed to defining the reasonable investor, his level of expertise, and his appetite for risk and for engaging in speculative behavior. Secondly, and perhaps more interestingly, according to the Commission possession of this type of "second-tier" inside information results in a prohibition on trading but will not trigger a disclosure requirement.[112] This appears eminently appropriate, bearing in mind that European law's wide definition of inside information carries the risk of catching imprecise or preliminary information, disclosure of which might well increase stock price volatility rather than foster information symmetry on the market.

C.   Concluding Remarks

European insider trading law has clearly been influenced by US law and closely continues to monitor the US debate. Topics such as the "probability/magnitude" or the "total mix of information" test, the "use versus possession" debate and the model person of the "reasonable investor" figure as prominently in the European discourse as they do in its US counterpart.[113]

Strikingly, the influence of US law is considerably stronger on a technical than at the policy level. While US law relies on the misappropriation theory, European law explains insider trading prohibitions from the perspective of promoting market integrity and

---

[109]   Proposal/regulation, supra note 15, at ¶ 3.4.2.1.
[110]   This is in line with the Commission arguing for a probability threshold in Geltl v. Daimler: see Opinion of GA Mengozzi, supra note 58, at ¶ 81.
[111]   See supra Section I.C.4.b.
[112]   See supra Section I.D.2.b.; see also text accompanying note 86.
[113]   See, e.g., supra text accompanying notes 34, 48, 59, 64, 69 and 101–102.

fairness to individual investors. Making use of an informational advantage is regarded as an unfair treatment of the insider's counterparty and at the same time a risk to smoothly functioning capital markets.[114] This accounts for European law's close linkage of trading prohibitions and disclosure requirements. The insider is barred from exploiting his superior information. Market mechanisms are enhanced by forcing disclosure as long as there is no legal basis for justifying a delay.[115]

This form of a more technical rather than policy-oriented influence of US law generates two lessons: from a US perspective, it is interesting to monitor the treatment of very similar issues under a fundamentally different policy. This is true especially with regard to the scope of insider trading prohibitions and the qualification of non-traditional insiders. The lesson to be learned for a European lawyer is caution to context when transplanting legal concepts and arguments. US law's scope of insider trading prohibitions is much narrower than that of European law and does not connect reporting requirements with the possession of inside information. This triggers a multiplying effect: whenever the findings of US research tend towards an expansion of the scope of insider trading law within the framework of § 10(b) and Rule 10b-5, the effect is considerably stronger when applying the very same arguments to the European context. Hence, this chapter has supported the Commission's newly formulated tendency to separate trading prohibitions from disclosure requirements.

---

[114] See supra Section II.A.
[115] See supra Section I.B.5.

23. Takeover bids and insider trading
Matthijs Nelemans and Michael Schouten

I. INTRODUCTION

No information is as price sensitive as information on pending takeover bids, rendering takeover bids a prime context within which insider trading occurs. The sentencing of former Goldman Sachs board member Rajat Gupta and of Raj Rajaratnam, the hedge fund manager, for example, was partly based on illicit trading on information regarding pending takeover bids. This chapter offers a positive analysis of the European regulatory framework with respect to insider trading in the context of takeover bids. We distinguish between trading by the bidder, by the target and by classical insiders such as officers and employees. Where relevant, we draw a comparison between EU law and US federal securities laws. The analysis suggests that European insider trading laws are insufficiently tailored for corporations, and that significant uncertainty remains as to the precise scope of the prohibition on insider trading in the context of takeover bids.

We start by addressing the issue of precisely *when* information about potential takeover bids qualifies as inside information (section 2). From that particular moment onwards, the prohibition on insider trading applies and an obligation to disclose the information without delay is triggered. Those who are in possession of inside information are generally prohibited from selectively sharing this information with others or giving recommendations (tipping), causing difficulties for potential bidders who wish to reach out to major shareholders of the target to obtain irrevocable undertakings or to their own shareholders to gauge whether they are willing to support the bid. We identify the circumstances under which information can be shared with such parties, and the conditions that need to be met. We also address the important question of when issuers are no longer entitled to keep inside information private and need to make public disclosure (section 3).

The fourth section of the chapter analyzes the extent to which bidders are permitted to build a stake in the target prior to announcement of the offer. Stake building is common and yields important financial benefits for bidders, as well as strategic advantage vis-à-vis other potential bidders and, in the case of hostile offers, target management. This section also addresses the prohibition for target companies and classical insiders to trade on information regarding a pending bid. Bidders can also have inside information relating to their own shares, potentially preventing them from repurchasing shares or issuing new shares in a secondary offering.

In the fifth section of the chapter, we discuss reporting obligations in respect of trades, distinguishing between reporting obligations for bidders and for classical insiders. We show that these obligations serve multiple purposes, including facilitating enforcement of the prohibition on insider trading and notifying target managers of pending offers. Perhaps most importantly, these reporting obligations serve the purpose of improving informational efficiency of the stock market, yet in doing so restrict potential bidders' profits from stake building, thereby negatively affecting their appetite to launch an offer. The chapter concludes with a brief discussion of policy implications.

II.   WHEN DOES INFORMATION ON A TAKEOVER BECOME INSIDE INFORMATION?

For the bidder, target and insiders it is essential to understand exactly *when* information about a potential offer qualifies as inside information. From that particular moment onwards, the prohibition on insider trading applies, as does the prohibition on selectively sharing inside information and tipping. At the same time, an obligation to publicly disclose the information to the market is triggered. Persons involved in the potential offer should thus be especially vigilant in their dealings from then on. Under EU law, inside information is defined as information (1) of a precise nature, (2) which, if it were made public, would be likely to have a significant effect on the price of financial instruments, and (3) that relates, directly or indirectly, to one or more issuers or financial instruments.[1] We briefly discuss each of these elements below.

A.   The "Precise Nature" Test

The basic idea behind the "precise nature" test is to exclude premature information from the definition of inside information. The test requires that an event such as a takeover bid should reasonably be expected to occur before it constitutes inside information.[2] The US federal securities laws contain a comparable condition to filter out premature information from the prohibition on insider trading: materiality, according to *SEC v. Texas Gulf Sulphur*, "will depend at any given time upon a balancing of both the indicated probability that the event will occur and the anticipated magnitude of the event in light of the totality of the company activity."[3] In *Basic v. Levinson*, this has been confirmed in a merger context: "materiality in the merger context depends on the probability that the transaction will be consummated, and its significance to the issuer of the securities."[4] Thus, under both EU law and US law, the probability that a future event such as a takeover bid will occur should exceed a certain minimum threshold.

In the European context, the "precise nature" test serves a particular purpose. Since EU issuers are bound by an affirmative disclosure obligation (discussed in the following section), they may be required to disclose ongoing merger negotiations.[5] The "precise nature" test precludes issuers from having to disclose information regarding takeovers if the information is not (yet) sufficiently precise. Indeed, the first purpose of the test is to confine the amount of information that issuers have to produce and the investors need

---

[1]   Section 2(1) Directive 2003/6/EC. We refer to the directive as "EU law"; however, directives need to be implemented by Member States and actual rules in force at the national level may therefore vary slightly.
[2]   Cf. Section 1(1) Commission Directive 2003/124/EC.
[3]   SEC v. Texas Gulf Sulphur Co., 401 F.2d 833, 849 (1968).
[4]   Basic, Inc. v. Levinson, 485 U.S. 224, 239 (1988).
[5]   Section 6(1) Directive 2003/6/EC.

to process before making an investment decision. As is well known, the adage "the more, the better" does not apply to information disclosure. At some point, the marginal benefits of increased availability of information no longer weigh up against the marginal costs of producing more information. In addition, information overload may make it more difficult for investors to make informed investment decisions. The *second* purpose of the test is to prevent issuers from having to make premature disclosures about possible events and then becoming exposed to claims that they have misinformed the market if such events do not materialize.[6]

According to the "precise nature" test, information on a future event such as a potential takeover bid should meet two conditions: (1) as noted earlier, it should reasonably be expected to come into existence or occur; and (2) the information should be sufficiently specific to draw a conclusion on the potential impact of the information on the share price.[7] As to the first condition, it is unclear when exactly an event may reasonably be expected to occur and whether the minimum probability is closer to, say, 30 percent or 70 percent.[8] This leaves market participants with a high degree of uncertainty. The European Securities Markets Authority (ESMA, formerly CESR) has so far done little to remove this uncertainty.[9] As a result, national regulators could be led to believe that any stage in a takeover process may qualify as sufficiently precise, even if the probability of a takeover at that time is close to zero. Contributing to this risk is that regulators' ex post assessment could be subject to hindsight bias. Regulators may be tempted to conclude that on T=1 the takeover must have been reasonably expected to occur, merely because of the fact that on T=2 the takeover actually occurred.

The second condition of the "precise nature" test prescribes that the information should be sufficiently specific to draw a conclusion on the potential price impact. This condition overlaps with the requirement that the information should be price sensitive (discussed below), and therefore is often not given full weight by regulators and sometimes simply ignored.[10] Nevertheless, it does have meaning in and of itself: the information should form a sufficient basis for drawing a conclusion on the possible impact on price. This may be the case if: (1) the information allows a reasonable investor to make an investment decision without, or at very low, financial risk; or (2) when it concerns information

---

[6]   To avoid this, issuers tend to provide the least amount of information possible, thereby exposing themselves to a different type of claim, based on the allegation that they have provided incomplete information.

[7]   Section 1(1) Commission Directive 2003/124/EC.

[8]   See CESR, Level 3—Second Set of CESR Guidance and Information on the Common Operation of the Directive to the Market, CESR/06-562b, July 7, 2007 at 4–5.

[9]   ESMA has so far only provided negatively framed guidance, stating that precise information may exist even if a proposed takeover might not actually occur, and that information can be of a precise nature even if a potential bidder has not yet decided the offer price or even if it has not finally decided which of two possible targets to make an offer for. CESR, supra note 8 at 5.

[10]   In a recent decision, the Financial Services Authority (FSA) has provided an explicit analysis of the possible impact on price and the direction of the price movement. FSA Decision Notice 12 January 2012 at 11–12. Available at: http://www.fsa.gov.uk/static/pubs/decisions/dn-einhorn-greenlight.pdf (last accessed Oct. 12, 2012). By contrast, a 2008 decision by the Dutch AFM lacks such a specific assessment. AFM decision of June 26, 2008, at 10–11. Available at: http://www.afm.nl/layouts/afm/default.aspx~/media/files/boete/2012/boete-muller.ashx (last accessed Oct. 12, 2012).

that is likely to be exploited immediately by the market.[11] Consequently, the information should enable an assessment of how the information, once publicly known, would affect the price. Since the investment decision should be almost riskless, it seems that the information should at least indicate a potential impact on the price and also provide insight into the direction thereof.[12]

Given the uncertainty on when information is to be considered of a precise nature, it is not surprising that the EU Court of Justice (ECJ) has been requested to provide clarity on the issue.[13] In the case of *Markus Geltl v. Daimler AG*, the ECJ has held that information relating to future circumstances or events can only be of a precise nature if "there is a *realistic prospect* that [the future circumstances or events] will come into existence or occur" [emphasis added].[14] It is remarkable, and commendable, that the ECJ has not followed the Advocate-General's opinion on this point. According to the Advocate-General, it would have been "sufficient that the occurrence of the future set of circumstances or event, albeit uncertain, be not impossible or improbable," provided that "the potential of the information for affecting share prices is significant."[15] Obviously, many potential events and potential takeover bids, regardless of how uncertain they are, may qualify as "not impossible or improbable," and the resulting disclosure obligation would therefore have likely been overbroad. This would have resulted in additional costs for issuers as well as increased liability risk, while the benefits for the investor community would have been doubtful given the information processing efforts that would need to be made and the risk of information overload.[16] Importantly, it would also have affected the European public merger and acquisition

---

[11]   See CESR, supra note 8 at 5.

[12]   Of course, investors can also benefit from price changes without knowing the direction of expected price movements, e.g. by purchasing straddles.

[13]   On January 14, 2011, the German Bundesgerichtshof referred a request for a preliminary ruling to the EU Court of Justice in the case Markus Geltl v. Daimler AG, revolving around the resignation of a CEO preceded by a series of consultations that were not disclosed to the market. The question was whether issuers have an ad-hoc disclosure duty for information on intermediate stages that precede a future event and whether information can be of a "precise nature" if occurrence of a particularly significant event is not unlikely. See also Katja Langenbucher, Insider Trading in European Law, Chapter 22 of this volume, at 436–440.

[14]   Case C-19/11, Markus Geltl v. Daimler AG, 2012. The ECJ also ruled that certain intermediate steps of a process to bring about a particular circumstance or event may qualify as precise information. However, this presupposes that the ultimate event is reasonably to be expected and at least not implausible. Otherwise, there is no ground for concluding that the information on the intermediate step is sufficiently specific and would have an impact on the price. Indeed, the second condition of the "precise nature" test would not be satisfied. According to the ECJ, "precise information is not to be considered as including information concerning circumstances and events the occurrence of which is implausible," because otherwise "issuers could believe that they are obliged to disclose information which is not specific or is unlikely to influence the prices of their financial instruments." See consideration 48.

[15]   See also Langenbucher, supra note 13 at 438–439.

[16]   For a critical assessment of the EU ad-hoc disclosure obligation, particularly the "precise nature" test, see Jesper Lau Hansen & David Moalem, The MAD Disclosure Regime and the Twofold Notion of Inside Information—The Available Solution, 4 Capital Markets L. J. 323 (2009); Carmine Di Noia & Matteo Gargantini, The Market Abuse Directive Disclosure Regime in Practice: Some Margins for Future Actions, Rivista Della Societa 782 (2009). On the proposed

market by hindering exploratory talks between public companies regarding potential business combinations.[17]

B.   The "Price Sensitivity" Test

Once it has been established that information is of a precise nature, the next step is to determine whether the information is likely to have a significant price effect were it made public.[18] In doing so, it should first be verified that the information is not already in the public domain. If it is, the information cannot qualify as inside information under EU law (the same applies in respect of US law). After all, public information is stale information without (news) value and disclosure therefore cannot be expected to have a price effect, at least not according to the efficient capital market hypothesis, which posits that public information will already be reflected in current market prices. As a result, it should be impossible for insiders to misuse such information.[19]

When should information be deemed price sensitive? There is no minimum threshold above which a price effect qualifies as "significant,"[20] nor is there a sub-definition that offers guidance in this respect.[21] As a result, market participants are confronted with another layer of uncertainty, in particular when they become involved in processes with intermediate stages preceding a future event, such as takeover negotiations, and need to assess at what particular moment information starts to become likely to have a significant price effect and thus starts to qualify as inside information. The European Commission, in an attempt to shed light on the issue, has stated that information should be considered likely to have a significant price effect if "a reasonable investor would be likely to use the information as part of the basis of his investment decisions."[22] While this criterion shows strong resemblance to the reasonable investor criterion that applies under US federal securities laws,[23] the Commission's approach ignores the fact that when reasonable investors consider information relevant in making their investment decisions, this does not

---

changes to the ad-hoc disclosure regime, see Carmine Di Noia, Pending Issues in the Review of the European Market Abuse Rules, 19 ECMI Policy Brief 1 (2012).

[17]   At least, companies engaging in such talks would be at risk that they have to make an unwanted, early disclosure should there be rumors or indications of a leak (see Section III.B. below on mandatory public disclosure). It is even conceivable that major shareholders or third parties, such as hedge funds, would intentionally release rumors on supposed merger talks if they had an interest in expediting the takeover or eliciting a takeover battle. This is because if the rumor were true, the target company would be required to make a public disclosure on its merger talks, thereby bringing the company in play.

[18]   Section 1(1) Directive 2003/6/EC.

[19]   See generally Andrei Shleifer, Inefficient Markets. An Introduction to Behavioral Finance (2000).

[20]   Cf. Mathias Siems, The EU Market Abuse Directive: A Case-Based Analysis, 2 Law & Financial Markets Rev. 39, 41 (2008).

[21]   Attempts to do so have merely resulted in tautological expressions and ambiguous guidance. See CESR, supra note 8 at 5.

[22]   Section 1(2) Commission Directive 2003/124/EC.

[23]   TSC Industries, Inc. v. Northway, Inc., 426 U.S. 438 (1976) (holding that there must be a substantial likelihood that a reasonable shareholder would consider the information important when buying or selling a financial instrument).

necessarily imply that the disclosure of such information would have a significant price effect. After all, the information may for example confirm the validity of expectations regarding the firm's prospects that are already reflected in the current share price. What is more, not all revaluations of the firm's prospects will result in a "significant" price effect.

Predictably, national regulators often rely solely on the "reasonable investor" criterion, since this criterion is met more easily than the "significant price effect" criterion. Sometimes, they treat the two criteria as if they were interchangeable, as the Commission has done. A case in point is the FSA's recent imposition of a fine on hedge fund manager David Einhorn for having traded on non-public information relating to Punch Taverns, Inc. shares. The FSA's decision was based in part on the reasoning that the information was likely to have a significant effect on price *(merely) because* a reasonable investor would likely have used the information as part of the basis of his investment decisions.[24]

In sum, the current state of play in the EU is that it may not require a lot for information to qualify as inside information and for the prohibition on insider trading and the disclosure obligation to kick in. Given the negative consequences of an overly broad scope of the disclosure obligation, the Commission arguably should consider abandoning the "reasonable investor" criterion and resorting only to the significant price effect criterion. Alternatively, the Commission could reframe the "reasonable investor" criterion such that it becomes clear that the information should at least cause the reasonable investor to significantly revalue the share.

C.   Information Relating to an Issuer of Shares or to Shares

The condition that the information should relate, directly or indirectly, to an issuer of shares or to shares is easily met.[25] Among other things, the condition implies that a bidder and a target can have inside information relating to one another's shares. To begin with, a potential bidder will often be in possession of information that is highly price sensitive as to the target's shares. As Figure 23.1 illustrates, the announcement of a takeover bid typically causes the target's share price to increase strongly.[26]

The strong positive price effect is primarily due to the anticipation of a bid premium to be paid by the bidder, and also to factors such as expected synergies between the companies, tax benefits and changes in board composition.[27] To be sure, the same price

---

[24]   FSA Decision Notice of 12 January 2012, paragraphs 4.6, 4.17–4.18. Available at http://www.fsa.gov.uk/static/pubs/decisions/dn-einhorn-greenlight.pdf (last accessed Oct. 12, 2012). See also, e.g., the Dutch AFM's penalty decision of March 9, 2011 at 11–14, available at http://www.afm.nl/layouts/afm/default.aspx~/media/files/boete/2011/wavin.ashx (last accessed Oct. 12, 2012).

[25]   Section 1(1) Directive 2003/6/EC.

[26]   See Marina Martynova & Luc Renneboog, Mergers and Acquisitions in Europe, in L. Renneboog (ed.), Advances in Corporate Finance and Asset Pricing (2006). See also Boyan Jovanovic & Serguey Braguinsky, Bidder Discounts and Target Premia in Takeovers, 94 Am. Econ. Rev. 46 (2004).

[27]   See Sayan Chatterjee, Sources of Value in Takeovers: Synergy or Restructuring—Implications for Target and Bidder Firms, 13 Strategic Manage. J. 269–272 (1992); Frank H. Easterbrook & Daniel R. Fischel, The Economic Structure of Corporate Law 163 (1991); Michael C. Jensen & R.S. Ruback, The Market for Corporate Control, 11 J. Fin. Econ. 23 (1983). The post-announcement share price typically remains below the offer price, reflecting the risk that the offer

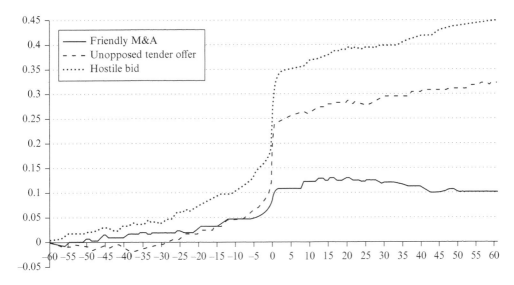

Source: Marina Martynova and Luc Renneboog (2006), Mergers and Acquisitions in Europe, in L. Renneboog (ed.), Advances in Corporate Finance and Asset Pricing.

Figure 23.1   EU target abnormal returns

effect would not necessarily occur at an earlier stage, when parties are merely exploring the possibility of a business combination and a takeover bid is not (yet) reasonably to be expected. What matters for present purposes, though, is that the potential bidder will possess information that, once it becomes sufficiently precise, may be highly price sensitive as to the target's shares and therefore qualify as inside information.

At the same time, the bidder may possess inside information regarding its *own* shares. As one would expect, the effect of a takeover announcement on the bidder's share price is far less pronounced than the effect on the target's shares, and the direction of the movement in the share price is not as predictable (see Figure 23.2).[28] Nevertheless, in individual cases regulators may well conclude that the bidder was in possession of inside information regarding its own shares, especially when the takeover is accompanied by a significant issuance of shares, either because it concerns an exchange offer or because the bidder will need to raise equity capital to finance the bid.

---

might not succeed. This is different when the market expects a competing offer to be launched, in which case the target's share price may exceed the offer price to reach a level that reflects the expected premium of the competing offer, again discounted for the probability that such offer may not succeed (or may not be launched after all).

[28]   Martynova & Renneboog, supra note 26. See also Jovanovic & Braguinsky, supra note 26 at 46. As Figure 23.2 shows, there can be upward and downward price pressure. There are various explanations for this. Downward price pressure can be caused by investors who believe that the bid premium is too high compared with potential synergies and that the bid would thus result in a wealth transfer from the bidder's shareholders to the target's shareholders. Upward price pressure can be attributed to investors who believe the present value of the synergies (and possibly of the strategic benefits) exceeds the premium.

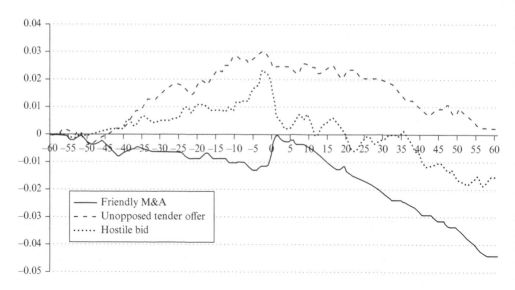

Source: Marina Martynova and Luc Renneboog (2006), Mergers and Acquisitions in Europe, in L. Renneboog (ed.), Advances in Corporate Finance and Asset Pricing.

Figure 23.2   EU bidder abnormal returns

Of course, in a friendly scenario in which the bidder and the target enter into negotiations regarding the terms of the offer, the target may have inside information to its own shares and may obtain inside information in relation to the bidder's shares.

III.   DISCLOSURE OF INSIDE INFORMATION

A.   Sharing Inside Information with Outsiders

A primary purpose of the prohibition on selectively sharing inside information is prevention of leakage. Leakage increases the number of people in possession of inside information and thereby the probability of insider trading. If there were not a sufficient downside to disclosing inside information, insiders could even start selling inside information to persons who would not be deterred by the risk of being prosecuted for insider trading violations. However, as a practical matter these prohibitions may also constitute obstacles in the preparation of a takeover, for example by preventing potential bidders from reaching out to the target's major shareholders to obtain irrevocable undertakings. In the USA, insiders disclosing inside information to outsiders can be held liable under Section 10(b) of the Securities Exchange Act 1934 and Rule 10b-5 if they do so for an improper purpose.[29] In terms of takeovers, pursuant to Section 14(e) and Rule 14e-3, it is unlawful for the bidder or target to communicate inside information relating to a tender offer

---

[29]   Dirks v. SEC, 463 U.S. 646, 662–664 (1983).

to any other person under circumstances in which it is reasonably foreseeable that such communication is likely to result in insider trading. Likewise, Regulation FD prohibits directors from disclosing inside information to certain recipients including shareholders, if it is reasonably foreseeable that they will purchase or sell the company's securities on the basis of that information (see Chapter 7 of this volume for a detailed discussion of Regulation FD).[30]

EU law similarly prohibits those who are in possession of inside information from selectively disclosing this information to others. They are also prohibited from recommending or inducing another person to purchase or sell shares on the basis of inside information (tipping).[31] A distinction is made between primary and secondary insiders.[32] Primary insiders are persons who possess inside information on a regular basis, including executive or non-executive directors and major shareholders. Persons who do not qualify as primary insiders qualify as *secondary* insiders. Primary insiders are deemed to be aware of the fact that they are in possession of inside information. By contrast, in cases where a secondary insider is suspected of selectively disclosing information or tipping, proof is required that he knew, or ought to have known, that he was in possession of inside information.

Absent nuances or exemptions, the prohibition on disclosing inside information would severely hinder issuers and their employees in conducting activities in the ordinary course of business. For example, a business secretary would not be able to circulate the minutes of a meeting when they include inside information. Also, the press officer would not be able to disclose inside information to the market. Since there is no reason to prohibit such activities, EU law permits disclosure of inside information "in the normal course of the exercise of employment, profession or duties." The scope of this exemption is not fully clear. In the matter of *Grøngaard & Bang*, the ECJ held that EU Member States should interpret the exemption in a restrictive manner.[33] Further guidance is typically offered at Member State level.

As a practical matter, when parties intend to share information with outsiders they typically enter into a confidentiality agreement prior to granting access to the information. The imposition of a duty of confidentiality on the receiving party is vital, for otherwise the disclosure to that party would trigger an obligation to publicly disclose the information without delay.[34] Yet even if a confidentiality agreement is put in place, the key question remains whether an exemption applies. Disclosing information to major shareholders of the target with a view to obtaining a commitment that they will tender their shares under the offer is allowed in most EU Member States, provided that the support of such shareholders is actually necessary for the offer to succeed and that no more information is

---

[30]   See Q&A 102.11, available at http://www.sec.gov/divisions/corpfin/guidance/regfd-interp. htm (last accessed Oct. 12, 2012).

[31]   Section 3 Directive 2003/6/EC.

[32]   Section 4 Directive 2003/6/EC.

[33]   Case C-384/02, 2005 E.C.R. I-9939. There should be a close link between the disclosure and the employment, profession or duties, and the disclosure should be strictly necessary for the exercise thereof. See Langenbucher, supra note 13 at 434.

[34]   Section 6(3) Directive 2003/6/EC. The FSA seems to take a slightly more flexible approach to the duty of confidentiality. FSA Market Conduct Sourcebook, MAR 1, 1.4.5.

disclosed than strictly necessary.[35] This exemption is justified from an efficiency perspective, since enabling the bidder to assess at an early stage whether major shareholders are willing to support the bid provides the bidder comfort that he will not waste resources (in the form of management time and advisors' fees) in connection with the preparation of a bid that is doomed to fail.

There are several other situations in which bidders and targets may want to share inside information with outsiders. A bidder may wish to consult some of its own major shareholders, for example if the bidder will need to raise equity to finance the bid or if the bidder requires shareholder approval for the takeover. A bidder may also want to reach out to other companies to form a bidder consortium or to discuss the possibility of a back-to-back sale of certain assets of the target. Target management, for its part, may also wish to reach out to its major shareholders to gauge their support or, in the case of a perceived threat of a hostile offer, to another preferred potential bidder (a so-called "white knight"). While there are efficiency reasons for facilitating the sharing of information for these various purposes, no specific exemptions apply under EU law and neither have the relevant authorities provided guidance in this respect, meaning that market participants rely solely on the use of confidentiality agreements. A certain degree of uncertainty therefore remains, which could restrain bidders or targets from sharing inside information, possibly resulting in fewer transactions than might be economically efficient. To the extent individual EU Member States have provided for exemptions, applicable standards may diverge across countries, discouraging cross-border acquisitions and thereby undermining the creation of a single European market.

B. Mandatory Public Disclosure

Under US federal securities laws, public companies do not have a general ongoing obligation to disclose material non-public information to the market.[36] In principle, the acquirer and the target could therefore choose to make a public announcement only after they have reached final agreement on a deal. Disclosure at an earlier stage may, however, be required by stock exchange rules. The New York Stock Exchange's listing rules, for example, require issuers to quickly release any news or information that might reasonably be expected to materially affect the market for their securities.[37] Issuers are also required to make an announcement if rumors or unusual market activity indicate that information on impending developments has leaked.[38]

EU law contains an ongoing obligation for issuers to disclose inside information without delay.[39] Consequently, from the moment information on a potential takeover bid

---

[35] See generally A.J. Nussbaum, C. Martin & S. Perry (eds.), Mergers & Acquisitions: Jurisdictional Comparisons (2012).

[36] D.M. Stuart & D.A. Wilson, Disclosure Obligations under the Federal Securities Laws in Government Investigations, 46 Bus. Law. 973, 977–982 (2009). See also Stephen M. Bainbridge, The Law and Economics of Insider Trading: A Comprehensive Primer 70 (2001). Available at http://papers.ssrn.com/sol3/papers.cfm?abstract_id=261277 (last accessed Oct. 12, 2012).

[37] NYSE Rule 202.05.

[38] NYSE Rule 202.03.

[39] Section 6(1) Directive 2003/6/EC.

qualifies as inside information, the issuer has an obligation to disclose the information—unless it is allowed to delay disclosure. Delay is permitted if three cumulative require-ments are met, the first being that the issuer must have a justified interest in doing so. Such an interest may exist, for example, if disclosure could negatively affect the outcome of pending negotiations, or when decisions taken by executives are still subject to board approval.[40] Accordingly, issuers will usually have a justified interest in delaying disclosure of the fact that merger negotiations are taking place.

The second requirement is that the delay of disclosure may not mislead the public. In theory, any delay of disclosure of material non-public information could result in the market being misled. This suggests that delay should never be possible, which is not the case.[41] It is generally understood that non-disclosure may mislead the market if the issuer discloses information that contradicts, or relates to, information that is being with-held. Also, the market could be misled if an issuer withholds information that would shine a different light on previously disclosed information. In determining whether the issuer is allowed to delay disclosure, previous disclosures will therefore have to be taken into account.

The third requirement that needs to be met for delay to be permitted is that the issuer guarantees the confidentiality of the information by controlling access to the relevant information and taking adequate measures (including preparing an insiders' list) to ensure access is limited to persons who need to have access as part of the normal exercise of their work, profession or responsibilities. The issuer should also take measures to be prepared to make the information generally available without delay as soon as confidentiality can no longer be guaranteed, such as drafting press releases.[42]

While there should normally be clear rumors to warrant the conclusion that confiden-tiality is no longer guaranteed,[43] courts sometimes consider irregular trading activity suf-ficient. For example, a Dutch court held that deviant share price movements or deviant trading volumes could be a signal that confidentiality is no longer guaranteed.[44] In the case at hand, the target, a Dutch supermarket chain, had received a bid letter from a potential bidder. Within a few days, trading volumes and the share price started to increase, without there being any clear rumors. A minority shareholders' association initiated civil proceed-ings and successfully claimed that the issuer had failed to make prompt disclosure. While ostensibly sound, the difficulty with this approach is that it seems to ignore the fact that price and volume movements could be caused by information or trades *unrelated* to the

---

[40]   Section 3(1) Commission Directive 2003/124/EC.
[41]   CESR, supra note 8 at 11.
[42]   Section 3(2) Commission Directive 2003/124/EC.
[43]   In general, if a bidder is preparing a hostile bid and rumors would cause the target's share price to increase, it is still only the bidder that has actual information on the potential hostile bid. The target, obviously, cannot make a disclosure in this respect for lack of information. If a bidder and target are negotiating a friendly deal, and rumors cause the target's share price to rise, the target may have a disclosure obligation. The information on the potential friendly deal should then at least qualify as inside information regarding the target's shares. The bidder may as well be required to make a disclosure if rumors were to spread. This can be the case if the bidder is a listed company and the information on the potential bid qualifies as inside information regarding the bidder's shares.
[44]   Super De Boer v. VEB, Utrecht District Court, LJN: BP9796, March 30, 2011.

takeover. If the court's decision, which is currently pending in appeal, were to be upheld, Dutch issuers may feel compelled to go public unless they have clear indications that the price and volume movements are caused by news or rumors unrelated to the takeover. In practice, this would result in a high degree of uncertainty. Issuers would have to monitor rumors unrelated to the takeover and, if there are any, determine whether these form a sufficient explanation for the price and volume movements. Also, major shareholders or hedge funds who wish to expedite a takeover or elicit a bidding contest may cause price and volume movements with a view to forcing the issuer to disclose any pending negotiations, thereby putting the company in play.

The current ad-hoc disclosure obligation is expected to become subject to changes in the short term. The European legislator has proposed several amendments to the current disclosure obligation.[45] Yet, as this stage it is unclear whether the legislative efforts will result in a more lenient disclosure regime for European issuers or not.

IV.   TRADING

A.   Trading by the Bidder

The acquisition of a minority stake, or "toehold," prior to announcing a bid may yield important financial benefits for bidders, since the price against which such shares can be purchased will not yet reflect the anticipated bid premium. Stake building may also create a strategic advantage vis-à-vis other potential bidders and, in the case of hostile offers, target management.[46] From an efficiency perspective, the bidder's gains from stake building can be considered a reward for the effort of searching for potential synergies.[47] Such gains can also be considered as a means to finance the relatively high bid premium that target shareholders will expect due to the free-rider problem associated with takeover bids.[48] As a result, the bidder will be able to profit from his monitoring efforts upon acquisition of the firm even after paying the premium. Even if the bidder does not succeed and a competing bidder were to end up realizing the synergy gains, sale of the toehold by the initial bidder to its competitor will ensure that search costs are covered.

In practice, bidders often do acquire a toehold. An empirical study by Betton et al. (2009) shows that in the period 1973–2001, 26.3 percent of bidders in their US sample acquired a toehold, with an average size of 20.3 percent.[49] For hostile offers, the percentage is much

---

[45]   Section 12(1) of the Presidency compromise on the Proposal for a Regulation on Insider Dealing and Market Manipulation (market abuse), 13313/12, September 3, 2012. See also Mathias Siems & Matthijs Nelemans, The Reform of the EU Market Abuse Law: Revolution or Evolution? 19 Maastricht J. Eur. & Comp. L. 195, 201 (2012).

[46]   See, generally, Jeremy Bulow, Ming Huang & Paul Klemperer, Toeholds and Takeovers, 107 J. Pol. Econ. 427, 427–454 (1999).

[47]   See Daniel Fischel, Efficient Capital Market Theory, the Market for Corporate Control, and the Regulation of Cash Tender Offers, 57 Tex. L. Rev. 1, 13 (1978).

[48]   Sanford J. Grossman & Oliver D. Hart, Takeover Bids, the Free-Rider Problem, and the Theory of the Corporation, 11 Bell J. Econ. 42, 45 (1980).

[49]   Sandra Betton, B. Espen Eckbo & Karin S. Thorburn, Merger Negotiations and the Toehold Puzzle, 91. J. Fin. Econ. 158, 166 (2009).

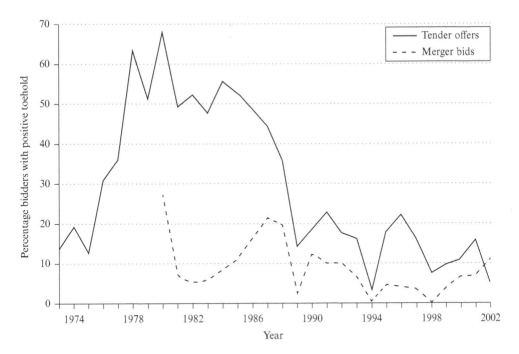

Source: Sandra Betton, B. Espen Eckbo & Karin S. Thorburn (2009), Merger Negotiations and the Toehold Puzzle, 91. J. Fin. Econ. 158, 166.

Figure 23.3   Annual frequency of toeholds in US targets (1973–2001)

higher, with 50.3 percent of bidders acquiring a toehold. As Figure 23.3 shows, the number of bidders for US companies that have been acquiring toeholds has been decreasing over time, which Betton et al. (2009) suggest may be explained by the availability of the "poison pill" as a defense mechanism for US target companies. While we are not aware of similar data regarding EU takeovers, it could well be that such data would show a different picture, given that in some jurisdictions such as the UK, target companies are limited in their ability to respond to stake building by taking defensive measures.

Under US federal securities laws, a bidder acquiring a toehold while in possession of material non-public information regarding the target would violate Rule 10b-5. However, if the bidder acquires a toehold prior to having conducted due diligence, the bidder will merely have knowledge of its own intentions to potentially launch an offer for the target's shares and the acquisition of a toehold generally does not constitute a breach of a duty of trust or confidence.[50] Rule 14e-3 also does not prevent such acquisition, since this rule merely prohibits persons other than the "offering person" from insider trading in the context of tender offers. Thus, even though there is no explicit exemption available for toehold acquisitions under US law, such acquisitions are generally permitted.

---

[50]   Chiarella v. United States, 445 U.S. 222 (1980); United States v. O'Hagan, 521 U.S. 642 (1997).

Under EU law, corporations and natural persons are prohibited from using inside information when trading in shares to which that information relates.[51] While this prohibition only applies to the extent inside information is actually "used," the ECJ's decision in the *Spector* case suggests that when a bidder trades while in possession of inside information with respect to the target, the authorities may simply presume that the bidder "used" the inside information.[52] This means that it is up to the bidder to rebut this presumption, and *Spector* can therefore hardly be considered a safe haven for toehold acquisitions. Be this as it may, individual EU Member States often use another ground to exclude toehold acquisitions from the prohibition on insider trading. This exclusion is based on the recitals of the Market Abuse Directive, which states that EU Member States may apply a milder regime in the context of public offers and that transactions are allowed if the trader merely has knowledge of its own intentions.[53] Indeed, most EU Member States have more or less explicitly allowed toehold acquisitions.[54] In the UK, for example, the FSA has indicated that trading in the context of a public takeover bid to gain control does not in and of itself amount to market abuse.[55] And in the Netherlands, legislators have declared that knowledge of one's own intentions should not be considered inside information.[56]

Again, once the bidder obtains material non-public information from the target, things become different and the bidder will generally be prevented from trading. This may be due not only to the statutory prohibition on insider trading, but also due to restrictions imposed by the target on the bidder through the confidentiality agreement that the parties will usually have entered into prior to the target granting the bidder access to information relating to the target. Obtaining such access is crucial for the bidder to conduct its due diligence and estimate potential synergies, but in exchange the target will typically insist on inclusion in the confidentiality agreement of a standstill provision, preventing the bidder from unilaterally purchasing target shares for a certain period of time. Indeed, as the Delaware Chancery Court's recent decision in the matter of *Martin Marrieta Inc. v. Vulcan Materials Company* reminds us, a standstill provision may be found to exist even if it has not been explicitly included in the agreement.[57]

Does this mean that the bidder has to cease the purchase of target shares upon approaching the target? We believe not necessarily, given that an approach in and of itself does not necessarily result in the bidder obtaining inside information. Indeed, EU law does not explicitly prescribe that the bidder should immediately cease purchasing target shares upon approaching the target, nor does it explicitly prescribe that the bidder should do so once it gains an impression of the target's willingness to cooperate (or lack thereof). This makes sense, given that a target's unwillingness to enter into talks may influence the bidder's course of action but not necessarily the outcome. After all, the bidder may carry on without the target's support.

---

[51]   Section 2(1) Directive 2003/6/EC.
[52]   Case C-45/08, Spector Photo Group, 2009 E.C.R. I-12073.
[53]   Recitals 29 and 30 of Directive 2003/6/EC.
[54]   See generally Nussbaum, Martin & Perry, supra note 35.
[55]   FSA Market Conduct Sourcebook, MAR 1, 1.3.17–1.319.
[56]   Parliamentary Papers II 1997/98, 25 095, no. 8, at 4, 8.
[57]   Martin Marrieta Inc. v. Vulcan Materials Co., No. 7102-CS, slip op. at 111 (Del. Ch. May 4, 2012).

Alternatively, suppose the target's CEO comes back with a specific, higher price at which the target board is willing to support a takeover. Again, this does not necessarily mean that the bidder has obtained inside information with respect to the target. Responding with a specific, higher price is often part of the target's negotiation tactics. It does not necessarily imply that the bidder can only be successful by raising the offer since ultimately, it is up to the target's shareholders to decide on whether or not to tender their shares. However, if it is apparent that the target's valuation is based on material non-public information, for example on unpublished half-yearly financial results or a material contract, the bidder may have to cease purchasing target shares.

B. Trading by Classical Insiders and Corporations

Under the US prohibition on insider trading, "classical" insiders such as directors and officers are not allowed to trade if they have material non-public information, and it is generally understood that corporations, too, are subject to this prohibition.[58] A major development in this regard has been the adoption of the misappropriation theory by the Supreme Court in 1997.[59] This has widened the scope of the prohibition by including outsiders who trade on the basis of material non-public information in breach of a duty of trust or confidence. Shortly thereafter, the "possession versus use" debate was settled. Until 2000, some courts took the view that the trader had to be in "knowing possession" of inside information while other courts required actual "use" of the inside information. In 2000, the Securities and Exchange Commission (SEC) effectively ended this debate by adopting Rule 10b5-1, which requires that the trader be "aware" of the inside information and which provides for a number of affirmative defenses.[60]

Under EU law, persons are prohibited from using inside information when trading in shares to which that information relates.[61] Accordingly, all legal and natural persons, irrespective of whether they are insiders or outsiders, are subject to the EU prohibition on insider trading. This already makes it a more sweeping prohibition than its US equivalent. The EU prohibition applies to the extent inside information is "used," which triggered a "possession versus use" debate comparable to that in the USA. The ECJ settled this debate by ruling in *Spector* that, if a primary insider trades while in possession of inside information, the regulator may simply presume that the inside information has been "used."[62] It is then up to the defendant to rebut the presumption and to motivate that he

---

[58] Mark J. Loewenstein & William K.S. Wang, The Corporation as Insider Trader, 30 Del. J. Corp. L. 45, 58 (2005).

[59] *United States v. O'Hagan*, 521 U.S. 642 (1997).

[60] Allan Horwich, The Origin, Application, Validity, and Potential Misuse of Rule 10b5-1, 62 Bus. L. 913, 917–920 (2007). Under Rule 10b5-1, corporations and individuals have, for example, an affirmative defense if they trade in accordance with a pre-existing trading plan, which should have been adopted prior to receiving any material non-public information.

[61] Section 2(1) Directive 2003/6/EC.

[62] Case C-45/08, *Spector Photo Group*, 2009 E.C.R. I-12073. See also Lars Klöhn, The European Insider Trading Regulation after the ECJ's Spector Photo Group-Decision, Eur. Comp. & Fin. L. Rev. 347 (2010); Katja Langenbucher, The "Use or Possession" Debate Revisited—Spector Photo Group and Insider Trading in Europe, 5 Cap. Mark. L. J. 452 (2010); Langenbucher, supra note 13 at 435–436.

did not use the inside information for his trades, for example, if he sold shares when the inside information indicated a price increase.[63]

The foregoing shows that the prohibitions on insider trading equally apply to corporations and natural persons, even though corporations operate in a more complex business environment than natural persons. In spite of this, EU law, and apparently also US law, lack constructive guidance on how corporations are supposed to act when they have material, non-public information, for example, on a takeover bid. There are no clear rules on trading by the corporation when having information on a takeover bid. Consequently, various questions may arise if a corporation wishes to make toehold acquisitions, obtain irrevocable undertakings, repurchase shares or issue new shares in a secondary offering. Of course, there are market practices and affirmative defenses, but these do not always provide the level of comfort that corporations seek.[64]

V.   REPORTING OF TRADES

A.   Toeholds

As we have seen, acquiring a toehold can be an attractive strategy for potential bidders for a variety of reasons. Yet the extent to which a potential bidder may discreetly purchase shares in the market is limited. Pursuant to the European Transparency Directive, shareholders acquiring in excess of 5 percent (or such lower threshold as set at national level) need to report their position, just as shareholders in US listed companies need to pursuant to Rule 13-D.[65] Once the market learns of the identity and stake of the potential bidder, the share price will rise in anticipation of a bid against a premium over the current share price (as illustrated in Figure 23.1), and the bidder will no longer be able to purchase shares cheaply. Thus, while ownership disclosure rules generally enhance market efficiency, they can also discourage bidders from making a bid in the first place.[66]

If the bidder intends to bypass target management and is covertly building a stake prior to launching a hostile offer, mandatory disclosure may also function as an early warning system to target management. By enabling target management to take defensive

---

[63]   Another potential defense exists if the contracting parties possessed the same information so that there was no information asymmetry (Case C-391/04, *Georgakis*, 2007 E.C.R. I-3741).

[64]   In the USA, corporations can limit the risk of insider trading liability by setting up a trading plan in accordance with Rule 10b5-1 prior to any share repurchases. See Loewenstein & Wang, supra note 58 at 71. And EU law provides a safe harbor for buy-back programs if certain transparency and trading conditions are met. Commission Regulation (EC) 2273/2003. These affirmative defenses, however, are rather limited. Besides, in terms of share offerings, neither the USA nor the EU rules stipulate under which conditions issuers may proceed with an intended secondary offering if they possess inside information. Indeed, Rule 10b5-1 may only be used in the context of certain secondary offerings. See also Horwich, supra note 60 at 929.

[65]   Directive 2004/109/EC. For a discussion of Rule 13-D, see, e.g., Lucian A. Bebchuk & Robert J. Jackson Jr., The Law and Economics of Blockholder Disclosure (2011), 2 Harv. Bus. L. Rev. (2012).

[66]   See Michael C. Schouten, The Case for Mandatory Ownership Disclosure, Stan. J. Bus., L. & Fin. (2010). The present section and the following section build on this article.

measures, mandatory disclosure potentially undermines the market for corporate control. At the same time, temporary defenses may benefit existing shareholders by strengthening the board's bargaining position in the case of a bid that undervalues the target and by enabling the board to reach out to other potential bidders to encourage them to launch a superior bid. The challenge for policymakers is to set a threshold for initial disclosure that strikes an optimal balance between these interests.

One way to make it possible for potential bidders to obtain a financial gain from buying shares at the pre-bid price while preserving target management's ability to adequately respond to an attempt to acquire control is by enabling bidders to obtain financial exposure to the target shares through cash-settled equity derivatives. The Transparency Directive currently does not require disclosure of cash-settled equity derivatives, only of physically settled equity derivatives such as call options. However, in many EU Member States, including the UK, France and Germany, the law has recently been amended to require disclosure of cash-settled equity derivatives as well. A major driver for these changes has been the desire to prevent creeping takeovers by bidders who enter into a derivative contract with a counterparty (usually a bank) stipulating cash settlement, yet upon termination of the contract nevertheless settle physically, thereby acquiring a sizeable stake while avoiding the price increases that open market purchases (and accompanying disclosure of the crossing of the 5 percent threshold) would have caused. Indeed, there have been several high-profile examples of this strategy, including the controversial takeover of tire manufacturer Continental by Schaeffler in Germany and more recently LVMH's acquisition of a large stake in luxury goods powerhouse Hermès.

The European Commission has recently proposed expanding the scope of the Transparency Directive along the same lines, and in the USA the SEC is considering doing the same. While there are strong arguments in favor of such a move, one possibly unintended effect is thus that it limits potential bidders' ability to exploit the information they have regarding their intention to launch an offer, making takeover bids costlier and discouraging bidders from making a bid in the first place. This is especially true if expanding the scope were combined with a lowering of the initial disclosure threshold from 5 percent to 3 percent, as has been done in EU Member States such as the UK and as has been proposed by the European Commission.[67]

B. Insider Trades

EU law requires all transactions by corporate insiders in the company's shares (or derivatives linked to them) to be reported to the national regulator, just as US law requires that transactions by corporate insiders be reported to the SEC.[68] In each case, the information is publicly disclosed by the regulator, enabling the market to learn of insider trades, albeit with a delay: the European Market Abuse Directive requires trades to be reported within

---

[67] See Michael C. Schouten & Mathias Siems, The Evolution of Ownership Disclosure Rules Around the World, J. Corp. L. Stud. 251 (2010).

[68] Section 6(4) Directive 2003/6/EC and Section 6 Commission Directive 2004/72/EC; Section 16 Securities Exchange Act 1934.

five days of the transaction date while in the USA trades are only required to be reported within two days after the end of the month in which they occurred.

In its recitals, the Market Abuse Directive states that the publication of transactions by insiders can be a highly valuable source of information to investors.[69] Indeed, as one of us has argued elsewhere, disclosure of transactions by insiders contributes to market efficiency by conveying to the market underlying fundamental information driving the transactions, thereby causing the share price to move closer toward the correct price.[70] Absent such disclosure, insider trading may still contribute to market efficiency, yet the derivatively informed trading mechanism of market efficiency will operate at a slower rate. As explained in Chapter 1 of this volume, the mechanism will then affect market prices, first (and only marginally) because of the trading itself, and subsequently because of leakage, tipping, observation of the insider's trades or by following the price fluctuations of securities. Mandatory disclosure of the insider's trades enables the market as a whole to respond by trading on the information—at least to the extent the information is not yet fully incorporated in the share price, which is why the time window between the trade and the reporting obligation matters.

Empirical studies confirm that insiders tend to purchase stock prior to an abnormal rise in stock prices and sell stock prior to an abnormal decline in stock prices, which suggests that these trades are motivated by the possession of non-public information about the company's prospects.[71] For example, a recent study by Malloy et al. (2012) that distinguishes between routine trades (e.g., trades for liquidity reasons) and "opportunistic" trades found that opportunistic trades yield abnormal returns of about 8 percent over a 12-month period, with no reversal following the price rise (see Figure 23.4). The study further shows that opportunistic trades (primarily buys) predict analyst information releases (recommendations and earnings forecasts), analyst earnings forecasts by themselves, management forecasts and firm-level earnings announcements.[72] This explains why markets tend to respond to the disclosure of such trades, as evidenced by this study and previous empirical studies.[73] Thus, mandatory disclosure of insider trades accelerates the speed at which fundamental information is incorporated in the share price, thereby contributing to market efficiency.

---

[69]   Recital 22 Directive 2003/6/EC.

[70]   See Schouten, supra note 66. See also Steven Huddart, John S. Hughes & Carolyn B. Levine, Public Disclosure of Insider Trades, 69 Econometrica 665 (2001).

[71]   See, e.g., H. Nejat Seyhun, Insiders' Profits, Costs of Trading, and Market Efficiency, 16 J. Fin. Econ. 189 (1986); Josef Lakonishok & Inmoo Lee, Are Insider Trades Informative?, 14 Rev. Fin. Stud. 79, 93 (2001).

[72]   Christopher Malloy, Lauren Cohen & Lukasz Pomorski, Decoding Inside Information, 67 J. Fin. 1009 (2012).

[73]   Id. See also, e.g., Jana P. Fidrmuc, Marc Goergen & Luc Renneboog, Insider Trading, News Releases, and Ownership Concentration, 61 J. Fin. 2931, 2949 (2006) (finding that UK directors' purchases and sales generate statistically significant abnormal returns of 3.12 percent and –0.37 percent respectively, measured over the two-day window starting with the announcement day); Jesse M. Fried, Reducing the Profitability of Corporate Insider Trading through Pretrading Disclosure, 71 S. Cal. L. Rev. 303, 354 (1998) (explaining how investors use information on insider trading to determine whether the company's insiders believe (based on their inside information) that the stock is over- or undervalued).

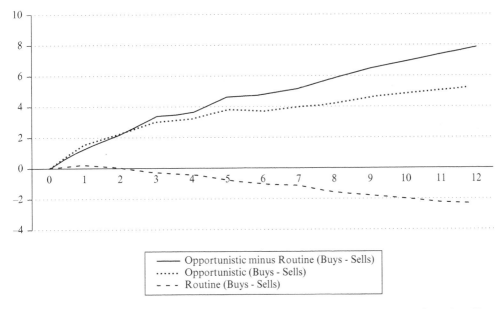

(legend)
——— Opportunistic minus Routine (Buys - Sells)
······ Opportunistic (Buys - Sells)
- - - Routine (Buys - Sells)

Source: Christopher Malloy, Lauren Cohen & Lukasz Pomorski (2012), Decoding Inside Information, 67 J. Fin. 1009.

Figure 23.4   Event-time returns for opportunistic trades

Interestingly, Malloy et al. (2012) do not find that opportunistic trades have predictive power for merger announcements. A possible explanation for this may be that corporate insiders are well aware that trading on non-public information about pending takeovers is illegal, and the risk of being caught once the takeover has become public is significant given that it will be easy to link the trades reported by the insider with the subsequent announcement of the takeover. In fact, this is precisely one of the effects intended by the Market Abuse Directive, which in its recitals states that the trading information to be reported by insiders constitutes a means for regulators to supervise markets.[74] This explanation is also consistent with a recent empirical study by Agrawal and Nasser,[75] who look at trades reported by insiders at US listed companies. They find no evidence that insiders increase their reported purchases in the period preceding takeover announcements, and suggest that this may be explained by the fact that the ban on short-swing trading (Section 16b of the Securities Exchange Act of 1934) is vigorously enforced by private attorneys. Interestingly, Agrawal and Nasser (2012) do find evidence that insiders reduce their sales during this period, thus increasing their *net* purchases. This "passive" insider trading often does not constitute a violation of insider trading laws, and is impossible to observe by the market since the decision not to sell does not (and could not possibly) trigger any disclosure obligation.

---

[74] Recital 26 Directive 2003/6/EC; Recital 7 Commission Directive 2004/72/EC.
[75] Anup Agrawal & Tareque Nasser, Insider Trading in Takeover Targets, 18 J. Corp. Fin. 598 (2012).

VI.   POLICY IMPLICATIONS

To facilitate a well-functioning market for corporate control, it is essential to have clear rules on how bidders, targets and classical insiders are supposed to act when in possession of inside information. Yet the present analysis has shown that the rules that are currently in place in the EU are insufficiently customized to corporations. Insider trading rules have historically been designed with classical insiders in mind, and as a result fail to take into account certain issues that arise when corporations possess inside information. While regulators sometimes attempt to alleviate this uncertainty with additional guidance, the guidance itself often leaves room for significant interpretation, justified by regulators on the ground that they do not wish to exclude any unforeseeable situations that may require regulatory action.

To be sure, any type of regulation will be accompanied with a level of uncertainty. However, EU law and apparently also US law lack constructive guidance on how bidders and targets are supposed to act when in possession of inside information. To the extent regulators have provided guidance, they have often done so on an ad-hoc basis rather than on the basis of a broader policy. From a policy perspective, the challenge is to strike an optimal balance between, on the one hand, effectively combating insider trading, and, on the other hand, observing the particularities of corporations as insiders and facilitating the market for corporate control.

In the EU, policymakers seem to have yielded to the temptation of a more instrumental approach against insider trading, without sufficient regard of the interests of corporations and the market for corporate control. This is not surprising, since insider trading laws and takeover laws are to a large extent discussed separately: the regulation of insider trading is considered a securities law matter, while takeover bids are classified as company law and are highly politicized. The lack of an integrated approach creates legal blind spots and uncertainties for corporations. Obviously, corporations may rely on market practices and certain affirmative defenses, but these do not always provide the corporation with sufficient comfort.

As to recent EU law developments, we believe it is positive that the ECJ has not followed the Advocate-General's opinion in the matter of *Markus Geltl v. Daimler AG*, which would have resulted in a broader disclosure obligation. Still, it remains uncertain how national regulators will apply the ECJ's judgment in practice and whether it will retain its relevance in light of the proposed EU market abuse regulation. This uncertainty comes on top of certain regulators applying the "reasonable investor" criterion and the "significant price effect" criterion as if they were interchangeable. Consequently, and given that deviating price and volume movements could be deemed a sufficient indication of a leak, corporations may still feel compelled to go public in premature situations, even if nothing really informative can be disclosed at such stage. Policymakers at the European and national level would therefore be well advised to ensure that they carefully consider the impact of contemplated changes to the current regulatory regime on the market for corporate control prior to making such changes.

Index

Wagner, Robert E. 262–3
Waksal, Sam 63, 64
Wall Street (film) 251
Wall Street Journal 130, 132, 251
  "Heard on the Street" 24–5, 86, 96
Warren, Chief Justice 45
Waterman, Judge Sterry 38, 40–44, 47
WebMediaBrands 128
websites, issuer 126–7
Webster, Daniel 172
Wei Jiang 236
Whaley, Robert E. 223
Wharton Research Database System 224
whistleblowing 262–3, 418, 441
White, Justice Byron 45–6
"white knight" 458
Whitney, Richard 33
Wikileaks 247
Williams, Justice 396
Williams Act 81
Wilson Neill 387, 392–3
Winans, R. Foster 24–5, 85, 96
winners, potential 268–9

wiretaps 217, 218
Wisniewski, Piotr 403–4
women
  role of gender in US insider trading law 15,
    191–207
  see also family; feminism; marriage
World Development Indicators 282, 285
Wurgler, Jeffrey 270–71

Xi Xiaoming 324
xuanzhu yingxiang 334, 339

Yazawa, Makoto 352
Yelp 99
Young, Justice 370–71

Zandford case 88–9
Zhejiang Hangxiao Steel Structure Co.
  Ltd. 327–8
Zhongda 334, 335
zhongyao 334–5
Ziobrowski, Alan 14, 169, 170
Zynga 99

Index